CLSA Duty Solicitors' Handbook

Third Edition

CLSA DUTY SOLICITOR'S HANDBOOK

Third Edition

Andrew Keogh

The Law Society

© Andrew Keogh 2006

ISBN 10: 1–85328–979–5
ISBN 13: 978–1–85328–979–8

Published in 2006 by Law Society
113 Chancery Lane, London WC2A 1PL

Typeset by J&L Composition, Filey, North Yorkshire
Printed by Antony Rowe Ltd, Chippenham, Wiltshire

Contents

CONTENTS

Preface to the third edition

The two years that have passed between the second edition and this one have seen an unprecedented degree of change to criminal practice and procedure. Much of the Criminal Justice Act 2003 that impacts upon sentencing and magistrates' court procedure has still to be implemented, and the Government's thirst for new law seems to know no bounds. Wherever possible I have tried to anticipate imminent change to law and procedure and incorporate it within the text.

Once again the emphasis has been on portability, which requires a selective approach to the materials that can be included. In this edition you will find the all important PACE codes and the popular sentencing toolkit. I have removed some text relating to remuneration from this edition, simply due to the pace of change and the fact that even at the time of writing the Legal Services Commission is consulting on April 2006 contract changes and Lord Carter is due to report on criminal legal aid before this edition hits the shelves, making any information mostly redundant by the time you buy the book. The law is as stated on 1 January 2006.

On a personal note the Keogh household has risen in number, and this edition is dedicated to our son Barnaby, who very kindly agreed to sleep long enough for me to finish the text.

Andrew Keogh
Manchester, January 2006

Foreword by Rodney Warren, CLSA

In the foreword to the first edition I said: 'Advising the suspect in the police station, or a defendant in the magistrates' court, can be a challenging experience in what is often a pressured environment. Complex issues can arise which require immediate answer. Sometimes even the most experienced may have doubts about simple points.'

Few could have believed then just how much change was on the way and yet much of the Criminal Justice Act 2003 is still to be implemented. The inclusion of the many changes, the revised PACE codes and the sentencing toolkit are most welcome and make this volume an ever more necessary aid for anyone involved in police station or magistrates court work.

Andrew is to be congratulated, not only for producing a most helpful work of reference, but also upon the birth of his son.

The Criminal Law Solicitors' Association is pleased to welcome the third edition of the CLSA Duty Solicitors' Handbook.

Rodney Warren
Director
Criminal Law Solicitors' Association
February 2006

Table of cases

Table of statutes

Table of secondary legislation, codes of practice and home office circulars

Home Office Circulars

Table of European legislation

CHAPTER 1

Duty solicitor practice

QUALIFYING AS A DUTY SOLICITOR

Introduction

Most criminal firms will require their lawyers to join at least one duty scheme, the simple reason being that membership of such schemes has been shown to give access to a substantial source of work.

Lawyers, however, will need to assess personally whether they are suited to such work. The disruption, particularly in out-of-hours participation in schemes, cannot be overestimated, and for many is simply unworkable. For others the remuneration makes such work unattractive, and there is no sign of any improvement in this respect. On a more involved level, a lawyer must feel capable of dispensing advice on a multitude of topics in difficult circumstances and with limitations on time and access to resources.

Changes have been introduced since the last edition, particularly in relation to decisions having to be made in relation to the admissibility and weight to be attached to evidence at a very early stage in the case. A more formal system of discounts for early plea has also added to the pressures of ensuring that the lawyer does not add delay to a case.

That having been said, duty slots often throw up some of the more serious work experienced by many lawyers, with opportunities to advise on terrorism, murder and other high profile offences. The heavy burden of responsibility acts as both a drain on the busy lawyer and at the same time the driver towards excellence, those with the energy will be assured of a varied and challenging diet of work and a career unmatched in variety.

Duty solicitor arrangements

The duty solicitor arrangements dictate that all members of the scheme must be accredited. Accreditation has been introduced in partnership with the Law

Society, which has set up the Criminal Litigation Accreditation Scheme (CLAS). Stage 1 of the scheme, which is in two parts, covers accreditation for court and police station duty work.

Employed barristers can qualify as duty solicitors, but are not allowed to participate in the Law Society's accreditation scheme. In order to qualify as duty solicitors, barristers must instead be accredited under the Police Station Accreditation Scheme and have passed the Magistrates' Court Qualification (MCQ). The MCQ is part two of Stage 1, and barristers therefore follow the same procedure as solicitors in this respect.

Accreditation

Membership of duty solicitor schemes is dependent upon accreditation, which, for the purposes of the duty solicitor arrangements (reproduced in Appendix B), means parts one and two of Stage 1 of the Law Society's CLAS. Part one covers a police station qualification, and part two a magistrates' court qualification. For most practitioners the local scheme will require membership of both court and police station schemes, necessitating a qualification in both parts. Where a solicitor is not willing to participate when so required on both police station and court schemes, the Legal Services Commission (LSC) can remove that person from the duty solicitor register.

For duty solicitors registered between all or part of the period 1 January to 1 April 2001, this in itself met the criteria, and all such solicitors were passported into CLAS Stage 1 membership. For those solicitors holding the police station representative qualification, similar rules allowed them to qualify automatically for part one of Stage 1.

Assessment criteria

Full scheme details, including application forms, can be accessed on the Internet via: **www.panels.lawsociety.org.uk**. The site contains not only the regulations but also useful guidance in relation to portfolio completion.

Police station qualification

The assessment is in two parts, submission of a portfolio, and a critical-incidents test. The portfolio comprises five cases, and the following information must be provided:

1. A brief description of the case, setting out what the case was about, describing what had to be done by the candidate, and what the result was.

2. Relevant information obtained from the police, the client and any relevant third party.
3. Description and analysis of how the solicitor assessed the information obtained, how they formulated their advice, and the advice given to the client.
4. Description and analysis of how the candidate dealt with the police and third parties including representations made, how they dealt with any issues or problems that arose.
5. Description of how the solicitor complied with relevant professional and ethical rules.

In addition, the standards of competence must be displayed to the satisfaction of the examiner.

The critical-incidents test is a role-play consisting of a number of issues or problems posed to the candidate, either verbally or in terms of behaviour, by a client, police officer or third party. An audio tape will indicate when a response is required.

Both parts of the examination must be successfully completed within 12 months of the date of first submission of the portfolio.

Magistrates' court qualification

The assessment is in two parts, a portfolio and an interview and advocacy assessment. A candidate must have 6 months' continuous experience of criminal defence work prior to submission of the portfolio. Newly-qualified solicitors are therefore able to be registered for the CLAS exams after a 6 month period, but duty solicitor rules preclude their admission on to rotas until 12 months' experience has been gained. In practice this poses no obstacle as it would generally take at least 6 months to satisfy all of the qualification requirements.

The portfolio consists of short notes on 20 cases and a detailed summary of a further five cases. The candidate must have personally represented the client in the cases submitted.

In addition to satisfying the standards of competence, the candidate must, in respect of cases included in the 'short notes', demonstrate:

(a) that the cases include a range of offences, of which at least five must be summary-only and at least five must be either-way. Indictable-only cases may be included, but are not required;
(b) that they have experience of appearing for more than one client during the course of a court session;
(c) that the cases include a range of applications and/or submissions, including at least one of each of a procedural application (e.g. an application for an adjournment), a venue submission, a bail application and a plea in mitigation;

3

(d) that they have appeared in more than one magistrates' court, and have represented a client in a youth court on at least one occasion.

For cases included in the 'detailed summary', the following (in addition to the standards of competence) must be demonstrated:

(a) that the cases include a range of offences, of which at least one must be a summary-only and at least one must be either-way. Indictable-only offences may be included, but are not required;

(b) that the cases include a range of applications or submissions, including at least one bail application, one advice on plea, one advice and/or representation on venue, one procedural adjournment application and one plea in mitigation. One case may involve more than one of these elements.

The following details must be provided:

1. Brief description of the case, setting out what the case was about, describing what had to be done by the candidate and what the result was.
2. Relevant information obtained from the prosecutor, the client and any relevant third party.
3. Description and analysis of how the candidate assessed the information obtained, how they formulated their advice, and the advice given to the client.
4. Description and analysis of the representations, applications and/or submissions made to the prosecution and/or the court by the candidate.
5. Evidence that the candidate complied with relevant professional and ethical rules.

The purpose of the interview and advocacy assessment is to assess a candidate's competence and effectiveness as a solicitor acting for a client in magistrates' court proceedings by reference to the standards of competence. The test takes the form of a simulated client interview and a simulated appearance in a magistrates' court. In respect of the simulated client interview, the assessment will last for a maximum of 15 minutes and the case will be used as the basis for one of the cases in the advocacy part of the assessment. The candidate must later make representations and/or submissions in respect of three cases, one of which will be a bail application.

It is notable that a large number of principals in practice complain loudly when their aspiring duty solicitors fail one or more component of the examinations. Whilst it is conceded that the accreditation process is far from perfect, as an examiner I can say that most of the people I fail do so because they make glaring errors in relation to even the most basic laws of evidence and procedure.

Re-accreditation

At the time of writing the Law Society is consulting on the form that re-accreditation will take. It is anticipated that re-accreditation will begin in 2006.

Transfer between firms

The LSC guidance provides for the following:

> The supplier that has been employing the solicitor may keep any slots allocated to that solicitor provided they still employ another duty solicitor. The solicitor/supplier must notify the CDSM [Regional Criminal Defence Service Manager] of the change in office (Arrangements 5.10(a) and (b)). The solicitor will need to ask the LSC to allocate slots on the next rota to him or her. The solicitor does not have to reapply for membership of a scheme of which he or she is already a member where he or she moves to another supplier or another office of the same supplier where the office complies with paragraph 4.8 of the Arrangements. However, the CDSM will need to check that the new office to which the solicitor moves complies with the geographical selection criteria (Arrangements 4.8, 4.9 or 4.10(b)).

PRACTICE GUIDANCE AND REMUNERATION

Practice as a duty solicitor is regulated by professional, ethical and contractual guidance, all of which must be adhered to in order to maintain duty solicitor status. For more detailed references refer to Part B of the Contract Specification (of the General Criminal Contract).

Duty to accept cases – police station

Cases referred by the call centre while one of a supplier's duty solicitors is on duty must be accepted unless the solicitor named on the rota is already engaged in connection with another client, either at the police station or at a hearing of an application for a warrant of further detention or an extension of such a warrant or at an armed forces custody hearing. If a conflict of interest arises, the case must be referred back to the call centre.

If the solicitor is already at the police station when the request is made, he shall notify the call centre if the request for advice is accepted.

In the event that the solicitor on rota is not available, the case can be accepted if another duty solicitor is available to undertake the case without delay, and that solicitor can if necessary attend the police station within 45 minutes.

A duty solicitor must use all reasonable endeavours to accept panel and back-up cases referred by the call centre service.

The call centre call can be taken by non-duty solicitor staff provided that the LSC is satisfied that such staff have been effectively trained to undertake such a role and there are clear procedures in place to ensure that referrals are not accepted unless there is a duty solicitor available who can make contact with the client immediately and attend at the police station within 45 minutes if necessary.

A duty solicitor must take all reasonable steps to contact the police within 30 minutes of a case being referred. A solicitor would be expected, if necessary, to make repeated calls in order to achieve this.

Scope of duty solicitor advice – police station

The following categories of suspects are covered:

(a) arrested suspects, including those detained by Customs and Excise,
(b) volunteers i.e. those who are free to leave the police station if they so wish,
(c) Services (Armed Forces) personnel unless an attendance takes place outside the UK,
(d) persons arrested under powers in the Immigration Acts,
(e) persons arrested for breach of a bail condition,
(f) persons arrested for breach of a matrimonial or domestic violence injunction,
(g) persons arrested under a warrant issued for default in paying a fine or maintenance,
(h) prisoners where the police are called into a prison to investigate an alleged offence by one prisoner upon another e.g. assaults,
(i) prisoners being investigated by the police other than for (h) above.

Suspects who are not covered:

1. The PACE Codes of Practice apply to a very wide range of investigations (see section 67(9) PACE 1984). Obvious examples are investigations by the Metropolitan and provincial constabularies, specialist police forces e.g. British Transport, Ministry of Defence, Services etc. Less obvious examples involve investigations by Immigration Officers, Customs and Excise, Serious Fraud Office but many also include consumer protection officers, Post Office investigators, store detectives and gas, water and electricity investigators. It does not follow that, simply because an investigation has to comply with the Codes of Practice, the advice at police stations scheme necessarily covers the suspect. In fact, where an investigation involves a non-police investigator who does not have a power of arrest, advice at police stations will not be available unless a constable (which include a Customs Officer) is present. The only alternative means of funding is Advice and Assistance which is means tested and subject to an upper limit which may not be exceeded without prior authority from the LSC. For full details see the Criminal Contract specification which sets out the position in more detail.

The following services must be provided (General Criminal Contract, Part B, para 8):

8.2 Service requirements for Police Station Duty Solicitor work

1. In Police Station Duty Solicitor cases the services set out in this Section shall be provided by a Police Station Duty Solicitor or an Accredited Representative in the full or part-time employment of, or a partner in the same firm or organisation as, the Duty Solicitor. You may deploy an Accredited Representative to undertake Police Station Duty Solicitor work in accordance with paragraph 8.2.11 below.

2. Cases referred by the Call Centre Service to you whilst one of your Duty Solicitors is on Rota duty must be accepted unless the Duty Solicitor named on the Rota is already engaged in connection with another Client at a Police Station or at a hearing of an application for a warrant of further detention or an extension of such a warrant or at an armed forces custody hearing or a conflict of interest arises. If the Duty Solicitor is already at the same Police Station when a Client requests the Duty Solicitor, he or she shall notify the Call Centre Service when a request for advice is accepted. If a conflict of interest arises the case must be referred back to the Call Centre Service.

3. You may accept a case referred by the Call Centre Service if the Duty Solicitor named on the Rota is unavailable for one of the reasons set out in paragraph 8.2.2 above but you have another Duty Solicitor available to accept the case without delay who is able to arrange attendance at the Police Station, if necessary, within 45 minutes.

4. You may accept Panel and Back-up cases referred by the Call Centre Service and must use all reasonable endeavours to do so.

5. With written prior approval from us you may use non-Duty Solicitor staff to receive calls from the Call Centre Service, and such staff may accept a referral from the Service provided that:

    (a) we are satisfied that the staff concerned have been effectively trained to undertake such a role; and

    (b) there are clear procedures in place for such staff to follow which ensure that referrals are not accepted unless there is a Duty Solicitor available to make first contact with the Client immediately and which ensure that referrals are passed to such Solicitors immediately; and

    (c) a Duty Solicitor is available to make first contact with the Client immediately and is able to arrange attendance at the Police Station, if necessary, within 45 minutes.

6. Subject to paragraph 8.2.8 below, the following services shall be provided once a case has been accepted:

    (a) initial advice by a Duty Solicitor personally by speaking directly to the Client on the telephone unless the Solicitor is at or adjacent to the Police Station and can immediately advise the Client in person, or the police refuse to permit the suspect to speak to the Duty Solicitor on the telephone, in which case he or she may attend the Police Station. If the Client is incapable by reason of drunkenness or violent behaviour of speaking to the Solicitor, initial advice may be postponed. Other circumstances in which initial advice may be postponed include sleep periods or where an interpreter is required. The Duty Solicitor shall make arrangements to provide initial advice as soon as the Client is capable of speaking to him or her;

(b) attendance at the Police Station to provide advice and to attend all police interviews with the Client during the Duty Period where the Client has been arrested in connection with an arrestable offence under section 24 of the Police and Criminal Evidence Act 1984;

(c) attendance at any identification parade, group or video identification or confrontation;

(d) attendance at the Police Station where the Client complains of serious maltreatment by the police;

(e) attendance at the Police Station where the Client is a youth or person at risk;

(f) the provision of advice where a Client is to be charged with an arrestable offence on the implications of the caution which will be given when the Client is charged. Consideration must also be given as to whether attendance should take place at that time bearing in mind whether it is possible to give confidential telephone advice and the possible consequences of not making a statement when being charged;

(g) representation in connection with an application for a warrant of further detention under Part A, paragraph 2.2.1(d) of this Specification;

(h) if a police interview and any identification parade, group or video identification or confrontation is postponed to a time when the Duty Solicitor is no longer on duty or, if on a Panel, where it is no longer convenient to act as Duty Solicitor, he or she must make arrangements to ensure that the Client continues to receive advice either by a Duty Solicitor or Own Solicitor. The Duty Solicitor may continue to act on an Own Solicitor basis.

7. The Duty Solicitor shall give initial advice. On giving initial advice under 8.2.6(a) above, the Duty Solicitor shall exercise his or her discretion whether it is in the interests of the Client for him or her or, if appropriate, an Accredited Representative to attend the Police Station. Attendance is mandatory under paragraphs 8.2.6(b) to (e) and (g) above, unless exceptional circumstances exist (see paragraph 8.2.8 below). In assessing whether attendance is necessary the Duty Solicitor shall consider whether advice can be given over the telephone with sufficient confidentiality and if he or she can communicate effectively with the Client by this means.

8. If exceptional circumstances exist which justify non-attendance at the Police Station, the Duty Solicitor shall record his or her decision not to attend, including details of the exceptional circumstances and the reasons for the decision on the case file. Exceptional circumstances could arise if a Client expressly instructs the Duty Solicitor not to attend. Exceptional circumstances are less likely to arise in the case of paragraphs 8.2.6(d) and (e).

9. If the Client is a Services Person at a services establishment or elsewhere assisting with an investigation by the Services Police and suspected of offences contrary to the Services Discipline Acts where:

(a) the investigation involves any offences which cannot be dealt with summarily; or

(b) the offence appears to the interviewing Services Police to be serious,

the Duty Solicitor shall attend personally upon the Client where he or she considers that such attendance is necessary for the protection of the Client's interests.

10. If the Client is a Services Person requiring representation at a custody hearing before a judicial officer under the Armed Forces Discipline Act 2000, the

Duty Solicitor shall attend personally upon the Client to provide Advice and Assistance (including Advocacy Assistance).

11. The services described in paragraph 8.2.6 above shall be provided as follows:

   (a) initial advice under paragraph 8.2.6(a) above shall be provided by a Duty Solicitor where the case has been referred by the Call Centre Service or accepted as a Duty Solicitor case at the Police Station;

   (b) the services referred to at paragraphs 8.2.6(b) to (f) above shall be provided by a Duty Solicitor or, where appropriate, by an Accredited Representative;

   (c) the services referred to at paragraphs 8.2.6(g) to (h), 8.2.9 and 8.2.10 above may only be provided by a Duty Solicitor or an Accredited Representative who is a Solicitor where the case has been referred by the Call Centre Service or accepted as a Duty Solicitor case at the Services establishment.

   If services are provided under (b) or (c) above by an Accredited Representative or Solicitor who is not an employee of the firm, the travel time claimed shall not exceed 45 minutes each way.

12. The Client shall be informed before advice is given of the status of the individual giving such advice.

13. Where required by local instructions, all staff undertaking Police Station Duty Solicitor work must carry an identification card as specified by us for production when attending Police Stations.

14. You shall only attend the Police Station when the Sufficient Benefit Test set out in Part B, Rule 2.5 is satisfied. The circumstances when this test will be satisfied include:

   (a) to provide advice prior to and during interview;

   (b) to advise at an identification procedure (including a video identification procedure when the Client is not present);

   (c) when appropriate, to advise a Client who is a youth or person at risk;

   (d) when appropriate, to advise on the implications of the caution when the Client is charged with an arrestable offence;

   (e) to advise when the advice may materially affect the outcome of the investigation and goes significantly beyond initial advice;

   (f) to advise a Client who complains of serious maltreatment by the police.

15. On Assessment of your Claims for Police Station Advice and Assistance we will take into account the factors above when determining whether it was reasonable for you to attend. If none of these are satisfied then further justification shall be provided on file. If one or more of the factors are met, then the attendance will normally be justified, however we may still reduce the Claim if we consider that the time spent was not reasonable.

16. Any attendance must be for the purposes of providing legal advice that could not be given over the telephone to the Client. You may not claim for an attendance when the advice could have been provided reasonably by way of telephone advice. If we consider that the advice could have been provided reasonably over the telephone, we may disallow the costs of any attendance at the Police Station, however, we will take into account any evidence on file that attendance was considered necessary at the time the decision to attend was made. The file must show that the attendance was expected to materially progress the case beyond initial advice. If you were already at the same Police Station, we may cap your Claim to no more than the value of the Police

Station Telephone Advice fixed fee if we consider that advice could have been provided reasonably over the telephone.

17. In the following cases, you may provide Police Station Telephone Advice only and you shall not claim from public funds for any Police Station Attendance unless one of the exceptions in paragraph 18 below applies:

(a) Client detained in relation to a non-imprisonable offence;

(b) Client arrested on a bench warrant for failing to appear and being held for production before the court, except where the solicitor has clear documentary evidence available that would result in the client being released from custody in which case attendance may be allowed provided that the reason is justified on file;

(c) Client arrested on suspicion of:

   (i) driving with excess alcohol who is taken to the Police Station to give a specimen (Section 5 Road Traffic Act 1988);

   (ii) failure to provide a specimen (Sections 6, 7 and 7A Road Traffic Act 1988);

   (iii) driving whilst unfit/drunk in charge of a motor vehicle (Section 4 Road Traffic Act 1988).

(d) Client detained in relation to breach of police or court bail conditions.

18. You may attend the Police Station to advise on any Matter falling within paragraph 17 above if one of the following exceptions applies and the Sufficient Benefit Test is satisfied:

(a) an interview or an identification procedure is going to take place;

(b) the Client is eligible for assistance from an appropriate adult under the PACE Codes of Practice;

(c) the Client requires an interpreter or is otherwise unable to communicate over the telephone;

(d) the Client complains of serious maltreatment by the police;

(e) the investigation includes another alleged offence which does not fall within paragraphs 17(a) to (d) above;

(f) you are already at the same Police Station, in which case you may attend the Client but may not claim more than the Police Station Telephone Advice fixed fee.

If any of the above exceptions apply then you must endorse the reasons for attendance on file, otherwise your Claim will be limited to the Police Station Telephone Advice fixed fee.

19. An attendance at the Police Station for an ineffective bail to return may be disallowed if telephone checks were not made prior to the attendance to establish whether it would be effective.

20. If the police indicate that an interview or identification procedure will take place at a specified time, Police Station Telephone Advice may be provided to the Client. You should attend the Police Station in sufficient time prior to the allotted time to undertake reasonable steps that directly relate to the interview or identification procedure e.g. taking instructions from the Client, obtaining disclosure of evidence, attending the officer in the case.

21. When you attend the Police Station you shall seek to minimise the travel, waiting and attendance time that you incur. In assessing whether your Claims are reasonable we may take into account the average costs incurred by other CDS Suppliers in your region.

22. You may provide further legal advice to the Client immediately following charge, but it will not be reasonable for you to continue to attend the Client thereafter whilst fingerprints, photographs and swabs are taken, except where the Client requires further assistance due to his or her particular circumstances, such as youth or vulnerability, in which case the relevant factors must be noted on file. It is reasonable to remain at the Police Station if you are required to make representations about bail provided that the justification is noted on file.

Enhanced rates for serious offences

Duty solicitor serious offence rates may be claimed for police station attendances provided that:

(a) the attendance is to advise a client under arrest for one or more of the following serious offences, either as a principal or as a secondary party, or who has been arrested on a warrant for failing to answer bail or an extradition warrant in respect of a case in which he or she is accused of such an offence:

    (i)   treason (common law);
    (ii)   murder (common law);
    (iii)   manslaughter (Homicide Act 1957 and common law);
    (iv)   causing death by dangerous driving (Section 1 Road Traffic Act 1988);
    (v)   rape (Section 1 Sexual Offences Act 2003);
    (vi)   assault by penetration (Section 2 Sexual Offences Act 2003);
    (vii)   rape of a child under 13 (Section 5 Sexual Offences Act 2003);
    (viii)   assault of a child under 13 by penetration (Section 6 Sexual Offences Act);
    (ix)   robbery (Section 8 Theft Act 1968);
    (x)   assault with intent to rob (common law);
    (xi)   arson (Section 1(1), 1(2) or 1(3) Criminal Damage Act 1971);
    (xii)   perverting the course of public justice (common law);
    (xiii)   conspiracy to defraud (common law);
    (xiv)   kidnapping (common law);
    (xv)   wounding or grievous bodily harm (Sections 18 and 20 Offences against the Person Act 1861);
    (xvi)   conspiracy to commit any of the above offences (Section 1 Criminal Law Act 1977);
    (xvii)   soliciting or inciting to commit any of the above offences (common law);
    (xviii)   attempting to commit any of the above offences (Sections 1 or 1A Criminal Attempts Act 1981);
    (xix)   any offence if the client is accused of possessing a firearm, shotgun or imitation firearm;
    (xx)   any offence if the client is detained under section 41 of the Terrorism Act 2000;

(b) the Matter has been referred to the firm by the Duty Solicitor Call Centre or the Duty Solicitor Call Centre has been notified if the case is accepted whilst the solicitor is already at the Police Station;

(c) the attendance is personally undertaken by a Duty Solicitor employed by the firm accepting the call from the Duty Solicitor Call Centre.

These rates only apply to claims relating to:

(a) attendances undertaken throughout a duty period; and
(b) attendances that take place after acceptance of a matter up until the point when the client is released from the initial continuous period of custody.

There are no serious offence rates for telephone advice, travelling or waiting. These rates remain the same whether or not serious offences are involved. These rates may not be claimed by CDS suppliers that have had their claims assessed at 'category 3' at the last audit prior to the police station attendance unless either:

(a) the time limit for appealing the assessment has yet to expire; or
(b) within that time limit, an appeal has been made but has not been finally determined.

The general criminal contract describes the above list of offences as 'exhaustive' it would therefore appear that historical sex offences, prosecuted under pre-Sexual Offences Act 2003 legislation would not be eligible.

Scope of duty solicitor advice – magistrates' court

A duty solicitor must provide the following services to any defendant who wishes to receive advice and assistance or advocacy assistance:

1. Advice to a client in custody.
2. The making of a bail application unless the client has received such assistance on a previous occasion.

The following services shall also be provided, save that advocacy assistance cannot be provided in committal proceedings, nor in a not-guilty trial. Further, neither advice and assistance nor advocacy assistance should be provided to a client in connection with a non-imprisonable offence, unless the duty solicitor considers the circumstances exceptional:

3. Assistance to a client in custody on a plea of guilty where the client wishes the case to be concluded at that appearance in court, unless the duty solicitor considers that the case should be adjourned in the interests of justice or of the client. Where the duty solicitor does believe the matter should be adjourned, he can of course still act and make the application for the adjournment.
4. Assistance to a client before the court in respect of failure to pay a sum ordered (whether a fine or other penalty), or a failure to obey an order of the court (e.g. breach of community penalty). Assistance can only be offered where the client is at risk of imprisonment. It is submitted that 'risk' means a real risk as opposed to theoretical, and the duty solicitor

should seek guidance from the clerk before agreeing to act. A first breach for example, where probation are asking for the order to continue would be unlikely to merit assistance being given.

5.   Assistance to a client who is not in custody, in connection with an imprisonable offence (unless exceptional circumstances apply), where the duty solicitor is of the opinion that the client requires such assistance. The duty solicitor could conclude that advice and assistance is sufficient and refuse advocacy assistance.

6.   Assistance with the making of an application for representation in relation to a future court appearance. The duty solicitor must inquire whether the client wishes to instruct another solicitor to act, and if the client does so wish, the duty solicitor must insert the name of that solicitor on the application form. Given that there is now a declaration to sign in relation to the solicitor's panel status, duty solicitors should take care only to sign such declarations in respect of firms which they know or believe meet the appropriate status.

7.   Assistance to parents who face being bound over, or are before the court in respect of breaching such orders.

8.   Assistance in respect of antisocial behaviour orders, sex offender orders and parenting orders, including proceedings to vary or discharge such orders. The scope of this rule covers interim orders.

9.   Assistance in respect of football-banning orders under s.14B Football Spectators Act 1989, including the variation or termination (s.14G) of such orders. Assistance to recipients of a notice under s.21(B)(2) of that Act.

10. Advice and assistance and, where appropriate, advocacy assistance to an individual applying to vary bail conditions imposed by police under s.47(1E) Police and Criminal Evidence Act 1984 (PACE), as amended by the Criminal Justice Act 2003 (CJA 2003).

A duty solicitor may advise in the following cases	A duty solicitor must not advise in these cases
Anyone in custody (must advise) Anyone applying for bail (unless they have used a duty solicitor for a previous bail application) Anyone charged or summonsed with an imprisonable offence (including defendants in extradition proceedings) Anyone at risk of imprisonment for • Failing to pay a fine or other sum (including council tax) • Failing to obey an order of the court (e.g. breach of community penalty)	Anyone in connection with • A trial • A hearing to commit a case to the Crown Court • A bail application (if they have used a duty solicitor for a previous application) • A non-imprisonable offence (unless they are in custody) Anyone who has their own representative or is expecting a representative to arrive (including anyone with a representation order)

Anyone at risk of, or applying to vary or discharge:
- Antisocial behaviour orders and sex offender orders
- Football banning orders

Anyone at risk of a parenting order or being bound over as the parent or guardian of a young offender

Including help to make an application for a representation order, to cover a subsequent appearance, for an individual in one or more of the above categories

Anyone at an adjourned hearing (if they used a duty solicitor for a previous hearing in this case) unless they are at risk of imprisonment for:
- Failing to pay a fine or other sum (including council tax)
- Failing to obey an order of the court (e.g. breach of community penalty)

Anyone to make an application for a representation order to cover a non-imprisonable offence (unless they are in custody)

Anyone at court for any other reason

Note: Subject to local rules, the person acting as Duty Solicitor may also act:
For a client of his/her own firm
For a client of another firm (if he is instructed by them as agent)
For any other person who is not already represented

Providing he/she does not claim for the above work under the Duty Solicitor scheme and as long as he/she remains available for duty solicitor work.

Imprisonable offences include

Obstructing a police officer
School non-attendance (parent at fault) s.444(1A) Education Act 1996
Social security – false representation to obtain benefit
Threatening behaviour (s.4 POA 1986)
Vehicle interference

Football related offences
- Possession of liquor while entering or trying to enter ground

Driving offences
- Dangerous driving
- Driving while disqualified
- Excess alcohol
- Failing to stop/report
- Fraudulent use/vehicle excise licence
- Refuse evidential specimen

Non-imprisonable offences include

Disorderly conduct (s.5 Public Order Act 1986 (POA 1986))
Drunk and disorderly
School non-attendance (parent not at fault) s.444(1) Education Act 1996
Taxi touting
TV licence payment evasion

Football related offences
- Being drunk in, or while trying to enter the ground
- Going onto playing area or adjacent area to which spectators are not admitted
- Throwing missiles
- Ticket touting/unauthorised sale of ticket

Driving Offences
- Careless driving
- No insurance
- Speeding

PREVIOUS ASSISTANCE

A duty solicitor may not act where duty solicitor services have been provided at an earlier hearing in connection with the same matter.

Exception
Where the client is before the court for failure to pay a fine or other sum ordered, or for failing to obey an order of the court, and such failure may lead to the client being at risk of imprisonment.

Golden rules

It is without doubt that the single largest complaint against duty solicitors is the allegation of poaching clients. The following rules are intended to guard against such complaints and, if followed, will leave the solicitor beyond reproach. It should, however, be remembered that the fact that a solicitor acts in relation to one set of proceedings does not mean that the client vests with him. A client properly informed of his right to choose is free to retain the services of a duty solicitor.

A duty solicitor must inform every client that he is not obliged to instruct the duty solicitor.

If a client wishes another solicitor to act, the duty solicitor shall not act unless the named solicitor is not available and the client asks the duty solicitor to act on that occasion only.

If the duty solicitor does not continue to act for the client, he must make available to any solicitor subsequently instructed any relevant information or papers.

Record keeping

Records of those persons assisted during a duty period, along with a note of the advice given should be retained for auditing purposes. A pro forma, used by Public Defender Service (PDS) offices, is available on the LSC website and can be downloaded in word format for the duty solicitor's own use (the PDS logo can be removed for example).

CHAPTER 2

Police station procedure

APPROPRIATE ADULTS

When there must be an appropriate adult

An appropriate adult must attend the police station in the following instances:

1. In the case of a juvenile (under 17 years of age). In the case of a person who appears to be under 17, they shall be treated as a juvenile for the purposes of PACE Code C in the absence of clear evidence that they are older.
2. In the case of a detainee who is mentally disordered or otherwise mentally vulnerable. If an officer has any suspicion, or is told in good faith, that a person of any age may be mentally disordered or otherwise mentally vulnerable, in the absence of clear evidence to dispel that suspicion, the person shall be treated as such for the purposes of Code C.

However, in *R. v. Stratford Youth Court, ex parte DPP* [2001] EWHC Admin 615, the following observation was made at paragraph 11 (words in square brackets added):

> a young man of 17, who, although not a juvenile for Code C purposes, is a juvenile for other legal purposes, has been interviewed both at his own election without representation and without an appropriate adult (because Code C does not apply to him) at a distance of time of 24 hours from his arrest . . . Nobody should underestimate, any more than they should overestimate, the kind of pressure to get things over and done with that a youngster may experience. That is part of the picture. So is the note for guidance at Code C, note C:11(b) *[note that this is different in the amended codes]*. . . It reminds everybody in the criminal justice process, not least those responsible for initiating and conducting interviews, that young people may be particularly prone in certain circumstances to provide information which is unreliable, misleading or self-incriminating.

The court remitted the case back for consideration as to whether the interview should be excluded under s.78 PACE. The judgment leaves open the possibility that the categories of detainees who might need the protections afforded by appropriate adults are not closed, and constant review of a detainee's needs is necessary at all stages of the investigative process.

The importance of an appropriate adult was highlighted (once again) in the case of *R. v. Aspinall* [1999] Crim LR 741 where it was said 'An appropriate adult played a significant role in respect of a vulnerable person whose condition rendered him liable to provide information which was unreliable, misleading or self-incriminating'.

The lack of an appropriate adult will not automatically lead to the exclusion of confession evidence, but will in many cases.

Who can be an appropriate adult?

Code C1.7 states that 'appropriate adult' means:

In the case of a juvenile:

(a) a juvenile's parent or guardian, or if in care (or otherwise being looked after under the Children Act 1989), a person representing the care authority or voluntary organisation;
(b) a social worker of a local authority social services department;
(c) failing either of the above, another responsible adult aged 18 or over who is not a police officer or employed by the police.

In the case of someone who is mentally disordered or mentally vulnerable:

(a) a relative, guardian or other person responsible for their care or custody;
(b) someone who has experience of dealing with mentally disordered or mentally vulnerable people but who is not a police officer or employed by the police (such as an approved social worker as defined by the Mental Health Act 1983 or a specialist social worker); or
(c) failing either of the above, some other responsible adult aged 18 or over who is not a police officer or employed by the police.

Regrettably, appropriate adults seldom have any training for dealing with the situation they face in the police station, in particular they are likely to be totally ignorant of the legal implications of their actions or inaction. In 1995 the Law Society submitted a response to the *Home Office Report of the Review Group on Appropriate Adults*, and called for a national scheme, with local panels of trained and experienced appropriate adults. It is disappointing that nothing has yet come of the idea.

Who cannot be an appropriate adult? (Code C, Note 1B–1D, 1F)

This category includes the following:

1. A police officer or person employed by the police.
2. A solicitor or independent custody visitor (formerly known as a lay visitor) who is present at the police station in that capacity.
3. Any person who is suspected of involvement in the offence, is the victim, is a witness, is involved in the investigation or has received admissions prior to attending to act as the appropriate adult. An estranged parent should not be asked to act if the juvenile expressly and specifically objects to his presence (*DPP* v. *Blake*, *The Times*, 2 January 1989).
4. Any person who would not be seen as impartial, for example an employee of a care home, if the offence was against another employee or to property there. Solicitors should be alert to these kinds of scenarios arising, as they occur frequently.

Role of appropriate adult

An appropriate adult should be present:

(a) during the giving (or repeating) of a detainee's rights and entitlements;
(b) during any interview;
(c) during a search if more than outer clothing is removed;
(d) when the detained person is asked to consent to any procedure;
(e) during charge, fingerprinting and photographing;
(f) when a review of detention takes place.

An appropriate adult is not a mere observer and should assist the detainee in understanding what is happening at the police station, what they are being asked and what their options are.

Interface of appropriate adult and solicitor

A detainee has the right to consult privately with a solicitor – which extends to a consultation without the appropriate adult being present (Code C, Note 1E). This is particularly important given the position with respect to legal privilege and appropriate adults. The right however belongs to the detainee, not the solicitor; it is therefore essential that the detainee knows what is being suggested and the reasons for it. It will be desirable for the solicitor to courteously explain the situation to the appropriate adult.

Legal privilege

The absence of legal privilege is a fundamental fact, which must be addressed by all solicitors in the police station. At the outset, instructions should be taken and advice should be tendered in the absence of the appropriate adult. However, it should be remembered that the appropriate adult is there to facilitate communication, and in cases where the client suffers from mental illness or handicap, the solicitor may not be trained to identify or remedy deficiencies in communication. In such situations it may be wise to take instructions and tender advice in the presence of the appropriate adult, but only with the client's consent, the client having been advised of the risks. It is the policy of many social workers not to disclose information, and they will say as much. However, there is no property in a witness and if the police discovered that a person had pertinent information they could seek to compel that person's evidence at trial. It should not be assumed that such evidence would be excluded, particularly if it was useful in rebuttal (a famous example of this was during the trial of Rosemary West, when the appropriate adult for Fred West gave evidence of what was said in private to her. The prosecution used this to rebut his assertions in interview, admitted at the behest of the defence under s.23 Criminal Justice Act 1988 (CJA 1988), that he was the only person involved in the killings).

Further information

Members of the Criminal Law Solicitors Association (CLSA) can download a fact sheet that can be given to appropriate adults, which explains their rights and role while at the police station (**www.clsa.co.uk**).

ARMED SERVICES PERSONNEL

The representation of armed services personnel raises issues peculiar to military life, and it is unlikely that duty solicitors will be called upon with any great frequency to deal with these types of cases unless their practice falls within the locality of a military base. Nonetheless, the General Criminal Contract provides for coverage of these cases in the scope rules, and all solicitors should be aware of the particular issues that may arise.

For solicitors undertaking this type of work in any quantity, reference should be made to the *Manual of Military Law* (available from TSO).

Contractual rules – own client

A representative who is not a solicitor shall not advise a client who is being investigated in connection with a serious service offence, or at an application to extend detention in military custody before a judicial officer under the Armed Forces Discipline Act 2000.

In particular:

1. Military suspects being investigated for military offences other than summary only must receive advice and assistance from a solicitor and shall not be advised by a non-solicitor representative.
2. The Armed Forces Discipline Act 2000 amends the relevant Service Acts by introducing an entitlement for services personnel to be legally represented at a pre-charge custody hearing. Representation at such hearings must be provided by a solicitor, not a non-solicitor representative.

Contractual rules – duty clients

In addition to initial telephone advice a duty solicitor is expected to undertake the following work in relation to armed services personnel:

1. If the client is a services person at a services establishment or elsewhere assisting with an investigation by the Services Police and suspected of offences contrary to the Services Discipline Acts where:

    (a) the investigation involves any offences which cannot be dealt with summarily; or
    (b) the offence appears to the interviewing Services Police to be serious.

2. The duty solicitor shall attend personally upon the client where he or she considers that such attendance is necessary for the protection of the client's interests.
3. If the client is a services person requiring representation at a custody hearing before a judicial officer under the Armed Forces Discipline Act 2000 the duty solicitor shall attend personally upon the client to provide advice and assistance (including advocacy assistance).

ARRESTABLE OFFENCES

On 1 January 2006 substantial changes to PACE took effect, rendering the old categories of arrestable and serious arrestable offences redundant. The changes are sweeping and now mean that any offence is, in theory, capable of resulting in arrest and detention.

A new power of arrest has been substituted for that previously contained in section 24 PACE, in the following terms:

24 Arrest without warrant: constables
(1) A constable may arrest without a warrant–

    (a) anyone who is about to commit an offence;
    (b) anyone who is in the act of committing an offence;
    (c) anyone whom he has reasonable grounds for suspecting to be about to commit an offence;
    (d) anyone whom he has reasonable grounds for suspecting to be committing an offence.

(2) If a constable has reasonable grounds for suspecting that an offence has been committed, he may arrest without a warrant anyone whom he has reasonable grounds to suspect of being guilty of it.

(3) If an offence has been committed, a constable may arrest without a warrant–

    (a) anyone who is guilty of the offence;

    (b) anyone whom he has reasonable grounds for suspecting to be guilty of it.

(4) But the power of summary arrest conferred by subsection (1), (2) or (3) is exercisable only if the constable has reasonable grounds for believing that for any of the reasons mentioned in subsection (5) it is necessary to arrest the person in question.

(5) The reasons are–

    (a) to enable the name of the person in question to be ascertained (in the case where the constable does not know, and cannot readily ascertain, the person's name, or has reasonable grounds for doubting whether a name given by the person as his name is his real name);

    (b) correspondingly as regards the person's address;

    (c) to prevent the person in question–

        (i) causing physical injury to himself or any other person;

        (ii) suffering physical injury;

        (iii) causing loss of or damage to property;

        (iv) committing an offence against public decency (subject to subsection (6)); or

        (v) causing an unlawful obstruction of the highway;

    (d) to protect a child or other vulnerable person from the person in question;

    (e) to allow the prompt and effective investigation of the offence or of the conduct of the person in question;

    (f) to prevent any prosecution for the offence from being hindered by the disappearance of the person in question.

(6) Subsection (5)(c)(iv) applies only where members of the public going about their normal business cannot reasonably be expected to avoid the person in question.

24A Arrest without warrant: other persons

(1) A person other than a constable may arrest without a warrant–

    (a) anyone who is in the act of committing an indictable offence;

    (b) anyone whom he has reasonable grounds for suspecting to be committing an indictable offence.

(2) Where an indictable offence has been committed, a person other than a constable may arrest without a warrant–

    (a) anyone who is guilty of the offence;

    (b) anyone whom he has reasonable grounds for suspecting to be guilty of it.

(3) But the power of summary arrest conferred by subsection (1) or (2) is exercisable only if–

(a) the person making the arrest has reasonable grounds for believing that for any of the reasons mentioned in subsection (4) it is necessary to arrest the person in question; and

(b) it appears to the person making the arrest that it is not reasonably practicable for a constable to make it instead.

(4) The reasons are to prevent the person in question–

(a) causing physical injury to himself or any other person;
(b) suffering physical injury;
(c) causing loss of or damage to property; or
(d) making off before a constable can assume responsibility for him.

Solicitors should be aware that there may be other legislative provisions which confer powers of arrest.

General arrest conditions (s.25 PACE)

Section 25 of PACE has been repealed. Section 24(5)(a) above replicates the previous power contained in s.25.

Definition of 'serious arrestable offence' (SAO)

This definition is now redundant and no regard need be given to s.116 PACE.

CHARGING, REPRIMANDS AND CAUTIONS

At the conclusion of an investigation the police have the following options:

(a) charge the suspect;
(b) discharge the suspect for summons;
(c) caution an adult;
(d) reprimand or warn a juvenile.

Charging

The decision as to whether there is sufficient evidence to charge a suspect lies with the custody officer or Crown Prosecution Service (CPS) (depending on the offence), and not the officer in the case. Statutory charging under the Criminal Justice Act 2003 is now being rolled out across England and Wales, ensuring that charging decisions are taken largely by the CPS, solicitors need to be familiar with the charging guidance reproduced in Appendix E.

Whilst in practice the officer in the case (OIC) will make representations to the custody officer/CPS, you should not assume that the issue is closed, and need to be able, in appropriate cases, to make representations as to why the suspect should not be charged at all, or be charged with a different offence. All solicitors should ensure therefore that they have a full understanding of the elements of the criminal offence with which they are dealing, and of any defences or statutory obstacles that may assist the suspect. However, it is not the custody officer's job to try the matter and a wide margin of appreciation in his decision-making is to be expected. It is the current practice of the CPS present at police stations for the purposes of giving charge advice not to engage with the defence in relation to whether or not to charge. This does not however stop you trying to make such representations, and the climate does appear to be changing in this respect, with a consultation proposed as to whether contact should be allowed on a formal basis.

In the event that the police are investigating more than one criminal offence, the suspect need not be brought before the custody officer for charge until Code C16.1 is satisfied in relation to all of the offences. He should, however, cease to question the suspect in relation to the offence for which there is sufficient evidence, provided that the officer is satisfied that all relevant questions have been put, the suspect has had an opportunity to give an innocent explanation and he has taken account of any other available evidence (C11.6).

Effect of 'sufficient evidence to charge' on the interview process

Code C11.6 states that the interview must cease when the officer in charge of the investigation:

    (a)   is satisfied all the questions they consider relevant to obtaining accurate and reliable information about the offence have been put to the suspect, this includes allowing the suspect an opportunity to give an innocent explanation and asking questions to test if the explanation is accurate and reliable; . . .

    (b)   has taken account of any other available evidence; and

    (c)   the officer in charge of the investigation, or in the case of a detained suspect, the custody officer, . . . reasonably believes there is sufficient evidence to provide a realistic prospect of conviction for that offence if the person was prosecuted for it.

***R. v. David Elliott* [2002] EWCA Crim 931** The appellant gave a no-comment interview. At trial, the investigating officer admitted that he had sufficient evidence to charge prior to the interview taking place. However, no fixed decision had been taken to charge the suspect, irrespective of his response in interview, and therefore the interview was not in breach of Code C. An interviewing officer was entitled to give an accused an opportunity to put forward his own account when there was sufficient evidence to charge and an account from the accused could serve to reduce or extinguish the prospects of a successful prosecution. Whether an offence had been committed depended as much on the availability of defences as it did on the proof of *actus reus* and *mens rea*. Accordingly, since s.34 Criminal Justice and Public Order Act 1994 (CJPOA 1994) applied where an officer was trying to discover whether or by whom the offence had been committed, the interview was justifiable and an adverse inference could be drawn.

***R. v. Pointer* [1997] Crim LR 676** In this case the interviewing officer stated that before he had interviewed the suspect he believed that there was sufficient evidence for a successful prosecution and that a prosecution should be brought. If the suspect chooses to say something, then an interview should be held for that purpose; if he declines, no interview should take place, or a current interview should cease. If an interview takes place for the purposes of allowing the suspect to say what he wishes, no inference should be drawn from any refusal to answer questions during that interview.

***R. v. Odeyemi* [1999] Crim LR 828** In this case *Pointer* was distinguished: it was desirable that officers should have the chance to question suspects in order that explanations could be put forward which showed that either no offence had been committed or that the offence had been committed by someone else so that the police in appropriate cases look in other directions before evidence disappeared and be sure that they were not accusing the wrong person. It was only where the officer was truly of the opinion that there was sufficient evidence for such a prosecution to succeed, that interviewing should be avoided or, if it was already in progress, stopped.

It is clear from this author's experience that the police have been quick to embrace the opportunities offered by *Odeyemi* and other cases, and now will rarely be drawn on the question of whether or not they have sufficient evidence to charge and succeed with a prosecution. A solicitor's view that the evidence is overwhelming should not now be the sole reason behind a decision to advise a client to make no comment in interview.

Responding to the caution on charge

When charging takes place, the suspect will be cautioned in the usual manner: 'you do not have to say anything. But it may harm your defence if you do not mention now something which you later rely on in court. Anything you do say should be given in evidence'.

In practice if an account is given in interview no point would be taken if no response was given at charge. Similarly, if a suspect made a no-comment interview, later silence would not in reality compound the matter. Nonetheless, solicitors should seek to protect their client from the strict letter of the law, and, in a case where an account has been given in interview, it is good practice to get a client to state on charge, words to the effect of 'I have given an account in interview which I now adopt'.

The question arises as to whether it is preferable to get a suspect to state his defence at charge, after giving a no-comment interview. Very often such statements will be prepared in writing and presented to the custody officer. The efficacy of this approach is considered in the later section on interviews.

Discharging for summons

This procedure tends to be used in relation to relatively minor road traffic offences. The police will initiate proceedings by the issue of a summons.

Adult cautions

Cautions are an alternative to charging and solicitors should be ready to propose their use in cases where the suspect has admitted or will admit his guilt. Solicitors should, however, be careful to ascertain that a client is admitting an offence of his own free will and not just because a caution will be available if guilt is admitted. Solicitors need to understand that the imposition of a caution may well have serious consequences in relation to some suspects, such as the operation of the notification requirement for sex offenders (see *R.* v. *Greater Manchester Police, ex parte R*, *The Independent*, 23 October 2000), and future good-character directions in criminal proceedings (see *R.* v. *David Martin* [2000] Crim LR 615).

Before a caution is administered, the police must be satisfied in relation to the following factors:

1. There is sufficient evidence on which to convict.
2. The suspect admits guilt. An admission of guilt will always support, but not necessarily conclusively, ground 1.

Cautions should be administered in accordance with Home Office guidance (Circular 30/2005).

Police forces often have their own policy guidance in relation to cautioning suggesting which offences might be suitable. Home Office guidance has been issued in relation to the new reprimand and warning scheme which will be of assistance in relation to adult cautions and should be relied upon by practitioners (see below).

A failure to consult a complainant in a criminal matter could render the subsequent caution of the offender unlawful. The imposition of a caution would not, save in exceptional circumstances, act as a bar to future criminal prosecution for the same offence (see *R. (on the application of Omar)* v. *Chief Constable of Bedford Police* [2002] EWHC 3060 and, more recently, *Jones* v. *Whalley* [2005] EWHC 931 (Admin) a case where a person brought a private prosecution following W's caution for an offence of assault).

Reprimands and warnings

Reprimands and warnings replaced cautioning for young offenders aged under 18. The scheme is detailed and solicitors are advised to obtain a copy of the full Home Office guidance, which is available from **www.homeoffice.gov.uk**. It is important to remember that a reprimand or warning is designed to be given at the police station following an admission of guilt. There is no requirement on the police, following charge, to administer a reprimand or warning to a young person who has had a change of heart in relation to the issue of guilt (*R. (F)* v. *Crown Prosecution Service* [2003] EWHC 3266 (Admin)).

The following criteria must be satisfied:

1. There is evidence against the young person sufficient to give a realistic prospect of conviction if he was prosecuted.
2. The young person admits the offence.
3. The young person has not previously been convicted of an offence (recordable or non-recordable).
4. It is not in the public interest for the offender to be prosecuted. In particular see points 4 and 5 in relation to adult cautions and indictable-only offences – these criteria similarly apply to young offenders.

Reprimand or warning?

The following should be borne in mind:

1. First-time offenders should normally receive a reprimand for a less serious offence.
2. Second-time offenders who have been reprimanded previously cannot be given a further reprimand – they should either be warned or, if the circumstances warrant it, charged.
3. Second-time offenders who have previously been warned cannot be given a reprimand and should not be further warned (therefore they should be charged); the only exception is where the new offence has been committed more than two years since the previous warning and the offence and its circumstances are not so serious to require a charge.
4. Third-time offenders who have already received a reprimand and a warning cannot be given a further reprimand and should not usually receive a further warning. They should be charged unless the new offence has been committed more than two years since the previous warning and the offence and its circumstances are not so serious as to require a charge.
5. Those offending for the fourth time or more, who have previously received a reprimand or warning, must be charged.

The Association of Chief Police Officers has produced guidance on assessing gravity factors, which will guide the police in deciding whether to reprimand, warn or charge.

DETENTION RULES

General

A suspect must be either charged or released within 24 hours (unless the period is extended, for which see below) of the time of his arrival at the police station, or the time of his arrest. The relevant time is the earlier of either his arrival at the police station or the time of his arrest.

There are a number of scenarios that require consideration as they impact upon how the release time is calculated (s.41 PACE).

In the case of a person arrested outside England and Wales the relevant time shall be whichever is the earlier of:

(a) the time at which that person arrives at the first police station to which he is taken in the police area in England and Wales in which the offence for which he was arrested is being investigated; or

(b) the time 24 hours after the time of that person's entry into England and Wales, whichever is the earlier.

Volunteers

In the case of a person who attends voluntarily at a police station or accompanies a constable to a police station without having been arrested, and is arrested at the police station, the time of his arrest is the 'relevant time'.

Arrests out of area

If a person's arrest is sought in one police area in England and Wales and he is arrested in another police area; and he is not questioned in the area in which he is arrested in order to obtain evidence in relation to an offence for which he is arrested, then the relevant time is the earlier of 24 hours after his arrival at a police station in the second area, or 24 hours after his arrest.

Hospitalisation

Where a person who is in police detention is removed to hospital because he is in need of medical treatment, any time during which he is being questioned in hospital or on the way there or back by a police officer for the purpose of obtaining evidence relating to an offence shall be included in any period which falls to be calculated, but any other time while he is in hospital or on his way there or back shall not be included. Essentially, hospitalisation has the effect of stopping the custody clock, provided that questioning is not taking place.

Detention can be extended beyond 24 hours in the circumstances outlined below.

Purpose of detention (s.37 PACE)

The custody officer must determine whether he has sufficient evidence to charge the suspect with the offence for which he was arrested. If there is sufficient evidence, he may detain him for such period as is necessary to charge. Post-charge detention can also be authorised; see below.

Where there is insufficient evidence to charge, the suspect shall be released either on bail or without bail, unless the custody officer has reasonable grounds for believing that his detention without charge is necessary to:

(a) secure or preserve evidence relating to an offence for which he is under arrest; or

(b) obtain such evidence by questioning him.

Where there is sufficient evidence to charge, the suspect shall be charged, or shall be released without charge, either on bail or without bail. Where a suspect has not been charged, because a decision as to whether or not to prosecute has yet to be made (or the charge is to be decided), the custody officer has a duty to inform the suspect of the situation.

Where a suspect is unfit to be charged he may be kept in detention until fit (s.37(9) PACE).

Fixed review periods (s.40 PACE)

Overview

First review no later than 6 hours	Second review no later than 15 hours	Third review no later than 24 hours, subsequent reviews no later than every 9 hours thereafter	Detention extending to 36 hours with authorisation	Detention beyond 36 hours with court authorisation, to a maximum of 96 hours (each single extension cannot exceed 36 hours, save in terrorist cases)

Detention must be reviewed (s.40 PACE):

(a) no later than six hours after detention was first authorised;

(b) second review not later than nine hours after the first;

(c) subsequent reviews at intervals of not more than nine hours.

28

A review may be postponed if, having regard to all the circumstances prevailing at the latest time for the review specified, it is not practicable to carry out the review. Where no review officer is available, or where a review did not take place because the suspect was in interview and it was believed that interrupting the interview would prejudice the investigation, the postponed review shall be carried out as soon as practicable afterwards.

Delayed review does not affect the timing of subsequent reviews.

A detainee produced from prison is not subject to review under s.40, nor is a person arrested for breach of bail or breach of the peace.

Rights on review

Before determining whether to authorise a person's continued detention, the review officer shall give the suspect (unless he is asleep or violent for example), or any solicitor representing him at the time of the review, an opportunity to make representations about the detention.

Continuing duty to monitor detention

If at any time a custody officer becomes aware that the grounds for the detention of a person have ceased to apply and he is not aware of any other grounds on which the continued detention of that person could be justified, then it shall be the duty of the officer to order his immediate release from custody (subject to there being no other lawful holding order) (s.34 PACE).

Detention beyond 24 hours but not exceeding 36 hours (s.42 PACE)

Where a police officer of at least the rank of superintendent has reasonable grounds for believing that:

(a) the detention of a person without charge is necessary to secure or preserve evidence relating to an offence for which he is under arrest or to obtain such evidence by questioning him;
(b) an offence for which he is under arrest is an arrestable offence; and
(c) the investigation is being conducted diligently and expeditiously

he may authorise the keeping of that person in police detention for a period expiring at or before 36 hours after the relevant time.

The extension should be for no longer than is absolutely necessary to achieve the objectives provided for. Subsequent extensions can be granted, subject to the overall limit of 36 hours.

The authorisation must be given before 24 hours after the relevant time has elapsed, and may not be given before the second review of detention (i.e. before 15 hours). A detained person or his solicitor must be given an opportunity to make representations.

Prior to CJA 2003, detention beyond 24 hours was only permissible for serious arrestable offences. The newly extended power is however to be used sparingly, and only where fully justified. The authorising officer must also be satisfied that alternatives to continued detention have been considered, for example bail, restorative justice, etc. and the reasons for their lack of appropriateness.

Home Office Circular 60/2003 states the following in relation to juveniles:

Detaining a juvenile or a mentally vulnerable person for longer than 24 hours without charge will only normally be justifiable where the offence is a *serious arrestable offence*. Any departure from this will need strong regard to their:

- special vulnerability;
- the legal obligation to provide an opportunity for representations to be made prior to a decision about extending detention;
- the need to consult and consider the views of any appropriate adult protecting the interests of a juvenile or mentally vulnerable person; and
- the alternatives to police custody.

Given that the term serious arrestable offence no longer has any meaning under PACE, solicitors will need to revert to pre-January 2006 definitions (for which see the repealed s.116).

Detention beyond 36 hours – warrant of further detention

The police cannot authorise detention beyond 36 hours: only a magistrates' court has such power, on an application for a warrant of further detention.

Timing of application

An application for a warrant of further detention may be made at any time before the expiry of 36 hours after the relevant time; or in a case where (a) it is not practicable for the magistrates' court to which the application will be made to sit at the expiry of 36 hours after the relevant time; but (b) the court will sit during the six hours following the end of that period, at any time before the expiry of the said six hours.

If an application for a warrant of further detention is made after the expiry of 36 hours after the relevant time and it appears to the court that it would have been reasonable for the police to have made it before the expiry of that period, the court shall dismiss the application (*R. v. Slough Justices, ex parte Stirling* [1987] Crim LR 576). The time of the application is the point at which the police begin to give evidence on oath, not the lodging of the information.

If the suspect has already been charged with one offence, it is submitted that it is not proper for an application for a warrant of further detention in relation to the remaining offence(s) to be made. The reasoning behind this is to be found in s.46(1) PACE, which states that a person charged (and who is

30

not going to be bailed) shall be brought before a magistrates' court as soon as is practicable. The proper method of dealing with this situation is to invite the court to remand the suspect into police custody (a three-day lie-down).

Contents of application

The application must state the following:

(a) the nature of the offence for which the person to whom the application relates has been arrested;
(b) the general nature of the evidence on which that person was arrested;
(c) what inquiries relating to the offence have been made by the police and what further inquiries are proposed by them;
(d) the reasons for believing the continued detention of that person to be necessary for the purposes of such further inquiries.

The detainee may be lawfully kept in custody until the application is heard.

Legal representation

The detainee has the right to legal representation and the hearing may be adjourned for that to be obtained. He may be legally held in custody during that adjournment. It should be noted that only those persons with a right of audience before the magistrates' court can appear on behalf of the accused.

Authorisation of continued detention

A court may authorise further detention where on an application on oath made by a constable and supported by an information, it is satisfied that there are reasonable grounds for believing that further detention of the person to whom the application relates is justified.

The court must be satisfied that:

(a) his detention without charge is necessary to secure or preserve evidence relating to an offence for which he is under arrest or to obtain such evidence by questioning him;
(b) an offence for which he is under arrest is an indictable offence; and
(c) the investigation is being conducted diligently and expeditiously.

The warrant can authorise further detention for a maximum period of 36 hours. A court should only grant an extension for the period necessary for the police to secure or preserve evidence or question the suspect. In determining the extension period, the court must have regard to the evidence before the court.

If the court is not satisfied as to the above criteria, it shall refuse the application, or adjourn the hearing of it until a time not later than 36 hours after

31

the relevant time. An adjournment could be granted where, for example, the court wished to hear from an officer not present at that hearing.

Resisting the application

The hearing allows the advocate an opportunity to have examined by the court the lawfulness of the suspect's current detention. Solicitors should take care to ensure that only relevant information is placed before a court – the suspect's antecedent history is of no relevance for example, as the questions the court needs to determine cannot in any way be answered by reference to it. An unlawful detention cannot be extended. In *Re an Application for a Warrant of Further Detention* [1988] Crim LR 296, it was successfully argued that the fact that custody had been extended to 36 hours, without hearing representations, is enough to vitiate the lawfulness of the current detention, and accordingly no extension could be granted.

It is frequently argued that, because a suspect has not answered questions in interview, there are no grounds for his continued detention and interview. It is submitted that this argument is flawed as the police still have the right to try to obtain such evidence. The argument carries more force, however, if it can be shown that no new areas of questioning are being pursued, or that the police are simply continuing to question on the same topics with the aim of 'breaking' the suspect. Professor Michael Zander QC cites the following response by the Home Office minister during the committee stage for PACE 1984:

> I do not doubt that in practice when interpreting the Bill, the court would ask questions and want to hear evidence on how fruitful interviews had been if the application for further detention were based on this ground.
> *Hansard*, February 16 1984, Cols. 1228–1229

Advocates should be able to cross-examine the police on the current stage of their inquiries, and particularly in relation to whether the inquiries are being carried out diligently and expeditiously. If the inquiries are other than the immediate interviewing of the suspect, the question arises as to why the suspect needs to be held in custody for the inquiries to take place, particularly in cases where there are no outstanding suspects and the alleged victim is unknown to the suspect. Any further interviewing as a result of information that may come to light could be carried out on the suspect's return to the police station.

Where further detention is refused, the detainee shall be charged forthwith or released either on bail or without bail. The release need not take place, however, before 24 hours after the relevant time, or, if the 24-hour period had been extended prior to the application for a warrant of further detention, before that extended time.

Following a dismissal of the application, no further applications can be made unless supported by evidence which has come to light since the refusal.

A copy of the information must be served on the person to whom the application relates and that person must be brought before the court for the hearing.

Following a successful application for a warrant of further detention, subsequent applications can be granted, provided the criteria are met, for periods not in excess of 36 hours. The maximum, cumulative period of detention cannot exceed 96 hours.

Funding

Duty solicitor representation at the hearing of a warrant of further detention is covered by the scheme. Own solicitors are similarly permitted to undertake this work.

Detention after charge (s.38 PACE)

Following charge, a suspect must be either bailed to appear before a court or held in custody in order to be produced before a court. Bail can only be withheld in the following circumstances:

Adults

(a) his name or address cannot be ascertained or the custody officer has reasonable grounds for doubting whether a name or address furnished by him is his real name or address;

(b) the custody officer has reasonable grounds for believing that the person arrested will fail to appear in court to answer to bail;

(c) in the case of a person arrested for an imprisonable offence, the custody officer has reasonable grounds for believing that the detention of the arrested person is necessary to prevent him committing an offence;

(d) in a case where a sample may be taken from the person under s.63B, the custody officer has reasonable grounds for believing that the detention of the person is necessary to enable the sample to be taken from him;

(e) in the case of a person arrested for an offence which is not an imprisonable offence, the custody officer has reasonable grounds for believing that the detention of the person arrested is necessary to prevent him from causing physical injury to any other person or from causing loss of or damage to property;

(f) the custody officer has reasonable grounds for believing that the detention of the person arrested is necessary to prevent him from interfering with the administration of justice or with the investigation of offences or of a particular offence; or

33

(g) the custody officer has reasonable grounds for believing that the detention of the person arrested is necessary for his own protection.

Juveniles

(a) any of the above grounds (a–g) apply (but subject to any minimum age
requirement for testing); or
(b) the custody officer has reasonable grounds for believing that he ought to
be detained in his own interests.

Making representations

Many of the exceptions listed above mirror those in the Bail Act. A custody
officer when considering those exceptions must have regard to the same considerations as those which a court is required to have regard to in taking the
corresponding decisions under the Bail Act (s.38(2A)). This would suggest that
he must take into account factors placed before him by the defence, although
it is submitted that he must still take the prosecution case at its highest.

Juveniles – place of detention

A detained juvenile must be moved to local authority accommodation unless
the custody officer certifies:

(a) it is not practicable for him to do so (for example because the local
authority refuses to take the juvenile); or
(b) that in the case of a juvenile who has attained the age of 12 years, that
no secure accommodation is available and that keeping him in other
local authority accommodation would not be adequate to protect the
public from serious harm from him.

A custody officer remains in overall charge of a juvenile, and if he is dissatisfied with the arrangements made by the local authority to receive the juvenile,
he is entitled to decide that the juvenile should remain in custody at a police
station (*R.* v. *Chief Constable of Cambridgeshire, ex parte Michel* [1991] Crim
LR 382).

It is important that duty solicitors are able to liaise independently with the
local authority, and it is desirable that such solicitors have with them a
contact number for the emergency duty team, at the local social services
department.

Appearing before a court

If the person charged is to be brought before a magistrates' court for the petty
sessions area in which the police station at which he was charged is situated,

he shall be brought before such a court as soon as is practicable and in any event not later than the first sitting after he is charged with the offence.

If no court is due to sit on the day he is charged or the next day the police must notify the clerk to the court, so that arrangements can be made for a court to sit (no later than the next day).

If the person charged is to be brought before a magistrates' court for a petty sessions area other than that in which the police station at which he was charged is situated, he shall be removed to that area as soon as is practicable and brought before such a court as soon as is practicable after his arrival in the area and in any event not later than the first sitting of a magistrates' court for that area after his arrival in the area. Again, if no court is scheduled to sit, arrangements must be made to convene an occasional court (to sit no later than the next day following his arrival in the area).

There is considerable debate in relation to courts' use of 'cut-off times', whereby defendants not delivered at court by, say noon, will not be accepted, and must be produced the following day. It is submitted that any rigid policy may well be *Wednesbury* unreasonable, but, nevertheless, it should be remembered that the court has an inherent discretion in the running of court business and is entitled to schedule and plan cases accordingly. The police discharge their duty by notifying the clerk to the justices of the existence of the prisoner (*R.* v. *Avon Magistrates' Court Committee, ex parte Broome* [1998] 1 WLR 1246). It is doubtful therefore whether a writ of *habeas corpus* could properly lie to challenge continued detention in circumstances where the prisoner is to be produced the next day.

Warrants

A typical scenario is the questioning of a person on a new matter at a time when there is an outstanding no-bail warrant. The police need not execute the warrant until their inquiries into the new offence are complete, even though this may have the effect of keeping a person in custody for a prolonged period, typically a weekend (*Henderson* v. *Chief Constable Cleveland Constabulary* [2001] 1 WLR 1103).

Detention in relation to those suspected of swallowing drugs

Section 152 of CJA 1988, permits a magistrates' court to commit a person charged with an offence under s.5(2) Misuse of Drugs Act 1971 (possession of a controlled drug) or a drug trafficking offence into the custody of a HMRC officer for a period of up to 192 hours to allow for drugs to be passed naturally and preserved as evidence. Section 8 Drugs Act 2005 will amend this power to allow for the remand of such people into police custody.

Effect of unlawful detention on court process

In *DPP* v. *Park* [2002] EWHC 1248 the Administrative Court held that the magistrates had no power to discharge proceedings on the ground that charging took place 30 minutes after the maximum time allowed, which meant that during charge he was unlawfully detained. In such circumstances any remedy would be civil in nature.

FINGERPRINTS, TAKING AND RETENTION

(See: Police and Criminal Evidence Act 1984 ss.61, 63A, 64, 65.)

Right to take fingerprints

With consent

The police can take fingerprints if a person consents. For a person under 14 years the consent must be of the parent or guardian. For someone aged 14 to 16 years the consent of the parent/guardian and juvenile are required. If the person is at the police station the consent must be in writing.

Without consent

Fingerprints can be taken without consent in the following circumstances:

- suspect detained at a police station as a result of arrest for a recordable offence and has not had fingerprints taken in the course of the investigation for that offence;
- suspect detained at a police station on being charged with or reported for a recordable offence, and has not had fingerprints taken in the course of the investigation for that offence;
- in the above cases where fingerprints have been taken but they are not of sufficient quality;
- where a person answers bail at the police station and there are reasonable grounds for disputing the identity of that person, or that person disputes identity (an officer of at least the rank of inspector must give authority); or
- following conviction, reprimand, caution or warning.

Use made of fingerprints

If a person has been arrested on suspicion of having committed a recordable offence, or has been convicted, charged or reported for summons, a speculative search can be carried out. If a person does not fall into the above cat-

36

egory consent must be given for the purposes of a speculative search, and once given cannot be withdrawn.

Destruction of fingerprints

The only instance where a person has the right to have fingerprint samples destroyed is where that person was not a suspect in an investigation and no-one has been convicted of the crime, e.g. elimination purposes. If a person was convicted, and that person also gave samples, the samples of the non-suspect can be retained.

If a person gave consent for retention that consent cannot be withdrawn.

FITNESS FOR DETENTION AND INTERVIEW

The custody officer must call the police surgeon or, if necessary, take more immediate action (for example by calling an ambulance) if a person brought to the police station or already detained there:

(a) appears to be suffering from physical illness or a mental disorder; or
(b) is injured; or
(c) fails to respond normally to questions or conversations (other than through drunkenness alone); or
(d) otherwise appears to be in need of medical attention.

It does not matter whether the detained person makes a request to see a doctor, nor does it matter that he has already received treatment elsewhere; if the above indicators are present the custody officer should act appropriately.

Disputes

If a request to see a doctor is refused by the custody officer, the solicitor should ensure that such refusal is recorded on the custody record. The detained person has the right to consult, at his own expense, a doctor of his own choosing. A solicitor should therefore consider in an appropriate case instructing a doctor to attend the police station to carry out an examination. Fees payable would be recoverable as a disbursement. In practice it is extremely difficult to access such doctors and it is to be hoped that this gap in medical provision will be filled in the near future.

If, despite an indication from a police surgeon that a detained person is fit for interview, the solicitor believes the contrary to be the case, this will almost certainly justify giving advice that questions should not be answered in interview. A solicitor should, however, be ready to justify his own assessment in later court proceedings should the issue arise, and it would be prudent to record in as much detail as possible the factors which were still of concern to the solicitor.

Substance misuse

One of the major areas of concern in relation to detainees arises as a result of the large numbers of detainees who enter custody suffering from the effects of drug misuse. Solicitors should obtain and consider Royal College of Psychiatrists guidelines on dealing with these cases, which can be obtained in PDF format (**www.rcpsych.ac.uk/publications/cr/cr81.htm**).

Urgent interviews (see C11.18)

No person, who is unfit through drink or drugs to the extent that he is unable to appreciate the significance of questions put to him and his answers, nor any person who requires an appropriate adult or interpreter but does not have one present may be questioned about an alleged offence in that condition, save when the exception in Code C applies. An interview can take place if an officer of the rank of superintendent or above considers that delay will lead to (a) interference with or harm to evidence connected with an offence or interference with or physical harm to other people, or (b) lead to the alerting of other people suspected of having committed an offence but not yet arrested for it, or (c) hindering the recovery of property obtained in consequence of the commission of an offence (see Code C11.18).

IDENTIFICATION PROCEDURES

Code D of PACE provides the framework for identification procedures and is reproduced at Appendix A. The code provides that where there is disputed identification evidence, and where the identity of the suspect is known to the police and he is available, the following identification procedures may be used:

1. Video identification, where the witness is shown images of a known suspect together with images of other people who resemble the suspect (commonly known as a VIPER procedure).
2. Identification parade, where the witness sees the suspect in a line of other people who resemble the suspect.
3. Group identification, where the witness sees the suspect in an informal group of people.
4. Confrontation, where the suspect is directly confronted by the witness. This procedure may be used when it has not proved possible to arrange any of the other means of identification.

The placing of video identification at the top of the identification hierarchy reflects the government's desire to move cases more quickly through the system. Most major police stations now have the technology required to conduct video-identification procedures within hours of arrest if necessary.

Known suspects

A suspect is known when there is sufficient information known to the police to justify the arrest of a particular person for suspected involvement in the offence (D3.4).

When suspect not available

If a suspect is known but not available a covert identification can take place (utilising a video-identification procedure). A group or photo-fit identification is also permissible. See Code D3.21.

Available suspect

A suspect is available if he can immediately take part in the procedure or he will become available within a reasonably short time. A known suspect who fails or refuses to take part in any identification procedure which it is practicable to arrange, or takes steps to prevent himself from being seen by a witness in such a procedure, may be treated as not being available for identification purposes, and the procedures above can be followed.

When parades must be held

If a suspect disputes an identification or the officer in charge of the investigation considers that an identification procedure would be useful, then an identification procedure must be carried out (see *R.* v. *Forbes* [2001] 1 Cr App R 430). Identification is not necessarily disputed simply by remaining silent in interview: it would be prudent in such cases for the solicitor to notify the police that an identification procedure is requested, otherwise a dock identification might well be allowed in some cases (*Karia* v. *DPP* [2002] EWHC 2175).

Which procedure?

The officer in the case may choose freely between a video identification and a parade, with a presumption that a video identification will be held where it could be completed sooner than a parade (D3.14). It is open to the suspect and his solicitor to make representations which must be considered; if, after consideration, the officer's decision stands, the reasons for that decision must be recorded. An officer may initially offer a group identification if it is considered more satisfactory in the circumstances, and it is practicable to arrange. It is difficult to see how the use of this procedure as a first resort can ever be justified.

If the suspect refuses to co-operate with the offered options, the identification officer has discretion to make arrangements for a covert video identification or a group identification.

As a last resort, the identification officer may arrange for the suspect to be confronted by the witness. No consent from the suspect is required, as it does not require his co-operation.

There is some evidence to suggest that video-identification procedures may be fairer to non-white suspects than a live line-up (Valentine *et al*, 'Are police video identifications fair to African-Caribbean suspects?', *Applied Cognitive Psychology*, (2003) 17, 459–76), and a solicitor should consider making appropriate representations in this respect.

Arranging the procedure

The suspect must be given a notice before a video identification, identification parade or group identification is arranged. The contents of the notice are detailed at Code D3.17.

Impartiality

No officer involved in the investigation may take part in any identification procedure. Breach of this rule is highly likely to render the procedure inadmissible (see *R. v. Gall* (1990) 90 Cr App R 64).

Detailed procedures

Guidance on the format of each procedure is given in the Annexes to Code D and should be consulted in detail.

It is incumbent on the solicitor to pay close attention to the operation of the parade to ensure that procedures are properly followed and documented. It is important that the seemingly insignificant details are not ignored, such as the wearing of shoes without laces by the suspect – if a police officer were to view the parade, he may well spot this and conclude that the person without laces was the suspect, not an unreasonable conclusion since a suspect held in custody would not have access to laces.

It is established that it is proper for two solicitors to attend upon an identification parade, and both can properly claim from the Criminal Defence Service fund for this purpose. This is to ensure that one solicitor can deal with the suspect, and that the other can properly monitor the conduct of the parade.

Steps should be taken to hide distinguishing features, such as scars or tattoos, in appropriate cases. This can be achieved by all participants in the procedure covering the offending item, for example by each wearing a plaster, or by the participants all wearing hats. The practice of all participants sitting significantly assists in equalising heights. Care should be taken, however, and hats should only be used when they were used by a person during the offence in question; extra caution should be taken before embarking on the use of make-up in case the witness viewing the parade is able to see that the suspect has not himself used it (*R.* v. *Marrin, The Times,* 5 March 2002).

A solicitor should seek to organise a procedure that contains participants who resemble the suspect, so far as that is practicable. Objection can be made to particular participants, and there is unlikely to be any problem with the identification officer unless the objection results in too few participants being available. Some police forces are adhering to the strict letter of Code D and only allowing representations on the administration of an identification procedure to be made by the suspect and not his solicitor.

A suspect can take any position on a parade but cannot interfere with the positioning of the other participants.

Solicitors have perhaps begun to feel that breaches of PACE rarely result in the exclusion of evidence; it is incumbent on the solicitor, in appropriate cases to make the challenge, and reference should be made to *Butterworths Police and Criminal Evidence Act Cases* or other publications. Appeals have been allowed for example in instances where the witness has failed to view the parade fully.

Advising the suspect

Suspects frequently want advice as to whether they should take part in an identification procedure. If the police already have a positive identification, in the street for example, the prosecution would be able to proceed regardless of any identification procedure, and it would generally be in the suspect's best interests to ask for a parade, as a failure to identify the suspect in those circumstances may well mean the end of the prosecution. However, a positive identification (at a later time) takes away the opportunity to challenge realistically an earlier street identification (on the basis of poor lighting, distance, intoxication of witness, etc.), and while it is suggested that they are only confirming their initial wrong identification, the argument is not so easily made in front of a jury. There is a very careful balancing exercise to be undertaken, which must only be done with the suspect's full consent after being informed of all the available options.

Where an identification procedure is necessary for the prosecution to continue it must be assumed that if co-operation is not forthcoming the police will resort to methods not requiring the suspect's involvement. The common view is that the lower down the identification hierarchy you go, the less protection is afforded to the suspect, with a confrontation being viewed as affording almost no protection.

Recognition

If the evidence of the witness is 'A man I know as Joe Smith stole my car', the question arises as to whether an identification parade is necessary. If the suspect disputes his association with the witness, then a parade should be held; similarly, if the association is weak or remote in time a parade may well be advantageous.

IMMIGRATION ISSUES

Introduction

> Immigration law is often complex and clients with immigration matters may be very vulnerable . . . It is anticipated that in all cases where the adviser who is not an immigration specialist, he or she will make efforts to refer the immigration case on to a specialist at the earliest opportunity. . . . However, given the nature of police station work at present, a police station adviser without specialist knowledge may need to take some initial steps in respect of the case and, in doing so, may need to negotiate with both the police and the immigration authorities.
>
> Brennan, R. *Immigration Advice at the Police Station* (3rd Edn),
> Law Society Publishing, 2006, p. 1.

The only way to be able to advise properly a detained person in relation to immigration issues is to become an expert in that field. Accordingly, unless you have the necessary expertise (i.e. you are an immigration law specialist) the case should be referred immediately to someone who has. The above book is an excellent *starting* point, and is required reading for all police station practitioners, but that book, albeit running to 400 pages is no substitute for specialist and detailed knowledge of the intricate and complicated procedures which apply and, as importantly, can be executed at speed, and should only be used as an emergency resource when a case cannot be referred on. All firms should have referral procedures in place to ensure that their staff are able to make appropriate arrangements at any time of day or night.

The reality of the situation is that the chances of getting a client referred on to an immigration specialist willing and able to attend at a police station at short notice is slim, even in the day. This is not however an excuse to 'make do and mend', and try to offer assistance, either you are an immigration specialist or you are not. If not, you have no place advising.

In relation to offences under the Immigration and other Acts, advice should of course be given, they are criminal offences just like any other.

Professional ethics

Irrespective of any perceived contractual requirement, a duty solicitor is not bound to accept a case outside his area of expertise. A solicitor shall not do anything in the course of practising as a solicitor which compromises or impairs the solicitor's duty to act in the best interests of the client, which includes in appropriate cases a duty not to act at all (Practice Rule 1, *The Guide to the Professional Conduct of Solicitors 1999*, published by the Law Society).

> It should be remembered that, if wrong or incomplete advice is given, it could result in a client being removed from the country and returned to a state where they have been persecuted – be under no illusion: many people enter this country as genuine victims of brutal and sadistic regimes.

The General Criminal Contract (Part B para. 3.6) states that:

1. Where it becomes apparent that an immigration offence has been committed or that an immigration issue arises, you shall give advice and assistance to the client up to the point where the immigration authorities take over conduct of the investigation.
2. You may continue to advise if the client remains in custody, however, you should consider whether it is practicable to refer the immigration offence or issue to a supplier with a contract in the immigration category of work.

You should not generally give police station advice and assistance where:

1. An individual is detained after entry and is served with illegal entry papers or a notice of intention to deport.
2. An individual is detained by the immigration authorities on entry.
3. An individual is arrested by police on behalf of the immigration authorities where no criminal allegations are made and is detained under the immigration authorities' administrative powers.

Duty solicitors have a contractual duty to accept all calls referred, even cases that relate to pure immigration law matters. In such circumstances the call should be accepted and the suspect spoken to; the extent of the advice though will simply be to try to arrange onward referral.

Interview problems

If you are satisfied that you are dealing with an immigration offence, which is unlikely to raise other immigration issues (for example a British national being investigated for conspiring to facilitate illegal entry), you can act and treat the offence as you would any other criminal offence. If the immigration authorities take over the investigation, however, you do need to consider referring it on, although you may conclude it is not practicable to do so given the circumstances.

The real difficulty arises where the immigration authorities take over a case at the outset and conduct the interview. The practice is to conduct a wide-ranging interview, which will seldom be limited to investigation of the criminal offence you are more likely to be concerned with. In such instances a two-part interview should be insisted upon, so that the matters can be kept separate. In practice, however, there will be considerable overlap, and you may not even know the significance of many of the questions asked of your client, nor are you likely to understand the geography or politics of regions being discussed – it is for this reason you should not act if you do not have the expertise.

INTERPRETERS

When interpreters are required

An interpreter will be required whenever there are communication difficulties, based on language differences, speech or hearing impediments. It should be remembered that detainees who appear to have a sound grasp of the English language may not properly understand localised expressions, specialist terminology or current idioms and dialects.

A person may not be interviewed in the absence of an interpreter if:

(a) they have difficulty understanding English;

(b) the interviewing officer cannot speak the person's own language; and

(c) the person wishes an interpreter to be present.

Clearly, in all cases where the officer can speak the detainee's language, an interpreter should be required and asked for, in order that the solicitor is able to understand what is being said and tender appropriate advice.

An interview can take place in the absence of an interpreter under C11.18 if the criteria in that provision are met.

Who arranges for an interpreter?

The following considerations should be borne in mind:

1. The police and defence should not use the same interpreter, unless this cannot be avoided. Whilst the police are responsible for providing an interpreter, they will generally only provide one for use by the police and detainee. A client must consent to the use of the same interpreter and it may be felt more appropriate to delay interview and wait for an interpreter than simply use the one who will be used by the police as well.

2. The fees of a second interpreter can be claimed as a disbursement.

3. It is the solicitor's duty to ensure that the interpretation needs of the client are adequately met, and the solicitor should ensure that the interpreter is properly trained and aware of his professional duties.

It is suggested in the guidance that a solicitor should discuss with the client the client's interpretation needs and preferences, including sex and ethnic origin. Care should be taken with this, as any requirement must be based on *real* need, not just preference, as the latter may well be discriminatory and unlawful (and in addition may amount to a breach of the General Criminal Contract).

An appropriate adult should never be used as an interpreter (*R*. v. *West London Youth Court, ex parte J, The Times*, 2 August 1999).

Legal privilege

A person acting as an interpreter between a solicitor and a detainee is bound by the rules of professional privilege (*R. (on the application of Bozhurt)* v. *Thames Magistrates' Court, The Daily Telegraph*, 22 May 2001). However, it should be remembered that many interpreters are likely to service particular police stations on a regular basis, and may well have frequent contact with particular police officers – careless talk can destroy a defence case, and interpreters should be reminded in all cases of their absolute duty of confidentiality.

It is good sense to arrange for an interpreter instructed by the defence at the police station also to be present at the next court hearing. Remember, however, to liaise with the police and the court to ensure that only one interpreter is actually instructed. If only one interpreter was used at the police station, then the same interpreter cannot act for the defendant at court.

INTERVIEWS

One of the most important roles of a solicitor attending upon clients at the police station is advising them in relation to the interview process. It ought to be remembered that the practice of law is not an exact science, and past experience, instinct and a small amount of good luck all combine to produce outcomes favourable to the client. It should be remembered, however, that your client should ultimately make the decisions that need to be made, after receiving appropriate advice.

Why no comment?

At the start of each interview a caution will be given which states: 'you do not have to say anything, but it may harm your defence if you do not mention when questioned something which you later rely on in court. Anything you do say may be given in evidence'.

Inferences can be drawn from the following:

1. Failing to mention facts when questioned which are later relied upon as part of a suspect's defence at court (s.34 CJPOA 1994).
2. Failing to account for any object, substance or mark (or mark on any

object) which is on his person, clothing or footwear or otherwise in his possession, or in any place in which he is at the time of his arrest (the officer must reasonably believe that the presence of the object, substance or mark may be attributable to the participation of the person arrested in the commission of the offence) (s.36 CJPOA 1994).

3.   Where a person arrested is found at a place at or about the time the offence is alleged to have been committed, failing to account for his presence at that place (s.37 CJPOA 1994).

The danger in failing to answer questions and put forward a fact known to the client at that time or account for presence, objects, substances or marks, will mean that there is a risk that a tribunal hearing the case will draw reasonable inferences from the failure to mention that fact or give an explanation (provided of course that the suspect does later give evidence on the point).

Balancing this danger with competing factors

The above-expressed danger must be balanced with competing factors, some of which are discussed below.

Lack of evidence

Is there sufficient evidence to charge at that stage? If there is insufficient evidence to charge or convict, then consideration should be given to a no-comment interview, as it may be the case that the situation can only get worse. Remember, however, that evidence may come to light at a later stage and the client may well have to answer for his earlier refusal. It is common therefore to refuse to answer questions pending the outcome of forensic tests. If the tests implicate the defendant and the only real option is a guilty plea, then no consequences from the silence will follow.

Consider, however, the situation where the client has been involved in a fight, is found near to the scene but there is no identification evidence, only the chance of forensics. The dilemma here is much more stark, as the police will send the clothing for forensics, and if, in a later interview, self-defence is advanced, a jury may well draw inferences from that silence. The same scenario arises in cases of violence in the home where it is thought that the complainant will retract or simply fail to come to court. However, thought must be given to what might happen if a witness summons were issued and the witness turned hostile to good effect. If a guilty plea followed, then again no harm done, but what of the case where the client has an arguable defence which he failed to put forward in interview?

The last scenario is where the evidence is strong and the client admits guilt. It may be thought that there is little point in saying anything, and this advice may well be correct. Consider, however, whether in appropriate cases true remorse can be evidenced on tape, and public money saved by not putting the prosecution to the trouble of obtaining forensic or other evidence. There are no right or wrong answers and each case must turn on its own facts.

Lack of disclosure

A client is entitled to be properly advised as to the case against him so that he can fairly answer it. Clients are frequently advised to make no comment on the back of a perceived failure by the police to disclose evidence to the defence. In *R. v. Imran and Hussain* [1997] Crim LR 754 the police failed to disclose to the defence prior to interview a video which purported to show the defendant committing the robbery. The court agreed with the comments of the trial judge, who said 'It is totally wrong to submit that a defendant should be prevented from lying by being presented with the whole of the evidence against him prior to the interview'. The court went on to say that 'to hold that the police have to play a form of cricket under one rigorous set of rules whereas the suspect can play under no rules whatever seems to us to lack reality'.

Solicitors therefore need to take care before advising no comment on this ground, and a file note should be prepared which details: (a) what information the solicitor needed to know; (b) why it impacted on the decision to advise the client to make no comment; and (c) the fact that a request was made to the police and the response to that request. It will be rare to justify a no comment interview on the basis of lack of disclosure.

Vulnerable clients

Fitness for interview does not equate to being able to understand the case being made against a person and that person's ability to answer properly for their action (if an answer is indeed required). A solicitor should be slow to allow a client who suffers from mental health or other significant difficulties, to answer questions. Serious thought should be given to: (a) taking a prepared statement instead; and (b) obtaining an independent assessment from a community psychiatric nurse prior to the interview. It should not be assumed that a police surgeon will have any of the necessary knowledge or training to assess properly such a person's ability to give proper instructions. The other side of the coin is of course not to necessarily assume that people with learning and other difficulties are not able to understand the process – an individual assessment must be made in every case.

Solicitor's advice

The following of a solicitor's advice to remain silent, simply to avoid giving an answer at that stage, will not prevent an inference being drawn. The high water mark of the solicitors shield can be found in *R.* v. *Betts and Hall* [2001] 2 Cr App R 16, in which it was said that:

> In the light of the judgment in *Condron* v. *United Kingdom* it is not the quality of the decision [i.e. not to answer questions] but the genuineness of the decision that matters. If it is a plausible explanation that the reason for not mentioning facts is that the particular appellant acted on the advice of his solicitor and not because he had no, or no satisfactory, answer to give then no inference can be drawn. That conclusion does not give a licence to a guilty person to shield behind the advice of his solicitor. The adequacy of the explanation advanced may well be relevant as to whether or not the advice was truly the reason for not mentioning the facts. A person, who is anxious not to answer questions because he has no or no adequate explanation to offer, gains no protection from his lawyer's advice because that advice is no more than a convenient way of disguising his true motivation for not mentioning facts.

Following this case many defendants took the witness stand with confidence that juries would have sympathy for someone simply following their solicitor's advice. After all, what is the point of having a statutory right to legal advice, taking advantage of that right, and then ignoring the advice of a professional? It soon became clear however that the standard Judicial Studies Board direction still allowed an inference in these circumstances if the jury believed that 'the defendant had no answer, and merely latched onto the legal advice as a convenient shield behind which to hide. . .'.

It is clear then that solicitors must have some proper basis for advising a client to remain silent. The Court of Appeal in *R.* v. *Howell* [2003] EWCA Crim 01, said the following:

> The kind of circumstance which may most likely justify silence will be such matters as the suspect's condition (ill-health, in particular mental disability; confusion; intoxication; shock, and so forth – of course we are not laying down an authoritative list), or his inability genuinely to recollect events without reference to documents which are not to hand, or communication with other persons who may be able to assist his recollection. There must always be soundly based objective reasons for silence, sufficiently cogent and telling to weigh in the balance against the clear public interest in an account being given by the suspect to the police. Solicitors bearing the important responsibility of giving advice to suspects at police stations must always have that in mind.

The prepared statement

It is not uncommon for clients to refuse to give any instructions at all to their solicitors; in such instances there is little more a solicitor can do. However, in cases where the client does have the bare bones of a defence, or a defence that he would rather not expand upon, then a prepared statement should be considered. The recording of instructions at least prevents a later accusation that the suspect has simply had time to think about the matter.

The timing of the statement is crucial and should rarely be prepared prior to the end of the interview. The simple reason for this is that by the end of the interview you are likely to know much more about the case than you did at the start. This will allow the client to address further points which may well be critical to his case. It is important to cover all important aspects of the case, to ensure that no critical facts are missed out. Provided that the statement covers the fundamental issues being relied upon by the suspect at trial, no inferences can be drawn (*R. v. Ali* [2001] EWCA Crim 885). The court in *Ali* was not able to resolve conclusively whether inferences could be drawn by virtue of the fact that the prepared statement meant that the defendant had not subjected his account to scrutiny in interview by the police (see *R. v. Daniel*, unreported, Case no. 971143Z2), but seemed to proceed on the basis that the inference should not be considered.

The situation has now been resolved following *R. v. Knight*, *The Times*, 20 August 2003, in which it was held to be improper to invite a jury to draw an inference when the defence went no further than the facts mentioned in the prepared statement.

Need you disclose the statement?

In *Knight* the prepared statement was read out at the start of the interview. There are disadvantages to this in that it allows the police to check on a defence early on in the proceedings. You are also putting forward a defence at a very early stage of the interrogation process: it should be remembered that, in serious cases at least, staged disclosure is now the norm. The question arises therefore as to whether a statement made to a solicitor, dated and timed, but not disclosed to the police until charge, or possibly not at all, will prevent inferences from being drawn. It is submitted that logically it should, but I would advise caution here. In *Knight* the court made particular reference to the purpose of s.34 being to secure disclosure of the accused's defence; presumably the intention of Parliament was to secure disclosure of the defence to the police. It still remains to be seen what sensible inferences could be drawn if recent fabrication is rebutted by a solicitor giving evidence on a voir dire, but I suspect that the last word on this topic has not yet been said. A solicitor will need to carefully balance the risks, but one tactic may be to wait until charge, indicate that the client wishes to be further interviewed and submit the statement then, or alternatively simply submit it at charge, having at that stage had all the disclosure he is going to get.

Adequacy of the statement

It is of paramount importance that the prepared statement covers all of the points to be relied upon in the accused's defence, as he can reasonably at that stage be expected to mention. The court in *Knight* commented 'We wish to make it crystal clear that of itself the making of a pre-prepared statement gives no automatic immunity against adverse inferences'.

Talk or make a statement?

Assuming a full defence is forthcoming, is there any advantage in participating in an interview if a prepared statement affords protection? It is a matter of judgment, but given the basic premise that a not insignificant number of people are in fact guilty of the offence for which they have been arrested, it would seem common sense to protect a client from having their account scrutinised at that stage. On the other hand, there are those rare cases where an experienced officer can be moved to investigate a defence put forward early in interview, leading to the proceedings being discontinued at a much earlier stage than they might otherwise be. The choice will remain difficult.

Interventions during interview

The solicitor has a duty to advise a client throughout the client's period of detention, and that extends to while he is in the interview room. The solicitor should be alert to multiple, illogical, improper and hypothetical questions being put to a client, and should advise a client not to answer such questions.

The police will frequently advise the client incorrectly as to the consequences which might flow from making no comment in interview. The solicitor can choose either to deal with this issue in advance with the client prior to interview, or intervene in such instances and state his opinion that the officer's assessment of the law is incorrect and that the advice remains the same.

The solicitor should not express any opinion whatsoever as to whether a client understands the caution, nor should he be drawn into agreeing with the officer on any subject at all during the interview. Some officers, when expressing a view, ask the solicitor for support – it should never be given.

Clients frequently begin to answer questions when they had earlier resolved to maintain silence. In such situations, the interview should either be stopped for further advice to be given, or the solicitor should remind the client that his advice not to answer is still the same. Such interjections often lead to objections from the police and it is appropriate to remind the officer of Code C Note for Guidance 6D, which deals with solicitor interventions and specifically states that a solicitor may 'advise their client not to reply to particular questions'. A solicitor should not adopt any other system of communicating with his client, however: nods and head shaking are not appropriate and will suggest to many officers that improper conduct is taking place during the interview, when in fact it is not.

PHOTOGRAPHS, TAKING OF

(See: Police and Criminal Evidence Act 1984 s.64A.)

A person who is detained at a police station may be photographed with the appropriate consent, or if the appropriate consent is withheld or it is not practicable to obtain it, without it. It is not likely that the courts will hold that the taking of a photograph in accordance with PACE and the codes, amounts to a breach of the European Convention on Human Rights (ECHR) (see: *Re McCullough's Application* [1997] NI 423). The taking of a photograph outside of the terms of PACE may well amount to a breach of Article 8, but the court will go on to consider whether the trial process itself was fair, regardless of the breach, and may well refuse to exercise its discretion to exclude the evidence (*R.* v. *Loveridge, The Times,* 3 May 2001).

The detained person may be required, for the purpose of taking the photograph, to remove any item or substance worn on or over the whole or any part of the head or face. If this requirement is not complied with the person proposing to take the photograph may remove the item or substance himself.

Photographs may be taken at locations other than police stations where a person has been (s.64A PACE):

(a) arrested by a constable for an offence;
(b) taken into custody by a constable after being arrested for an offence by a person other than a constable;
(c) made subject to a requirement to wait with a community support officer under paragraph 2(3) or (3B) of Schedule 4 to the Police Reform Act 2002 (the 2002 Act);
(d) given a penalty notice by a constable in uniform under Chapter 1 of Part 1 of the Criminal Justice and Police Act 2001, a penalty notice by a constable under section 444A of the Education Act 1996, or a fixed penalty notice by a constable in uniform under section 54 of the Road Traffic Offenders Act 1988;
(e) given a notice in relation to a relevant fixed penalty offence (within the meaning of paragraph 1 of Schedule 4 to the 2002 Act) by a community support officer by virtue of a designation applying that paragraph to him; or
(f) given a notice in relation to a relevant fixed penalty offence (within the meaning of paragraph 1 of Schedule 5 to the 2002 Act) by an accredited person by virtue of accreditation specifying that that paragraph applies to him.

References to taking a photograph include references to using any process by means of which a visual image may be produced (digital camera for example), and references to photographing a person shall be construed accordingly. Moving images fall within the definition.

Use of photographs

A photograph taken under s.64A may be used by, or disclosed to, any person for any purpose related to the prevention or detection of crime, the investigation of an offence or the conduct of a prosecution.

The reference to crime includes a reference to any conduct which constitutes one or more criminal offences (whether under the law of a part of the United Kingdom or of a country or territory outside the United Kingdom); or is, or corresponds to, any conduct, which, if it all took place in any one part of the United Kingdom, would constitute one or more criminal offences.

References to an investigation and to a prosecution include references, respectively, to any investigation outside the United Kingdom of any crime or suspected crime and to a prosecution brought in respect of any crime in a country or territory outside the United Kingdom.

Retention of photographs

A photograph can be retained but may not be used or disclosed except for a purpose as outlined above.

POLICE BAIL

Pre-charge

Where a person is arrested and taken to the police station, it is the duty of the custody officer to determine whether there is sufficient evidence to charge (s.37(1) PACE). If the custody officer determines that he does not have such evidence before him, the suspect can either be:

(a) detained without charge if it is necessary to secure or preserve evidence relating to the offence for which he is under arrest or to obtain such evidence by questioning; or
(b) released either on bail or without bail (s.37(2)).

A custody officer can release a person without charge, either on bail or without where he does have sufficient evidence to charge, but has chosen not to, for whatever reason (s.37(7)).

Effect of bail

If pre-charge bail is imposed it must be unconditional (s.47(1A)), save for satisfaction of any pre-release conditions, namely the provision of a surety or security. Bail is, however, with a duty to attend at such police station at such time as the custody officer may appoint (s.47(3)(b)). Such bail can be cancelled if notice is given in writing (s.47(4)).

The grant of bail does not prevent re-arrest if new evidence comes to light justifying a further arrest (s.57(2)).

Failing to surrender to police bail

It is an offence to fail without reasonable excuse to surrender to bail at the appointed time (s.6 Bail Act 1976), and a constable can arrest without warrant any person who has failed to surrender (s.46A). The offence is punishable with three months' imprisonment and/or a fine not exceeding level 5 on the standard scale.

Bail for the purposes of deciding what offence to charge (CPS advice)

Pre-charge bail conditions can be imposed where a suspect is being released for the police to determine what to charge, as opposed to whether to charge at all. If a person is arrested for breach of a bail condition imposed he may either be charged with the offence, or further bailed. The Director of Public Prosecution's guidance is reproduced at Appendix E.

Post-charge

When a person is charged with an offence, he should be released either on bail or without bail, unless:

In the case of an adult (s.38(1)(a))

(a) his name or address cannot be ascertained, or the custody officer has reasonable grounds for doubting its accuracy;
(b) there are reasonable grounds for believing that the detainee will fail to answer bail;
(c) there are reasonable grounds for believing that a person arrested for an imprisonable offence will commit new offences;
(d) where a sample may be taken from the person under section 63B and the custody officer has reasonable grounds for believing that the detention of the person is necessary to enable the sample to be taken from him;
(e) where a person is arrested for an offence which is not an imprisonable offence and the custody officer has reasonable grounds for believing that the detention of the person arrested is necessary to prevent him from causing physical injury to any other person or from causing loss of or damage to property;
(f) detention is necessary to prevent interference with the administration of justice or with the investigation of offences or of a particular offence;
(g) detention is necessary for the person's own protection.

Normal Bail Act considerations apply to (b)–(c) and (e)–(f), and the custody officer should approach the matter in a similar way to how a court would. It is proper for the custody officer to consider the suspect's current disposition if violent, and threats he may have made and antecedent history (so far as relevant) (Home Office Circular 111/92).

A solicitor should be ready to provide the custody officer with details of his client's personal circumstances, family and community ties, employment, and mitigating circumstances in relation to any previous failures to surrender or offences on bail. Whilst the representations do not take the form of a formal application of the type that might be made to a court, care should be put in to the representations, and your client's case should be ably argued before the police, pointing out weaknesses or contradictions in evidence, and how suitable conditions might allay police fears.

In the case of a juvenile (s.38(1)(b))

(a) any of the above requirements are satisfied; or
(b) the custody officer has reasonable grounds for believing that he ought to be detained in his own interests.

If a juvenile is denied bail, he should be moved to local authority accommodation unless it is impracticable for him to do so or in the case of an arrested juvenile who has attained the age of 12, that no secure accommodation is available and that keeping him in other local authority accommodation would not be adequate to protect the public from serious harm from him.

Custody officers frequently ignore this provision and solicitors should always be alert to the fact. All solicitors should know the telephone number of their local social services emergency duty team so that appropriate representation can be made to them direct, as opposed to relying on the police, who are unlikely to want to force the issue.

A custody officer should do: 'everything practicable to ensure that the place of detention was with the local authority and not the police station but if the only accommodation was insufficient to avoid the very consequences which led to the refusal of bail, the officer was entitled to decide that the local authority arrangements were impracticable' (*R*. v. *Chief Constable of Cambridgeshire, ex parte Michel* [1991] Crim LR 382).

Section 25 CJPOA 1994

If a defendant is charged with or convicted of murder, attempted murder, manslaughter, rape or attempted rape *and* he has a previous conviction (by or before a court in any part of the United Kingdom) for any one of those offences (not necessarily the same offence with which he is now charged) or for culpable homicide, he shall only be granted bail if the officer granting bail is satisfied that there are exceptional circumstances which justify it (s.25 CJPOA 1994).

Conditional bail

Bail conditions can be imposed to ensure that the defendant: (a) surrenders to his bail; (b) does not commit offences while on bail; and (c) does not interfere with witnesses or otherwise obstruct the course of justice (s.3A(5)).

A requirement to reside in a bail hostel cannot be imposed by the police (s.3A(2)), nor can the new electronic-monitoring provisions be utilised.

Varying police bail

Any custody officer at the police station where bail was granted can at the request of the person to whom bail was granted, vary that bail. A solicitor can undertake this work under CDS 1 and 2 provided the client meets the financial eligibility criteria. The officer can impose conditions or more onerous conditions (s.3A(8)). An application can also be made to a magistrates' court, under s.43B Magistrates' Courts Act 1980 (MCA 1980), a useful device where the police are refusing to vary bail. As in the case of a variation 'hearing' before a custody officer, the court enjoys the same right to impose more onerous conditions of bail (s.43B(2)).

RIGHT TO HAVE SOMEONE INFORMED WHEN ARRESTED

(See: Police and Criminal Evidence Act 1984 s.56, Code C.)

Nature of the right

The detained person has the right, if he so requests, to have one friend or relative or other person who is known to him or who is likely to take an interest in his welfare told, as soon as is practicable except to the extent that delay is permitted as detailed below, that he has been arrested and is being detained at the police station (or other place). If the person nominated cannot be contacted, he can nominate up to a further two people. Subsequent attempts are thereafter at the discretion of the custody officer. In the event that the detained person knows of no person to notify, the officer should have regard to any local voluntary organisations that may be able to offer suitable support.

Delay

Delay is only permitted:

(a) in the case of a person who is in police detention for an indictable offence; and if
(b) an officer of at least the rank of inspector authorises it; and
(c) the officer has reasonable grounds to believe that telling the named person of the arrest will lead to interference with or harm to evidence connected with an indictable offence or interference with or physical injury to other persons; or will lead to the alerting of other persons suspected of having committed such an offence but not yet arrested for it; or will hinder the recovery of any property obtained as a result of such an offence.

If delay is authorised, the detained person shall be told the reason for it and the reason shall be noted on his custody record. The authorisation can be given orally, but in that event it shall be confirmed in writing as soon as is practicable.

Period of delay

This right cannot be delayed beyond 36 hours from the relevant time (which is normally the time of arrival at the police station – but see s.41(2) PACE). Once the reason for authorising the delay ends, the detained person must at that point be allowed to exercise the right.

Children and young persons

It is the duty of the police (see s.34(2) Children and Young Persons Act 1933) to ascertain the identity of a person responsible for the welfare of the child or young person and inform them as soon as practicable of the fact of the young person's arrest, reasons for it and place of detention. This right subsists irrespective of the nature of the offence, including terrorist offences.

If it appears that, at the time of arrest of the child or young person, a supervision order, as defined in s.11 Children and Young Persons Act 1969 or Part IV Children Act 1989, is in force in respect of him, the person responsible for his supervision shall also be informed as soon as it is reasonably practicable to do so (s.34(7) Children and Young Persons Act 1933).

If it appears that at the time of his arrest the child or young person is being provided with accommodation by or on behalf of a local authority under s.20 Children Act 1989, the local authority shall be informed as soon as it is reasonably practicable to do so (s.34(7A) Children and Young Persons Act 1933).

RIGHT TO LEGAL ADVICE

(See: Police and Criminal Evidence Act 1984 s.58.)

Exception in relation to terrorism and service offences

This section does not apply in relation to those detained under terrorism provisions (s.58(12) PACE). In the event of dealing with a person detained under terrorist provisions, the solicitor should take care in applying the codes of practice, since they are not wholly in accordance with the provisions of Schedule 8 Terrorism Act 2000, which provides for an alternative arrangement.

In relation to the investigation of service offences under the Army Act 1955, the Air Force Act 1955 or the Naval Discipline Act 1957, regard should be had to the codes of practice in force for the military (last amended 30 September 2003).

Nature of right

A person held in custody at a police station or other premises shall be entitled, if he so requests, to consult a solicitor – see bullet point below – privately at any time. The right is exercisable as soon as is reasonably practicable, except to the extent that delay is authorised. The detained person will be told of this right when being booked in at the custody desk. The right is exercisable at any time during detention. If the detained person does not know of a solicitor, and does not want a duty solicitor, he should be allowed to consult a list of those solicitors who have indicated a willingness to offer legal advice to those detained at police stations. The police must not advise the detained person about any particular firm of solicitors. Nor should the police make mention of any other organisation charged with providing legal services (for example Public Defender Service), other than the duty solicitor scheme.

- Solicitor means a solicitor who holds a current practising certificate, a trainee solicitor, duty solicitor representative or accredited representative. Code C6.12A deals with refusal to allow other persons, including probationary representatives, access to the police station.

The right to be informed of the right to free legal advice did not extend to trading standards officers as they were not bound by PACE (*R. (on the application of Beale)* v. *South East Wiltshire Magistrates* [2002] EWHC 2961 (Admin).

Delay

Delay is only permitted (Code C, Annex B):

(a) in the case of a person who is in police detention for an indictable offence; and

(b) if an officer of at least the rank of superintendent authorises it; and

(c) if the officer has reasonable grounds for believing that access to legal advice will lead to interference with or harm to evidence connected with an indictable offence or interference with or physical injury to other persons; or will lead to the alerting of other persons suspected of having committed such an offence but not yet arrested for it; or will hinder the recovery of any property obtained as a result of such an offence.

An officer may also authorise delay where the offence is a drug-trafficking offence or an offence to which Part VI Criminal Justice Act 1988 applies and the officer has reasonable grounds for believing:

(a) where the offence is a drug-trafficking offence, that the detained person has benefited from drug-trafficking and that the recovery of the value of that person's proceeds of drug-trafficking will be hindered by the exercise of the right to legal advice; and

(b) where the offence is one to which Part VI Criminal Justice Act 1988 applies, that the detained person has benefited from the offence and that the recovery of the value of the property obtained by that person from or in connection with the offence or of the pecuniary advantage derived by him from or in connection with it will be hindered by the exercise of the right to legal advice.

If delay is authorised, the detained person shall be told the reason for it and the reason shall be noted on his custody record. The authorisation can be given orally, but in that event shall be confirmed in writing as soon as is practicable. If access to a solicitor is delayed there are restrictions on the drawing of inferences (see Code C, Annex C).

Period of delay

This right cannot be delayed beyond 36 hours from the relevant time (which is normally the time of arrival at the police station – but see s.41(2) PACE). Once the reason for authorising the delay ends, the detained person must at that point be allowed to exercise the right.

Effect on interviews

A person who wants legal advice may not be interviewed or continue to be interviewed until he has received it unless:

1. Delay has been authorised (as set out above). Or
2. An officer of at least the rank of superintendent or above has reasonable grounds for believing that:

   (a) delay will involve an immediate risk of harm to persons or serious loss of, or damage to, property (once sufficient information to avert the risk has been obtained, questioning must cease until the person has obtained legal advice unless one or more other exceptions apply); or

   (b) where a solicitor, including a duty solicitor, has been contacted and has agreed to attend, awaiting his arrival would cause unreasonable delay to the process of the investigation; or

   (c) the solicitor nominated by the person, or selected by him from a list:

      (i) cannot be contacted; or
      (ii) has previously indicated that he does not wish to be contacted; or
      (iii) having been contacted, has declined to attend;

      and the person has been advised of the duty solicitor scheme but has declined to ask for the duty solicitor, or the duty solicitor is unavailable. (In these circumstances, the interview may be started or continued without further delay provided that an officer of the rank of inspector or above has given agreement for the interview to proceed in those circumstances.);

   (d) the person who wanted legal advice changes his mind.

Where a person has been permitted to consult a solicitor and the solicitor is available (i.e. present at the station or on his way to the station or easily contactable by telephone) at the time the interview begins or is in progress, the solicitor must be allowed to be present while he is being interviewed.

If an interview takes place and the right to legal advice is delayed then see Code C, Annex C for the effect this will have in relation to the drawing of adverse inferences.

Drink driving cases

In *R. (Kennedy)* v. *CPS* [2003] Crim LR 120, it was said:

> ... in this jurisdiction the public interest requires that the obtaining of breath specimens part of the investigation cannot be delayed to any significant extent in order to enable a suspect to take legal advice. That, to my mind, means this – that if there happens to be a solicitor in the charge office whom the suspect says that he wants to consult for a couple of minutes before deciding whether or not to provide specimens of breath he must be allowed to do so. Similarly, if the suspect asks at that stage to speak on the telephone for a couple of minutes to his own solicitor or the duty solicitor, and the solicitor in question is immediately available. But where,

as here, the suspect does no more than indicate a general desire to have legal advice, I see no reason why the custody officer should not simply continue to take details, and alert the solicitors' call centre at the first convenient opportunity.

There have been a number of cases subsequent to *Kennedy*, but they do not alter the fundamental position as outlined above.

Removal of solicitor (Code C6.9)

The solicitor may only be required to leave the interview if his conduct is such that the investigating officer is unable to put questions properly to the suspect. But regard should be had to the note of guidance which a solicitor should not hesitate in reminding an interview officer of:

> The solicitor's only role in the police station is to protect and advance the legal rights of their client. On occasions this may require the solicitor to give advice which has the effect of the client avoiding giving evidence which strengthens a prosecution case. The solicitor may intervene in order to seek clarification, challenge an improper question to their client or the manner in which it is put, advise their client not to reply to particular questions, or if they wish to give their client further legal advice. Paragraph 6.9 only applies if the solicitor's approach or conduct prevents or unreasonably obstructs proper questions being put to the suspect or the suspect's response being recorded. Examples of unacceptable conduct include answering questions on a suspect's behalf or providing written replies for the suspect to quote.

A solicitor should always advise his client to wait a few seconds before answering any question in order to give the solicitor a chance to advise him not to respond, should such advice be necessary. This approach is unobjectionable, since it does not prevent the question being asked, nor does it attempt to obstruct a client's response. There is nothing wrong with an approach whereby a client asks his solicitor whether he should answer the question or not. However, any system of 'nods and winks' will inevitably lead to misunderstanding and conflict between the solicitor and the police, which should be avoided wherever possible.

If the investigating officer considers that a solicitor is acting improperly, he will stop the interview and consult an officer not below the rank of superintendent, if one is readily available, and otherwise an officer not below the rank of inspector who is not connected with the investigation. After speaking to the solicitor, the officer who has been consulted will decide whether or not the interview should continue in the presence of that solicitor. If he decides it should not, the suspect will be given the opportunity to consult another solicitor before the interview continues and that solicitor will be given an opportunity to be present at the interview.

In a case where an officer takes the decision to exclude a solicitor, he must be in a position to satisfy the court that the decision was properly made. The exclusion of a solicitor is a serious step to take and a superintendent should consider whether to report the removal to the Law Society and the LSC (in the case of a duty solicitor). It follows that a solicitor should always be in a position to be able to defend his stance.

Given the pressures of the interview situation, particularly in serious cases, things are sometimes said which in hindsight could be judged inappropriate. A solicitor should be able to stand back quickly from a situation and if appropriate rectify any conduct which falls below the required standard. A timely apology, delivered out of earshot of the client, is much better for all concerned, particularly the client who would otherwise suffer from a lengthier period of detention.

When a client's rights are being robustly and properly defended, however, a solicitor must never fold under the threat of removal.

TAKING OF SAMPLES

(See: Police and Criminal Evidence Act 1984 s.62.)

Samples are defined as either intimate or non-intimate (s.65):

Intimate samples	Non-intimate samples
blood	hair other than pubic hair
semen	sample taken from a nail, or under a nail
any other tissue fluid	swab taken from any part of a person's body,
urine	other than a part from which a swab taken
pubic hair	would be an intimate sample
dental impression	saliva
swab taken from a person's	skin impression
genitals or from a person's body	
orifice other than the mouth	

Criteria for taking of intimate sample

An intimate sample can only be taken if an officer of at least the rank of inspector authorises it to be taken. Such authorisation can only be given where that officer has reasonable grounds to suspect the involvement of the person from whom the sample is to be taken in a recordable offence and for believing that the sample will tend to confirm or disprove his involvement. In respect of persons not in police custody, see s.62(1A) PACE.

Use of force

An intimate sample cannot be taken by force, appropriate consent must be given. The consent must be fully informed and in particular the suspect should be warned of the inferences which might be drawn from a refusal. The suspect should be reminded of his right to independent legal advice.

Authorisation can be given orally or in writing, but if given orally shall be confirmed in writing as soon as is practicable. The officer shall inform the person from whom the sample is to be taken of the grounds on which that officer has authorised it. The suspect must be informed that the sample may be used for the purposes of a speculative search.

Effect of a refusal to consent to taking of an intimate sample

Where consent has been withheld without good cause, a judge or jury can draw such inferences from the refusal as appear proper.

Where the sample being sought is for DNA purposes, there appears to be little point in refusing to give a sample, and thereby risking inferences, given that a non-intimate sample, which can be taken by force, will in all likelihood be taken.

Criteria for taking of non-intimate sample

Such samples can be taken either with or without consent. If the suspect refuses his consent to the taking of the sample, it can be taken by using reasonable force provided that an officer of at least the rank of inspector authorises it. Authorisation can be given in the following situations.

1. Suspect charged with a recordable offence or informed that he will be reported for such an offence, and either he has not had a non-intimate sample taken from him in the course of the investigation of the offence by the police or he has had a non-intimate sample taken from him but either it was not suitable for the same means of analysis or, though so suitable, the sample proved insufficient.

2. Suspect is being held in custody by the police on the authority of a court; and an officer of at least the rank of inspector authorises the sample to be taken without the appropriate consent. An officer may only give an authorisation under this power if he has reasonable grounds:

   (a) for suspecting the involvement of the person from whom the sample is to be taken has been involved in a [recordable offence]; and
   (b) for believing that the sample will tend to confirm or disprove his involvement.

3. Suspect has been charged with a recordable offence or informed that he will be reported for such an offence; and either he has not had a non-intimate sample taken from him in the course of the investigation of the offence by the police or he has had a non-intimate sample taken from him but either it was not suitable for the same means of analysis or, though so suitable, the sample proved insufficient.

4. Suspect has been convicted of a recordable offence.

5. Suspect is a person to whom s.2 of the Criminal Evidence (Amendment) Act 1997 applies (persons detained following acquittal on grounds of insanity or finding of unfitness to plead).

Destruction of samples, s.64 PACE

(1A) Where–

  (a) fingerprints, impressions of footwear or samples are taken from a person in connection with the investigation of an offence, and
  (b) subsection (3) below does not require them to be destroyed,

the fingerprints, impressions of footwear or samples may be retained after they have fulfilled the purposes for which they were taken but shall not be used by any person except for purposes related to the prevention or detection of crime, the investigation of an offence, the conduct of a prosecution or the identification of a deceased person or of the person from whom a body part came.

(1B) In subsection (1A) above–

  (a) the reference to using a fingerprint or an impression of footwear includes a reference to allowing any check to be made against it under section 63A(1) or (1C) above and to disclosing it to any person;
  (b) the reference to using a sample includes a reference to allowing any check to be made under section 63A(1) or (1C) above against it or against information derived from it and to disclosing it or any such information to any person;
  (c) the reference to crime includes a reference to any conduct which–

  (i) constitutes one or more criminal offences (whether under the law of a part of the United Kingdom or of a country or territory outside the United Kingdom); or
  (ii) is, or corresponds to, any conduct which, if it all took place in any one part of the United Kingdom, would constitute one or more criminal offences;

  and
  (d) the references to an investigation and to a prosecution include references, respectively, to any investigation outside the United Kingdom of any crime or suspected crime and to a prosecution brought in respect of any crime in a country or territory outside the United Kingdom.

(1BA) Fingerprints taken from a person by virtue of section 61(6A) above must be destroyed as soon as they have fulfilled the purpose for which they were taken.

(2) [. . .]

(3) If–

  (a) fingerprints, impressions of footwear or samples are taken from a person in connection with the investigation of an offence; and
  (b) that person is not suspected of having committed the offence,

they must, except as provided in the following provisions of this section, be destroyed as soon as they have fulfilled the purpose for which they were taken.

(3AA) Samples, fingerprints and impressions of footwear are not required to be destroyed under subsection (3) above if–

    (a)   they were taken for the purposes of the investigation of an offence of which a person has been convicted; and

    (b)   a sample, fingerprint, (or as the case may be) an impression of footwear was also taken from the convicted person for the purposes of that investigation.

(3AB) Subject to subsection (3AC) below, where a person is entitled under subsection (3) subsection (1BA) or (3) above to the destruction of any fingerprint, impression of footwear or sample taken from him (or would be but for subsection (3AA) above), neither the fingerprint, nor the impression of footwear, nor the sample, nor any information derived from the sample, shall be used–

    (a)   in evidence against the person who is or would be entitled to the destruction of that fingerprint, impression of footwear or sample; or

    (b)   for the purposes of the investigation of any offence;

and subsection (1B) above applies for the purposes of this subsection as it applies for the purposes of subsection (1A) above.

(3AC) Where a person from whom a fingerprint, impression of footwear or sample has been taken consents in writing to its retention–

    (a)   that fingerprint, impression of footwear or sample need not be destroyed under subsection (3) above;

    (b)   subsection (3AB) above shall not restrict the use that may be made of the fingerprint, impression of footwear or sample or, in the case of a sample, of any information derived from it; and

    (c)   that consent shall be treated as comprising a consent for the purposes of section 63A(1C) above;

and a consent given for the purpose of this subsection shall not be capable of being withdrawn. This subsection does not apply to fingerprints taken from a person by virtue of section 61(6A) above.

(3AD) For the purposes of subsection (3AC) above it shall be immaterial whether the consent is given at, before or after the time when the entitlement to the destruction of the fingerprint, impression of footwear or sample arises.

(4)   [. . .]

(5)   If fingerprints or impressions of footwear are destroyed–

    (a)   any copies of the fingerprints or impressions of footwear shall also be destroyed; and

    (b)   any chief officer of police controlling access to computer data relating to the fingerprints or impressions of footwear shall make access to the data impossible, as soon as it is practicable to do so.

(6)   A person who asks to be allowed to witness the destruction of his fingerprints or impressions of footwear or copies of them shall have a right to witness it.

(6A) If–

    (a)   subsection (5)(b) above falls to be complied with; and

    (b)   the person to whose fingerprints or impressions of footwear the data relate asks for a certificate that it has been complied with, such a certificate shall be issued to him, not later than the end of the period of three months beginning with the day on which he asks for it, by the responsible chief officer of police or a person authorised by him or on his behalf for the purposes of this section.

(6B) In this section–

[. . .]

'the responsible chief officer of police' means the chief officer of police in whose police area the computer data were put on to the computer.

(7) Nothing in this section–

(a) affects any power conferred by paragraph 18(2) of Schedule 2 to the Immigration Act 1971 or section 20 of the Immigration and Asylum Act 1999 (c 33) (disclosure of police information to the Secretary of State for use for immigration purposes); or

(b) applies to a person arrested or detained under the terrorism provisions.

Human rights

The new statutory scheme in relation to the retention of fingerprints and other samples has been held to be compatible with the European Convention (*R.* v. *Chief Constable of South Yorkshire and others, ex parte Marper* [2002] EWHC Admin 478). This decision has been affirmed by the House of Lords ([2004] UKHL 39).

TERRORIST SUSPECTS

Terrorism legislation has now been put on a more permanent footing, with primary provisions being contained in the Terrorism Act 2000 (TA 2000). The 2000 Act replaces the Prevention of Terrorism (Temporary Provisions) Act 1989.

Under the 2000 Act, two forms of detention arise which will be of concern to duty solicitors, those being detention under Schedules 7 and 8.

Overview

Schedule 7 detention is a procedure for holding persons who are suspected of terrorist activity but in respect of whom there is insufficient evidence to arrest at that stage; the powers are only exercisable in relation to persons who are at a port (different considerations apply in relation to Northern Ireland).

Schedule 8 detention covers all situations where persons are arrested and detained for terrorist offences, and is of critical importance to solicitors advising at the police station. The Police and Criminal Evidence Act 1984 has very little application in relation to such detainees, and regard must always be had to the Terrorism Act 2000 codes of practice and Schedule 8.

Definitions

Terrorism

This is defined as an action (listed below), the use or threat of which is designed to influence the government or to intimidate the public or a section of the public, and the use or threat is made for the purpose of advancing a political, religious or ideological cause (s.1 TA 2000).

The actions mentioned are:

1. Serious violence against a person, serious damage to property, endangering another person's life, creating a serious risk to the health or safety of the public or a section of the public, an act designed seriously to interfere with or seriously to disrupt an electronic system (s.1(2) TA 2000).
2. A use or threat of an action which involves the use of firearms or explosives is terrorism whether or not it involves serious damage to property. An action includes activity outside the United Kingdom, and references to the public and government include the public or government of a country other than the United Kingdom.

Terrorist

A person is a terrorist if he commits an offence under:

(a) any of ss.11, 12, 15 to 18, 54 and 56 to 63 TA 2000 (s.40(1)(a) TA 2000); or
(b) is or has been concerned in the commission, preparation or instigation of acts of terrorism (s.40(1)(b) TA 2000), whether before or after the passing of the Terrorism Act 2000 (s.40(2) TA 2000).

Detention under Schedule 7

Officers entitled to exercise powers

These are referred to as 'examining officers' and include: a constable, immigration officer or customs officer designated for the purpose by the Secretary of State.

Detention period

A person may be detained for a period not in excess of nine hours, in order that the following power can be exercised:

*   questioning of a person for the purpose of determining whether he is a person who is or has been concerned in the commission, preparation or

instigation of acts of terrorism. The questioning officer need not suspect that the person falls into this category.

The nine hours runs from the time the 'examination begins' (Sched. 7, para. 6(4)). It is not clear as to precisely what is meant by this term, but it is submitted that the time runs from initial detention, not initial questioning, and this is important since it may take some time for a person to be conveyed to a police station and for questioning to begin. Where an examining officer carries out other investigations under Schedule 7, for example the searching of a vehicle, and then decides to detain for questioning, it is arguable that the time runs from the time of the initial search.

Obligations on detained person

The detained person must give the examining officer any information in his possession which the officer requests (Sched. 7, para. 5(a)). It is a summary offence, punishable with three months' imprisonment to withhold wilfully such information (Sched. 7, para. 18).

There are additional obligations in relation to the surrender of documents.

Intervening arrest

Should evidence come to light which justifies an arrest, the nine-hour detention limit shall cease to have effect (although it does count in respect of further detention under Schedule 8).

Rights while detained

Detained persons are entitled to the same protections afforded to persons arrested and detained under Schedule 8, for which see below.

Detention under Schedule 8

Section 41(1) TA 2000 states that a person may arrest without warrant a person whom he reasonably suspects to be a terrorist. Where a person is so arrested, the provisions of Schedule 8 shall apply.

Length of detention

A person detained shall be released not later than the end of 48 hours beginning with the time of his arrest under s.41 TA 2000, or if he was being detained under Schedule 7 when he was arrested under s.41, with the time when his examination under that schedule began.

Review of detention

Detention must be reviewed as soon as reasonably practicable following a person's arrest, and thereafter at intervals of at least 12 hours (Sched. 8, para. 21).

If, on a review of a person's detention, the review officer does not authorise continued detention, the person shall (unless detained in accordance with s.41(5) or (6) or under any other enactment) be released.

Where a police officer intends to make an application for a warrant of further detention under Sched. 8, para. 29, the person may be detained pending the making of the application, and, where an application has been made, he may be detained pending the conclusion of the proceedings for the application (s.41(5) and (6)).

Delay in review (Sched. 8, para. 22)

A review may be postponed if at the latest time at which it should have been carried out:

(a) the detained person is being questioned by a police officer and an officer is satisfied than an interruption of the questioning to carry out the review would prejudice the investigation in connection with which the person is being detained;
(b) no review officer is readily available; or
(c) it is not practicable for any other reason to carry out the review.

Where a review is postponed, it shall be carried out as soon as reasonably practicable thereafter.

Grounds for continued detention (Sched. 8, para. 23)

A review officer may only authorise a person's continued detention if satisfied that it is necessary:

(a) to obtain relevant evidence whether by questioning him or otherwise;
(b) to preserve relevant evidence;
(c) pending a decision whether to apply to the Secretary of State for a deportation notice to be served on the detained person;
(d) pending the making of an application to the Secretary of State for a deportation notice to be served on the detained person;
(e) pending consideration by the Secretary of State whether to serve a deportation notice on the detained person; or
(f) pending a decision whether the detained person should be charged with an offence.

Before granting an extension under (a) or (b) above, the review officer must be satisfied that the investigation in connection with which the person is being detained is being conducted diligently and expeditiously (Sched. 8, para. 23(2)). Similarly, the process pending completion under (c)–(f) above must be being conducted diligently and expeditiously.

The review officer must be an officer who has not been directly involved in the investigation. Reviews within the first 24 hours must be carried out by an officer of at least the rank of inspector. Later reviews must be carried out by an officer of at least the rank of superintendent.

The review officer, before determining whether to authorise a person's continued detention, must give the detained person or a solicitor available at the time of the review an opportunity to make written or oral representations. A detained person may be refused the opportunity to make oral representations on account of his condition or behaviour (e.g. drunkenness or violence).

Warrant of further detention

A police officer of at least the rank of superintendent may apply to a judicial authority for the issue of a warrant of further detention, to authorise the continued detention of the suspect for a period no later than the end of the period of seven days beginning with his arrest under s.41, or if he was being detained under Schedule 7 when he was arrested under s.41, with the time when his examination under that schedule began.

The application must be heard only before designated district judges.

Timing of application

The application must be made within the period of 48 hours following arrest (or Schedule 7 detention), or within six hours of the end of that period. The six-hour period of grace allows for delay in convening a suitable court.

If the judge holds it to have been reasonably practicable to have made the application during the 48-hour period, he shall dismiss the application. It follows therefore that, where it is apparent that inquiries will extend beyond the 48-hour period, an application should be made as soon as possible thereafter.

Grounds for extension (Sched. 8, para. 32)

A warrant of further detention may be issued only if the judge is satisfied that:

(a) there are reasonable grounds for believing that the further detention of the person to whom the application relates is necessary to obtain relevant evidence whether by questioning him or otherwise to preserve relevant evidence; and

(b) the investigation in connection with which the person is detained is being conducted diligently and expeditiously.

Representation (Sched. 8, para. 33)

The detained person may make oral or written representations and has the right to be legally represented. Where a person is not legally represented and wishes to be, the application must be adjourned for legal representation to be arranged.

The judge has the right to exclude both the person to whom the application relates and anyone representing him, from any part of the hearing (para. 33(3)). This rule is to enable sensitive information to be given to the judge *ex parte* (see Sched. 8, para. 34). This discretion must be exercised with care, and solicitors should have careful regard to the criteria specified in para. 34.

There is provision for applications to be made via video link. Where such a direction is made, all parties will make submissions via video link.

Further extensions

An extension should only be for the period necessary to continue with the investigation. It follows that further extensions may be necessary, and provision for such applications is contained in Sched. 8, para. 36. The maximum period of detention must not exceed seven days.

Identification

An authorised person (see Sched. 8, para. 2(2)), may take any steps which are reasonably necessary for identifying, measuring or photographing the detained person. The power contained in para. 2 does not, however, extend to the taking of fingerprints or intimate or non-intimate samples.

Basic rights

A detained person has the following basic rights while detained (note, however, that rights may be delayed as detailed below):

1. To have one named person informed as soon as is reasonably practicable that he is being detained there.
2. To consult a solicitor as soon as is reasonably practicable, privately and at any time.

Rights can be delayed (Sched. 8, para. 8) only where an officer of at least the rank of superintendent believes that exercising the right will have any of the following consequences:

(a) interference with or harm to evidence of an indictable offence;
(b) interference with or physical injury to any person;
(c) the alerting of persons who are suspected of having committed a serious arrestable offence but who have not been arrested for it;
(d) the hindering of the recovery of property obtained as a result of an indictable offence or in respect of which a forfeiture order could be made under s.23;
(e) interference with the gathering of information about the commission, preparation or instigation of acts of terrorism;
(f) the alerting of a person and thereby making it more difficult to prevent an act of terrorism; and
(g) the alerting of a person and thereby making it more difficult to secure a person's apprehension, prosecution or conviction in connection with the commission, preparation or instigation of an act of terrorism.

There is a further right of delay under Sched. 8, para. 7(5) in relation to proceeds of crime.

Once the reason for the delay ceases to subsist, there may be no further delay in permitting the exercise of the right in the absence of a further authorisation.

The right to consult privately with a solicitor can be curtailed under Sched. 8, para. 9 for any of the above reasons (and in limited circumstances in relation to proceeds of crime). Where this paragraph is applied, a detained person who wishes to exercise his right to consult with a solicitor may only do so in the sight and hearing of a police officer (referred to as a qualified officer).

Guidance on when the police should exercise the right to remain within sight and hearing can be found in Home Office Circular 42/2003 issued on 5 September 2003. The circular states that '. . .the restriction should only be used exceptionally after a careful assessment encompassing applicability and proportionality. This will involve balancing the consequences set out in paragraph 8(4), or the necessity in terms of paragraphs 17(1) and (3), against the effect on the suspect of denying him access to the solicitor other than in the presence of a police officer.'

There are no circumstances under which instructions from a client should be taken within the hearing of an officer, and it might be better to see whether the same limitations would be imposed if there were to be a change of representative.

An authorisation under Sched. 8, para. 9 can only be given by an officer of at least the rank of commander or assistant chief constable.

Taking of fingerprints

Fingerprints may be taken either with the detained person's consent or without it in limited circumstances. Before fingerprints are taken, the detainee must be informed of the reason for the taking of the fingerprints and that they may be the subject of a speculative search. Where finger-prints are taken without consent, the detainee must be informed that an authorisation has been given, the grounds on which it was given and, where relevant, the nature of the offence in which it is suspected he has been involved.

Taking of fingerprints without consent

Fingerprints can be taken with the use of reasonable force if the following criteria are satisfied:

1. The person is detained at a police station and a police officer of at least the rank of superintendent authorises the fingerprints to be taken, or the person has been convicted of a recordable offence and was convicted of the offence on or after 10 April 1995.
2. In the case of a person detained under s.41, the officer reasonably suspects that the person has been involved in an offence under any of the provisions mentioned in s.40(1)(a) and the officer reasonably believes that the fingerprints will tend to confirm or disprove his involvement, or, in any case, the officer is satisfied that the taking of the fingerprints from the person is necessary in order to assist in determining whether he falls within s.40(1)(b).

An officer may also give authorisation for the taking of fingerprints if:

(a) he is satisfied that the fingerprints of the detained person will facilitate the ascertainment of that person's identity; and
(b) the person has refused to identify himself or the officer has reasonable grounds for suspecting that that person is not who he claims to be.

Retention of fingerprints

Fingerprints may be retained but shall not be used by any person except for the purposes of a terrorist investigation or for purposes related to the prevention or detection of crime, the investigation of an offence, or the conduct of a prosecution. A speculative check may not be made *against* the fingerprints except for the purpose of a terrorist investigation or for purposes related to the prevention or detection of crime, the investigation of an offence or the conduct of a prosecution.

Taking of non-intimate samples

Non-intimate samples may be taken either with the detained person's consent or without it in limited circumstances. Before non-intimate samples are taken, the detainee must be informed of the reason for the taking of such samples and that he may be the subject of a speculative search. Where a non-intimate sample is taken without consent, the detainee must be informed that an authorisation has been given, the grounds on which it was given and, where relevant, the nature of the offence in which it is suspected he has been involved.

Taking of non-intimate samples without consent

Non-intimate samples can be taken with the use of reasonable force if the following criteria are satisfied:

1. The person is detained at a police station and a police officer of at least the rank of superintendent authorises the non-intimate samples to be taken, or the person has been convicted of a recordable offence and was convicted of the offence on or after 10 April 1995.
2. In the case of a person detained under s.41, the officer reasonably suspects that the person has been involved in an offence under any of the provisions mentioned in s.40(1)(a) and the officer reasonably believes that the non-intimate sample will tend to confirm or disprove his involvement, or, in any case, the officer is satisfied that the taking of the non-intimate sample from the person is necessary in order to assist in determining whether he falls within s.40(1)(b).

Retention of non-intimate samples

Non-intimate samples may be retained but shall not be used by any person except for the purposes of a terrorist investigation or for purposes related to the prevention or detection of crime, the investigation of an offence or the conduct of a prosecution. A speculative check may not be made against the non-intimate sample except for the purpose of a terrorist investigation or for purposes related to the prevention or detection of crime, the investigation of an offence or the conduct of a prosecution.

Intimate samples

An intimate sample can only ever be taken with the consent of the suspect, and then only when the following criteria are satisfied:

1. In the case of a person detained under s.41, the officer (of at least the rank of superintendent) reasonably suspects that the person has been involved in an offence under any of the provisions mentioned in s.40(1)(a) and the officer reasonably believes that the intimate sample will tend to confirm or disprove his involvement, or, in any case, the officer is satisfied that the taking of the intimate sample from the person is

necessary in order to assist in determining whether he falls within section 40(1)(b). Or

2. Two or more non-intimate samples suitable for the same means of analysis have been taken from a person who has been released from detention, and those samples have proved insufficient, *and* the officer (of at least the rank of superintendent) reasonably suspects that the person has been involved in an offence under any of the provisions mentioned in s.40(1)(a) and the officer reasonably believes that the intimate sample will tend to confirm or disprove his involvement, or, in any case, the officer is satisfied that the taking of the intimate sample from the person is necessary in order to assist in determining whether he falls within s.40(1)(b).

Consequences of withholding consent

Where consent is refused without good cause, in any proceedings against that person for an offence:

(a) the court, in determining whether to commit him for trial or whether there is a case to answer, may draw such inferences from the refusal as appear proper; and

(b) the court or jury, in determining whether that person is guilty of the offence charged, may draw such inferences from the refusal as appear proper.

TESTING FOR PRESENCE OF CLASS-A DRUGS

(See: Police and Criminal Evidence Act 1984 s.63B.)

A sample of urine or a non-intimate sample can be taken for the purpose of ascertaining whether a person has any specified Class-A drug in his body. This provision is in force to complement new bail provisions, which can take account of a person's drug-use status. Solicitors should note that as of 1 December 2005 a new scheme operates in pilot areas resulting in the testing of suspects prior to charge, this scheme is to be rolled out nationally. Persons are requested to give a sample for testing and cannot be forced to do so. However, persons commit an offence under ss.63B and 63C PACE where they refuse without good cause to provide a sample for which they are liable, on summary conviction, to imprisonment for a term not exceeding three months or a fine not exceeding level 4 on the standard scale (£2,500) or both. If a person who has tested positive refuses to undergo further assessment they commit a criminal offence, even if they are not charged with the matter for which they were originally arrested.

Before such a sample can be taken the following conditions must be met:

(a) the person concerned has been arrested (if a pilot area) or charged with a 'trigger' offence (trigger offences are detailed in Schedule 6 Criminal Justice and Court Services Act 2000); or

(b) the person concerned has been arrested or charged with an offence and a police officer of inspector rank or above, who has reasonable grounds to suspect that the misuse by the person of any specified Class-A drug caused or contributed to the offence, has authorised the taking of the sample.

It should be noted that post-charge drug testing operates for those aged 14 years and above, but at the present time testing on arrest only applies to those aged 18 years or over.

A custody officer may authorise continued detention for up to six hours from the time of charge to enable a sample to be taken.

Table 2.3 Class-A drugs and trigger offences

Specified Class-A drugs

Class-A drugs as defined in the Misuse of Drugs Act 1971, specified by the Secretary of State (in SI 2001/1816) as:

Cocaine, its salts and any preparation or other product containing cocaine or its salts.

Diamorphine (commonly known as heroin), its salts and any preparation or other product containing diamorphine or its salts.

Trigger offences

1. Offences under the following provisions of the Theft Act 1968 are trigger offences:

section 1 (theft)
section 8 (robbery)
section 9 (burglary)
section 10 (aggravated burglary)
section 12 (taking motor vehicle or other conveyance without authority)
section 12A (aggravated vehicle-taking)
section 15 (obtaining property by deception)
section 22 (handling stolen goods)
section 25 (going equipped for stealing, etc.)

2. Offences under the following provisions of the Misuse of Drugs Act 1971 are trigger offences if committed in respect of a specified Class-A drug:

section 4 (restriction on production and supply of controlled drugs)
section 5(2) (possession of controlled drug)
section 5(3) (possession of controlled drug with intent to supply)

Table 2.3 Class-A drugs and trigger offences (cont.)

---

3. **An offence under section 1(1) of the Criminal Attempts Act 1981 is a trigger offence, if committed in respect of an offence under any of the following provisions of the Theft Act 1968:**

   section 1 (theft)
   section 8 (robbery)
   section 9 (burglary)
   section 15 (obtaining property by deception)
   section 22 (handling stolen goods)

4. **Offences under the following provisions of the Vagrancy Act 1824 are trigger offences:**

   section 3 (begging)
   section 4 (persistent begging)

Refusal

A person who refuses, without good cause, to give a sample is guilty of an offence punishable on summary conviction by imprisonment for a term not exceeding three months, or by a fine not exceeding level 4 on the standard scale, or both.

Clients may ask whether a refusal is better than a positive sample. In reality a refusal will simply lead to an inevitable inference by the court, so little is to be gained apart from a conviction. A solicitor can only advise his client of the available options and likely consequences; it is never proper to suggest that a criminal offence be committed.

Use of samples

Information obtained from a sample may be disclosed:

(a) for the purpose of informing decisions about bail;
(b) where a person is detained or otherwise remanded, or has been granted bail, for the purpose of informing any decision about his supervision;
(c) where the person is convicted of an offence, for the purpose of informing any decision about the appropriate sentence to be passed by a court and any decision about his supervision or release;
(d) for the purpose of ensuring that appropriate advice and treatment is made available to the person concerned.

It follows that a negative sample should always be emphasised to the court.

Interview

Solicitors who do not already advise their clients to stay away from the topic of drug use in interviews will now need to exercise even greater caution given that information received under this new power may well result in the refusal of bail in the magistrates' courts.

Codes of practice

See Code C17.

Scanning for drugs

Section 55A(1) enables a police officer of at least the rank of inspector to authorise an x-ray or ultrasound scan (or both) of a person suspected of swallowing a Class-A drug which he had in his possession with intent to supply or export unlawfully, where the person has been arrested for an offence and is in police detention.

Section 55A(2) provides that an x-ray may not be taken or an ultrasound scan undertaken without the suspect's consent which must be in writing. Section 55A(3) requires that the person be informed that the x-ray or ultrasound has been authorised and the grounds on which it has been authorised. Section 55A(4) provides that the x-ray or ultrasound scan may only be taken at a hospital, registered medical practitioner's surgery or other place used for medical purposes and only by a registered medical practitioner or nurse. Section 55A(5) and (6) requires that the authorisation for the x-ray or ultrasound, grounds for that authorisation and consent of the person to be searched is recorded in the custody record as soon as practicable after the x-ray has been taken or ultrasound carried out. Section 55A(9) provides that appropriate inferences may be drawn by a court or jury where a person refuses without good cause to consent to an x-ray or ultrasound scan.

VOLUNTARY ATTENDANCE

(See: Police and Criminal Evidence Act 1984 s.29.)

Where, for the purpose of assisting with an investigation, a person attends voluntarily at a police station or at any other place where a constable is present or accompanies a constable to a police station or any other such place without having been arrested:

1. He shall be entitled to leave at will unless he is placed under arrest.
2. He shall be informed at once that he is under arrest if a decision is taken by a constable to prevent him from leaving at will.

Cautioning

In the first instance, the volunteer will not necessarily have been cautioned, normally because they are not suspected at that stage of having committed an offence. If later the officer believes that there are grounds to suspect that a volunteer has committed an offence, the officer must caution the volunteer before questions or further questions are put (see Code C10.1).

Whenever a person who is not under arrest is initially cautioned or is reminded that he is under caution he must at the same time be told that he is not under arrest and is not obliged to remain with the officer. He must also be told that he may obtain free legal advice and assistance if he wishes, which includes the right to speak with a solicitor on the telephone. Once informed of this additional right, the volunteer must be asked whether or not he wants legal advice.

Treatment

Code C, Note for Guidance 1A provides that 'those there voluntarily to assist with an investigation should be treated with no less consideration [than those formally detained], e.g. offered refreshments at appropriate times, and enjoy an absolute right to obtain legal advice or communicate with anyone outside the police station'.

Particular issues

Since the person is at liberty to leave the police station seemingly without consequence it might be wondered what the advantages of assisting the police are. Apart from civic obligations, more likely to be adhered to by the truly innocent, there is arguably little point in assisting. A person may reason that their behaviour was justified or non-criminal in nature, yet, as solicitors know, the interpretation of the police may be different. It could be argued that it will avoid arrest, but if the offence is of any gravity, and is an arrestable offence, it is likely that as soon as any admissions are made an arrest will follow in any event; by forcing the arrest at least the custody clock has been set ticking. It should also be remembered that a person may feel a false sense of security in not having been arrested; such situations frequently lead to a tissue of lies being told which are only too easy to disprove subsequently to the severe detriment of the, now, defendant. It is a difficult balancing exercise but in any case where a solicitor is asked for advice he would be wise to stress to his client that only the truly innocent should attend as volunteers; anyone else should keep their distance.

CHAPTER 3

Magistrates' court procedure

ADVANCE DISCLOSURE

Overview

Advance disclosure of the prosecution case must be made in all either-way matters, prior to plea before venue and mode of trial (*R. v. Calderdale Magistrates' Court, ex parte Donahue and others* [2001] Crim LR 141). The purpose of disclosure is to ensure that the defendant can make an informed decision in relation to plea and venue. The prosecutor must give the defendant written notice of his right to see advance disclosure as soon as practicable after charge but in any event prior to plea before venue and mode of trial being determined. The court must be satisfied that the defendant has had an opportunity to see advance disclosure before proceeding further. It is now often the case that the police charge sheet will make reference to the right, and it is rare that one must actually ask to exercise it before the prosecution act. It is invariably the case that the prosecution will prepare a disclosure bundle in each and every either-way case.

Youths

In the youth court, the issue of plea before venue and mode of trial does not arise in the same way. A notice must be served in the same way, and a court, before taking a plea should ensure that the defendant has had an opportunity to receive and consider advance disclosure.

Summary or indictable-only matters

No obligation arises in respect of summary-only matters, nor those triable only on indictment. Despite there being no legal compulsion for disclosure most CPS prosecutors make voluntary disclosure in line with internal CPS guidance. This practice is in line with paragraph 43 of the Attorney-General's guidelines on disclosure.

Extent of the obligation

Magistrates' Courts (Advance Information) Rules 1985 (SI 1985/601) state that the prosecutor shall furnish the defendant with: 'a copy of those parts of every written statement which contains information as to the facts and matters of which the prosecution proposes to adduce in evidence in the proceedings, or, a summary of the facts and matters which the prosecutor proposes to adduce evidence in the proceedings' (rule 4).

Where further documents are referred to within statements (i.e. documentary exhibits), the prosecutor must also furnish a copy of those exhibits or such information as may be necessary to enable the person making the request to inspect the document or copy document.

Information can be withheld when the prosecutor is of the opinion that the disclosure of any particular fact or matter might lead to any person on whose evidence he proposes to rely in the proceedings being intimidated, to an attempt to intimidate him being made or otherwise to the course of justice being interfered with (rule 5). When a prosecutor withholds such disclosure, he shall give a notice in writing to the person who made the request for disclosure to the effect that certain evidence is being withheld. The prosecutor need not state the nature or source of that evidence. There has been much debate over the last few years as to the extent of disclosure required, particularly in relation to other documents referred to either in disclosed witness statements or summaries of evidence. In *R. v. Calderdale Magistrates' Court, ex parte Donahue and others* [2001] Crim LR 141, the Administrative Court held that a video should have been disclosed to the defence (either by providing a copy of it or by allowing it to be viewed) before plea and venue procedures had been entered into (it should be noted that in a later case (see below) the Crown, while acknowledging the correctness of this decision, wished to leave open for argument the question of whether a video was a document; defence lawyers should not therefore be surprised if at some point in the future they are faced with this argument). In the case of a video that the Crown is not seeking to rely upon there would be no such duty.

In *R. v. Croydon Magistrates' Court, ex parte DPP* [2001] Crim LR 980, the court stated that there was no duty to serve details of DNA profiles as no document had been referred to in the case summary, and the scientific case had been spelled out fully in the summary. Brooke LJ revisited the 'document' question raised in the *Calderdale* case and hinted that a later court may take a different view.

If the defence are seeking disclosure in order to decide whether or not to advise a client to accept a police caution, it should be given (*DPP* v. *Ara, The Times*, 16 July 2001).

Adjournments in default of advance disclosure

Rule 7 states that: '[If rule 4] has not been complied with, the court shall adjourn the proceedings pending compliance with the requirements unless the court is satisfied that the conduct of the case for the accused will not be substantially prejudiced by non-compliance with the requirement'.

A court has no power to dismiss a case if advance disclosure is not given (*King* v. *Kucharz, The Times*, 2 February 1989). Repeated failure to serve advance disclosure in defiance of a direction of the court may found a basis upon which to apply to stay the case for abuse of process (however, given the current authorities on abuse of process, this would have to be an extreme case). Any solicitor contemplating an abuse of process application on the grounds of non-disclosure should refer to the full transcript in *R.* v. *Leeds Youth Court, ex parte AP and others* (2001) 165 JP 684.

BAIL

Presumption in favour of bail

Although it is common to speak of a presumption in favour of bail, in fact, under the Bail Act 1976 (BA 1976) the language used is much stronger than that; there is a statutory right to bail, in all but a few cases. The distinction is not without importance given the significance for the defendant of a refusal of bail. Recent changes in the Criminal Justice Act 2003 (see below) create reverse burdens for offenders with drug-related problems.

Bail applications

Every defendant has the right to apply for bail when appearing before the court for the first time in custody. A second application, based on the same grounds is permitted at the next hearing. Technically, if no application is made at the first or second hearing that opportunity is lost. Therefore to maximise a defendant's chances of bail, applications should be made at the first and second hearings. A remand due to insufficient information (under BA 1976, Sched. 1, pt. 1, para. 5) should be disregarded, as a remand under para. 5 is not a decision to refuse bail (*R.* v. *Calder Justices, ex parte Kennedy, The Times*, 18 February 1992). A remand in absence is also disregarded in considering the 'subsequent hearing rule' (*R.* v. *Dover and East Kent Justices, ex parte Dean, The Times*, 22 August 1991).

Repeated applications for bail

Subsequent applications for bail can be made only where there is a change in circumstances. The following may amount to a change:

1. A lapse of 28 days since the last application (a recommendation of the Law Commission).
2. Service of committal documents may amount to a change in circumstances, particularly if the case against the defendant appears to be much different from what the defence believed it to be on an earlier occasion (*R. v. Reading Crown Court, ex parte Malik* [1981] QB 451).
3. Increased surety (*R. v. Isleworth Crown Court, ex parte Commissioners of Customs and Excise, The Times*, 27 July 1990).
4. Illness of defendant's relative (in this case mother): *R v. Barking Justices, ex parte Shankshaft* (1983) 147 JP 399.

On a renewed application for bail the court must consider not only the new circumstances, but all those circumstances that applied before. The court has to bear wholly in mind the facts of the previous applications, how they were put and what the objections were at that particular time (per Comyn, J. *ex parte Shankshaft*).

Applications to the Crown Court

Once magistrates' court bail applications have been exhausted (or before if the defendant prefers, provided you have a certificate of full argument) an application can be made to a judge in chambers in the Crown Court. To maximise the chances of success, it is generally preferable to make two applications in the magistrates' court before turning to the Crown Court, as it is extremely unlikely that a magistrates' court would grant bail following a refusal by the Crown Court.

If a case is sent to the Crown Court by virtue of s.51 Crime and Disorder Act 1998, the second bail application before the magistrates' court is lost. Before an application can be made to the Crown Court it is essential to have received a certificate of full argument, which should be lodged with the application.

Applications to the High Court

High Court jurisdiction in respect to bail in criminal proceedings has now been abolished (s.17 CJA 2003). A defendant aggrieved at the refusal of bail, or the imposition of conditions has now to make his application to the Crown Court.

Applications to the Crown Court to vary conditional bail

Appeals against the imposition of certain bail conditions can be made (s.16 CJA 2003) provided that the condition appealed relates to:

(a) the person concerned residing away from a particular place or area;

(b) the person concerned residing at a particular place other than a bail hostel;

(c) the provision of a surety or sureties or the giving of a security;

(d) the person concerned remaining indoors between certain hours;

(e) requirements with respect to electronic monitoring (imposed under s.3(6ZAA) Bail Act 1976); or

(f) the person concerned making no contact with another person.

If the Crown Court refuses bail, or refuses to vary conditions of bail, an application by way of judicial review is possible (see **www.crimeline.info/ issue130.doc** for an article discussing judicial review of bail refusals).

Exceptions to the right to bail

These include the following:

1. A magistrates' court cannot grant bail to a defendant charged with treason. Bail can only be granted by a Justice of the High Court or by order of the Secretary of State. Given that a High Court bail application can be listed and heard within 24 hours, there would appear to be no infringement of the ECHR.

2. If a defendant is charged with or convicted of murder, attempted murder, manslaughter, rape or attempted rape and he has a previous conviction (by or before a court in any part of the United Kingdom) for any one of those offences (not necessarily the same offence with which he is now charged) or for culpable homicide, he shall only be granted bail if the court is satisfied that there are exceptional circumstances which justify it (s.25 Criminal Justice and Public Order Act 1994 (CJPOA 1994)). It remains doubtful whether this section is compatible with the ECHR. The Law Commission (paper no. 157 *Bail and the Human Rights Act 1998*) expressed grave reservations about its operation in practice and solicitors should read and consider paras. 27–40 of the report. Section 25 also operates on the expiry of custody time limits, thereby preventing the release of the defendant (*R. (On the application of 'O') v. (1) Harrow Crown Court (2) Governor of HM Prison Wormwood Scrubbs, The Times*, 29 May 2003).

3. A defendant committed for sentence does not enjoy a statutory right to bail, nor does a defendant who has been convicted of an offence (even when appealing the conviction or sentence), save where his case has been adjourned for reports before sentencing. However, even in the absence of a statutory right to bail it would be wrong of a court to consider that it could simply remand a defendant in custody without good reason, as this would offend Article 5 ECHR. It is generally accepted practice that a defendant who has been on bail in proceedings and then enters a guilty

plea and is committed to the Crown Court for sentence, should remain on bail.

4. The court can refuse bail if it has substantial grounds for believing that a person charged with or convicted of an imprisonable offence would, if released on bail, with or without conditions:

   (a) fail to surrender to custody;
   (b) commit an offence while on bail;
   (c) interfere with witnesses or otherwise obstruct the course of justice.

5. The court can refuse bail in respect of a person charged with or convicted of an imprisonable offence, if:

   (a) custody is required for the protection of the defendant or, in the case of a defendant under 17 years, his own welfare;
   (b) he is already serving a sentence;
   (c) the court has insufficient information, due to the want of time since proceedings were initiated;
   (d) he has breached his bail conditions or absconded (see below);
   (e) the court wishes to receive a report or make inquiries and it would not be practicable to complete that task without the defendant being in custody.

6. In the case of a person charged with or convicted of an offence which is not imprisonable, bail can be denied if he has failed to surrender to bail in those proceedings and the court believes that due to that failure he would not surrender to bail (with or without conditions) in the future, and also under grounds 5(a), (b) and (d) above.

7. A defendant need not be granted bail if the offence is not triable summarily only and he was already on bail for another offence at the date the new offence was allegedly committed. The Law Commission felt that this rule was not compatible with Article 5 ECHR.

Section 19 CJA 2003 provides for a presumption against the grant of bail in the following circumstances:

1. The defendant is aged 18 or over.
2. A sample taken under s.63B PACE or s.161 CJA 2003 has revealed the presence of a Class-A drug in the body.
3. Either the offence is possession (or possession with intent) of any specified Class-A drug, or the court is satisfied that there are substantial grounds for believing that misuse by the defendant of any specified Class-A drug caused or contributed to the offence or (even if it did not) that the offence was motivated wholly or partly by intended misuse of such drug.
4. A relevant assessment has been offered to the defendant but the defendant has refused it or the defendant has undergone a relevant

assessment, and relevant follow-up has been proposed, but the defendant does not agree to it.

If all the above factors are present the defendant may not be granted bail unless the court is satisfied that there is no significant risk of the commission of an offence while on bail; but this does not require the court, if so satisfied, to grant bail.

Where the court does grant bail to an offender meeting the criteria above, it must impose a condition that the offender undergo the relevant assessment, or as the case may be, participate in the relevant follow up.

Home Office circular 22/2004 provides more details of the scheme and also lists the current pilot areas.

Imposition of conditions

Unconditional bail should be the starting point for all bail decisions. Conditional bail may be imposed if the court believes that there is a risk that the defendant will:

(a) fail to surrender to bail;
(b) commit offences while on bail;
(c) interfere with witnesses or otherwise obstruct the course of justice;
(d) not co-operate with the making of pre-sentence or other reports;
(e) not attend appointments with his legal adviser.

There is a requirement in relation to a person granted bail on a charge of murder, to impose a condition of bail that the defendant undergo examination by two medical practitioners, one of whom must be approved under s.12 Mental Health Act 1983 (MHA 1983). For the difficulties that can arise from the ordering of such reports see *R.* v. *Reid and Others* [2002] 1 Cr App R 21.

Solicitors should always examine closely the necessity for any given bail condition. Defendants frequently appear before the court laden with conditions which the Crown seek to have reimposed, but which are often unnecessary and not founded on any real risks; this is particularly so in relation to defendants with no antecedent history.

Doorstep curfews have been held to be compliant with the Bail Act and do not violate Articles 5 or 8 ECHR (*R. (DPP)* v. *Chorley Justices*, *The Times*, 22 October 2002).

Electronic monitoring as a condition of bail

Electronic tagging is available in pilot areas as part of the government's street crime initiative.

The use of tagging on bail is intended to act as an alternative to custody, and therefore should be suggested in cases where custody seems likely, in order to avoid a remand into the adult custody estate. In addition to tagging, voice verification can be utilised (full guidance is available from **www.homeoffice.gov.uk**).

Prosecution applying to amend conditions of bail or remand defendant in custody

A common scenario is a defendant arriving at court for his first appearance and the prosecution wanting to add to the conditions of bail imposed by the police. There are less frequently cases where a prosecutor wishes to revisit the question of conditional bail and ask for a remand into custody, at either a first or a subsequent hearing (or even before the first hearing in some instances).

Section 5B Bail Act 1976 allows a prosecutor to invite the court to reconsider the question of bail and either:

(a) vary the conditions of bail;
(b) impose conditions in respect of bail which has been granted uncondi-
     tionally; or
(c) withhold bail.

Such applications cannot be made in respect of offences triable summarily only, and no application for reconsideration of a previous decision on bail can be made unless it is based on information which was not available to the court or constable when the decision to grant bail was made (s.5B(3)). It would appear that if a prosecutor exercises his rights under s.5B and bail is still granted, the prosecutor can, if the other conditions are met, appeal the grant of bail to the Crown Court (for which see below).

If a court refuses to withhold bail after being invited to do so by the Crown, it must state the reasons for so refusing (s.5B(8B)).

The powers available to the prosecution under s.5B are often mistaken for those under s.3(8). Section 5B acts as a mechanism by which the Crown can move quickly to oppose bail granted by the police in circumstances where the Crown feel that either bail should not have been granted at all, or should have been granted with different conditions. Such an application must be made in writing and contain a statement of the grounds on which it is made (see rule 93B(2) MCR 1981). Section 3(8) allows applications to be made by the prosecutor to vary or impose conditions of bail already granted by a court, without a requirement that there be a change of circumstances.

Prosecution appeals against the grant of bail

The Bail (Amendment) Act 1993 allows a prosecutor to appeal the grant of bail in the following circumstances:

1. The offence must be punishable with imprisonment.
2. The prosecution must be conducted by or on behalf of the Director of Public Prosecutions (DPP) or other authorised prosecutors (Serious Fraud Office, Department of Trade and Industry, Customs and Excise, Department of Work and Pensions (former DSS), Post Office, The Director of Revenue and Customs Prosecutions and any person designated under s.37(1) Commissioners for Revenue and Customs Act 2005 (SI 1994/1438 and SI 2005/1129)).
3. The prosecution must have made representations that bail should not be granted, before the time it was actually granted.

Procedure

The prosecutor must give oral notice of the appeal to the court at the conclusion of the proceedings and before the defendant is released, and within two hours thereafter serve a written appeal notice on the defendant and the court. In *R.* v. *Isleworth Crown Court, ex parte Clarke* [1998] 1 Cr App R 257, oral notice was given to the clerk five minutes after the court rose, but before the defendant had been released, this was deemed to comply with the requirements of the Act. Similarly in *R.* v. *Warwick Crown Court, ex parte Jeffrey* [2003] Crim LR 190, a delay in actual service of the written notice of three minutes in circumstances where the prosecution delayed even attempting to serve the notice for some considerable period of time, was held to be valid.

If written notice is served within the two hours, the defendant will remain in custody and be brought before the Crown Court for the appeal to be heard. Service is satisfied if the prosecutor hands the notice to the jailer to pass to the defendant (*ex parte Clarke*).

The appeal must be heard within 48 hours (excluding weekends and public holidays); the time runs from the end of the day on which notice was given (*R.* v. *Middlesex Crown Court, ex parte Okoli* [2001] 1 Cr App R 1).

Defence appeal against conditional bail

If a defendant is dissatisfied with the conditions of bail imposed by a magistrates' court, his remedy is to apply to the Crown Court (see above). A representation order covers related bail proceedings in the Crown Court.

Breaches of bail

Section 7 Bail Act 1976 (BA 1976) states that a person who has been released on bail in criminal proceedings and is under a duty to surrender into the custody of a court may be arrested without warrant by a constable:

1. If the constable has reasonable grounds for believing that that person is not likely to surrender to custody.
2. If the constable has reasonable grounds for believing that that person is likely to break any of the conditions of his bail or has reasonable grounds for suspecting that that person has broken any of those conditions. Or
3. In a case where that person was released on bail with one or more surety or sureties, if a surety notifies a constable in writing that that person is unlikely to surrender to custody and that for that reason the surety wishes to be relieved of his obligations as a surety.

Procedure

The person must be brought before the court as soon as practicable after arrest and in any event within 24 hours after his arrest. The person must be brought before a court within the petty sessions area in which he was arrested, or in the case of a person who was due in any event to surrender to custody within 24 hours of arrest (i.e. next appearance only a day away) he shall be brought before the court at which he was to have surrendered to custody. In calculating the 24 hours, no account shall be taken of Christmas Day, Good Friday or Sunday.

If the breach is admitted, the court will move on to consider bail in the normal way; if it is denied, the court will determine the breach.

Hearing to determine whether bail breached

Magistrates' courts must determine alleged breaches of bail imposed by the Crown Court, they cannot remand the defendant in custody so that a judge can determine the breach (*R.* v. *Teesside Magistrates' Court, ex parte Ellison, The Times*, 20 February 2001).

There is no power to adjourn the breach hearing to another day, but in *R.* v. *Derby Magistrates' Court and another, ex parte Jamil Hussain* [2001] 1 WLR 2454 it was held lawful for a bench to adjourn the case to an afternoon list where another bench would hear the matter, in order that further evidence could be gathered.

The general procedure to be followed was decided in *R.* v. *Liverpool Justices, ex parte DPP* (1992) 95 Cr App R 222, and reaffirmed as being correct and Human Rights Act compatible in *R.* v. *Havering Magistrates' Court, ex parte DPP* [2001] Cr App R 2, and can be summarised as follows:

(a) the strict rules of evidence did not apply, hearsay evidence could be permitted;

(b) the court would take regard of the type of evidence advanced, and take account of the fact that evidence has not been subjected to cross-examination;

(c) the prosecution can call witnesses to give evidence, and those witnesses can be cross-examined by the defence;

(d) the defendant may be allowed to give oral evidence.

In practice, prosecutors rarely have witness statements from arresting officers, and mainly rely upon matters detailed on the MG5. It is this author's practice to take a detailed witness statement from a defendant denying a breach and submit it as evidence after the prosecution has outlined its case. There is no requirement to put the Crown on notice of this practice. A powerful submission can then be made as to how the court could possibly favour one version over another. Of course, the balance changes if there is more than one officer's evidence or there is other compelling evidence, but frequently the prosecution will take their case for granted and be ill-equipped to deal with this kind of challenge. There is no requirement to subject a defendant to cross-examination on his statement and he is not a compellable witness. If the court is not satisfied that a breach has occurred, the defendant must be released on the same conditions as before.

Arguably, the fact of an earlier admitted or proven breach could be admitted under the bad character provisions to show a propensity to breach bail.

Bail if breach proved

If a breach of bail is admitted or proved, the court must then go on to consider whether to grant bail or remand into custody. A breach of bail cannot of itself justify a remand into custody, but may well lend support to other objections to bail. For example, if an alleged burglar, subject to a night-time curfew, were found in a back garden in the middle of the night, the court may justifiably feel that there are now substantial grounds for believing that if he were to be released on bail he would commit further offences, as their fears could no longer be alleviated by conditional bail.

The Law Commission has stated that:

We conclude that a refusal to grant bail on the ground that the defendant has been arrested is likely to violate article 5 unless it can be justified on one of the other exceptions to the right to bail. Paragraph 9 already requires a court to have regard to 'the defendant's record as respects the fulfilment of his obligations under previous grants of bail' as a factor in assessing whether paragraph 2 grounds are made out. That is all that need be said.

Bail Act offences

The following are offences:

(a) to fail, without reasonable excuse, to surrender to bail;

(b) having failed with reasonable cause to surrender to bail, failing to surrender to custody as soon as reasonably practicable thereafter.

The defence of 'reasonable excuse' falls upon the defendant to prove on the balance of probabilities. Getting the date wrong (*Laidlaw* v. *Atkinson, The Times*, 2 August 1986), and not being given a copy of the bail notice (s.6(4) BA 1976), do not amount to a reasonable excuse, although query whether there might be exceptional circumstances prevailing which may justify 'forgetting' the date, such as the death of a defendant's child at or around the date he was due to surrender. A reliance on what was said by a legal adviser could amount to a reasonable excuse, but whether a solicitor's mistake was or was not a reasonable excuse is a question to be determined in every case in the light of all the circumstances (*R.* v. *Liverpool Stipendiary Magistrate, ex parte Santos* [1996] EWHC Admin 235, at para. 11).

The designated date of surrender can be proved by production of a certified copy of the court register (s.6 BA 1976) or bail sheet. It should be remembered, however, that it must still be proved that the person in the dock is the person referred to in the register; this is a classic scenario, more often utilised by the defence in driving-while-disqualified cases, but of no less importance in this situation; cases can easily be won by taking this point (*R.* v. *Derwentside Justices, ex parte Heaviside* [1996] RTR 354). However, if the Bail Act trial takes place after the substantive matter (and it should), and the defendant has acknowledged bail in his name at a previous hearing, that would be sufficient to prove identity; similarly, if there was a conviction on the substantive matter, it could be admitted pursuant to s.74 PACE to support identity.

It is a matter for the prosecution to decide whether to proceed with a failure to answer bail set by the police. Any information must be laid within six months of the failure to attend, or alternatively no later than three months after that person's surrender, arrest or being brought before the court (s.15 CJA 2003). Solicitors should always check that the charge has been entered on to the court register within the limitation; the fact that a note exists on the prosecution file is irrelevant. In respect of court bail, the court has discretion as to whether or not to proceed, and a decision not to proceed with a Bail Act offence is binding on subsequent benches (*France* v. *Dewsbury Magistrates' Court* [1988] Crim LR 295). The maximum penalty for failing to surrender to bail is three months' imprisonment, although the magistrates' court can commit the matter for sentence, with 12 months' imprisonment being available to the Crown Court (s.6(7) BA 1976).

Penalty

A Crown Court ought not to impose a sentence of imprisonment of less than five days (as is the case in the magistrates' court by virtue of statute) (*R.* v. *Hourigan* [2003] EWCA Crim 2306). Sentences imposed for Bail Act offences should generally be consecutive to any other custodial sentence imposed (*R.* v. *White and McKinnon, The Times*, 9 December 2002).

BAIL – YOUNG OFFENDERS

Children and Young Persons Act 1969 (CYPA 1969) s.23

The bail framework in relation to juveniles is as for adults, save for two differences:

1. The age of the defendant determines the fate for a person denied bail, with differing provisions for boys and girls.
2. Electronic monitoring of bail conditions is now available whether as part of an intensive supervision and surveillance programme or stand alone (ss.3(6ZAA) and 3AA BA 1976).

Electronic monitoring of bail conditions

Section 3(6ZAA) provides that a child or young person may be required to comply with requirements imposed for the purpose of securing the electronic monitoring of his compliance with any other requirement imposed on him as a condition of bail.

The following criteria must be satisfied under s.3AA:

1. Child or young person must be at least 12 years of age.
2. The youth must be charged with or have been convicted of a violent or sexual offence, or an offence punishable in the case of an adult with imprisonment for a term of 14 years or more; *or*, is charged with or has been convicted of one or more imprisonable offences which, together with any other imprisonable offences of which he has been convicted in any proceedings amount to (or would amount to if he were convicted of the offences with which he is charged) a recent history of repeatedly committing imprisonable offences while remanded on bail or to local authority accommodation.
3. The court must have been notified that electronic-monitoring arrangements are in force.
4. The youth offending team must have informed the court that in its opinion the imposition of such a requirement will be suitable in the case of the child or young person.

Table 3.1 Disposal on refusal of bail
Note: Once bail has been refused, disposal will be as set out below. (Note CA 1989 = Children Act 1989.)

Boys and girls aged 10 and 11	Boys and girls aged 12–14	Girls aged 15 and 16	Boys aged 15 and 16	Boys and girls aged 17 years
Remand to local authority accommodation with or without conditions***	Remand to local authority accommodation with or without conditions***	Remand to local authority accommodation with or without conditions***	Remand to local authority accommodation with or without conditions***	Remand to prison, as in the case of an adult
LA can apply for Secure Accommodation order (s.25 CA 1989)****	LA can apply for Secure Accommodation order (s.25 CA 1989)****	LA can apply for Secure Accommodation order (s.25 CA 1989)****	LA can apply for Secure Accommodation order (s.25 CA 1989)****	
Court can require the LA to report to the court (s.23B CYPA 1969)	Court can remand to LA accommodation with a require-ment that he be kept in secure accommodation, if criteria met (the security requirement)*	Court can remand to LA accommodation with a require-ment that she be kept in secure accommodation, if criteria met (the security requirement)*	If the criteria is met (the security requirement)*, the remand in the case of a boy aged 15 to 16 will be to a remand centre if available or prison, unless the boy is deemed 'vulnerable'.** If deemed vulnerable, the remand will be to LA accom-modation with a requirement that he be kept in secure accommodation *but* only if the court has been notified that secure accom-modation is available (If there is none available then the remand will be to a remand centre if a place is available or to a prison if it is not) The reason for this distinction is the simple lack of available places in LA secure accom-modation units	

*Criteria for imposition of security requirement when remanding to LA accommodation (s.23 CYPA 1969):

1. The defendant (who must have attained 12 years) is convicted of or is charged with a *violent offence* or *sexual offence* (Part 1 CJA 1991) or *offence which for an adult is punishable with imprisonment of 14 years or more* (s.23(5)(a) CYPA 1969).

    Or:

2. Is charged with or has been convicted of one or more imprisonable offences, which, together with any other imprisonable offences of which he has been convicted in any proceedings, amount to (or would amount to if he were convicted of the offences with which he is charged) a recent history of repeatedly committing imprisonable offences while remanded on bail or to LA accommodation.

    And:

    In either case the court is of the opinion, after considering all the options for the remand of the person, that only remanding him to LA accommodation with a security requirement would be adequate: (a) to protect the public from really serious harm from him; or (b) to prevent the commission by him of imprisonable offences.

The court must consult the designated authority before imposing the security requirement (s.23(4) CYPA 1969).

A court shall not impose a security requirement in respect of a person who is not legally represented in the court unless he was granted a right to representation which was withdrawn because of his conduct or having been informed of his right to apply for representation and had the opportunity to do so, he refused or failed to apply.

** Vulnerability criteria

The effect of the criteria being established in the case of a boy aged 15 or 16 will be to prevent a remand into the prison estate, and mean a remand into LA accommodation, with a security requirement instead. Advocates should never underestimate the severe detrimental effect a remand into prison may have upon a young child.

Section 23(5A) CYPA 1969 states that a person will be deemed vulnerable if the court is of the opinion that, by reason of his physical or emotional immaturity or a propensity of his to harm himself, it would be undesirable for him to be remanded to a remand centre or prison.

It is important to remember that the Youth Justice Board has been working to produce bail assessment material which will heavily influence the decision-making process in respect of the assessment of vulnerability. Advocates should ensure that a full assessment is available to the court as soon as possible; this can be done by early liaison with the youth offending team at court.

*** Imposition of conditions

When remanding to LA accommodation without a security requirement, the court can impose conditions in the same manner as it might consider in the case of an adult. In addition, electronic monitoring can be imposed (ss.23(7)(b) and 23AA CYPA 1969), the criteria for which are outlined above.

Conditions can be imposed on the defendant (s.23(7) CYPA 1969), after consulting with the local authority.

Conditions can be imposed on the LA (s.23(9) CYPA 1969), after consulting with the LA. The conditions must be such as to assist in securing compliance by the defendant with the conditions imposed on him, and may stipulate that he shall not be placed with a named person.

**** LA applications for secure accommodation

These applications are civil in nature and not covered under a representation order. Children under 13 cannot be made subject to such orders without the permission of the Secretary of State. Note, however, that this restriction does not apply to remands ordered in criminal proceedings in the case of children aged 13 or over.

No remand shall exceed 28 days.

Criteria:

Accommodation other than secure accommodation is inappropriate because the child is likely to abscond from such other accommodation, or the child is likely to injure himself or other people if he is kept in any such other accommodation (s.23(5)(a) and (b) CYPA 1969).

Meaning of serious harm

The court must examine the nature of the offences of which the youth has been charged or convicted; the chance that further such offences might be committed is not of itself enough (*R.* v. *Croydon Youth Court, ex parte G, The Times*, 3 May 1995).

Meaning of violent offence

Violent offence means any offence which leads or is intended or likely to lead to a person's death or physical injury. Aggravated vehicle taking is a violent offence (*R.* v. *Calder Justices, ex parte Coleman* [1993] COD 459).

Practical considerations

It is important to understand that there are a large number of options available to the court before resorting to secure remand. The options are:

- unconditional bail;
- conditional bail;
- conditional bail with tagging;
- bail supervision and support;
- bail supervision and support with tagging;
- bail, Intensive Supervision and Surveillance Programme (ISSP);
- bail ISSP with voice verification;
- bail ISSP with tagging;
- remand into LA accommodation (with conditions);
- remand into LA accommodation with tagging;
- secure remand.

At every bail hearing it is incumbent on the advocate to draw the court back to the beginning and analyse each option carefully before allowing it to be dismissed; a remand into secure accommodation is a last-resort measure and ought to be regarded as a failure if other methods have not at least been proposed and discussed at length.

Human Rights Act compliance

The provisions in relation to the imprisonment of boys aged 15 and 16 years differ greatly from those affecting girls of the same age. The provisions have however been held ECHR compliant (*R. (SR)* v. *Nottingham Magistrates' Court* [2001] EWHC Admin 802).

COMMITTAL FOR TRIAL AND ALTERNATIVES

Trial at the Crown Court can take place in the following scenarios:

(a) indictable-only matters which must go to the Crown Court;
(b) either-way matters where jurisdiction has been declined or the defendant has elected Crown Court trial (or in the case of a youth where he is to be tried according to the adult offender's choice);
(c) transferred proceedings;
(d) voluntary bill of indictment (outside the scope of this book).

Table 3.2 Transfer of cases

Method of transferring case to the Crown Court	Notes
Committal proceedings	Jurisdiction under s.6 MCA 1980. Defendant can concede a prima facie case exists (s.6(2)), or ask to challenge the evidence by having the evidence read out to the court and making submissions (s.6(1)).
	Prosecution can decide which evidence to rely upon during committal proceedings and serve additional evidence at a later stage.
	There is no right to have oral evidence presented during a s.6(1) committal, nor do the defence have the right to call any evidence whatsoever.
	The test is whether there is 'sufficient evidence' on which to commit, commonly referred to as a 'prima facie' case.
	The court has no power to exercise discretion under ss.76 and 78 PACE.
	The court can commit on any indictable offence, although if the offence is different from the one charged and triable either way, the court may revert to trying the offence summarily (with consent), provided that the original offence was not itself triable only on indictment (see *R.* v. *Cambridge Justices, ex parte Fraser* [1985] 1 All ER 667 and s.25 MCA 1980). Certain summary-only offences can be included on an indictment provided that the criteria are satisfied. The offences are not committed to the Crown Court, simply added to the indictment (see s.40 CJA 1988). If the offences have been charged in the lower court they are simply adjourned *sine die*.
	Other purely summary offences provided that they are either imprisonable or carry discretionary or obligatory disqualification from driving can also be included provided that the offence being committed is triable either way and the offences are related (see s.41 CJA 1988). There is no power to attach s.41 offences to an indictable-only matter.
	A committal can take place in the absence of the defendant (*R.* v. *Liverpool City Magistrates' Court, ex parte Quantrell* [1999] Crim LR 734).
Sending cases for trial	Jurisdiction under s.51 Crime and Disorder Act 1998.
	The court shall send any indictable-only offence, along with any related either-way

	offence, to the Crown Court. There is no plea before venue issue or mode of trial to determine. The court must also send any related summary-only offence which is punishable with imprisonment or discretionary or mandatory disqualification. Related offences need not be sent on the same occasion. Others jointly charged will similarly be sent. Again, it does not matter whether they appear on the same occasion or not, and will be sent even if only charged with a related either-way matter. A youth jointly charged with an adult (whether on the same occasion or not) will be subject to s.51 if it is in the interests of justice to try him with the adult. If a defendant is charged with an either-way offence and the offence is later changed to an indictable-only offence, the s.51 procedure will still apply (*R.* v. *Bow Street Magistrates' Court, ex parte Salubi and another (and conjoined cases)*, *The Times*, 4 June 2002).
Transferred cases involving allegations of fraud and cases involving children	Jurisdiction under s.4 Criminal Justice Act 1987 (fraud cases) and s.53 Criminal Justice Act 1991 (child cases). These provisions have the effect of immediately moving the case to the Crown Court. Plea before venue and mode of trial do not arise, although the transfer could take place afterwards. If a youth court has decided to hear a matter summarily, a notice of transfer has no effect, since the powers of the DPP do not have the effect of overriding a lawful order of the court (*R.* v. *Fareham Youth Court, ex parte CPS* [1999] Crim LR 325), and the presumption is in favour of summary justice for youths (s.24 MCA 1980). It is only where the grave-crime provisions operate and the youth court has declined jurisdiction that the transfer provisions can arise. There is nothing that can be done to challenge a notice of transfer provided it is procedurally correct, as the decision to transfer is not open to question or challenge in any court.

Anticipated changes to sending provisions

When brought into force, Schedule 3 CJA 2003 will abolish committal proceedings and allow all offences to be sent immediately to the Crown Court once a court has declined jurisdiction, or the defendant has elected Crown Court trial.

EVIDENCE IN CIVIL CASES

Duty solicitors can now be called upon to deal with cases which are civil in nature. The civil evidence rules differ greatly from the usual criminal rules, and will be encountered in applications for antisocial behaviour orders, football-banning orders, and the like.

Evidential framework

Civil complaints are dealt with under Part II MCA 1980 and statutory rules made thereunder.

The main rules are:

Section 51 Court's power to issue summons on complaint. Solicitors should check that the summons is procedurally correct, in particular that the complainant is a named person as opposed to a body corporate.

Section 52 Defines the court's jurisdiction to deal with complaints arising in its commission area.

Section 53 The nature of the complaint must be put to the defendant if he appears. The court must thereafter hear evidence (if the complaint is denied). The court can dismiss the complaint or grant the order sought.

Section 54 Court's power to adjourn. The court cannot resume a hearing unless it is satisfied that the parties have had adequate notice. Adjournment period is unlimited, subject to s.55.

Section 55 If the defendant does not appear, the court may proceed in his absence, adjourn the hearing or issue a warrant. The court can only issue a warrant if the complaint is substantiated on oath (or in any other prescribed manner), and the court is satisfied that the summons was served on the defendant within what appears to the court to be a reasonable time and that the notice given of the new date is adequate. The latter criteria must also be satisfied before a court proceeds in absence. It should be noted that a summons may well have been served in good time, but the notice period is still inadequate, for example in the case of a doctor with fixed surgery commitments.

If the defendant was present on the last occasion, then he is deemed to have known of the new date (unless it was later changed) and therefore no issue of service of an adjournment notice arises.

If a defendant appears on an executed warrant, he may be further remanded; no single remand may exceed eight days (see s.128(3)). A warrant may not be issued, nor may a further remand be authorised after the defendant has given evidence in the proceedings.

If the complainant does not appear, the court may dismiss the complaint, or in the case where the complainant's evidence has already been heard, proceed in the complainant's absence.

A defendant represented by solicitor or counsel is deemed to be present, unless required to be there on any condition of a recognisance expressly requiring his attendance (see s.122 MCA 1980).

Order of evidence

Rule 14 Magistrates' Court Rules 1981 lays down the following framework for contested cases:

1. Complainant may make opening speech.
2. Complainant calls evidence. Since this is a civil matter, the statements will have been served in advance and either agreed or rejected. If rejected, the witness will be called to give evidence, but does not give evidence-in-chief in the usual way, since the witness statement stands as that evidence. The complainant will call the witness, show the witness his statement and confirm that that witness made the statement. The complainant should only ask supplementary questions to clarify any points in the witness statement. Any attempt to lead the witness through the evidence should be resisted. The defendant can, of course, cross-examine in the usual way.
3. Defendant may address the court, whether or not he calls evidence.
4. Defendant may call evidence.
5. Complainant may call evidence in rebuttal.
6. Defendant may make closing speech, unless he made an opening speech.
7. Either party may seek leave to address the court further; if one party is granted leave the other must also be given leave to make a further speech. If leave is granted at the behest of the defendant, then he will make his second speech before the complainant makes his. However, where the complainant asks to make a second speech, the defendant will follow, thereby having the last word.

Hearsay rules

It is the admissibility of hearsay evidence which will have the potential to cause the most confusion among criminal practitioners, since the criminal rules of evidence are centred around an avoidance of anything other than first-hand knowledge.

Solicitors will need to consider SI 1999/681 (as amended), but the position can be summarised as follows:

1. A party seeking to rely on hearsay evidence must give a notice, not less than 21 days before the hearing, signifying his intention. The hearsay notice must:

(a) state that it is a hearsay notice;

(b) identify the proceedings;

(c) state that the party proposes to call hearsay evidence;

(d) identify the hearsay evidence;

(e) identify the person who made the statement which is to be given in evidence; and

(f) state why that person will not be called to given oral evidence.

So, for example, a local authority in an antisocial behaviour order case may serve notice that a police officer will give evidence of what a resident has told him, relying on the fact that the resident refuses himself to give evidence. Alternatively, the complainant may serve a witness statement written by a resident who is not willing to attend court.

2. A notice may deal with the hearsay evidence of more than one witness.

3. The other party may seek to get round the hearsay notice by attempting to call that witness themselves (i.e. in the above example requiring the resident to give evidence). See rule 4 for this power, and the procedural formalities. There is a significant difference in this scenario with a criminal case, since a witness so called can be cross-examined by the party calling. There is a discretion in the rules as to whether the court will allow such a witness to be called, but there are no criteria upon which the discretion is to be exercised. The rule stems from s.3 Civil Evidence Act 1995 (CEA 1995). It may, however, be wiser tactically to leave the evidence, and instead comment on its credibility and the weight to be attached to it.

4. If a hearsay notice is served, then that evidence will be admitted (subject to the other party making an application to call the witness as outlined above).

5. If an attack is to be made on the credibility of a witness whose hearsay evidence is to be admitted, or it is to be alleged that the person who made the statement made another statement inconsistent with it, that party must give notice to the other side. So, in the example above, a defendant may wish to call evidence of bad character on the part of the resident, or admit evidence that he has on a previous occasion praised the defendant's community spirit.

6. If notice is given that such an attack on credibility is to be made, the other party may then choose to call the witness. Notice may be given. If the other party still decides not to call the witness there is little that that party can do to repair the damage.

It should be remembered that hearsay notices can be used by both sides. It is also not essential that a live witness introduce the hearsay (i.e. you do not have to produce a witness to say what another person told them), you can simply serve that person's statement. Use can also be made of other sources of hearsay, for example, newspaper articles quoting anonymous residents. The weight to be attached to such evidence is outlined below.

Weight attached to hearsay evidence

If hearsay evidence is used, it can be challenged by the other party either by seeking to call the witness for cross-examination or by attacking the maker's credibility. If an attack is made on credibility, it would be unwise not to call the witness to deal with the matter, but in the case of reluctant witnesses the LA/police often have no choice. It is important that defence solicitors fully exploit the rules in relation to the weight to be attached to this evidence.

Section 4 CEA 1995 provides the following (italicised comments in brackets added by author):

(1) In estimating the weight (if any) to be given to hearsay evidence in civil proceedings, the court shall have regard to any circumstances from which any inference can reasonably be drawn as to the reliability or otherwise of the evidence.

(2) Regard may be had, in particular, to the following:

(a) whether it would have been reasonable and practicable for the party by whom the evidence was adduced to have produced the maker of the original statement as a witness; [*challenge why the witness was not called. It does not matter that you yourself did not request the witness's attendance, it was a matter for the party seeking to rely on the hearsay evidence to decide tactically whether to call or not. If the witness is not called, there is considerable scope for comment – is there evidence to support fear for example?*];

(b) whether the original statement was made contemporaneously with the occurrence or existence of the matters stated; [*check when the statement was made, if it was made verbally to a person introducing it in evidence, for example a police officer, when was it recorded? Was it read back to the maker? Has identification been proved, or is that itself a further level of hearsay?*];

(c) whether the evidence involves multiple hearsay; [*the more levels of hearsay, the more unreliable; in addition, have all the makers been identified?*];

(d) whether any person involved had any motive to conceal or misrepresent matters; [*with newspaper articles, consideration should be given to whether the author of the article is only portraying one particular side of the story. In addition, comment should be made as to whether contributors to the story have been asked leading questions. It is fair comment that people may lie to get their viewpoint in print; they may also exaggerate – particularly when they do not have in mind the prospect that what they have to say will be used in a court case. An application could be made for disclosure of journalistic sources – a complex legal matter outside the scope of this book, but an avenue that should not be ignored*];

(e) whether the original statement was an edited account, or was made in collaboration with another or for a particular purpose;

(f) whether the circumstances in which the evidence is adduced as hearsay are such as to suggest an attempt to prevent proper evaluation of its weight.

Undermining credibility and proving previous inconsistent statements

Section 5(2) CEA 1995 provides:

> Where in civil proceedings hearsay evidence is adduced and the maker of the original statement, or of any statement relied upon to prove another statement, is not called as a witness:
>
> (a) evidence which if he had been so called would be admissible for the purpose of attacking or supporting his credibility as a witness is admissible for that purpose in the proceedings; and
>
> (b) evidence tending to prove that, whether before or after he made the statement, he made any other statement inconsistent with it is admissible for the purpose of showing that he had contradicted himself.
>
> Provided that evidence may not be given of any matter of which, if he had been called as a witness and had denied that matter in cross-examination, evidence could not have been adduced by the cross-examining party.

Requirement for leave

Leave to adduce a previous inconsistent statement must be sought (s.6 CEA 1995).

HANDCUFFING OF DEFENDANTS

Applications to handcuff defendants in the dock are regrettably becoming commonplace, with those responsible for prisoner escort routinely making applications based on police-assessed risk indicators, rarely supported by evidence.

Suspects appearing before courts may be handcuffed or otherwise restrained in the dock, where there is a danger that they may escape or to prevent a violent breach of the peace (*Lockley* (1864) 4F & F 155). These are the only two factors which may be taken into account when deciding whether or not to restrain a defendant in the courtroom (*R. v. Vrastides* [1998] Crim LR 251, CA). Where a defendant appears before a court, it is a matter for the court whether or not s/he should be handcuffed. It is not a matter for the police or security staff to decide (*R. v. Cambridge Justices, ex parte Peacock* (1992) 161 JP 113, DC).

The presumption that prevails is that a defendant should be unfettered *unless* there are reasonable grounds for restraint. The onus is on the prosecution to show the reasonable grounds for the use of handcuffs.

Any application that the defendant should be restrained should be heard *inter partes* (*R. v. Rollinson* (1996) 161 JP 107, CA).

Where handcuffs are unjustifiably resorted to, their use will constitute a civil trespass even though the arrest itself is lawful (*Taylor* (1895) 59 JP 393;

Bibby v. Chief Constable of Essex (2000) 164 JP 297). It may also violate Articles 3 (degrading treatment) and 6 (the right to a fair trial, and the presumption of innocence) of the ECHR. The rights of the suspects need to be balanced against public safety, and legitimate reasons put forward for handcuffing in court. Any derogations from these principles must be strictly justified. Consistent with this approach, other methods of countering any risk of escape or violence should be explored to ensure the least risk of prejudice to the suspect. This may include, for example, the presence of covertly armed police officers in court or the use of a specially protected dock.

Prosecutor's role

The following guidance is taken from the CPS operational manual:

> It is the role of the prosecutor to make representations to the court for the handcuffing of a prisoner based on information provided by the police or court security officers.
>
> It would not be appropriate for a prosecutor to comment upon the decision to seek an order or to advise on the safety of a particular person, other than to advise on the legal parameters of the court's discretion.
>
> Therefore, a prosecutor should not advise whether a particular defendant should be handcuffed but may refuse to assist the police or security staff where an application would be outside the court's discretion.
>
> A prosecutor may also refuse to make an application where s/he is not satisfied about the nature or extent of information provided by the police or Securicor when requested to make an application.
>
> It is not appropriate for anyone other than the prosecutor to make a direct application to the court.
>
> To maintain consistency of approach, all requests should be channelled through the prosecutor and the application should be made, wherever possible, before the defendant is brought into court. There is nothing, however, to prevent an application being made once the court is sitting or the suspect is in the dock.
>
> Prosecutors need to carefully examine requests to make applications for handcuffs to be worn in court, and to ensure that there are sufficient grounds for making such applications.

FITNESS TO PLEAD

In the magistrates' court (which includes a youth court) there is a less defined fitness to plead procedure than exists in the Crown Court. Section 11(1) Powers of Criminal Courts (Sentencing) Act 2000 (PCC(S)A 2000) and s.37(3) Mental Health Act 1983 (MHA 1983) do however prescribe the following powers:

- Under s.37(3) MHA 1983 the court may hear evidence in order to satisfy itself that the defendant did the act or made the omission charged. If so satisfied, the court can, without convicting the defendant, make a

hospital order. In exceptional cases, where a defendant is represented, the court can dispense with hearing evidence (*R.* v. *Lincoln Justices, ex parte O'Connor* [1983] 1 WLR 335).
* Section 11(1) PCC(S)A 2000 allows for the making of medical reports.

As an alternative to a hospital order, particularly where the offence is minor in nature, the reports may indicate to the CPS that a prosecution is not necessary in the public interest.

A court should not be tempted to adopt a modified version of the Crown Court procedure, if it does so any resulting order may be quashed (*R. (P)* v. *Barking Youth Court* [2002] Crim LR 657).

HUMAN RIGHTS ACT

The European Convention on Human Rights now has statutory recognition by virtue of the Human Rights Act 1988. The following rights are the ones mainly affecting criminal practice in the lower courts:

ARTICLE 3

PROHIBITION OF TORTURE

No one shall be subjected to torture or to inhuman or degrading treatment or punishment.

ARTICLE 5

RIGHT TO LIBERTY AND SECURITY

1. Everyone has the right to liberty and security of person. No one shall be deprived of his liberty save in the following cases and in accordance with a procedure prescribed by law:

(a) the lawful detention of a person after conviction by a competent court;
(b) the lawful arrest or detention of a person for non-compliance with the lawful order of a court or in order to secure the fulfilment of any obligation prescribed by law;
(c) the lawful arrest or detention of a person effected for the purpose of bringing him before the competent legal authority on reasonable suspicion of having committed an offence or when it is reasonably considered necessary to prevent his committing an offence or fleeing after having done so;
(d) the detention of a minor by lawful order for the purpose of educational supervision or his lawful detention for the purpose of bringing him before the competent legal authority;
(e) the lawful detention of persons for the prevention of the spreading of infectious diseases, of persons of unsound mind, alcoholics or drug addicts or vagrants;
(f) the lawful arrest or detention of a person to prevent his effecting an unauthorised entry into the country or of a person against whom action is being taken with a view to deportation or extradition.

2. Everyone who is arrested shall be informed promptly, in a language which he understands, of the reasons for his arrest and of any charge against him.

3. Everyone arrested or detained in accordance with the provisions of paragraph 1(c) of this Article shall be brought promptly before a judge or other officer authorised by law to exercise judicial power and shall be entitled to trial within a reasonable time or to release pending trial. Release may be conditioned by guarantees to appear for trial.

4. Everyone who is deprived of his liberty by arrest or detention shall be entitled to take proceedings by which the lawfulness of his detention shall be decided speedily by a court and his release ordered if the detention is not lawful.

5. Everyone who has been the victim of arrest or detention in contravention of the provisions of this Article shall have an enforceable right to compensation.

ARTICLE 6

RIGHT TO A FAIR TRIAL

1. In the determination of his civil rights and obligations or of any criminal charge against him, everyone is entitled to a fair and public hearing within a reasonable time by an independent and impartial tribunal established by law. Judgment shall be pronounced publicly but the press and public may be excluded from all or part of the trial in the interest of morals, public order or national security in a democratic society, where the interests of juveniles or the protection of the private life of the parties so require, or to the extent strictly necessary in the opinion of the court in special circumstances where publicity would prejudice the interests of justice.

2. Everyone charged with a criminal offence shall be presumed innocent until proved guilty according to law.

3. Everyone charged with a criminal offence has the following minimum rights:

(a) to be informed promptly, in a language which he understands and in detail, of the nature and cause of the accusation against him;

(b) to have adequate time and facilities for the preparation of his defence;

(c) to defend himself in person or through legal assistance of his own choosing or, if he has not sufficient means to pay for legal assistance, to be given it free when the interests of justice so require;

(d) to examine or have examined witnesses against him and to obtain the attendance and examination of witnesses on his behalf under the same conditions as witnesses against him;

(e) to have the free assistance of an interpreter if he cannot understand or speak the language used in court.

ARTICLE 7

NO PUNISHMENT WITHOUT LAW

1. No one shall be held guilty of any criminal offence on account of any act or omission which did not constitute a criminal offence under national or international law at the time when it was committed. Nor shall a heavier penalty be imposed than the one that was applicable at the time the criminal offence was committed.

2. This Article shall not prejudice the trial and punishment of any person for any act or omission which, at the time when it was committed, was criminal according to the general principles of law recognised by civilised nations.

ARTICLE 8

RIGHT TO RESPECT FOR PRIVATE AND FAMILY LIFE

1. Everyone has the right to respect for his private and family life, his home and his correspondence.
2. There shall be no interference by a public authority with the exercise of this right except such as is in accordance with the law and is necessary in a democratic society in the interests of national security, public safety or the economic well-being of the country, for the prevention of disorder or crime, for the protection of health or morals, or for the protection of the rights and freedoms of others.

ARTICLE 9

FREEDOM OF THOUGHT, CONSCIENCE AND RELIGION

1. Everyone has the right to freedom of thought, conscience and religion; this right includes freedom to change his religion or belief and freedom, either alone or in community with others and in public or private, to manifest his religion or belief, in worship, teaching, practice and observance.
2. Freedom to manifest one's religion or beliefs shall be subject only to such limitations as are prescribed by law and are necessary in a democratic society in the interests of public safety, for the protection of public order, health or morals, or for the protection of the rights and freedoms of others.

ARTICLE 10

FREEDOM OF EXPRESSION

1. Everyone has the right to freedom of expression. This right shall include freedom to hold opinions and to receive and impart information and ideas without interference by public authority and regardless of frontiers. This Article shall not prevent States from requiring the licensing of broadcasting, television or cinema enterprises.
2. The exercise of these freedoms, since it carries with it duties and responsibilities, may be subject to such formalities, conditions, restrictions or penalties as are prescribed by law and are necessary in a democratic society, in the interests of national security, territorial integrity or public safety, for the prevention of disorder or crime, for the protection of health or morals, for the protection of the reputation or rights of others, for preventing the disclosure of information received in confidence, or for maintaining the authority and impartiality of the judiciary.

ARTICLE 11

FREEDOM OF ASSEMBLY AND ASSOCIATION

1. Everyone has the right to freedom of peaceful assembly and to freedom of association with others, including the right to form and to join trade unions for the protection of his interests.
2. No restrictions shall be placed on the exercise of these rights other than such as are prescribed by law and are necessary in a democratic society in the interests of national security or public safety, for the prevention of disorder or crime, for the protection of health or morals or for the protection of the rights and freedoms of others. This Article shall not prevent the imposition of lawful restrictions on

the exercise of these rights by members of the armed forces, of the police or of the administration of the State.

ARTICLE 14

PROHIBITION OF DISCRIMINATION

The enjoyment of the rights and freedoms set forth in this Convention shall be secured without discrimination on any ground such as sex, race, colour, language, religion, political or other opinion, national or social origin, association with a national minority, property, birth or other status.

MISBEHAVIOUR AT COURT

Magistrates' courts have a variety of powers available to deal with defendants and others who might be intent on disturbing the smooth running of the court. Statute provides specific remedy in the case of disturbances during committal proceedings (s.4(4) MCA 1980), mode of trial and summary trial (s.18(4) MCA 1980). There are a number of other powers, arguably still exercisable at common law, but it is submitted that the Contempt of Court Act 1981 should be used to deal with serious cases of contempt, as per guidance given in the practice direction below.

Duty solicitors are, however, more likely to have to deal with the more serious contempt of court, which could result in a person's imprisonment.

Definition of 'contempt'

Contempt of court is defined under s.12 Contempt of Court Act 1981 as:

12 Offences of contempt of magistrates' courts

(1) A magistrates' court has jurisdiction under this section to deal with any person who–

  (a) wilfully insults the justice or justices, any witness before or officer of the court or any solicitor or counsel having business in the court, during his or their sitting or attendance in court or in going to or returning from the court; or
  (b) wilfully interrupts the proceedings of the court or otherwise misbehaves in court.

(2) In any such case the court may order any officer of the court, or any constable, to take the offender into custody and detain him until the rising of the court; and the court may, if it thinks fit, commit the offender to custody for a specified period not exceeding one month or impose on him a fine not exceeding £2,500 on the standard scale, or both.

[. . .]

(4) A magistrates' court may at any time revoke an order of committal made under subsection (2) and, if the offender is in custody, order his discharge.

Procedure

The court, when seeking to deal with cases of alleged contempt, should adhere to the following practice direction:

PRACTICE DIRECTION: (MAGISTRATES' COURTS: CONTEMPT IN THE FACE OF THE COURT OR REFUSAL TO GIVE EVIDENCE)

General

1. Magistrates' courts have power to detain someone, whether a defendant or another person present in court, who wilfully insults or interrupts proceedings under s.12 Contempt of Court Act 1981 until the court rises. In any such case, the court may order any officer of the court, or any constable, to take the offender into custody and detain him until the rising of the court; and the court may, if it thinks fit, commit the offender to custody for a specified period not exceeding one month or impose on him a fine not exceeding level 4 on the standard scale, or both. This power can be used to stop disruption of their proceedings. Detention is until the person can be conveniently dealt with without disruption of the proceedings. Prior to the court using the power, the offender should be warned to desist or face the prospect of being detained.
2. Magistrates' courts also have power to commit to custody any person attending or brought before a magistrates' court who refuses without just cause to be sworn or give evidence under s.97(4) Magistrates' Court Act 1980 until the expiration of such period not exceeding one month as may be specified in the warrant or until he sooner gives evidence or produces the document or thing or impose on him a fine not exceeding level 4 on the standard scale or both.
3. In the exercise of any of these powers, as soon as practical, and in any event prior to an offender being proceeded against, an offender should be told the conduct which is alleged to constitute his offending in clear terms. When making an order under s.12 of the 1981 Act, the justices should state their findings of fact as to the contempt.
4. Exceptional situations require exceptional treatment. While the Practice Direction deals with the generality of situations, there will be a minority of situations where the application of the Practice Direction will not be consistent with achieving justice in the special circumstances of the particular case. Where this is the situation, the compliance with the Practice Direction should be modified so far as is necessary so as to accord with the interests of justice.
5. The power to bind persons over to be of good behaviour in respect to their conduct in court should cease to be exercised.

Contempt consisting of wilfully insulting or interrupting proceedings

6. In the case of someone who wilfully insults or interrupts proceedings, if an offender expresses a willingness to apologise for his misconduct, he or she should be brought back before the court at the earliest convenient moment in order to make the apology and to give undertakings to the court to refrain from further misbehaviour.
7. In the majority of cases, an apology and a promise as to future conduct should be sufficient for justices to order an offender's release. However, there are likely to be certain cases where the nature and seriousness of the miscon-

duct requires the justices to consider using their powers under s.12(2) of the 1981 Act to either fine or order the offender's committal to custody.

Where an offender is detained for contempt of court

8. Anyone detained under either of these provisions in paragraphs 1 or 2, above, should be seen by the duty solicitor or another legal representative and be represented in proceedings if they so wish. Legal aid should generally be granted to cover representation. The offender must be afforded adequate time and facilities in order to prepare his case. The matter should be resolved the same day if at all possible.
9. The offender should be brought back before the court before the justices conclude their daily business. The justices should ensure that he understands the nature of the proceedings, including his opportunity to apologise or give evidence and the alternative of them exercising their powers.
10. Having heard from the offender's solicitor the justices should decide whether to take further action.

Sentencing of an offender who admits being in contempt

11. If an offence of contempt is admitted, the justices should consider whether they are able to proceed on the day or whether to adjourn to allow further reflection. The matter should be dealt with on the same day if at all possible. If the justices are of the view to adjourn they should generally grant the offender bail unless one or more of the exceptions to the right to bail in the Bail Act 1976 are made out.
12. When they come to sentence the offender where the offence has been admitted, the justices should first ask the offender if he has any objection to them dealing with the matter. If there is any objection to the justices dealing with the matter, a differently constituted panel should hear the proceedings. If the offender's conduct was directed to the magistrates, it will not be appropriate for the same bench to deal with the matter. If the offender's conduct was not directed to the magistrates, it may be in order for the same bench to deal with the matter.
13. The justices should consider whether an order for the offender's discharge is appropriate, taking into account any time spent on remand, whether the offence was admitted and the nature and seriousness of the contempt. Any period of committal should be for the shortest period of time commensurate with the interests of preserving good order in the administration of justice.

Trial of the issue where the contempt is not admitted

14. Where the contempt is not admitted the justices' powers are limited to making arrangements for a trial to take place. They should not at this stage make findings against the offender.
15. In the case of a contested contempt, the trial should take place at the earliest opportunity and should be before a bench of magistrates other than those justices before whom the alleged contempt took place. If trial of the issue can take place on the day such arrangements should be made taking into account the offender's rights under Art. 6 European Convention on Human Rights. If the trial cannot take place that day, the justices should again bail the offender unless there are grounds under the 1976 Act to remand him in custody.
16. The offender is entitled to call and examine witnesses where evidence is relevant. If the offender is found by the court to have committed contempt the court should again consider first whether an order for his discharge from

custody is sufficient to bring proceedings to an end. The justices should also allow the offender a further opportunity to apologise for his contempt or to make representations. If the justices are of the view that they must exercise their powers to commit to custody under s.12(2) of the 1981 Act, they must take into account any time spent on remand and the nature and seriousness of the contempt. Any period of committal should be for the shortest period of time commensurate with the interests of preserving good order in the administration of justice.

MODE OF TRIAL (MCA 1980)

Overview

Venue must be determined in relation to offences triable either way. The first stage is to invite the defendant to indicate his plea (plea-before-venue procedure). If the defendant indicates a guilty plea, that is the end of mode-of-trial considerations, with the court then deciding whether to retain the case or commit the defendant to the Crown Court for sentence. In the event of a not-guilty indication, or a defendant declining to give any indication of plea, the court must move on to consider whether the case should be tried in the magistrates' court or on indictment.

Where a youth is jointly charged with an adult, the procedures documented below are only invoked in respect of the adult; the youth has no independent choice.

When Sched. 3 CJA 2003 comes in to force new allocation guidelines and procedures will substantially alter the procedure to be followed.

Exceptions

Some offences are triable either way, but fall to have jurisdiction determined in relation to 'value' ('scheduled offences').

If the offence is one of criminal damage (save arson), or aggravated vehicle-taking where the aggravating element is damage alone, the case must be tried in the magistrates' court if the value of the damage is less than £5,000.

Where the accused is charged on the same occasion with two or more scheduled offences and it appears to the court that they constitute or form part of a series of two or more offences of the same or a similar character, or the offence charged consists in incitement to commit two or more scheduled offences, any reference to value is a reference to the aggregate of the values involved (s.22(11) MCA 1980).

In determining value, the court must have regard to any representations made by the prosecution and defence. There is no obligation on the court to hear evidence as to the value, but there is discretion to do so (*R.* v. *Canterbury*

Justices, ex parte Klisiak [1981] 2 All ER 129). A court should be concerned only with damage to the property itself, not any consequential loss flowing from its damage or destruction (*R. v. Colchester Magistrates' Court, ex parte Abbott* [2001] Crim LR 564). There are no grounds of appeal on the basis that the court's assessment of value was later found to be wrong (s.22(8)).

If the court determines the value involved to be greater than £5,000, the court moves on to consider plea before venue and, if appropriate, mode of trial.

In the event that it is not clear as to whether the value exceeds £5,000, the defendant must be invited to state his preference in relation to trial. If he consents to summary trial, that is where the trial will take place; if he does not so consent, the court will proceed with plea before venue and mode of trial in the normal way (s.22(4)).

Advance disclosure

This subject is dealt with in a separate chapter, but is mentioned at this point due to the fact that for some time it was unclear as to whether the issue of advance disclosure arose prior to mode of trial being carried out. There is now no doubt that advance disclosure is necessary prior to plea before venue, following the case of *R. v. Calderdale Magistrates' Court, ex parte Donahue and others* [2001] Crim LR 141, where a court's refusal to adjourn the taking of an indication of plea so that the defence could view a video was quashed. The court stated that: 'one of the purposes of the prosecution providing advance information was to enable a defendant to make an informed choice as to his plea and mode of trial at the plea before venue hearing'.

Plea before venue (s.17A)

The charge is read to the defendant and he is invited to indicate his plea. If he pleads guilty, the court will go on to consider sentence (s.17A(6)).

In the event of a not-guilty indication or a refusal to indicate plea the court proceeds to consider mode of trial (s.17A(7), (8)).

In the case of an unruly defendant who has been removed from the court, there is a discretion to invite the defendant's legal representative to indicate a plea on his client's behalf (s.17B).

Effect on sentence of early indication of plea

Where a defendant pleads guilty at the plea-before-venue stage, a reduction in sentence of greater than the usual one-third can be granted (*R. v. Barber* [2001] Crim LR 998); this applied the judgment in *R. v. Rafferty* [1998] 2 Cr App R (s) 450, where it was stated:

111

when a defendant pleads guilty before venue at the magistrates' court, the judge at the Crown Court must have regard to the fact that the plea has been made at that early stage. In the usual case therefore a defendant who enters a guilty plea before venue should be entitled to a greater discount than a person who delays making a plea until he pleads to the indictment in respect of those offences at the Crown Court.

Legitimate expectation

Difficulties arise where a defendant pleads guilty and is not immediately either sentenced or committed to the Crown Court for sentence. Before deciding whether to commit a defendant for sentence the court is entitled to hear from the Crown and receive guidance in relation to sentencing authorities. The court is also entitled to first adjourn for pre-sentence reports before considering whether to commit for sentence.

If the court adjourns sentence, it should make it abundantly clear that all sentencing options including custody remain open. Where a court has indicated prior to a plea being entered that it would retain jurisdiction, the subsequent warning that it may commit for sentence will not be enough to avoid a legitimate expectation in the mind of the defendant (for a most unusual case where the advocate stated that his client would plead if the court gave an indication that they would not commit for sentence, and later did, see: *R.* v. *Wirral Magistrates' Court, ex parte Jermyn* [2001] Crim LR 45). Where an expectation is given that is outside the bounds of reasonableness, the court would not interfere with a later decision to commit for sentence (*R. (White)* v. *Barking Magistrates' Court* [2004] EWHC 417 (Admin)).

Mode of trial

The court should satisfy itself that a defendant has had an opportunity to consider any advance disclosure; this is particularly important in relation to unrepresented defendants.

The court then goes on to consider representation from both prosecution and defence before determining whether the case is more suitably tried in the magistrates' court or Crown Court.

The court must have regard to the following factors (s.19(3)):

(a) nature of the case;

(b) whether the circumstances make the offence one of a serious character;

(c) whether the punishment which a magistrates' court would have power to inflict for it would be adequate;

(d) any other circumstances which appear to the court to make it more suitable for the offence to be tried in one way rather than the other. The court shall not have regard to any previous convictions of the defendant.

If the offence is being carried on (personally) by the Attorney-General, the Solicitor-General or the DPP, and he applies for the offence to be tried on indictment the court shall proceed to inquire into the information as examining justices.

For mode-of-trial purposes the prosecution case must be assumed to be correct, but this does not prevent the defence from exposing weaknesses in the prosecution case evident on the face of the papers.

The defendant's antecedent history and matters of personal mitigation are not relevant to the mode-of-trial decision, nor is the fact that the defendant may wish other offences to be taken into consideration (this may be a matter, though, which would lead to the magistrates deciding to commit for sentence). Note however that previous convictions may be relevant in cases where the Crown are seeking to rely upon dangerous offender provisions (for which see Chapter 4).

National Mode of Trial Guidelines have been issued dealing with the more common either-way offences; they are reproduced below.

Declining jurisdiction

If the court declines to hear the case, it will be adjourned for committal proceedings to take place. When Sched. 3 CJA 2003 comes into force, such cases will be sent to the Crown Court forthwith, thereby negating the need for committal proceedings.

Accepting jurisdiction

If the court deems the case as being suitable for summary trial, the defendant is then given a choice as to where the case should be tried. If he consents to summary trial, the matter will be adjourned for trial; if he elects trial on indictment or refuses to elect at all, the case will be adjourned for committal proceedings to take place. When Sched. 3 CJA 2003 comes into force, such cases will be sent to the Crown Court forthwith, thereby negating the need for committal proceedings.

In a case where more than one defendant is charged with the same offence, each defendant enjoys an individual right of election, so in the event that the case is deemed suitable for summary trial, one could elect summary trial, the other trial on indictment (*R. v. Wigan Magistrates' Court, ex parte Layland* (1995) 160 JP 223).

Changing the venue decision

A court, having declined jurisdiction, can, at any stage prior to the defendant having been committed, seek to have the case tried summarily. In order for the case to be tried in this way, the defendant must consent (s.25 MCA 1980).

A defendant, having decided to have a matter tried summarily, can only change the venue if he can show that he did not understand the nature and significance of the election decision (*R.* v. *Birmingham Justices, ex parte Hodgson and another* [1985] 2 WLR 630).

National Mode of Trial Guidelines

These have been issued to deal with the more common either-way offences.

The purpose of these guidelines is to help magistrates decide whether or not to commit either way offences for trial in the Crown Court. Their object is to provide guidance not direction. They are not intended to impinge upon a magistrate's duty to consider each case individually and on its own particular facts.

These guidelines apply to all defendants aged 18 and above.

General mode of trial considerations

Section 19 of the Magistrates' Courts Act 1980 requires magistrates to have regard to the following matters in deciding whether an offence is more suitable for summary trial or trial on indictment: (1) the nature of the case; (2) whether the circumstances make the offence one of a serious character; (3) whether the punishment which a magistrates' court would have power to inflict for it would be adequate; (4) any other circumstances which appear to the court to make it more suitable for the offence to be tried in one way rather than the other; (5) any representations made by the prosecution or the defence.

Certain general observations can be made

(a)   the court should never make its decision on the grounds of convenience or expedition;

(b)   the court should assume for the purpose of deciding mode of trial that the prosecution version of the facts is correct;

(c)   the fact that the offences are alleged to be specimens is a relevant consideration; the fact that the defendant will be asking for other offences to be taken into consideration, if convicted, is not;

(d)   where cases involve complex questions of fact or difficult questions of law, the court should consider transfer for trial;

(e)   where two or more defendants are jointly charged with an offence each has an individual right to elect his mode of trial;

(f)   in general, except where otherwise stated, either-way offences should be tried summarily unless the court considers that the particular case has one or more of the features set out in the following pages and that its sentencing powers are insufficient;

(g)   the court should also consider its powers to commit an offender for sentence, under the PCC(S)A 2000, s.3 [Powers of Criminal Courts (Sentencing) Act], if information emerges during the course of the hearing which leads them to conclude that the offence is so serious, or the offender such a risk to the public, that their powers to sentence him are inadequate. This amendment means that committal for sentence is no longer determined by reference to the character or antecedents of the defendant.

Features relevant to the individual offences

Note: Where reference is made in these guidelines to property or damage of 'high value' it means a figure equal to at least twice the amount of the limit (currently £5,000) imposed by statute on a magistrates' court when making a compensation order.

Burglary

1. Dwelling-house

(1) Entry in the daytime when the occupier (or another) is present.
(2) Entry at night of a house which is normally occupied, whether or not the occupier (or another) is present.
(3) The offence is alleged to be one of a series of similar offences.
(4) When soiling, ransacking, damage or vandalism occurs.
(5) The offence has professional hallmarks.
(6) The unrecovered property is of high value [see above for definition of 'high value'].

Note: Attention is drawn to para. 28(c) of Schedule 1 to the Magistrates' Courts Act 1980, by which offences of burglary in a dwelling cannot be tried summarily if any person in the dwelling was subjected to violence or the threat of violence.

2. Non-dwellings

(1) Entry of a pharmacy or doctor's surgery.
(2) Fear is caused or violence is done to anyone lawfully on the premises (e.g. night watchman; security guard).
(3) The offence has professional hallmarks.
(4) Vandalism on a substantial scale.
(5) The unrecovered property is of high value [see above for definition of 'high value'].

Theft and fraud

(1) Breach of trust by a person in a position of substantial authority, or in whom a high degree of trust is placed.
(2) Theft or fraud which has been committed or disguised in a sophisticated manner.
(3) Theft or fraud committed by an organised gang.
(4) The victim is particularly vulnerable to theft or fraud (e.g. the elderly or infirm).
(5) The unrecovered property is of high value [see above for definition of 'high value'].

Handling

(1) Dishonest handling of stolen property by a receiver who has commissioned the theft.
(2) The offence has professional hallmarks.
(3) The property is of high value [see above for definition of 'high value'].

Social security frauds

(1) Organised fraud on a large scale.
(2) The frauds are substantial and carried out over a long period of time.

Violence (sections 20 and 47 of the Offences against the Person Act 1861)

(1) The use of a weapon of a kind likely to cause serious injury.
(2) A weapon is used and serious injury is caused.
(3) More than minor injury is caused by kicking, head-butting or similar forms of assault.
(4) Serious violence is caused to those whose work has to be done in contact with the public or who are likely to face violence in the course of their work.
(5) Violence to vulnerable people (e.g. the elderly and infirm).
(6) The offence has clear racial motivation.

Note: The same considerations apply to cases of domestic violence.

Public Order Act offences

1. Cases of violent disorder should generally be committed for trial.

2. Affray.

(1) Organised violence or use of weapons.
(2) Significant injury or substantial damage.
(3) The offence has clear racial motivation.
(4) An attack upon police officers, prison officers, ambulancemen, firemen and the like.

Violence to and neglect of children

(1) Substantial injury.
(2) Repeated violence or serious neglect, even if the physical harm is slight.
(3) Sadistic violence (e.g. deliberate burning or scalding).

Indecent assault

(1) Substantial disparity in age between victim and defendant, and the assault is more than trivial.
(2) Violence or threats of violence.
(3) Relationship of trust or responsibility between defendant and victim.
(4) Several similar offences, and the assaults are more than trivial.
(5) The victim is particularly vulnerable.
(6) Serious nature of the assault.

Unlawful sexual intercourse

(1) Wide disparity of age.
(2) Breach of position of trust.
(3) The victim is particularly vulnerable.

Note: Unlawful sexual intercourse with a girl under 13 is triable only on indictment.

Drugs

1.   Class A

(a)   Supply; possession with intent to supply: these cases should be committed for trial.
(b)   Possession: should be committed for trial unless the amount is consistent only with personal use.

2.   Class B

(a)   Supply; possession with intent to supply: should be committed for trial unless there is only small scale supply for no payment.
(b)   Possession: should be committed for trial when the quantity is substantial and not consistent only with personal use.

Dangerous driving

(1)   Alcohol or drugs contributing to dangerousness.
(2)   Grossly excessive speed.
(3)   Racing.
(4)   Prolonged course of dangerous driving.
(5)   Degree of injury or damage sustained.
(6)   Other related offences.

Criminal damage

(1)   Deliberate fire-raising.
(2)   Committed by a group.
(3)   Damage of a high value [see above for definition of 'high value'].
(4)   The offence has clear racial motivation.

Note: Offences set out in Schedule 2 to the Magistrates' Courts Act 1980 (which includes offences of criminal damage which do not amount to arson) must be tried summarily if the value of the property damaged or destroyed is £5,000 or less.

REMAND PERIODS

A court can remand a defendant either on bail or in custody. The maximum remand periods are dictated by statute.

On bail

Prior to conviction

No period longer than eight days unless both defence and prosecution consent (s.128(6) MCA 1980).

If committed for sentence or to stand trial at the Crown Court the remand will be to the date fixed by the Crown Court.

Post-conviction

An adjournment not exceeding four weeks (s.10(3) MCA 1980).

In custody

Prior to conviction

Remand to a police station for up to three days, or one day in respect of a youth (s.128(7) MCA 1980, s.23(12) CYPA 1969).

Maximum remand eight days, unless: (a) he has previously been remanded into custody for the same offence; (b) he is before the court; (c) both parties have been afforded the opportunity to make representations; and (d) it will be possible for the next stage in the proceedings, other than a hearing relating only to a further remand to take place. If the criteria are met, he may be remanded for a period ending not later than that date, or for a period of 28 clear days, whichever is less (s.128A MCA 1980).

A legally represented person, present in court, may give his consent to be remanded in his absence on future occasions (s.128(3A) MCA 1980).

A court can remand an accused person who is already in custody serving a sentence for a period of up to 28 days. If he is to be released before the period of eight days, the maximum remand period is eight days; if he is to be released after eight days, the remand period will be to that date or 28 days whichever is shorter (s.131 MCA 1980).

A defendant whose case is sent, transferred or committed to the Crown Court can be remanded until the case is heard at the Crown Court.

Post-conviction

An adjournment not exceeding three weeks (s.10(3) MCA 1980).

Further remands

Further remands, again not exceeding any of the maximum periods above, may take place.

Remands when defendant not produced

If a defendant is not produced from custody for whatever reason, there is a danger that the remand process will break down and that a defendant would be liable to release, as he would be held without legal authority. Similarly, if there is good reason for a defendant on bail not to appear, it is important that the bail process does not break down.

Bail

A court has the power to enlarge bail to a new date.

Custody

A court can remand in absence for a further period if the defendant is unable to appear by reason of illness or accident (s.129 MCA 1980). A finding of fact in respect of 'illness or accident' must be based on solid grounds on which a court could reasonably found a reliable opinion (*R.* v. *Liverpool Justices, ex parte Grogan, The Times*, 8 October 1990). A breakdown of a prisoner van is not to be regarded as an 'accident'. Accident included the situation where another court had remanded a defendant in custody on the same day (*Jenkins* [1997] COD 38).

If a defendant is unlawfully detained, appears before the court and is further remanded, the unlawfulness of the original detention does not have any effect in relation to the later remand (*R.* v. *Governor of Winchester Prison and Southampton Justices, ex parte Cato*, 16 July 1999, unreported).

REOPENING CASES

Statutory declarations

A statutory declaration has the effect of making void a summons and all subsequent proceedings. The purpose of the procedure is to notify the court that the applicant has had no notice of the proceedings against him.

Where the grievance is lack of knowledge of the proceedings, the statutory declaration procedure should be adopted as opposed to seeking redress by way of judicial review (*R.* v. *Brighton Justices, ex parte Robinson* [1973] 1 WLR 69).

The law

MCA 1980 s.14 provides:

(1) Where a summons has been issued under section 1 above and a magistrates' court has begun to try the information to which the summons relates, then, if—

    (a) the accused, at any time during or after the trial, makes a statutory declaration that he did not know of the summons or the proceedings until a date specified in the declaration, being a date after the court has begun to try the information; and

(b) within 21 days of that date the declaration is served on the justices' chief executive for the court, without prejudice to the validity of the information, the summons and all subsequent proceedings shall be void.

(2) For the purposes of subsection (1) above a statutory declaration shall be deemed to be duly served on the justices' chief executive if it is delivered to him, or left at his office, or is sent in a registered letter or by the recorded delivery service addressed to him at his office.

(3) If on the application of the accused it appears to a magistrates' court (which for this purpose may be composed of a single justice) that it was not reasonable to expect the accused to serve such a statutory declaration as is mentioned in subsection (1) above within the period allowed by that subsection, the court may accept service of such a declaration by the accused after that period has expired; and a statutory declaration accepted under this subsection shall be deemed to have been served as required by that subsection.

(4) Where any proceedings have become void by virtue of subsection (1) above, the information shall not be tried again by any of the same justices.

Application

A sworn statutory declaration must be made and served on the court within 21 days of the accused knowing of the proceedings against him. If the 21 days have expired, it will be for the accused to show good reason as to why the period should be extended. A declaration will have no effect unless the court has proceeded to hear evidence on the matter. At the point in time that the declaration is accepted by the court, the proceedings become a nullity, with any penalties thereunder having no effect. A prosecutor may issue process immediately in court if the accused is present (a summons returnable *instanter*), otherwise a summons can be reissued in the normal manner. If the offence is triable summarily only, the 'new' prosecution will not be time-barred.

With the new relaxed s.142 (see below), it may be thought more expedient to use that avenue. However, a defence solicitor should be alert to the possibility that the prosecution will fail to reissue process – there is no good reason to assist the prosecution in its pursuit of your client.

Form of statutory declaration

STATUTORY DECLARATIONS ACT 1835

I, Paul Smith of 123 Taneytown, Bedfordshire, do solemnly and sincerely declare that:

Until 1 October 2005 I had no knowledge of the summons or proceedings against me, alleging an offence/offences of:

(1) Driving otherwise than in accordance with a licence
(2) No insurance

Alleged to have been committed on 1 March 2005.

And I make this solemn declaration conscientiously believing the same to be true, and by virtue of the provisions of the Statutory Declarations Act 1835.

[SIGNATURE]

Declared before me [JUSTICE OF THE PEACE/SOLICITOR], THIS [   ] DAY OF [   ], [2005]

DATE

Section 142 procedure

MCA 1980 s.142 provides:

(1) A magistrates' court may vary or rescind a sentence or other order imposed or made by it when dealing with an offender if it appears to the court to be in the interests of justice to do so; and it is hereby declared that this power extends to replacing a sentence or order which for any reason appears to be invalid by another which the court has power to impose or make.

(1A) The power conferred on a magistrates' court by subsection (1) above shall not be exercisable in relation to any sentence or order imposed or made by it when dealing with an offender if –

    (a)   the Crown Court has determined an appeal against –

        (i)   that sentence or order;

        (ii)   the conviction in respect of which that sentence or order was imposed or made; or

> (iii) any other sentence or order imposed or made by the magistrates' court when dealing with the offender in respect of that conviction (including a sentence or order replaced by that sentence or order); or
>
> (b) the High Court has determined a case stated for the opinion of that court on any question arising in any proceeding leading to or resulting from the imposition or making of the sentence or order.

(2) Where a person is convicted by a magistrates' court and it subsequently appears to the court that it would be in the interests of justice that the case should be heard again by different justices, the court may so direct.

(2A) The power conferred on a magistrates' court by subsection (2) above shall not be exercisable in relation to a conviction if –

> (a) the Crown Court has determined an appeal against –
>
> > (i) the conviction; or
> > (ii) any sentence or order imposed or made by the magistrates' court when dealing with the offender in respect of the conviction; or
>
> (b) the High Court has determined a case stated for the opinion of that court on any question arising in any proceeding leading to or resulting from the conviction.

(3) Where a court gives a direction under subsection (2) above –

> (a) the conviction and any sentence or other order imposed or made in consequence thereof shall be of no effect; and
> (b) section 10(4) above shall apply as if the trial of the person in question had been adjourned.

(5) Where a sentence or order is varied under subsection (1) above, the sentence or other order, as so varied, shall take effect from the beginning of the day on which it was originally imposed or made, unless the court otherwise directs.

Application

The application can be made orally or in writing, there is no requirement for the applicant to be present. The power is open to the Crown or other prosecuting authority, private prosecutor or defendant, and the opposing party in the proceedings should be afforded an opportunity to make representations.

It is clear that the applicant should not attempt to overturn a conviction or sentence merely because he was dissatisfied with the outcome. While a convicted applicant with new evidence may (exceptionally) have grounds for an application to reopen, it is clear that the Crown in the same position could not seek to reopen an acquittal, as this would offend against the double-jeopardy rule.

An applicant who has appealed to the Crown Court or proceeded by way of case stated cannot use the s.142 procedure, but he may be able to make an application to the Criminal Cases Review Commission.

The purpose of s.142 is to enable the court to rectify mistakes, and it is to be regarded as a slip rule. Accordingly, the section has no application where there has been an unequivocal guilty plea (*R*. v. *Croydon Youth Court, ex parte DPP* [1997] 2 Cr App R 411).

A defendant made subject to a hospital order under s.37(3) Mental Health Act 1983 is allowed to make an application under s.142 as he falls within the definition of 'offender' (*R*. v. *Thames Magistrates' Court, ex parte Ramadan* [1999] 1 Cr App R 386).

A court should not allow a reopening because there has been a change in the law, as such a reopening offends against having certainty of justice. However, there may be Human Rights Act challenges to this ground and a solicitor should explore them fully before dismissing the idea.

Whilst the previous 28-day time limit has been removed, the former 28-day limit should be regarded as a salutary guideline (*R*. v. *Ealing Magistrates' Court, ex parte Sahota*, *The Times*, 9 December 1997).

Interests of justice

The court may reopen the matter where it is in the interests of justice to do so. A court must consider all the surrounding circumstances including:

1. Why the convicted person did not appear at the original trial (if that was the case).
2. Timeliness of the application.
3. Reason (if any) for delay.
4. Importance of the decision being questioned.
5. Inconvenience caused to the opposing parties.
6. Whether a more appropriate remedy is available.

Justices are given a very wide discretion in determining what are relevant factors (*R*. v. *Gwent Magistrates' Court, ex parte Carey* (1996) 160 JP 613). They must act judicially, and the fact, for example, that a defendant arrived late at court has been held not to be a proper ground for refusing a rehearing (*R*. v. *Camberwell Green Magistrates' Court, ex parte Ibrahim* (1984) 148 JP 400).

Effect of reopening

In respect of a conviction, the reopening has the effect of setting aside the conviction and any sentence or order made pursuant to it. The matter is then treated as if it had been adjourned prior to trial.

The new trial must be heard before different justices from those: (a) hearing the reopening; and (b) who sat during the original trial.

In respect of orders other than conviction, the court may vary or rescind the original finding, with the power extending to the replacing of a sentence or order, which for any reason appears invalid, with any other lawful order. A sentence or order varied takes effect from the date on which the original order was imposed, unless the court directs otherwise. A court may increase an order, but must take care not to offend against any legitimate expectation given to the offender (*Jane* v. *Broome, The Times*, 2 November 1988).

SPECIAL MEASURES APPLICATIONS

Introduction

The special measures provisions came into force on 24 July 2002, and applications for their use are now commonplace. The previous memorandum of good practice in relation to child witnesses has been replaced by a comprehensive three volume work that provides guidance for dealing with vulnerable or intimidated witnesses including children. It is essential that the guidance, entitled 'Achieving Best Evidence in Criminal Proceedings' is obtained and understood by all criminal lawyers. Special measures applications are covered in volume one, which is available from: **www.homeoffice. gov.uk/documents/achieving-best-evidence.**

Special measures directions under the Youth Justice and Criminal Evidence Act 1999 are not available to defendants, but do apply to other defence witnesses. It is unlikely that an Article 6 challenge would succeed on the basis that special measures direction under statute do not apply to defendants, and the wider statutory scheme has been held to be Article 6 compliant. In *R. (D and others)* v. *Camberwell Green Youth Court and others, The Times*, 13 February 2003, the court commented that:

> [safeguards for defendants] include the Code of Practice for Crown Prosecutors' requirements for sufficient evidence before prosecuting; the presumption of innocence; the burden and standard of proof; the defendant's ability to choose whether to give evidence and the right to legal representation; the general requirement that prosecution witnesses give oral evidence, subject to cross-examination; the overriding duty of a judge to ensure a fair trial; the power, in the interests of justice, to stay proceedings as an abuse, dismiss a case and direct an acquittal; and the powers to exclude prejudicial evidence, evidence obtained unfairly and evidence which would have an adverse effect on the fairness of the proceedings.

The court does however have a wide inherent jurisdiction to adapt procedures to ensure fairness; this might include allowing intermediaries, and even the reading of a defence statement to form part of the defendant's own evidence in the case (*R.* v. *S.H.* [2003] EWCA Crim 1208).

Overview of eligibility

Age	Eligibility	Notes
Is witness under 17 at time of application, or was under 17 when video interviewed?	Automatically eligible for special measures. If a court makes a special measures direction in respect of a child witness who was eligible on grounds of youth only, and the witness turns 17 before beginning to give evidence, the direction no longer has effect. If such a witness turns 17 after beginning to give evidence the direction continues to apply. If evidence-in-chief or cross-examination recorded when witness under 17 years, it is still admissible if the witness turns 17 during the proceedings.	If the child is a victim of or eyewitness to an offence involving sex, neglect, cruelty, actual or threatened violence or kidnapping then the primary rule applies. If not in the above category then the primary rule still applies unless it is unlikely to maximise quality of witness' evidence so far as is practicable. *The primary rule* Mandatory admission of video interview as evidence-in-chief. If sex offence: mandatory video recorded pre-trial cross-examination or re-examination (subject to availability of facilities) (provided that the witness consents). If not sex offence: mandatory live link for any non-video testimony if facilities available, unless optional order for video cross-examination is made. Consider additional measures and whether they would be likely to maximise quality of testimony, e.g. communication aids, intermediary, removal of wigs/gowns, and evidence in private. *If not subject to primary rule* Consider screens. Consider whether other measures would be likely to maximise quality of testimony, e.g. communication aids, intermediary, removal of wigs/gown, evidence in private.
Witness 17 or over	Complainant of a sexual offence is automatically eligible unless the witness declines. The following categories of witness are	Once a witness is deemed eligible the court should go on to consider what special measures are appropriate, e.g. screens, live link, evidence in private (for sex offences or intimidated witnesses), video interview of evidence-in-chief (and pre-recorded cross-examination). The court must take into account the views of the witness, and whether the use

Age	Eligibility	Notes
	eligible, provided that the quality of their evidence would be diminished by their 'condition' and they wish to take advantage of special measures: (a) Witnesses affected by mental disorder or impairment of intelligence and social functioning. (b) Witnesses affected by physical disability or disorder. (c) Witnesses in fear or distress about testifying.	of the special measure might inhibit the testing of the evidence. In assessing whether special measures are appropriate for a witness in fear or distress the court must consider the following factors: • Nature and circumstances of the offence • Age of the witness • Social and cultural background and ethnic origins of the witness • Any religious beliefs or political opinions of the witness • Any behaviour towards the witness on the part of the accused, his or her family or associates, or any other witness or co-accused.

Availability in criminal proceedings at magistrates' courts (England & Wales) at 3 October 2005 (see Home Office Circular 39/2005)

	Section 16 witnesses (children & vulnerable adults)	Section 17 witnesses (intimidated/fear or distress)
Section 23 screening witness from accused	Full availability (note 2)	Full availability (note 2)
Section 24 evidence by live link	Full availability (notes 3 & 4)	Full availability (note 4)
Section 25 evidence given in private	Full availability (note 2)	Full availability (note 2)
Section 26 removal of wigs and gowns	Not applicable	Not applicable
Section 27 video recorded evidence in chief	Partial availability – for child witnesses in need of special protection *only*) (notes 3 & 6)	*Not* available (note 6)
Section 28 video recorded cross-examination/ re-examination	*Not* available (note 7)	*Not* available (note 7)

Section 29 examination through an intermediary	Partial availability – *pilot areas* (note 8)	Not applicable
Section 30 aids to communication	Full availability (note 9)	Not applicable

Note 1: [. . .]

Note 2: Full availability for these witnesses in these courts since 3 June 2004.

Note 3: available for 'child witnesses in need of special protection' (defined by s.21 of the 1999 Act) only since 24 July 2002.

Note 4: Available since 1 September 2004 in West London magistrates' court and full availability across magistrates' courts from 3 October 2005.

Note 5: [. . .]

Note 6: No decision on the extension of video-recorded evidence in chief to all vulnerable and intimidated witnesses will be made until after the final evaluation report of the ROVI pilot has been received in September 2005. This will inform the development of implementation plans for extending the availability of video-recorded evidence in chief. The implementation plan will incorporate a suitable period of notice to enable criminal justice agencies to prepare.

Note 7: Home Office is currently reviewing the workability of this measure in the context of a review of child evidence.

Note 8: Intermediaries are being piloted in preparation for national roll out (planned 2006/07) – Merseyside pilot went live 23 February 2004, Thames Valley 2 October 2004, West Midlands 1 November 2004 (from 13 September 2004 in Black Country area), Norfolk 1 February 2005, S Wales 1 February 2005 (Cardiff Crown Court and related magistrates' courts in S Wales) and Devon and Cornwall 20 June 2005 (Plymouth Crown Court and magistrates' court).

Note 9: Available in Merseyside since 23 February 2004; full availability across magistrates' courts since 3 June 2004.

Discharge of orders

Section 20(2) Youth Justice and Criminal Evidence Act 1999 provides for the discharge of orders, and is an important consideration for defence lawyers. For example, it may be clearly disclosed during the proceedings, whether by demeanor or questioning that a witness is not afraid. In such a case there is a proper basis for an application to discharge the order.

Warnings in relation to evidence

Section 32 Youth Justice and Criminal Evidence Act 1999 provides for a direction be given if necessary, to a jury, to counteract any prejudice that may be caused to the accused. There is no such requirement on summary trial but it is suggested that in all cases magistrates should be reminded that the order is not be held against the accused in any way. There is always a danger that magistrates will be swayed by witnesses who claim to be in fear some time after an alleged incident, and will use this to bolster the veracity of the witness.

TIME LIMITS

Custody time limits

Custody time limits attach to individual offences. An all too common problem is the charging of new offences at a later stage of the proceedings, thereby triggering a new custody time limit. The following principles can be derived from the case law:

1. Each offence attracts its own limit. There was no new time limit when the constituent elements of the new offence were in substance the same as those of the original offence, so that the offences were substantially the same. The fact that the new offence was a legal alternative to the old offence does not mean that the offences are essentially the same, so, for example, the laying of a charge of manslaughter in place of murder attracted a new custody time limit (*R.* v. *Leeds Crown Court, ex parte Wardle* [2001] 1 Crim LR 468).
2. If a new charge is brought simply to keep the accused in custody, it will amount to an abuse of process and will not attract a new custody time limit.
3. It was desirable that the Crown should review all of the evidence in a case at the earliest possible stage, so as to ensure that wherever possible they were able to comply with the initial custody time limit (*R.* v. *Stafford Crown Court, ex parte UPPAL* [1995] Crim LR 223).

Indictable-only cases, sent by virtue of s.51 Crime and Disorder Act (CDA) 1998	Maximum period of custody between the accused being sent to the Crown Court for trial by a magistrates' court for an offence and the start of the trial in relation to it, shall be 182 days less any period, or the aggregate of any periods, during which the accused has, since that first appearance for the offence, been in the custody of the magistrates' court	Prosecution of Offences (Custody Time Limits) (Amendment) Regulations 2000 (SI 2000/3284)

Indictable-only cases, committed for trial, or transferred to the Crown Court by way of a notice of transfer	Maximum period of 70 days between first appearance and the court hearing evidence in committal proceedings, committing under s.6(2) MCA 1980, or transferring the case for trial	Prosecution of Offences (Custody Time Limits) Regulations 1987 (as amended) (SI 1987/299)
Either-way offences	70 days if jurisdiction is declined or defendant elects Crown Court trial (see above), otherwise 56 days in relation to the start of a summary trial (provided that the decision to proceed to summary trial was itself made within the first 56 days, if it was not, then the 70-day limit applies)	
Summary-only offences	56 days in relation to the start of a summary trial	
Youths	As above, save that indictable-only cases that are tried summarily in the youth court (i.e. not grave crimes), are subject to the same time limits as either-way cases (*R.* v. *Stratford Youth Court, ex parte S* (*a minor*) [1998] 1 WLR 1758)	

First appearance

The first appearance is deemed to be:

1. In a case where that person has made an application under s.43B MCA 1980 (to vary or remove bail conditions), a reference to the time when he appears before the court on the hearing of that application.
2. In a case where that person appears or is brought before the court in pursuance of s.5B Bail Act 1976 and the decision which is to be, or has been, reconsidered under that section is the decision of a constable, a reference to the time when he so appears or is brought (prosecution challenge to grant of police bail). And
3. In any other case, a reference to the time when first he appears or is brought before the court on an information charging him with that offence.

Common scenarios

A defendant who escapes from custody before the expiry of a custody time limit will not have the protection of the custody time limits (for the current stage of the proceedings) once he is re-arrested.

A defendant released on bail, following the expiry of a custody time limit, will not have the protection of the custody time limits (for the current stage of the proceedings) if he is later remanded into custody for failing to surrender to bail, or breaching bail conditions.

If bail is granted to a defendant, the custody time limit clock stops. It will restart, however, should the defendant be later remanded into custody. The period remaining at the time bail was granted will stand as the maximum period of time for completion of the current stage of the proceedings.

The custody time limit takes effect from the end of the first day of remand, until midnight of the last day of the relevant time limit. A custody time limit expiring on any of the following days: Saturday, Sunday, Christmas Day, Good Friday and any day which under the Banking and Financial Dealings Act 1971 is a bank holiday in England and Wales, shall be treated as expiring on the next preceding day which is not one of those days.

Extending custody time limits

If a time limit expires, the defendant is entitled to be released on bail (save where s.25 CJPOA 1994 applies: *R. (On the application of 'O')* v. *(1) Harrow Crown Court (2) Governor of HM Prison Wormwood Scrubs, The Times*, 29 May 2003). All solicitors should be in a position to calculate their own custody time limits in order to act quickly should they expire. Any detention beyond a custody time limit will be unlawful.

The prosecution can apply (on notice or in certain circumstances without) to extend custody time limits. They must satisfy the court, on a balance of probabilities that:

(a) there is good and sufficient cause for doing so; and
(b) the prosecution has acted with all due diligence and expedition.

The prosecution should be in a position to inform the court fully as to the history of the matter and all steps taken, along with dates, in order to meet the time limit.

Case law in relation to the statutory criteria is evolving at a fast pace, and the current position can be summarised as follows:

1. The court must make its own findings on the evidence available to it.
2. Difficulties with court listing, absent special circumstances, amount to a good and sufficient cause to extend time limits; to find otherwise would emasculate the primary legislative purpose and would be wrong. The court must examine rigorously listing difficulties and investigate whether

cases can in fact be heard earlier, for example by moving a bail case (*R.* v. *Birmingham Crown Court, ex parte Cunningham* [2002] EWHC Admin 527).

3. Bail Act considerations could not properly be taken into account as a factor capable of giving rise to a good and reasonable cause for extending custody time limits. So, for example, a defendant's appalling record of failing to surrender to bail is of no relevance to the custody time limit argument (*R.* v. *Reading Crown Court, ex parte Eliot* [2001] Crim LR 811).

4. The prosecution should take steps to notify other relevant agencies that a defendant is in custody, in order to speed up work on cases. The forensic science service is able to upgrade work from a status of 'standard' to 'critical'. If forensic evidence would have been available to the court, but for the failure to notify, or the late notification of a defendant's custody status, that failure might amount to grounds for finding that the prosecution had not acted with all due expedition (*R.* v. *Sheffield Crown Court, ex parte Webster*, 22 June 2000, unreported).

5. The seriousness of the offence, or the need to protect the public, or that the extension was for a short period are not of themselves a good and sufficient cause for extending custody time limits (*R.* v. *Manchester Crown Court, ex parte McDonald* [1999] Crim LR 736).

Appeals

The prosecution can appeal against a refusal to extend a custody time limit, and must do so before the time limit expires. A defendant can similarly appeal against a decision to extend a custody time limit. In both instances, the appeal lies to the Crown Court.

Youth court time limits

By virtue of ss.22 and 29 Prosecution of Offences Act 1985 and the Prosecution of Offences (Youth Courts Time Limits) Regulations 1999 (SI 1999/2743), time limits apply to certain youth court stages. This legislation has now been repealed, and only has effect on cases that were subject to the time limits prior to the repeal.

TRIAL OF YOUTHS

Duty solicitors will need to consider the trial options available to a court in relation to youths. The options available to the court will differ depending on whether the youth is charged alone (or with other youths) or jointly charged with an adult.

Offences of homicide

For the exceptional case where a youth is charged with an offence of homicide, the court must adjourn for committal proceedings (s.24(1) MCA 1980). There is no statutory definition of homicide, but murder, attempted murder and manslaughter fall clearly into this category. The author also believes that offences of infanticide and genocide (where death is caused) also meet the criteria. The ingredients of infanticide are the death of the child in circumstances amounting to murder but for the defendant's state of mind (see: *R. v. K. A. Smith* [1983] Crim LR 739). Most practitioners now accept that causing death by dangerous driving is not an offence of homicide, and support for this can be found within the list of grave crimes where the offence appears – its entry is otiose if the offence is one of homicide.

Committal for other offences

If a court commits a youth for an offence of homicide, it can, at the same time, commit him for trial for any other offence with which he is charged at the same time if the charges for both offences could be joined in the same indictment (s.24(1A) MCA 1980).

Firearms offences

A young person must be tried at the Crown Court if:

- s/he is charged with an offence under subsections (1)(a), (ab), (aba), (ac), (ad), (af) or (c) of s.5 Firearms Act 1968 (prohibited weapons) or under subsection (1A)(a) of that section; and
- the offence was committed on or after 22 January 2004; and
- at the time of the offence s/he was aged 16 or over.

Section 287 CJA 2003 inserted amendments to the Firearms Act and created a minimum 3-year sentence of s.91 detention in these circumstances.

There is no need for a mode of trial hearing and the matter will proceed to committal. When Sched. 3 CJA 2003 is fully in force such cases will be sent as opposed to being committed.

Youth charged with an adult

Indictable-only offences

In the case of a youth jointly charged with an adult for an offence which is indictable only, the youth will be sent for trial to the Crown Court if it is necessary in the interests of justice to do so (for which see below). It matters not whether the youth is produced in court at the same time as the adult, nor does it matter that the adult's case has already been sent on an earlier occasion (s.51(5) CDA 1998). The youth should be charged to appear in the adult court.

In the event that the court does not feel it in the interests of justice to send the youth for trial, the case should be remitted to a youth court.

Committal for other offences

If a youth is sent for trial alongside an adult, he may also be sent for trial for any either-way offence provided that it could be joined in the same indictment as the indictable-only offence, and for any summary offence if it arises out of circumstances which are the same as or connected with those giving rise to the indictable-only offence.

Offences triable either-way

For all other cases, the youth will in the same way appear before the magistrates' court with the adult.

If the adult pleads guilty at plea before venue, the youth should be put to his plea. The youth has no independent right to seek election. If a guilty plea is entered by the youth the adult court may discharge or fine him (or bind over a parent), or alternatively remit the case to the youth court for sentence. If a not-guilty plea is entered by the youth the case will be remitted to the youth court for trial.

Once again, the grave-crime scenario arises. If the offence is a grave crime the court must consider whether summary trial is appropriate or not.

If the youth has pleaded guilty prior to consideration of whether the offence is a grave crime, the court must retain jurisdiction (*R.* v. *Herefordshire Youth Court, ex parte J* (*a minor*), *The Times*, 4 May 1998). If the youth has pleaded not guilty, the court may be able to decline jurisdiction at a later point (s.25(6) MCA 1980), if at any time before the conclusion of evidence for the prosecution the case is one which should not after all be tried summarily. Other circumstances, such as the youth being charged later with another serious offence should not impact upon the venue decision (*R.* v. *Hammersmith Juvenile Court, ex parte O* (*a minor*) (1988) 86 Cr App R 343, QB).

If the adult pleads not guilty or otherwise declines to indicate a plea, the court will consider mode of trial. In the event that the adult is tried in the magistrates' court, the youth will be tried alongside. A subsequent change of plea by the adult (to guilty) will enable the youth to be remitted to the youth court (s.29(2)). If, however, the court declines jurisdiction, or the adult elects trial on indictment, the court then must go on to consider where the youth should be tried. A court can change its decision prior to committal having taken place (s.25(7) MCA 1980); this may occur when the case against the adult is discharged at committal or other change of circumstances occurs.

133

Interests of justice

The following factors are relevant to the issue of whether a youth should be committed to stand joint trial with an adult:

1. Age of the youth.
2. Age of the adult.
3. Seriousness of offence.
4. Vulnerability of the youth and whether trial on indictment would be unduly prejudicial to the welfare of the child. Prosecutors will often argue that, since this is a matter which the Crown Court can take into consideration, justices ought not to be concerned with it. This approach is flawed: the issue of vulnerability should be assessed and decided upon at the earliest possible stage; it is wrong for justices to abdicate responsibility for this to Crown Court judges.
5. Presumption that youths should be dealt with quickly.
6. Desirability or otherwise of two separate trials.
7. Whether the adult is likely to plead guilty.

It is often helpful to consider guidance given by the Lord Chief Justice in *Practice Direction* (*Crown Court: Trial of Children and Young Persons*) [2000] 1 Cr App R 483, which gave effect to the European Court of Human Rights judgment in the *Thompson and Venables* case (the 'Jamie Bulger murder').

Committal for other offences

The court may also commit the youth for trial for any other indictable offence with which he is charged at the same time (whether jointly with the adult or not) if the charges for both offences could be joined in the same indictment.

Youth – dangerous offender provisions

The youth court shall 'send' a child or young person for trial at the Crown Court if (s.51A(2) and (3)(d) Crime and Disorder Act 1998):

- the offence was committed on or after 4 April 2005; and
- the offence is a specified offence; and
- it appears to the court that if s/he is found guilty of the offence the criteria for the imposition of detention for public protection or extended detention would be met.

To impose detention for public protection or extended detention the court must consider there is a significant risk to members of the public of serious harm occasioned by the commission by the offender of further specified offences.

Specified offence

A violent or sexual offence listed in Sched.15 CJA 2003 (see Appendix D).

Serious harm

Defined as 'death or serious person injury, whether physical or psychological' (s.224(3) CJA 2003).

Assessment of dangerousness

The court:

- must take into account all such information as is available to it about the nature and circumstances of the offence;
- may take into account any information which is before it about any pattern of behaviour of which the offence forms part; and
- may take into account any information about the offender that is before it.

How should the court approach the dangerous offender provisions?

In *R. (on the application of the DPP)* v. *South East Surrey Youth Court*, Administrative Court, 8 December 2005 it was stated that in deciding whether a crime is grave, or that the dangerous offender provisions require the defendant to be sent to the Crown Court forthwith, the court must consider the following:

- that the policy of the legislature is that those who are under 18 should, wherever possible, be tried in a youth court, which is best designed for their specific needs;
- the guidance given by the Court of Appeal Criminal Division particularly in relation to non-serious specified offences;
- the need, in relation to those under 18, to be particularly rigorous before concluding that there is a significant risk of serious harm by the commission of further offences: such a conclusion is unlikely to be appropriate in the absence of a pre-sentence report following assessment by a young offender team; and
- in most cases where a non-serious specified offence is charged, an assessment of dangerousness will not be appropriate until after conviction, when, if the dangerousness criteria are met, the defendant can be committed to the Crown Court for sentence.

Post-conviction committal for sentence

If a youth court concludes that an offender convicted of a specified offence presents a significant risk of serious harm to members of the public from the commission of further specified offences, it must commit him/her to the Crown Court for sentence (s.3C PCC(S)A 2000 as inserted by Sched.3 para.23 CJA 2003).

Youths charged alone or with other youths

Trial will take place in the youth court save where the offence amounts to a grave crime (s.24(1)(a) MCA 1980).

It is imperative that a court considers the grave-crime provisions before taking a plea, as a guilty plea will deprive the court of the later exercising of its powers in that regard (*R. v. Herefordshire Youth Court, ex parte J (a minor)*, *The Times*, 4 May 1998). Conversely, defence lawyers, *in appropriate cases*, should never miss an opportunity to take advantage of entering a guilty plea if the opportunity arises before venue has been considered, thereby depriving the court of its power to commit for trial on indictment.

Grave crimes

A youth should be tried summarily unless the offence is one listed in sub-section (1) or (2) of s.91 PCC(S)A 2000, *and*, the court considers that if he is found guilty of the offence it ought to be possible to sentence him in pursuance of s.91(3) of that Act.

Offences which are grave

These include the following:

- an offence punishable in the case of an adult with imprisonment for 14 years or more;
- firearms possession (if subject to mandatory minimum sentence under s.51A Firearms Act 1968);
- various sexual offences under the Sexual Offences Act 2003;
- indecent assault upon a female contrary to s.14 Sexual Offences Act 1956;
- indecent assault upon a male contrary to s.15 Sexual Offences Act 1956;
- (for offenders who have attained the age of 14) offences of causing death by dangerous driving or whilst under the influence of drink or drugs.

The following sexual offences may be treated as grave crimes notwithstanding the fact that the maximum sentence is less than 14 years:

(a) for offences committed before 1 May 2004:

- indecent assault upon a woman, contrary to s.14 Sexual Offences Act 1956; and
- indecent assault upon a man, contrary to s.15 Sexual Offences Act 1956 (only for offences committed on or after 1 October 1997).

(b) for offences committed on or after 1 May 2004:

- sexual assault contrary to s.3 Sexual Offences Act 2003;
- child sex offences committed by children and young persons contrary to s.13 Sexual Offences Act 2003;
- sexual activity with a child family member contrary to s.25 Sexual Offences Act 2003; and
- inciting a child family member to engage in sexual activity contrary to s.26 Sexual Offences Act 2003.

Likely sentence

Essentially, the court will be considering whether there is more than a vague or theoretical possibility (*R. (CPS)* v. *Redbridge Youth Court* [2005] EWHC 1390 (Admin)) that the Crown Court is likely to impose a sentence greater than two years on the youth; if not, the court should retain jurisdiction whatever the limitations on its own powers might be. Both prosecution and defence are entitled to make representations and it will be important to have access to recent sentencing decisions.

In *R.* v. *Manchester Youth Court, ex parte D* [2002] Crim LR 149, the court stated that:

> a court should not decline jurisdiction unless the offence, the circumstances surrounding it and the offender were such that it was more than just a vague or theoretical possibility that a sentence of detention for a long period might be passed. Section 91 of the 2000 Act was primarily applicable to cases of such gravity that a court might consider a sentence of at least two years and anything less fell primarily to be dealt with as a detention and training order.

In this case, the district judge would have been unable to impose a custodial sentence on the youth as he was 12 years of age and not a persistent offender, however, he considered that the Crown Court may wish to impose a period of detention of less than two years. In answer to this scenario the court said:

> There was no statutory restriction on a court using its powers ... to pass a sentence of less than two years but it would only do so in very exceptional and restricted circumstances. The fact than an offender did not qualify for a detention and training order because he was not a persistent offender was not an exceptional circumstance that justified passing a period of detention of less than two years under s. 91 of the Act.

137

Considerations

The court must consider the full facts of the case as outlined by the prosecution, but cannot be informed of the youth's antecedent history if he has one. Following *ex parte D*, it would appear that the court should have regard to all of the surrounding circumstances from a defence perspective, including, if appropriate, good character, conduct since time of alleged offence and any other factors peculiar to the youth which might mitigate the sentence (see *R. v. South Hackney Juvenile Court, ex parte RB and another (minors)* (1984) 77 Cr App R 294). Support for this approach is to be found in *R. (on the application of C and D) and (of N) v. Sheffield Youth Court, The Times*, 3 February 2003, Administrative Court, where it was said that in making a decision as to whether a youth should be sent to the Crown Court with a view to him being sentenced pursuant to s.91 PCC(S)A 2000, the court should take into account any mitigation not in dispute, such as good character. It was entitled to reject mitigation which was in dispute.

In *R. v. H*, Court of Appeal, 20 January 2003, unreported, it was said that courts should think 'long and hard' before imposing sentences of more than two years on offenders aged 15–17 years.

Further guidance can be found in *R. (W) v. Thetford Youth Court; R. v. Waltham Forest Youth Court* [2002] Crim LR 681.

Committal for other offences

If a court commits a youth for a grave crime, it can, at the same time, commit him for trial for any other offence with which he is charged at the same time if the charges for both offences could be joined in the same indictment.

Relevance of age

Offenders aged 17 or younger are tried in the youth court, subject to the exceptions above (offence of homicide, jointly charged with an adult or grave crime). The following are common scenarios arising in relation to the question of age:

1. If an offender is charged when aged under 18, but will be 18 years old when surrendering to bail (or otherwise appearing at court for the first time), he should be bailed to the adult court (*R. v. Amersham Juvenile Court, ex parte Wilson* [1981] 2 All ER 315). The same situation applies if a new charge is laid when the offender has attained 18 years of age during youth court proceedings – the new charge must be dealt with in the adult magistrates' court (*R. v. Chelsea Justices, ex parte DPP* [1963] 1 WLR 1138).
2. In the case of an offender who was believed to be 18 years of age or over when proceedings began, but later transpires to have actually been aged

under 18, the court has a discretion to retain the case or remit to the youth court. If the adult court retains the case it can only sentence the youth to a discharge, fine or referral order (or make a parent the subject of a parental bind-over) (CYPA 1963 s.18).

3. In the case of an offender who was believed to be under 18 years of age, but in fact was older than 18 years, the youth court retains a discretion to continue with the case or remit it to the adult court (CYPA 1933 s.48(1)).

4. If a youth attains 18 years of age during the proceedings the court can retain the case or remit it to the adult court. If it retains the case, it can make any order it could have made if the defendant had not reached that age (CYPA 1963 s.29).

5. A person who attains 18 years of age before venue has been determined has the right to elect jury trial (*R.* v. *Islington North Juvenile Court, ex parte Daley* (1982) 75 Cr App R 280). Venue will generally have been determined if the defendant has entered a not-guilty plea or the issue of venue has been adjudicated upon by the court (in relation to a grave crime). It is good practice for the court file to be marked clearly as to the intention of the court. If a defendant did not intend his not-guilty plea to prejudice any rights he might otherwise have as a result of a change of age, the solicitor acting for the defendant should clearly state this to the court.

6. Many sentencing provisions are determined by reference to age. The date of conviction (i.e. finding of guilt or entering of a guilty plea) is the relevant date. So, for example, a defendant who pleaded guilty to an offence when aged 15, but attained 16 years before the date of sentence, could not be sentenced to a community rehabilitation order since that order is only available to offenders aged 16 or over at the date of conviction. Similarly, an offender convicted when 17 years of age, but attaining 18 years before the date of sentence could still be sentenced to a detention and training order (*R.* v. *Cassidy, The Times*, 13 October 2000).

Composition of the youth bench

The court must include both a male and female, save in unforeseen circumstances (*R.* v. *Birmingham Justices, ex parte F* (2000) 164 JP 523).

Attendance of parents

The court must require the attendance of a parent or guardian of a youth under the age of 16 years unless to do so would be unreasonable. The court may require the attendance of a parent or guardian if the youth is 16 or 17 years. The court has the power to issue a summons against a parent.

Reporting restrictions

No juvenile may be identified unless reporting restrictions are lifted. Restrictions should only be lifted:

(a) to avoid injustice to the young offender;

(b) in the case of a youth charged with an offence punishable with imprisonment (in the case of an adult) with 14 years or more, if necessary to bring the youth before a court or return him to custody (i.e. publicise absconding); or

(c) following conviction if it is in the public interest.

It is regrettably becoming more common to name convicted youths, and the High Court has issued guidance in *McKerry* v. *Teesdale and Wear Valley Justices* [2000] Crim LR 594:

> (1) . . . there was clearly a conflict between: (i) the need to avoid injustice to a young person and the great weight to be given to his or her welfare, particularly in light of Art.8 European Convention on Human Rights ('ECHR'); and (ii) the legitimate interests of the public in receiving fair and accurate reports of criminal proceedings and the right to freedom of expression (Art.10 ECHR). The power to dispense with anonymity of a young person was to be exercised with very great care and it would be very wrong to dispense with anonymity in order to add to the punishment of the young person. The court was to be satisfied and clear in its mind that the statutory criteria under which anonymity could be dispensed with were satisfied, which would very rarely be the case.

> (2) There was nothing that prevented the magistrates from hearing representations from the press. In practical terms hearing such representations might be of value and save the court falling into error.

> [. . .]

Antisocial behaviour orders

As antisocial behaviour orders cannot be made in the youth court, there is no automatic bar on reporting and advocates should always ensure that an application is made to prevent reporting.

It should be noted that s.141 Serious Organised Crime and Police Act 2005 disapplies automatic reporting restrictions in the youth court for those facing proceedings for breach of an antisocial behaviour order, but the court still has a discretion to prevent reporting and advocates should always seek to have restrictions imposed.

CHAPTER 4

Sentencing

(See: Appendix C for the Sentencing Toolkit, including Magistrates' Association sentencing guidelines.)

ACTION PLAN ORDERS

(See: Powers of Criminal Courts (Sentencing) Act 2000 ss.69–71)

The government intended this order to be a starting point for community-based penalties in respect of young offenders. The stated aim of the order was to provide: 'a short but intensive individually tailored response to offending behaviour which will, by means of a series of requirements placed on the young person, address the causes of his offending behaviour and nip it in the bud' (Home Office).

Criteria

An action plan order can be made in respect of a person:

(a) under 18 years;
(b) who has been convicted of an offence, and that offence or the combination of that offence and one or more offences associated with it, is serious enough to warrant a community penalty (other than an offence for which the sentence is fixed by law);
(c) provided that the court is of the opinion that such an order is desirable in the interests of securing the rehabilitation of the offender or preventing the commission by him of further offences.

The restrictions on liberty in the order must be commensurate with the seriousness of the offence or combination of offences.

A court can only make the order if it has been notified that arrangements for implementing such orders are in force.

Scope of the order

Such an order requires the offender to comply with an action plan. An action plan is a series of requirements with respect to the offender's actions and whereabouts during the period of the order. The offender is placed under the supervision of a responsible officer and requires the offender to comply with any directions given by the responsible officer with a view to the implementation of the action plan.

Length of order

The order is for a period of three months, beginning with the date of the order.

Restrictions on making order

An order cannot be made if the offender is already subject to an action plan order, or the court proposes to sentence him to a custodial sentence or make him subject to a community order under s.177 CJA 2003, an attendance centre order, a supervision order or a referral order.

Requirement for reports

Before making such an order, the court must obtain and consider a report detailing the requirements that it is proposed to make the offender subject to, the benefits to be achieved and the attitude of a parent or guardian of the offender to the proposed requirements. Where the offender is under 16, the court must receive information of the offender's family circumstances and the likely effect of the order on those circumstances. National standards that operate in respect of pre-sentence reports stipulate that reports should be prepared within 15 days, or 10 days for persistent young offenders. Since the report required for the making of an action plan order is less detailed than a pre-sentence report, it is expected that an adjournment should generally be for not more than 10 days.

Requirements which may be included in action plan orders and directions

The following requirements can be included in an action plan order, or directions given by a responsible officer:

(a) participate in activities at a time or times specified;
(b) present himself to a person or persons at a place or places at a time or times so specified;
(c) to attend at an attendance centre for a specified number of hours (this can only be imposed where the offence in question is an offence punishable with imprisonment);

(d) to stay away from a place or places;

(e) to comply with arrangements for his education;

(f) to make reparation to a person or persons or to the community at large (other than by way of compensation). A person shall not be specified without his consent to the making of reparation. It is expected that reparation shall be a component in most action plan orders since it is seen as an important part of the process of allowing the offender to take responsibility for his actions and understand the consequences of his offending;

(g) to attend any hearing fixed by the court under s.71 of the Act.

Drug treatment and testing

A pilot programme for drug treatment and testing is now in operation. A sentencing court may include a requirement for the offender to undergo drug treatment and testing where it is satisfied:

- that the offender is dependent on, or has a propensity to misuse, drugs; and
- that his/her dependency or propensity is such as requires and may be susceptible to treatment.

A drug-testing requirement may not be included in an action plan order unless:

- the offender is aged 14 or over and s/he consents to its inclusion; and
- the court has been notified by the Secretary of State that arrangements for implementing such requirements are in force in the area proposed to be specified in the order.

A drug treatment requirement may not be included in an action plan order:

(a) in any case, unless:

- the court is satisfied that arrangements have been or can be made for the treatment intended to be specified in the order (including arrangements for the reception of the offender where s/he is to be required to submit to treatment as a resident); and
- the requirement has been recommended to the court as suitable for the offender by an officer of a local probation board or a member of a youth offending team; and

(b) in the case of an order made in respect of an offender aged 14 or over, unless s/he consents to its inclusion.

A testing requirement is a requirement that, for the purpose of ascertaining whether s/he has any drug in his/her body during the treatment period, the offender shall during that period, at such times or in such circumstances as may be determined by the responsible officer or the treatment provider, provide a sample of such description as may be so determined.

Compatibility of order with religious, educational and other community orders

Requirements and directions shall, as far as practicable, be such as to avoid:

(a) any conflict with the offender's religious beliefs or with the requirements of any other community order to which he may be subject; and
(b) any interference with the times, if any, at which he normally works or attends school or any other educational establishment.

Court-ordered review

Under s.71 of the Act, the court, immediately after making an action plan order may fix a further hearing for a date not more than 21 days after the making of the order, and direct the responsible officer to make, at that hearing, a report as to the effectiveness of the order and the extent to which it has been implemented.

Variation of the order

At that hearing, on the application of the responsible officer or offender, the court may amend the order, by cancelling any provision in it, or by inserting in it (either in addition to or as substitution for any of its provisions) any provision that the court could originally have included in it.

Breaches

A breach is failure without reasonable excuse to comply with any requirement or direction included in the order. If a breach is admitted or proved the court may:

(a) order the offender to pay a fine of an amount not exceeding £1,000;
(b) make an attendance centre order in respect of the offender;
(c) make a curfew order in respect of the offender;
(d) revoke the order and deal with the offender in any other way that would have been open to the court had the order not been made. If the order was made by a Crown Court, the order can only be revoked by a Crown Court. If revocation is proposed, the offender should be committed either on bail or in custody to the Crown Court for sentence. The court, when resentencing, must have regard to the extent of compliance prior to the breach.

Revocation or variation

Any party can apply to revoke or vary the order while it is in force. If it appears appropriate to the court to do so, it may:

(a) revoke the order;
(b) cancel any provision in the order;
(c) insert any provision which could have been included in the order if the court had then had the power to make it and were exercising the power.

Further applications for revocation

If an application to revoke the order is refused by the court, then no further applications can be made without permission of the court.

ANTISOCIAL BEHAVIOUR ORDERS (ASBOs)

(See: Crime and Disorder Act 1998 s.1.)

Overview of funding and duty solicitor's obligation

Duty solicitors are liable to deal with respondents to applications for anti-social behaviour orders. The court does not have power to grant a representation order in these cases, an application must be made to the LSC. The LSC has indicated that such applications are unlikely to succeed given the availability of advocacy assistance. Own solicitors need to apply a merits test to the self-grant of advocacy assistance (using form CDS3). There is no upper limit on the work that can be performed by a duty solicitor, but a £1,500 limit applies to own client work.

Orders can be made in freestanding proceedings or following conviction.

Procedure – freestanding applications

The application is dealt with in the same way as any other complaint under s.53 MCA 1980, with the court hearing evidence on oath if the matter is contested. There is no prohibition on using evidence that previously formed the basis of a criminal conviction (*S* v. *Poole Borough Council* [2002] EWHC Admin 244). Hearsay evidence is admissible subject to the weight to be attached to that evidence, and this will represent a wholly different evidential emphasis from that which duty solicitors are generally used to. The application must be made within six months of the conduct complained of (s.127 MCA 1980), but other conduct, outside of that six months can be used to support the application.

Chapter 3 of this book deals with civil evidence in the magistrates' court, but the following is of specific relevance to these orders. The proceedings are civil in nature and often therefore somewhat alien to criminal practitioners. Solicitors need to be aware that hearsay evidence is not only permitted in these proceedings, but will often amount to the entirety of the evidence to be presented. It is commonplace for neighbourhood incident logs to be produced as well as statements from police officers reporting what others have told them. A most powerful piece of evidence can be a person's antecedent history, particularly if it shows frequent offending over a limited period, of an antisocial nature (criminal damage, drunk and disorderly, harassment, etc.). There is no issue of double jeopardy involved when basing an application on prior criminal conduct (*S* v. *Poole Borough Council*). Other real evidence, particularly CCTV evidence can be properly utilised.

There is no statutory framework for the disclosure of evidence in these proceedings, as the Civil Procedure Rules do not apply, nor does the Criminal Procedure and Investigations Act 1996. Home Office guidance is clear in stating that evidence not disclosed cannot be relied upon.

The Civil Evidence Act 1995 controls the admissibility of hearsay evidence, and crucially the weight to be attached to it. The Act applies to the magistrates' court. There are stringent rules in relation to giving the other party notice of hearsay evidence, and solicitors should be careful to ensure that the rules are followed. It should also be remembered that the respondent to the application can also use hearsay evidence in his defence – the opportunity, in appropriate cases, should not be missed. It is essential that solicitors are familiar with the House of Lords case of *Clingham* and *McCann* (*R. (McCann and others)* v. *Crown Court at Manchester and another*; *Clingham* v. *Kensington and Chelsea Royal London Borough Council* [2002] 3 WLR 1313), that confirmed the admissibility of hearsay evidence and commented at some length about the probative value of it in these proceedings. The defence have the right to apply for direct evidence of the facts to be adduced, and refusal will lend support to a submission that the weight to be attached to admitted hearsay, in circumstances where the maker was available to give direct evidence to the court, is less than might have been attached to oral evidence. Clearly, if the hearsay is based on anonymous reports the defence will want to examine motives and make strong submissions on the fact that the evidence has not been subject to cross-examination designed to test its true strength.

Procedure – applications following conviction

These applications will be made either on the court's own motion or by relevant authorities. The evidential provisions are as for freestanding applications (but note that there is no requirement to issue any summons, and in many cases the fact of conviction may be enough in itself to justify the making of the order). The court has power to adjourn proceedings for the purposes of making an order. There is a growing body of case law in relation to the making of antisocial behaviour orders and how breaches should be dealt with. At the time of writing there were also a number of irreconcilable authorities leaving both practitioners and courts confused as to the correct approach: for a link to all relevant cases follow the link on **www.crimeline.info**.

Effect of Human Rights Act 1998

Human Rights Act considerations have been analysed in *R.* v. *Manchester Crown Court, ex parte McCann* [2002] 3 WLR 1313. The Court of Appeal concluded that proceedings in respect of applications for antisocial behaviour orders are civil in nature and do not offend the European Convention on Human Rights.

Criteria

The following criteria must be satisfied:

1. The order must be made by the 'relevant authority'.
2. That the person, being a person 10 years or over, has acted since the commencement date (1 April 1999), in an antisocial manner, that is to say, in a manner that caused or was likely to cause harassment, alarm or distress to one or more persons not of the same household as himself. And
3. That such an order is necessary to protect persons in the local government area in which the harassment, alarm or distress was caused or was likely to be caused from further antisocial acts by him.

Reasonable actions

If it is proved that the above conditions are met, the court can make the order. In deciding on whether the conditions are met, the court shall disregard any act of the defendant which he shows was reasonable in the circumstances (for example, an act of self-defence).

Standard of proof

Although the civil standard of proof applies, that standard is flexible and has to reflect the consequences that would follow if an antisocial behaviour order were made. This should lead magistrates to apply an exacting standard of proof which, in practice, would be hard to distinguish from the criminal one (*R.* v. *Manchester Crown Court, ex parte McCann* [2002] 3 WLR 1313).

Effect of order

The order can contain such prohibitions as are necessary for the purpose of protecting persons in the local government area (or adjoining that area), from further antisocial acts by the defendant. Common prohibitions include:

(a) entering specific areas;
(b) threatening or engaging in violence or damage against any person or property within a given area;
(c) encouraging any other person to engage in the above acts.

Duration of order

The order shall be for a period not less than two years, or until further order. A person subject to such an order can apply to vary or discharge it. No order can be discharged earlier than two years without the consent of both parties.

Interim orders

An interim order can be applied for under s.1D Crime and Disorder Act 1998, for a fixed period. The court must be satisfied that 'it is just to make an order under this section pending the determination of [the main application]'. A person subject to such an order has the same rights to apply for variation or discharge as a person subject to a full order. In appropriate cases an interim order can be applied for without notice, but such cases will be rare. An interim order will only take effect once served on the respondent (so always check this in breach proceedings), and if service does not take place within seven days the order will lapse. Interim orders should not be consented to lightly: if the risk to the community is so great one might have thought that criminal proceedings would have been justified; it should also be noted that breach of an interim order carries the same severe punishment as breach of a full order.

Breach

A person who, without reasonable excuse, does anything which he is prohibited from doing by an antisocial behaviour order is guilty of an offence triable either way and shall be liable on summary conviction to imprisonment not exceeding six months or a fine not exceeding the statutory maximum (or both). On indictment, the offence carries five years' imprisonment.

A court may not conditionally discharge an offender found in breach of the order. The criminal standard of proof applies to breach proceedings.

Appeals

An appeal shall lie to the Crown Court (s.4 CDA 1998).

ATTENDANCE CENTRE ORDERS

(See: Powers of Criminal Courts (Sentencing) Act 2000 s.60.)

Criteria

An attendance centre order can be made in respect of a person:

(a) under 21 years of age,
(b) who has been convicted of an offence, and that offence or the combination of that offence and one or more offences associated with it, is serious enough to warrant a community penalty (other than an offence for which the sentence is fixed by law).

In limited circumstances, the court can also make this order in respect of an offender no older than 24 years of age, for default in paying financial penalties.

Scope

The order requires the offender to attend at a specified centre for a fixed number of hours. The court need not consider a pre-sentence report before making such an order, but it is good practice to do so.

Length of order

The court should normally specify a period not less than 12 hours except where the offender is aged under 14 and the court is of the opinion that 12 hours would be excessive having regard to his age and all other circumstances.

The aggregate number of hours shall not exceed 12 except where the court is of the opinion, having regard to all the circumstances, that 12 hours would be inadequate, and in such a case the court can impose hours not exceeding 24 hours where the person is aged under 16, and not exceeding 36 hours where the person is aged over 16 but under 21 years.

Limits on daily attendance

Attendance cannot exceed three hours on any one day, nor may attendance fall on more than one occasion per day.

Existing attendance centre orders

New orders can be made where an existing order is in force. The court need not have regard to hours remaining on the uncompleted order when imposing the new order.

Accessibility of attendance centre

The attendance centre must be reasonably accessible to the person concerned having regard to his age, the means of access available to him and any other circumstances. If such a centre is not reasonably accessible, then the court cannot make the order. Home Office Circular 135/79 suggests travel of 10 miles or 45 minutes for offenders under 14 years, and 15 miles or 90 minutes in the case of older offenders.

Compatibility of order with religious, educational and other community orders

Times of attendance at the centre should not conflict with the offender's religious beliefs, any other community order to which he may be subject, and schooling.

Breaches

If it is proved that an offender has failed without reasonable excuse to attend the centre, or has committed a breach of the attendance centre rules, the court may deal with him in one of the following ways:

1. Impose a fine not exceeding £1,000, and allow the order to continue.
2. Where the attendance centre order was made by a magistrates' court, it may deal with him, for any offence in respect of which the order was made, in any way in which he could have been dealt with for that offence by the court which made the order if the order had not been made. When such an order is made the attendance centre order must be revoked if it is still in force.
3. Where the order was made by the Crown Court, it may commit him to custody or release him on bail until he can be brought to appear before the Crown Court.

Extent of compliance

If a court chooses to resentence the offender, it shall take into account the extent to which the offender has complied with the requirements of the order. In the case of an offender who has wilfully and persistently failed to comply with the requirements of the order, a court may impose a custodial sentence notwithstanding anything in s.79(2) of the Act (which states that custody should not be imposed unless the offence(s) are so serious that only a custodial sentence can be justified).

Applying to revoke the order

An offender or officer in charge of an attendance centre may apply to the court to revoke a current attendance centre order. A magistrates' court can hear an application in respect of an order made by the Crown Court, save when there is included in the order a direction that the power to revoke is reserved to the Crown Court.

An application shall be made to the magistrates' court acting for the petty sessions area in which the attendance centre is situated, or to the court that made the order.

Powers on revocation

The court has the power, having revoked an order under these provisions, to resentence as outlined above (which can include making an attendance centre order for fewer hours).

Application to vary order

The court has power on an application being made by the offender or attendance centre officer, to vary the day or hour specified for the offender's first attendance at the centre, or to substitute for the centre specified an alternative centre provided that it is reasonably accessible in accordance with the criteria outlined above.

BIND OVER

The power to bind over a defendant remains a frequently used order in the magistrates' court. The power to bind over is derived from common law and statute (Justices of the Peace Act 1361, s.115 MCA 1980).

Scope

A person can be bound over to keep the peace, or to be of good behaviour only.

Initiating process

A complaint can be laid to bring a person before the court, but no new complaint need be laid if a person is already before the court on another matter.

If the matter is dealt with under s.115 MCA 1980, it should be remembered that, contrary to common belief, there is a power of arrest following a failure to appear at the adjourned hearing, by virtue of s.55 MCA 1980.

Test to be applied and burden of proof

The court must be satisfied beyond reasonable doubt that a breach of the peace occurred, which means that the court must be sure that violence or threat of violence was used, which was unreasonable (i.e. unlawful). It is arguable that the usual circumstances which bring many defendants before the court would not satisfy this test, as officers very often arrive after the event, and in circumstances where no one who was present wishes to make a complaint. In addition, the court must believe that such an order is necessary to prevent a further breach of the peace: the risk must be real. On a strict interpretation, it is not surprising that many district judges refuse to bind over defendants of good character who have appeared before the court on a charge of, for example, drunk and disorderly, where the justification for binding over as opposed to proceeding to trial, is that the behaviour was a 'one-off event and out of character'.

Agitation or excitement, including hysterical waving of a handbag in front of a police officer who was dealing with another member of the public did not amount to a breach of the peace (*Jarrett* v. *Chief Constable of West Midlands*, *The Times*, 28 February 2003).

Costs

If the matter proceeds to trial, and the magistrates do not find that a breach of the peace was committed, costs can be awarded. The complainant, who will normally be the chief officer of police, pays costs.

Compatibility with European Convention

It is doubtful whether an order to be of good behaviour should now be made in light of the ruling in *Hashman* v. *United Kindgom* (2000) 30 EHRR 241, which involved a complaint in respect of hunt saboteurs who were bound over in the sum of £100 to be of good behaviour. The court held by a majority of 16:1 that there had been a violation of Article 10. In essence, the court felt that the term was too vague.

Binding over parties to proceedings

In addition to proceedings on complaint, the court has the power to bind over any witness appearing in proceedings before them. This caters for the trial situations where all persons have been deemed to be as bad as one another. It is submitted, however, that justices should proceed with great care before binding over a witness in proceedings, to ensure that appropriate findings of fact have been made, which the party is in a position to challenge if he so wishes. It is unlikely that this power will survive the Human Rights Act 1998. A witness who has not given evidence cannot be bound over.

Setting the recognisance

The recognisance entered into can be with or without sureties. The court must assess a person's means before fixing the level of surety.

Consequences of refusing to enter into a recognisance

If a person refuses to enter into a recognisance, the court may commit him to custody for a period not exceeding six months or until he sooner complies with the order. A person under 21 years, until recently, could not be so detained, as 'custody' is not available, but by virtue of s.108(1)(c) PCC(S)A 2000, there is a power to commit a person aged at least 18 but under 21 to prison for contempt of court or any kindred offence. It has been held that a refusal to enter into a recognisance is such a kindred offence (*Howley* v. *Oxford* [1985] Crim LR 724).

Breach of recognisance

Proceedings for breaking the order are commenced by summons. If the person is already before the court, this gives the court appropriate jurisdiction. The court must be satisfied to the civil standard that the order has been breached, and on so finding can order part or the entire recognisance to be forfeit.

COMMITTAL FOR SENTENCE

(See: Powers of Criminal Courts (Sentencing) Act 2000 ss.3–4.)

Committal for sentence following conviction after trial

The power to commit for sentence applies to any triable either-way offence, save those that because of their value fall to be tried summarily only.

Excluded offences

Excluded offences, by virtue of the value of damage being less than £5,000 are:

- Offences under s.1 Criminal Damage Act 1971, excluding any offence committed by damaging or destroying property by fire.
- Aiding, abetting, counselling or procuring; attempting to commit; inciting another to commit; offences under s.1 Criminal Damage Act 1971.
- Offences under s.12A Theft Act 1968 where no allegation is made under subsection (1)(b) other than of damage, whether to the vehicle or other property or both.

Conditions to be satisfied

A court can commit for sentence if the following conditions are satisfied:

(a) the offender is aged at least 18 years, or the defendant in question is a corporation; and
(b) the offence or the combination of the offence and one or more offences associated with it was so serious that greater punishment should be inflicted for the offence than the court has the power to impose (this also covers a situation where the sentence proposed is not available to the court, for example a hospital restriction order); or
(c) in the case of a violent or sexual offence, that a custodial sentence for a term longer than the court has power to impose is necessary to protect the public from serious harm from the offender.

Associated offences and violent offences are defined by s.161 PCC(S)A 2000.

Committal for sentence following plea before venue

The court can commit for sentence if the following criteria are satisfied:

(a) the offender is aged at least 18 years, or the defendant in question is a corporation; and
(b) the offence or the combination of the offence and one or more offences associated with it was so serious that greater punishment should be inflicted for the offence than the court has the power to impose (this also covers a situation where the sentence proposed is not available to the court, for example a hospital restriction order); or
(c) in the case of a violent or sexual offence, that a custodial sentence for a term longer than the court has power to impose is necessary to protect the public from serious harm from the offender.

Committal for sentence in relation to indictable offences when defendant committed for trial

If the court has committed the defendant for trial in relation to one or more related offences, then the court can commit the defendant for sentence in respect of an indictable offence to which a guilty plea has been entered. The court should certify whether it believes its powers of punishment are sufficient. If it so certifies, then in the event of the charges in respect of which the defendant was committed for trial being resolved in the defendant's favour, the sentencing powers of the Crown Court are restricted to the powers the magistrates would have had, had the defendant not been so committed. If, however, a conviction follows on the other matter, or the magistrates would have committed for sentence in any event then the powers are those of the Crown Court as if it had been a matter tried on indictment.

Adjournment to await committal for trial

The court can adjourn to await committal for trial, in order that offences to which a guilty plea has been entered at plea before venue can be tied up.

Committal for other offences

In the event that the court commits an offender for sentence to the Crown Court for an offence, it can at the same time commit for sentence in relation to any other indictable offence, regardless of whether or not it is related. It can also commit for sentence in relation to any other offence that the committing court has convicted the offender, being either:

(a) an offence punishable with imprisonment; or
(b) an offence in respect of which the committing court has a power or duty to order him to be disqualified under ss.34, 35 or 36 Road Traffic Offenders Act 1988; or
(c) any suspended sentence in respect of which the committing court has power under s.120(1) of the Act to deal with him.

Committal for Bail Act offences

The court can commit an offender for a Bail Act offence if it feels that its powers of punishment (six months) are insufficient (s.6(6) Bail Act 1976), or it is committing an offender for trial in respect of another offence, and it would be appropriate for him to be dealt with in respect of both matters together.

Mentally disordered offenders

If a court is of the opinion that a restriction order is appropriate in the case of an offender aged at least 14 years, it can commit that offender for sentence to the Crown Court, which has the power to make such a sentence (s.43 Mental Health Act 1983).

Bail status

Generally, bail should not be taken away because an offender has been committed to the Crown Court for sentence (*R. v. Rafferty* [1998] Crim LR 433).

COMMUNITY SENTENCES

Definitions

Statutory references in this chapter are to the CJA 2003 unless otherwise stated. A community sentence is defined as a sentence which consists of or includes a community order or one or more youth community orders (s.147(1)). Youth community orders will come in to force in April 2007.

Community order

A community order can be made in respect of a person aged 16 or over convicted of an offence. The order, for a maximum length of three years, comprises one or more of the following requirements:

- an unpaid work requirement (s.199);
- an activity requirement (s.201);
- a programme requirement (s.202);
- a prohibited activity requirement (s.203);
- a curfew requirement (s.204);
- an exclusion requirement (s.205);
- a residence requirement (s.206);
- a mental health treatment requirement (s.207);
- a drug rehabilitation requirement (s.209);
- an alcohol treatment requirement (s.212);
- a supervision requirement (s.213); or
- an attendance centre requirement (s.214) (for offenders below 25 years of age).

The specific requirements of these orders are set out below.

Youth community order

This order, for a maximum period of three years comprises one of:

- a curfew order (s.163 PCC(S)A 2000);
- an exclusion order (s.40A(1) PCC(S)A 2000);
- an attendance centre order (s.163 PCC(S)A 2000);
- a supervision order (s.63(1) PCC(S)A 2000); or
- an action plan order (s.69(1) PCC(S)A 2000).

A drug treatment and testing requirement can be imposed as a requirement of an action plan or supervision order, in accordance with Schedule 24 CJA 2003. The offender must be aged 14 years or over and consent.

Restrictions on imposing community sentences

Seriousness criteria

A court must not pass a community sentence unless of the opinion that the offence, or the combination of the offence and one or more offences associated with it, was serious enough to warrant such a sentence (s.148(1)).

The community sentence must comprise elements that are suitable for the offender (s.148(2)(a)) and restrictions on liberty imposed must be commensurate with the seriousness of the offence, or the combination of the offence and one or more offences associated with it (s.148(2)(b)).

Community order for persistent offender previously fined

A community sentence can be passed, regardless of the fact that the seriousness criteria are not met, in the following circumstances (s.151):

- person aged 16 years or over convicted of an offence;
- on three or more previous occasions has been convicted by a court in the United Kingdom of an offence after attaining the age of 16, and has had passed on him a sentence consisting only of a fine;
- the current offence would not otherwise be serious enough to warrant a community sentence; and
- having considered the nature of the previous offences and their relevance to the current offence, and the time that has elapsed since the offender's conviction of each of those offences, it is in all of the circumstances in the interests of justice to make such an order.

Effect of previous remand in custody on length of community sentence

The court must have regard to any period served on remand in custody prior to sentence for the offence or any other offence the charge for which was

157

founded on the same facts or evidence (s.149). This section reflects current sentencing practice.

Effect of mandatory sentences

A court cannot pass a community sentence in respect of an offence for which the sentence is fixed by law, including where the offender falls to be sentenced under s.51A(2) of the Firearms Act 1968 (required custodial sentence for certain firearms offences), or falls to receive a minimum sentence for a third drug trafficking offence or third burglary (ss.110(2) and 111(2) PCC(S)A 2000). Nor can a community sentence be imposed where a sentence under ss.225–228 CJA 2003 falls to be imposed.

Requirement for pre-sentence report before passing community sentence

Adults

The court must order and consider a pre-sentence report unless, having consideration to the circumstances of the case, it is of the opinion that a report is unnecessary (s.156).

Youths

Unless the youth falls to be sentenced for an indictable only offence (whether on its own or in combination with one or more other offences of any description), the court must not dispense with a pre-sentence report unless there exists a previous pre-sentence report which the court has had regard to (s.156). If there is more than one previous report the court must consider the most recent.

Effect of failure to obtain a pre-sentence report

A sentence is not invalidated by the failure of a court to obtain a pre-sentence report, but a court on appeal should order and consider such a report unless it agrees that such a report was unnecessary or is at the time of the appeal unnecessary. In the case of a youth the appeal court should consider any earlier report.

Disclosure of pre-sentence reports

Section 159 details the parties who must receive any written report. A copy must be given to the offender, his legal representative and the prosecutor. A report in respect to an unrepresented youth offender should be given to his parent or guardian if present in court.

The report is only to be used for formulating and making representations to the court in relation to its contents.

Other reports, such as those prepared by a member of the youth offending team, must be similarly disclosed if given to a court other than a youth court.

Pre-sentence drug testing

A court can order a convicted offender aged 14 years or over, in respect of whom it is considering passing a community sentence, to provide samples for the purpose of ascertaining whether the offender has any specified Class-A drug in his body (s.161).

If the offender is under 17 years of age such samples must be provided in the presence of an appropriate adult, and the order should reflect this fact.

A failure to comply with such an order, without reasonable excuse is an offence punishable with a fine not exceeding level 4 on the standard scale.

Specified Class-A Drugs

- Cocaine, its salts and any preparation or other product containing cocaine or its salts.
- Diamorphine (commonly known as heroin), its salts and any preparation or other product containing diamorphine or its salts.

Types of community order

Overview

A community sentence can be made up of a combination of different orders (see Table 4.1), but the court must consider when combining orders whether the requirements are compatible with each other. Some orders carry an electronic monitoring requirement, unless exceptions are met. Reference is made to other penalties such as custody plus, this is because these community orders can now be combined with various types of custodial sentence and licence conditions.

Table 4.1 Types of community order

Name	Nature of order	Min length/ hours (no minimum period unless otherwise specified)	Max length/ hours (note the maximum of 3 years for community orders, unless otherwise specified)	Comments
Unpaid work requirement	Performance of unpaid work	40 hours	300 hours. Must be completed within 12 months unless the period is extended	Court must be satisfied that offender a suitable person to perform such work Concurrent orders must not exceed 300 hours Court may impose electronic monitoring requirement unless prevented from doing so by s.215
Activity requirement	To present himself to a person at such place and time as specified, and/or participate in specified activities. Such activities to include reparative schemes	N/A	60 days, comprising attendance and/or activities	Court must consult officer of local probation board before imposing such a requirement, or in the case of an offender aged under 18 years either an officer of the local probation board or a member of a youth offending team Following consultation court must be satisfied that it is feasible to ensure compliance with the requirement(s) to be imposed If the requirement involves the cooperation of a person other than the offender (for example a victim

Name	Nature of order	Min length/ hours (no minimum period unless otherwise specified)	Max length/ hours (note the maximum of 3 years for community orders, unless otherwise specified)	Comments
				in a reparative scheme) the person concerned must consent before the requirement can be imposed Court may impose electronic monitoring requirement unless prevented from doing so by s.215
Programme requirement	Participation in an accredited programme of activities	Not specified This order will generally be in addition to a supervision requirement, and would include courses such as 'Think First' and domestic violence programmes	Not specified	If the requirement involves the cooperation of a person other than the offender, the person concerned must consent before the requirement can be imposed Court must consult officer of local probation board before imposing such a requirement, or in the case of an offender aged under 18 years either an officer of the local probation board or a member of a youth offending team Following consultation court must be satisfied that it is feasible to ensure compliance with the requirement(s) to be imposed

161

Name	Nature of order	Min length/ hours (no minimum period unless otherwise specified)	Max length/ hours (note the maximum of 3 years for community orders, unless otherwise specified)	Comments
				Court may impose electronic monitoring requirement unless prevented from doing so by s.215
Prohibited activity requirement	An order refraining the offender from participating in activities specified in the order, on a day or days so specified, or during a period so specified	Not specified	Not specified	An order requiring the offender not to possess, use or carry a firearm (within the meaning of the Firearms Act 1968) can be included in such an order Court must consult officer of local probation board before imposing such a requirement, or in the case of an offender aged under 18 years either an officer of the local probation board or a member of a youth offending team. Following consultation court must be satisfied that it is feasible to ensure compliance with the requirement(s) to be imposed Court may impose electronic monitoring requirement unless prevented from doing so by s.215

Name	Nature of order	Min length/ hours (no minimum period unless otherwise specified)	Max length/ hours (note the maximum of 3 years for community orders, unless otherwise specified)	Comments
Curfew requirement	An order requiring the offender to remain at a place specified in the order	2 hours per day	12 hours per day (see additional notes)	The court must also impose an electronic monitoring requirement unless it is prevented from doing so by s.215 or in the particular circumstances of the case it considers it inappropriate to do so A community order or suspended custody order which imposes a curfew requirement may not specify periods which fall outside the period of 6 months beginning with the day on which the order is made. If imposed as part of a custody plus order the 6 month period starts with the first day of the licence period If the order is made as part of an intermittent custody order the aggregate number of days on which the offender is subject to the requirement for any part of the day must not exceed 182 days The court must obtain and consider information about

Name	Nature of order	Min length/ hours (no minimum period unless otherwise specified)	Max length/ hours (note the maximum of 3 years for community orders, unless otherwise specified)	Comments
				the place proposed to be specified in the order, including information as to the attitude of persons likely to be affected by the enforced presence there of the offender
Exclusion requirement	An order prohibiting the offender from entering a place specified in the order	Not specified	Not exceeding a 2 year period where the relevant order is a community order	The court must also impose an electronic monitoring requirement unless it is prevented from doing so by s.215 or in the particular circumstances of the case it considers it inappropriate to do so Exclusions can operate for certain defined periods and may specify different places for different periods or days
Residence requirement	In relation to a community order or a suspended sentence order means a requirement that, during a period specified, the offender must reside at a particular place	Not specified	Not specified	The court must consider the home surroundings of the offender before making an order A court may not specify a hostel or other institution except on the recommendation of an officer of the local probation board Court may impose electronic monitoring

Name	Nature of order	Min length/ hours (no minimum period unless otherwise specified)	Max length/ hours (note the maximum of 3 years for community orders, unless otherwise specified)	Comments
				requirement unless prevented from doing so by s.215
Mental health treatment requirement	Order requiring offender to submit to treatment by or under the direction of a registered medical practitioner or a chartered psychologist or both. The order must be made with a view to the improvement of the offender's mental condition	Not specified	Not specified	Court must be satisfied on the evidence of a person approved under s.12 Mental Health Act 1983 that the mental condition of the offender is (i) such as requires and may be susceptible to treatment, but (ii) is not such as to warrant the making of a hospital order or guardianship order within the meaning of the Mental Health Act 1983 Court may impose electronic monitoring requirement unless prevented from doing so by s.215
Drug rehabilitation requirement	An order requiring the offender to submit to treatment, with a view to the reduction or elimination of the offender's dependency on or propensity to misuse drugs, and, for the purpose of ascertaining	Treatment and testing period must be for a minimum of 6 hours	Not specified	Can only impose the order if satisfied that the offender is dependent on, or has propensity to misuse drugs, and that his dependency or propensity is such as requires and may be susceptible to treatment Mandatory court review for orders of more that 12 months, otherwise

165

Name	Nature of order	Min length/ hours (no minimum period unless otherwise specified)	Max length/ hours (note the maximum of 3 years for community orders, unless otherwise specified)	Comments
	whether he has drugs in his body may impose a requirement to supply samples for analysis			discretionary (s.210) Court may impose electronic monitoring requirement unless prevented from doing so by s.215 Court must consult officer of local probation board before imposing such a requirement, or in the case of an offender aged under 18 years either an officer of the local probation board or a member of a youth offending team Following consultation court must be satisfied that it is feasible to ensure compliance with the requirement(s) to be imposed
Alcohol treatment requirement	Order requiring offender to submit to treatment, with a view to the reduction or elimination of the offender's dependency on alcohol	6 months minimum	Not specified	Court must be satisfied that the offender is dependent on alcohol, that his dependency is such as requires and may be susceptible to treatment, and, that suitable arrangements have been made, or can be made for the reception of the offender

Name	Nature of order	Min length/ hours (no minimum period unless otherwise specified)	Max length/ hours (note the maximum of 3 years for community orders, unless otherwise specified)	Comments
				Court may impose electronic monitoring requirement unless prevented from doing so by s.215
Supervision requirement	Order requiring that the offender attend appointments with the 'responsible officer', in order to promote the offender's rehabilitation	See notes	See notes	The order will apply during the 'relevant period', which is the period that the community order remains in force (i.e. for up to 3 years), or in relation to a custody plus order, the licence period as defined by s.181(3)(b). In relation to an intermittent custody order the period is the licence period specified by s.183(3), and for a suspended sentence order it is the supervision period as specified by s.189(1)(a) Court may impose electronic monitoring requirement unless prevented from doing so by s.215
Attendance centre requirement	Requirement to attend at an attendance centre	12 hours	36 hours Cannot be required to attend on more than one occasion on any one day	Offender must be under 25 years of age Court must have regard to whether the centre is reasonably

Name	Nature of order	Min length/ hours (no minimum period unless otherwise specified)	Max length/ hours (note the maximum of 3 years for community orders, unless otherwise specified)	Comments
			Cannot be required to attend for more than 3 hours on any one day.	accessible to the offender, having regard to the means of access available to him and any other circumstances Court may impose electronic monitoring requirement unless prevented from doing so by s.215

Electronic monitoring

Electronic monitoring is to ensure compliance with various orders, as outlined above. Any other person, whose cooperation is necessary to make the order work, must consent to the order.

Religious beliefs and other conflicts

A court must ensure as far as practicable that a community order does not conflict with an offender's religious beliefs or schooling (s.217).

Review of community orders

The Secretary of State can, by order, enable or require a court to provide for the review or amendment of community orders, and make provision for the timing and conduct of such reviews and the powers of the court on review (s.178). Such an order from the Secretary of State can have the effect of repealing or amending any provision of Part 12 CJA 2003.

Breach, revocation and amendment of community orders

Schedule 8 deals with breach, revocation and amendment of community orders, and provides for a warning system in relation to offenders. Generally, unless the breach is serious or cannot be remedied by a warning, a first warning will be given to the offender, outlining the circumstances of the failure to comply with the order and that the failure is unacceptable, and informing the offender that a further failure within 12 months will lead to the offender being brought before the court for breach proceedings.

Effect of previous warning

If a warning has previously been given, and within 12 months of that warning the responsible officer is of the opinion that the offender has since that date failed without reasonable excuse to comply with any of the requirement of the order, the officer must cause court proceedings to be taken in respect to the breach.

Crown Court orders

Orders made by the Crown Court will be dealt with at first instance by a Crown Court unless the order included a requirement that failure to comply with the order was to be dealt with by the magistrates' court. This power recognises that in many instances a Crown Court will be content for justices to decide whether a breach should be sent to the Crown Court for re-sentencing, or whether it can be dealt with in the lower court.

Powers of magistrates' court if breach proved

If a person fails, without reasonable excuse, to comply with any of the requirements of the community order, it can be dealt with in any one of the following ways, taking into account beforehand the extent of compliance with the order aside from the breach:

1. Amending the order to include more onerous requirements.
2. Where the order is one made by the magistrates' court: by dealing with the offender in any way in which the court could have dealt with him if he had just been convicted of the offence (i.e. re-sentencing). The original order must be revoked.
3. Where the community order was made by a magistrates' court and the offence was not an offence punishable by imprisonment, the court has the power to impose a term of imprisonment not exceeding 51 weeks, provided the offender is aged 18 or over and has wilfully and persistently failed to comply with the requirements of the order. The original order must be revoked.

If the community order was made by the Crown Court, instead of dealing with the offender in one of the three ways specified above, the magistrates' court can commit him to the Crown Court to be dealt with, either on bail or in custody. The Crown Court can deal with the offender in any one of the three ways specified above.

Effect of certain breaches

An offender required under a mental health, drug rehabilitation or alcohol treatment requirement to submit to treatment, is not to be treated as having failed to comply with that requirement on the ground only that he had refused to undergo any surgical, electrical or other treatment if, in the opinion of the court, his refusal was reasonable having regard to all of the circumstances.

Revocation of orders

A court can revoke the order, or revoke the order and re-sentence and deal with the offender in any way which it could have dealt with him had he just been convicted. Orders can be revoked on the grounds of good progress or satisfactory response to treatment or supervision.

Amendment of orders

Schedule 8, para.16 contains provision for the amendment of orders.

Effect of subsequent conviction

An offender convicted of an offence during the currency of a community order may have his order revoked. On revoking an order the court can go on to re-sentence for the original offence and deal with him in any way it could have when he was first convicted. The provisions for the Crown Court and magistrates' court are the same, and reflect current practice.

CUSTODIAL PENALTIES

Availability

Different custodial disposals are available, dependent upon the offender's age:

21 years and over	Imprisonment
18–20 years	Young offender institution (YOI)*
Under 18 years	Detention and training order (DTO) – not in force for 10 and 11 year olds.

*When s.61 Criminal Justice and Court Services Act 2000 is implemented, sentences of detention in a young offender institution will be abolished. All offenders aged 18 years and above will be sentenced as adult offenders.

General limits on custodial sentences in the magistrates' court

The following limits apply:

Imprisonment	Minimum five days (save exceptions under ss.135 and 136 MCA 1980).
	Maximum six months for any one offence.
	Maximum 12 months if two or more either-way offences.
	Subject always to the statutory maximum for the offences in question.
YOI	Minimum 21 days (save exception under s.97(3) MCA 1980).
	Maximum: as above.
DTO	Minimum four months.
	Maximum 24 months in respect of any one or more offences, subject only to the statutory maximums that apply.

Statutory criteria for imposition of custodial sentences

The offence, or combination of the offence and one or more offences associated with it, must be so serious that only such a sentence can be justified for the offence, or, where the offence is a violent or sexual offence, that only such a sentence would be adequate to protect the public from serious harm from the offender.

Custody where offender fails to express willingness to comply with requirement of a community penalty

Nothing in the above criteria shall prevent the court from passing a custodial sentence on the offender if he fails to express his willingness to comply with a requirement that is proposed by the court to be included in a community rehabilitation order, supervision order or drug treatment and testing order. In the case of community rehabilitation orders and supervision orders the requirement sought to be imposed must have required the offender's consent.

Requirements for making of detention and training orders

The following point from *R. v. C*, *The Times*, 11 October 2000 should be noted:

- A court shall not make a detention and training order in the case of an offender under the age of 15 at the time of the conviction, unless it is of the opinion that he is a persistent offender. There is no statutory definition of 'persistent offender': it is a matter of fact to be determined by the sentencing court. The following cases will be of assistance in determining whether or not an offender is likely to be regarded as persistent.

***R. v. C, The Times,* 11 October 2000** An offender of previous good character was convicted of offences of burglary and theft; while on bail for those offences he committed two further burglaries. The Court of Appeal rejected the suggestion that there was any nexus between persistency and court appearances, and held that the sequence of criminal behaviour showed a sufficient degree of persistence for the offender to be considered a persistent offender within the meaning of the PCC(S)A 2000.

***R. v. D* [2000] Crim LR 867** A court is able to have regard to cautions recorded against an offender when making a determination as to whether that offender is a persistent offender within the meaning of the PCC(S)A 2000. Cautions require three preconditions: (a) evidence sufficient to warrant a prosecution; (b) the offender admits his guilt; and (c) the offender and his parents/guardian are aware that the caution may be cited in court in the event of future offending. In relation to this case though, it should be remembered that even though an offender has previous cautions they could be so distanced in time or similarity to lack any assistance with the definition of persistent. In *R.* v. *L*, 11 April 2001, unreported, the Court of Appeal, while not expressly ruling that the persistence threshold had been met, substituted a supervision order in place of a 10-month detention and training order, noting that the previous cautions amounted to an encounter with the law which was not for extremely serious or dishonest offences.

- In addition a court shall not make a detention and training order in the case of an offender under the age of 12 years unless it is of the opinion that only a custodial sentence would be adequate to protect the public from further offending by him.

Pre-sentence reports and medical reports

A court shall obtain and consider a pre-sentence report before passing a custodial sentence unless the court is of the opinion that it is unnecessary.

Young offenders

In a case where the offender is aged under 18 and the offence is not triable only on indictment, and there is no other offence associated with it that is triable only on indictment, the court can only deem a report to be unnecessary if there exists a previous pre-sentence report in respect of the offender, and the court has had regard to the information contained in that report before assessing necessity.

Effect of failing to obtain a pre-sentence report when one was required

No custodial sentence shall be invalidated by the failure of a court to obtain and consider a pre-sentence report.

Mentally disordered offenders

In any case where the offender is or appears to be mentally disordered, the court shall obtain and consider a medical report before passing a custodial sentence, unless, in the circumstances of the case, the court is of the opinion that such a report is unnecessary.

Consideration of reports

Before passing a custodial sentence, the court shall consider any information before it which relates to the offender's mental condition (whether given in a medical report, a pre-sentence report or otherwise) and the likely effect of such a sentence on that condition and on any treatment which may be available for it.

Legal representation

A magistrates' court shall not pass a sentence of imprisonment, detention in a young offender institution or a detention and training order, on a person who is not legally represented and has not previously been sentenced to imprisonment by a court in any part of the United Kingdom, unless he was granted a right to representation, but the right was withdrawn due to his conduct, or having been informed of his right to apply for such representation and having had the opportunity to do so, he refused or failed to apply.

For the purposes of the requirement to have legal representation, the term 'sentence of imprisonment' does not include a committal for contempt of court or any kindred offence (for example, refusing to be bound over).

Detention and training orders – period of detention

A detention and training order shall be either 4, 6, 8, 10, 12, 18 or 24 months. It may be appropriate to impose the maximum term of two years, notwithstanding a guilty plea, but this should only be done in rare cases of exceptional seriousness (*R.* v. *March, The Independent,* 22 February 2002). Similarly, in cases where a period of long-term detention could be appropriate, the court can conclude that a sentence of 24 months is a proper sentence even where the offender had pleaded guilty and had spent a significant period of time in custody (*R.* v. *Fieldhouse and Watts* [2000] Crim LR 1020).

Limits on individual sentences

The term of detention shall not exceed the maximum term of imprisonment that the Crown Court could impose on an offender aged 21 or over for the offence. So, for example, it is not possible to sentence a young offender to a term of detention for an offence of obstructing a constable in the execution of his duty, as this offence carries a maximum of one month's imprisonment.

Effect of exceeding maximum sentence

If consecutive terms exceeding 24 months are made, the excess shall be deemed to be remitted. This is another example of Parliament expressly catering for errors in sentencing, and ensuring that an otherwise proper sentence is not quashed.

Limit on consecutive sentencing

A court making a detention and training order shall not order that it commence on the expiry of a term of a detention and training order under which the period of supervision has already begun.

Offenders on supervision

Where a new detention and training order is made in respect of an offender who is subject to a detention and training order under which the period of supervision has begun ('the old order'), the old order shall be disregarded in determining whether the period of detention ordered exceeds 24 months. So, for example, a person serving the last three months of his supervision period under the order can still be sentenced to a period of 24 months' detention and training.

Effect of earlier remand time

In determining the term of a detention and training order for an offence, the court shall take into account any period for which the offender has been remanded in custody in connection with the offence, or any other offence the charge for which was founded on the same facts or evidence.

Where a court proposes to make a detention and training order in respect of an offender for two or more offences, it shall, for the purposes of determining the total term of detention, take into account the total period (if any) for which he has been remanded in custody in connection with any of those offences, or any other offence which was founded on the same facts or evidence.

However, the court need not carry out an exact arithmetical deduction. In *R. v. March, The Independent*, 22 February 2002, the court, having reduced a two-year detention and training order to 18 months, on the sole ground that no credit had been given for a guilty plea, declined to make any further deduction for the eight months that the offender had spent on remand. The court observed that to take account of the time spent on remand did not mean reflecting it in some specific way in the sentence passed. This authority needs to be considered with some care, as, on the facts, the court expressed a great deal of displeasure, as did the judge at first instance, at the limitations on sentencing powers (the judge having been deprived, wrongly, in his view, of the opportunity to pass a sentence under s.91 PCC(S)A 2000); this may explain why earlier authorities were not followed.

Breach of supervision requirement

Once an offender has been released from custody (halfway through the sentence), he shall remain on supervision for the remainder of the sentence period.

Where an offender fails to comply with the terms of the supervision, the court may order the offender to be detained for such period, not exceeding the shorter of three months or the remainder of the term of detention and training order, or may impose a fine not exceeding level 3 on the standard scale.

Offences during currency of the order

If a person, subject to a detention and training order, after his release and before the date on which the term of the order ends, commits an offence punishable with imprisonment in the case of a person aged 21 or over ('the new offence'), and whether before or after that date he is convicted of the new offence, the court may order him to be detained for whole or part of any period which begins with the date of the court's order and is equal in length to the period between the date on which the new offence was committed and the date the order ends.

Miscellaneous custodial sentences

The following points should also be noted:

- Section 135 MCA 1980 allows for the detention of an offender for one day in a courthouse or police station.
- Section 136 MCA 1980 allows for overnight detention for non-payment of fines, and similar offences.

CHANGES TO CUSTODIAL SENTENCES – CRIMINAL JUSTICE ACT 2003

Overview

The Criminal Justice Act 2003 completely overhauls custodial penalties, providing for novel sentencing options in relation to short term prisoners, and the introduction of intermittent custody as a means of dealing with offenders for whom a prison sentence is called for, but would otherwise have particularly counterproductive effects (loss of employment for example). More stringent licensing conditions will become the norm, as will severe sentences for dangerous offenders. Sentencing penalties in relation to firearms offences have been radically altered. All prison sentences of less than 12 months will be either 'custody plus' or 'intermittent custody' orders as outlined below.

A key change is the removal of the maximum penalty of six months imprisonment for any one offence in the magistrates' court. These provisions do not have effect in the youth court.

Magistrates' new sentencing powers

Section 154 of the Act will allow a magistrates' court to impose a sentence of up to 12 months in respect to any one offence (provided of course that it does not exceed the statutory maximum). As a result of this increased sentencing power the magistrates' court will lose its power to commit for sentence having accepted jurisdiction for a case.

Some summary only offences which previously carried short terms of imprisonment are taken away from the custodial scheme, and only a community penalty can be passed in relation to those offences (see Sched.25).

Some other summary offences (involving violence, public health, cruelty, etc.), typically those that carried three months imprisonment (but in some cases only one month), have had their maximum penalties increased to 51 weeks (which will mean a maximum 13 week custodial term under the new scheme detailed below).

For all other summary only offences currently carrying a maximum sentence of six months imprisonment, the penalties are raised to 51 weeks (to keep punishment within the new scheme).

Example 1: D is charged with the theft from his employer of £20 from the till. Under previous rules the court would not have known about any antecedent history of D, and may well have declined jurisdiction. Under the new rules the court can accept jurisdiction (and it will be able to hear of any antecedent history before doing so), in the knowledge that it can impose custody of up to 12 months for this single offence.

The court, having accepted jurisdiction will not be able to commit D for sentence thereafter.

If the sentence imposed is less that 12 months, it will be expressed as either a custody plus or intermittent custody sentence (for which see below).

Example 2: D is charged with common assault (maximum now 51 weeks). The magistrates wish to imprison him for 32 weeks. This sentence is not available; the court will have to sentence him under the new rules below.

Example 3: D is charged with two offences of common assault, that each carry 51 weeks maximum penalty. In order to avoid a custody plus sentence, the magistrates wish to sentence D to six months in respect of each offence, to run consecutively. The clerk advises that this is possible since s.133 MCA 1980 has been amended to provide for consecutive sentences of up to 65 weeks. This sentence is not available, since the two individual sentences are less than 12 months, sentencing falls within s.181 CJA 2003, and the court will have to impose a custody plus or intermittent custody sentence for D. Note that under the old rules two offences of common assault could only ever have received a sentence of six months imprisonment, of which only half would have been served (12 weeks), under the new custody plus regime, two summary offences consecutively sentenced can be met with up to 26 weeks imprisonment which will not be subject to any remission.

Prison sentences of less than 12 months

All custodial sentences of less than 12 months, imposed by a magistrates' court or Crown Court will be a 'custody plus order' or 'intermittent custody order'. Intermittent custody is in force in pilot areas.

Custody plus order

A custody plus order is a term of custody and stringent licence period that must be expressed in weeks. Various parts of a community order can be attached to the licence period to allow for unpaid work and other activities to be completed during the licence period. The order is made up as follows:

Custodial period	Licence period	Notes
Minimum 2 weeks, maximum 13 weeks in respect of any one offence (for multiple offences that are to be sentenced consecutively see below).	Minimum of 26 weeks.	The minimum combined sentence must be 28 weeks. The combined custody and licence period must not exceed 51 weeks in relation to any one offence, nor may it exceed the maximum penalty for the offence in question. Many summary only offences have been increased to 51 weeks to cater for this new sentence.

Example: A court wishing to impose a custodial sentence of four weeks duration, and the minimum 26 weeks licence period would sentence the offender to a custody plus order of 30 weeks.

Whilst many summary only offences now carry 51 weeks imprisonment, the effect of the custody plus order is that the offender cannot ever serve more than 13 weeks in prison for more than one offence, the same period he would have served when receiving the previous maximum sentence of six months imprisonment. Prisoners are still eligible for release on licence.

Consecutive sentences

In respect of an offender who falls to be sentenced for more than one offence, and where the court wishes to impose consecutive sentences, the following provisions apply:

Custodial period	Licence period	Notes
Custodial period not to exceed 26 weeks in respect of 2 or more offences	Licence period must for a minimum of 26 weeks	The combined custody and licence period cannot exceed 65 weeks.

Licence conditions

Save where the court imposes a suspended sentence, it may require the offender to be subject to a licence with one or more requirements attached. Those requirements, which must be compatible with each other, are:

- unpaid work;
- activity
- programme;
- prohibited activity;
- curfew (with electronic monitoring if appropriate under s.215);
- exclusion (with electronic monitoring if appropriate under s.215);
- supervision;
- attendance centre (for offender under 25 years).

Intermittent custody

Intermittent custody allows the offender to serve the custodial element of the sentence over a longer period of time, and not on consecutive days. The effect of this sentence would be to allow those working for example to serve their prison sentence at weekends, allowing them to keep their normal jobs and therefore protect against the wider family losing their home.

Length of order

Custodial period	Licence period	Notes
14 days minimum, 90 days maximum (The same applies if sentencing concurrently for offences, i.e. the maximum term for the longest period must not exceed 90 days). For consecutive sentences see below	The period required to ensure that the minimum sentence of 28 weeks is served, up to a maximum of 51 weeks e.g. If the court imposed a 28 day custodial period (4 weeks) a licence period of at least 24 weeks would be required to ensure a minimum overall sentence of 28 weeks was imposed	Minimum combined sentence of 28 weeks, maximum of 51 weeks for any one offence, or the longest of any of the offences sentenced concurrently

Consecutive sentences

Custodial period	Licence period	Notes
Minimum 14 days for each offence. Maximum consecutive sentence of 180 days	The period required to ensure that the minimum sentence of 28 weeks is served, up to a maximum of 65 weeks e.g. An offender is sentenced to 70 days custodial period (10 weeks), the licence period would have to be a minimum of 18 weeks	A court in specifying licence periods may specify (a) periods of a prescribed duration, (b) periods beginning or ending at prescribed times or (c) periods including, or not including, specified parts of the week

Licence conditions

An intermittent custody order can contain the following additional requirements:

- unpaid work;
- activity;
- programme; and
- prohibited activity.

179

Revocation or amendment of custody plus and intermittent custody orders

Schedule 10 provides for the revocation and amendment of the licence conditions attached to these orders, including alterations to the pattern of temporary release in relation to intermittent custody orders.

Suspended sentences

Short term sentences of between 28 and 51 (65 in relation to consecutively sentenced offences) weeks, which would otherwise be custody plus or intermittent custody sentences, can be suspended if it is in the interests of justice to do so (s.189).

The court must specify a supervision period and an operational period (of not less than six months and not exceeding two years). During the supervision period the offender can be made subject to one or more additional requirements. The supervision period must not exceed the operational period of the order, which is the period during which the offender can be re-sentenced for the offence should he commit a further offence in that period. The additional requirements that can be imposed are (s.190):

- unpaid work;
- activity;
- programme;
- prohibited activity;
- curfew (including electronic monitoring, provided not excluded under s.215);
- exclusion (including electronic monitoring, provided not excluded under s.215);
- residence;
- mental health;
- drug rehabilitation;
- alcohol;
- supervision;
- attendance centre (for offenders aged under 25 years).

Effect of suspension

The sentence of imprisonment will not take effect unless either during the supervision period the offender fails to comply with a requirement imposed in the order, or, the offender commits an offence (whether or not punishable with imprisonment) during the operational period of the order.

Review of order

The order can be reviewed at periodic intervals, and the court can order that it be given a report on the offender's progress in complying with the community requirements of the order. Drug rehabilitation requirements are reviewed as part of the provisions under s.210.

The powers of the court on review are specified in s.191.

Breach, revocation or amendment of a suspended sentence order

Schedule 12 details the powers of the court in relation to breach, revocation and amendment.

DANGEROUS OFFENDERS

Life sentence or imprisonment for public protection for serious offences

A person aged 18 or over, convicted of a serious offence committed after the commencement of s.225 is liable to be detained either for life (if the offence carries that sentence and the judge feels that a sentence of imprisonment for life is justified), or a period of indeterminate imprisonment for the purpose of public protection. Before invoking this power the court must be of the opinion that there is a significant risk to members of the public of serious harm occasioned by the commission, by him, of further specified offences (see below).

Date of commission of offence

Section 232 states that where an offence is alleged to have been committed over a period of two or more days, it shall be taken to have been committed on the last of those days.

Specified offences

Specified offences are violent or sexual in nature and listed in Schedule 15, reproduced in Appendix D.

Serious offence

An offence is a serious offence if it is a specified offence and it would be punishable in the case of a person aged 18 or over, with imprisonment for life, or a determinate period of imprisonment exceeding 10 years.

Example 1: The offender is convicted of assault occasioning actual bodily harm and the judge considers that there is a significant risk to members of the public of serious harm occasioned by the commission by him of further specified offences (which need not be the same offence as he was convicted of).

A judge could not impose a life sentence as the maximum period of imprisonment for this offence is five years. Nor could the judge impose an indeterminate sentence for public protection, as the offence must carry 10 years or more for this provision to be invoked.

Example 2: If the offence were one of wounding contrary to s.18 Offences Against the Person Act 1861 (an offence carrying life), the judge would either be able to impose life imprisonment if that were justified, or imprisonment for an indeterminate period if there was a serious risk to the public.

Overview

Is the offender aged 18 or over and convicted of a serious offence committed after the commencement of this section?

If no, normal sentencing provisions apply (if no by reason of age alone then see below).

Is the court of the opinion that there is a significant risk to members of the public of serious harm occasioned by the commission by him of further specified offences?

If no, normal sentencing provisions apply.

Does the offence carry a maximum penalty of life imprisonment?

If no, the court must pass a sentence of imprisonment for public protection.

If yes, the court must pass a sentence of imprisonment for public protection, unless it considers that the seriousness of the offence, or the offence and one or more offences associated with it, is such as to justify the imposition of imprisonment for life – when it must impose a sentence of imprisonment for life.

Offenders under 18 years

Section 226 mirrors the scheme above, save that before imposing a sentence for public protection the court must first consider whether an extended sentence would be adequate to protect the public. Only if such a sentence would be inadequate should a sentence under this section be imposed. If a court is of the view that a sentence of detention for life should be imposed, it must be imposed (s.226(2)).

Assessment of serious harm ('dangerousness')

See below.

What is a sentence of imprisonment for public protection?

A sentence of imprisonment for public protection is a sentence of imprisonment for an indeterminate period. Release from such sentences is governed by the provisions of Chapter 2 of Part 2 of the Crime (Sentences) Act 1997 (which is amended by CJA 2003), and Schedule 18 to the CJA 2003. A sentencing judge will, at the time of sentencing, determine the tariff period (to reflect punishment and deterrence, but not the factors in s.142 CJA 2003 to be served before release can be considered by the parole board.

Extended sentences for certain violent or sexual offences

Offences which are not classified as serious specified offences (because they do not carry a maximum sentence of 10 years or more) are dealt with under s.227.

An extended sentence can be imposed in relation to a person aged 18 years or over, convicted of a specified offence (other than a serious offence), committed after the commencement of this section, provided that the court considers that there is a significant risk to members of the public of serious harm occasioned by the commission by the offender of further specified offences.

Specified offence has the same meaning as outlined above.

Offenders aged less than 18 years

Mirror provisions apply by virtue of s.228, but there is one important difference. In the case of an adult, a serious specified offence must always be dealt with by virtue of section 225. For those under 18 years an extended sentence can be imposed for serious specified offences as an alternative to a detention for public protection, save where detention for life or for public protection is needed.

Effect of extended sentence

The court must pass on the offender an extended term of imprisonment comprising:

> The appropriate custodial term for the offence in question (which must be at least 12 months minimum, and not exceed the maximum for the offence in question) and an extension period for which the offender is to be subject to a licence, to be of such length as the court considers necessary for the purpose of protecting members of the public from serious harm occasioned by the commission by him of further specified offences.

Maximum length of extension period

The extension period must not exceed five years in the case of a specified violent offence, and eight years in the case of a specified sexual offence.

The aggregate sentence must not exceed the maximum term permitted for the offence. For example, a custodial sentence of three years, followed by an extension period of four years would not be permissible for an offence of assault occasioning actual bodily harm, as the maximum sentence for that offence is five years. The maximum extension period in that instance would be two years.

Assessing dangerousness

A court must determine whether there is a significant risk to members of the public of serious harm occasioned by the commission by him of further such offences (s.229).

In the case of a person aged under 18 or an offender not previously convicted of any relevant offence (i.e. in England a specified offence) the court must take into account all such information as is available to it about the nature and circumstances of the offence, any pattern of behaviour of which the offence forms part and any information about the offender which is before it.

It is questionable as to whether patterns of behaviour are necessarily to be confined to matters recorded as convictions. It is further arguable that this provision violates Articles 5 and 6 of the European Convention on Human Rights.

The two strikes presumption

In the case of an offender aged over 18 when the offence was committed, who had previously been convicted of one or more relevant offences (i.e. in England a specified offence) the court must assume that there is a 'significant risk to members of the public of serious harm occasioned by the commission by him of further such offences', unless having taken into consideration all such information as is available to the court about the nature and circumstances of the offence, pattern of behaviour and offender, that it would be unreasonable to conclude that there is such a risk (s.229(3)). It will be clear to practitioners that this provision allows for the repeal of s.109 PCC(S)A 2000 (s.303(d)(iv)).

It has been argued by Liberty that the test of 'unreasonable' is a straitjacketing provision which is 'an affront to the role of an independent and skilled judiciary. . . [This] could result in unfairness in individual cases'.

Offences committed prior to the commencement of CJA 2003

Whilst the second offence must have been committed after the commencement of this section, the first offence can pre-date the coming into force of these provisions, as was the case under s.109 PCC(S)A 2000.

Case law

The Court of Appeal gave detailed guidance in relation to dangerous offender provisions in the case of *R.* v. *Lang and others* [2005] EWCA Crim 2864.

DEFERRED SENTENCE

Schedule 23 of the CJA 2003 lays down a framework for the deferment of sentences. A Crown Court or magistrates' court can defer sentence on any offender who consents and undertakes to comply with any conditions of deferment.

Purpose of deferment

Deferment is for the purposes of assessing an offender's conduct post conviction, including the making (if appropriate) by him of reparation for his offence, and any change in his circumstances. The court will further be able to assess adherence to any requirements imposed.

Conditions

A wide range of conditions can be imposed, as at present. Paragraph 1A of Schedule 23 allows for the imposition of a condition of residence during the deferment period, and the appointment of the probation service to supervise the offender.

Period of deferment

Deferment cannot exceed six months, nor can a sentence be further deferred.

Breach

A magistrates' court, in dealing with an offender for a new offence during a period of deferment may not deal with the deferred sentence if it was passed by a Crown Court. A Crown Court may deal with a sentence deferred by a magistrates' court but may not pass a greater penalty than that which could have been imposed in the lower court.

DEPRIVATION AND FORFEITURE

(See: Powers of Criminal Courts (Sentencing) Act 2000 s.143.)

Deprivation

A deprivation order allows the court to deprive an offender of property used for the purpose of committing, or facilitating the commission of any offence, and was intended by him to be used for that purpose. In the magistrates' court, these orders are commonly but incorrectly referred to as forfeiture orders.

The item in question must have been lawfully seized from the defendant, or must have been in his possession or under his control at the time when he was apprehended for the offence.

Considerations

In considering whether or not to make an order, the court shall have regard to the value of the property and to the likely financial and other effects on the offender of the making of the order; failure to take these matters into account could lead to the quashing of the order (*R. v. Highbury Corner Magistrates' Court, ex parte Di Matteo* (1991) 92 Cr App R 263). The court must take into account any other order it makes at the same time. The order should not be out of proportion to the offence. Where one offender had driven with two co-accused in his car for the purpose of committing a joint-enterprise offence, a deprivation order in respect of the car (worth £4,000) would not necessarily result in a disparity between otherwise similar sentences (*R. v. Burgess, The Times*, 28 November 2000).

Third-party interests

A person whose property was in the possession of an offender may make an application for the return of the forfeit property in accordance with s.144 PCC(S)A 2000 and the Police Property Act 1897.

Discount for early guilty plea

The following discount regime is to be applied to all offenders, and discount should not be withheld simply because the evidence was overwhelming leaving them with little option but to plead guilty.

First reasonable opportunity	Maximum 1 third
After trial date is set	Maximum 1 quarter
Door of the court/after trial begun	Maximum 1 tenth

Forfeiture

Drugs offences

Section 27 Misuse of Drugs Act 1971 provides that the court by or before which a person is convicted of an offence under the 1971 Act, or a drug-trafficking offence, may order anything shown to the satisfaction of the court to relate to the offence, to be forfeited and either destroyed or dealt with in such other manner as the court may direct. Inchoate forms of these above offences qualify under the 1971 Act.

Third-party interests

A person who owns or has any other interest in the property in question must be afforded an opportunity to be heard before such an order is made.

DISCHARGES

(See: Powers of Criminal Courts (Sentencing) Act 2000 ss.12–15.)

A court which takes the view that it is inexpedient to inflict punishment may instead discharge the offender absolutely or, if the court thinks fit, discharge him subject to the condition that he commit no offence during a period not exceeding three years from the date of the order.

Provisions in relation to young offenders

Where a youth offender has received a warning (s.65 CDA 1998) and is convicted of an offence within two years of that warning, a court may not impose a conditional discharge in respect of the offence unless it is of the opinion that there are exceptional circumstances relating to the offender which justify its doing so.

Warning to be given to those conditionally discharged

A person made subject to a conditional discharge must be warned that if he commits an offence during the discharge period he may be sentenced for the new offence and the original offence.

Effect of resentencing

If a person is sentenced in respect of an offence for which he was originally conditionally discharged, that discharge shall cease to have effect.

Generally a court will be aware of a conditional discharge when it sentences for the new offence. In the event that the discharged matter should come to light later, there is power under s.13 PCC(S)A 2000 to bring a person before the court in order that the matter for which he was conditionally discharged can be dealt with.

Discharges imposed by Crown Court

A magistrates' court cannot deal with a conditional discharge imposed by the Crown Court, but may instead commit the offender in custody or on bail to the Crown Court.

Consent from court that imposed discharge before resentencing

In the event that the new offence comes before a different court from the one that dealt with the discharged matter, the court must seek the consent of the original sentencing court before dealing with the breach.

Where a conditional discharge has been imposed on an offender under the age of 18 in respect of an offence, which in the case of an adult would have been triable only on indictment, and the discharge is breached after the offender has attained the age of 18, the following punishments are available:

(a) imposition of a fine not exceeding £5,000;
(b) imprisonment not exceeding six months.

Effect of discharge

A discharge is not a conviction save for the purposes of the proceedings during which the order is made, and any subsequent breach proceedings. However, where a person over the age of 18 years is subsequently sentenced for a breach of a discharge the offence at that point becomes a conviction for all purposes.

DISQUALIFICATION AND ENDORSEMENT

General scheme

Disqualification from driving arises as a result of a mandatory or discretionary power to disqualify for any individual offence; as a result of accumulating 12 or more penalty points; or under other powers to deprive a person of the privilege of being able to drive a motor vehicle (notably ss.146–147 PCC(S)A 2000).

Obligatory disqualification (s.34 Road Traffic Offenders Act 1988 (RTO Act 1988))

In relation to the following offences the court must disqualify following conviction unless there are special reasons for either not disqualifying (or disqualifying for a shorter period):

- manslaughter;
- causing death by dangerous driving;
- causing death by careless driving while under the influence of drink or drugs;
- dangerous driving;
- aggravated vehicle-taking;
- driving or attempting to drive with excess alcohol;
- driving or attempting to drive while unfit;
- failing to provide a specimen for analysis in relation to driving/attempting to drive;
- motor racing and speed trials.

In the event that special reasons are found, the court, if exercising its discretion not to disqualify, must endorse the requisite penalty points.

Minimum period

The following points should be noted.

1. In the case of manslaughter, causing death by dangerous driving and causing death by careless driving while under the influence of drink or drugs, the minimum period of disqualification is two years. The court must order the defendant to take an extended retest.
2. In the case of an offender who, in the three years preceding the commission of the new offence, has been twice disqualified for a period of 56 days or more, the minimum disqualification is two years.
3. In the case of an offender convicted of an excess-alcohol offence, who has been convicted in the last 10 years of an excess-alcohol offence, the minimum period is three years. This provision covers the offence of failing to provide a specimen for analysis.
4. In all other cases the minimum period is 12 months.

Retests

Save where the court must make an order that the offender pass an extended test before regaining his licence, the court can in any other case order an offender to retake his driving test.

Penalty points following mandatory disqualification

No penalty points are awarded when mandatory disqualification is imposed.

Penalty points and discretionary disqualification (s.34 RTO Act 1988)

In cases where the offence allows for discretionary disqualification, the court must consider disqualifying before it considers the question of points. This is so, even if the offender would 'tot'. In the event that the court disqualifies under this provision, no points are awarded.

Practical effect of discretionary disqualification

The effect of a discretionary disqualification is that any points on the licence remain there. The period of disqualification can be for any length, commensurate with the seriousness of the offence.

Endorsement of penalty points

If the court does not exercise its power to disqualify under the discretionary regime, it must endorse penalty points. The court has discretion not to award points if there are special reasons for so deciding (see below). Each offence attracts its own range of points, and reference should be made to the offence guide in Chapter 5.

Imposing penalty points for more than one offence

Where a person is convicted of two or more offences committed on the same occasion and involving obligatory endorsement, the total number of penalty points to be attributed to them is the number or highest number that would be attributed on a conviction of one of them. For example, a person convicted of speeding (3–6 points) and driving without insurance (6–8 points), could only have a maximum of 8 points endorsed. However, advocates should be aware that the court has power to disapply this provision if it thinks fit.

Special provisions in respect of new drivers

Special provisions apply in respect of drivers in the first two years following the passing of the driving test (see below).

Totting-up (s.35 RTO Act 1988)

Penalty points are effective for a period of three years. For the purposes of the totting-up provisions, the court is concerned with points accumulated within three years of the date of the offences in question, not the date of conviction.

An offender accumulating 12 or more points is liable to disqualification under these provisions. The court should ignore points imposed for an offence that led to a totting-up disqualification. The disqualification has the effect of removing all points from the offender's licence that were on the licence prior to the disqualification. The court need not disqualify, or can disqualify for a lesser period if the court thinks there are grounds for mitigating the normal consequences of the conviction (see below).

Minimum periods of disqualification

In determining the length of any disqualification, the court must have regard to any previous periods of disqualification within the three years preceding the current offence.

The minimum periods are:

- 6 months if no previous disqualifications;
- 12 months if one previous disqualification;
- 2 years if 2 or more previous disqualifications.

Special reasons

If special reasons are established, the court has discretion not to endorse points, and to reduce or not impose a mandatory period of disqualification. The court, having found special reasons, is not bound to exercise its discretion in the offender's favour. If a mandatory disqualification is not imposed, the court must endorse the appropriate penalty points.

Burden of proof

The burden of proof falls upon the defendant, and the civil standard applies.

Definition

There is no statutory definition of special reasons, but it must not amount to a defence in law, must be directly connected with the offence in question (as opposed to the offender), and must be a mitigating or extenuating circumstance, which the court should take into account.

Typical reasons

Special reasons include:

1. Spiked drinks/mistake as to item consumed.
2. Shortness of distance driven (*Chatters* v. *Burke* [1986] All ER 168). The court can consider not only the actual distance driven, but also whether the defendant intended to drive any further (*Crown Prosecution Service* v. *Humphries* [2000] RTR 52). Driving a distance of only 500 yards may be too far to justify special reasons (*DPP* v. *Bristow* [1998] RTR 100).
3. Medical or other emergencies. A solicitor called out by his clerk at 5 a.m. in the morning could not rely on special reasons to escape disqualification for an offence of speeding. The clerk could have dealt with the emergency (*Robinson* v. *DPP* [1989] RTR 42).

It is difficult to establish these and other special reasons, and regard should be had to the considerable body of case law that exists in this area. Advocates should make reference to *Wilkinson's* in such cases. It is incumbent on justices to approach the evidence of an expert critically, even if no expert is called on the other side, and reject it in appropriate cases (*DPP* v. *Wynne, The Independent*, 19 February 2001).

Mitigating circumstances

In cases where the totting-up provisions are invoked, the court is able to order disqualification for a reduced time, or to not disqualify at all, if mitigating circumstances are established by the defendant.

Definition

In deciding what is a mitigating circumstance, the court shall not have regard to:

(a) any circumstances that are alleged to make the offence or any of the offences not a serious one;
(b) hardship, other than exceptional hardship; or
(c) any circumstances, which, within the three years immediately preceding the conviction, have been taken into account in deciding not to disqualify an offender or disqualify him for a shorter period.

New drivers

By virtue of the Road Traffic (New Drivers) Act 1995, drivers passing a test for the first time are deemed probationary drivers for the first two years. If a probationary driver accumulates six or more penalty points within that two-year period, that driver falls to have his licence revoked by the DVLA. The effect of this is that a driving test will have to be retaken. Such drivers are not disqualified, but can only drive subject to the rules in force for learner drivers. Penalty points imposed prior to the full licence being granted count. For example, a learner driver who incurs a fixed penalty for speeding (three penalty points) goes on the next month to pass his driving test, and 12 months later a further fixed penalty speeding ticket is issued – as six points are now on the licence, the Secretary of State is bound to revoke it.

For a full description of the scheme see: Keogh, A.W., 'Britain welcomes careful drivers' S.J. 1996, 140(11), 274–5.

Other powers of disqualification

General power to disqualify as a punishment in respect of any offence

Section 146 PCC(S)A 2000 gives a court the power to disqualify an offender from holding a driving licence following conviction for any offence. There need be no nexus between driving and the offence in question.

Availability

A court cannot use this power unless it has been notified of its availability by the Secretary of State.

Disqualification where vehicle used for purpose of crime

Section 147 PCC(S)A 2000 provides that, where a person is convicted of common assault or any other offence involving assault (including aiding, abetting, counselling, inciting or procuring the commission of an offence), and the court is satisfied that the assault was committed by driving a motor vehicle, the court may order the person convicted to be disqualified, for such period as the court thinks fit, from holding or obtaining a driving licence.

Interim disqualification

An interim disqualification can be imposed when the court commits an offender for sentence to the Crown Court, remits the case to another court, or defers or adjourns sentence. More than one interim disqualification can be made, but the total term must not exceed six months.

Suspension of disqualification pending appeal (s.40 RTO Act 1988)

The court has the power to suspend a disqualification pending an appeal to the Crown Court. In respect of appeals by way of case stated, or applications for judicial review only the High Court has power to suspend the disqualification.

Provisions in respect of new drivers whose licence has been revoked

In respect of a new driver who appeals a conviction that led to the Secretary of State revoking his licence, provision is made for the applicant being allowed to drive pending the outcome of the appeal. The magistrates' court has no jurisdiction in this regard, and reference should be had to the New Drivers (Appeal Procedure) Regulations 1997 (SI 1997/1098), for the procedure to be followed.

EXCLUSION ORDERS

This section considers the following orders:

- exclusion orders under s.40A PCC(S)A 2000;
- exclusion from licensed premises.

Exclusion orders under s.40A PCC(S)A 2000

Powers of Criminal Courts (Sentencing) Act 2000 s.40A

Section 40A provides that where a person aged under 16 years is convicted of an offence, the court by or before which he is convicted may (provided the usual criteria for the impositions of community penalties are met (seriousness, etc.)) make an exclusion order.

Effect of order

The order prohibits the defendant from entering a place specified in the order for a period of no more than three months.

The order may provide for the prohibition to operate only during the periods specified in the order, and may specify different places for different periods or days.

Avoiding conflicts

The order should be framed so as to avoid conflict with the offender's religious beliefs, requirements of any other community order and interference with schooling.

The court shall obtain and consider information about the offender's family circumstances and the likely effect of such an order on those circumstances.

Electronic monitoring

This order may be electronically monitored under the provisions of s.36B PCC(S)A 2000.

Breach

If it is proved to the satisfaction of the court that an offender has failed without reasonable excuse to comply with any of the requirements of the relevant order, the court may deal with him in respect of the failure in any one of the following ways:

1. It may impose a fine not exceeding £1,000.
2. It may make an attendance order in respect of him.
3. Or, where the relevant order was made by a magistrates' court, it may deal with him, for the offence in respect of which the order was made, in any way in which it could deal with him if he had just been convicted by the court of the offence. The court shall take into account the extent to which the offender has complied with the requirements of the relevant order, and in the case of an offender who has wilfully and persistently failed to comply with those requirements may impose a custodial sentence, notwithstanding anything in s.79(2) PCC(S)A 2000 (the 'so serious' criteria). If a court deals with an offender in this way, it must revoke the order.

Crown Court orders

A magistrates' court cannot revoke and resentence in relation to an order made by the Crown Court; in such instances it must commit the offender, in custody or on bail to the Crown Court. A magistrates' court can deal with an offender in breach of a Crown Court order in the other ways outlined, but may choose to commit him to the Crown Court instead, and generally will do so.

Licensed Premises (Exclusion of Certain Persons) Act 1980 s.1

Where a court by or before which a person is convicted of an offence committed on licensed premises is satisfied that in committing that offence he resorted to violence or offered or threatened to resort to violence, the court may make an order prohibiting him from entering those or any other specified premises, without the express consent of the licensee of the premises or his servant or agent.

Imposing other sentences at the same time

The order can be made in addition to any other sentence, including an absolute or conditional discharge.

Length of order

An exclusion order shall be for a period not less than three months and not exceeding two years.

Offence committed by breach of the order

It is an offence to enter excluded premises, carrying a sentence of a fine not exceeding level 3, or imprisonment for a term not exceeding one month, or both. At the same time, the court shall consider whether or not the exclusion order should continue in force, and may, if it thinks fit, by order terminate the exclusion order or vary it by deleting the name of any specified premises, but an exclusion order shall not otherwise be affected by a person's conviction for such an offence.

Definition of licensed premises for purposes of the order

Licensed premises means premises in respect of which there is in force a justices' on-licence, within the meaning of s.1 Licensing Act 1974.

The premises must be specified by reference to their name and address.

FINANCIAL ORDERS (FINES, COMPENSATION AND COSTS)

Obtaining information in relation to means

Where an individual has been convicted of an offence, the court may, before sentencing him, make a financial circumstances order in respect of him. Similarly, if a person desires to plead guilty to an offence without appearing before the court (s.12(4) MCA 1980), the court may make a financial circumstances order in respect of him. The order requires an offender to furnish the court with a statement of his financial circumstances, in as much detail as the court requires. Most courts have a standard means assessment form for this purpose. It is an offence to fail, without reasonable excuse, to comply with a financial circumstances order, or make false or reckless statements in pursuance of such orders, or to fail to disclose material facts. Duty solicitors will often become involved in either the imposition, or default in payment, of fines, compensation and costs.

Maximum fines

Maximum fine levels are as follows:

- Level 1 = £200
- Level 2 = £500
- Level 3 = £1,000
- Level 4 = £2,500
- Level 5 = £5,000

Maximum compensation

A court cannot order compensation exceeding £5,000 for an offence or any other offences associated with it. A compensation order is a sentence in itself and need not be imposed alongside a fine, community penalty or any other sentence.

Young persons

Persons under the age of 14 can only be ordered to pay a maximum of £250. For those aged 14–17, the maximum is £1,000. In both cases, if the statutory maximum is less then the lower amount applies.

For offenders aged 16 and 17, the court may order that a parent or guardian pay financial penalties imposed. For those aged under 16, the court must make such an order, unless the parent or guardian cannot be found, or it would be unreasonable to make an order for payment having regard to the circumstances of the case (s.137 PCC(S)A 2000).

Children in local authority care

In the case of a child or young person for whom the local authority have parental responsibility and who is in their care, or, is provided with accommodation by them, references to parent or guardian shall be construed as references to that authority.

A parent's or guardian's means must be assessed in place of those of the child or young person, and they must be given an opportunity to be heard. An order can be made in their absence if, having been given an opportunity to attend, they fail to do so.

Fixing the amount

The amount of any fine shall be such as, in the opinion of the court, reflects the seriousness of the offence (s.128(2) PCC(S)A 2000).

In fixing the amount of any fine to be imposed, the court shall take into account the circumstances of the case including, among other things, the financial circumstances of the offender so far as they are known, or appear, to the court (s.128(3) PCC(S)A 2000).

Compensation

Compensation shall be of such amount as the court considers appropriate, having regard to the evidence and to any representations that are made by or on behalf of the accused or prosecutor. The court must have regard to the offender's means.

Precedence of payment

If the court would have imposed both a fine and compensation, but feels unable to do so due to the offender's means, the court shall give preference to the compensation (s.130(12) PCC(S)A 2000).

Payment

Financial penalties are payable forthwith, but time to pay can be given. How long should be given will depend on the level of the penalty and the offender's ability to pay (*R. v. Olliver (Richard George) Joined Cases*: *R. v. Olliver (Michael Andrew)* (1989) 11 Cr App R (S) 10, CA). The court has the power to transfer the penalty to another court for collection (s.89(1) MCA 1980).

Searches

A court who believes an offender has money on his person can order that he be searched and any money seized applied to payment of the financial penalty, save where it is satisfied that the money does not belong to him or that the loss of the money would be more injurious to his family than would be his detention (s.80(1) MCA 1980).

Attachment of earnings

The court at the request of the offender, or by its own volition with the offender's consent may order attachment of earnings (see ss.6, 7 Attachment of Earnings Act 1971 for the effect of such an order).

Money payment supervision order

The court can impose a money payment supervision order, without the offender's consent. Where a person under 21 having not been committed to detention forthwith, later appears before the court in default, or for want of distress, the court shall not commit him for such default without first trying a money payment supervision order, unless he has already been under such supervision or it is impracticable or undesirable to place him under supervision (s.88 MCA 1980).

Distress warrant

The court may issue a distress warrant in order to enforce payment (s.76 MCA 1980). The issue of the warrant can be conditionally postponed, to allow, for example, weekly payments (s.77 MCA 1980).

Local detention

The court can order detention at a police station or within the court precincts. Detention must not extend beyond 8 p.m., and is usually until the court rises for the day. This default provision can only be ordered for offenders aged at least 18 years (s.135 MCA 1980). The court can also order detention in a police station overnight (s.136 MCA 1980).

Immediate imprisonment

As an alternative to allowing time to pay, the court can commit a person aged at least 18 years to a prison or detention centre. Committal wipes out the sum owed.

Committal can only be imposed where the offence is imprisonable and the offender appears to have the means to pay the sum forthwith, or it appears that the offender is unlikely to remain in the United Kingdom long enough to pay, or has been sentenced on that occasion to a custodial sentence, or is already serving a custodial sentence. For other occasions where these criteria are not met (e.g. non-payment of a fine in relation to failing to have a TV licence, resort can be had to local detention (for which see above)).

Committal periods:

- Not exceeding £200   7 days;
- Exceeding £200   < £500   14 days;
- Exceeding £500   < £1,000   28 days;
- Exceeding £1,000 < £2,500   45 days;
- Exceeding £2,500 < £5,000   3 months;
- Exceeding £5,000 < £10,000   6 months;
- Exceeding £10,000   12 months.

Default in payment

If an offender is in default with payment, the following methods of enforcement, described above can be attempted:

- money payment supervision;
- distress warrant;
- transfer of fines;
- warrant for local detention;
- attachment of earnings.

In addition, the following methods can be tried:

1. Remission of whole or part of the outstanding amount (only a fine can be remitted). Consent from the Crown Court will be needed if the penalty was imposed by a Crown Court. The purpose of this is generally to reduce the amount outstanding to a more realistic level, in the hope of giving the offender the sight of light at the end of the tunnel. It is good practice if an offender is sentenced to clear up outstanding fines while he is serving a sentence.
2. Attachment of benefits (subject to the social security department consenting, and the offender being aged at least 18 years).
3. Attendance centre order for between 12 and 36 hours for offenders below 25 years of age (s.60 PCC(S)A 2000).
4. Courts can make orders against parents or guardians in the case of a default by an offender below 18 years of age. The court with the parent's or guardian's consent can order them to enter into a recognisance to ensure the continued payment of the penalty, or can order that the sum remaining unpaid be transferred for payment to the parent or guardian. Reference should be made to s.81(1) MCA 1980 if the court is considering either of these options.
5. If an offender turns 18 years with a financial penalty outstanding, the previous immunity from committal to custody ceases to apply.

Custody in default

The default option that will most commonly exercise duty solicitors is that of committal to prison. Full consideration should be given to s.82 MCA 1980. Given the large number of successful judicial reviews in relation to committals in default, it appears to be the case that many courts ignore the strict statutory tests contained within s.82. Committal in default can take place in the following circumstances:

1. If the offender is already serving a sentence of imprisonment or detention. A means inquiry is not needed, but the court should first consider the practicality of a distress warrant as an alternative.

200

2. When the court has held a means inquiry in the offender's presence and the offence is imprisonable and the offender appears to have the means to pay forthwith, or the court is satisfied that default is due to the offender's wilful refusal or culpable neglect and it has considered or tried all other methods of enforcement and it appears that they are inappropriate or unsuccessful (s.82 MCA 1980).

The warrant can take effect immediately or its effect can be suspended.

Compensation orders – general principles

A court may award compensation instead of (with some exceptions which would not apply in the magistrates' court) or in addition to dealing with an offender in any other way. He may be required to pay compensation in respect of any personal injury, loss or damage resulting from an offence, or any other offence taken into consideration; or to make payments for funeral expenses or bereavement in respect of death resulting from any such offence, other than a death due to an accident arising out of the presence of a motor vehicle on a road.

In the case of an offence under the Theft Act 1968, where the property in question is recovered, any damage to that property which occurred while it was out of the owner's possession shall be deemed to have resulted from the offence, regardless of who or what caused the damage.

A compensation order may only be made in respect of injury, loss or damage (other than loss suffered by a person's dependants in consequence of his death) which was due to an accident arising out of the presence of a motor vehicle on a road, if: (a) it is in respect of damage which is treated as resulting from an offence under the Theft Act 1968 (but note that this would only apply to the unlawfully taken vehicle); or (b) it is in respect of injury, loss or damage for which the offender is uninsured and compensation is not payable under any arrangements to which the Secretary of State is a party. The latter provision takes account of uninsured loss payable by the Motor Insurers' Bureau, but orders can still be made in respect of the first £175 and any amount exceeding £25,000. Compensation can include the loss of any preferential insurance rates.

The amount of compensation sought should either be agreed by the defence or proved to the satisfaction of the court. Where there are complex or prolonged arguments in relation to liability it is not the function of a criminal court to try to decide the issue; compensation should be refused, leaving the parties to resolve the issue in the civil jurisdiction.

Costs – general principles

A defendant, who stands convicted of any charge, can generally expect to have to pay a contribution toward prosecution costs. The award of costs should be in such amount as the court determines to be just and reasonable, having regard to all the circumstances of the case, including the means of the defendant. Where a defendant is under 17 years, the amount of costs should not exceed the amount of any fine imposed on him. In the case of adults, a costs order can greatly exceed a fine, in an appropriate case.

If the defendant is ordered to pay costs, compensation or any other financial penalty not exceeding £5, then the court shall not make a costs order unless in the particular circumstances of the case it considers it right to do so.

In cases where the costs are likely to be more than nominal, frequently the case with prosecutions involving private prosecutors (RSPCA, FACT, etc.), the prosecutor should serve a full schedule of costs at the earliest opportunity, to allow the defendant to challenge properly the claim should he wish to.

Advocates should have regard to a practice direction of 3 May 1991 on costs, reported at [1991] 1 WLR 498 and to *R.* v. *Northallerton Magistrates' Court, ex parte Dove* [2000] 1 Cr App R (S) 136, where the following principles were established:

1. An order to pay costs to the prosecutor should never exceed the sum which, having regard to the defendant's means and any other financial order imposed upon him, the defendant was able to pay and which it was reasonable to order the defendant to pay.
2. Such an order should never exceed the sum that the prosecutor had actually and reasonably incurred.
3. The purpose of such an order was to compensate the prosecutor and not punish the defendant. Where the defendant had by his conduct put the prosecutor to avoidable expense he might, subject to his means, be ordered to pay some or all of that sum to the prosecutor. However, he was not to be punished for exercising a constitutional right to defend himself.
4. While there was no requirement that any sum ordered by justices to be paid to a prosecutor by way of costs should stand in any arithmetical relationship to any fine imposed, the costs ordered to be paid should not in any ordinary way be grossly disproportionate to the fine. Justices should ordinarily begin by deciding on the appropriate fine to reflect the criminality of the defendant's offence, always bearing in mind his means and his ability to pay, and then consider what, if any, costs he should be ordered to pay to the prosecutor. If, when the costs sought by the prosecutor were added to the proposed fine, the total exceeded the sum which in the light of the defendant's means and all other relevant circumstances the defendant could reasonably be ordered to pay, it was preferable to achieve an acceptable total by reducing the sum of costs which the defendant was ordered to pay rather than by reducing the fine.

5. If the offender fails to disclose properly his means to the court, reasonable inferences can be drawn as to his means from evidence they had heard and all the circumstances of the case.

FOOTBALL ORDERS

(See: Football Spectators Act 1989 s.14.)

The Football Spectators Act 1989 (FSA 1989), as substantially amended by the Football (Disorder) Act 2000 (F(D)A 2000), makes provision for banning orders to be made following conviction and on a freestanding basis.

Effect of orders

A banning order in relation to regulated football matches in England and Wales prohibits the person subject to the order from entering any premises for the purposes of attending such matches. In relation to regulated matches outside England and Wales the order requires that person to report at a police station in accordance with the terms of the order.

Civil orders

While the freestanding orders are civil in nature and not 'sentences', they are included in this book due to the high likelihood that a duty solicitor will be called to deal with such an application at short notice. Solicitors will need to give careful consideration to the civil evidence rules in relation to these orders.

Reference is made throughout to 'relevant offence'; see Schedule 1 FSA 1989 for a full list. Regulated football matches are association football matches whether in England and Wales or elsewhere.

Banning orders made on conviction of an offence (s.14A)

Where a person is convicted of a relevant offence and the court is satisfied that there are reasonable grounds to believe that making a banning order would help to prevent violence or disorder at or in connection with any regulated football matches, it must make an order in respect of the offender. If the court is not so satisfied, it must in open court state its reasons. See below for the definitions of violence and disorder.

Banning orders made on a complaint (s.14B)

This is the civil order, and provides that an application for a banning order can be made in respect of any person, and may be made by the chief officer of police for the area in which the person resides or appears to reside.

Justification in applying for the order

Before making the application, the officer must be satisfied that the respondent has at any time caused or contributed to any violence or disorder in the UK or elsewhere. If it is proved to the satisfaction of the court that the respondent has contributed to any violence in the UK or elsewhere, and the court is satisfied that there are reasonable grounds to believe that making a banning order would help to prevent violence or disorder at or in connection with any regulated football matches, then the court must make a banning order in respect of the respondent.

Evidence

The proceedings in connection with the making of these orders will not be familiar to many duty solicitors; hearsay evidence may be admitted, for example. Solicitors should consider the separate section on civil evidence in Chapter 3 to gain an understanding of the procedures.

Standard of proof

Although the civil standard of proof applies, that standard is flexible and has to reflect the consequences that would follow if a banning order were made out. This should lead magistrates to apply an exacting standard of proof which, in practice, would be hard to distinguish from the criminal one (*R.* v. *Manchester Crown Court, ex parte McCann* [2002] 3 WLR 1313, in relation to other civil orders, and approved in later cases).

Compatibility with European law and human rights jurisprudence

The orders have been held not to infringe European law on the right to free movement, nor any convention rights (particularly Article 8), as any interference with Article 8 rights would be justified under Article 8(2) as it was necessary for the prevention of disorder (*Gough* v. *Chief Constable of Derbyshire*, *The Times*, 10 April 2002).

Definitions

Violence means violence against persons or property and includes threatening violence and doing anything which endangers the life of any person.

Disorder includes stirring up hatred against a group of persons defined by reference to colour, race, nationality (including citizenship) or ethnic or national origins, or against an individual as a member of such a group. It further includes using threatening, abusive or insulting words or behaviour or disorderly behaviour, and displaying any writing or other thing which is threatening, abusive or insulting.

Violence and disorder are not limited to violence or disorder in connection with football.

Matters to be taken into account

The magistrates' court, when deciding whether to make a banning order under s.14B, may take into account the following matters (among others):

(a) any decision of a court or tribunal outside the UK;
(b) deportation or exclusion from a country outside the UK;
(c) removal or exclusion from premises used for playing football matches, whether in the UK or elsewhere;
(d) conduct recorded on video or by any other means.

The court may not take into account anything done by the respondent before the beginning of the period of 10 years ending with the application under s.14B, except circumstances ancillary to a conviction.

Appeal of banning order made on a complaint

An appeal lies to the Crown Court.

Duration of banning orders

The following points should be noted:

(a) order under s.14A imposed at the same time as a sentence of imprisonment taking immediate effect: minimum 5 years, maximum 10 years;
(b) order under s.14A in any other case: minimum 3 years, maximum 5 years;
(c) order under s.14B: minimum 2 years, maximum 3 years.

Effect of order

The order prohibits entry to regulated football matches in England and Wales and imposes reporting requirements in relation to international

205

football matches. The order must, unless there are exceptional circumstances, make provision for the surrender of the respondent's or offender's passport, in order to curtail travel abroad. Careful reference should be made to the proposed order to ensure that it complies with FSA 1989 and does no more than is necessary in all of the circumstances. Section 19 FSA 1989 details the powers of the enforcing authority and local police in respect of these orders.

Variation and discharge

The applicant or respondent can apply to the court to vary the order so as to impose, replace or omit any requirements.

A person subject to a banning order can apply for its discharge provided that it has had effect for at least two-thirds of the period imposed by the court.

The court, in considering whether to discharge an order, must have regard to the person's character, his conduct since the banning order was made, the nature of the offence or conduct which led to it and any other circumstances, which appear to it to be relevant.

Repeated applications

Where an application to discharge the order is refused, a fresh application cannot be made within the period of six months beginning with the day of the refusal.

Costs

The court may order the applicant to pay all or any of the costs of an application to discharge.

Failing to comply with banning order

A person who fails to comply with a banning order is liable on summary conviction to imprisonment for a term not exceeding six months, or a fine not exceeding level 5, or both.

FOSTER PARENT REQUIREMENT

(See Anti-social Behaviour Act 2003, Sched. 2, para 4(5).)

A court in a pilot area may impose a requirement that an offender live for a specified period with a local authority foster parent, for a period not exceeding 12 months (this could be varied to up to 18 months) if:

(a) the offence is punishable with imprisonment in the case of an offender aged 18 or over;

(b) the offence, or the combination of the offence and one or more offences associated with it, was so serious that a custodial sentence would normally be appropriate (or, if the offender is aged 10 or 11, would normally be appropriate if the offender were aged 12 or over); and

(c) the court is satisfied that:

(i) the behaviour which constituted the offence was due to a significant extent to the circumstances in which the offender was living; and

(ii) the imposition of a foster parent residence requirement will assist in his/her rehabilitation.

A foster parent residence requirement may be imposed at the same time as an order enforcing any of the following:

- participation in non-specified activities;
- participation in specified activities or an intensive supervision and surveillance programme (ISSP);
- a reparation requirement;
- refraining from specified activities;
- a requirement as to education; and
- a requirement as to psychiatric treatment.

A court may not impose a foster parent residence requirement on an offender who is not legally represented at the relevant time unless:

- s/he was granted a representation order but this was later withdrawn because of his/her behaviour; or
- s/he was informed of her/his right to apply for a representation order but nevertheless refused or failed to do so.

INTENSIVE SUPERVISION AND SURVEILLANCE PROGRAMME (ISSP)

Nature of ISSP

The ISSP is not a sentence in its own right, but a set of conditions that can be attached as part of a supervision order, supervision order and a curfew order, community rehabilitation order, detention and training order (supervision element) or bail. Electronic monitoring was expressly provided for in s.36B PCC(S)A 2000, as amended.

Target group

The programme is aimed at those young offenders who fit the eligibility criteria and the current offence before the court is of sufficient gravity for the court to be considering actively a custodial sentence or remand in custody or secure accommodation.

The programme is in effect a last-ditch attempt to divert the most prevalent young offenders away from custody, yet at the same time making the offender subject to stringent and sophisticated surveillance and monitoring, through electronic tagging and other devices.

Eligibility criteria

An eligibility flowchart is reproduced on page 209 (see Figure 4.1). The following are to be noted:

1. The offender must be aged 10–17 years, appearing in court either charged with (in relation to bail ISSPs) or convicted of an offence.
2. The offender must have been charged or warned on four or more separate occasions within the last 12 months in respect of an imprisonable offence, and must have previously received at least one community or custodial penalty. Or
3. The offender is charged with or convicted of an offences or offences that carry in the case of an adult a sentence of 14 years or more. Or
4. The offender has a history of repeat offending on bail and is at risk of secure remand under s.23(5) Children and Young Persons Act 1969.

Provided that all these criteria are met, and on the current occasion the court is actively considering a custodial sentence or remand, the ISSP criteria are met.

Programme components

The programme will involve the tailoring of an individual package of measures, dependent upon the risks posed by the offender, and whether the programme is being used to support bail, or is post-conviction. At least one of the following methods of surveillance will be used:

1. Tracking: staff accompanying offenders to their appointments, providing support and advice and immediately following up any non-attendance.
2. Tagging: electronic monitoring to ensure compliance with the primary order, for example, a curfew or bail.
3. Voice verification: works by checking the voiceprint of the offender in order to confirm that he is where he is supposed to be. Provides a more flexible framework than a simple curfew option.
4. The surveillance will involve a minimum of two contacts per day.
5. Intelligence-led policing: police will overtly monitor the movements of the offender at key times. Information will be shared with the youth offending team (YOT).

Figure 4.1 ISSP eligibility criteria

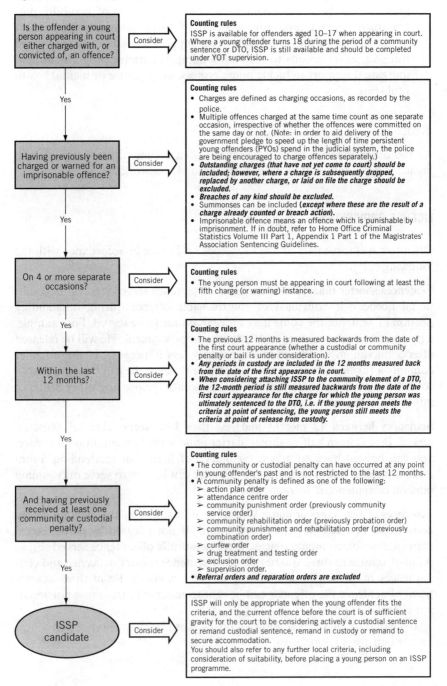

Note: Items marked in bold italics added January 2002.

6. Supervision: rigorous assessment of the offender's background, behaviour and needs. A minimum of 25 hours per week of carefully programmed contact time, for a period of three months, with support during evenings and weekends. The support includes education and training, interventions to tackle offending, reparative programmes and individual support to tackle homelessness, drug misuse or mental health problems.

Breach

As the order is imposed as a condition of a community penalty or bail, breach is dealt with within the corresponding framework.

LICENCE PROVISIONS

Offenders will serve part of their sentence on licence in accordance with the following scale:

Sentences shorter than 12 months: Half of sentence served (rest on unconditional licence); if convicted of imprisonable offence during outstanding portion of sentence the court may order that time to be served. For example, a person receives a sentence of 10 months' imprisonment. He will be released after a maximum of five months (possibly less if tagged). If the offender commits a further offence at the end of month seven, he can be sentenced to serve the remaining three months of his licence, before any other sentence imposed for the new offence.

Sentences between 12 months and less than four years: Half of sentence served. Period from half to three-quarter point served on conditional licence, and can be sent back to prison for breach of licence or reoffending. From three-quarter point of sentence the offender can be sent to serve outstanding portion of sentence if he reoffends.

Sentences of four years or more: Will serve at least half of the sentence before considered for release by the parole board. If not released by parole board then eligible for automatic release after two-thirds of sentence served. From point of release to three-quarter point of sentence subject to licence and consequences of breach or reoffending as set out above. From three-quarter point of sentence the offender can be sent to re-serve outstanding portion of sentence if he reoffends.

Note that for offences committed post 4 April 2005, the licence period will be one half for all sentences.

MENTALLY DISORDERED OFFENDERS

Overview

There are a wide range of orders available in respect of offenders suffering from mental illness. It is vital that such offenders are identified at the very earliest opportunity, as this affords the maximum prospect of either diverting the offender (or suspected offender) away from the criminal justice system entirely, or being able to obtain appropriate treatment in a shorter timeframe. All advocates need to have in mind Home Office guidance on dealing with mentally disordered offenders, and should remember that most courts have access to community psychiatric services, which can often make the difference between a remand in custody and a suitable bail package.

Availability of orders

It is important to note that not all orders available to the Crown Court are available to magistrates' courts. These include restriction orders and remands for hospital reports or psychiatric reports. A court that considers a restriction order to be an appropriate sentence should consider committal for sentence. The magistrates' court has a power under s.43 Mental Health Act 1983 to commit a person aged 14 or above to the Crown Court in order that such a sentence can be passed.

Obtaining reports

Remand on bail

The court can remand an offender on bail for the purposes of obtaining appropriate medical reports, normally obtained at the behest of the defence.

Remand to a hospital

The court can remand an accused person to a hospital specified by the court for a report on his mental condition (s.35 MHA 1983). The following criteria must be satisfied:

1. The person must have been convicted of an offence punishable on summary conviction with imprisonment, or be charged with such an offence and the court is satisfied that he did the act or made the omission charged, or he has consented to the exercise by the court of these powers.
2. The court must be satisfied, on the written or oral evidence of a registered medical practitioner, that there is reason to suspect that the accused is suffering from mental illness, psychopathic disorder, severe mental impairment or mental impairment.

211

3. The court must be satisfied that it would be impracticable for a report on his mental condition to be made if he were remanded on bail.
4. Arrangements must have been made for the person's reception into hospital within the period of seven days beginning with the date of the remand. In such cases the court can direct for the interim conveyance to, and detention in, a place of safety. The court must have oral or written evidence of these arrangements.

Further remand

A further remand can take place, but no remand shall exceed 28 days, nor shall the total remand period exceed 12 weeks in all.

Power to arrest absconders

A person who absconds from a hospital after being so remanded can be arrested by a constable without warrant.

Psychiatric community rehabilitation order

This is a community rehabilitation order, satisfying the normal criteria for the imposition of a community penalty, but with a condition that the offender submit to treatment during that order. Paragraph 5 of Schedule 2 PCC(S)A 2000 provides that such an order can be made where:

(a) a court proposes to make a community rehabilitation order;
(b) the court is satisfied on the evidence of a practitioner approved under s.12 MHA 1983 that the offender's medical condition is such as requires and may be susceptible to treatment; but
(c) is not such as to warrant the making of a hospital order or guardianship order.

Terms of order

The order will be such as to require the offender to submit, during the whole or part of the community rehabilitation period or during such part or parts of that period as may be specified in the order, to treatment, with a view to improving the offender's mental condition.

Forms of treatment

The treatment may be in any of the following forms:

1. As a resident patient in a hospital or mental nursing home within the meaning of the MHA 1983, but not hospital premises at which high security psychiatric services are provided.
2. Treatment as a non-resident patient at such institution or place as may be specified in the order.
3. Treatment by or under the direction of such registered medical practitioner or chartered psychologist (or both) as may be so specified.

Availability of treatment

A court shall not make such a requirement in the order unless it is satisfied that arrangements have been or can be made for the treatment intended to be specified in the order.

Consent

The requirement cannot be imposed in the order unless the offender has expressed his willingness to comply with such a requirement.

Hospital and guardianship orders (MHA 1983 s.37)

The effect of these orders is to make the offender a patient of an appropriate mental health care provider. In the case of guardianship orders, the offender will normally be under the supervision of local social services.

Criteria

The offender must have been convicted of an offence punishable with imprisonment. Guardianship orders can only be made in respect of offenders aged 16 and over.

The court must be satisfied on the written or oral evidence of two registered medical practitioners that the offender is suffering from mental illness, psychopathic disorder, severe mental impairment or mental impairment and that either: (a) the mental disorder from which the offender is suffering is of a nature or degree which makes it appropriate for him to be detained in a hospital for medical treatment and, in the case of a psychopathic disorder or mental impairment, that such treatment is likely to alleviate or prevent a deterioration of his condition; or (b) in the case of an offender who has attained the age of 16 years, the mental disorder is of a nature or degree which warrants his reception into guardianship under MHA 1983.

Interim orders

A court has the power to make an interim hospital order (s.38 MHA 1983) where an immediate place is available. The initial order must not exceed 12 weeks, but can be renewed thereafter for periods of no more than 28 days, and must not in total exceed 12 months.

MINIMUM SENTENCES FOR FIREARMS OFFENCES

The Criminal Justice Act 2003 (s.287) makes substantial changes to the mode of trial and sentencing of certain firearms offences, including minimum terms for some offences committed after the commencement of this section. The minimum sentence must be imposed unless the court is of the opinion that there are exceptional circumstances relating to the offence or to the offender which justify the court not imposing such a sentence. The Secretary of State can, by order, exclude the application of minimum sentences to those under 18 if he so wishes.

Overview

Section of Firearms Act 1968	Offence	Place of trial	Maximum sentence	Minimum sentence
5(1)(a), (ab), (aba), (ac), (ad), (ae), (af) or (c)	Possessing or distributing prohibited weapons or ammunition	On indictment	10 years or a fine or both	In the case of an offender who was aged 18 or over when he committed the offence 5 years In the case of an offender under 18 years at the time of committing the offence but aged at least 16 years, 3 years
5(1)(b)	Possessing or distributing prohibited weapon designed for discharge of noxious liquid etc	(a) summary (b) on indictment	6 months or a fine of the statutory maximum or both 10 years or a fine or both	Not applicable

214

Section of Firearms Act 1968	Offence	Place of trial	Maximum sentence	Minimum sentence
5(1A)(a)	Possessing or distributing firearm disguised as other object	On indictment	10 years or a fine or both	In the case of an offender who was aged 18 or over when he committed the offence 5 years In the case of an offender under 18 years at the time of committing the offence but aged at least 16 years, 3 years
5(1A)(b), (c), (d), (e), (f) or (g)	Possessing or distributing other prohibited weapons	(a) summary (b) on indictment	6 months or a fine of the statutory maximum or both 10 years or a fine or both	Not applicable

MISCELLANEOUS ORDERS

This section covers some of the less frequently encountered orders available to the magistrates' court.

Company director – disqualification

Company Directors Disqualification Act 1986 ss.1, 2

An order for a maximum period of five years can be made preventing an offender from being a director, administrator, liquidator, receiver or manager of property (in relation to a company), or otherwise being involved in the promotion, formation or management of a company.

The order can be made following conviction for an offence related to the formation, promotion, liquidation, receivership or management of a company.

For a discussion as to the reason behind the making of such orders, and the appropriate sentencing brackets see: *R.* v. *Anthony Glen Edwards* [1998] Crim LR 298.

Breach

It is an offence punishable with up to two years' imprisonment to act in a prohibited way in relation to company activity.

Deportation order

Immigration Act 1971 s.6 and Schedule 3

A court may give a convicted person over the age of 17 (by the date of conviction), notice (at least seven days) that they are proposing to make a deportation order. An order should only be made if the offender's continued presence in the UK will represent a potential detriment to the interests of the UK. There are complicated exceptions to the making of the order in relation to nationality rules, and full regard should be had to the current legislation.

ORDERS AGAINST PARENTS

This section deals with parenting orders and parental bind-over.

Parenting orders (Crime and Disorder Act 1998 s.8)

The court may make a parenting order in respect of a person who is a parent or guardian of a child or young person, or is the person convicted of the offence under ss.443 or 444 Education Act 1996.

Criteria

To make the order, one of the following conditions must be met:

1. A child safety order is made in respect of a child.
2. An antisocial behaviour order or sex offender order is made in respect of a child or young person.
3. A child or young person is convicted of an offence.
4. A person is convicted of an offence under s.443 (failing to comply with school attendance order) or s.444 (failing to secure regular attendance at school of a registered pupil) of the Education Act 1996.

And, that the parenting order would be desirable in the interests of preventing any repetition of the kind of behaviour which led to the making of a child safety order, antisocial behaviour order or sex offender order; or the commission of any further offence by the child or young person or any further offence under ss.443 or 444 of the Education Act 1996.

216

Scope of the order

A parenting order is an order which requires the parent to comply for a period not exceeding 12 months with such requirements as are specified in the order and to attend for a concurrent period not exceeding three months and not more than once a week, such counselling or guidance sessions as may be specified (the second requirement may be dispensed with if the parent has been made subject to an earlier order).

Mandatory nature of order

In the case of a person under the age of 16 years, the court, if satisfied that the conditions above are met, must make the order; if it is not so satisfied, must state in open court that it is not and why it is not.

Avoiding conflict

The order should be framed to avoid conflict with religious beliefs and educational or work commitments.

Discharge

There is provision for discharging the order.

Breach

If, while the order is in force, the parent, without reasonable excuse, fails to comply with any requirement included in the order, or specified in directions given by the responsible officer, that parent shall be liable on summary conviction to a fine not exceeding level 3 on the standard scale.

Other parenting order provisions

A person named in a referral order can be summonsed to appear before the court if they fail to attend the referral sessions. The court can, if it thinks appropriate, make a parenting order .

A freestanding parenting order is also available by virtue of s.27 Anti-social Behaviour Act 2003.

Parental bind-over

(See: Powers of Criminal Courts (Sentencing) Act 2000 s.150.)

The power to bind over arises where a person under 18 years of age is convicted of an offence. If the person is under 16 years of age, the power shall be exercised if it would be desirable in the interests of preventing the commission of further offences by that person.

Power to impose recognisance

With the parent or guardian's consent, a recognisance (max. £1,000) will be entered into to take proper care of the young person and exercise proper control over him. If consent is not given, and the court considers such refusal to give consent to be unreasonable, the court can order the parent or guardian to pay a fine not exceeding £1,000.

Duration of bind-over

The recognisance must not last for more than three years, nor must the period extend beyond the eighteenth birthday of the young person.

Appeals

An appeal lies to the Crown Court.

PRE-SENTENCE DRUG TESTING

A court can order a convicted offender aged 14 years or over, in respect of whom it is considering passing a community sentence, to provide samples for the purpose of ascertaining whether the offender has any specified Class-A drug in his body (s.161 CJA 2003).

If the offender is under 17 years of age such samples must be provided in the presence of an appropriate adult, and the order should reflect this fact.

A failure to comply with such an order, without reasonable excuse is an offence punishable with a fine not exceeding level 4 on the standard scale.

Specified Class-A drugs

- Cocaine, its salts and any preparation or other product containing cocaine or its salts.
- Diamorphine (commonly known as heroin), its salts and any preparation or other product containing diamorphine or its salts.

RACIALLY OR RELIGIOUSLY AGGRAVATED OFFENCES

Overview

There are two different sentencing considerations in relation to racially or religiously aggravated offences:

(a) offences actually charged as racially or religiously aggravated, by virtue of the Crime and Disorder Act 1998 (CDA 1998); and

(b) other offences, which are deemed to be racially or religiously aggravated as a result of conduct during the commission of the offence.

Definition of racially and religiously aggravated (s.28 CDA 1998)

An offence is racially or religiously aggravated if:

(a) at the time of committing the offence, or immediately before or after doing so, the offender demonstrates towards the victim of the offence hostility based on the victim's membership (or presumed membership) of a racial or religious group; or

(b) the offence is motivated (wholly or partly) by hostility towards members of a racial or religious group based on their membership of that group.

Membership includes association with members of that group, and presumed means presumed by the offender.

Racial group means a group of persons defined by reference to race, colour, nationality (including citizenship) or ethnic or national origins.

Religious group means a group of persons defined by reference to religious belief or lack of religious belief.

Intent

The fact that a defendant only used racist words out of frustration as opposed to an intention to insult is not relevant (see s.28(3) CDA 1998), neither is it relevant that the 'victim' is not bothered by the comments and does not regard them as racially offensive (*DPP* v. *Woods* [2002] EWHC Admin 85).

Specific aggravated offences (ss.29–32 CDA 1998)

The following offences can be charged as racially or religiously aggravated offences. When the offence is so charged it carries the penalty stated:

Section 20 Offences Against the Person Act (OAPA) 1861	6 months summarily, 7 years on indictment.
Section 47 OAPA 1861	6 months summarily, 7 years on indictment.
Common assault	6 months summarily, 2 years on indictment.
Criminal damage	6 months summarily, 14 years on indictment.
Section 4 Public Order Act (POA) 1986	6 months summarily, 2 years on indictment.
Section 4A POA 1986	6 months summarily, 2 years on indictment.
Section 5 POA 1986	Fine not exceeding level 4.
Section 2 Protection from Harassment Act (PFHA) 1997	6 months summarily, 2 years on indictment.
Section 4 PFHA 1997	6 months summarily, 7 years on indictment.

Other offences

A court must regard any other offence as being aggravated if the above definition is met. Section 153 PCC(S)A 2000 applies to offences other than those listed above and it is submitted that if an offence listed above was not charged as racially or religiously aggravated s.153 cannot be relied upon.

If it is stated in open court that an offence was so aggravated, the court must treat that fact as a factor that increases the seriousness of the offence.

Approach to sentencing

R. v. *Kelly and Donnelly* [2001] Crim LR 411, suggests the following approach should be adopted by courts.

Arrive at the appropriate sentence without the element of racial or religious aggravation, but including any other aggravating or mitigating factors:

1. Enhance that sentence to take account of the racial or religious aggravation.
2. Declare to the court what the appropriate sentence would have been for the offence without the aggravation so that the sentence for the racial or religious element of the offence could be clearly seen.

The amount to be added to the sentence would differ according to the circumstances of the individual case, but the following factors ought to be taken into account:

(a) planning or pattern of racist/religious offending;
(b) membership of a group promoting such unlawful activity;
(c) deliberately exposing the victim to offence or humiliation;
(d) offences within the victim's home;
(e) particularly vulnerable victims or victim performing public service;
(f) if the timing of the offence was calculated to maximise harm (e.g. during a religious festival);
(g) repeated or prolonged expressions of hostility;
(h) fear or distress within the community flowing from the offence.

It is likely that most aggravated offences will not be suitable for summary trial.

REFERRAL ORDER

(See: Powers of Criminal Courts (Sentencing) Act 2000 s.16.)

Overview

Referral orders arise in the case of persons under 18 years who are being dealt with for an offence (or connected offences) for which the sentence is not fixed by law, and the court is not proposing to impose a custodial sentence or make a hospital order, and the court is not proposing to absolutely discharge him in respect of the offence. Once a referral order has been successfully completed the conviction is immediately spent. An overview of the sentencing process can be found at the end of this section: see Figure 4.2.

The order may be mandatory or discretionary depending upon the circumstances.

Mandatory referral

The court must make the order if the offender:

(a) pleaded guilty to an offence punishable with imprisonment and to any connected offence (the connected offence(s) need not be imprisonable);
(b) has never been convicted by or before a court in the UK of any offence other than the offence and the connected offence; and
(c) has never been bound over in criminal proceedings in England and Wales or Northern Ireland to keep the peace and be of good behaviour.

Discretionary referral

Discretionary referral – non-imprisonable offences

The court may make the order if the offender pleads guilty to a non-imprisonable and any connected offence (which need not be imprisonable) and the criteria in paragraphs (b) and (c) above in relation to mandatory referral are met.

The effect of this change is to remove offences that might otherwise have been met with discharges or fines from the referral scheme in appropriate cases. The Home Office accepted that the minimum three-month referral period might be disproportionate for some offences.

Discretionary referral – mixed pleas

The court may make the order if the offender:

(a) is being dealt with by the court for the offence and one or more connected offences (whether or not any of them is an offence punishable with imprisonment);
(b) although he pleaded guilty to at least one of the offences mentioned above, he also pleaded not guilty to at least one of them;

(c) has never been convicted by or before a court in the UK of any offence other than the offence above; and

(d) has never been bound over in criminal proceedings in England and Wales or Northern Ireland to keep the peace and be of good behaviour.

Nature of the order

The offender will be referred to a youth offender panel for a period not less than three and not more than 12 months. This is the actual sentence, although costs, compensation, forfeiture may follow, as may an absolute discharge in relation to related offences. The court may disqualify from driving and endorse driving licences. The court may not make a parenting order, nor can it bind over a parent.

Attendance of parent

Section 20 PCC(S)A 2000 permits the court to order the attendance of a parent at a youth offender panel meeting. Unless it is thought unreasonable to do so, the court shall order the attendance of a parent, guardian or other appropriate person in the case of a youth under 16 years of age. The court must have regard to what would be reasonable attendance (s.20(3)(b)), and may take into account all factors it thinks are appropriate, for example, disability of a parent.

Remitting supervision

Where a youth is convicted before a court outside his area of residence the court can nominate his home youth offending team as the supervising authority. This avoids the need to remit the case to the home court, thereby avoiding delay and unnecessary court proceedings.

Length of order

The length of the order is set by the court, and will be commensurate with the seriousness of the offence. The term of the order begins to run from the date of the first successful meeting between the panel and the offender, which should usually be within 20 days of the sentencing hearing. Levels of seriousness are banded as follows:

Low   3–4 months referral order
Medium 5–7 months referral order
High   8–9 months referral order

A list of offences along with recommended banding has been issued by the government, and is reproduced in Table 4.2 below.

The 'ceiling' of nine months is to allow for orders of 9–12 months to be made in the following circumstances:

(a) in the most serious cases of offending (but where custody is not suitable);
(b) in the case of subsequent offending (allowing the three-month period to be used for a consecutive order, which otherwise would not be available);
(c) following mixed pleas (recognising that the offender has denied the offence and been found guilty as opposed to pleading and admitting guilt);
(d) following a guilty plea at a late stage.

Breach

The panel has power to refer the offender back to the court, and if the court agrees with the decision to refer back, it can sentence the offender by dealing with him in any way in which (assuming the mandatory referral provisions did not apply) he could have been dealt with for that offence by the court which made the order. A breach may occur where an offender fails to make contact with the panel, fails to agree a contract with the panel, or otherwise fails to complete the order.

Further offending

Further offences committed pre-referral

The referral order can be extended if:

(a) the occasion on which the offender was referred to the panel is the only other occasion on which it has fallen to a court in the UK to deal with the offender for any offence or offences; and
(b) the offence was committed before the referral order was made; and
(c) the offender pleaded guilty; and
(d) the original order was less than 12 months (one of the reasons for the nine-month ceiling); and
(e) the offender is still under 18 years old.

Further offences committed after referral

The referral order can be extended if the new offence was committed after the offender was referred to the panel, if:

(a) the occasion on which the offender was referred to the panel is the only other occasion on which it has fallen to a court in the UK to deal with the offender for any offence or offences; and

(b) the court is satisfied, on the basis of a report made to it by the relevant body, that there are *exceptional circumstances*, which indicate that, even though the offender has reoffended since being referred to the panel, extending his compliance period is likely to help prevent further reoffending by him.

The total referral period must not exceed 12 months.

Alternatives to extending the referral period

If the court decides not to extend the referral period when dealing with further offending, or it is unable to because of the 12-month restriction, it must decide on an alternative sentencing option. Any option, save for an absolute discharge, will mean that the referral order in respect of the original offence is automatically brought to an end, and the court has the power to resentence in respect of it.

Further guidance

It is vital that any solicitor undertaking youth court work should have a full understanding of the processes involved in respect of referral orders. Full guidance can be found in *Referral Orders and Youth Offender Panels, Guidance for Courts, Youth Offending Teams and Youth Offender Panels* (which can be downloaded from: **www.homeoffice.gov.uk**).

Figure 4.2 Referral order process

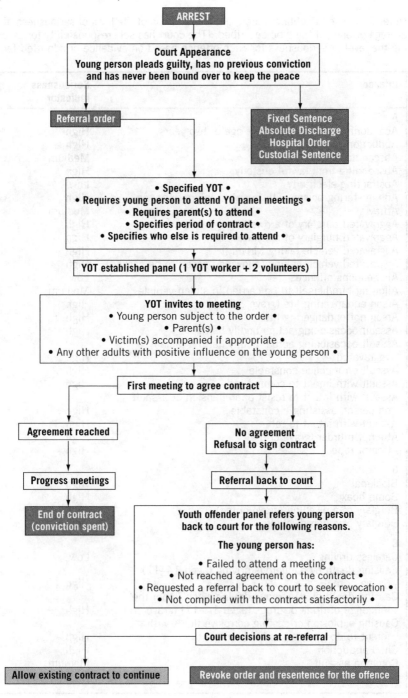

Table 4.2 Offence-seriousness indicators

Note: To be used to obtain a preliminary indication of the level of seriousness of an average offence of the type described. (The court has sole responsibility for assessing the level of seriousness for each offence based on evidence or admitted facts)

Offence	Seriousness indicator
A	
Abandoning a child under the age of two years	High
Abduction of female	High
Absconding from bail	Medium
Absconding from lawful custody	High
Abstracting electricity	Low
Administering poison with intent to injure or annoy	High
Affray	Medium
Aggravated burglary of a dwelling (grave crime)	High
Aggravated burglary of non-dwelling	High
Aggravated vehicle-taking (driving)	High
Aggravated vehicle-taking (allowing oneself to be carried)	High
Air weapons offences	Low
Allowing him/herself to be carried in stolen vehicle	Medium
Arson endangering life (grave crime)	High
Arson not endangering life	High
Assault occasioning actual bodily harm	High
Assault occasioning actual bodily harm – racially aggravated	High
Assault on a police constable	High
Assault with intent to commit rape	High
Assault with intent to resist apprehension or assault on person assisting a constable	High
Assault with intent to rob	High
Attempt murder (grave crime)	High
Attempt rape	High
B	
Blackmail	High
Bomb hoax	High
Burglary of a dwelling (grave crime)	High
Burglary of a non-dwelling	High
C	
Careless driving	Low
Causing death by dangerous driving (aged 14–17) (grave crime)	High
Causing death by dangerous driving when under the influence of drink or drugs (aged 14–17) (grave crime)	High
Causing explosion or casting corrosive fluids with intent to do grievous bodily harm	High
Child abduction	High
Common assault	Medium
Common assault – racially aggravated	High

Offence	Seriousness indicator
Conspiracy to defraud	High
Conspiring or soliciting to commit murder	High
Counterfeiting	High
Criminal damage	Low
Criminal damage – racially aggravated	High
Criminal damage endangering life	High
Cultivation of cannabis	Medium
D	
Demanding money with menaces (grave crime)	High
Driving whilst disqualified	Medium
Drunk and disorderly	Low
Drunkenness	Low
E	
Endangering life or causing harm by administering poison	High
Endangering railway passenger by placing anything on rail, taking up rail, changing points or signals	High
Endangering railway passenger by throwing anything at railway carriage	High
Excess alcohol – driving	Medium
Excess alcohol – in charge	Medium
F	
False fire alarm	Medium
False imprisonment	High
Forgery	High
Forgery of prescription	Medium
G	
Genocide (grave crime)	High
Going equipped to steal	Medium
Grievous bodily harm with intent (grave crime)	High
Gross indecency with children	High
H	
Handling stolen goods	High
Harassment	Medium
Harassment – racially aggravated	High
Harassment with intent	High
Harassment with intent – racially aggravated	High
Hijacking	High
I	
Importation/exportation of controlled drug	High
Incest with female under 13 years	High
Inciting female aged under 16 years to have incestuous sexual intercourse	High
Indecent photographs – making or possession	High
Indecent assault on female aged 16 or over (grave crime)	High
Indecent assault on female under 16 (grave crime)	High
Indecent assault on male aged 16 or over (grave crime)	High
Indecent assault on male aged under 16 (grave crime)	High

Offence	Seriousness indicator
Indecent exposure	Medium
Infanticide (grave crime)	High
Interfering with a motor vehicle	Medium
K	
Kidnapping	High
M	
Making off without payment	Low
Making written or verbal threats to kill	High
Malicious wounding/grievous bodily harm	High
Malicious wounding/grievous bodily harm – racially aggravated	High
Manslaughter (grave crime)	High
Murder (grave crime)	High
O	
Obstruct police	Low
Obtaining pecuniary advantage by deception	Medium
Obtaining property by deception	Medium
Offensive weapon	Medium
P	
Permitting use of premises for use of Class-A drug	High
Permitting use of premises for use of Class-B drug	Low
Perverting the course of justice	High
Possession of an article with a blade or point	Medium
Possession firearm/imitation firearm with intent to commit an indictable offence or resist arrest	High
Possession firearm/imitation firearm with intent to endanger life or injure property	High
Possession firearm/imitation firearm with intent to cause violence	High
Possession of Class-A drug	Medium
Possession of Class-B drug	Low
Possession of Class-C drug	Low
Possession of controlled drug with intent to supply it to another (grave crime)	High
Possession of explosive weapon	High
Possession of explosive weapon with intent to endanger life (grave crime)	High
Possession of firearm/imitation firearm at time of committing or being arrested for an offence under Schedule 1 of Firearms Act 1968 (grave crime)	High
Production of Class-A or -B drugs (grave crime)	High
Prostitution	Low
R	
Railway frauds	Low
Rape – female (grave crime)	High
Rape – male (grave crime)	High
Riot	High
Robbery (grave crime)	High

Offence	Seriousness indicator
S	
s.4 Public Order Act	Medium
s.4 Public Order Act – racially aggravated	High
s.4(a) Public Order Act	Low
s.4(a) Public Order Act – racially aggravated	Medium
s.5 Public Order Act	Low
s.5 Public Order Act – racially aggravated	Low
Sending articles – offensive/indecent	Medium
Supplying or offering to supply controlled drug or being concerned in the doing of either activity by another (grave crime)	High
T	
Telephone calls – making obscene	Low
Theft by an employee	High
Theft	Medium
Theft from the person	High
Theft from a shop	Low
Theft or unauthorised taking of mail	Medium
Threat or conspiracy to murder	High
Threat to commit criminal damage	Low
Trespass on a railway	Low
Taking a vehicle without consent (TWOC)	Medium
U	
Unlawful sexual intercourse with female under 13	High
Using false prescription	Medium
V	
Violent disorder	High
W	
Wasting police time	Medium
Witness intimidation	High
Wounding with intent to do grievous bodily harm	High

REHABILITATION OF OFFENDERS

Rehabilitation periods

Rehabilitation periods subject to reduction by half for persons under 18	
Imprisonment or youth custody exceeding 6 months but not exceeding 30 months	10 years
Imprisonment or youth custody not exceeding 6 months	7 years

Fine or other sentence subject to rehabilitation under PCC(S)A 2000, not being a sentence in the table below	5 years
Absolute discharge	6 months from date of conviction
Conditional discharge or bind-over	1 year from date of conviction or a period beginning with that date and ending when the order for conditional discharge or recognisance for good behaviour ceases or ceased to have effect, whichever is the longer

Rehabilitation periods for certain offences confined to young offenders	
Sentence of detention for a term exceeding 6 months but not exceeding 30 months passed under s.91 PCC(S)A 2000	5 years
Sentence of detention for a term not exceeding 6 months, pursuant to s.91 PCC(S)A 2000	3 years

REPARATION ORDER

(See: Powers of Criminal Courts (Sentencing) Act 2000 s.73.)

When a person under the age of 18 years is convicted of an offence other than one for which the sentence is fixed by law, the court by or before which he is convicted may make an order requiring him to make reparation specified in the order, to a person or persons so specified or to the community at large. The person or persons specified must be identified by the court as a victim of the offence or a person otherwise affected by it.

Compatibility with other orders

The court shall not make such an order if it proposes to pass on the offender a custodial sentence or make in respect of him a community sentence with an unpaid work or supervision requirement, an action plan order or a referral order.

Requirement for reports

Before making such an order the court shall obtain and consider a written report indicating the type of work that is suitable for the offender and the attitude of the victim or victims to the requirements proposed to be included in the order.

Scope of the order

The order shall not require the offender to work more than 24 hours in aggregate, or make reparation to any person without the consent of that person.

Conflict

The order should avoid conflict with religious beliefs, other community orders and schooling.

Breach

A breach is failure without reasonable excuse to comply with any require-ment or direction included in the order. If a breach is admitted or proved the court may:

(a) order the offender to pay a fine of an amount not exceeding £1,000;
(b) make an attendance centre order in respect of the offender;
(c) make a curfew order in respect of the offender;
(d) revoke the order and deal with the offender in any other way that would have been open to the court had the order not been made. If the order was made by a Crown Court, the order can only be revoked by a Crown Court. If revocation is proposed, the offender should be committed either on bail or in custody to the Crown Court for sentence. The court, when resentencing, must have regard to the extent of compliance prior to the breach.

Revocation or variation

Any party can apply to revoke or vary the order while it is in force. If it appears appropriate to the court to do so, it may:

(a) revoke the order;
(b) cancel any provision in the order;
(c) insert any provision which could have been included in the order if the court had then had the power to make it and were exercising the power.

Further applications for revocation

If an application to revoke the order is refused by the court, no further applications can be made without permission of the court.

SEXUAL OFFENCES PREVENTION ORDERS

Sections 104–113 Sexual Offences Act 2003 deal with the making of sexual offences prevention orders. In order to make such an order the following must be satisfied:

* The offender must be convicted of an offence listed in Schedules 3 or 5 to the Sexual Offences Act 2003, or been found not guilty by reason of disability.
* Such an order must be necessary to protect the public or any particular members of the public from serious sexual harm from him.

Orders can also be applied for in freestanding proceedings that fall within duty solicitor scope.

SUPERVISION ORDER

(See: Powers of Criminal Courts (Sentencing) Act 2000 s.63.)

Criteria

A supervision order can be made in respect of a person:

(a) under 18 years of age;
(b) who has been convicted of an offence, and the offence or the combination of the offence and one or more offences associated with it, is serious enough to warrant a community penalty (other than an offence for which the sentence is fixed by law).

A pre-sentence report should be obtained before making such an order, unless the court is of the opinion that it is unnecessary.

Scope

The order places the offender under the supervision of a local authority, officer of a local probation board or a member of a youth offending team.

The following requirements may be included in an attendance centre order (see Schedule 6 PCC(S)A 2000):

(a) to reside with a named individual;
(b) to comply with directions of supervisor;
(c) to undertake specified activities, or refrain from activities;
(d) to make reparation;
(e) to comply with curfew for specified periods between 6 p.m. and 6 a.m.

The maximum period that can be specified in relation to the above requirements is 90 days (with the exception of refraining from activities).

Further requirements may require the offender to:

(a) live for a specified period in local authority accommodation (maximum
     period of six months);
(b) undergo treatment for a mental condition;
(c) participate in education.

Length of order

The order will cease to have effect at the end of the period of three years,
unless a shorter period has been specified. It is good practice for a court to
specify the length of the order at sentencing.

Breaches

If a court is satisfied that an offender has failed without reasonable excuse to
comply with the order, it may *whether or not it revokes or amends the order*:

(a) fine the offender an amount not exceeding £1,000;
(b) make a curfew order (see Schedule 7 para. 3);
(c) make an attendance centre order (see Schedule 7 para. 4).

The court may also:

(a) revoke the order (if it was made by a magistrates' court) and deal with
     the offender, for the offence in respect of which the order was made, in
     any way in which he could have been dealt with for that offence by the
     court which made the order if the order had not been made; or
(b) if the supervision order was made by the Crown Court, commit the
     offender in custody or release him on bail until he can be brought or
     appear before the Crown Court.

Extent of compliance

If a court chooses to resentence the offender, it shall take into account the
extent to which the offender has complied with the requirements of the order,
and, in the case of an offender who has wilfully and persistently failed to
comply with the requirements of the order, may impose a custodial sentence

notwithstanding anything in s.79(2) PCC(S)A 2000 (which states that custody should not be imposed unless the offence(s) are so serious that only a custodial sentence can be justified).

Applying to revoke or amend the order

The supervisor or offender can apply to the court to revoke or amend the order. If the court feels that the application is appropriate, it can:

(a) revoke the supervision order; or
(b) amend it by cancelling or including any requirements.

There are certain restrictions in relation to adding additional requirements (see Schedule 7 para. 5(3)). Regard should also be had to para. 8.

Further applications

Where an application for revocation is dismissed, no further application can be made within three months of the dismissal except with leave of the court.

CHAPTER 5

Offences, definitions and sentences

ROAD TRAFFIC OFFENCES – STATUTORY DEFINITIONS AND PENALTIES

Road Traffic Act 1988

The following sections of the Act should be noted:

1 Causing death by dangerous driving

A person who causes the death of another person by driving a mechanically propelled vehicle dangerously on a road or other public place is guilty of an offence.

2 Dangerous driving

A person who drives a mechanically propelled vehicle dangerously on a road or other public place is guilty of an offence.

2A Meaning of dangerous driving

(1) For the purposes of sections 1 and 2 above a person is to be regarded as driving dangerously if (and, subject to subsection (2) below, only if)—

    (*a*)   the way he drives falls far below what would be expected of a competent and careful driver, and

    (*b*)   it would be obvious to a competent and careful driver that driving in that way would be dangerous.

(2) A person is also to be regarded as driving dangerously for the purposes of sections 1 and 2 above if it would be obvious to a competent and careful driver that driving the vehicle in its current state would be dangerous.

(3) In subsections (1) and (2) above 'dangerous' refers to danger either of injury to any person or of serious damage to property; and in determining for the purposes of those subsections what would be expected of, or obvious to, a competent and careful driver in a particular case, regard shall be had not only to the circumstances of which he could be expected to be aware but also to any circumstances shown to have been within the knowledge of the accused.

(4) In determining for the purposes of subsection (2) above the state of a vehicle, regard may be had to anything attached to or carried on or in it and to the manner in which it is attached or carried.

3 Careless, and inconsiderate, driving

If a person drives a mechanically propelled vehicle on a road or other public place without due care and attention, or without reasonable consideration for other persons using the road or place, he is guilty of an offence.

3A Causing death by careless driving when under influence of drink or drugs

(1) If a person causes the death of another person by driving a mechanically propelled vehicle on a road or other public place without due care and attention, or without reasonable consideration for other persons using the road or place, and—

    (*a*)   he is, at the time when he is driving, unfit to drive through drink or drugs, or

    (*b*)   he has consumed so much alcohol that the proportion of it in his breath, blood or urine at that time exceeds the prescribed limit, or

    (*c*)   he is, within 18 hours after that time, required to provide a specimen in pursuance of section 7 of this Act, but without reasonable excuse fails to provide it,

he is guilty of an offence.

(2) For the purposes of this section a person shall be taken to be unfit to drive at any time when his ability to drive properly is impaired.

(3) Subsection (1)(*b*) and (*c*) above shall not apply in relation to a person driving a mechanically propelled vehicle other than a motor vehicle.

4 Driving, or being in charge, when under influence of drink or drugs

(1) A person who, when driving or attempting to drive a mechanically propelled vehicle on a road or other public place, is unfit to drive through drink or drugs is guilty of an offence.

(2) Without prejudice to subsection (1) above, a person who, when in charge of a mechanically propelled vehicle which is on a road or other public place, is unfit to drive through drink or drugs is guilty of an offence.

(3) For the purposes of subsection (2) above, a person shall be deemed not to have been in charge of a mechanically propelled vehicle if he proves that at the material time the circumstances were such that there was no likelihood of his driving it so long as he remained unfit to drive through drink or drugs.

(4) The court may, in determining whether there was such a likelihood as is mentioned in subsection (3) above, disregard any injury to him and any damage to the vehicle.

(5) For the purposes of this section, a person shall be taken to be unfit to drive if his ability to drive properly is for the time being impaired.

5 Driving or being in charge of a motor vehicle with alcohol concentration above prescribed limit

(1) If a person—

    (*a*)   drives or attempts to drive a motor vehicle on a road or other public place, or

    (*b*)   is in charge of a motor vehicle on a road or other public place after consuming so much alcohol that the proportion of it in his breath, blood or urine exceeds the prescribed limit he is guilty of an offence.

(2) It is a defence for a person charged with an offence under subsection (1)(*b*) above to prove that at the time he is alleged to have committed the offence the circumstances were such that there was no likelihood of his driving the vehicle while the proportion of alcohol in his breath, blood or urine remained likely to exceed the prescribed limit.

(3) The court may, in determining whether there was such a likelihood as is mentioned in subsection (2) above, disregard any injury to him and any damage to the vehicle.

6 Power to administer preliminary tests

(1) If any of subsections (2) to (5) applies a constable may require a person to co-operate with any one or more preliminary tests administered to the person by that constable or another constable.

(2) This subsection applies if a constable reasonably suspects that the person—

- (*a*) is driving, is attempting to drive or is in charge of a motor vehicle on a road or other public place, and
- (*b*) has alcohol or a drug in his body or is under the influence of a drug.

(3) This subsection applies if a constable reasonably suspects that the person—

- (*a*) has been driving, attempting to drive or in charge of a motor vehicle on a road or other public place while having alcohol or a drug in his body or while unfit to drive because of a drug, and
- (*b*) still has alcohol or a drug in his body or is still under the influence of a drug.

(4) This subsection applies if a constable reasonably suspects that the person—

- (*a*) is or has been driving, attempting to drive or in charge of a motor vehicle on a road or other public place, and
- (*b*) has committed a traffic offence while the vehicle was in motion.

(5) This subsection applies if—

- (*a*) an accident occurs owing to the presence of a motor vehicle on a road or other public place, and
- (*b*) a constable reasonably believes that the person was driving, attempting to drive or in charge of the vehicle at the time of the accident.

(6) A person commits an offence if without reasonable excuse he fails to co-operate with a preliminary test in pursuance of a requirement imposed under this section.

(7) A constable may administer a preliminary test by virtue of any of subsections (2) to (4) only if he is in uniform.

(8) In this section—

- (*a*) a reference to a preliminary test is to any of the tests described in sections 6A to 6C, and
- (*b*) 'traffic offence' means an offence under—
  - (i) a provision of Part II of the Public Passenger Vehicles Act 1981 (c. 14),
  - (ii) a provision of the Road Traffic Regulation Act 1984 (c. 27),

      (iii) a provision of the Road Traffic Offenders Act 1988 (c. 53) other than a provision of Part III, or

      (iv) a provision of this Act other than a provision of Part V.

6A   Preliminary breath test

(1) A preliminary breath test is a procedure whereby the person to whom the test is administered provides a specimen of breath to be used for the purpose of obtaining, by means of a device of a type approved by the Secretary of State, an indication whether the proportion of alcohol in the person's breath or blood is likely to exceed the prescribed limit.

(2) A preliminary breath test administered in reliance on section 6(2) to (4) may be administered only at or near the place where the requirement to co-operate with the test is imposed.

(3) A preliminary breath test administered in reliance on section 6(5) may be administered—

      (a) at or near the place where the requirement to co-operate with the test is imposed, or

      (b) if the constable who imposes the requirement thinks it expedient, at a police station specified by him.

6B   Preliminary impairment test

(1) A preliminary impairment test is a procedure whereby the constable administering the test—

      (a) observes the person to whom the test is administered in his performance of tasks specified by the constable, and

      (b) makes such other observations of the person's physical state as the constable thinks expedient.

(2) The Secretary of State shall issue (and may from time to time revise) a code of practice about—

      (a) the kind of task that may be specified for the purpose of a preliminary impairment test,

      (b) the kind of observation of physical state that may be made in the course of a preliminary impairment test,

      (c) the manner in which a preliminary impairment test should be administered, and

      (d) the inferences that may be drawn from observations made in the course of a preliminary impairment test.

(3) In issuing or revising the code of practice the Secretary of State shall aim to ensure that a preliminary impairment test is designed to indicate—

      (a) whether a person is unfit to drive, and

      (b) if he is, whether or not his unfitness is likely to be due to drink or drugs.

(4) A preliminary impairment test may be administered—

      (a) at or near the place where the requirement to co-operate with the test is imposed, or

      (b) if the constable who imposes the requirement thinks it expedient, at a police station specified by him.

(5) A constable administering a preliminary impairment test shall have regard to the code of practice under this section.

(6) A constable may administer a preliminary impairment test only if he is approved for that purpose by the chief officer of the police force to which he belongs.

(7) A code of practice under this section may include provision about—

    (*a*)   the giving of approval under subsection (6), and

    (*b*)   in particular, the kind of training that a constable should have undergone, or the kind of qualification that a constable should possess, before being approved under that subsection.

7   Provision of specimens for analysis

(1) In the course of an investigation into whether a person has committed an offence under section 3A, 4 or 5 of this Act a constable may, subject to the following provisions of this section and section 9 of this Act, require him—

    (*a*)   to provide two specimens of breath for analysis by means of a device of a type approved by the Secretary of State, or

    (*b*)   to provide a specimen of blood or urine for a laboratory test.

(2) A requirement under this section to provide specimens of breath can only be made—

    (*a*)   at a police station,

    (*b*)   at a hospital, or

    (*c*)   at or near a place where a relevant breath test has been administered to the person concerned or would have been so administered but for his failure to co-operate with it.

(2A) For the purposes of this section 'a relevant breath test' is a procedure involving the provision by the person concerned of a specimen of breath to be used for the purpose of obtaining an indication whether the proportion of alcohol in his breath or blood is likely to exceed the prescribed limit.

(2B) A requirement under this section to provide specimens of breath may not be made at or near a place mentioned in subsection (2)(*c*) above unless the constable making it—

    (*a*)   is in uniform, or

    (*b*)   has imposed a requirement on the person concerned to co-operate with a relevant breath test in circumstances in which section 6(5) of this Act applies.

(2C) Where a constable has imposed a requirement on the person concerned to co-operate with a relevant breath test at any place, he is entitled to remain at or near that place in order to impose on him there a requirement under this section.

(2D) If a requirement under subsection (1)(*a*) above has been made at a place other than at a police station, such a requirement may subsequently be made at a police station if (but only if)—

    (*a*)   a device or a reliable device of the type mentioned in subsection (1)(*a*) above was not available at that place or it was for any other reason not practicable to use such a device there, or

(b)   the constable who made the previous requirement has reasonable cause to believe that the device used there has not produced a reliable indication of the proportion of alcohol in the breath of the person concerned.

(3) A requirement under this section to provide a specimen of blood or urine can only be made at a police station or at a hospital; and it cannot be made at a police station unless—

(a)   the constable making the requirement has reasonable cause to believe that for medical reasons a specimen of breath cannot be provided or should not be required, or

(b)   specimens of breath have not been provided elsewhere and at the time the requirement is made a device or a reliable device of the type mentioned in subsection (1)(a) above is not available at the police station or it is then for any other reason not practicable to use such a device there, or

(bb) a device of the type mentioned in subsection (1)(a) above has been used (at the police station or elsewhere) but the constable who required the specimens of breath has reasonable cause to believe that the device has not produced a reliable indication of the proportion of alcohol in the breath of the person concerned, or

(bc) as a result of the administration of a preliminary drug test, the constable making the requirement has reasonable cause to believe that the person required to provide a specimen of blood or urine has a drug in his body, or

(c)   the suspected offence is one under section 3A or 4 of this Act and the constable making the requirement has been advised by a medical practitioner that the condition of the person required to provide the specimen might be due to some drug;

but may then be made notwithstanding that the person required to provide the specimen has already provided or been required to provide two specimens of breath.

(4) If the provision of a specimen other than a specimen of breath may be required in pursuance of this section the question whether it is to be a specimen of blood or a specimen of urine and, in the case of a specimen of blood, the question who is to be asked to take it shall be decided (subject to subsection (4A)) by the constable making the requirement.

(4A) Where a constable decides for the purposes of subsection (4) to require the provision of a specimen of blood, there shall be no requirement to provide such a specimen if—

(a)   the medical practitioner who is asked to take the specimen is of the opinion that, for medical reasons, it cannot or should not be taken; or

(b)   the registered health care professional who is asked to take it is of that opinion and there is no contrary opinion from a medical practitioner;

and, where by virtue of this subsection there can be no requirement to provide a specimen of blood, the constable may require a specimen of urine instead.

(5) A specimen of urine shall be provided within one hour of the requirement for its provision being made and after the provision of a previous specimen of urine.

(6) A person who, without reasonable excuse, fails to provide a specimen when required to do so in pursuance of this section is guilty of an offence.

(7) A constable must, on requiring any person to provide a specimen in pursuance of this section, warn him that a failure to provide it may render him liable to prosecution.

8 Choice of specimens of breath

(1) Subject to subsection (2) below, of any two specimens of breath provided by any person in pursuance of section 7 of this Act that with the lower proportion of alcohol in the breath shall be used and the other shall be disregarded.

(2) If the specimen with the lower proportion of alcohol contains no more than 50 microgrammes of alcohol in 100 millilitres of breath, the person who provided it may claim that it should be replaced by such specimen as may be required under section 7(4) of this Act and, if he then provides such a specimen, neither specimen of breath shall be used.

(2A) If the person who makes a claim under subsection (2) above was required to provide specimens of breath under section 7 of this Act at or near a place mentioned in subsection (2)(*c*) of that section, a constable may arrest him without warrant.

(3) The Secretary of State may by regulations substitute another proportion of alcohol in the breath for that specified in subsection (2) above.

9 Protection for hospital patients

(1) While a person is at a hospital as a patient he shall not be required to co-operate with a preliminary test or to provide a specimen under section 7 of this Act unless the medical practitioner in immediate charge of his case has been notified of the proposal to make the requirement; and—

    (*a*) if the requirement is then made, it shall be for co-operation with a test administered, or for the provision of a specimen, at the hospital, but

    (*b*) if the medical practitioner objects on the ground specified in subsection (2) below, the requirement shall not be made.

(1A) While a person is at a hospital as a patient, no specimen of blood shall be taken from him under section 7A of this Act and he shall not be required to give his permission for a laboratory test of a specimen taken under that section unless the medical practitioner in immediate charge of his case—

    (*a*) has been notified of the proposal to take the specimen or to make the requirement; and

    (*b*) has not objected on the ground specified in subsection (2).

(2) The ground on which the medical practitioner may object is—

    (*a*) in a case falling within subsection (1), that the requirement or the provision of the specimen or (if one is required) the warning required by section 7(7) of this Act would be prejudicial to the proper care and treatment of the patient; and

    (*b*) in a case falling within subsection (1A), that the taking of the specimen, the requirement or the warning required by section 7A(5) of this Act would be so prejudicial.

[. . .]

12   Motor racing on public ways

(1) A person who promotes or takes part in a race or trial of speed between motor vehicles on a public way is guilty of an offence.

(2) In this section 'public way' means, in England and Wales, a highway and, in Scotland, a public road.

[. . .]

22   Leaving vehicles in dangerous positions

If a person in charge of a vehicle causes or permits the vehicle or a trailer drawn by it to remain at rest on a road in such a position or in such condition or in such circumstances as to involve a danger of injury to other persons using the road, he is guilty of an offence.

22A   Causing danger to road-users

(1) A person is guilty of an offence if he intentionally and without lawful authority or reasonable cause—

> (*a*)   causes anything to be on or over a road, or
> (*b*)   interferes with a motor vehicle, trailer or cycle, or
> (*c*)   interferes (directly or indirectly) with traffic equipment,

in such circumstances that it would be obvious to a reasonable person that to do so would be dangerous.

(2) In subsection (1) above 'dangerous' refers to danger either of injury to any person while on or near a road, or of serious damage to property on or near a road; and in determining for the purposes of that subsection what would be obvious to a reasonable person in a particular case, regard shall be had not only to the circumstances of which he could be expected to be aware but also to any circumstances shown to have been within the knowledge of the accused.

(3) In subsection (1) above 'traffic equipment' means—

> (*a*)   anything lawfully placed on or near a road by a highway authority;
> (*b*)   a traffic sign lawfully placed on or near a road by a person other than a highway authority;
> (*c*)   any fence, barrier or light lawfully placed on or near a road—
>
> > (i)   in pursuance of section 174 of the Highways Act 1980, section 8 of the Public Utilities Street Works Act 1950 or section 65 of the New Roads and Street Works Act 1991 (which provide for guarding, lighting and signing in streets where works are undertaken), or
> > (ii)   by a constable or a person acting under the instructions (whether general or specific) of a chief officer of police.

(4) For the purposes of subsection (3) above anything placed on or near a road shall unless the contrary is proved be deemed to have been lawfully placed there.

(5) In this section 'road' does not include a footpath or bridleway.

[. . .]

103 Obtaining licence, or driving, while disqualified

(1) A person is guilty of an offence if, while disqualified for holding or obtaining a licence, he—

    (*a*) obtains a licence, or

    (*b*) drives a motor vehicle on a road.

(2) A licence obtained by a person who is disqualified is of no effect (or, where the disqualification relates only to vehicles of a particular class, is of no effect in relation to vehicles of that class).

(3) A constable in uniform may arrest without warrant any person driving a motor vehicle on a road whom he has reasonable cause to suspect of being disqualified.

(4) Subsections (1) and (3) above do not apply in relation to disqualification by virtue of section 101 of this Act.

(5) Subsections (1)(*b*) and (3) above do not apply in relation to disqualification by virtue of section 102 of this Act.

(6) In the application of subsections (1) and (3) above to a person whose disqualification is limited to the driving of motor vehicles of a particular class by virtue of—

    (*a*) section 102, 117 or 117A of this Act, or

    (*b*) subsection (9) of section 36 of the Road Traffic Offenders Act 1988 (disqualification until test is passed),

the references to disqualification for holding or obtaining a licence and driving motor vehicles are references to disqualification for holding or obtaining a licence to drive and driving motor vehicles of that class.

[. . .]

143 Users of motor vehicles to be insured or secured against third-party risks

(1) Subject to the provisions of this Part of this Act—

    (*a*) a person must not use a motor vehicle on a road or other public place unless there is in force in relation to the use of the vehicle by that person such a policy of insurance or such a security in respect of third party risks as complies with the requirements of this Part of this Act, and

    (*b*) a person must not cause or permit any other person to use a motor vehicle on a road or other public place unless there is in force in relation to the use of the vehicle by that other person such a policy of insurance or such a security in respect of third party risks as complies with the requirements of this Part of this Act.

(2) If a person acts in contravention of subsection (1) above he is guilty of an offence.

(3) A person charged with using a motor vehicle in contravention of this section shall not be convicted if he proves—

    (*a*) that the vehicle did not belong to him and was not in his possession under a contract of hiring or of loan,

    (*b*) that he was using the vehicle in the course of his employment, and (*c*) that he neither knew nor had reason to believe that there was not in force in relation to the vehicle such a policy of insurance or security as is mentioned in subsection (1) above.

(4) This Part of this Act does not apply to invalid carriages.

[. . .]

170   Duty of driver to stop, report accident and give information or documents

(1) This section applies in a case where, owing to the presence of a mechanically propelled vehicle on a road, or other public place an accident occurs by which—

(*a*) personal injury is caused to a person other than the driver of that mechanically propelled vehicle, or

(*b*) damage is caused—

(i) to a vehicle other than that mechanically propelled vehicle or a trailer drawn by that mechanically propelled vehicle, or

(ii) to an animal other than an animal in or on that mechanically propelled vehicle or a trailer drawn by that mechanically propelled vehicle, or

(iii) to any other property constructed on, fixed to, growing in or otherwise forming part of the land on which the road or place in question is situated or land adjacent to such land.

(2) The driver of the mechanically propelled vehicle must stop and, if required to do so by any person having reasonable grounds for so requiring, give his name and address and also the name and address of the owner and the identification marks of the vehicle.

(3) If for any reason the driver of the mechanically propelled vehicle does not give his name and address under subsection (2) above, he must report the accident.

(4) A person who fails to comply with subsection (2) or (3) above is guilty of an offence.

(5) If, in a case where this section applies by virtue of subsection (1)(*a*) above, the driver of a motor vehicle does not at the time of the accident produce such a certificate of insurance or security, or other evidence, as is mentioned in section 165(2) of this Act—

(*a*) to a constable, or

(*b*) to some person who, having reasonable grounds for so doing, has required him to produce it,

the driver must report the accident and produce such a certificate or other evidence.

This subsection does not apply to the driver of an invalid carriage.

(6) To comply with a duty under this section to report an accident or to produce such a certificate of insurance or security, or other evidence, as is mentioned in section 165(2)(*a*) of this Act, the driver—

(*a*) must do so at a police station or to a constable, and

(*b*) must do so as soon as is reasonably practicable and, in any case, within twenty-four hours of the occurrence of the accident.

(7) A person who fails to comply with a duty under subsection (5) above is guilty of an offence, but he shall not be convicted by reason only of a failure to produce a certificate or other evidence if, within seven days after the occurrence of the accident, the certificate or other evidence is produced at a police station that was specified by him at the time when the accident was reported.

(8) In this section 'animal' means horse, cattle, ass, mule, sheep, pig, goat or dog.

171 Duty of owner of motor vehicle to give information for verifying compliance with requirement of compulsory insurance or security

(1) For the purpose of determining whether a motor vehicle was or was not being driven in contravention of section 143 of this Act on any occasion when the driver was required under section 165(1) or 170 of this Act to produce such a certificate of insurance or security, or other evidence, as is mentioned in section 165(2)(a) of this Act, the owner of the vehicle must give such information as he may be required, by or on behalf of a chief officer of police, to give.

(2) A person who fails to comply with the requirement of subsection (1) above is guilty of an offence.

(3) In this section 'owner', in relation to a vehicle which is the subject of a hiring agreement, includes each party to the agreement.

172 Duty to give information as to identity of driver etc. in certain circumstances

(1) This section applies—

    (a)   to any offence under the preceding provisions of this Act except—

        (i)   an offence under Part V, or
        (ii) an offence under section 13, 16, 51(2), 61(4), 67(9), 68(4), 96 or 120, and to an offence under section 178 of this Act,

    (b)   to any offence under sections 25, 26 or 27 of the Road Traffic Offenders Act 1988,
    (c)   to any offence against any other enactment relating to the use of vehicles on roads, and
    (d)   to manslaughter, or in Scotland culpable homicide, by the driver of a motor vehicle.

(2) Where the driver of a vehicle is alleged to be guilty of an offence to which this section applies—

    (a)   the person keeping the vehicle shall give such information as to the identity of the driver as he may be required to give by or on behalf of a chief officer of police, and
    (b)   any other person shall if required as stated above give any information which it is in his power to give and may lead to identification of the driver.

(3) Subject to the following provisions, a person who fails to comply with a requirement under subsection (2) above shall be guilty of an offence.

(4) A person shall not be guilty of an offence by virtue of paragraph (a) of subsection (2) above if he shows that he did not know and could not with reasonable diligence have ascertained who the driver of the vehicle was.

(5) Where a body corporate is guilty of an offence under this section and the offence is proved to have been committed with the consent or connivance of, or to be attributable to neglect on the part of, a director, manager, secretary or other similar officer of the body corporate, or a person who was purporting to act in any such capacity, he, as well as the body corporate, is guilty of that offence and liable to be proceeded against and punished accordingly.

(6) Where the alleged offender is a body corporate, or in Scotland a partnership or an unincorporated association, or the proceedings are brought against him by virtue of subsection (5) above or subsection (11) below, subsection (4) above shall not apply unless, in addition to the matters there mentioned, the alleged offender shows that no record was kept of the persons who drove the vehicle and that the failure to keep a record was reasonable.

(7) A requirement under subsection (2) may be made by written notice served by post; and where it is so made—

    (*a*)   it shall have effect as a requirement to give the information within the period of 28 days beginning with the day on which the notice is served, and

    (*b*)   the person on whom the notice is served shall not be guilty of an offence under this section if he shows either that he gave the information as soon as reasonably practicable after the end of that period or that it has not been reasonably practicable for him to give it.

(8) Where the person on whom a notice under subsection (7) above is to be served is a body corporate, the notice is duly served if it is served on the secretary or clerk of that body.

(9) For the purposes of section 7 of the Interpretation Act 1978 as it applies for the purposes of this section the proper address of any person in relation to the service on him of a notice under subsection (7) above is—

    (*a*)   in the case of the secretary or clerk of a body corporate, that of the registered or principal office of that body or (if the body corporate is the registered keeper of the vehicle concerned) the registered address, and

    (*b*)   in any other case, his last known address at the time of service.

(10) In this section—

        'registered address', in relation to the registered keeper of a vehicle, means the address recorded in the record kept under the Vehicles Excise and Registration Act 1994 with respect to that vehicle as being that person's address, and
        'registered keeper', in relation to a vehicle, means the person in whose name the vehicle is registered under that Act;

and references to the driver of a vehicle include references to the rider of a cycle.

(11) Where, in Scotland, an offence under this section is committed by a partnership or by an unincorporated association other than a partnership and is proved to have been committed with the consent or connivance or in consequence of the negligence of a partner in the partnership or, as the case may be, a person concerned in the management or control of the association, he (as well as the partnership or association) shall be guilty of the offence.

Prosecution and punishment of offences

Table 5.1 Part I: Offences under the Traffic Acts

(1) Provision creating offence	(2) General nature of offence	(3) Mode of prosecution	(4) Punishment	(5) Disqualification	(6) Endorsement	(7) Penalty points
Offences under the Road Traffic Regulation Act 1984						
RTRA 115(1)	Mishandling or faking parking documents	(a) Summarily (b) On indictment	(a) The statutory maximum (b) 2 years			
Offences under the Road Traffic Act 1988						
RTA s.1	Causing death by dangerous driving	On indictment	14 years	Obligatory	Obligatory	3–11
RTA s.2	Dangerous driving	(a) Summarily (b) On indictment	(a) 6 months or the statutory maximum or both (b) 2 years or a fine or both	Obligatory	Obligatory	3–11
RTA s.3	Careless, and inconsiderate, driving	Summarily	Level 4 on the standard scale	Discretionary	Obligatory	3–9
RTA s.3A	Causing death by careless driving when under influence of drink or drugs	On indictment	14 years or a fine or both	Obligatory	Obligatory	3–11
RTA s.4(1)	Driving or attempting to drive when unfit to drive through drink or drugs	Summarily	6 months or level 5 on the standard scale or both	Obligatory	Obligatory	3–11
RTA s.4(2)	Being in charge of a mechanically propelled vehicle when unfit to drive through drink or drugs	Summarily	3 months or level 4 on the standard scale or both	Discretionary	Obligatory	10
RTA s.5(1)(a)	Driving or attempting to drive with excess alcohol in breath, blood or urine	Summarily	6 months or level 5 on the standard scale or both	Obligatory	Obligatory	3–11
RTA s.5(1)(b)	Being in charge of a motor vehicle with excess alcohol in breath, blood or urine	Summarily	3 months or level 4 on the standard scale or both	Discretionary	Obligatory	10

(1) Provision creating offence	(2) General nature of offence	(3) Mode of prosecution	(4) Punishment	(5) Disqualification	(6) Endorsement	(7) Penalty points
RTA s.6	Failing to provide a specimen of breath for a breath test	Summarily	Level 3 on the standard scale	Discretionary	Obligatory	4
RTA s.7	Failing to provide specimen for analysis or laboratory test	Summarily	(a) Where the specimen was required to ascertain ability to drive or proportion of alcohol at the time offender was driving or attempting to drive, 6 months or level 5 on the standard scale or both	(a) Obligatory in case mentioned in column 4(a)	Obligatory	(a) 3–11 in case mentioned in column 4(a)
			(b) In any other case, 3 months or level 4 on the standard scale or both	(b) Discretionary in any other case		(b) 10 in any other case
RTA s.22A	Causing danger to road-users	(a) Summarily (b) On indictment	(a) 6 months or the statutory maximum or both (b) 7 years or a fine or both			
RTA s.172	Failure of person keeping vehicle and others to give police information as to identity of driver, etc., in the case of certain offences	Summarily	Level 3 on the standard scale	Discretionary, if committed otherwise than by virtue of subsection (5) or (11)	Obligatory, if committed otherwise than by virtue of subsection (5) or (11)	
RTA s.173	Forgery etc., of licences, counterparts of Community licences, test certificates, certificates of insurance and other documents and things	(a) Summarily (b) On indictment	(a) The statutory maximum (b) 2 years			

OTHER CRIMINAL OFFENCES

Children and Young Persons Act 1933

The following sections of the Act should be noted:

1 Cruelty to persons under sixteen [6 months/10 years]

(1) If any person who has attained the age of sixteen years and has responsibility for any child or young person under that age, wilfully assaults, ill-treats, neglects, abandons, or exposes him, or causes or procures him to be assaulted, ill-treated, neglected, abandoned, or exposed, in a manner likely to cause him unnecessary suffering or injury to health (including injury to or loss of sight, or hearing, or limb, or organ of the body, and any mental derangement) that person shall be guilty of an offence. [. . .]

(2) For the purposes of this section—

    (*a*) a parent or other person legally liable to maintain a child or young person, or the legal guardian of a child or young person, shall be deemed to have neglected him in a manner likely to cause injury to his health if he has failed to provide adequate food, clothing, medical aid or lodging for him, or if, having been unable otherwise to provide such food, clothing, medical aid or lodging, he has failed to take steps to procure it to be provided under the enactments applicable in that behalf;

    (*b*) where it is proved that the death of an infant under three years of age was caused by suffocation (not being suffocation caused by disease or the presence of any foreign body in the throat or air passages of the infant) while the infant was in bed with some other person who has attained the age of sixteen years, that other person shall, if he was, when he went to bed, under the influence of drink, be deemed to have neglected the infant in a manner likely to cause injury to its health.

(3) A person may be convicted of an offence under this section—

    (*a*) notwithstanding that actual suffering or injury to health, or the likelihood of actual suffering or injury to health, was obviated by the action of another person;

    (*b*) notwithstanding the death of the child or young person in question.

Criminal Attempts Act 1981

The following sections of the Act should be noted:

9 Interference with vehicles [3 months]

(1) A person is guilty of the offence of vehicle interference if he interferes with a motor vehicle or trailer or with anything carried in or on a motor vehicle or trailer with the intention that an offence specified in subsection (2) below shall be committed by himself or some other person.

(2) The offences mentioned in subsection (1) above are—

    (*a*) theft of the motor vehicle or trailer or part of it;

    (*b*) theft of anything carried in or on the motor vehicle or trailer; and (*c*)   an offence under section 12(1) of the Theft Act 1968 (taking and driving away without consent);

and, if it is shown that a person accused of an offence under this section intended that one of those offences should be committed, it is immaterial that it cannot be shown which it was.

Criminal Damage Act 1971

The following sections of the Act should be noted:

1   Destroying or damaging property

(1) A person who without lawful excuse destroys or damages any property belonging to another intending to destroy or damage any such property or being reckless as to whether any such property would be destroyed or damaged shall be guilty of an offence.

(2) A person who without lawful excuse destroys or damages any property, whether belonging to himself or another—

(*a*)   intending to destroy or damage any property or being reckless as to whether any property would be destroyed or damaged; and

(*b*)   intending by the destruction or damage to endanger the life of another or being reckless as to whether the life of another would be thereby endangered;

shall be guilty of an offence.

(3) An offence committed under this section by destroying or damaging property by fire shall be charged as arson.

2   Threats to destroy or damage property

A person who without lawful excuse makes to another a threat, intending that that other would fear it would be carried out—

(*a*)   to destroy or damage any property belonging to that other or a third person; or

(*b*)   to destroy or damage his own property in a way which he knows is likely to endanger the life of that other or a third person.

3   Possessing anything with intent to destroy or damage property

A person who has anything in his custody or under his control intending without lawful excuse to use it or cause or permit another to use it—

(*a*)   to destroy or damage any property belonging to some other person; or

(*b*)   to destroy or damage his own or the user's property in a way which he knows is likely to endanger the life of some other person.

4   Punishment of offences

(1) A person guilty of arson under section 1 above or of an offence under section 1(2) above (whether arson or not) shall on conviction on indictment be liable to imprisonment for life.

(2) A person guilty of any other offence under this Act shall on conviction on indictment be liable to imprisonment for a term not exceeding ten years.

5 'Without lawful excuse'

(1) This section applies to any offence under section 1(1) above and any offence under section 2 or 3 above other than one involving a threat by the person charged to destroy or damage property in a way which he knows is likely to endanger the life of another or involving an intent by the person charged to use or cause or permit the use of something in his custody or under his control so to destroy or damage property.

(2) A person charged with an offence to which this section applies shall, whether or not he would be treated for the purposes of this Act as having a lawful excuse apart from this subsection, be treated for those purposes as having a lawful excuse—

    (*a*) if at the time of the act or acts alleged to constitute the offence he believed that the person or persons whom he believed to be entitled to consent to the destruction of or damage to the property in question had so consented, or would have so consented to it if he or they had known of the destruction or damage and its circumstances; or

    (*b*) if he destroyed or damaged or threatened to destroy or damage the property in question or, in the case of a charge of an offence under section 3 above, intended to use or cause or permit the use of something to destroy or damage it, in order to protect property belonging to himself or another or a right or interest in property which was or which he believed to be vested in himself or another, and at the time of the act or acts alleged to constitute the offence he believed—

        (i) that the property, right or interest was in immediate need of protection; and

        (ii) that the means of protection adopted or proposed to be adopted were or would be reasonable having regard to all the circumstances.

(3) For the purposes of this section it is immaterial whether a belief is justified or not if it is honestly held.

[. . .]

10 Interpretation

[. . .]

(2) Property shall be treated for the purposes of this Act as belonging to any person—

    (*a*) having the custody or control of it;

    (*b*) having in it any proprietary right or interest (not being an equitable interest arising only from an agreement to transfer or grant an interest); or

    (*c*) having a charge on it.

Criminal Justice Act 1988

The following sections of the Act should be noted:

39 Common assault and battery to be summary offences

Common assault and battery shall be summary offences and a person guilty of either of them shall be liable to a fine not exceeding level 5 on the standard scale, to imprisonment for a term not exceeding six months, or to both.

[. . .]

139 Offence of having article with blade or point in public place [6 months/2 years]

(1) Subject to subsections (4) and (5) below, any person who has an article to which this section applies with him in a public place shall be guilty of an offence.

(2) Subject to subsection (3) below, this section applies to any article which has a blade or is sharply pointed except a folding pocketknife.

(3) This section applies to a folding pocketknife if the cutting edge of its blade exceeds 3 inches.

(4) It shall be a defence for a person charged with an offence under this section to prove that he had good reason or lawful authority for having the article with him in a public place.

(5) Without prejudice to the generality of subsection (4) above, it shall be a defence for a person charged with an offence under this section to prove that he had the article with him—

    (a)   for use at work;
    (b)   for religious reasons; or
    (c)   as part of any national costume.

[. . .]

(7) In this section 'public place' includes any place to which at the material time the public have or are permitted access, whether on payment or otherwise.

139A Offence of having article with blade or point (or offensive weapon) on school premises [6 months/2 years or 4 years for offence under subsection (2)]

(1) Any person who has an article to which section 139 of this Act applies with him on school premises shall be guilty of an offence.

(2) Any person who has an offensive weapon within the meaning of section 1 of the Prevention of Crime Act 1953 with him on school premises shall be guilty of an offence.

(3) It shall be a defence for a person charged with an offence under subsection (1) or (2) above to prove that he had good reason or lawful authority for having the article or weapon with him on the premises in question.

(4) Without prejudice to the generality of subsection (3) above, it shall be a defence for a person charged with an offence under subsection (1) or (2) above to prove that he had the article or weapon in question with him—

    (a)   for use at work,
    (b)   for educational purposes,

(*c*) for religious reasons, or

(*d*) as part of any national costume.

[. . .]

141   Offensive weapons [6 months]

(1) Any person who manufactures, sells or hires or offers for sale or hire, exposes or has in his possession for the purpose of sale or hire, or lends or gives to any other person, a weapon to which this section applies shall be guilty of an offence.

[. . .]

160   Summary offence of possession of indecent photograph of child [6 months]

(1) Subject to subsection (1A), it is an offence for a person to have any indecent photograph or pseudo-photograph of a child in his possession.

(1A) [. . .]

(2) Where a person is charged with an offence under subsection (1) above, it shall be a defence for him to prove—

(*a*) that he had a legitimate reason for having the photograph or pseudo-photograph in his possession; or

(*b*) that he had not himself seen the photograph or pseudo-photograph and did not know, nor had any cause to suspect, it to be indecent; or

(*c*) that the photograph or pseudo-photograph was sent to him without any prior request made by him or on his behalf and that he did not keep it for an unreasonable time.

(2A) A person shall be liable on conviction on indictment of an offence under this section to imprisonment for a term not exceeding five years or a fine, or both.

(3) A person shall be liable on summary conviction of an offence under this section to imprisonment for a term not exceeding six months or a fine not exceeding level 5 on the standard scale, or both.

(4) Sections 1(3), 2(3), 3 and 7 of the Protection of Children Act 1978 shall have effect as if any reference in them to that Act included a reference to this section.

Criminal Law Act 1977

The following sections of the Act should be noted:

6   Violence for securing entry [6 months]

(1) Subject to the following provisions of this section, any person who, without lawful authority, uses or threatens violence for the purpose of securing entry into any premises for himself or for any other person is guilty of an offence, provided that—

(*a*) there is someone present on those premises at the time who is opposed to the entry which the violence is intended to secure; and

(*b*) the person using or threatening the violence knows that that is the case.

[. . .]

(4) It is immaterial for the purposes of this section—

(*a*)   whether the violence in question is directed against the person or against property; and

(*b*)   whether the entry which the violence is intended to secure is for the purpose of acquiring possession of the premises in question or for any other purpose.

[. . .]

51   Bomb hoaxes [6 months/7 years]

(1) A person who—

(*a*)   places any article in any place whatever; or

(*b*)   dispatches any article by post, rail or any other means whatever of sending things from one place to another,

with the intention (in either case) of inducing in some other person a belief that it is likely to explode or ignite and thereby cause personal injury or damage to property is guilty of an offence.

In this subsection 'article' includes substance.

(2) A person who communicates any information which he knows or believes to be false to another person with the intention of inducing in him or any other person a false belief that a bomb or other thing liable to explode or ignite is present in any place or location whatever is guilty of an offence.

(3) For a person to be guilty of an offence under subsection (1) or (2) above it is not necessary for him to have any particular person in mind as the person in whom he intends to induce the belief mentioned in that subsection.

Customs and Excise Management Act 1979

The following sections of the Act should be noted:

170   Penalty for fraudulent evasion of duty, etc.

(1) Without prejudice to any other provision of the Customs and Excise Acts 1979, if any person—

(*a*)   knowingly acquires possession of any of the following goods, that is to say—

(i)   goods which have been unlawfully removed from a warehouse or Queen's warehouse;

(ii)   goods which are chargeable with a duty which has not been paid;

(iii)   goods with respect to the importation or exportation of which any prohibition or restriction is for the time being in force under or by virtue of any enactment; or

(*b*)   is in any way knowingly concerned in carrying, removing, depositing, harbouring, keeping or concealing or in any manner dealing with any such goods,

and does so with intent to defraud Her Majesty of any duty payable on the goods or to evade any such prohibition or restriction with respect to the goods he shall be guilty of an offence under this section and may be arrested.

(2) Without prejudice to any other provision of the Customs and Excise Acts 1979, if any person is, in relation to any goods, in any way knowingly concerned in any fraudulent evasion or attempt at evasion—

(a) of any duty chargeable on the goods;

(b) of any prohibition or restriction for the time being in force with respect to the goods under or by virtue of any enactment; or

(c) of any provision of the Customs and Excise Acts 1979 applicable to the goods,

he shall be guilty of an offence under this section and may be arrested.

(3) Subject to subsection (4), (4A) or (4B) below, a person guilty of an offence under this section shall be liable—

(a) on summary conviction, to a penalty of the prescribed sum or of three times the value of the goods, whichever is the greater, or to imprisonment for a term not exceeding 6 months, or to both; or

(b) on conviction on indictment, to a penalty of any amount, or to imprisonment for a term not exceeding 7 years, or to both.

(4) In the case of an offence under this section in connection with a prohibition or restriction on importation or exportation having effect by virtue of section 3 of the Misuse of Drugs Act 1971, subsection (3) above shall have effect subject to the modifications specified in Schedule 1 to this Act.

(4A) In the case of—

(a) an offence under subsection (2) or (3) above committed in Great Britain in connection with a prohibition or restriction on the importation or exportation of any weapon or ammunition that is of a kind mentioned in section 5(1)(a), (ab), (aba), (ac), (ad), (ae), (af) or (c) or (1A)(a) of the Firearms Act 1968,

(b) any such offence committed in Northern Ireland in connection with a prohibition or restriction on the importation or exportation of any weapon or ammunition that is of a kind mentioned in Article 6(1)(a), (ab), (ac), (ad), (ae) or (c) or (1A)(a) of the Firearms (Northern Ireland) Order 1981, or

(c) any such offence committed in connection with the prohibitions contained in sections 20 and 21 of the Forgery and Counterfeiting Act 1981,

subsection (3)(b) above shall have effect as if for the words '7 years' there were substituted the words '10 years'.

(4B) In the case of an offence under subsection (1) or (2) above in connection with the prohibition contained in regulation 2 of the Import of Seal Skins Regulations 1996, subsection (3) above shall have effect as if—

(a) for paragraph (a) there were substituted the following—

'(a) on summary conviction, to a fine not exceeding the statutory maximum or to imprisonment for a term not exceeding three months, or to both'; and

(b) in paragraph (b) for the words '7 years' there were substituted the words '2 years'.

(5) In any case where a person would, apart from this subsection, be guilty of—

(a) an offence under this section in connection with a prohibition or restriction; and

(b) a corresponding offence under the enactment or other instrument imposing the prohibition or restriction, being an offence for which a fine or other penalty is expressly provided by that enactment or other instrument,

he shall not be guilty of the offence mentioned in paragraph (a) of this subsection.

(6) Where any person is guilty of an offence under this section, the goods in respect of which the offence was committed shall be liable to forfeiture.

170B   Offence of taking preparatory steps for evasion of excise duty

(1) If any person is knowingly concerned in the taking of any steps with a view to the fraudulent evasion, whether by himself or another, of any duty of excise on any goods, he shall be liable—

(a) on summary conviction, to a penalty of the prescribed sum or of three times the amount of the duty, whichever is the greater, or to imprisonment for a term not exceeding six months or to both; and

(b) on conviction on indictment, to a penalty of any amount or to imprisonment for a term not exceeding seven years or to both.

(2) Where any person is guilty of an offence under this section, the goods in respect of which the offence was committed shall be liable to forfeiture.

Dangerous Dogs Act 1991

The following sections of the Act should be noted:

1   Dogs bred for fighting

(1) This section applies to—

(a) any dog of the type known as the pit bull terrier;

(b) any dog of the type known as the Japanese tosa; and

(c) any dog of any type designated for the purposes of this section by an order of the Secretary of State, being a type appearing to him to be bred for fighting or to have the characteristics of a type bred for that purpose.

(2) No person shall—

(a) breed, or breed from, a dog to which this section applies;

(b) sell or exchange such a dog or offer, advertise or expose such a dog for sale or exchange;

(c) make or offer to make a gift of such a dog or advertise or expose such a dog as a gift;

(d) allow such a dog of which he is the owner or of which he is for the time being in charge to be in a public place without being muzzled and kept on a lead; or

(e) abandon such a dog of which he is the owner or, being the owner or for the time being in charge of such a dog, allow it to stray.

[. . .]

(7) Any person who contravenes this section is guilty of an offence and liable on summary conviction to imprisonment for a term not exceeding six months or a fine not exceeding level 5 on the standard scale or both except that a person who publishes an advertisement in contravention of subsection (2)(*b*) or (*c*)—

> (*a*) shall not on being convicted be liable to imprisonment if he shows that he published the advertisement to the order of someone else and did not himself devise it; and
>
> (*b*) shall not be convicted if, in addition, he shows that he did not know and had no reasonable cause to suspect that it related to a dog to which this section applies.

[. . .]

3 Keeping dogs under proper control

(1) If a dog is dangerously out of control in a public place—

> (*a*) the owner; and
>
> (*b*) if different, the person for the time being in charge of the dog,

is guilty of an offence, or, if the dog while so out of control injures any person, an aggravated offence, under this subsection.

(2) In proceedings for an offence under subsection (1) above against a person who is the owner of a dog but was not at the material time in charge of it, it shall be a defence for the accused to prove that the dog was at the material time in the charge of a person whom he reasonably believed to be a fit and proper person to be in charge of it.

(3) If the owner or, if different, the person for the time being in charge of a dog allows it to enter a place which is not a public place but where it is not permitted to be and while it is there—

> (*a*) it injures any person; or
>
> (*b*) there are grounds for reasonable apprehension that it will do so,

he is guilty of an offence, or, if the dog injures any person, an aggravated offence, under this subsection.

(4) A person guilty of an offence under subsection (1) or (3) above other than an aggravated offence is liable on summary conviction to imprisonment for a term not exceeding six months or a fine not exceeding level 5 on the standard scale or both; and a person guilty of an aggravated offence under either of those subsections is liable—

> (*a*) on summary conviction, to imprisonment for a term not exceeding six months or a fine not exceeding the statutory maximum or both;
>
> (*b*) on conviction on indictment, to imprisonment for a term not exceeding two years or a fine or both.

[. . .]

(6) If it appears to a court on a complaint under section 2 of the said Act of 1871 that the dog to which the complaint relates is a male and would be less dangerous if neutered the court may under that section make an order requiring it to be neutered.

(7) The reference in section 1(3) of the Dangerous Dogs Act 1989 (penalties) to failing to comply with an order under section 2 of the said Act of 1871 to keep a dog under proper control shall include a reference to failing to comply with any other order made under that section; but no order shall be made under that section by virtue of subsection (6) above where the matters complained of arose before the coming into force of that subsection.

4 Destruction and disqualification orders

(1) Where a person is convicted of an offence under section 1 or 3(1) or (3) above or of an offence under an order made under section 2 above the court—

   (*a*) may order the destruction of any dog in respect of which the offence was committed and, subject to subsection (1A) below, shall do so in the case of an offence under section 1 or an aggravated offence under section 3(1) or (3) above; and

   (*b*) may order the offender to be disqualified, for such period as the court thinks fit, for having custody of a dog.

(1A) Nothing in subsection (1)(*a*) above shall require the court to order the destruction of a dog if the court is satisfied—

   (*a*) that the dog would not constitute a danger to public safety; and

   (*b*) where the dog was born before 30 November 1991 and is subject to the prohibition in section 1(3) above, that there is a good reason why the dog has not been exempted from that prohibition.

Education Act 1996

The following sections of the Act should be noted:

443   Offence: failure to comply with school attendance order

(1) If a parent on whom a school attendance order is served fails to comply with the requirements of the order, he is guilty of an offence, unless he proves that he is causing the child to receive suitable education otherwise than at school.

(2) If, in proceedings for an offence under this section, the parent is acquitted, the court may direct that the school attendance order shall cease to be in force.

(3) A direction under subsection (2) does not affect the duty of the local education authority to take further action under section 437 if at any time the authority are of the opinion that, having regard to any change of circumstances, it is expedient to do so.

(4) A person guilty of an offence under this section is liable on summary conviction to a fine not exceeding level 3 on the standard scale.

444   Offence: failure to secure regular attendance at school of registered pupil

(1) If a child of compulsory school age who is a registered pupil at a school fails to attend regularly at the school, his parent is guilty of an offence.

(1A) If in the circumstances mentioned in subsection (1) the parent knows that his child is failing to attend regularly at the school and fails without reasonable justification to cause him to do so, he is guilty of an offence.

(2) Subsections (3) to (6) below apply in proceedings for an offence under this section in respect of a child who is not a boarder at the school at which he is a registered pupil.

(3) The child shall not be taken to have failed to attend regularly at the school by reason of his absence from the school—

(a)   with leave,

(b)   at any time when he was prevented from attending by reason of sickness or any unavoidable cause, or

(c)   on any day exclusively set apart for religious observance by the religious body to which his parent belongs.

(4) The child shall not be taken to have failed to attend regularly at the school if the parent proves—

(a)   that the school at which the child is a registered pupil is not within walking distance of the child's home, and

(b)   that no suitable arrangements have been made by the local education authority for any of the following—

(i)   his transport to and from the school,

(ii)   boarding accommodation for him at or near the school, or

(iii)   enabling him to become a registered pupil at a school nearer to his home.

(5) In subsection (4) 'walking distance'—

(a)   in relation to a child who is under the age of eight, means 3.218688 kilometres (two miles), and

(b)   in relation to a child who has attained the age of eight, means 4.828032 kilometres (three miles),

in each case measured by the nearest available route.

(6) If it is proved that the child has no fixed abode, subsection (4) shall not apply, but the parent shall be acquitted if he proves—

(a)   that he is engaged in a trade or business of such a nature as to require him to travel from place to place,

(b)   that the child has attended at a school as a registered pupil as regularly as the nature of that trade or business permits, and

(c)   if the child has attained the age of six, that he has made at least 200 attendances during the period of 12 months ending with the date on which the proceedings were instituted.

(7) In proceedings for an offence under this section in respect of a child who is a boarder at the school at which he is a pupil, the child shall be taken to have failed to attend regularly at the school if he is absent from it without leave during any part of the school term at a time when he was not prevented from being present by reason of sickness or any unavoidable cause.

(8) A person guilty of an offence under this section is liable on summary conviction to a fine not exceeding level 3 on the standard scale.

(8A) A person guilty of an offence under subsection (1A) is liable on summary conviction—

(a)   to a fine not exceeding level 4 on the standard scale, or

(b)   to imprisonment for a term not exceeding three months,

or both.

Firearms Act 1968

The following sections of the Act should be noted:

1 Requirement of firearm certificate

(1) Subject to any exemption under this Act, it is an offence for a person—

- (*a*) to have in his possession, or to purchase or acquire a firearm to which this section applies without holding a firearm certificate in force at the time, or otherwise than as authorised by such a certificate;
- (*b*) to have in his possession, or to purchase or acquire, any ammunition to which this section applies without holding a firearm certificate in force at the time, or otherwise than as authorised by such a certificate, or in quantities in excess of those so authorised.

(2) It is an offence for a person to fail to comply with a condition subject to which a firearm certificate is held by him.

(3) This section applies to every firearm except—

- (*a*) a shot gun within the meaning of this Act, that is to say a smooth-bore gun (not being an air gun) which—

  - (i) has a barrel not less than 24 inches in length and does not have any barrel with a bore exceeding 2 inches in diameter;
  - (ii) either has no magazine or has a non-detachable magazine incapable of holding more than two cartridges; and
  - (iii) is not a revolver gun; and

- (*b*) an air weapon (that is to say, an air rifle, air gun or air pistol not of a type declared by rules made by the Secretary of State under section 53 of this Act to be specially dangerous).

(3A) A gun which has been adapted to have such a magazine as is mentioned in subsection (3)(*a*)(ii) above shall not be regarded as falling within that provision unless the magazine bears a mark approved by the Secretary of State for denoting that fact and that mark has been made, and the adaptation has been certified in writing as having been carried out in a manner approved by him, either by one of the two companies mentioned in section 58(1) of this Act or by such other person as may be approved by him for that purpose.

(4) This section applies to any ammunition for a firearm, except the following articles, namely:

- (*a*) cartridges containing five or more shot, none of which exceeds .36 inch in diameter;
- (*b*) ammunition for an air gun, air rifle or air pistol; and
- (*c*) blank cartridges not more than one inch in diameter measured immediately in front of the rim or cannelure of the base of the cartridge.

[See Schedule 6 for sentencing.]

2 Requirement of certificate for possession of shot guns

(1) Subject to any exemption under this Act, it is an offence for a person to have in his possession, or to purchase or acquire, a shot gun without holding a certificate under this Act authorising him to possess shot guns.

(2) It is an offence for a person to fail to comply with a condition subject to which a shot gun certificate is held by him.

[See Schedule 6 for sentencing.]

[. . .]

4 Conversion of weapons

(1) Subject to this section, it is an offence to shorten the barrel of a shot gun to a length less than 24 inches.

(2) It is not an offence under subsection (1) above for a registered firearms dealer to shorten the barrel of a shot gun for the sole purpose of replacing a defective part of the barrel so as to produce a barrel not less than 24 inches in length.

(3) It is an offence for a person other than a registered firearms dealer to convert into a firearm anything which, though having the appearance of being a firearm, is so constructed as to be incapable of discharging any missile through its barrel.

(4) A person who commits an offence under section 1 of this Act by having in his possession, or purchasing or acquiring, a shot gun which has been shortened contrary to subsection (1) above or a firearm which has been converted as mentioned in subsection (3) above (whether by a registered firearms dealer or not), without holding a firearm certificate authorising him to have it in his possession, or to purchase or acquire it, shall be treated for the purposes of provisions of this Act relating to the punishment of offences as committing that offence in an aggravated form.

[See Schedule 6 for sentencing.]

5 Weapons subject to general prohibition

(1) A person commits an offence if, without the authority of the Defence Council, he has in his possession, or purchases or acquires, or manufactures, sells or transfers—

- (*a*) any firearm which is so designed or adapted that two or more missiles can be successively discharged without repeated pressure on the trigger;
- (*ab*) any self-loading or pump-action rifled gun other than one which is chambered for .22 rim-fire cartridges;
- (*aba*) any firearm which either has a barrel less than 30 centimetres in length or is less than 60 centimetres in length overall, other than an air weapon, a muzzle-loading gun or a firearm as signalling apparatus;
- (*ac*) any self-loading or pump-action smooth-bore gun which is not an air weapon or chambered for .22 rim-fire cartridges and either has a barrel less than 24 inches in length or an air weapon or is less than 40 inches in length overall;
- (*ad*) any smooth-bore revolver gun other than one which is chambered for 9 mm rim-fire cartridges or a muzzle-loading gun;
- (*ae*) any rocket launcher, or any mortar, for projecting a stabilised missile, other than a launcher or mortar designed for line-throwing or pyrotechnic purposes or as signalling apparatus;
- (*b*) any weapon of whatever description designed or adapted for the discharge of any noxious liquid, gas or other thing; and
- (*c*) any cartridge with a bullet designed to explode on or immediately before impact, any ammunition containing or designed or adapted to contain

261

any such noxious thing as is mentioned in paragraph (*b*) above and, if capable of being used with a firearm of any description, any grenade, bomb (or other like missile), or rocket or shell designed to explode as aforesaid.

(1A) Subject to section 5A of this Act, a person commits an offence if, without the authority of the Secretary of State, he has in his possession, or purchases or acquires, or sells or transfers—

(*a*)   any firearm which is disguised as another object;

(*b*)   any rocket or ammunition not falling within paragraph (*c*) of subsection (1) of this section which consists in or incorporates a missile designed to explode on or immediately before impact and is for military use;

(*c*)   any launcher or other projecting apparatus not falling within paragraph (*ae*) of that subsection which is designed to be used with any rocket or ammunition falling within paragraph (*b*) above or with ammunition which would fall within that paragraph but for its being ammunition falling within paragraph (*c*) of that subsection;

(*d*)   any ammunition for military use which consists in or incorporates a missile designed so that a substance contained in the missile will ignite on or immediately before impact;

(*e*)   any ammunition for military use which consists in or incorporates a missile designed, on account of its having a jacket and hard-core, to penetrate armour plating, armour screening or body armour;

(*f*)   any ammunition which incorporates a missile designed or adapted to expand on impact;

(*g*)   anything which is designed to be projected as a missile from any weapon and is designed to be, or has been, incorporated in—

(i)   any ammunition falling within any of the preceding paragraphs; or

(ii)   any ammunition which would fall within any of those paragraphs but for its being specified in subsection (1) of this section.

(2) The weapons and ammunition specified in subsections (1) and (1A) of this section (including, in the case of ammunition, any missiles falling within subsection (1A)(*g*) of this section) are referred to in this Act as 'prohibited weapons' and 'prohibited ammunition' respectively.

[See Schedule 6 for sentencing.]

[. . .]

16   Possession of firearm with intent to injure

It is an offence for a person to have in his possession any firearm or ammunition with intent by means thereof to endanger life, or to enable another person by means thereof to endanger life, whether any injury has been caused or not.

[See Schedule 6 for sentencing.]

16A   Possession of firearm with intent to cause fear of violence

It is an offence for a person to have in his possession any firearm or imitation firearm with intent—

(*a*)   by means thereof to cause, or

(*b*)   to enable another person by means thereof to cause,

any person to believe that unlawful violence will be used against him or another person.

[See Schedule 6 for sentencing.]

17   Use of firearm to resist arrest

(1) It is an offence for a person to make or attempt to make any use whatsoever of a firearm or imitation firearm with intent to resist or prevent the lawful arrest or detention of himself or another person.

(2) If a person, at the time of his committing or being arrested for an offence specified in Schedule 1 to this Act, has in his possession a firearm or imitation firearm, he shall be guilty of an offence under this subsection unless he shows that he had it in his possession for a lawful object.

[. . .]

(4) For the purposes of this section, the definition of 'firearm' in section 57(1) of this Act shall apply without paragraphs (b) and (c) of that subsection, and 'imitation firearm' shall be construed accordingly.

[See Schedule 6 for sentencing.]

18   Carrying firearms with criminal intent

(1) It is an offence for a person to have with him a firearm or imitation firearm with intent to commit an indictable offence, or to resist arrest or prevent the arrest of another, in either case while he has the firearm or imitation firearm with him.

(2) In proceedings for an offence under this section proof that the accused had a firearm or imitation firearm with him and intended to commit an offence, or to resist or prevent arrest, is evidence that he intended to have with him while doing so.

[See Schedule 6 for sentencing.]

19   Carrying firearm in a public place

A person commits an offence if, without lawful authority or reasonable excuse (the proof whereof lies on him) he has with him in a public place a loaded shot gun or loaded air weapon, or any other firearm (whether loaded or not) together with ammunition suitable for use in that firearm.

[See Schedule 6 for sentencing.]

20   Trespassing with firearm

(1) A person commits an offence if, while he has a firearm or imitation firearm with him, he enters or is in any building or part of a building as a trespasser and without reasonable excuse (the proof whereof lies on him).

(2) A person commits an offence if, while he has a firearm or imitation firearm with him, he enters or is on any land as a trespasser and without reasonable excuse (the proof whereof lies on him).

(3) In subsection (2) of this section the expression 'land' includes land covered with water.

[See Schedule 6 for sentencing.]

21 Possession of firearms by persons previously convicted of crime

(1) A person who has been sentenced to custody for life or to preventative detention, or to imprisonment or to corrective training for a term of three years or more or to youth custody or detention in a young offender institution for such a term, or who has been sentenced to be detained for such a term in a young offenders institution in Scotland, shall not at any time have a firearm or ammunition in his possession.

(2) A person who has been sentenced to imprisonment for a term of three months or more but less than three years or to youth custody or detention in a young offender institution for such a term, or who has been sentenced to be detained for such a term in a detention centre or in a young offenders institution in Scotland or who has been subject to a secure training order or a detention and training order, shall not at any time before the expiration of the period of five years from the date of his release have a firearm or ammunition in his possession.

(2A) For the purposes of subsection (2) above, 'the date of his release' means—

    (*a*) in the case of a person sentenced to imprisonment with an order under section 47(1) of the Criminal Law Act 1977 (prison sentence partly served and partly suspended), the date on which he completes service of so much of the sentence as was by that order required to be served in prison;

    (*b*) in the case of a person who has been subject to a secure training order—

        (i) the date on which he is released from detention under the order;

        (ii) the date on which he is released from detention ordered under section 4 of the Criminal Justice and Public Order Act 1994; or

        (iii) the date halfway through the total period specified by the court in making the order,

      whichever is the later;

    (*c*) in the case of a person who has been subject to a detention and training order—

        (i) the date on which he is released from detention under the order;

        (ii) the date on which he is released from detention ordered under section 104 of the Powers of Criminal Courts (Sentencing) Act 2000; or

        (iii) the date of the halfway point of the term of the order,

      whichever is the later.

(3) A person who—

    (*a*) is the holder of a licence issued under section 53 of the Children and Young Persons Act 1933, or section 57 of the Children and Young Persons (Scotland) Act 1937 (which sections provide for the detention of children and young persons convicted of serious crime, but enable them to be discharged on licence by the Secretary of State); or

    (*b*) is subject to a recognisance to keep the peace or to be of good behaviour, a condition of which is that he shall not possess, use or carry a firearm, or is subject to a probation order containing a requirement that he shall not possess, use or carry a firearm; or

    [. . .]

shall not, at any time during which he holds the licence or is so subject or has been so ordained, have a firearm or ammunition in his possession.

(4) It is an offence for a person to contravene any of the foregoing provisions of this section.

(5) It is an offence for a person to sell or transfer a firearm or ammunition to, or to repair, test or prove a firearm or ammunition for, a person whom he knows or has reasonable ground for believing to be prohibited by this section from having a firearm or ammunition in his possession.

(6) A person prohibited under subsection (1), (2), (3) or (3A) of this section from having in his possession a firearm or ammunition may apply to the Crown Court or, in Scotland, in accordance with Act of Sederunt to the sheriff for a removal of the prohibition; and if the application is granted that prohibition shall not then apply to him.

[See Schedule 6 for sentencing.]

SCHEDULE 6

Section of this Act creating offence	General nature of offence	Mode of prosecution	Punishment	Additional provisions
s.1(1)	Possessing etc. firearm or ammunition without firearm certificate	(a) Summary (b) On indictment	6 months or a fine of £400; or both (i) Where the offence is committed in an aggravated form within the meaning of s.4(4) of this Act, 7 years, or a fine; or both (ii) In any other case, 5 years or a fine; or both	Paragraph 1 of Part II of this Schedule applies
s.1(2)	Non-compliance with condition of firearm certificate	Summary	6 months or a fine of level 5 on the standard scale; or both	Paragraph 1 of Part II of this Schedule applies
s.2(1)	Possessing, etc., shot gun without shot gun certificate	(a) Summary (b) On indictment	6 months or the statutory maximum or both 5 years or a fine; or both	Paragraph 1 of Part II of this Schedule applies
s.2(2)	Non-compliance with condition of shot gun certificate	Summary	6 months or a fine of level 5 on the standard scale; or both	Paragraph 1 of Part II of this Schedule applies

Section of this Act creating offence	General nature of offence	Mode of prosecution	Punishment	Additional provisions
s.3(1)	Trading in firearms without being registered as firearms dealer	(a) Summary (b) On indictment	6 months or a fine of £400; or both 5 years or a fine; or both	
s.3(2)	Selling firearms to person without a certificate	(a) Summary (b) On indictment	6 months or a fine of £400; or both 5 years or a fine; or both	
s.3(3)	Repairing, testing etc. firearm for person without a certificate	(a) Summary (b) On indictment	6 months or a fine of £400; or both 5 years or a fine; or both	
s.3(5)	Falsifying certificate, etc., with view to acquisition of firearm	(a) Summary (b) On indictment	6 months or a fine of £400; or both 5 years or a fine; or both	
s.3(6)	Pawnbroker taking firearm in pawn	Summary	3 months or a fine of level 3 on the standard scale; or both	
s.4(1)(3)	Shortening a shot gun; conversion of firearms	(a) Summary (b) On indictment	6 months or a fine of £400; or both 7 years or a fine; or both	
s.5(1)(a), (ab), (aba), (ac), (ad), (ae), (af) or (c)	Possessing or distributing prohibited weapons or ammunition.	On indictment	10 years or a fine, or both	
s.5(1)(b)	Possessing or distributing prohibited weapon designed for discharge of noxious liquid etc.	(a) Summary (b) On indictment	6 months or a fine of the statutory maximum, or both 10 years or a fine or both	
s.5(1A)(a)	Possessing or distributing firearm disguised as other object.	On indictment	10 years or a fine, or both	
s.5(1A)(b) (c), (d), (e), (f) or (g)	Possessing or distributing other prohibited weapons.	(a) Summary (b) On indictment	6 months or a fine of the statutory maximum, or both 10 years or a fine, or both	
s.5(5)	Non-compliance with condition of Secretary of State authority	Summary	6 months or a fine of level 5 on the standard scale; or both	
s.5(6)	Non-compliance with requirements to surrender authority to possess, etc., prohibited weapon or ammunition	Summary	A fine of level 3 on the standard scale	

Section of this Act creating offence	General nature of offence	Mode of prosecution	Punishment	Additional provisions
s.6(3)	Contravention of order under s.6 (or corresponding Northern Irish order) restricting removal of arms	Summary	3 months or, for each firearm or parcel of ammunition in respect of which the offence is committed, a fine of level 3 on the standard scale or both	Paragraph 2 of Part II of this Schedule applies
s.7(2)	Making false statement in order to obtain police permit	Summary	6 months or a fine of level 5 on the standard scale; or both	
s.9(3)	Making false statement in order to obtain permit for auction of firearms, etc.	(a) Summary	6 months or a fine not exceeding level 5 on the standard scale; or both	
		(b) On indictment	3 years or a fine; or both	
s.13(2)	Making false statement in order to obtain permit for removal of signalling apparatus	Summary	6 months or a fine of level 5 on the standard scale; or both	
s.16	Possession of firearm with intent to endanger life or injure property	On indictment	Life imprisonment or a fine; or, both	
s.16A	Possession of firearm with intent to cause fear of violence	On indictment	10 years or a fine; or both	
s.17(1)	Use of firearms to resist arrest	On indictment	Life imprisonment or a fine; or both	Paragraphs 3 to 5 of Part II of this Schedule apply
s.17(2)	Possessing firearms while committing an offence specified in Schedule I or, in Scotland, an offence specified in Schedule 2	On indictment	Life imprisonment or a fine; or both	Paragraphs 3 and 6 of Part II of this Schedule apply
s.18(1)	Carrying firearms or imitation firearms with intent to commit indictable offence (or, in Scotland, an offence specified in Schedule 2) or to resist arrest	On indictment	Life imprisonment; or a fine; or both	
s.19	Carrying firearm or imitation firearm in public place	(a) Summary	6 months or a fine of £400; or both	
		(b) On indictment (but not in the case of an imitation firearm if the firearm is an air weapon)	7 years or a fine; or both	

267

Section of this Act creating offence	General nature of offence	Mode of prosecution	Punishment	Additional provisions
s.20(1)	Trespassing with firearm or imitation firearm in a building	(a) Summary (b) On indictment (but not in the case of an imitation firearm or if the firearm is an air weapon)	6 months or a fine of £400; or both 5 years or a fine; or both	
s.20(2)	Trespassing with firearm or imitation firearm on land	Summary	3 months or a fine of level 4 on the standard scale; or both	
s.21(4)	Contravention of provisions denying firearms to ex-prisoners and the like	(a) Summary (b) On indictment	6 months or a fine of £400; or both 5 years or a fine; or both	
s.21(5)	Supplying firearms to person denied them under s.21	(a) Summary (b) On indictment	6 months or a fine of £400; or both 5 years or a fine; or both	
s.22(1)	Person under 17 acquiring firearm	Summary	6 months or a fine of level 5 on the standard scale; or both	
s.22(1A)	Person under 18 using certificated firearm for unauthorised purpose	Summary	3 months or a fine of level 5 on the standard scale; or both	
s.22(2)	Person under 14 having firearms in his possession without lawful authority	Summary	6 months or a fine of level 5 on the standard scale; or both	
s.22(3)	Person under 15 having with him a shot gun without adult supervision	Summary	A fine of level 3 on the standard scale	Paragraph 8 of Part II of this Schedule applies
s.22(4)	Person under 14 having with him an air weapon or ammunition therefor	Summary	A fine of level 3 on the standard scale	Paragraphs 7 and 8 of Part II of this Schedule apply
s.23(1)	Persons under 17 making improper use of air weapon when under supervision; person supervising him permitting such use	Summary	A fine of level 3 on the standard scale	Paragraphs 7 and 8 of Part II of this Schedule apply
s.23(4)	Person under 17 making improper use of air weapon on private premises	Summary	A fine of level 3 on the standard scale	Paragraphs 7 and 8 of Part II of this Schedule apply

Section of this Act creating offence	General nature of offence	Mode of prosecution	Punishment	Additional provisions
s.24(1)	Selling or letting on hire a firearm to person under 17	Summary	6 months or a fine of level 5 on the standard scale; or both	
s.24(2)	Supplying firearm or ammunition (being of a kind to which s.1 of this Act applies) to person under 14	Summary	6 months or a fine of level 5 on the standard scale; or both	
s.24(3)	Making gift of shot gun to person under 15	Summary	A fine of level 3 on the standard scale	Paragraph 9 of Part II of this Schedule applies
s.24(4)	Supplying air weapon to person under 17	Summary	A fine of level 3 on the standard scale	Paragraphs 7 and 8 of Part II of this Schedule apply
s.25	Supplying firearm to person drunk or insane	Summary	3 months or a fine of level 3 on the standard scale; or both	
s.28A(7)	Making false statement in order to procure grant or renewal of a firearm or shot gun certificate	Summary	6 months or a fine of level 5 on the standard scale; or both	
s.29(3)	Making false statement in order to procure variation of a firearm certificate	Summary	6 months or a fine of level 5 on the standard scale; or both	
s.30D(3)	Failing to surrender certificate on revocation	Summary	A fine of level 3 on the standard scale	
s.32B(5)	Failure to surrender expired European firearms pass	Summary	A fine of level 3 on the standard scale	
s.32C(6)	Failure to produce European firearms pass or Article 7 authority for variation or cancellation etc.; failure to notify loss or theft of firearm identified in pass or to produce pass for endorsement	Summary	3 months or a fine of level 5 on the standard scale; or both	
s.38(8)	Failure to surrender certificate of registration or register of transactions on removal of firearms dealer's name from register	Summary	A fine of level 3 on the standard scale	
s.39(1)	Making false statement in order to secure registration or entry in register of a place of business	Summary	6 months or a fine of level 5 on the standard scale; or both	

Section of this Act creating offence	General nature of offence	Mode of prosecution	Punishment	Additional provisions
s.39(2)	Registered firearms dealer having place of business not entered in the register	Summary	6 months or a fine of level 5 on the standard scale; or both	
s.39(3)	Non-compliance with condition of registration	Summary	6 months or a fine of level 5 on the standard scale; or both	
s.40(5)	Non-compliance by firearms dealer with provisions as to register of transactions; making false entry in register	Summary	6 months or a fine of level 5 on the standard scale; or both	
s.42A	Failure to report transaction authorised by visitor's shot gun permit	Summary	3 months or a fine of level 5 on the standard scale; or both	
s.46	Obstructing constable or civilian officer in exercise of search powers	Summary	6 months or a fine of level 5 on the standard scale; or both	
s.47(2)	Failure to hand over firearm or ammunition on demand by constable	Summary	3 months, or a fine of level 4 on the standard scale; or both	
s.48(3)	Failure to comply with requirement of a constable that a person shall declare his name and address	Summary	A fine of level 3 on the standard scale	
s.48(4)	Failure to produce firearms pass issued in another member State	Summary	A fine of level 3 on the standard scale	
s.49(3)	Failure to give constable facilities for examination of firearms in transit, or to produce papers	Summary	3 months or, for each firearm or parcel of ammunition in respect of which the offence is committed, a fine of level 3 on the standard scale; or both	Paragraph 2 of Part II of this Schedule applies
s.52 (2)(c)	Failure to surrender firearm or shot gun certificate cancelled by court on conviction	Summary	A fine of level 3 on the standard scale	

270

Football (Offences) Act 1991

The following sections of the Act should be noted:

2   Throwing of missiles [level 3 fine]

It is an offence for a person at a regulated football match to throw anything at or towards—

(*a*)   the playing area, or any area adjacent to the playing area to which spectators are not generally admitted, or

(*b*)   any area in which spectators or other persons are or may be present,

without lawful authority or lawful excuse (which shall be for him to prove).

3   Indecent or racialist chanting [level 3 fine]

(1) It is an offence to engage or take part in chanting of an indecent or racialist nature at a regulated football match.

(2) For this purpose—

(*a*)   'chanting' means the repeated uttering of any words or sounds (whether alone or in concert with one or more others); and

(*b*)   'of a racialist nature' means consisting of or including matter which is threatening, abusive or insulting to a person by reason of his colour, race, nationality (including citizenship) or ethnic or national origins.

4   Going onto the playing area [level 3 fine]

It is an offence for a person at a regulated football match to go onto the playing area, or any area adjacent to the playing area to which spectators are not generally admitted, without lawful authority or lawful excuse (which shall be for him to prove).

Forgery and Counterfeiting Act 1981

The following sections of the Act should be noted:

1   The offence of forgery

A person is guilty of forgery if he makes a false instrument, with the intention that he or another shall use it to induce somebody to accept it as genuine, and by reason of so accepting it to do or not to do some act to his own or any other person's prejudice.

2   The offence of copying a false instrument

It is an offence for a person to make a copy of an instrument which is, and which he knows or believes to be, a false instrument, with the intention that he or another shall use it to induce somebody to accept it as a copy of a genuine instrument, and by reason of so accepting it to do or not to do some act to his own or any other person's prejudice.

3   The offence of using a false instrument

It is an offence for a person to use an instrument which is, and which he knows or believes to be, false, with the intention of inducing somebody to accept it as genuine, and by reason of so accepting it to do or not to do some act to his own or any other person's prejudice.

271

4   The offence of using a copy of a false instrument

It is an offence for a person to use a copy of an instrument which is, and which he knows or believes to be, a false instrument, with the intention of inducing somebody to accept it as a copy of a genuine instrument, and by reason of so accepting it to do or not to do some act to his own or any other person's prejudice.

5   Offences relating to money orders, share certificates, passports, etc.

(1) It is an offence for a person to have in his custody or under his control an instrument to which this section applies which is, and which he knows or believes to be, false, with the intention that he or another shall use it to induce somebody to accept it as genuine, and by reason of so accepting it to do or not to do some act to his own or any other person's prejudice.

(2) It is an offence for a person to have in his custody or under his control, without lawful authority or excuse, an instrument to which this section applies which is, and which he knows or believes to be, false.

(3) It is an offence for a person to make or to have in his custody or under his control a machine or implement, or paper or any other material, which to his knowledge is or has been specially designed or adapted for the making of an instrument to which this section applies, with the intention that he or another shall make an instrument to which this section applies which is false and that he or another shall use the instrument to induce somebody to accept it as genuine, and by reason of so accepting it to do or not to do some act to his own or any other person's prejudice.

(4) It is an offence for a person to make or to have in his custody or under his control any such machine, implement, paper or material, without lawful authority or excuse.

(5) The instruments to which this section applies are—

- (a)   money orders;
- (b)   postal orders;
- (c)   United Kingdom postage stamps;
- (d)   Inland Revenue stamps;
- (e)   share certificates;
- (f)   passports and documents which can be used instead of passports;
- (g)   cheques;
- (h)   travellers' cheques;
- (j)   cheque cards;
- (k)   credit cards;
- (l)   credited copies relating to an entry in a register of births, adoptions, marriages or deaths and issued by the Registrar General, the Registrar General for Northern Ireland, a registration officer or a person lawfully authorised to register marriages; and
- (m)   certificates relating to entries in such registers.

(6) In subsection (5)(e) above 'share certificate' means an instrument entitling or evidencing the title of a person to a share or interest—

- (a)   in any public stock, annuity, fund or debt of any government or state, including a state which forms part of another state; or
- (b)   in any stock, fund or debt of a body (whether corporate or unincorporated) established in the United Kingdom or elsewhere.

6   Penalties for offences under Part I

(1) A person guilty of an offence under this Part of this Act shall be liable on summary conviction—

    (*a*)   to a fine not exceeding the statutory maximum; or

    (*b*)   to imprisonment for a term not exceeding six months; or

    (*c*)   to both.

(2) A person guilty of an offence to which this subsection applies shall be liable on conviction on indictment to imprisonment for a term not exceeding ten years.

(3) The offences to which subsection (2) above applies are offences under the following provisions of this Part of this Act—

    (*a*)   section 1;

    (*b*)   section 2;

    (*c*)   section 3;

    (*d*)   section 4;

    (*e*)   section 5(1); and

    (*f*)   section 5(3).

(4) A person guilty of an offence under section 5(2) or (4) above shall be liable on conviction on indictment to imprisonment for a term not exceeding two years.

[. . .]

14   Offences of counterfeiting notes and coins

(1) It is an offence for a person to make a counterfeit of a currency note or of a protected coin, intending that he or another shall pass or tender it as genuine.

(2) It is an offence for a person to make a counterfeit of a currency note or of a protected coin without lawful authority or excuse.

15   Offences of passing etc. counterfeit notes and coins

(1) It is an offence for a person—

    (*a*)   to pass or tender as genuine any thing which is, and which he knows or believes to be, a counterfeit of a currency note or of a protected coin; or

    (*b*)   to deliver to another any thing which is, and which he knows or believes to be such a counterfeit, intending that the person to whom it is delivered or another shall pass or tender it as genuine.

(2) It is an offence for a person to deliver to another, without lawful authority or excuse, any thing which is, and which he knows or believes to be, a counterfeit of a currency note or of a protected coin.

16   Offences involving the custody or control of counterfeit notes and coins

(1) It is an offence for a person to have in his custody or under his control any thing which is, and which he knows or believes to be, a counterfeit of a currency note or of a protected coin, intending either to pass or tender it as genuine or to deliver it to another with the intention that he or another shall pass or tender it as genuine.

(2) It is an offence for a person to have in his custody or under his control, without lawful authority or excuse, any thing which is, and which he knows or believes to be, a counterfeit of a currency note or of a protected coin.

(3) It is immaterial for the purposes of subsections (1) and (2) above that a coin or note is not in a fit state to be passed or tendered or that the making or counterfeiting of a coin or note has not been finished or perfected.

17 Offences involving the making or custody or control of counterfeiting materials and implements

(1) It is an offence for a person to make, or to have in his custody or under his control, any thing which he intends to use, or to permit any other person to use, for the purpose of making a counterfeit of a currency note or of a protected coin with the intention that it be passed or tendered as genuine.

(2) It is an offence for a person without lawful authority or excuse—

    (*a*)   to make; or
    (*b*)   to have in his custody or under his control

any thing which, to his knowledge, is or has been specially designed or adapted for the making of a counterfeit of a currency note.

(3) Subject to subsection (4) below, it is an offence for a person to make, or to have in his custody or under his control, any implement which, to his knowledge, is capable of imparting to any thing a resemblance—

    (*a*)   to the whole or part of either side of a protected coin; or
    (*b*)   to the whole or part of the reverse of the image on either side of a protected coin.

(4) It shall be a defence for a person charged with an offence under subsection (3) above to show—

    (*a*)   that he made the implement or as the case may be, had it in his custody or under his control, with the written consent of the Treasury; or
    (*b*)   that he had lawful authority otherwise than by virtue of paragraph (*a*) above, or a lawful excuse, for making it or having it in his custody or under his control.

18 The offence of reproducing British currency notes

(1) It is an offence for any person, unless the relevant authority has previously consented in writing, to reproduce on any substance whatsoever, and whether or not on the correct scale, any British currency note or any part of a British currency note.

(2) In this section—

'British currency note' means any note which—

    (*a*)   has been lawfully issued in England and Wales, Scotland or Northern Ireland; and
    (*b*)   is or has been customarily used as money in the country where it was issued; and
    (*c*)   is payable on demand; and

'the relevant authority', in relation to a British currency note of any particular description, means the authority empowered by law to issue notes of that description.

19 Offences of making etc. imitation British coins

(1) It is an offence for a person—

    (*a*) to make an imitation British coin in connection with a scheme intended to promote the sale of any product or the making of contracts for the supply of any service; or

    (*b*) to sell or distribute imitation British coins in connection with any such scheme, or to have imitation British coins in his custody or under his control with a view to such sale or distribution,

unless the treasury have previously consented in writing to the sale or distribution of such imitation British coins in connection with that scheme.

[. . .]

22 Penalties for offences under Part II

(1) A person guilty of an offence to which this subsection applies shall be liable—

    (*a*) on summary conviction—

        (i) to a fine not exceeding the statutory maximum; or
        (ii) to imprisonment for a term not exceeding six months; or
        (iii) to both; and

    (*b*) on conviction on indictment—

        (i) to a fine; or
        (ii) to imprisonment for a term not exceeding ten years; or
        (iii) to both.

(2) The offences to which subsection (1) above applies are offences under the following provisions of this Part of this Act—

    (*a*) section 14(1);
    (*b*) section 15(1);
    (*c*) section 16(1); and
    (*d*) section 17(1).

(3) A person guilty of an offence to which this subsection applies shall be liable—

    (*a*) on summary conviction—

        (i) to a fine not exceeding the statutory maximum; or
        (ii) to imprisonment for a term not exceeding six months; or
        (iii) to both; and

    (*b*) on conviction on indictment—

        (i) to a fine; or
        (ii) to imprisonment for a term not exceeding two years; or
        (iii) to both.

(4) The offences to which subsection (3) above applies are offences under the following provisions of this Part of this Act—

    (*a*) section 14(2);
    (*b*) section 15(2);
    (*c*) section 16(2);
    (*d*) section 17(2); and
    (*e*) section 17(3).

(5) A person guilty of an offence under section 18 or 19 above shall be liable—

    (*a*) on summary conviction, to a fine not exceeding the statutory maximum; and

    (*b*) on conviction on indictment, to a fine.

Immigration Act 1971

The following sections of the Act should be noted:

24 Illegal entry and similar offences

(1) A person who is not a British citizen shall be guilty of an offence punishable on summary conviction with a fine of not more than level 5 on the standard scale or with imprisonment for not more than six months or with both, in any of the following cases:

    (*a*) if contrary to this Act he knowingly enters the United Kingdom in breach of a deportation order or without leave;

    (*b*) if, having only a limited leave to enter or remain in the United Kingdom, he knowingly either—

        (i) remains beyond the time limited by the leave; or
        (ii) fails to observe a condition of the leave;

    (*c*) if, having lawfully entered the United Kingdom without leave by virtue of section 8(1) above, he remains without leave beyond the time allowed by section 8(1);

    (*d*) if, without reasonable excuse, he fails to comply with any requirement imposed on him under Schedule 2 to this Act to report to a medical officer of health, or to attend, or submit to a test or examination, as required by such an officer;

    (*e*) if, without reasonable excuse, he fails to observe any restriction imposed on him under Schedule 2 or 3 to this Act as to residence, as to his employment or occupation or as to reporting to the police or to an immigration officer;

    (*f*) if he disembarks in the United Kingdom from a ship or aircraft after being placed on board under Schedule 2 or 3 to this Act with a view to his removal from the United Kingdom;

    (*g*) if he embarks in contravention of a restriction imposed by or under an Order in Council under section 3(7) of this Act.

(1A) A person commits an offence under subsection (1)(*b*)(i) above on the day when he first knows that the time limited by his leave has expired and continues to commit it throughout any period during which he is in the United Kingdom thereafter; but a person shall not be prosecuted under that provision more than once in respect of the same limited leave.

24A Deception [6 months/2 years]

(1) A person who is not a British citizen is guilty of an offence if, by means which include deception by him—

    (*a*) he obtains or seeks to obtain leave to enter or remain in the United Kingdom; or

    (*b*) he secures or seeks to secure the avoidance, postponement or revocation of enforcement action against him.

(2) 'Enforcement action', in relation to a person, means—

    (*a*)   the giving of directions for his removal from the United Kingdom ('directions') under Schedule 2 to this Act or section 10 of the Immigration and Asylum Act 1999;

    (*b*)   the making of a deportation order against him under section 5 of this Act; or

    (*c*)   his removal from the United Kingdom in consequence of directions or a deportation order.

25   Assisting illegal entry, and harbouring [6 months/10 years]

(1) Any person knowingly concerned in making or carrying out arrangements for securing or facilitating

    (*a*)   the entry into the United Kingdom of anyone whom he knows or has reasonable cause for believing to be an illegal entrant;

    (*b*)   the entry into the United Kingdom of anyone whom he knows or has reasonable cause for believing to be an asylum claimant; or

    (*c*)   the obtaining by anyone of leave to remain in the United Kingdom by means which he knows or has reasonable cause for believing to include deception,

shall be guilty of an offence.

Indecency with Children Act 1960

The following section of the Act should be noted:

1   Indecent conduct towards young child

(1) Any person who commits an act of gross indecency with or towards a child under the age of sixteen, or who incites a child under that age to such an act with him or another, shall be liable on conviction on indictment to imprisonment for a term not exceeding ten years, or on summary conviction to imprisonment for a term not exceeding six months, to a fine not exceeding the statutory maximum, or to both.

Misuse of Drugs Act 1971

The following sections of the Act should be noted:

3   Restriction of importation and exportation of controlled drugs

(1) Subject to subsection (2) below—

    (*a*)   the importation of a controlled drug; and

    (*b*)   the exportation of a controlled drug,

are hereby prohibited.

(2) Subsection (1) above does not apply—

    (*a*)   to the importation or exportation of a controlled drug which is for the time being excepted from paragraph (*a*) or, as the case may be, paragraph (*b*) of subsection (1) above by regulations under section 7 of this Act; or (*b*)   to the importation or exportation of a controlled drug under and in accordance with the terms of a licence issued by the Secretary of State and in compliance with any conditions attached thereto.

4   Restriction of production and supply of controlled drugs

(1) Subject to any regulations under section 7 of this Act for the time being in force, it shall not be lawful for a person—

(*a*)   to produce a controlled drug; or
(*b*)   to supply or offer to supply a controlled drug to another.

(2) Subject to section 28 of this Act, it is an offence for a person—

(*a*)   to produce a controlled drug in contravention of subsection (1) above; or
(*b*)   to be concerned in the production of such a drug in contravention of that subsection by another.

(3) Subject to section 28 of this Act, it is an offence for a person—

(*a*)   to supply or offer to supply a controlled drug to another in contravention of subsection (1) above; or
(*b*)   to be concerned in the supplying of such a drug to another in contravention of that subsection; or
(*c*)   to be concerned in the making to another in contravention of that subsection of an offer to supply such a drug.

5   Restriction of possession of controlled drugs

(1) Subject to any regulations under section 7 of this Act for the time being in force, it shall not be lawful for a person to have a controlled drug in his possession.

(2) Subject to section 28 of this Act and to subsection (4) below, it is an offence for a person to have a controlled drug in his possession in contravention of subsection (1) above.

(3) Subject to section 28 of this Act, it is an offence for a person to have a controlled drug in his possession, whether lawfully or not, with intent to supply it to another in contravention of section 4(1) of this Act.

(4) In any proceedings for an offence under subsection (2) above in which it is proved that the accused had a controlled drug in his possession, it shall be a defence for him to prove—

(*a*)   that, knowing or suspecting it to be a controlled drug, he took possession of it for the purpose of preventing another from committing or continuing to commit an offence in connection with that drug and that as soon as possible after taking possession of it he took all such steps as were reasonably open to him to destroy the drug or to deliver it into the custody of a person lawfully entitled to take custody of it; or
(*b*)   that, knowing or suspecting it to be a controlled drug, he took possession of it for the purpose of delivering it into the custody of a person lawfully entitled to take custody of it and that as soon as possible after taking possession of it he took all such steps as were reasonably open to him to deliver it into the custody of such a person.

(6) Nothing in subsection (4) above shall prejudice any defence which it is open to a person charged with an offence under this section to raise apart from that subsection.

6 Restriction of cultivation of cannabis plant

(1) Subject to any regulations under section 7 of this Act for the time being in force, it shall not be lawful for a person to cultivate any plant of the genus *Cannabis*.

(2) Subject to section 28 of this Act, it is an offence to cultivate any such plant in contravention of subsection (1) above.

[. . .]

8 Occupiers etc. of premises to be punishable for permitting certain activities to take place there

A person commits an offence if, being the occupier or concerned in the management of any premises, he knowingly permits or suffers any of the following activities to take place on those premises, that is to say—

    (*a*)   producing or attempting to produce a controlled drug in contravention of section 4(1) of this Act;

    (*b*)   supplying or attempting to supply a controlled drug to another in contravention of section 4(1) of this Act, or offering to supply a controlled drug to another in contravention of section 4;

    (*c*)   preparing opium for smoking;

    (*d*)   smoking cannabis, cannabis resin or prepared opium.

9 Prohibition of certain activities etc. relating to opium

Subject to section 28 of this Act, it is an offence for a person—

    (*a*)   to smoke or otherwise use prepared opium; or

    (*b*)   to frequent a place used for the purpose of opium smoking; or

    (*c*)   to have in his possession—

        (i)   any pipes or other utensils made or adapted for use in connection with the smoking of opium, being pipes or utensils which have been used by him or with his knowledge and permission in that connection or which he intends to use or permit others to use in that connection; or

        (ii)   any utensils which have been used by him or with his knowledge and permission in connection with the preparation of opium for smoking.

9A Prohibition of supply etc., of articles for administering or preparing controlled drugs

(1) A person who supplies or offers to supply any article which may be used or adapted to be used (whether by itself or in combination with another article or other articles) in the administration by any person of a controlled drug to himself or another, believing that the article (or the article as adapted) is to be so used in circumstances where the administration is unlawful, is guilty of an offence.

(2) It is not an offence under subsection (1) above to supply or offer to supply a hypodermic syringe, or any part of one.

(3) A person who supplies or offers to supply any article which may be used to prepare a controlled drug for administration by any person to himself or another believing that the article is to be used in circumstances where the administration is unlawful is guilty of an offence.

(4) For the purposes of this section, any administration of a controlled drug is unlawful except—

(*a*) the administration by any person of a controlled drug to another in circumstances where the administration of the drug is not unlawful under section 4(1) of this Act, or

(*b*) the administration by any person of a controlled drug to himself in circumstances where having the controlled drug in his possession is not unlawful under section 5(1) of this Act.

(5) In this section, references to administration by any person of a controlled drug to himself include a reference to his administering it to himself with the assistance of another.

[. . .]

18 Miscellaneous offences

(1) It is an offence for a person to contravene any regulations made under this Act other than regulations made in pursuance of section 10(2)(*h*) or (*i*).

(2) It is an offence for a person to contravene a condition or other term of a licence issued under section 3 of this Act or of a licence or other authority issued under regulations made under this Act, not being a licence issued under regulations made in pursuance of section 10(2)(*i*).

(3) A person commits an offence if, in purported compliance with any obligation to give information to which he is subject under or by virtue of regulations made under this Act, he gives any information which he knows to be false in a material particular or recklessly gives any information which is so false.

(4) A person commits an offence if, for the purpose of obtaining, whether for himself or another, the issue or renewal of a licence or other authority under this Act or under any regulations made under this Act, he—

(*a*) makes any statement or gives any information which he knows to be false in a material particular or recklessly gives any information which is so false; or

(*b*) produces or otherwise makes use of any book, record or other document which to his knowledge contains any statement or information which he knows to be false in a material particular.

[. . .]

28 Proof of lack of knowledge etc. to be a defence in proceedings for certain offences

(1) This section applies to offences under any of the following provisions of this Act, that is to say section 4(2) and (3), section 5(2) and (3), section 6(2) and section 9.

(2) Subject to subsection (3) below, in any proceedings for an offence to which this section applies it shall be a defence for the accused to prove that he neither knew of nor suspected nor had reason to suspect the existence of some fact alleged by the prosecution which it is necessary for the prosecution to prove if he is to be convicted of the offence charged.

(3) Where in any proceedings for an offence to which this section applies it is necessary, if the accused is to be convicted of the offence charged, for the prosecution

to prove that some substance or product involved in the alleged offence was the controlled drug which the prosecution alleges it to have been, and it is proved that the substance or product in question was that controlled drug, the accused—

(a) shall not be acquitted of the offence charged by reason only of proving that he neither knew nor suspected nor had reason to suspect that the substance or product in question was the particular controlled drug alleged; but

(b) shall be acquitted thereof—

(i) if he proves that he neither believed nor suspected nor had reason to suspect that the substance or product in question was a controlled drug; or

(ii) if he proves that he believed the substance or product in question to be a controlled drug, or a controlled drug of a description, such that, if it had in fact been that controlled drug or a controlled drug of that description, he would not at the material time have been committing any offence to which this section applies.

(4) Nothing in this section shall prejudice any defence which it is open to a person charged with an offence to which this section applies to raise apart from this section.

SCHEDULE 4 – Punishments

Section Creating Offence	General Nature of Offence	Mode of prosecution	Punishment Class A-drug involved	Class B-drug involved	Class C-drug involved	General
s.4(2)	Production, or being concerned in the production, of a controlled drug	(a) Summary	6 months or the prescribed sum, or both	6 months or the prescribed sum, or both	3 months or £2,500, or both	
		(b) On indictment	Life or a fine, or both	14 years or a fine, or both	14 years or a fine, or both	
s.4(3)	Supplying or offering to supply a controlled drug or being concerned in the doing of either activity by another	(a) Summary	6 months or the prescribed sum, or both	6 months or the prescribed sum, or both	3 months or £2,500, or both	
		(b) On indictment	Life or a fine, or both	14 years or a fine, or both	14 years or a fine, or both	
s.5(2)	Having possession of a controlled drug	(a) Summary	6 months or the prescribed sum, or both	3 months or £2,500, or both	3 months or £1,000 or both	
		(b) On indictment	7 years or a fine, or both	5 years or a fine, or both	2 years or a fine, or both	

Section Creating Offence	General Nature of Offence	Mode of prosecution	Punishment Class A- drug involved	Class B- drug involved	Class C- drug involved	General
s.5(3)	Having possession of a controlled drug with intent to supply to it another	(a) Summary	6 months or the prescribed sum, or both	6 months or the prescribed sum, or both	3 months or £2,500, or both	
		(b) On indictment	Life or a fine, or both	14 years or a fine, or both	5 years or a fine, or both	
s.6(2)	Cultivation of cannabis plant	(a) Summary	–	–	–	6 months or the prescribed sum or both
		(b) On indictment	–	–	–	14 years or a fine, or both
s.8	Being the occupier, or concerned in the management, of premises and permitting or suffering certain activities to take place there	(a) Summary	6 months or the prescribed sum, or both	6 months or the prescribed sum, or both	3 months or £2,500, or both	
		(b) On indictment	14 years or a fine, or both	14 years or a fine, or both	14 years or a fine, or both	6 months or the prescribed sum, or both
s.9	Offences relating to opium	(a) Summary	–	–	–	
		(b) On indictment	–	–	–	14 years or a fine, or both
s.9A	Prohibition of supply etc. of articles for administering or preparing controlled drugs	Summary				
s.11(2)	Contravention of directions relating to safe custody of controlled drugs	(a) Summary	–	–	–	6 months or the prescribed sum, or both
		(b) On indictment	–	–	–	2 years or a fine, or both
s.12(6)	Contravention of direction prohibiting practitioner etc. from possessing, supplying etc. controlled drugs	(a) Summary	6 months or the prescribed sum, or both	6 months or the prescribed sum, or both	3 months or £2,500, or both	

Section Creating Offence	General Nature of Offence	Mode of prosecution	Punishment Class A- drug involved	Class B- drug involved	Class C- drug involved	General
		(b) On indictment	14 years or a fine, or both	14 years or a fine, or both	14 years or a fine, or both	
s.13(3)	Contravention of direction prohibiting practitioner etc. from prescribing, supplying etc. controlled drugs	(a) Summary	6 months or the prescribed sum or both	6 months or the prescribed sum or both	3 months or £2,500, or both	
		(b) On indictment	14 years or a fine, or both	14 years or a fine, or both	14 years or a fine, or both	
s.17(3)	Failure to comply with notice requiring information relating to prescribing, supply etc. of drugs	Summary	–	–	–	Level 3 on the standard scale
s.17(4)	Giving false information in purported compliance with notice requiring information relating to prescribing, supply etc. of drugs	(a) Summary	–	–	–	6 months or the prescribed sum, or both
		(b) On indictment	–	–	–	2 years or a fine, or both
s.18(1)	Contravention of regulations (other than regulations relating to addicts)	(a) Summary	–	–	–	6 months or the prescribed sum, or both
		(b) On indictment	–	–	–	2 years or a fine, or both
s.18(2)	Contravention of terms of licence or other authority (other than licence issued under regulations relating to addicts)	(a) Summary	–	–	–	6 months or the prescribed sum, or both
		(b) On indictment	–	–	–	2 years or a fine, or both
s.18(3)	Giving false information in purported compliance with obligation to give information	(a) Summary	–	–	–	6 months or the prescribed sum, or both

283

Section Creating Offence	General Nature of Offence	Mode of prosecution	Punishment Class A- drug involved	Class B- drug involved	Class C- drug involved	General
	imposed under or by virtue of regulations	(b) On indictment	–	–	–	2 years or a fine, or both
s.18(4)	Giving false information, or producing document etc. containing false statement etc., for purposes of obtaining issue or renewal of a licence or other authority	(a) Summary	–	–	–	6 months or the prescribed sum, or both
		(b) On indictment	–	–	–	2 years or a fine, or both.
s.20	Assisting in or inducing commission outside United Kingdom of an offence punishable under a corresponding law	(a) Summary	–	–	–	6 months or the prescribed sum or both
		(b) On indictment	–	–	–	14 years or a fine, or both.
s.23(4)	Obstructing exercise of powers of search etc. or concealing books, drugs etc.	(a) Summary	–	–	–	6 months or the prescribed sum, or both
		(b) On indictment	–	–	–	2 years or a fine, or both

Offences Against the Person Act 1861

The following sections of the Act should be noted:

4   Soliciting to commit murder

Whosoever shall solicit, encourage, persuade, or endeavour to persuade, or shall propose to any person, to murder any other person, whether he be a subject of Her Majesty or not, and whether he be within the Queen's Dominions or not, shall be guilty of an offence and being convicted thereof shall be liable to imprisonment for life.

[. . .]

16 Threats to kill

A person who without lawful excuse makes to another a threat, intending that that other would fear it would be carried out, to kill that other or a third person shall be guilty of an offence and liable on conviction on indictment to imprisonment for a term not exceeding ten years.

[. . .]

18 Wounding with intent to do grievous bodily harm

Whosoever shall unlawfully and maliciously by any means whatsoever, wound or cause any grievous bodily harm to any person with intent to do some grievous bodily harm to any person, or with intent to resist or prevent the lawful apprehension or detainer of any person, shall be guilty of an offence and being convicted thereof shall be liable to imprisonment for life. [Triable only on indictment.]

[. . .]

20 Inflicting bodily injury, with or without weapon

Whosoever shall unlawfully and maliciously wound or inflict any grievous bodily harm upon any other person, either with or without any weapon or instrument shall be guilty of an offence and being convicted thereof shall be liable to imprisonment not exceeding five years. [Not exceeding 6 months if tried summarily.]

21 Attempting to choke etc. in order to commit indictable offence

Whosoever shall by any means whatsoever attempt to choke, suffocate, or strangle any other person, or shall by any means calculated to choke, suffocate, or strangle, attempt to render any other person insensible, unconscious, or incapable of resistance, with intent in any of such cases thereby to enable himself or any other person to commit or with intent in any of such cases thereby to assist any other person in committing any indictable offence shall be guilty of an offence and being convicted thereof shall be liable to imprisonment for life.

[. . .]

23 Maliciously administering poison etc. so as to endanger life etc.

Whosoever shall unlawfully and maliciously administer to, or cause to be administered to, or taken by, any other person, any poison, or other destructive or noxious thing, so as thereby to endanger the life of such person, or so as thereby to inflict upon any such person any grievous bodily harm shall be guilty of an offence, and being convicted thereof shall be liable to imprisonment for any term not exceeding ten years.

24 Maliciously administering poison etc. with intent to injure, aggrieve or annoy

Whosoever shall unlawfully and maliciously administer to, or cause to be administered to or taken by any other person, any poison or other destructive or noxious thing, with intent to injure, aggrieve, or annoy such person shall be guilty of an offence, and being convicted thereof shall be liable to imprisonment not exceeding five years.

[. . .]

27 Exposing child whereby life is in danger

Whosoever shall unlawfully abandon or expose any child, being under the age of two years, whereby the life of such child shall be endangered, or the health of such child shall have been or shall be likely to be permanently injured shall be guilty of an offence and being convicted hereof shall be liable to imprisonment not exceeding five years.

[. . .]

38 Assault with intent to resist apprehension, etc.

Whosoever shall assault any person with intent to resist or prevent the lawful apprehension or detainer of himself or of any other person for any offence, shall be guilty of misdemeanour, and being convicted thereof shall be liable, at the discretion of the Court, to be imprisoned for any term not exceeding two years.

[. . .]

47 Assault occasioning bodily harm

Whosoever shall be convicted upon an indictment of any assault occasioning actual bodily harm shall be liable to be imprisoned for any term not exceeding 5 years.

Police Act 1996

The following sections of the Act should be noted:

89 Assaults on constables

(1) Any person who assaults a constable in the execution of his duty, or a person assisting a constable in the execution of his duty, shall be guilty of an offence and liable on summary conviction to imprisonment for a term not exceeding six months or to a fine not exceeding level 5 on the standard scale, or to both.

(2) Any person who resists or wilfully obstructs a constable in the execution of his duty, or a person assisting a constable in the execution of his duty, shall be guilty of an offence and liable on summary conviction to imprisonment for a term not exceeding one month or to a fine not exceeding level 3 on the standard scale, or to both.

Prevention of Crime Act 1953

The following section of the Act should be noted:

1 Prohibition of the carrying of offensive weapons without lawful authority or reasonable excuse

(1) Any person who without lawful authority or reasonable excuse, the proof whereof shall lie on him, has with him in any public place any offensive weapon shall be guilty of an offence, and shall be liable—

    (a) on summary conviction, to imprisonment for a term not exceeding six months or a fine not exceeding the statutory maximum, or both;

(*b*)   on conviction on indictment, to imprisonment for a term not exceeding four years or a fine or both.

(2) Where any person is convicted of an offence under subsection (1) of this section the court may make an order for the forfeiture or disposal of any weapon in respect of which the offence was committed.

Prison Act 1952

The following section of the Act should be noted:

40   Unlawful conveyance of spirits or tobacco into prisons, etc.

Any person who contrary to the regulations of a prison brings or attempts to bring into the prison or to a prisoner any spirituous or fermented liquor or tobacco, or places any such liquor or any tobacco anywhere outside the prison with intent that it shall come into the possession of a prisoner, and any officer who contrary to those regulations allows any such liquor or any tobacco to be sold or used in the prison, shall be liable on summary conviction to imprisonment for a term not exceeding six months or a fine not exceeding level 3 on the standard scale or both.

Protection from Eviction Act 1977

The following sections of the Act should be noted:

1   Unlawful eviction and harassment of occupier

(1) In this section 'residential occupier', in relation to any premises, means a person occupying the premises as a residence, whether under a contract or by virtue of any enactment or rule of law giving him the right to remain in occupation or restricting the right of any other person to recover possession of the premises.

(2) If any person unlawfully deprives the residential occupier of any premises of his occupation of the premises or any part thereof, or attempts to do so, he shall be guilty of an offence unless he proves that he believed, and had reasonable cause to believe, that the residential occupier had ceased to reside in the premises.

(3) If any person with intent to cause the residential occupier of any premises—

(*a*)   to give up the occupation of the premises or any part thereof; or
(*b*)   to refrain from exercising any right or pursuing any remedy in respect of the premises or part thereof;

does acts likely to interfere with the peace or comfort of the residential occupier or members of his household, or persistently withdraws or withholds services reasonably required for the occupation of the premises as a residence, he shall be guilty of an offence.

(3A) Subject to subsection (3B) below, the landlord of a residential occupier or an agent of the landlord shall be guilty of an offence if—

(*a*)   he does acts likely to interfere with the peace or comfort of the residential occupier or members of his household, or
(*b*)   he persistently withdraws or withholds services reasonably required for the occupation of the premises in question as a residence,

and (in either case) he knows, or has reasonable cause to believe, that that conduct is likely to cause the residential occupier to give up the occupation of the whole or part of the premises or to refrain from exercising any right or pursuing any remedy in respect of the whole or part of the premises.

(3B) A person shall not be guilty of an offence under subsection (3A) above if he proves that he had reasonable grounds for doing the acts or withdrawing or withholding the services in question.

(4) A person guilty of an offence under this section shall be liable—

(*a*) on summary conviction, to a fine not exceeding the prescribed sum or to imprisonment for a term not exceeding 6 months or to both;

(*b*) on conviction on indictment, to a fine or to imprisonment for a term not exceeding 2 years or to both.

Protection from Harassment Act 1997

The following sections of the Act should be noted:

1 Prohibition of harassment

(1) A person must not pursue a course of conduct—

(*a*) which amounts to harassment of another, and

(*b*) which he knows or ought to know amounts to harassment of the other.

(2) For the purposes of this section, the person whose course of conduct is in question ought to know that it amounts to harassment of another if a reasonable person in possession of the same information would think the course of conduct amounted to harassment of the other.

(3) Subsection (1) does not apply to a course of conduct if the person who pursued it shows—

(*a*) that it was pursued for the purpose of preventing or detecting crime,

(*b*) that it was pursued under any enactment or rule of law or to comply with any condition or requirement imposed by any person under any enactment, or

(*c*) that in the particular circumstances the pursuit of the course of conduct was reasonable.

2 Offence of harassment

(1) A person who pursues a course of conduct in breach of section 1 is guilty of an offence.

(2) A person guilty of an offence under this section is liable on summary conviction to imprisonment for a term not exceeding six months, or a fine not exceeding level 5 on the standard scale, or both.

[. . .]

4 Putting people in fear of violence

(1) A person whose course of conduct causes another to fear, on at least two occasions, that violence will be used against him is guilty of an offence if he knows or ought to know that his course of conduct will cause the other so to fear on each of those occasions.

(2) For the purposes of this section, the person whose course of conduct is in question ought to know that it will cause another to fear that violence will be used against him on any occasion if a reasonable person in possession of the same information would think the course of conduct would cause the other so to fear on that occasion.

(3) It is a defence for a person charged with an offence under this section to show that—

(*a*) his course of conduct was pursued for the purpose of preventing or detecting crime,

(*b*) his course of conduct was pursued under any enactment or rule of law or to comply with any condition or requirement imposed by any person under any enactment, or

(*c*) the pursuit of his course of conduct was reasonable for the protection of himself or another or for the protection of his or another's property.

(4) A person guilty of an offence under this section is liable—

(*a*) on conviction on indictment, to imprisonment for a term not exceeding five years, or a fine, or both, or

(*b*) on summary conviction, to imprisonment for a term not exceeding six months, or a fine not exceeding the statutory maximum, or both.

5 Restraining orders

(1) A court sentencing or otherwise dealing with a person ('the defendant') convicted of an offence under section 2 or 4 may (as well as sentencing him or dealing with him in any other way) make an order under this section.

(2) The order may, for the purpose of protecting the victim of the offence, or any other person mentioned in the order, from further conduct which—

(*a*) amounts to harassment, or

(*b*) will cause a fear of violence,

prohibit the defendant from doing anything described in the order.

(3) The order may have effect for a specified period or until further order.

(4) The prosecutor, the defendant or any other person mentioned in the order may apply to the court which made the order for it to be varied or discharged by a further order.

(5) If without reasonable excuse the defendant does anything which he is prohibited from doing by an order under this section, he is guilty of an offence.

(6) A person guilty of an offence under this section is liable—

(*a*) on conviction on indictment, to imprisonment for a term not exceeding five years, or a fine, or both, or

(*b*) on summary conviction, to imprisonment for a term not exceeding six months, or a fine not exceeding the statutory maximum, or both.

Protection of Animals Act 1911

The following sections of the Act should be noted:

1 Cruelty

(1) If any person—

    (*a*) shall cruelly beat, kick, ill-treat, over-ride, over-drive, over-load, torture, infuriate, or terrify any animal, or shall cause or procure, or, being the owner, permit any animal to be so used, or shall, by wantonly or unreasonably doing or omitting to do any act, or causing or procuring the commission or omission of any act, cause any unnecessary suffering, or, being the owner, permit any unnecessary suffering to be so caused to any animal; or

    (*b*) shall convey or carry, or cause or procure, or, being the owner, permit to be conveyed or carried, any animal in such manner or position as to cause that animal any unnecessary suffering; or

    (*c*) shall cause, procure, or assist at the fighting or baiting of any animal; or shall keep, use, manage, or act or assist in the management of, any premises or place for the purpose, or partly for the purpose, of fighting or baiting any animal, or shall permit any premises or place to be so kept, managed, or used, or shall receive, or cause or procure any person to receive, money for the admission of any person to such premises or place; or

    (*d*) shall wilfully, without any reasonable cause or excuse, administer, or cause or procure, or being the owner permit, such administration of, any poisonous or injurious drug or substance to any animal, or shall wilfully, without any reasonable cause or excuse, cause any such substance to be taken by any animal; or

    (*e*) shall subject, or cause or procure, or being the owner permit, to be subjected, any animal to any operation which is performed without due care and humanity; or

    (*f*) shall tether any horse, ass or mule under such conditions or in such manner as to cause that animal unnecessary suffering;

such person shall be guilty of an offence of cruelty within the meaning of this Act and shall be liable on summary conviction to imprisonment for a term not exceeding six months or to a fine not exceeding level 5 on the standard scale, or both.

(2) For the purposes of this section, an owner shall be deemed to have permitted cruelty within the meaning of this Act if he shall have failed to exercise reasonable care and supervision in respect of the protection of the animal therefrom:

Provided that, where an owner is convicted of permitting cruelty within the meaning of this Act by reason only of his having failed to exercise such care and supervision, he shall not be liable to imprisonment without the option of a fine.

2 Destruction of animal

Where the owner of an animal is convicted of an offence of cruelty within the meaning of this Act, it shall be lawful for the court, if the court is satisfied that it would be cruel to keep the animal alive, to direct that the animal be destroyed, and to assign the animal to any suitable person for that purpose; and the person to whom such animal is so assigned shall, as soon as possible, destroy such animal, or cause or procure such animal to be destroyed, in his presence without unnecessary suffering. Any reasonable expenses incurred in destroying the animal may be ordered by the court to be paid by the owner, and thereupon shall be recoverable summarily as a civil debt:

Provided that, unless the owner assent, no order shall be made under this section except upon the evidence of a duly registered veterinary surgeon.

3 Deprivation of ownership

If the owner of any animal shall be guilty of cruelty within the meaning of this Act to the animal, the court, upon his conviction thereof, may, if they think fit, in addition to any other punishment, deprive such person of the ownership of the animal, and may make such order as to the disposal of the animal as they think fit under the circumstances:

Provided that no order shall be made under this section, unless it is shown by evidence as to a previous conviction, or as to the character of the owner, or otherwise, that the animal, if left with the owner, is likely to be exposed to further cruelty.

Protection of Animals (Amendment) Act 1954

The following section of the Act should be noted:

1 Power to disqualify persons convicted of cruelty to animals

(1) Where a person has been convicted under the Protection of Animals Act 1911 or the Protection of Animals (Scotland) Act 1912 of an offence of cruelty to any animal the court by which he is convicted may, if it thinks fit, in addition to or in substitution for any other punishment, order him to be disqualified, for such period as it thinks fit, for having custody of any animal or any animal of a kind specified in the order.

(2) A court which has ordered the disqualification of a person in pursuance of this section may, if it thinks fit, suspend the operation of the order—

   (a) for such period as the court thinks necessary for enabling arrangements to be made for the custody of any animal or animals to which the disqualification relates; or

   (b) pending an appeal.

(3) A person who is disqualified by virtue of an order under this section may, at any time after the expiration of twelve months from the date of the order, and from time to time apply to the court by which the order was made to remove the disqualification, and on any such application the court may, as it thinks proper, having regard to the character of the applicant and his conduct subsequent to the order, the nature of the offence of which he was convicted, and any other circumstances of the case, either—

   (a) direct that, as from such date as may be specified in the direction, the disqualification be removed or the order be so varied as to apply only to animals of a kind specified in the direction; or

   (b) refuse the application:

Provided that where on an application under this section the court directs the variation of the order or refuses the application, a further application thereunder shall not be entertained if made within twelve months after the date of the direction or, as the case may be, the refusal.

Protection of Children Act 1978

The following sections of the Act should be noted:

1   Indecent photographs of children

(1) It is an offence for a person—

  (a)   to take, or permit to be taken or to make, any indecent photograph or pseudo-photograph of a child; or

  (b)   to distribute or show such indecent photographs or pseudo-photographs; or

  (c)   to have in his possession such indecent photographs or pseudo-photographs, with a view to their being distributed or shown by himself or others; or

  (d)   to publish or cause to be published any advertisement likely to be understood as conveying that the advertiser distributes or shows such indecent photographs or pseudo-photographs, or intends to do so.

(2) For the purposes of this Act, a person is to be regarded as distributing an indecent photograph or pseudo-photographs if he parts with possession of it to, or exposes or offers it for acquisition by, another person.

(3) Proceedings for an offence under this Act shall not be instituted except by or with the consent of the Director of Public Prosecutions.

(4) Where a person is charged with an offence under subsection (1)(b) or (c), it shall be a defence for him to prove—

  (a)   that he had a legitimate reason for distributing or showing the photographs or pseudo-photographs or (as the case may be) having them in his possession; or

  (b)   that he had not himself seen the photographs or pseudo-photographs and did not know, nor had any cause to suspect, them to be indecent.

[. . .]

6   Punishments

(1) Offences under this Act shall be punishable either on conviction on indictment or on summary conviction.

(2) A person convicted on indictment of any offence under this Act shall be liable to imprisonment for a term of not more than ten years, or to a fine or to both.

(3) A person convicted summarily of any offence under this Act shall be liable—

  (a)   to imprisonment for a term not exceeding six months; or

  (b)   to a fine not exceeding the prescribed sum for the purposes of section 32 of the Magistrates' Courts Act 1980 (punishment on summary conviction of offences triable either way: £1,000 or other sum substituted by order under that Act), or to both.

Public Order Act 1986

The following sections of the Act should be noted:

1 Riot

(1) Where 12 or more persons who are present together use or threaten unlawful violence for a common purpose and the conduct of them (taken together) is such as would cause a person of reasonable firmness present at the scene to fear for his personal safety, each of the persons using unlawful violence for the common purpose is guilty of riot.

(2) It is immaterial whether or not the 12 or more use or threaten unlawful violence simultaneously.

(3) The common purpose may be inferred from conduct.

(4) No person of reasonable firmness need actually be, or be likely to be, present at the scene.

(5) Riot may be committed in private as well as in public places.

(6) A person guilty of riot is liable on conviction on indictment to imprisonment for a term not exceeding ten years or a fine or both.

2 Violent disorder

(1) Where 3 or more persons who are present together use or threaten unlawful violence and the conduct of them (taken together) is such as would cause a person of reasonable firmness present at the scene to fear for his personal safety, each of the persons using or threatening unlawful violence is guilty of violent disorder.

(2) It is immaterial whether or not the 3 or more use or threaten unlawful violence simultaneously.

(3) No person of reasonable firmness need actually be, or be likely to be, present at the scene.

(4) Violent disorder may be committed in private as well as in public places.

(5) A person guilty of violent disorder is liable on conviction on indictment to imprisonment for a term not exceeding 5 years or a fine or both, or on summary conviction to imprisonment for a term not exceeding 6 months or a fine not exceeding the statutory maximum or both.

3 Affray [6 months/3 years]

(1) A person is guilty of affray if he uses or threatens unlawful violence towards another and his conduct is such as would cause a person of reasonable firmness present at the scene to fear for his personal safety.

(2) Where 2 or more persons use or threaten the unlawful violence, it is the conduct of them taken together that must be considered for the purposes of subsection (1).

(3) For the purposes of this section a threat cannot be made by the use of words alone.

(4) No person of reasonable firmness need actually be, or be likely to be, present at the scene.

(5) Affray may be committed in private as well as in public places.

293

4 Fear or provocation of violence

(1) A person is guilty of an offence if he—

    (*a*) uses towards another person threatening, abusive or insulting words or behaviour, or

    (*b*) distributes or displays to another person any writing, sign or other visible representation which is threatening, abusive or insulting,

with intent to cause that person to believe that immediate unlawful violence will be used against him or another by any person, or to provoke the immediate use of unlawful violence by that person or another, or whereby that person is likely to believe that such violence will be used or it is likely that such violence will be provoked.

(2) An offence under this section may be committed in a public or a private place, except that no offence is committed where the words or behaviour are used, or the writing, sign or other visible representation is distributed or displayed, by a person inside a dwelling and the other person is also inside that or another dwelling.

(3) A constable may arrest without warrant anyone he reasonably suspects is committing an offence under this section.

(4) A person guilty of an offence under this section is liable on summary conviction to imprisonment for a term not exceeding 6 months or a fine not exceeding level 5 on the standard scale or both.

4A Intentional harassment, alarm or distress

(1) A person is guilty of an offence if, with intent to cause a person harassment, alarm or distress, he—

    (*a*) uses threatening, abusive or insulting words or behaviour, or disorderly behaviour, or

    (*b*) displays any writing, sign or other visible representation which is threatening, abusive or insulting,

thereby causing that or another person harassment, alarm or distress.

(2) An offence under this section may be committed in a public or a private place, except that no offence is committed where the words or behaviour are used, or the writing, sign or other visible representation is displayed, by a person inside a dwelling and the person who is harassed, alarmed or distressed is also inside that or another dwelling.

(3) It is a defence for the accused to prove—

    (*a*) that he was inside a dwelling and had no reason to believe that the words or behaviour used, or the writing, sign or other visible representation displayed, would be heard or seen by a person outside that or any other dwelling, or

    (*b*) that his conduct was reasonable.

(4) A constable may arrest without warrant anyone he reasonably suspects is committing an offence under this section.

(5) A person guilty of an offence under this section is liable on summary conviction to imprisonment for a term not exceeding 6 months or a fine not exceeding level 5 on the standard scale or both.

5 Harassment, alarm or distress

(1) A person is guilty of an offence if he—

    (*a*) uses threatening, abusive or insulting words or behaviour, or disorderly behaviour, or

    (*b*) displays any writing, sign or other visible representation which is threatening, abusive or insulting,

within the hearing or sight of a person likely to be caused harassment, alarm or distress thereby.

(2) An offence under this section may be committed in a public or a private place, except that no offence is committed where the words or behaviour are used, or the writing, sign or other visible representation is displayed, by a person inside a dwelling and the other person is also inside that or another dwelling.

(3) It is a defence for the accused to prove—

    (*a*) that he had no reason to believe that there was any person within hearing or sight who was likely to be caused harassment, alarm or distress, or

    (*b*) that he was inside a dwelling and had no reason to believe that the words or behaviour used, or the writing, sign or other visible representation displayed, would be heard or seen by a person outside that or any other dwelling, or

    (*c*) that his conduct was reasonable.

(4) A constable may arrest a person without warrant if—

    (*a*) he engages in offensive conduct which a constable warns him to stop, and

    (*b*) he engages in further offensive conduct immediately or shortly after the warning.

(5) In subsection (4) 'offensive conduct' means conduct the constable reasonably suspects to constitute an offence under this section, and the conduct mentioned in paragraph (*a*) and the further conduct need not be of the same nature.

(6) A person guilty of an offence under this section is liable on summary conviction to a fine not exceeding level 3 on the standard scale.

6 Mental element: miscellaneous

(1) A person is guilty of riot only if he intends to use violence or is aware that his conduct may be violent.

(2) A person is guilty of violent disorder or affray only if he intends to use or threaten violence or is aware that his conduct may be violent or threaten violence.

(3) A person is guilty of an offence under section 4 only if he intends his words or behaviour, or the writing, sign or other visible representation, to be threatening, abusive or insulting, or is aware that it may be threatening, abusive or insulting.

(4) A person is guilty of an offence under section 5 only if he intends his words or behaviour, or the writing, sign or other visible representation, to be threatening, abusive or insulting, or is aware that it may be threatening, abusive or insulting or (as the case may be) he intends his behaviour to be or is aware that it may be disorderly.

(5) For the purposes of this section a person whose awareness is impaired by intoxication shall be taken to be aware of that of which he would be aware if not

intoxicated, unless he shows either that his intoxication was not self-induced or that it was caused solely by the taking or administration of a substance in the course of medical treatment.

(6) In subsection (5) 'intoxication' means any intoxication, whether caused by drink, drugs or other means, or by a combination of means.

[. . .]

17 Meaning of 'racial hatred'

In this Part 'racial hatred' means hatred against a group of persons defined by reference to colour, race, nationality (including citizenship) or ethnic or national origins.

18 Use of words or behaviour or display of written material

(1) A person who uses threatening, abusive or insulting words or behaviour, or displays any written material which is threatening, abusive or insulting, is guilty of an offence if—

> (a) he intends thereby to stir up racial hatred, or
> (b) having regard to all the circumstances racial hatred is likely to be stirred up thereby.

(2) An offence under this section may be committed in a public or a private place, except that no offence is committed where the words or behaviour are used, or the written material is displayed, by a person inside a dwelling and are not heard or seen except by other persons in that or another dwelling.

(3) A constable may arrest without warrant anyone he reasonably suspects is committing an offence under this section.

(4) In proceedings for an offence under this section it is a defence for the accused to prove that he was inside a dwelling and had no reason to believe that the words or behaviour used, or the written material displayed, would be heard or seen by a person outside that or any other dwelling.

(5) A person who is not shown to have intended to stir up racial hatred is not guilty of an offence under this section if he did not intend his words or behaviour, or the written material, to be, and was not aware that it might be, threatening, abusive or insulting.

(6) This section does not apply to words or behaviour used, or written material displayed, solely for the purpose of being included in a programme included in a programme service.

19 Publishing or distributing written material

(1) A person who publishes or distributes written material which is threatening, abusive or insulting is guilty of an offence if—

> (a) he intends thereby to stir up racial hatred, or
> (b) having regard to all the circumstances racial hatred is likely to be stirred up thereby.

(2) In proceedings for an offence under this section it is a defence for an accused who is not shown to have intended to stir up racial hatred to prove that he was not aware of the content of the material and did not suspect, and had no reason to suspect, that it was threatening, abusive or insulting.

(3) References in this Part to the publication or distribution of written material are to its publication or distribution to the public or a section of the public.

[. . .]

23 Possession of racially inflammatory material

(1) A person who has in his possession written material which is threatening, abusive or insulting, or a recording of visual images or sounds which are threatening, abusive or insulting, with a view to—

  (a) in the case of written material, its being displayed, published, distributed, or included in a programme service whether by himself or another, or
  (b) in the case of a recording, its being distributed, shown, played, or included in a programme service whether by himself or another,

is guilty of an offence if he intends racial hatred to be stirred up thereby or, having regard to all the circumstances, racial hatred is likely to be stirred up thereby.

(2) For this purpose regard shall be had to such display, publication, distribution, showing, playing, or inclusion in a programme service as he has, or it may reasonably be inferred that he has, in view.

(3) In proceedings for an offence under this section it is a defence for an accused who is not shown to have intended to stir up racial hatred to prove that he was not aware of the content of the written material or recording and did not suspect, and had no reason to suspect, that it was threatening, abusive or insulting.

27 Procedure and punishment

(1) No proceedings for an offence under this Part may be instituted in England and Wales except by or with the consent of the Attorney General.

(2) For the purposes of the rules in England and Wales against charging more than one offence in the same count or information, each of sections 18 to 23 creates one offence.

(3) A person guilty of an offence under this Part is liable—

  (a) on conviction on indictment to imprisonment for a term not exceeding seven years or a fine or both;
  (b) on summary conviction to imprisonment for a term not exceeding six months or a fine not exceeding the statutory maximum or both.

Sexual Offences Act 2003

The following section of the Act should be noted:

1 Rape

(1) A person (A) commits an offence if—

  (a) he intentionally penetrates the vagina, anus or mouth of another person (B) with his penis,
  (b) B does not consent to the penetration, and
  (c) A does not reasonably believe that B consents.

(2) Whether a belief is reasonable is to be determined having regard to all the circumstances, including any steps A has taken to ascertain whether B consents.

(3) Sections 75 and 76 apply to an offence under this section.

(4) A person guilty of an offence under this section is liable, on conviction on indictment, to imprisonment for life.

2   Assault by penetration

(1) A person (A) commits an offence if—

    (*a*)   he intentionally penetrates the vagina or anus of another person (B) with a part of his body or anything else,

    (*b*)   the penetration is sexual,

    (*c*)   B does not consent to the penetration, and

    (*d*)   A does not reasonably believe that B consents.

(2) Whether a belief is reasonable is to be determined having regard to all the circumstances, including any steps A has taken to ascertain whether B consents.

(3) Sections 75 and 76 apply to an offence under this section.

(4) A person guilty of an offence under this section is liable, on conviction on indictment, to imprisonment for life.

3   Sexual assault

(1) A person (A) commits an offence if—

    (*a*)   he intentionally touches another person (B),

    (*b*)   the touching is sexual,

    (*c*)   B does not consent to the touching, and

    (*d*)   A does not reasonably believe that B consents.

(2) Whether a belief is reasonable is to be determined having regard to all the circumstances, including any steps A has taken to ascertain whether B consents.

(3) Sections 75 and 76 apply to an offence under this section.

(4) A person guilty of an offence under this section is liable—

    (*a*)   on summary conviction, to imprisonment for a term not exceeding 6 months or a fine not exceeding the statutory maximum or both;

    (*b*)   on conviction on indictment, to imprisonment for a term not exceeding 10 years.

4   Causing a person to engage in sexual activity without consent

(1) A person (A) commits an offence if—

    (*a*)   he intentionally causes another person (B) to engage in an activity,

    (*b*)   the activity is sexual,

    (*c*)   B does not consent to engaging in the activity, and

    (*d*)   A does not reasonably believe that B consents.

(2) Whether a belief is reasonable is to be determined having regard to all the circumstances, including any steps A has taken to ascertain whether B consents.

(3) Sections 75 and 76 apply to an offence under this section.

(4) A person guilty of an offence under this section, if the activity caused involved—

    (*a*)   penetration of B's anus or vagina,

    (*b*)   penetration of B's mouth with a person's penis,

(c)   penetration of a person's anus or vagina with a part of B's body or by B with anything else, or

(d)   penetration of a person's mouth with B's penis,

is liable, on conviction on indictment, to imprisonment for life.

(5) Unless subsection (4) applies, a person guilty of an offence under this section is liable—

(a)   on summary conviction, to imprisonment for a term not exceeding 6 months or to a fine not exceeding the statutory maximum or both;

(b)   on conviction on indictment, to imprisonment for a term not exceeding 10 years.

5   Rape of a child under 13

(1) A person commits an offence if—

(a)   he intentionally penetrates the vagina, anus or mouth of another person with his penis, and

(b)   the other person is under 13.

(2) A person guilty of an offence under this section is liable, on conviction on indictment, to imprisonment for life.

6   Assault of a child under 13 by penetration

(1) A person commits an offence if—

(a)   he intentionally penetrates the vagina or anus of another person with a part of his body or anything else,

(b)   the penetration is sexual, and

(c)   the other person is under 13.

(2) A person guilty of an offence under this section is liable, on conviction on indictment, to imprisonment for life.

7   Sexual assault of a child under 13

(1) A person commits an offence if—

(a)   he intentionally touches another person,

(b)   the touching is sexual, and

(c)   the other person is under 13.

(2) A person guilty of an offence under this section is liable—

(a)   on summary conviction, to imprisonment for a term not exceeding 6 months or a fine not exceeding the statutory maximum or both;

(b)   on conviction on indictment, to imprisonment for a term not exceeding 14 years.

8   Causing or inciting a child under 13 to engage in sexual activity

(1) A person commits an offence if—

(a)   he intentionally causes or incites another person (B) to engage in an activity,

(b)   the activity is sexual, and

(c)   B is under 13.

(2) A person guilty of an offence under this section, if the activity caused or incited involved—

- (*a*)   penetration of B's anus or vagina,
- (*b*)   penetration of B's mouth with a person's penis,
- (*c*)   penetration of a person's anus or vagina with a part of B's body or by B with anything else, or
- (*d*)   penetration of a person's mouth with B's penis,

is liable, on conviction on indictment, to imprisonment for life.

(3) Unless subsection (2) applies, a person guilty of an offence under this section is liable—

- (*a*)   on summary conviction, to imprisonment for a term not exceeding 6 months or to a fine not exceeding the statutory maximum or both;
- (*b*)   on conviction on indictment, to imprisonment for a term not exceeding 14 years.

9   Sexual activity with a child

(1) A person aged 18 or over (A) commits an offence if—

- (*a*)   he intentionally touches another person (B),
- (*b*)   the touching is sexual, and
- (*c*)   either—

  - (i)   B is under 16 and A does not reasonably believe that B is 16 or over, or
  - (ii)   B is under 13.

(2) A person guilty of an offence under this section, if the touching involved—

- (*a*)   penetration of B's anus or vagina with a part of A's body or anything else,
- (*b*)   penetration of B's mouth with A's penis,
- (*c*)   penetration of A's anus or vagina with a part of B's body, or
- (*d*)   penetration of A's mouth with B's penis,

is liable, on conviction on indictment, to imprisonment for a term not exceeding 14 years.

(3) Unless subsection (2) applies, a person guilty of an offence under this section is liable—

- (*a*)   on summary conviction, to imprisonment for a term not exceeding 6 months or to a fine not exceeding the statutory maximum or both;
- (*b*)   on conviction on indictment, to imprisonment for a term not exceeding 14 years.

10   Causing or inciting a child to engage in sexual activity

(1) A person aged 18 or over (A) commits an offence if—

- (*a*)   he intentionally causes or incites another person (B) to engage in an activity,
- (*b*)   the activity is sexual, and
- (*c*)   either—

  - (i)   B is under 16 and A does not reasonably believe that B is 16 or over, or
  - (ii)   B is under 13.

(2) A person guilty of an offence under this section, if the activity caused or incited involved—

- (*a*) penetration of B's anus or vagina,
- (*b*) penetration of B's mouth with a person's penis,
- (*c*) penetration of a person's anus or vagina with a part of B's body or by B with anything else, or
- (*d*) penetration of a person's mouth with B's penis,

is liable, on conviction on indictment, to imprisonment for a term not exceeding 14 years.

(3) Unless subsection (2) applies, a person guilty of an offence under this section is liable—

- (*a*) on summary conviction, to imprisonment for a term not exceeding 6 months or to a fine not exceeding the statutory maximum or both;
- (*b*) on conviction on indictment, to imprisonment for a term not exceeding 14 years.

11   Engaging in sexual activity in the presence of a child

(1) A person aged 18 or over (A) commits an offence if—

- (*a*) he intentionally engages in an activity,
- (*b*) the activity is sexual,
- (*c*) for the purpose of obtaining sexual gratification, he engages in it—
  - (i) when another person (B) is present or is in a place from which A can be observed, and
  - (ii) knowing or believing that B is aware, or intending that B should be aware, that he is engaging in it, and
- (*d*) either—
  - (i) B is under 16 and A does not reasonably believe that B is 16 or over, or
  - (ii) B is under 13.

(2) A person guilty of an offence under this section is liable—

- (*a*) on summary conviction, to imprisonment for a term not exceeding 6 months or a fine not exceeding the statutory maximum or both;
- (*b*) on conviction on indictment, to imprisonment for a term not exceeding 10 years.

12   Causing a child to watch a sexual act

(1) A person aged 18 or over (A) commits an offence if—

- (*a*) for the purpose of obtaining sexual gratification, he intentionally causes another person (B) to watch a third person engaging in an activity, or to look at an image of any person engaging in an activity,
- (*b*) the activity is sexual, and
- (*c*) either—
  - (i) B is under 16 and A does not reasonably believe that B is 16 or over, or
  - (ii) B is under 13.

(2) A person guilty of an offence under this section is liable—

    (*a*) on summary conviction, to imprisonment for a term not exceeding 6 months or a fine not exceeding the statutory maximum or both;

    (*b*) on conviction on indictment, to imprisonment for a term not exceeding 10 years.

13   Child sex offences committed by children or young persons

(1) A person under 18 commits an offence if he does anything which would be an offence under any of sections 9 to 12 if he were aged 18.

(2) A person guilty of an offence under this section is liable—

    (*a*) on summary conviction, to imprisonment for a term not exceeding 6 months or a fine not exceeding the statutory maximum or both;

    (*b*) on conviction on indictment, to imprisonment for a term not exceeding 5 years.

14   Arranging or facilitating commission of a child sex offence

(1) A person commits an offence if—

    (*a*) he intentionally arranges or facilitates something that he intends to do, intends another person to do, or believes that another person will do, in any part of the world, and

    (*b*) doing it will involve the commission of an offence under any of sections 9 to 13.

(2) A person does not commit an offence under this section if—

    (*a*) he arranges or facilitates something that he believes another person will do, but that he does not intend to do or intend another person to do, and

    (*b*) any offence within subsection (1)(*b*) would be an offence against a child for whose protection he acts.

(3) For the purposes of subsection (2), a person acts for the protection of a child if he acts for the purpose of—

    (*a*) protecting the child from sexually transmitted infection,

    (*b*) protecting the physical safety of the child,

    (*c*) preventing the child from becoming pregnant, or

    (*d*) promoting the child's emotional well-being by the giving of advice,

and not for the purpose of obtaining sexual gratification or for the purpose of causing or encouraging the activity constituting the offence within subsection (1)(b) or the child's participation in it.

(4) A person guilty of an offence under this section is liable—

    (*a*) on summary conviction, to imprisonment for a term not exceeding 6 months or a fine not exceeding the statutory maximum or both;

    (*b*) on conviction on indictment, to imprisonment for a term not exceeding 14 years.

15   Meeting a child following sexual grooming etc.

(1) A person aged 18 or over (A) commits an offence if—

    (*a*) having met or communicated with another person (B) on at least two earlier occasions, he—

        (i) intentionally meets B, or

       (ii) travels with the intention of meeting B in any part of the world,

  (*b*) at the time, he intends to do anything to or in respect of B, during or after the meeting and in any part of the world, which if done will involve the commission by A of a relevant offence,

  (*c*) B is under 16, and

  (*d*) A does not reasonably believe that B is 16 or over.

(2) In subsection (1)—

  (*a*) the reference to A having met or communicated with B is a reference to A having met B in any part of the world or having communicated with B by any means from, to or in any part of the world;

  (*b*) 'relevant offence' means–

        (i) an offence under this Part,

       (ii) an offence within any of paragraphs 61 to 92 of Schedule 3, or

      (iii) anything done outside England and Wales and Northern Ireland which is not an offence within sub-paragraph (i) or (ii) but would be an offence within sub-paragraph (i) if done in England and Wales.

(3) In this section as it applies to Northern Ireland—

  (*a*) subsection (1) has effect with the substitution of '17' for '16' in both places;

  (*b*) subsection (2)(*b*)(iii) has effect with the substitution of 'sub-paragraph (ii) if done in Northern Ireland' for ' sub-paragraph (i) if done in England and Wales'.

(4) A person guilty of an offence under this section is liable—

  (*a*) on summary conviction, to imprisonment for a term not exceeding 6 months or a fine not exceeding the statutory maximum or both;

  (*b*) on conviction on indictment, to imprisonment for a term not exceeding 10 years.

16   Abuse of position of trust: sexual activity with a child

(1) A person aged 18 or over (A) commits an offence if—

  (*a*) he intentionally touches another person (B),

  (*b*) the touching is sexual,

  (*c*) A is in a position of trust in relation to B,

  (*d*) where subsection (2) applies, A knows or could reasonably be expected to know of the circumstances by virtue of which he is in a position of trust in relation to B, and

  (*e*) either—

        (i) B is under 18 and A does not reasonably believe that B is 18 or over, or

       (ii) B is under 13.

(2) This subsection applies where A—

  (*a*) is in a position of trust in relation to B by virtue of circumstances within section 21(2), (3), (4) or (5), and

  (*b*) is not in such a position of trust by virtue of other circumstances.

(3) Where in proceedings for an offence under this section it is proved that the other person was under 18, the defendant is to be taken not to have reasonably believed that that person was 18 or over unless sufficient evidence is adduced to raise an issue as to whether he reasonably believed it.

(4) Where in proceedings for an offence under this section—

    (*a*)   it is proved that the defendant was in a position of trust in relation to the other person by virtue of circumstances within section 21(2), (3), (4) or (5), and

    (*b*)   it is not proved that he was in such a position of trust by virtue of other circumstances,

it is to be taken that the defendant knew or could reasonably have been expected to know of the circumstances by virtue of which he was in such a position of trust unless sufficient evidence is adduced to raise an issue as to whether he knew or could reasonably have been expected to know of those circumstances.

(5) A person guilty of an offence under this section is liable—

    (*a*)   on summary conviction, to imprisonment for a term not exceeding 6 months or a fine not exceeding the statutory maximum or both;

    (*b*)   on conviction on indictment, to imprisonment for a term not exceeding 5 years.

17   Abuse of position of trust: causing or inciting a child to engage in sexual activity

(1) A person aged 18 or over (A) commits an offence if—

    (*a*)   he intentionally causes or incites another person (B) to engage in an activity,

    (*b*)   the activity is sexual,

    (*c*)   A is in a position of trust in relation to B,

    (*d*)   where subsection (2) applies, A knows or could reasonably be expected to know of the circumstances by virtue of which he is in a position of trust in relation to B, and

    (*e*)   either—

        (i)   B is under 18 and A does not reasonably believe that B is 18 or over, or

        (ii)   B is under 13.

(2) This subsection applies where A—

    (*a*)   is in a position of trust in relation to B by virtue of circumstances within section 21(2), (3), (4) or (5), and

    (*b*)   is not in such a position of trust by virtue of other circumstances.

(3) Where in proceedings for an offence under this section it is proved that the other person was under 18, the defendant is to be taken not to have reasonably believed that that person was 18 or over unless sufficient evidence is adduced to raise an issue as to whether he reasonably believed it.

(4) Where in proceedings for an offence under this section—

    (*a*)   it is proved that the defendant was in a position of trust in relation to the other person by virtue of circumstances within section 21(2), (3), (4) or (5), and (*b*) it is not proved that he was in such a position of trust by virtue of other circumstances,

it is to be taken that the defendant knew or could reasonably have been expected to know of the circumstances by virtue of which he was in such a position of trust unless sufficient evidence is adduced to raise an issue as to whether he knew or could reasonably have been expected to know of those circumstances.

(5) A person guilty of an offence under this section is liable—

    (*a*) on summary conviction, to imprisonment for a term not exceeding 6 months or a fine not exceeding the statutory maximum or both;

    (*b*) on conviction on indictment, to imprisonment for a term not exceeding 5 years.

18 Abuse of position of trust: sexual activity in the presence of a child

(1) A person aged 18 or over (A) commits an offence if—

    (*a*) he intentionally engages in an activity,

    (*b*) the activity is sexual,

    (*c*) for the purpose of obtaining sexual gratification, he engages in it—

        (i) when another person (B) is present or is in a place from which A can be observed, and

        (ii) knowing or believing that B is aware, or intending that B should be aware, that he is engaging in it,

    (*d*) A is in a position of trust in relation to B,

    (*e*) where subsection (2) applies, A knows or could reasonably be expected to know of the circumstances by virtue of which he is in a position of trust in relation to B, and

    (*f*) either—

        (i) B is under 18 and A does not reasonably believe that B is 18 or over, or

        (ii) B is under 13.

(2) This subsection applies where A—

    (*a*) is in a position of trust in relation to B by virtue of circumstances within section 21(2), (3), (4) or (5), and

    (*b*) is not in such a position of trust by virtue of other circumstances.

(3) Where in proceedings for an offence under this section it is proved that the other person was under 18, the defendant is to be taken not to have reasonably believed that that person was 18 or over unless sufficient evidence is adduced to raise an issue as to whether he reasonably believed it.

(4) Where in proceedings for an offence under this section—

    (*a*) it is proved that the defendant was in a position of trust in relation to the other person by virtue of circumstances within section 21(2), (3), (4) or (5), and

    (*b*) it is not proved that he was in such a position of trust by virtue of other circumstances,

it is to be taken that the defendant knew or could reasonably have been expected to know of the circumstances by virtue of which he was in such a position of trust unless sufficient evidence is adduced to raise an issue as to whether he knew or could reasonably have been expected to know of those circumstances.

(5) A person guilty of an offence under this section is liable—

    (*a*) on summary conviction, to imprisonment for a term not exceeding 6 months or a fine not exceeding the statutory maximum or both;

    (*b*) on conviction on indictment, to imprisonment for a term not exceeding 5 years.

19   Abuse of position of trust: causing a child to watch a sexual act

(1) A person aged 18 or over (A) commits an offence if—

    (*a*) for the purpose of obtaining sexual gratification, he intentionally causes another person (B) to watch a third person engaging in an activity, or to look at an image of any person engaging in an activity,

    (*b*) the activity is sexual,

    (*c*) A is in a position of trust in relation to B,

    (*d*) where subsection (2) applies, A knows or could reasonably be expected to know of the circumstances by virtue of which he is in a position of trust in relation to B, and

    (*e*) either—

        (i) B is under 18 and A does not reasonably believe that B is 18 or over, or

        (ii) B is under 13.

(2) This subsection applies where A—

    (*a*) is in a position of trust in relation to B by virtue of circumstances within section 21(2), (3), (4) or (5), and

    (*b*) is not in such a position of trust by virtue of other circumstances.

(3) Where in proceedings for an offence under this section it is proved that the other person was under 18, the defendant is to be taken not to have reasonably believed that that person was 18 or over unless sufficient evidence is adduced to raise an issue as to whether he reasonably believed it.

(4) Where in proceedings for an offence under this section—

    (*a*) it is proved that the defendant was in a position of trust in relation to the other person by virtue of circumstances within section 21(2), (3), (4) or (5), and

    (*b*) it is not proved that he was in such a position of trust by virtue of other circumstances,

it is to be taken that the defendant knew or could reasonably have been expected to know of the circumstances by virtue of which he was in such a position of trust unless sufficient evidence is adduced to raise an issue as to whether he knew or could reasonably have been expected to know of those circumstances.

(5) A person guilty of an offence under this section is liable—

    (*a*) on summary conviction, to imprisonment for a term not exceeding 6 months or a fine not exceeding the statutory maximum or both;

    (*b*) on conviction on indictment, to imprisonment for a term not exceeding 5 years.

[. . .]

25 Sexual activity with a child family member

(1) A person (A) commits an offence if—

- (*a*) he intentionally touches another person (B),
- (*b*) the touching is sexual,
- (*c*) the relation of A to B is within section 27,
- (*d*) A knows or could reasonably be expected to know that his relation to B is of a description falling within that section, and
- (*e*) either—

  - (i) B is under 18 and A does not reasonably believe that B is 18 or over, or
  - (ii) B is under 13.

(2) Where in proceedings for an offence under this section it is proved that the other person was under 18, the defendant is to be taken not to have reasonably believed that that person was 18 or over unless sufficient evidence is adduced to raise an issue as to whether he reasonably believed it.

(3) Where in proceedings for an offence under this section it is proved that the relation of the defendant to the other person was of a description falling within section 27, it is to be taken that the defendant knew or could reasonably have been expected to know that his relation to the other person was of that description unless sufficient evidence is adduced to raise an issue as to whether he knew or could reasonably have been expected to know that it was.

(4) A person guilty of an offence under this section, if aged 18 or over at the time of the offence, is liable—

- (*a*) where subsection (6) applies, on conviction on indictment to imprisonment for a term not exceeding 14 years;
- (*b*) in any other case—

  - (i) on summary conviction, to imprisonment for a term not exceeding 6 months or a fine not exceeding the statutory maximum or both;
  - (ii) on conviction on indictment, to imprisonment for a term not exceeding 14 years.

(5) Unless subsection (4) applies, a person guilty of an offence under this section is liable—

- (*a*) on summary conviction, to imprisonment for a term not exceeding 6 months or a fine not exceeding the statutory maximum or both;
- (*b*) on conviction on indictment, to imprisonment for a term not exceeding 5 years.

(6) This subsection applies where the touching involved—

- (*a*) penetration of B's anus or vagina with a part of A's body or anything else,
- (*b*) penetration of B's mouth with A's penis,
- (*c*) penetration of A's anus or vagina with a part of B's body, or
- (*d*) penetration of A's mouth with B's penis.

26 Inciting a child family member to engage in sexual activity

(1) A person (A) commits an offence if—

- (*a*) he intentionally incites another person (B) to touch, or allow himself to be touched by, A, (*b*)   the touching is sexual,

   (*c*)   the relation of A to B is within section 27,

   (*d*)   A knows or could reasonably be expected to know that his relation to B is of a description falling within that section, and

   (*e*)   either—

      (i) B is under 18 and A does not reasonably believe that B is 18 or over, or

      (ii) B is under 13.

(2) Where in proceedings for an offence under this section it is proved that the other person was under 18, the defendant is to be taken not to have reasonably believed that that person was 18 or over unless sufficient evidence is adduced to raise an issue as to whether he reasonably believed it.

(3) Where in proceedings for an offence under this section it is proved that the relation of the defendant to the other person was of a description falling within section 27, it is to be taken that the defendant knew or could reasonably have been expected to know that his relation to the other person was of that description unless sufficient evidence is adduced to raise an issue as to whether he knew or could reasonably have been expected to know that it was.

(4) A person guilty of an offence under this section, if he was aged 18 or over at the time of the offence, is liable—

   (*a*)   where subsection (6) applies, on conviction on indictment to imprisonment for a term not exceeding 14 years;

   (*b*)   in any other case—

      (i) on summary conviction, to imprisonment for a term not exceeding 6 months or a fine not exceeding the statutory maximum or both;

      (ii) on conviction on indictment, to imprisonment for a term not exceeding 14 years.

(5) Unless subsection (4) applies, a person guilty of an offence under this section is liable—

   (*a*)   on summary conviction, to imprisonment for a term not exceeding 6 months or a fine not exceeding the statutory maximum or both;

   (*b*)   on conviction on indictment, to imprisonment for a term not exceeding 5 years.

(6) This subsection applies where the touching to which the incitement related involved—

   (*a*)   penetration of B's anus or vagina with a part of A's body or anything else,

   (*b*)   penetration of B's mouth with A's penis,

   (*c*)   penetration of A's anus or vagina with a part of B's body, or

   (*d*)   penetration of A's mouth with B's penis.

[. . .]

30 Sexual activity with a person with a mental disorder impeding choice

(1) A person (A) commits an offence if—

   (*a*)   he intentionally touches another person (B),

   (*b*)   the touching is sexual,

(c) B is unable to refuse because of or for a reason related to a mental disorder, and

(d) A knows or could reasonably be expected to know that B has a mental disorder and that because of it or for a reason related to it B is likely to be unable to refuse.

(2) B is unable to refuse if—

(a) he lacks the capacity to choose whether to agree to the touching (whether because he lacks sufficient understanding of the nature or reasonably foreseeable consequences of what is being done, or for any other reason), or

(b) he is unable to communicate such a choice to A.

(3) A person guilty of an offence under this section, if the touching involved—

(a) penetration of B's anus or vagina with a part of A's body or anything else,

(b) penetration of B's mouth with A's penis,

(c) penetration of A's anus or vagina with a part of B's body, or

(d) penetration of A's mouth with B's penis,

is liable, on conviction on indictment, to imprisonment for life.

(4) Unless subsection (3) applies, a person guilty of an offence under this section is liable—

(a) on summary conviction, to imprisonment for a term not exceeding 6 months or to a fine not exceeding the statutory maximum or both;

(b) on conviction on indictment, to imprisonment for a term not exceeding 14 years.

[. . .]

49 Controlling a child prostitute or a child involved in pornography

(1) A person (A) commits an offence if—

(a) he intentionally controls any of the activities of another person (B) relating to B's prostitution or involvement in pornography in any part of the world, and

(b) either—

(i) B is under 18, and A does not reasonably believe that B is 18 or over, or

(ii) B is under 13.

(2) A person guilty of an offence under this section is liable—

(a) on summary conviction, to imprisonment for a term not exceeding 6 months or a fine not exceeding the statutory maximum or both;

(b) on conviction on indictment, to imprisonment for a term not exceeding 14 years.

50 Arranging or facilitating child prostitution or pornography

(1) A person (A) commits an offence if—

(a) he intentionally arranges or facilitates the prostitution or involvement in pornography in any part of the world of another person (B), and

309

(*b*) either—

    (i) B is under 18, and A does not reasonably believe that B is 18 or over, or

    (ii) B is under 13.

(2) A person guilty of an offence under this section is liable—

    (*a*) on summary conviction, to imprisonment for a term not exceeding 6 months or a fine not exceeding the statutory maximum or both;

    (*b*) on conviction on indictment, to imprisonment for a term not exceeding 14 years.

[. . .]

61   Administering a substance with intent

(1) A person commits an offence if he intentionally administers a substance to, or causes a substance to be taken by, another person (B)—

    (*a*) knowing that B does not consent, and

    (*b*) with the intention of stupefying or overpowering B, so as to enable any person to engage in a sexual activity that involves B.

(2) A person guilty of an offence under this section is liable—

    (*a*) on summary conviction, to imprisonment for a term not exceeding 6 months or a fine not exceeding the statutory maximum or both;

    (*b*) on conviction on indictment, to imprisonment for a term not exceeding 10 years.

[. . .]

66   Exposure

(1) A person commits an offence if—

    (*a*) he intentionally exposes his genitals, and

    (*b*) he intends that someone will see them and be caused alarm or distress.

(2) A person guilty of an offence under this section is liable—

    (*a*) on summary conviction, to imprisonment for a term not exceeding 6 months or a fine not exceeding the statutory maximum or both;

    (*b*) on conviction on indictment, to imprisonment for a term not exceeding 2 years.

67   Voyeurism

(1) A person commits an offence if—

    (*a*) for the purpose of obtaining sexual gratification, he observes another person doing a private act, and

    (*b*) he knows that the other person does not consent to being observed for his sexual gratification.

(2) A person commits an offence if—

    (*a*) he operates equipment with the intention of enabling another person to observe, for the purpose of obtaining sexual gratification, a third person (B) doing a private act, and (*b*) he knows that B does not consent to his operating equipment with that intention.

(3) A person commits an offence if—

    (*a*) he records another person (B) doing a private act,

    (*b*) he does so with the intention that he or a third person will, for the purpose of obtaining sexual gratification, look at an image of B doing the act, and

    (*c*) he knows that B does not consent to his recording the act with that intention.

(4) A person commits an offence if he instals equipment, or constructs or adapts a structure or part of a structure, with the intention of enabling himself or another person to commit an offence under subsection (1).

(5) A person guilty of an offence under this section is liable—

    (*a*) on summary conviction, to imprisonment for a term not exceeding 6 months or a fine not exceeding the statutory maximum or both;

    (*b*) on conviction on indictment, to imprisonment for a term not exceeding 2 years

Social Security Administration Act 1992

The following sections of the Act should be noted:

111A   Dishonest representations for obtaining benefit etc.

(1) If a person dishonestly—

    (*a*) makes a false statement or representation;

    (*b*) produces or furnishes, or causes or allows to be produced or furnished, any document or information which is false in a material particular;

    (*c*) fails to notify a change of circumstances which regulations under this Act require him to notify; or

    (*d*) causes or allows another person to fail to notify a change of circumstances which such regulations require the other person to notify,

with a view to obtaining any benefit or other payment or advantage under the relevant social security legislation (whether for himself or for some other person), he shall be guilty of an offence.

[. . .]

(3) A person guilty of an offence under this section shall be liable—

    (*a*) on summary conviction, to imprisonment for a term not exceeding six months, or to a fine not exceeding the statutory maximum, or to both; or

    (*b*) on conviction on indictment, to imprisonment for a term not exceeding seven years, or to a fine, or to both.

112   False representations for obtaining benefit etc.

(1) If a person for the purpose of obtaining any benefit or other payment under the relevant social security legislation whether for himself or some other person, or for any other purpose connected with that legislation—

311

(a) makes a statement or representation which he knows to be false; or

(b) produces or furnishes, or knowingly causes or knowingly allows to be produced or furnished, any document or information which he knows to be false in a material particular,

he shall be guilty of an offence.

(1A) If a person without reasonable excuse—

(a) fails to notify a change of circumstances which regulations under this Act require him to notify; or

(b) knowingly causes or knowingly allows another person to fail to notify a change of circumstances which such regulations require the other person to notify,

and he knows that he, or the other person, is required to notify the change of circumstances, he shall be guilty of an offence.

(2) A person guilty of an offence under this section shall be liable on summary conviction to a fine not exceeding level 5 on the standard scale, or to imprisonment for a term not exceeding 3 months, or to both.

[. . .]

114   Offences relating to contributions

(1) Any person who is knowingly concerned in the fraudulent evasion of any contributions which he or any other person is liable to pay shall be guilty of an offence.

(2) A person guilty of an offence under this section shall be liable—

(a) on conviction on indictment, to imprisonment for a term not exceeding seven years or to a fine or to both;

(b) on summary conviction, to a fine not exceeding the statutory maximum.

Terrorism Act 2000

The following sections of the Act should be noted:

11   Membership

(1) A person commits an offence if he belongs or professes to belong to a proscribed organisation.

(2) It is a defence for a person charged with an offence under subsection (1) to prove—

(a) that the organisation was not proscribed on the last (or only) occasion on which he became a member or began to profess to be a member, and

(b) that he has not taken part in the activities of the organisation at any time while it was proscribed.

(3) A person guilty of an offence under this section shall be liable—

(a) on conviction on indictment, to imprisonment for a term not exceeding ten years, to a fine or to both, or

(b) on summary conviction, to imprisonment for a term not exceeding six months, to a fine not exceeding the statutory maximum or to both.

(4) In subsection (2) 'proscribed' means proscribed for the purposes of any of the following—

    (*a*)   this Act;
    (*b*)   the Northern Ireland (Emergency Provisions) Act 1996;

    [. . .]

    (*e*)   the Prevention of Terrorism (Temporary Provisions) Act 1984;
    (*f*)   the Northern Ireland (Emergency Provisions) Act 1978;
    (*g*)   the Prevention of Terrorism (Temporary Provisions) Act 1976;
    (*h*)   the Prevention of Terrorism (Temporary Provisions) Act 1974;
    (*i*)   the Northern Ireland (Emergency Provisions) Act 1973.

12 Support

(1) A person commits an offence if—

    (*a*)   he invites support for a proscribed organisation, and
    (*b*)   the support is not, or is not restricted to, the provision of money or other property (within the meaning of section 15).

(2) A person commits an offence if he arranges, manages or assists in arranging or managing a meeting which he knows is—

    (*a*)   to support a proscribed organisation,
    (*b*)   to further the activities of a proscribed organisation, or
    (*c*)   to be addressed by a person who belongs or professes to belong to a proscribed organisation.

(3) A person commits an offence if he addresses a meeting and the purpose of his address is to encourage support for a proscribed organisation or to further its activities.

(4) Where a person is charged with an offence under subsection (2)(*c*) in respect of a private meeting it is a defence for him to prove that he had no reasonable cause to believe that the address mentioned in subsection (2)(*c*) would support a proscribed organisation or further its activities.

(5) In subsections (2) to (4)—

    (*a*)   'meeting' means a meeting of three or more persons, whether or not the public are admitted, and
    (*b*)   a meeting is private if the public are not admitted.

(6) A person guilty of an offence under this section shall be liable—

    (*a*)   on conviction on indictment, to imprisonment for a term not exceeding ten years, to a fine or to both, or
    (*b*)   on summary conviction, to imprisonment for a term not exceeding six months, to a fine not exceeding the statutory maximum or to both.

[. . .]

15 Fund-raising

(1) A person commits an offence if he—

    (*a*)   invites another to provide money or other property, and
    (*b*)   intends that it should be used, or has reasonable cause to suspect that it may be used, for the purposes of terrorism.

(2) A person commits an offence if he—

    (*a*)   receives money or other property, and

    (*b*)   intends that it should be used, or has reasonable cause to suspect that it may be used, for the purposes of terrorism.

(3) A person commits an offence if he—

    (*a*)   provides money or other property, and

    (*b*)   knows or has reasonable cause to suspect that it will or may be used for the purposes of terrorism.

(4) In this section a reference to the provision of money or other property is a reference to its being given, lent or otherwise made available, whether or not for consideration.

[Sentencing: 14 years and/or unlimited fine on indictment, 6 months and/or fine not exceeding statutory maximum if tried summarily.]

16   Use and possession

(1) A person commits an offence if he uses money or other property for the purposes of terrorism.

(2) A person commits an offence if he—

    (*a*)   possesses money or other property, and

    (*b*)   intends that it should be used, or has reasonable cause to suspect that it may be used, for the purposes of terrorism.

[Sentencing: 14 years and/or unlimited fine on indictment, 6 months and/or fine not exceeding statutory maximum if tried summarily.]

17   Funding arrangements

A person commits an offence if—

    (*a*)   he enters into or becomes concerned in an arrangement as a result of which money or other property is made available or is to be made available to another, and

    (*b*)   he knows or has reasonable cause to suspect that it will or may be used for the purposes of terrorism.

[Sentencing: 14 years and/or unlimited fine on indictment, 6 months and/or fine not exceeding statutory maximum if tried summarily.]

18   Money laundering

(1) A person commits an offence if he enters into or becomes concerned in an arrangement which facilitates the retention or control by or on behalf of another person of terrorist property—

    (*a*)   by concealment,

    (*b*)   by removal from the jurisdiction,

    (*c*)   by transfer to nominees, or

    (*d*)   in any other way.

(2) It is a defence for a person charged with an offence under subsection (1) to prove that he did not know and had no reasonable cause to suspect that the arrangement related to terrorist property.

[Sentencing: 14 years and/or unlimited fine on indictment, 6 months and/or fine not exceeding statutory maximum if tried summarily.]

[. . .]

54 Weapons training

(1) A person commits an offence if he provides instruction or training in the making or use of—

- (*a*) firearms,
- (*aa*) radioactive material or weapons designed or adapted for the discharge of any radioactive material,
- (*b*) explosives, or
- (*c*) chemical, biological or nuclear weapons.

(2) A person commits an offence if he receives instruction or training in the making or use of—

- (*a*) firearms,
- (*aa*) radioactive material or weapons designed or adapted for the discharge of any radioactive material,
- (*b*) explosives, or
- (*c*) chemical, biological or nuclear weapons.

(3) A person commits an offence if he invites another to receive instruction or training and the receipt—

- (*a*) would constitute an offence under subsection (2), or
- (*b*) would constitute an offence under subsection (2) but for the fact that it is to take place outside the United Kingdom.

(4) For the purpose of subsections (1) and (3)—

- (*a*) a reference to the provision of instruction includes a reference to making it available either generally or to one or more specific persons, and
- (*b*) an invitation to receive instruction or training may be either general or addressed to one or more specific persons.

(5) It is a defence for a person charged with an offence under this section in relation to instruction or training to prove that his action or involvement was wholly for a purpose other than assisting, preparing for or participating in terrorism.

(6) A person guilty of an offence under this section shall be liable—

- (*a*) on conviction on indictment, to imprisonment for a term not exceeding ten years, to a fine or to both, or
- (*b*) on summary conviction, to imprisonment for a term not exceeding six months, to a fine not exceeding the statutory maximum or to both.

[. . .]

56 Directing terrorist organisation

(1) A person commits an offence if he directs, at any level, the activities of an organisation which is concerned in the commission of acts of terrorism.

(2) A person guilty of an offence under this section is liable on conviction on indictment to imprisonment for life.

315

57   Possession for terrorist purposes

(1) A person commits an offence if he possesses an article in circumstances which give rise to a reasonable suspicion that his possession is for a purpose connected with the commission, preparation or instigation of an act of terrorism.

(2) It is a defence for a person charged with an offence under this section to prove that his possession of the article was not for a purpose connected with the commission, preparation or instigation of an act of terrorism.

(3) In proceedings for an offence under this section, if it is proved that an article—

  (*a*)   was on any premises at the same time as the accused, or
  (*b*)   was on premises of which the accused was the occupier or which he habitually used otherwise than as a member of the public,

the court may assume that the accused possessed the article, unless he proves that he did not know of its presence on the premises or that he had no control over it.

(4) A person guilty of an offence under this section shall be liable—

  (*a*)   on conviction on indictment, to imprisonment for a term not exceeding 10 years, to a fine or to both, or
  (*b*)   on summary conviction, to imprisonment for a term not exceeding six months, to a fine not exceeding the statutory maximum or to both.

58   Collection of information

(1) A person commits an offence if—

  (*a*)   he collects or makes a record of information of a kind likely to be useful to a person committing or preparing an act of terrorism, or
  (*b*)   he possesses a document or record containing information of that kind.

(2) In this section 'record' includes a photographic or electronic record.

(3) It is a defence for a person charged with an offence under this section to prove that he had a reasonable excuse for his action or possession.

(4) A person guilty of an offence under this section shall be liable—

  (*a*)   on conviction on indictment, to imprisonment for a term not exceeding 10 years, to a fine or to both, or
  (*b*)   on summary conviction, to imprisonment for a term not exceeding six months, to a fine not exceeding the statutory maximum or to both.

59   England and Wales

(1) A person commits an offence if—

  (*a*)   he incites another person to commit an act of terrorism wholly or partly outside the United Kingdom, and
  (*b*)   the act would, if committed in England and Wales, constitute one of the offences listed in subsection (2).

(2) Those offences are—

  (*a*)   murder,
  (*b*)   an offence under section 18 of the Offences against the Person Act 1861 (wounding with intent),
  (*c*)   an offence under section 23 or 24 of that Act (poison),

316

(*d*) an offence under section 28 or 29 of that Act (explosions), and

(*e*) an offence under section 1(2) of the Criminal Damage Act 1971 (endangering life by damaging property).

(3) A person guilty of an offence under this section shall be liable to any penalty to which he would be liable on conviction of the offence listed in subsection (2) which corresponds to the act which he incites.

(4) For the purposes of subsection (1) it is immaterial whether or not the person incited is in the United Kingdom at the time of the incitement.

(5) Nothing in this section imposes criminal liability on any person acting on behalf of, or holding office under, the Crown.

[. . .]

62   Terrorist bombing: jurisdiction

(1) If—

(*a*) a person does anything outside the United Kingdom as an act of terrorism or for the purposes of terrorism, and

(*b*) his action would have constituted the commission of one of the offences listed in subsection (2) if it had been done in the United Kingdom,

he shall be guilty of the offence.

(2) The offences referred to in subsection (1)(*b*) are—

(*a*) an offence under section 2, 3 or 5 of the Explosive Substances Act 1883 (causing explosions, etc.),

(*b*) an offence under section 1 of the Biological Weapons Act 1974 (biological weapons), and

(*c*) an offence under section 2 of the Chemical Weapons Act 1996 (chemical weapons).

63   Terrorist finance: jurisdiction.

(1) If—

(a) a person does anything outside the United Kingdom, and

(b) his action would have constituted the commission of an offence under any of sections 15 to 18 if it had been done in the United Kingdom,

he shall be guilty of the offence.

[. . .]

Theft Act 1968

The following sections of the Act should be noted:

1   Basic definition of theft

(1) A person is guilty of theft if he dishonestly appropriates property belonging to another with the intention of permanently depriving the other of it; and 'thief' and 'steal' shall be construed accordingly.

(2) It is immaterial whether the appropriation is made with a view to gain, or is made for the thief's own benefit.

317

(3) The five following sections of this Act shall have effect as regards the interpretation and operation of this section (and, except as otherwise provided by this Act, shall apply only for purposes of this section).

2 'Dishonestly'

(1) A person's appropriation of property belonging to another is not to be regarded as dishonest—

(*a*)   if he appropriates the property in the belief that he has in law the right to deprive the other of it, on behalf of himself or of a third person; or

(*b*)   if he appropriates the property in the belief that he would have the other's consent if the other knew of the appropriation and the circumstances of it; or

(*c*)   (except where the property came to him as trustee or personal representative) if he appropriates the property in the belief that the person to whom the property belongs cannot be discovered by taking reasonable steps.

(2) A person's appropriation of property belonging to another may be dishonest notwithstanding that he is willing to pay for the property.

3 'Appropriates'

(1) Any assumption by a person of the rights of an owner amounts to an appropriation, and this includes, where he has come by the property (innocently or not) without stealing it, any later assumption of a right to it by keeping or dealing with it as owner.

(2) Where property or a right or interest in property is or purports to be transferred for value to a person acting in good faith, no later assumption by him of rights which he believed himself to be acquiring shall, by reason of any defect in the transferor's title, amount to theft of the property.

4 'Property'

(1) 'Property' includes money and all other property, real or personal, including things in action and other intangible property.

[. . .]

5 'Belonging to another'

(1) Property shall be regarded as belonging to any person having possession or control of it, or having in it any proprietary right or interest (not being an equitable interest arising only from an agreement to transfer or grant an interest).

(2) Where property is subject to a trust, the persons to whom it belongs shall be regarded as including any person having a right to enforce the trust, and an intention to defeat the trust shall be regarded accordingly as an intention to deprive of the property any person having that right.

(3) Where a person receives property from or on account of another, and is under an obligation to the other to retain and deal with that property or its proceeds in a particular way, the property or proceeds shall be regarded (as against him) as belonging to the other.

(4) Where a person gets property by another's mistake, and is under an obligation to make restoration (in whole or in part) of the property or its proceeds or of the value thereof, then to the extent of that obligation the property or proceeds shall

be regarded (as against him) as belonging to the person entitled to restoration, and an intention not to make restoration shall be regarded accordingly as an intention to deprive that person of the property or proceeds.

(5) Property of a corporation sole shall be regarded as belonging to the corporation notwithstanding a vacancy in the corporation.

6 'With the intention of permanently depriving the other of it'

(1) A person appropriating property belonging to another without meaning the other permanently to lose the thing itself is nevertheless to be regarded as having the intention of permanently depriving the other of it if his intention is to treat the thing as his own to dispose of regardless of the other's rights; and a borrowing or lending of it may amount to so treating it if, but only if, the borrowing or lending is for a period and in circumstances making it equivalent to an outright taking or disposal.

(2) Without prejudice to the generality of subsection (1) above, where a person, having possession or control (lawfully or not) of property belonging to another, parts with the property under a condition as to its return which he may not be able to perform, this (if done for purposes of his own and without the other's authority) amounts to treating the property as his own to dispose of regardless of the other's rights.

7 Theft

A person guilty of theft shall on conviction on indictment be liable to imprisonment for a term not exceeding seven years. [6 months summarily]

8 Robbery

(1) A person is guilty of robbery if he steals, and immediately before or at the time of doing so, and in order to do so, he uses force on any person or puts or seeks to put any person in fear of being then and there subjected to force.

(2) A person guilty of robbery, or of an assault with intent to rob, shall on conviction on indictment be liable to imprisonment for life.

9 Burglary

(1) A person is guilty of burglary if—

- (*a*) he enters any building or part of a building as a trespasser and with intent to commit any such offence as is mentioned in subsection (2) below; or
- (*b*) having entered any building or part of a building as a trespasser he steals or attempts to steal anything in the building or that part of it or inflicts or attempts to inflict on any person therein any grievous bodily harm.

(2) The offences referred to in subsection (1)(*a*) above are offences of stealing anything in the building or part of a building in question, of inflicting on any person therein any grievous bodily harm or raping any person therein, and of doing unlawful damage to the building or anything therein.

(3) A person guilty of burglary shall on conviction on indictment be liable to imprisonment for a term not exceeding—

- (*a*) where the offence was committed in respect of a building or part of a building which is a dwelling, fourteen years;
- (*b*) in any other case, ten years.

(4) References in subsections (1) and (2) above to a building, and the reference in subsection (3) above to a building which is a dwelling, shall apply also to an inhabited vehicle or vessel, and shall apply to any such vehicle or vessel at times when the person having a habitation in it is not there as well as at times when he is.

10   Aggravated burglary

(1) A person is guilty of aggravated burglary if he commits any burglary and at the time has with him any firearm or imitation firearm, any weapon of offence, or any explosive; and for this purpose—

(a) 'firearm' includes an airgun or air pistol, and 'imitation firearm' means anything which has the appearance of being a firearm, whether capable of being discharged or not; and

(b) 'weapon of offence' means any article made or adapted for use for causing injury to or incapacitating a person, or intended by the person having it with him for such use; and

(c) 'explosive' means any article manufactured for the purpose of producing a practical effect by explosion, or intended by the person having it with him for that purpose.

(2) A person guilty of aggravated burglary shall on conviction on indictment be liable to imprisonment for life.

[. . .]

12   Taking motor vehicle or other conveyance without authority

(1) Subject to subsections (5) and (6) below, a person shall be guilty of an offence if, without having the consent of the owner or other lawful authority, he takes any conveyance for his own or another's use or, knowing that any conveyance has been taken without such authority, drives it or allows himself to be carried in or on it.

(2) A person guilty of an offence under subsection (1) above shall be liable on summary conviction to a fine not exceeding level 5 on the standard scale, to imprisonment for a term not exceeding six months, or to both.

[. . .]

(5) Subsection (1) above shall not apply in relation to pedal cycles; but, subject to subsection (6) below, a person who, without having the consent of the owner or other lawful authority, takes a pedal cycle for his own or another's use, or rides a pedal cycle knowing it to have been taken without such authority, shall on summary conviction be liable to a fine not exceeding level 3 on the standard scale.

(6) A person does not commit an offence under this section by anything done in the belief that he has lawful authority to do it or that he would have the owner's consent if the owner knew of his doing it and the circumstances of it.

12A   Aggravated vehicle-taking

(1) Subject to subsection (3) below a person is guilty of aggravated taking of a vehicle if—

(a) he commits an offence under section 12(1) above (in this section referred to as a 'basic offence') in relation to a mechanically propelled vehicle; and (*b*)   it is proved that, at any time after the vehicle was unlawfully taken (whether by him or another) and before it was recovered, the vehicle was driven, or injury or damage was caused, in one or more of the circumstances set out in paragraphs (*a*) to (*d*) of subsection (2) below.

(2) The circumstances referred to in subsection (1)(*b*) above are—

(*a*)   that the vehicle was driven dangerously on a road or other public place;

(*b*)   that, owing to the driving of the vehicle, an accident occurred by which injury was caused to any person;

(*c*)   that, owing to the driving of the vehicle, an accident occurred by which damage was caused to any property, other than the vehicle;

(*d*)   that damage was caused to the vehicle.

(3) A person is not guilty of an offence under this section if he proves that, as regards any such proven driving, injury or damage as is referred to in subsection (1)(*b*) above, either—

(*a*)   the driving, accident or damage referred to in subsection (2) above occurred before he committed the basic offence; or

(*b*)   he was neither in nor on nor in the immediate vicinity of the vehicle when that driving, accident or damage occurred.

(4) A person guilty of an offence under this section shall be liable on conviction on indictment to imprisonment for a term not exceeding two years or, if it is proved that, in circumstances falling within subsection (2)(*b*) above, the accident caused the death of the person concerned, five years.

[. . .]

(7) For the purposes of this section a vehicle is driven dangerously if—

(*a*)   it is driven in a way which falls far below what would be expected of a competent and careful driver; and

(*b*)   it would be obvious to a competent and careful driver that driving the vehicle in that way would be dangerous.

13   Abstracting of electricity

A person who dishonestly uses without due authority, or dishonestly causes to be wasted or diverted, any electricity shall on conviction on indictment be liable to imprisonment for a term not exceeding five years.

[. . .]

15   Obtaining property by deception

(1) A person who by any deception dishonestly obtains property belonging to another, with the intention of permanently depriving the other of it, shall on conviction on indictment be liable to imprisonment for a term not exceeding ten years.

(2) For purposes of this section a person is to be treated as obtaining property if he obtains ownership, possession or control of it, and 'obtain' includes obtaining for another or enabling another to obtain or to retain.

(3) Section 6 above shall apply for purposes of this section, with the necessary adaptation of the reference to appropriating, as it applies for purposes of section 1.

(4) For purposes of this section 'deception' means any deception (whether deliberate or reckless) by words or conduct as to fact or as to law, including a deception as to the present intentions of the person using the deception or any other person.

15A Obtaining a money transfer by deception

(1) A person is guilty of an offence if by any deception he dishonestly obtains a money transfer for himself or another.

(2) A money transfer occurs when—

    (*a*) a debit is made to one account,
    (*b*) a credit is made to another, and
    (*c*) the credit results from the debit or the debit results from the credit.

(3) References to a credit and to a debit are to a credit of an amount of money and to a debit of an amount of money.

(4) It is immaterial (in particular)—

    (*a*) whether the amount credited is the same as the amount debited;
    (*b*) whether the money transfer is effected on presentment of a cheque or by another method;
    (*c*) whether any delay occurs in the process by which the money transfer is effected;
    (*d*) whether any intermediate credits or debits are made in the course of the money transfer;
    (*e*) whether either of the accounts is overdrawn before or after the money transfer is effected.

(5) A person guilty of an offence under this section shall be liable on conviction on indictment to imprisonment for a term not exceeding ten years.

15B Section 15A: supplementary

(1) The following provisions have effect for the interpretation of section 15A of this Act.

(2) 'Deception' has the same meaning as in section 15 of this Act.

(3) 'Account' means an account kept with—

    (*a*) a bank; or
    (*b*) a person carrying on a business which falls within subsection (4) below.

(4) A business falls within this subsection if—

    (*a*) in the course of the business money received by way of deposit is lent to others; or
    (*b*) any other activity of the business is financed, wholly or to any material extent, out of the capital of or the interest on money received by way of deposit;

and 'deposit' here has the same meaning as in section 35 of the Banking Act 1987 (fraudulent inducement to make a deposit).

(5) For the purposes of subsection (4) above—

    (*a*) all the activities which a person carries on by way of business shall be regarded as a single business carried on by him; and (*b*) 'money' includes money expressed in a currency other than sterling or in the European currency unit (as defined in Council Regulation No. 3320/94/EC or any Community instrument replacing it).

16 Obtaining pecuniary advantage by deception

(1) A person who by any deception dishonestly obtains for himself or another any pecuniary advantage shall on conviction on indictment be liable to imprisonment for a term not exceeding five years.

(2) The cases in which a pecuniary advantage within the meaning of this section is to be regarded as obtained for a person are cases where—

(*a*) [. . .]
(*b*) he is allowed to borrow by way of overdraft, or to take out any policy of insurance or annuity contract, or obtains an improvement of the terms on which he is allowed to do so; or
(*c*) he is given the opportunity to earn remuneration or greater remuneration in an office or employment, or to win money by betting.

(3) For purposes of this section 'deception' has the same meaning as in section 15 of this Act.

17 False accounting

(1) Where a person dishonestly with a view to gain for himself or another or with intent to cause loss to another—

(*a*) destroys, defaces, conceals or falsifies any account or any record or document made or required for any accounting purpose; or
(*b*) in furnishing information for any purpose produces or makes use of any account, or any such record or document as aforesaid, which to his knowledge is or may be misleading, false or deceptive in a material particular

he shall, on conviction on indictment, be liable to imprisonment for a term not exceeding seven years.

(2) For purposes of this section a person who makes or concurs in making in an account or other document an entry which is or may be misleading, false or deceptive in a material particular, or who omits or concurs in omitting a material particular from an account or other document, is to be treated as falsifying the account or document.

[. . .]

19 False statements by company directors, etc.

(1) Where an officer of a body corporate or unincorporated association (or person purporting to act as such), with intent to deceive members or creditors of the body corporate or association about its affairs, publishes or concurs in publishing a written statement or account which to his knowledge is or may be misleading, false or deceptive in a material particular, he shall on conviction on indictment be liable to imprisonment for a term not exceeding seven years.

(2) For purposes of this section a person who has entered into a security for the benefit of a body corporate or association is to be treated as a creditor of it.

[. . .]

21   Blackmail

(1) A person is guilty of blackmail if, with a view to gain for himself or another or with intent to cause loss to another, he makes any unwarranted demand with menaces; and for this purpose a demand with menaces is unwarranted unless the person making it does so in the belief—

    (*a*)   that he has reasonable grounds for making the demand; and
    (*b*)   that the use of the menaces is a proper means of reinforcing the demand.

(2) The nature of the act or omission demanded is immaterial, and it is also immaterial whether the menaces relate to action to be taken by the person making the demand.

(3) A person guilty of blackmail shall on conviction on indictment be liable to imprisonment for a term not exceeding fourteen years.

22   Handling stolen goods

(1) A person handles stolen goods if (otherwise than in the course of the stealing) knowing or believing them to be stolen goods he dishonestly receives the goods, or dishonestly undertakes or assists in their retention, removal, disposal or realisation by or for the benefit of another person, or if he arranges to do so.

(2) A person guilty of handling stolen goods shall on conviction on indictment be liable to imprisonment for a term not exceeding fourteen years.

[. . .]

24A   Dishonestly retaining a wrongful credit

(1) A person is guilty of an offence if—

    (*a*)   a wrongful credit has been made to an account kept by him or in respect of which he has any right or interest;
    (*b*)   he knows or believes that the credit is wrongful; and
    (*c*)   he dishonestly fails to take such steps as are reasonable in the circumstances to secure that the credit is cancelled.

(2) References to a credit are to a credit of an amount of money.

(3) A credit to an account is wrongful if it is the credit side of a money transfer obtained contrary to section 15A of this Act.

(4) A credit to an account is also wrongful to the extent that it derives from—

    (*a*)   theft;
    (*b*)   an offence under section 15A of this Act;
    (*c*)   blackmail; or
    (*d*)   stolen goods.

(5) In determining whether a credit to an account is wrongful, it is immaterial (in particular) whether the account is overdrawn before or after the credit is made.

(6) A person guilty of an offence under this section shall be liable on conviction on indictment to imprisonment for a term not exceeding ten years.

(7) Subsection (8) below applies for purposes of provisions of this Act relating to stolen goods (including subsection (4) above).

(8) References to stolen goods include money which is dishonestly withdrawn from an account to which a wrongful credit has been made, but only to the extent that the money derives from the credit.

(9) In this section 'account' and 'money' shall be construed in accordance with section 15B of this Act.

25 Going equipped for stealing, etc.

(1) A person shall be guilty of an offence if, when not at his place of abode, he has with him any article for use in the course of or in connection with any burglary, theft or cheat.

(2) A person guilty of an offence under this section shall on conviction on indictment be liable to imprisonment for a term not exceeding three years.

(3) Where a person is charged with an offence under this section, proof that he had with him any article made or adapted for use in committing a burglary, theft or cheat shall be evidence that he had it with him for such use.

[. . .]

(5) For purposes of this section an offence under section 12(1) of this Act of taking a conveyance shall be treated as theft, and 'cheat' means an offence under section 15 of this Act.

Theft Act 1978

The following sections of this Act should be noted:

1 Obtaining services by deception

(1) A person who by any deception dishonestly obtains services from another shall be guilty of an offence.

(2) It is an obtaining of services where the other is induced to confer a benefit by doing some act, or causing or permitting some act to be done, on the understanding that the benefit has been or will be paid for.

(3) Without prejudice to the generality of subsection (2) above, it is an obtaining of services where the other is induced to make a loan, or to cause or permit a loan to be made, on the understanding that any payment (whether by way of interest or otherwise) will be or has been made in respect of the loan.

2 Evasion of liability by deception

(1) Subject to subsection (2) below, where a person by any deception—

    (*a*) dishonestly secures the remission of the whole or part of any existing liability to make a payment, whether his own liability or another's; or

    (*b*) with intent to make permanent default in whole or in part on any existing liability to make a payment, or with intent to let another do so, dishonestly induces the creditor or any person claiming payment on behalf of the creditor to wait for payment (whether or not the due date for payment is deferred) or to forgo payment; or (*c*)   dishonestly obtains any exemption from or abatement of liability to make a payment;

he shall be guilty of an offence.

(2) For purposes of this section 'liability' means legally enforceable liability; and subsection (1) shall not apply in relation to a liability that has not been accepted or established to pay compensation for a wrongful act or omission.

(3) For purposes of subsection (1)(*b*) a person induced to take in payment a cheque or other security for money by way of conditional satisfaction of a pre-existing liability is to be treated not as being paid but as being induced to wait for payment.

(4) For purposes of subsection (1)(*c*) 'obtains' includes obtaining for another or enabling another to obtain.

3   Making off without payment

(1) Subject to subsection (3) below, a person who, knowing that payment on the spot for any goods supplied or service done is required or expected from him, dishonestly makes off without having paid as required or expected and with intent to avoid payment of the amount due shall be guilty of an offence.

(2) For purposes of this section 'payment on the spot' includes payment at the time of collecting goods on which work has been done or in respect of which service has been provided.

(3) Subsection (1) above shall not apply where the supply of the goods or the doing of the service is contrary to law, or where the service done is such that payment is not legally enforceable.

(4) Any person may arrest without warrant anyone who is or whom he, with reasonable cause, suspects to be, committing or attempting to commit an offence under this section.

4   Punishments

(1) Offences under this Act shall be punishable either on conviction on indictment or on summary conviction.

(2) A person convicted on indictment shall be liable—

    (*a*)   for an offence under section 1 or section 2 of this Act, to imprisonment for a term not exceeding five years; and

    (*b*)   for an offence under section 3 of this Act, to imprisonment for a term not exceeding two years.

(3) A person convicted summarily of any offence under this Act shall be liable—

    (*a*)   to imprisonment for a term not exceeding six months; or

    (*b*)   to a fine not exceeding the prescribed sum for the purposes of section 32 of the Magistrates' Courts Act 1980 (punishment on summary conviction of offences triable either way: £1,000 or other sum substituted by order under that Act), or to both.

APPENDIX A

Police and Criminal Evidence Act 1984 (s.60(1)(a), s.60A(1) and s.66(1)): Codes of Practice A–G revised edition (effective 1 January 2006)

FOREWORD

This booklet contains revised Codes of Practice A–G. Sections 60 and 66 (as amended) of the Police and Criminal Evidence Act 1984 (PACE) provide for the Secretary of State to issue Codes of Practice governing certain key areas of police procedure. The existing Codes are:

- Code A: Stop and Search and recording of public encounters. The exercise by police officers of statutory powers of stop and search and requirements for police officers and other police staff to record public encounters. This Code was last revised on 1 August 2004. [pp. 328–345.]
- Code B: Searching of premises and seizure of property. This Code governs the exercise of police powers in respect of the searching of premises and the seizure of property found by police officers on persons or premises. This Code was last revised on 1 August 2004. [pp. 346–361.]
- Code C: Detention, treatment and questioning. The purpose of this Code is to ensure that all persons suspected of being involved in crime, and others who are in police custody, are dealt with fairly and properly in accordance with the law. This Code was last revised on 1 August 2004. The Code outlines powers in respect of testing for the presence of class A drugs in specified police areas. [pp. 362–420.]
- Code D: Identification. This Code concerns the principal methods used by police for identifying persons in connection with the investigation of offences and the keeping of accurate and reliable criminal records. This Code was last revised on 1 August 2004. [pp. 421–459.]
- Code E: Audio recording of interviews with suspects. This Code deals with the audio recording of interviews with persons suspected of certain types of criminal offences and governs the way in which audio recorded interviews are carried out. This Code was last revised on 1 August 2004. [pp. 460–466.]
- Code F: Visual recording of interviews. This Code sets out the procedure by which police may consider carrying out a visual recording of an interview with a suspect. There is no statutory requirement on police to visually record interviews. The Code was introduced in April 2002. [pp. 467–475.]
- Code G: Power of arrest. This Code sets out the criteria the police must consider when exercising their power of arrest under section 24 of PACE as amended by section 110 of the Serious Organised Crime and Police Act 2005. [pp. 476–480.]

[...]

CODE A: FOR THE EXERCISE BY:
POLICE OFFICERS OF STATUTORY POWERS OF STOP AND SEARCH

POLICE OFFICERS AND POLICE STAFF OF REQUIREMENTS TO RECORD PUBLIC ENCOUNTERS

Commencement – Transitional Arrangements

This code applies to any search by a police officer and the requirement to record public encounters taking place after midnight on 31 December 2005.

GENERAL

This code of practice must be readily available at all police stations for consultation by police officers, detained persons and members of the public.

The notes for guidance included are not provisions of this code, but are guidance to police officers and others about its application and interpretation. Provisions in the annexes to the code are provisions of this code.

This code governs the exercise by police officers of statutory powers to search a person or a vehicle without first making an arrest. The main stop and search powers to which this code applies are set out in Annex A, but that list should not be regarded as definitive. See Note 1.

In addition, it covers requirements on police officers and police staff to record encounters not governed by statutory powers. This code does not apply to:

(a)   the powers of stop and search under;

    (i)   Aviation Security Act 1982, section 27(2);

    (ii) Police and Criminal Evidence Act 1984, section 6(1) (which relates specifically to powers of constables employed by statutory undertakers on the premises of the statutory undertakers).

(b)   searches carried out for the purposes of examination under Schedule 7 to the Terrorism Act 2000 and to which the Code of Practice issued under paragraph 6 of Schedule 14 to the Terrorism Act 2000 applies.

1   PRINCIPLES GOVERNING STOP AND SEARCH

1.1   Powers to stop and search must be used fairly, responsibly, with respect for people being searched and without unlawful discrimination. The Race Relations (Amendment) Act 2000 makes it unlawful for police officers to discriminate on the grounds of race, colour, ethnic origin, nationality or national origins when using their powers.

1.2   The intrusion on the liberty of the person stopped or searched must be brief and detention for the purposes of a search must take place at or near the location of the stop.

1.3   If these fundamental principles are not observed the use of powers to stop and search may be drawn into question. Failure to use the powers in the proper manner reduces their effectiveness. Stop and search can play an important role in the detection and prevention of crime, and using the powers fairly makes them more effective.

1.4   The primary purpose of stop and search powers is to enable officers to allay or confirm suspicions about individuals without exercising their power of arrest. Officers may be required to justify the use or authorisation of such powers, in relation both to individual searches and the overall pattern of their activity in this regard, to their supervisory officers or in court. Any misuse of the powers is likely to be harmful to policing and lead to mistrust of the police. Officers must also be able to explain their actions to the member of the public searched. The misuse of these powers can lead to disciplinary action.

1.5 An officer must not search a person, even with his or her consent, where no power to search is applicable. Even where a person is prepared to submit to a search voluntarily, the person must not be searched unless the necessary legal power exists, and the search must be in accordance with the relevant power and the provisions of this Code. The only exception, where an officer does not require a specific power, applies to searches of persons entering sports grounds or other premises carried out with their consent given as a condition of entry.

2 EXPLANATION OF POWERS TO STOP AND SEARCH

2.1 This code applies to powers of stop and search as follows:

(a) powers which require reasonable grounds for suspicion, before they may be exercised; that articles unlawfully obtained or possessed are being carried, or under section 43 of the Terrorism Act 2000 that a person is a terrorist;

(b) authorised under section 60 of the Criminal Justice and Public Order Act 1994, based upon a reasonable belief that incidents involving serious violence may take place or that people are carrying dangerous instruments or offensive weapons within any locality in the police area;

(c) authorised under section 44(1) and (2) of the Terrorism Act 2000 based upon a consideration that the exercise of one or both powers is expedient for the prevention of acts of terrorism;

(d) powers to search a person who has not been arrested in the exercise of a power to search premises (see Code B paragraph 2.4).

Searches requiring reasonable grounds for suspicion

2.2 Reasonable grounds for suspicion depend on the circumstances in each case. There must be an objective basis for that suspicion based on facts, information, and/or intelligence which are relevant to the likelihood of finding an article of a certain kind or, in the case of searches under section 43 of the Terrorism Act 2000, to the likelihood that the person is a terrorist. Reasonable suspicion can never be supported on the basis of personal factors alone without reliable supporting intelligence or information or some specific behaviour by the person concerned. For example, a person's race, age, appearance, or the fact that the person is known to have a previous conviction, cannot be used alone or in combination with each other as the reason for searching that person. Reasonable suspicion cannot be based on generalisations or stereotypical images of certain groups or categories of people as more likely to be involved in criminal activity. A person's religion cannot be considered as reasonable grounds for suspicion and should never be considered as a reason to stop or stop and search an individual.

2.3 Reasonable suspicion can sometimes exist without specific information or intelligence and on the basis of some level of generalisation stemming from the behaviour of a person. For example, if an officer encounters someone on the street at night who is obviously trying to hide something, the officer may (depending on the other surrounding circumstances) base such suspicion on the fact that this kind of behaviour is often linked to stolen or prohibited articles being carried. Similarly, for the purposes of section 43 of the Terrorism Act 2000, suspicion that a person is a terrorist may arise from the person's behaviour at or near a location which has been identified as a potential target for terrorists.

2.4   However, reasonable suspicion should normally be linked to accurate and current intelligence or information, such as information describing an article being carried, a suspected offender, or a person who has been seen carrying a type of article known to have been stolen recently from premises in the area. Searches based on accurate and current intelligence or information are more likely to be effective. Targeting searches in a particular area at specified crime problems increases their effectiveness and minimises inconvenience to law-abiding members of the public. It also helps in justifying the use of searches both to those who are searched and to the public. This does not however prevent stop and search powers being exercised in other locations where such powers may be exercised and reasonable suspicion exists.

2.5   Searches are more likely to be effective, legitimate, and secure public confidence when reasonable suspicion is based on a range of factors. The overall use of these powers is more likely to be effective when up to date and accurate intelligence or information is communicated to officers and they are well-informed about local crime patterns.

2.6   Where there is reliable information or intelligence that members of a group or gang habitually carry knives unlawfully or weapons or controlled drugs, and wear a distinctive item of clothing or other means of identification to indicate their membership of the group or gang, that distinctive item of clothing or other means of identification may provide reasonable grounds to stop and search a person. See Note 9.

2.7   A police officer may have reasonable grounds to suspect that a person is in innocent possession of a stolen or prohibited article or other item for which he or she is empowered to search. In that case the officer may stop and search the person even though there would be no power of arrest.

2.8   Under section 43(1) of the Terrorism Act 2000 a constable may stop and search a person whom the officer reasonably suspects to be a terrorist to discover whether the person is in possession of anything which may constitute evidence that the person is a terrorist. These searches may only be carried out by an officer of the same sex as the person searched.

2.9   An officer who has reasonable grounds for suspicion may detain the person concerned in order to carry out a search. Before carrying out a search the officer may ask questions about the person's behaviour or presence in circumstances which gave rise to the suspicion. As a result of questioning the detained person, the reasonable grounds for suspicion necessary to detain that person may be confirmed or, because of a satisfactory explanation, be eliminated. See Notes 2 and 3. Questioning may also reveal reasonable grounds to suspect the possession of a different kind of unlawful article from that originally suspected. Reasonable grounds for suspicion however cannot be provided retrospectively by such questioning during a person's detention or by refusal to answer any questions put.

2.10   If, as a result of questioning before a search, or other circumstances which come to the attention of the officer, there cease to be reasonable grounds for suspecting that an article is being carried of a kind for which there is a power to stop and search, no search may take place. See Note 3. In the absence of any other lawful power to detain, the person is free to leave at will and must be so informed.

2.11   There is no power to stop or detain a person in order to find grounds for a search. Police officers have many encounters with members of the public which do not involve detaining people against their will. If reasonable grounds for suspicion emerge during such an encounter, the officer may search the person, even though no grounds existed when the encounter began. If an officer is detaining someone for the purpose of a search, he or she should inform the person as soon as detention begins.

Searches authorised under section 60 of the Criminal Justice and Public Order Act 1994

2.12 Authority for a constable in uniform to stop and search under section 60 of the Criminal Justice and Public Order Act 1994 may be given if the authorising officer reasonably believes:

(a) that incidents involving serious violence may take place in any locality in the officer's police area, and it is expedient to use these powers to prevent their occurrence, or

(b) that persons are carrying dangerous instruments or offensive weapons without good reason in any locality in the officer's police area.

2.13 An authorisation under section 60 may only be given by an officer of the rank of inspector or above, in writing, specifying the grounds on which it was given, the locality in which the powers may be exercised and the period of time for which they are in force. The period authorised shall be no longer than appears reasonably necessary to prevent, or seek to prevent incidents of serious violence, or to deal with the problem of carrying dangerous instruments or offensive weapons. It may not exceed 24 hours. See Notes 10–13.

2.14 If an inspector gives an authorisation, he or she must, as soon as practicable, inform an officer of or above the rank of superintendent. This officer may direct that the authorisation shall be extended for a further 24 hours, if violence or the carrying of dangerous instruments or offensive weapons has occurred, or is suspected to have occurred, and the continued use of the powers is considered necessary to prevent or deal with further such activity. That direction must also be given in writing at the time or as soon as practicable afterwards. See Note 12.

Powers to require removal of face coverings

2.15 Section 60AA of the Criminal Justice and Public Order Act 1994 also provides a power to demand the removal of disguises. The officer exercising the power must reasonably believe that someone is wearing an item wholly or mainly for the purpose of concealing identity. There is also a power to seize such items where the officer believes that a person intends to wear them for this purpose. There is no power to stop and search for disguises. An officer may seize any such item which is discovered when exercising a power of search for something else, or which is being carried, and which the officer reasonably believes is intended to be used for concealing anyone's identity. This power can only be used if an authorisation under section 60 or an authorisation under section 60AA is in force.

2.16 Authority for a constable in uniform to require the removal of disguises and to seize them under section 60AA may be given if the authorising officer reasonably believes that activities may take place in any locality in the officer's police area that are likely to involve the commission of offences and it is expedient to use these powers to prevent or control these activities.

2.17 An authorisation under section 60AA may only be given by an officer of the rank of inspector or above, in writing, specifying the grounds on which it was given, the locality in which the powers may be exercised and the period of time for which they are in force. The period authorised shall be no longer than appears reasonably necessary to prevent, or seek to prevent the commission of offences. It may not exceed 24 hours. See Notes 10–13.

2.18   If an inspector gives an authorisation, he or she must, as soon as practicable, inform an officer of or above the rank of superintendent. This officer may direct that the authorisation shall be extended for a further 24 hours, if crimes have been committed, or is suspected to have been committed, and the continued use of the powers is considered necessary to prevent or deal with further such activity. This direction must also be given in writing at the time or as soon as practicable afterwards. See Note 12.

Searches authorised under section 44 of the Terrorism Act 2000

2.19   An officer of the rank of assistant chief constable (or equivalent) or above, may give authority for the following powers of stop and search under section 44 of the Terrorism Act 2000 to be exercised in the whole or part of his or her police area if the officer considers it is expedient for the prevention of acts of terrorism:

   (a)   under section 44(1) of the Terrorism Act 2000, to give a constable in uniform power to stop and search any vehicle, its driver, any passenger in the vehicle and anything in or on the vehicle or carried by the driver or any passenger; and

   (b)   under section 44(2) of the Terrorism Act 2000, to give a constable in uniform power to stop and search any pedestrian and anything carried by the pedestrian.

An authorisation under section 44(1) may be combined with one under section 44(2).

2.20   If an authorisation is given orally at first, it must be confirmed in writing by the officer who gave it as soon as reasonably practicable.

2.21   When giving an authorisation, the officer must specify the geographical area in which the power may be used, and the time and date that the authorisation ends (up to a maximum of 28 days from the time the authorisation was given). See Notes 12 and 13.

2.22   The officer giving an authorisation under section 44(1) or (2) must cause the Secretary of State to be informed, as soon as reasonably practicable, that such an authorisation has been given. An authorisation which is not confirmed by the Secretary of State within 48 hours of its having been given, shall have effect up until the end of that 48 hour period or the end of the period specified in the authorisation (whichever is the earlier). See Note 14.

2.23   Following notification of the authorisation, the Secretary of State may:

   (i)   cancel the authorisation with immediate effect or with effect from such other time as he or she may direct;

   (ii)   confirm it but for a shorter period than that specified in the authorisation; or

   (iii) confirm the authorisation as given.

2.24   When an authorisation under section 44 is given, a constable in uniform may exercise the powers:

   (a)   only for the purpose of searching for articles of a kind which could be used in connection with terrorism (see paragraph 2.25);

   (b)   whether or not there are any grounds for suspecting the presence of such articles.

2.24A   When a Community Support Officer on duty and in uniform has been conferred powers under Section 44 of the Terrorism Act 2000 by a Chief Officer of their force, the exercise of this power must comply with the requirements of this Code of Practice, including the recording requirements.

2.25 The selection of persons stopped under section 44 of Terrorism Act 2000 should reflect an objective assessment of the threat posed by the various terrorist groups active in Great Britain. The powers must not be used to stop and search for reasons unconnected with terrorism. Officers must take particular care not to discriminate against members of minority ethnic groups in the exercise of these powers. There may be circumstances, however, where it is appropriate for officers to take account of a person's ethnic origin in selecting persons to be stopped in response to a specific terrorist threat (for example, some international terrorist groups are associated with particular ethnic identities). See Notes 12 and 13.

2.26 The powers under sections 43 and 44 of the Terrorism Act 2000 allow a constable to search only for articles which could be used for terrorist purposes. However, this would not prevent a search being carried out under other powers if, in the course of exercising these powers, the officer formed reasonable grounds for suspicion.

Powers to search in the exercise of a power to search premises

2.27 The following powers to search premises also authorise the search of a person, not under arrest, who is found on the premises during the course of the search:

(a) section 139B of the Criminal Justice Act 1988 under which a constable may enter school premises and search the premises and any person on those premises for any bladed or pointed article or offensive weapon; and

(b) under a warrant issued under section s.23(3) of the Misuse of Drugs Act 1971 to search premises for drugs or documents but only if the warrant specifically authorises the search of persons found on the premises.

2.28 Before the power under section 139B of the Criminal Justice Act 1988 may be exercised, the constable must have reasonable grounds to believe that an offence under section 139A of the Criminal Justice Act 1988 (having a bladed or pointed article or offensive weapon on school premises) has been or is being committed. A warrant to search premises and persons found therein may be issued under section s.23(3) of the Misuse of Drugs Act 1971 if there are reasonable grounds to suspect that controlled drugs or certain documents are in the possession of a person on the premises.

2.29 The powers in paragraph 2.27(a) or (b) do not require prior specific grounds to suspect that the person to be searched is in possession of an item for which there is an existing power to search. However, it is still necessary to ensure that the selection and treatment of those searched under these powers is based upon objective factors connected with the search of the premises, and not upon personal prejudice.

3 CONDUCT OF SEARCHES

3.1 All stops and searches must be carried out with courtesy, consideration and respect for the person concerned. This has a significant impact on public confidence in the police. Every reasonable effort must be made to minimise the embarrassment that a person being searched may experience. See Note 4.

3.2 The co-operation of the person to be searched must be sought in every case, even if the person initially objects to the search. A forcible search may be made only if it has been established that the person is unwilling to co-operate or resists. Reasonable force may be used as a last resort if necessary to conduct a search or to detain a person or vehicle for the purposes of a search.

3.3   The length of time for which a person or vehicle may be detained must be reasonable and kept to a minimum. Where the exercise of the power requires reasonable suspicion, the thoroughness and extent of a search must depend on what is suspected of being carried, and by whom. If the suspicion relates to a particular article which is seen to be slipped into a person's pocket, then, in the absence of other grounds for suspicion or an opportunity for the article to be moved elsewhere, the search must be confined to that pocket. In the case of a small article which can readily be concealed, such as a drug, and which might be concealed anywhere on the person, a more extensive search may be necessary. In the case of searches mentioned in paragraph 2.1(b), (c), and (d), which do not require reasonable grounds for suspicion, officers may make any reasonable search to look for items for which they are empowered to search. See Note 5.

3.4   The search must be carried out at or near the place where the person or vehicle was first detained. See Note 6.

3.5   There is no power to require a person to remove any clothing in public other than an outer coat, jacket or gloves except under section 45(3) of the Terrorism Act 2000 (which empowers a constable conducting a search under section 44(1) or 44(2) of that Act to require a person to remove headgear and footwear in public) and under section 60AA of the Criminal Justice and Public Order Act 1994 (which empowers a constable to require a person to remove any item worn to conceal identity). See Notes 4 and 6. A search in public of a person's clothing which has not been removed must be restricted to superficial examination of outer garments. This does not, however, prevent an officer from placing his or her hand inside the pockets of the outer clothing, or feeling round the inside of collars, socks and shoes if this is reasonably necessary in the circumstances to look for the object of the search or to remove and examine any item reasonably suspected to be the object of the search. For the same reasons, subject to the restrictions on the removal of headgear, a person's hair may also be searched in public (see paragraphs 3.1 and 3.3).

3.6   Where on reasonable grounds it is considered necessary to conduct a more thorough search (e.g. by requiring a person to take off a T-shirt), this must be done out of public view, for example, in a police van unless paragraph 3.7 applies, or police station if there is one nearby. See Note 6. Any search involving the removal of more than an outer coat, jacket, gloves, headgear or footwear, or any other item concealing identity, may only be made by an officer of the same sex as the person searched and may not be made in the presence of anyone of the opposite sex unless the person being searched specifically requests it. See Notes 4, 7 and 8.

3.7   Searches involving exposure of intimate parts of the body must not be conducted as a routine extension of a less thorough search, simply because nothing is found in the course of the initial search. Searches involving exposure of intimate parts of the body may be carried out only at a nearby police station or other nearby location which is out of public view (but not a police vehicle). These searches must be conducted in accordance with paragraph 11 of Annex A to Code C except that an intimate search mentioned in paragraph 11(f) of Annex A to Code C may not be authorised or carried out under any stop and search powers. The other provisions of Code C do not apply to the conduct and recording of searches of persons detained at police stations in the exercise of stop and search powers. See Note 7.

Steps to be taken prior to a search

3.8   Before any search of a detained person or attended vehicle takes place the officer must take reasonable steps to give the person to be searched or in charge of the vehicle the following information:

(a)   that they are being detained for the purposes of a search;

(b)   the officer's name (except in the case of enquiries linked to the investigation of terrorism, or otherwise where the officer reasonably believes that giving his or her name might put him or her in danger, in which case a warrant or other identification number shall be given) and the name of the police station to which the officer is attached;

(c)   the legal search power which is being exercised; and

(d)   a clear explanation of:

 (i)   the purpose of the search in terms of the article or articles for which there is a power to search; and

 (ii)   in the case of powers requiring reasonable suspicion (see paragraph 2.1(a)), the grounds for that suspicion; or

 (iii)   in the case of powers which do not require reasonable suspicion (see paragraph 2.1(b), and (c)), the nature of the power and of any necessary authorisation and the fact that it has been given.

3.9   Officers not in uniform must show their warrant cards. Stops and searches under the powers mentioned in paragraphs 2.1(b), and (c) may be undertaken only by a constable in uniform.

3.10   Before the search takes place the officer must inform the person (or the owner or person in charge of the vehicle that is to be searched) of his or her entitlement to a copy of the record of the search, including his entitlement to a record of the search if an application is made within 12 months, if it is wholly impracticable to make a record at the time. If a record is not made at the time the person should also be told how a copy can be obtained (see section 4). The person should also be given information about police powers to stop and search and the individual's rights in these circumstances.

3.11   If the person to be searched, or in charge of a vehicle to be searched, does not appear to understand what is being said, or there is any doubt about the person's ability to understand English, the officer must take reasonable steps to bring information regarding the person's rights and any relevant provisions of this Code to his or her attention. If the person is deaf or cannot understand English and is accompanied by someone, then the officer must try to establish whether that person can interpret or otherwise help the officer to give the required information.

4   RECORDING REQUIREMENTS

4.1   An officer who has carried out a search in the exercise of any power to which this Code applies, must make a record of it at the time, unless there are exceptional circumstances which would make this wholly impracticable (e.g. in situations involving public disorder or when the officer's presence is urgently required elsewhere). If a record is not made at the time, the officer must do so as soon as practicable afterwards. There may be situations in which it is not practicable to obtain the information necessary to complete a record, but the officer should make every reasonable effort to do so. See Note 21.

4.2   A copy of a record made at the time must be given immediately to the person who has been searched. The officer must ask for the name, address and date of birth of the person searched, but there is no obligation on a person to provide these details and no power of detention if the person is unwilling to do so.

4.3   The following information must always be included in the record of a search even if the person does not wish to provide any personal details:

    (i)   the name of the person searched, or (if it is withheld) a description;

    (ii)   a note of the person's self-defined ethnic background; see Note 18;

    (iii)   when a vehicle is searched, its registration number; see Note 16;

    (iv)   the date, time, and place that the person or vehicle was first detained;

    (v)   the date, time and place the person or vehicle was searched (if different from (iv));

    (vi)   the purpose of the search;

    (vii)   the grounds for making it, or in the case of those searches mentioned in paragraph 2.1(b) and (c), the nature of the power and of any necessary authorisation and the fact that it has been given; see Note 17;

    (viii)   its outcome (e.g. arrest or no further action);

    (ix)   a note of any injury or damage to property resulting from it;

    (x)   subject to paragraph 3.8(b), the identity of the officer making the search. See Note 15.

4.4   Nothing in paragraph 4.3 (x) or 4.10A requires the names of police officers to be shown on the search record or any other record required to be made under this code in the case of enquiries linked to the investigation of terrorism or otherwise where an officer reasonably believes that recording names might endanger the officers. In such cases the record must show the officers' warrant or other identification number and duty station.

4.5   A record is required for each person and each vehicle searched. However, if a person is in a vehicle and both are searched, and the object and grounds of the search are the same, only one record need be completed. If more than one person in a vehicle is searched, separate records for each search of a person must be made. If only a vehicle is searched, the name of the driver and his or her self-defined ethnic background must be recorded, unless the vehicle is unattended.

4.6   The record of the grounds for making a search must, briefly but informatively, explain the reason for suspecting the person concerned, by reference to the person's behaviour and/or other circumstances.

4.7   Where officers detain an individual with a view to performing a search, but the search is not carried out due to the grounds for suspicion being eliminated as a result of questioning the person detained, a record must still be made in accordance with the procedure outlined in paragraph 4.12.

4.8   After searching an unattended vehicle, or anything in or on it, an officer must leave a notice in it (or on it, if things on it have been searched without opening it) recording the fact that it has been searched.

4.9   The notice must include the name of the police station to which the officer concerned is attached and state where a copy of the record of the search may be obtained and where any application for compensation should be directed.

4.10   The vehicle must if practicable be left secure.

4.10A   When an officer makes a record of the stop electronically and is unable to produce a copy of the form at the time, the officer must explain how the person can obtain a full copy of the record of the stop or search and give the person a receipt which contains:

- a unique reference number and guidance on how to obtain a full copy of the stop or search;
- the name of the officer who carried out the stop or search (unless paragraph 4.4 applies); and
- the power used to stop and search them. See Note 21.

Recording of encounters not governed by Statutory Powers

4.11   Not used.

4.12   When an officer requests a person in a public place to account for themselves, i.e. their actions, behaviour, presence in an area or possession of anything, a record of the encounter must be completed at the time and a copy given to the person who has been questioned. The record must identify the name of the officer who has made the stop and conducted the encounter. This does not apply under the exceptional circumstances outlined in paragraph 4.1 of this code.

4.13   This requirement does not apply to general conversations such as when giving directions to a place, or when seeking witnesses. It also does not include occasions on which an officer is seeking general information or questioning people to establish background to incidents which have required officers to intervene to keep the peace or resolve a dispute.

4.14   A separate record need not be completed when:

- stopping a person in a vehicle when an HORT/1 form, a Vehicle Defect Rectification Scheme Notice, or a Fixed Penalty Notice is issued. It also does not apply when a specimen of breath is required under Section 6 of the Road Traffic Act 1988.
- stopping a person when a Penalty Notice is issued for an offence.

4.15   Officers must inform the person of their entitlement to a copy of a record of the encounter.

4.16   The provisions of paragraph 4.4 of this code apply equally when the encounters described in 4.12 and 4.13 are recorded.

4.17   The following information must be included in the record

     (i)   the date, time and place of the encounter;
     (ii)   if the person is in a vehicle, the registration number;
     (iii) the reason why the officer questioned that person; See Note 17;
     (iv) a note of the person's self-defined ethnic background; See Note 18;
     (v)   the outcome of the encounter.

4.18   There is no power to require the person questioned to provide personal details. If a person refuses to give their self-defined ethnic background, a form must still be completed, which includes a description of the person's ethnic background. See Note 18.

4.19   A record of an encounter must always be made when the criteria set out in 4.12 have been met. If the criteria are not met but the person requests a record, the officer should provide a copy of the form but record on it that the encounter did not meet the criteria. The officer can refuse to issue the form if he or she reasonably believes that the purpose of the request is deliberately aimed at frustrating or delaying legitimate police activity. See Note 20.

4.20   All references to officers in this section include police staff designated as Community Support Officers under section 38 of the Police Reform Act 2002.

5   MONITORING AND SUPERVISING THE USE OF STOP AND SEARCH POWERS

5.1   Supervising officers must monitor the use of stop and search powers and should consider in particular whether there is any evidence that they are being exercised on the basis of stereotyped images or inappropriate generalisations. Supervising officers should satisfy themselves that the practice of officers under their supervision in stopping, searching and recording is fully in accordance with this Code. Supervisors must also examine whether the records reveal any trends or patterns which give cause for concern, and if so take appropriate action to address this.

5.2   Senior officers with area or force-wide responsibilities must also monitor the broader use of stop and search powers and, where necessary, take action at the relevant level.

5.3   Supervision and monitoring must be supported by the compilation of comprehensive statistical records of stops and searches at force, area and local level. Any apparently disproportionate use of the powers by particular officers or groups of officers or in relation to specific sections of the community should be identified and investigated.

5.4   In order to promote public confidence in the use of the powers, forces in consultation with police authorities must make arrangements for the records to be scrutinised by representatives of the community, and to explain the use of the powers at a local level. See Note 19.

Notes for Guidance

Officers exercising stop and search powers

1   This code does not affect the ability of an officer to speak to or question a person in the ordinary course of the officer's duties without detaining the person or exercising any element of compulsion. It is not the purpose of the code to prohibit such encounters between the police and the community with the co-operation of the person concerned and neither does it affect the principle that all citizens have a duty to help police officers to prevent crime and discover offenders. This is a civic rather than a legal duty; but when a police officer is trying to discover whether, or by whom, an offence has been committed he or she may question any person from whom useful information might be obtained, subject to the restrictions imposed by Code C. A person's unwillingness to reply does not alter this entitlement, but in the absence of a power to arrest, or to detain in order to search, the person is free to leave at will and cannot be compelled to remain with the officer.

2   In some circumstances preparatory questioning may be unnecessary, but in general a brief conversation or exchange will be desirable not only as a means of avoiding unsuccessful searches, but to explain the grounds for the stop/search, to gain co-operation and reduce any tension there might be surrounding the stop/search.

3   Where a person is lawfully detained for the purpose of a search, but no search in the event takes place, the detention will not thereby have been rendered unlawful.

4   Many people customarily cover their heads or faces for religious reasons – for example, Muslim women, Sikh men, Sikh or Hindu women, or Rastarfarian men or women. A police officer cannot order the removal of a head or face covering except where there is reason to believe that the item is being worn by the individual wholly or mainly for the purpose of disguising identity, not simply because it disguises identity. Where there may be religious sensitivities about ordering the removal of such an item, the officer should permit the item to be removed out of public view. Where practicable, the item should be removed in the presence of an officer of the same sex as the person and out of sight of anyone of the opposite sex.

5   A search of a person in public should be completed as soon as possible.

6   A person may be detained under a stop and search power at a place other than where the person was first detained, only if that place, be it a police station or elsewhere, is nearby. Such a place should be located within a reasonable travelling distance using whatever mode of travel (on foot or by car) is appropriate. This applies to all searches under stop and search powers, whether or not they involve the removal of clothing or exposure of intimate parts of the body (see paragraphs 3.6 and 3.7) or take place in or out of public view. It means, for example, that a search under the stop and search power in section 23 of the Misuse of Drugs Act 1971 which involves the compulsory removal of more than a person's outer coat, jacket or gloves cannot be carried out unless a place which is both nearby the place they were first detained and out of public view, is available. If a search involves exposure of intimate parts of the body and a police station is not nearby, particular care must be taken to ensure that the location is suitable in that it enables the search to be conducted in accordance with the requirements of paragraph 11 of Annex A to Code C.

7   A search in the street itself should be regarded as being in public for the purposes of paragraphs 3.6 and 3.7 above, even though it may be empty at the time a search begins. Although there is no power to require a person to do so, there is nothing to prevent an officer from asking a person voluntarily to remove more than an outer coat, jacket or gloves (and headgear or footwear under section 45(3) of the Terrorism Act 2000) in public.

8   Where there may be religious sensitivities about asking someone to remove headgear using a power under section 45(3) of the Terrorism Act 2000, the police officer should offer to carry out the search out of public view (for example, in a police van or police station if there is one nearby).

9   Other means of identification might include jewellery, insignias, tattoos or other features which are known to identify members of the particular gang or group.

Authorising officers

10   The powers under section 60 are separate from and additional to the normal stop and search powers which require reasonable grounds to suspect an individual of carrying an offensive weapon (or other article). Their overall purpose is to prevent serious violence and the widespread carrying of weapons which might lead to persons being seriously injured by disarming potential offenders in circumstances where other powers would not be sufficient. They should not therefore be used to replace or circumvent the normal powers for dealing with routine crime problems. The purpose of the powers under section 60AA is to prevent those involved in intimidatory or violent protests using face coverings to disguise identity.

11   Authorisations under section 60 require a reasonable belief on the part of the authorising officer. This must have an objective basis, for example: intelligence or relevant information such as a history of antagonism and violence between particular groups; previous incidents of violence at, or connected with, particular events or locations; a significant increase in knife-point robberies in a limited area; reports that individuals are regularly carrying weapons in a particular locality; or in the case of section 60AA previous incidents of crimes being committed while wearing face coverings to conceal identity.

12   It is for the authorising officer to determine the period of time during which the powers mentioned in paragraph 2.1 (b) and (c) may be exercised. The officer should set the minimum period he or she considers necessary to deal with the risk of violence, the carrying of knives or offensive weapons, or terrorism. A direction to extend the period authorised under the powers mentioned in paragraph 2.1(b) may be given only once. Thereafter further use of the powers requires a new authorisation. There is no provision to extend an authorisation of the powers mentioned in paragraph 2.1(c); further use of the powers requires a new authorisation.

13   It is for the authorising officer to determine the geographical area in which the use of the powers is to be authorised. In doing so the officer may wish to take into account factors such as the nature and venue of the anticipated incident, the number of people who may be in the immediate area of any possible incident, their access to surrounding areas and the anticipated level of violence. The officer should not set a geographical area which is wider than that he or she believes necessary for the purpose of preventing antici-pated violence, the carrying of knives or offensive weapons, acts of terrorism, or, in the case of section 60AA, the prevention of commission of offences. It is particularly impor-tant to ensure that constables exercising such powers are fully aware of where they may be used. If the area specified is smaller than the whole force area, the officer giving the authorisation should specify either the streets which form the boundary of the area or a divisional boundary within the force area. If the power is to be used in response to a threat or incident that straddles police force areas, an officer from each of the forces con-cerned will need to give an authorisation.

14   An officer who has authorised the use of powers under section 44 of the Terrorism Act 2000 must take immediate steps to send a copy of the authorisation to the National Joint Unit, Metropolitan Police Special Branch, who will forward it to the Secretary of State. The Secretary of State should be informed of the reasons for the authorisation. The National Joint Unit will inform the force concerned, within 48 hours of the author-isation being made, whether the Secretary of State has confirmed or cancelled or altered the authorisation.

Recording

15   Where a stop and search is conducted by more than one officer the identity of all the officers engaged in the search must be recorded on the record. Nothing prevents an officer who is present but not directly involved in searching from completing the record during the course of the encounter.

16   Where a vehicle has not been allocated a registration number (e.g. a rally car or a trials motorbike) that part of the requirement under 4.3(iii) does not apply.

17   It is important for monitoring purposes to specify whether the authority for exer-cising a stop and search power was given under section 60 of the Criminal Justice and Public Order Act 1994, or under section 44(1) or 44(2) of the Terrorism Act 2000.

18   Officers should record the self-defined ethnicity of every person stopped according to the categories used in the 2001 census question listed in Annex B. Respondents should be asked to select one of the five main categories representing broad ethnic groups and then a more specific cultural background from within this group. The ethnic classification should be coded for recording purposes using the coding system in Annex B. An addi-tional 'Not stated' box is available but should not be offered to respondents explicitly. Officers should be aware and explain to members of the public, especially where concerns are raised, that this information is required to obtain a true picture of stop and search activity and to help improve ethnic monitoring, tackle discriminatory practice, and promote effective use of the powers. If the person gives what appears to the officer to be an 'incorrect' answer (e.g. a person who appears to be white states that they are black), the officer should record the response that has been given. Officers should also record their own perception of the ethnic background of every person stopped and this must be done by using the PNC/Phoenix classification system. If the 'Not stated' category is used the reason for this must be recorded on the form.

19 Arrangements for public scrutiny of records should take account of the right to confidentiality of those stopped and searched. Anonymised forms and/or statistics generated from records should be the focus of the examinations by members of the public.

20 Where an officer engages in conversation which is not pertinent to the actions or whereabouts of the individual (e.g. does not relate to why the person is there, what they are doing or where they have been or are going) then issuing a form would not meet the criteria set out in paragraph 4.12. Situations designed to impede police activity may arise, for example, in public order situations where individuals engage in dialogue with the officer but the officer does not initiate or engage in contact about the person's individual circumstances.

21 In situations where it is not practicable to provide a written record of the stop or stop and search at that time, the officer should consider providing the person with details of the station to which the person may attend for a record. This may take the form of a simple business card, adding the date of the stop or stop and search.

ANNEX A   SUMMARY OF MAIN STOP AND SEARCH POWERS

THIS TABLE RELATES TO STOP AND SEARCH POWERS ONLY. INDIVIDUAL STATUTES BELOW MAY CONTAIN OTHER POLICE POWERS OF ENTRY, SEARCH AND SEIZURE

Power	Object of Search	Extent of Search	Where Exercisable
Unlawful articles general			
1. Public Stores Act 1875, s6	HM Stores stolen or unlawfully obtained	Persons, vehicles and vessels	Anywhere where the constabulary powers are exercisable
2. Firearms Act 1968, s47	Firearms	Persons and vehicles	A public place, or anywhere in the case of reasonable suspicion of offences of carrying firearms with criminal intent or trespassing with firearms
3. Misuse of Drugs Act 1971, s23	Controlled drugs	Persons and vehicles	Anywhere
4. Customs and Excise Management Act 1979, s163	Goods: (a) on which duty has not been paid; (b) being unlawfully removed, imported or exported; (c) otherwise liable to forfeiture to HM Customs and Excise	Vehicles and vessels only	Anywhere
5. Aviation Security Act 1982, s27(1)	Stolen or unlawfully obtained goods	Airport employees and vehicles carrying airport employees or aircraft or any vehicle in a cargo area whether or not carrying an employee	Any designated airport

Power	Object of Search	Extent of Search	Where Exercisable
6. Police and Criminal Evidence Act 1984, s1	Stolen goods; articles for use in certain Theft Act offences; offensive weapons, including bladed or sharply-pointed articles (except folding pocket knives with a bladed cutting edge not exceeding 3 inches); prohibited possession of a category 4 (display grade) firework, any person under 18 in possession of an adult firework in a public place	Persons and vehicles	Where there is public access
	Criminal Damage: Articles made, adapted or intended for use in destroying or damaging property	Persons and vehicles	Where there is public access
Police and Criminal Evidence Act 1984, s6(3) (by a constable of the United Kingdom Atomic Energy Authority Constabulary in respect of property owned or controlled by British Nuclear Fuels plc)	HM Stores (in the form of goods and chattels belonging to British Nuclear Fuels plc)	Persons, vehicles and vessels	Anywhere where the constabulary powers are exercisable
7. Sporting events (Control of Alcohol etc.) Act 1985, s7	Intoxicating liquor	Persons, coaches and trains	Designated sports grounds or coaches and trains travelling to or from a designated sporting event
8. Crossbows Act 1987, s4	Crossbows or parts of crossbows (except crossbows with a draw weight of less than 1.4 kilograms)	Persons and vehicles	Anywhere except dwellings
9. Criminal Justice Act 1988 s139B	Offensive weapons, bladed or sharply pointed article	Persons	School premises
Evidence of game and wildlife offences			
10. Poaching Prevention Act 1862, s2	Game or poaching equipment	Persons and vehicles	A public place
11. Deer Act 1991, s12	Evidence of offences under the Act	Persons and vehicles	Anywhere except dwellings
12. Conservation of Seals Act 1970, s4	Seals or hunting equipment	Vehicles only	Anywhere
13. Badgers Act 1992, s11	Evidence of offences under the Act	Persons and vehicles	Anywhere
14. Wildlife and Countryside Act 1981, s19	Evidence of wildlife offences	Persons and vehicles	Anywhere except dwellings
Other			
15. Terrorism Act 2000, s.43	*Evidence of liability to arrest under section 14 of the Act*	Persons	Anywhere
16. Terrorism Act 2000, s.44(1)	Articles which could be used for a purpose connected with the commission, preparation or instigation of acts of terrorism	Vehicles, driver and passengers	Anywhere within the area or locality authorised under subsection (1)
17. Terrorism Act 2000, s.44(2)	*Articles which could be used for a purpose connected with the commission, preparation or instigation of acts of terrorism*	Pedestrians	Anywhere within the area of locality authorised

Power	Object of Search	Extent of Search	Where Exercisable
18. Paragraphs 7 and 8 of Schedule 7 to the Terrorism Act 2000	*Anything relevant to determining if a person being examined falls within paragraph 2(1)(a) to (c) of Schedule 5*	Persons, vehicles, vessels etc.	Ports and airports
19. Section 60 Criminal Justice and Public Order Act 1994, as amended by s.8 of the Knives Act 1997	Offensive weapons or dangerous instruments to prevent incidents of serious violence or to deal with the carrying of such items	Persons and vehicles	Anywhere within a locality authorised under subsection (1)

ANNEX B SELF-DEFINED ETHNIC CLASSIFICATION CATEGORIES

White	*W*
A. *White – British*	*W1*
B. *White – Irish*	*W2*
C. *Any other White background*	*W9*

Mixed	*M*
D. *White and Black Caribbean*	*M1*
E. *White and Black African*	*M2*
F. *White and Asian*	*M3*
G. *Any other Mixed Background*	*M9*

Asian/Asian – British	*A*
H. *Asian – Indian*	*A1*
I. *Asian – Pakistani*	*A2*
J. *Asian – Bangladeshi*	*A3*
K. *Any other Asian background*	*A9*

Black/Black – British	*B*
L. *Black – Caribbean*	*B1*
M. *Black African*	*B2*
N. *Any other Black background*	*B9*

Other	*O*
O. *Chinese*	*O1*
P *Any other*	*O9*

Not Stated **NS**

ANNEX C SUMMARY OF POWERS OF COMMUNITY SUPPORT OFFICERS TO SEARCH AND SEIZE

The following is a summary of the search and seizure powers that may be exercised by a community support officer (CSO) who has been designated with the relevant powers in accordance with Part 4 of the Police Reform Act 2002.

When exercising any of these powers, a CSO must have regard to any relevant provisions of this Code, including section 3 governing the conduct of searches and the steps to be taken prior to a search.

1. Power to stop and search not requiring consent

Designation	Power conferred	Object of Search	Extent of Search	Where Exercisable
Police Reform Act 2002 Schedule 4, paragraph 15	(a) Terrorism Act 2000, s.44(1)(a) and (d) and 45(2); (b) Terrorism Act 2000, s.44(2)(b) and 45(2)	Items intended to be used in connection with terrorism	(a) Vehicles or anything carried in or on the vehicle and anything carried by driver or passenger. (b) Anything carried by a pedestrian.	Anywhere within area of locality authorised and in the company and under the supervision of a constable

2. Powers to search requiring the consent of the person and seizure

A CSO may detain a person using reasonable force where necessary as set out in Part 1 of Schedule 4 to the Police Reform Act 2002. If the person has been lawfully detained, the CSO may search the person provided that person gives consent to such a search in relation to the following:

Designation	Powers conferred	Object of Search	Extent of Search	Where Exercisable
Police Reform Act 2002, Schedule 4, paragraph 7A	(a) Criminal Justice and Police Act 2001, s.12(2) (b) Confiscation of Alcohol (Young Persons) Act 1997, s.1 (c) Children and Young Persons Act 1933, section 7(3)	a) Alcohol or a container for alcohol b) Alcohol c) Tobacco or cigarette papers	a) Persons b) Persons under 18 years old c) Persons under 16 years old found smoking	a) Designated public place b) Public place c) Public place

3. Powers to search not requiring the consent of the person and seizure

A CSO may detain a person using reasonable force where necessary as set out in Part 1 of Schedule 4 to the Police Reform Act 2002. If the person has been lawfully detained, the CSO may search the person without the need for that person's consent in relation to the following:

Designation	Power conferred	Object of Search	Extent of Search	Where Exercisable
Police Reform Act 2002, Schedule 4, paragraph 2A	Police and Criminal Evidence Act 1984, s.32	a) Objects that might be used to cause physical injury to the person or the CSO b) Items that might be used to assist escape.	Persons made subject to a requirement to wait.	Any place where the requirement to wait has been made.

4. Powers to seize without consent

This power applies when drugs are found in the course of any search mentioned above.

Designation	Power conferred	Object of Seizure	Where Exercisable
Police Reform Act 2002, Schedule 4, paragraph 7B	*Police Reform Act 2002, Schedule 4, paragraph 7B*	Controlled drugs in a person's possession.	Any place where the person is in possession of the drug.

CODE B: FOR SEARCHES OF PREMISES BY POLICE OFFICERS AND THE SEIZURE OF PROPERTY FOUND BY POLICE OFFICERS ON PERSONS OR PREMISES

Commencement – Transitional Arrangements

This Code applies to applications for warrants made after midnight 31 December 2005 and to searches and seizures taking place after midnight on 31 December 2005.

1 INTRODUCTION

1.1 This Code of Practice deals with police powers to:
- search premises;
- seize and retain property found on premises and persons.

1.1A These powers may be used to find:
- property and material relating to a crime;
- wanted persons;
- children who abscond from local authority accommodation where they have been remanded or committed by a court.

1.2 A justice of the peace may issue a search warrant granting powers of entry, search and seizure, e.g. warrants to search for stolen property, drugs, firearms and evidence of serious offences. Police also have powers without a search warrant. The main ones provided by the Police and Criminal Evidence Act 1984 (PACE) include powers to search premises:
- to make an arrest;
- after an arrest.

1.3 The right to privacy and respect for personal property are key principles of the Human Rights Act 1998. Powers of entry, search and seizure should be fully and clearly justified before use because they may significantly interfere with the occupier's privacy. Officers should consider if the necessary objectives can be met by less intrusive means.

1.4 In all cases, police should:
- exercise their powers courteously and with respect for persons and property;
- only use reasonable force when this is considered necessary and proportionate to the circumstances.

1.5 If the provisions of PACE and this Code are not observed, evidence obtained from a search may be open to question.

2 GENERAL

2.1 This Code must be readily available at all police stations for consultation by:
- police officers;
- police staff;
- detained persons;
- members of the public.

2.2 The Notes for Guidance included are not provisions of this Code.

2.3 This Code applies to searches of premises:
    (a) by police for the purposes of an investigation into an alleged offence, with the occupier's consent, other than:
- routine scene of crime searches;

- calls to a fire or burglary made by or on behalf of an occupier or searches following the activation of fire or burglar alarms or discovery of insecure premises;
- searches when paragraph 5.4 applies;
- bomb threat calls;

(b) under powers conferred on police officers by PACE, sections 17, 18 and 32;

(c) undertaken in pursuance of search warrants issued to and executed by constables in accordance with PACE, sections 15 and 16. See Note 2A;

(d) subject to paragraph 2.6, under any other power given to police to enter premises with or without a search warrant for any purpose connected with the investigation into an alleged or suspected offence. See Note 2B.

For the purposes of this Code, 'premises' as defined in PACE, section 23, includes any place, vehicle, vessel, aircraft, hovercraft, tent or movable structure and any offshore installation as defined in the Mineral Workings (Offshore Installations) Act 1971, section 1. See Note 2D.

2.4   A person who has not been arrested but is searched during a search of premises should be searched in accordance with Code A. See Note 2C.

2.5   This Code does not apply to the exercise of a statutory power to enter premises or to inspect goods, equipment or procedures if the exercise of that power is not dependent on the existence of grounds for suspecting that an offence may have been committed and the person exercising the power has no reasonable grounds for such suspicion.

2.6   This Code does not affect any directions of a search warrant or order, lawfully executed in England or Wales that any item or evidence seized under that warrant or order be handed over to a police force, court, tribunal, or other authority outside England or Wales. For example, warrants and orders issued in Scotland or Northern Ireland, see Note 2B(f) and search warrants issued under the Criminal Justice (International Co-operation) Act 1990, section 7.

2.7   When this Code requires the prior authority or agreement of an officer of at least inspector or superintendent rank, that authority may be given by a sergeant or chief inspector authorised to perform the functions of the higher rank under PACE, section 107.

2.8   Written records required under this Code not made in the search record shall, unless otherwise specified, be made:

- in the recording officer's pocket book ('pocket book' includes any official report book issued to police officers) or
- on forms provided for the purpose

2.9   Nothing in this Code requires the identity of officers (or anyone accompanying them during a search of premises) to be recorded or disclosed:

(a) in the case of enquiries linked to the investigation of terrorism; or

(b) if officers reasonably believe recording or disclosing their names might put them in danger.

In these cases officers should use warrant or other identification numbers and the name of their police station. See Note 2E.

2.10   The 'officer in charge of the search' means the officer assigned specific duties and responsibilities under this Code. Whenever there is a search of premises to which this Code applies one officer must act as the officer in charge of the search. See Note 2F.

2.11   In this Code:

   (a)   'designated person' means a person other than a police officer, designated under the Police Reform Act 2002, Part 4 who has specified powers and duties of police officers conferred or imposed on them. See Note 2G.

   (b)   any reference to a police officer includes a designated person acting in the exercise or performance of the powers and duties conferred or imposed on them by their designation.

   (c)   a person authorised to accompany police officers or designated persons in the execution of a warrant has the same powers as a constable in the execution of the warrant and the search and seizure of anything related to the warrant. These powers must be exercised in the company and under the supervision of a police officer. See Note 3C.

2.12   If a power conferred on a designated person:

   (a)   allows reasonable force to be used when exercised by a police officer, a designated person exercising that power has the same entitlement to use force;

   (b)   includes power to use force to enter any premises, that power is not exercisable by that designated person except:

      (i)   in the company and under the supervision of a police officer; or
      (ii)   for the purpose of:

         • saving life or limb; or
         • preventing serious damage to property.

2.13   Designated persons must have regard to any relevant provisions of the Codes of Practice.

Notes for Guidance

2A   PACE sections 15 and 16 apply to all search warrants issued to and executed by constables under any enactment, e.g. search warrants issued by a:

   (a)   justice of the peace under the:

      • *Theft Act 1968, section 26 – stolen property;*
      • *Misuse of Drugs Act 1971, section 23 – controlled drugs;*
      • *PACE, section 8 – evidence of an indictable offence;*
      • *Terrorism Act 2000, Schedule 5, paragraph 1;*

   (b)   judge of the High Court, a circuit judge, a Recorder or a District Judge under:

      • *PACE, Schedule 1;*
      • *Terrorism Act 2000, Schedule 5, paragraph 11.*

2B   Examples of the other powers in paragraph 2.3(d) include:

   (a)   Road Traffic Act 1988, section 6E(1) giving police power to enter premises under section 6E(1) to:

      • *require a person to provide a specimen of breath; or*
      • *arrest a person following:*

         ~ *a positive breath test;*
         ~ *failure to provide a specimen of breath;*

   (b)   Transport and Works Act 1992, section 30(4) giving police powers to enter premises mirroring the powers in (a) in relation to specified persons working on transport systems to which the Act applies;

(c) Criminal Justice Act 1988, section 139B giving police power to enter and search school premises for offensive weapons, bladed or pointed articles;

(d) Terrorism Act 2000, Schedule 5, paragraphs 3 and 15 empowering a superintendent in urgent cases to give written authority for police to enter and search premises for the purposes of a terrorist investigation;

(e) Explosives Act 1875, section 73(b) empowering a superintendent to give written authority for police to enter premises, examine and search them for explosives;

(f) search warrants and production orders or the equivalent issued in Scotland or Northern Ireland endorsed under the Summary Jurisdiction (Process) Act 1881 or the Petty Sessions (Ireland) Act 1851 respectively for execution in England and Wales.

2C The Criminal Justice Act 1988, section 139B provides that a constable who has reasonable grounds to believe an offence under the Criminal Justice Act 1988, section 139A has or is being committed may enter school premises and search the premises and any persons on the premises for any bladed or pointed article or offensive weapon. Persons may be searched under a warrant issued under the Misuse of Drugs Act 1971, section 23(3) to search premises for drugs or documents only if the warrant specifically authorises the search of persons on the premises.

2D The Immigration Act 1971, Part III and Schedule 2 gives immigration officers powers to enter and search premises, seize and retain property, with and without a search warrant. These are similar to the powers available to police under search warrants issued by a justice of the peace and without a warrant under PACE, sections 17, 18, 19 and 32 except they only apply to specified offences under the Immigration Act 1971 and immigration control powers. For certain types of investigations and enquiries these powers avoid the need for the Immigration Service to rely on police officers becoming directly involved. When exercising these powers, immigration officers are required by the Immigration and Asylum Act 1999, section 145 to have regard to this Code's corresponding provisions. When immigration officers are dealing with persons or property at police stations, police officers should give appropriate assistance to help them discharge their specific duties and responsibilities.

2E The purpose of paragraph 2.9(b) is to protect those involved in serious organised crime investigations or arrests of particularly violent suspects when there is reliable information that those arrested or their associates may threaten or cause harm to the officers or anyone accompanying them during a search of premises. In cases of doubt, an officer of inspector rank or above should be consulted.

2F For the purposes of paragraph 2.10, the officer in charge of the search should normally be the most senior officer present. Some exceptions are:

(a) a supervising officer who attends or assists at the scene of a premises search may appoint an officer of lower rank as officer in charge of the search if that officer is:

- *more conversant with the facts;*
- *a more appropriate officer to be in charge of the search;*

(b) when all officers in a premises search are the same rank. The supervising officer if available must make sure one of them is appointed officer in charge of the search, otherwise the officers themselves must nominate one of their number as the officer in charge;

(c) a senior officer assisting in a specialist role. This officer need not be regarded as having a general supervisory role over the conduct of the search or be appointed or expected to act as the officer in charge of the search.

Except in (c), nothing in this Note diminishes the role and responsibilities of a supervisory officer who is present at the search or knows of a search taking place.

2G   An officer of the rank of inspector or above may direct a designated investigating officer not to wear a uniform for the purposes of a specific operation.

3   SEARCH WARRANTS AND PRODUCTION ORDERS

(a)   Before making an application

3.1   When information appears to justify an application, the officer must take reasonable steps to check the information is accurate, recent and not provided maliciously or irresponsibly. An application may not be made on the basis of information from an anonymous source if corroboration has not been sought. See Note 3A.

3.2   The officer shall ascertain as specifically as possible the nature of the articles concerned and their location.

3.3   The officer shall make reasonable enquiries to:

    (i)   establish if:

- anything is known about the likely occupier of the premises and the nature of the premises themselves;
- the premises have been searched previously and how recently;

    (ii)   obtain any other relevant information.

3.4   An application:

    (a)   to a justice of the peace for a search warrant or to a judge of the High Court, a circuit judge, a Recorder or a District Judge for a search warrant or production order under PACE, Schedule 1 must be supported by a signed written authority from an officer of inspector rank or above:
Note: If the case is an urgent application to a justice of the peace and an inspector or above is not readily available, the next most senior officer on duty can give the written authority.

    (b)   to a circuit judge under the Terrorism Act 2000, Schedule 5 for

- a production order;
- search warrant; or
- an order requiring an explanation of material seized or produced under such a warrant or production order

must be supported by a signed written authority from an officer of superintendent rank or above.

3.5   Except in a case of urgency, if there is reason to believe a search might have an adverse effect on relations between the police and the community, the officer in charge shall consult the local police/community liaison officer:

- before the search; or
- in urgent cases, as soon as practicable after the search

(b)   Making an application

3.6   A search warrant application must be supported in writing, specifying:

    (a)   the enactment under which the application is made, see Note 2A;

    (b)   (i)   whether the warrant is to authorise entry and search of:

- one set of premises; or
- if the application is under PACE section 8, or Schedule 1, paragraph 12, more than one set of specified premises or all premises occupied or controlled by a specified person, and

(ii) the premises to be searched;

(c) the object of the search, see Note 3B;

(d) the grounds for the application, including, when the purpose of the proposed search is to find evidence of an alleged offence, an indication of how the evidence relates to the investigation;

(da) where the application is under PACE section 8, or Schedule 1, paragraph 12 for a single warrant to enter and search:

(i) more than one set of specified premises, the officer must specify each set of premises which it is desired to enter and search

(ii) all premises occupied or controlled by a specified person, the officer must specify;

- as many sets of premises which it is desired to enter and search as it is reasonably practicable to specify
- the person who is in occupation or control of those premises and any others which it is desired to search
- why it is necessary to search more premises than those which can be specified
- why it is not reasonably practicable to specify all the premises which it is desired to enter and search

(db) whether an application under PACE section 8 is for a warrant authorising entry and search on more than one occasion, and if so, the officer must state the grounds for this and whether the desired number of entries authorised is unlimited or a specified maximum.

(e) there are no reasonable grounds to believe the material to be sought, when making application to a:

(i) justice of the peace or a judge of the High Court, a circuit judge, a Recorder or a District Judge, consists of or includes items subject to legal privilege;

(ii) justice of the peace, consists of or includes excluded material or special procedure material;

Note: this does not affect the additional powers of seizure in the Criminal Justice and Police Act 2001, Part 2 covered in paragraph 7.7, see Note 3B;

(f) if applicable, a request for the warrant to authorise a person or persons to accompany the officer who executes the warrant, see Note 3C.

3.7 A search warrant application under PACE, Schedule 1, paragraph 12(a), shall if appropriate indicate why it is believed service of notice of an application for a production order may seriously prejudice the investigation. Applications for search warrants under the Terrorism Act 2000, Schedule 5, paragraph 11 must indicate why a production order would not be appropriate.

3.8 If a search warrant application is refused, a further application may not be made for those premises unless supported by additional grounds.

Notes for Guidance

3A The identity of an informant need not be disclosed when making an application, but the officer should be prepared to answer any questions the magistrate or judge may have about:

- *the accuracy of previous information from that source*
- *any other related matters*

3B   The information supporting a search warrant application should be as specific as possible, particularly in relation to the articles or persons being sought and where in the premises it is suspected they may be found. The meaning of 'items subject to legal privilege', 'excluded material' and 'special procedure material' are defined by PACE, sections 10, 11 and 14 respectively.

3C   Under PACE, section 16(2), a search warrant may authorise persons other than police officers to accompany the constable who executes the warrant. This includes, e.g. any suitably qualified or skilled person or an expert in a particular field whose presence is needed to help accurately identify the material sought or to advise where certain evidence is most likely to be found and how it should be dealt with. It does not give them any right to force entry, but it gives them the right to be on the premises during the search and to search for or seize property without the occupier's permission.

4   ENTRY WITHOUT WARRANT – PARTICULAR POWERS

(a)   Making an arrest etc

4.1   The conditions under which an officer may enter and search premises without a warrant are set out in PACE, section 17. It should be noted that this section does not create or confer any powers of arrest. See other powers in Note 2B(a).

(b)   Search of premises where arrest takes place or the arrested person was immediately before arrest

4.2   When a person has been arrested for an indictable offence, a police officer has power under PACE, section 32 to search the premises where the person was arrested or where the person was immediately before being arrested.

(c)   Search of premises occupied or controlled by the arrested person

4.3   The specific powers to search premises occupied or controlled by a person arrested for an indictable offence are set out in PACE, section 18. They may not be exercised, except if section 18(5) applies, unless an officer of inspector rank or above has given written authority. That authority should only be given when the authorising officer is satisfied the necessary grounds exist. If possible the authorising officer should record the authority on the Notice of Powers and Rights and, subject to paragraph 2.9, sign the Notice. The record of the grounds for the search and the nature of the evidence sought as required by section 18(7) of the Act should be made in:

- the custody record if there is one, otherwise
- the officer's pocket book, or
- the search record

5   SEARCH WITH CONSENT

5.1 Subject to paragraph 5.4, if it is proposed to search premises with the consent of a person entitled to grant entry the consent must, if practicable, be given in writing on the Notice of Powers and Rights before the search. The officer must make any necessary enquiries to be satisfied the person is in a position to give such consent. See Notes 5A and 5B.

5.2　Before seeking consent the officer in charge of the search shall state the purpose of the proposed search and its extent. This information must be as specific as possible, particularly regarding the articles or persons being sought and the parts of the premises to be searched. The person concerned must be clearly informed they are not obliged to consent and anything seized may be produced in evidence. If at the time the person is not suspected of an offence, the officer shall say this when stating the purpose of the search.

5.3　An officer cannot enter and search or continue to search premises under paragraph 5.1 if consent is given under duress or withdrawn before the search is completed.

5.4　It is unnecessary to seek consent under paragraphs 5.1 and 5.2 if this would cause disproportionate inconvenience to the person concerned. See Note 5C.

Notes for Guidance

5A　In a lodging house or similar accommodation, every reasonable effort should be made to obtain the consent of the tenant, lodger or occupier. A search should not be made solely on the basis of the landlord's consent unless the tenant, lodger or occupier is unavailable and the matter is urgent.

5B　If the intention is to search premises under the authority of a warrant or a power of entry and search without warrant, and the occupier of the premises co-operates in accordance with paragraph 6.4, there is no need to obtain written consent.

5C　Paragraph 5.4 is intended to apply when it is reasonable to assume innocent occupiers would agree to, and expect, police to take the proposed action, e.g. if:

- *a suspect has fled the scene of a crime or to evade arrest and it is necessary quickly to check surrounding gardens and readily accessible places to see if the suspect is hiding*
- *police have arrested someone in the night after a pursuit and it is necessary to make a brief check of gardens along the pursuit route to see if stolen or incriminating articles have been discarded*

6　SEARCHING PREMISES – GENERAL CONSIDERATIONS

(a)　Time of searches

6.1　Searches made under warrant must be made within three calendar months of the date of the warrant's issue.

6.2　Searches must be made at a reasonable hour unless this might frustrate the purpose of the search.

6.3　When the extent or complexity of a search mean it is likely to take a long time, the officer in charge of the search may consider using the seize and sift powers referred to in section 7.

6.3A　A warrant under PACE, section 8 may authorise entry to and search of premises on more than one occasion if, on the application, the justice of the peace is satisfied that it is necessary to authorise multiple entries in order to achieve the purpose for which the warrant is issued. No premises may be entered or searched on any subsequent occasions without the prior written authority of an officer of the rank of inspector who is not involved in the investigation. All other warrants authorise entry on one occasion only.

6.3B   Where a warrant under PACE section 8, or Schedule 1, paragraph 12 authorises entry to and search of all premises occupied or controlled by a specified person, no premises which are not specified in the warrant may be entered and searched without the prior written authority of an officer of the rank of inspector who is not involved in the investigation.

(b)   Entry other than with consent

6.4   The officer in charge of the search shall first try to communicate with the occupier, or any other person entitled to grant access to the premises, explain the authority under which entry is sought and ask the occupier to allow entry, unless:

  (i)   the search premises are unoccupied;
  (ii) the occupier and any other person entitled to grant access are absent;
  (iii) there are reasonable grounds for believing that alerting the occupier or any other person entitled to grant access would frustrate the object of the search or endanger officers or other people.

6.5   Unless sub-paragraph 6.4(iii) applies, if the premises are occupied the officer, subject to paragraph 2.9, shall, before the search begins:

  (i)   identify him or herself, show their warrant card (if not in uniform) and state the purpose of and grounds for the search;
  (ii) identify and introduce any person accompanying the officer on the search (such persons should carry identification for production on request) and briefly describe that person's role in the process.

6.6   Reasonable and proportionate force may be used if necessary to enter premises if the officer in charge of the search is satisfied the premises are those specified in any warrant, or in exercise of the powers described in paragraphs 4.1 to 4.3, and if:

  (i)   the occupier or any other person entitled to grant access has refused entry;
  (ii) it is impossible to communicate with the occupier or any other person entitled to grant access; or
  (iii) any of the provisions of paragraph 6.4 apply.

(c)   Notice of Powers and Rights

6.7   If an officer conducts a search to which this Code applies the officer shall, unless it is impracticable to do so, provide the occupier with a copy of a Notice in a standard format:

  (i)   specifying if the search is made under warrant, with consent, or in the exercise of the powers described in paragraphs 4.1 to 4.3. Note: the notice format shall provide for authority or consent to be indicated, see paragraphs 4.3 and 5.1;
  (ii) summarising the extent of the powers of search and seizure conferred by PACE;
  (iii) explaining the rights of the occupier, and the owner of the property seized;
  (iv) explaining compensation may be payable in appropriate cases for damages caused entering and searching premises, and giving the address to send a compensation application, see Note 6A;
  (v)   stating this Code is available at any police station.

6.8   If the occupier is:

- present, copies of the Notice and warrant shall, if practicable, be given to them before the search begins, unless the officer in charge of the search reasonably believes this would frustrate the object of the search or endanger officers or other people;
- not present, copies of the Notice and warrant shall be left in a prominent place on the premises or appropriate part of the premises and endorsed, subject to paragraph 2.9 with the name of the officer in charge of the search, the date and time of the search;

The warrant shall be endorsed to show this has been done.

(d) Conduct of searches

6.9   Premises may be searched only to the extent necessary to achieve the object of the search, having regard to the size and nature of whatever is sought.

6.9A   A search may not continue under:

- a warrant's authority once all the things specified in that warrant have been found;
- any other power once the object of that search has been achieved;

6.9B   No search may continue once the officer in charge of the search is satisfied whatever is being sought is not on the premises. See Note 6B. This does not prevent a further search of the same premises if additional grounds come to light supporting a further application for a search warrant or exercise or further exercise of another power. For example, when, as a result of new information, it is believed articles previously not found or additional articles are on the premises.

6.10   Searches must be conducted with due consideration for the property and privacy of the occupier and with no more disturbance than necessary. Reasonable force may be used only when necessary and proportionate because the co-operation of the occupier cannot be obtained or is insufficient for the purpose. See Note 6C.

6.11   A friend, neighbour or other person must be allowed to witness the search if the occupier wishes unless the officer in charge of the search has reasonable grounds for believing the presence of the person asked for would seriously hinder the investigation or endanger officers or other people. A search need not be unreasonably delayed for this purpose. A record of the action taken should be made on the premises search record including the grounds for refusing the occupier's request.

6.12   A person is not required to be cautioned prior to being asked questions that are solely necessary for the purpose of furthering the proper and effective conduct of a search, see Code C, paragraph 10.1(c). For example, questions to discover the occupier of specified premises, to find a key to open a locked drawer or cupboard or to otherwise seek co-operation during the search or to determine if a particular item is liable to be seized.

6.12A   If questioning goes beyond what is necessary for the purpose of the exemption in Code C, the exchange is likely to constitute an interview as defined by Code C, paragraph 11.1A and would require the associated safeguards included in Code C, section 10.

(e) Leaving premises

6.13   If premises have been entered by force, before leaving the officer in charge of the search must make sure they are secure by:

- arranging for the occupier or their agent to be present
- any other appropriate means

(f) Searches under PACE Schedule 1 or the Terrorism Act 2000, Schedule 5

6.14 An officer shall be appointed as the officer in charge of the search, see paragraph 2.10, in respect of any search made under a warrant issued under PACE Act 1984, Schedule 1 or the Terrorism Act 2000, Schedule 5. They are responsible for making sure the search is conducted with discretion and in a manner that causes the least possible disruption to any business or other activities carried out on the premises.

6.15 Once the officer in charge of the search is satisfied material may not be taken from the premises without their knowledge, they shall ask for the documents or other records concerned. The officer in charge of the search may also ask to see the index to files held on the premises, and the officers conducting the search may inspect any files which, according to the index, appear to contain the material sought. A more extensive search of the premises may be made only if:

- the person responsible for them refuses to:
  ~ produce the material sought; or
  ~ allow access to the index
- it appears the index is:
  ~ inaccurate; or
  ~ incomplete
- for any other reason the officer in charge of the search has reasonable grounds for believing such a search is necessary in order to find the material sought

Notes for Guidance

6A Whether compensation is appropriate depends on the circumstances in each case. Compensation for damage caused when effecting entry is unlikely to be appropriate if the search was lawful, and the force used can be shown to be reasonable, proportionate and necessary to effect entry. If the wrong premises are searched by mistake everything possible should be done at the earliest opportunity to allay any sense of grievance and there should normally be a strong presumption in favour of paying compensation.

6B It is important that, when possible, all those involved in a search are fully briefed about any powers to be exercised and the extent and limits within which it should be conducted.

6C In all cases the number of officers and other persons involved in executing the warrant should be determined by what is reasonable and necessary according to the particular circumstances.

7 SEIZURE AND RETENTION OF PROPERTY

(a) Seizure

7.1 Subject to paragraph 7.2, an officer who is searching any person or premises under any statutory power or with the consent of the occupier may seize anything:
  (a) covered by a warrant;
  (b) the officer has reasonable grounds for believing is evidence of an offence or has been obtained in consequence of the commission of an offence but only

if seizure is necessary to prevent the items being concealed, lost, disposed of, altered, damaged, destroyed or tampered with;

(c) covered by the powers in the Criminal Justice and Police Act 2001, Part 2 allowing an officer to seize property from persons or premises and retain it for sifting or examination elsewhere.

See Note 7B

7.2 No item may be seized which an officer has reasonable grounds for believing to be subject to legal privilege, as defined in PACE, section 10, other than under the Criminal Justice and Police Act 2001, Part 2.

7.3 Officers must be aware of the provisions in the Criminal Justice and Police Act 2001, section 59, allowing for applications to a judicial authority for the return of property seized and the subsequent duty to secure in section 60, see paragraph 7.12(iii).

7.4 An officer may decide it is not appropriate to seize property because of an explanation from the person holding it but may nevertheless have reasonable grounds for believing it was obtained in consequence of an offence by some person. In these circumstances, the officer should identify the property to the holder, inform the holder of their suspicions and explain the holder may be liable to civil or criminal proceedings if they dispose of, alter or destroy the property.

7.5 An officer may arrange to photograph, image or copy, any document or other article they have the power to seize in accordance with paragraph 7.1. This is subject to specific restrictions on the examination, imaging or copying of certain property seized under the Criminal Justice and Police Act 2001, Part 2. An officer must have regard to their statutory obligation to retain an original document or other article only when a photograph or copy is not sufficient.

7.6 If an officer considers information stored in any electronic form and accessible from the premises could be used in evidence, they may require the information to be produced in a form:

- which can be taken away and in which it is visible and legible; or
- from which it can readily be produced in a visible and legible form

(b) Criminal Justice and Police Act 2001: Specific procedures for seize and sift powers

7.7 The Criminal Justice and Police Act 2001, Part 2 gives officers limited powers to seize property from premises or persons so they can sift or examine it elsewhere. Officers must be careful they only exercise these powers when it is essential and they do not remove any more material than necessary. The removal of large volumes of material, much of which may not ultimately be retainable, may have serious implications for the owners, particularly when they are involved in business or activities such as journalism or the provision of medical services. Officers must carefully consider if removing copies or images of relevant material or data would be a satisfactory alternative to removing originals. When originals are taken, officers must be prepared to facilitate the provision of copies or images for the owners when reasonably practicable. See Note 7C.

7.8 Property seized under the Criminal Justice and Police Act 2001, sections 50 or 51 must be kept securely and separately from any material seized under other powers. An examination under section 53 to determine which elements may be retained must be carried out at the earliest practicable time, having due regard to the desirability of allowing the person from whom the property was seized, or a person with an interest in the property, an opportunity of being present or represented at the examination.

7.8A   All reasonable steps should be taken to accommodate an interested person's request to be present, provided the request is reasonable and subject to the need to prevent harm to, interference with, or unreasonable delay to the investigatory process. If an examination proceeds in the absence of an interested person who asked to attend or their representative, the officer who exercised the relevant seizure power must give that person a written notice of why the examination was carried out in those circumstances. If it is necessary for security reasons or to maintain confidentiality officers may exclude interested persons from decryption or other processes which facilitate the examination but do not form part of it. See Note 7D.

7.9   It is the responsibility of the officer in charge of the investigation to make sure property is returned in accordance with sections 53 to 55. Material which there is no power to retain must be:

- separated from the rest of the seized property;
- returned as soon as reasonably practicable after examination of all the seized property.

7.9A   Delay is only warranted if very clear and compelling reasons exist, e.g. the:

- unavailability of the person to whom the material is to be returned;
- need to agree a convenient time to return a large volume of material.

7.9B   Legally privileged, excluded or special procedure material which cannot be retained must be returned:

- as soon as reasonably practicable;
- without waiting for the whole examination.

7.9C   As set out in section 58, material must be returned to the person from whom it was seized, except when it is clear some other person has a better right to it. See Note 7E.

7.10   When an officer involved in the investigation has reasonable grounds to believe a person with a relevant interest in property seized under section 50 or 51 intends to make an application under section 59 for the return of any legally privileged, special procedure or excluded material, the officer in charge of the investigation should be informed as soon as practicable and the material seized should be kept secure in accordance with section 61. See Note 7C.

7.11   The officer in charge of the investigation is responsible for making sure property is properly secured. Securing involves making sure the property is not examined, copied, imaged or put to any other use except at the request, or with the consent, of the applicant or in accordance with the directions of the appropriate judicial authority. Any request, consent or directions must be recorded in writing and signed by both the initiator and the officer in charge of the investigation. See Notes 7F and 7G.

7.12   When an officer exercises a power of seizure conferred by sections 50 or 51 they shall provide the occupier of the premises or the person from whom the property is being seized with a written notice:

- (i)   specifying what has been seized under the powers conferred by that section;
- (ii) specifying the grounds for those powers;
- (iii) setting out the effect of sections 59 to 61 covering the grounds for a person with a relevant interest in seized property to apply to a judicial authority for its return and the duty of officers to secure property in certain circumstances when an application is made;
- (iv) specifying the name and address of the person to whom:
  - notice of an application to the appropriate judicial authority in respect of any of the seized property must be given;

- an application may be made to allow attendance at the initial examination of the property.

7.13   If the occupier is not present but there is someone in charge of the premises, the notice shall be given to them. If no suitable person is available, so the notice will easily be found it should either be:

- left in a prominent place on the premises;
- attached to the exterior of the premises.

(c)   Retention

7.14   Subject to paragraph 7.15, anything seized in accordance with the above provisions may be retained only for as long as is necessary. It may be retained, among other purposes:

(i)   for use as evidence at a trial for an offence;
(ii)   to facilitate the use in any investigation or proceedings of anything to which it is inextricably linked, see Note 7H;
(iii)   for forensic examination or other investigation in connection with an offence;
(iv)   in order to establish its lawful owner when there are reasonable grounds for believing it has been stolen or obtained by the commission of an offence.

7.15   Property shall not be retained under paragraph 7.14(i), (ii) or (iii) if a copy or image would be sufficient.

(d)   Rights of owners etc

7.16   If property is retained, the person who had custody or control of it immediately before seizure must, on request, be provided with a list or description of the property within a reasonable time.

7.17   That person or their representative must be allowed supervised access to the property to examine it or have it photographed or copied, or must be provided with a photograph or copy, in either case within a reasonable time of any request and at their own expense, unless the officer in charge of an investigation has reasonable grounds for believing this would:

(i)   prejudice the investigation of any offence or criminal proceedings; or
(ii)   lead to the commission of an offence by providing access to unlawful material such as pornography;

A record of the ground shall be made when access is denied.

Notes for Guidance

7A   Any person claiming property seized by the police may apply to a magistrates' court under the Police (Property) Act 1897 for its possession and should, if appropriate, be advised of this procedure.

7B   The powers of seizure conferred by PACE, sections 18(2) and 19(3) extend to the seizure of the whole premises when it is physically possible to seize and retain the premises in their totality and practical considerations make seizure desirable. For example, police may remove premises such as tents, vehicles or caravans to a police station for the purpose of preserving evidence.

7C Officers should consider reaching agreement with owners and/or other interested parties on the procedures for examining a specific set of property, rather than awaiting the judicial authority's determination. Agreement can sometimes give a quicker and more satisfactory route for all concerned and minimise costs and legal complexities.

7D What constitutes a relevant interest in specific material may depend on the nature of that material and the circumstances in which it is seized. Anyone with a reasonable claim to ownership of the material and anyone entrusted with its safe keeping by the owner should be considered.

7E Requirements to secure and return property apply equally to all copies, images or other material created because of seizure of the original property.

7F The mechanics of securing property vary according to the circumstances; 'bagging up', i.e. placing material in sealed bags or containers and strict subsequent control of access is the appropriate procedure in many cases.

7G When material is seized under the powers of seizure conferred by PACE, the duty to retain it under the Code of Practice issued under the Criminal Procedure and Investigations Act 1996 is subject to the provisions on retention of seized material in PACE, section 22.

7H Paragraph 7.14 (ii) applies if inextricably linked material is seized under the Criminal Justice and Police Act 2001, sections 50 or 51. Inextricably linked material is material it is not reasonably practicable to separate from other linked material without prejudicing the use of that other material in any investigation or proceedings. For example, it may not be possible to separate items of data held on computer disk without damaging their evidential integrity. Inextricably linked material must not be examined, imaged, copied or used for any purpose other than for proving the source and/or integrity of the linked material.

8 ACTION AFTER SEARCHES

8.1 If premises are searched in circumstances where this Code applies, unless the exceptions in paragraph 2.3(a) apply, on arrival at a police station the officer in charge of the search shall make or have made a record of the search, to include:

    (i)   the address of the searched premises;

    (ii)   the date, time and duration of the search;

    (iii) the authority used for the search:

- if the search was made in exercise of a statutory power to search premises without warrant, the power which was used for the search;
- if the search was made under a warrant or with written consent:
  - ~ a copy of the warrant and the written authority to apply for it, see paragraph 3.4; or
  - ~ the written consent;

shall be appended to the record or the record shall show the location of the copy warrant or consent.

    (iv) subject to paragraph 2.9, the names of:

- the officer(s) in charge of the search;
- all other officers and any authorised persons who conducted the search;

    (v)   the names of any people on the premises if they are known;

    (vi) any grounds for refusing the occupier's request to have someone present during the search, see paragraph 6.11;

(vii) a list of any articles seized or the location of a list and, if not covered by a warrant, the grounds for their seizure;

(viii) whether force was used, and the reason;

(ix) details of any damage caused during the search, and the circumstances;

(x) if applicable, the reason it was not practicable:

    (a) to give the occupier a copy of the Notice of Powers and Rights, see paragraph 6.7;

    (b) before the search to give the occupier a copy of the Notice, see paragraph 6.8;

(xi) when the occupier was not present, the place where copies of the Notice of Powers and Rights and search warrant were left on the premises, see paragraph 6.8.

8.2 On each occasion when premises are searched under warrant, the warrant authorising the search on that occasion shall be endorsed to show:

(i) if any articles specified in the warrant were found and the address where found;

(ii) if any other articles were seized;

(iii) the date and time it was executed and if present, the name of the occupier or if the occupier is not present the name of the person in charge of the premises;

(iv) subject to paragraph 2.9, the names of the officers who executed it and any authorised persons who accompanied them;

(v) if a copy, together with a copy of the Notice of Powers and Rights was:

- handed to the occupier; or
- endorsed as required by paragraph 6.8; and left on the premises and where.

8.3 Any warrant shall be returned within three calendar months of its issue or sooner on completion of the search(es) authorised by that warrant, if it was issued by a:

- justice of the peace, to the designated officer for the local justice area in which the justice was acting when issuing the warrant; or
- judge, to the appropriate officer of the court concerned.

9 SEARCH REGISTERS

9.1 A search register will be maintained at each sub-divisional or equivalent police station. All search records required under paragraph 8.1 shall be made, copied, or referred to in the register. See Note 9A.

Note for Guidance

9A Paragraph 9.1 also applies to search records made by immigration officers. In these cases, a search register must also be maintained at an immigration office. See also Note 2D.

CODE C: FOR THE DETENTION, TREATMENT AND QUESTIONING OF PERSONS BY POLICE OFFICERS

Commencement – Transitional Arrangements

This Code applies to people in police detention after midnight on 31 December 2005, notwithstanding that their period of detention may have commenced before that time.

1   GENERAL

1.1   All persons in custody must be dealt with expeditiously, and released as soon as the need for detention no longer applies.

1.1A   A custody officer must perform the functions in this Code as soon as practicable. A custody officer will not be in breach of this Code if delay is justifiable and reasonable steps are taken to prevent unnecessary delay. The custody record shall show when a delay has occurred and the reason. See Note 1H.

1.2   This Code of Practice must be readily available at all police stations for consultation by:

- police officers;
- police staff;
- detained persons;
- members of the public.

1.3   The provisions of this Code:

- include the Annexes;
- do not include the Notes for Guidance.

1.4   If an officer has any suspicion, or is told in good faith, that a person of any age may be mentally disordered or otherwise mentally vulnerable, in the absence of clear evidence to dispel that suspicion, the person shall be treated as such for the purposes of this Code. See Note 1G.

1.5   If anyone appears to be under 17, they shall be treated as a juvenile for the purposes of this Code in the absence of clear evidence that they are older.

1.6   If a person appears to be blind, seriously visually impaired, deaf, unable to read or speak or has difficulty orally because of a speech impediment, they shall be treated as such for the purposes of this Code in the absence of clear evidence to the contrary.

1.7   'The appropriate adult' means, in the case of a:

  (a) juvenile:

     (i) the parent, guardian or, if the juvenile is in local authority or voluntary organisation care, or is otherwise being looked after under the Children Act 1989, a person representing that authority or organisation;

    (ii) a social worker of a local authority social services department;

  (iii) failing these, some other responsible adult aged 18 or over who is not a police officer or employed by the police.

  (b) person who is mentally disordered or mentally vulnerable; see Note 1D:

     (i) a relative, guardian or other person responsible for their care or custody;

    (ii) someone experienced in dealing with mentally disordered or mentally vulnerable people but who is not a police officer or employed by the police;

        (iii) failing these, some other responsible adult aged 18 or over who is not a police officer or employed by the police.

1.8   If this Code requires a person be given certain information, they do not have to be given it if at the time they are incapable of understanding what is said, are violent or may become violent or in urgent need of medical attention, but they must be given it as soon as practicable.

1.9   References to a custody officer include any:

- police officer; or
- designated staff custody officer acting in the exercise or performance of the powers and duties conferred or imposed on them by their designation,

performing the functions of a custody officer. See Note 1J.

1.9A   When this Code requires the prior authority or agreement of an officer of at least inspector or superintendent rank, that authority may be given by a sergeant or chief inspector authorised to perform the functions of the higher rank under the Police and Criminal Evidence Act 1984 (PACE), section 107.

1.10   Subject to paragraph 1.12, this Code applies to people in custody at police stations in England and Wales, whether or not they have been arrested, and to those removed to a police station as a place of safety under the Mental Health Act 1983, sections 135 and 136. Section 15 applies solely to people in police detention, e.g. those brought to a police station under arrest or arrested at a police station for an offence after going there voluntarily.

1.11   People in police custody include anyone detained under the Terrorism Act 2000, Schedule 8 and section 41, having been taken to a police station after being arrested under the Terrorism Act 2000, section 41. In these cases, reference to an offence in this Code includes the commission, preparation and instigation of acts of terrorism.

1.12   This Code's provisions do not apply to people in custody:

      (i) arrested on warrants issued in Scotland by officers under the Criminal Justice and Public Order Act 1994, section 136(2), or arrested or detained without warrant by officers from a police force in Scotland under section 137(2). In these cases, police powers and duties and the person's rights and entitlements whilst at a police station in England or Wales are the same as those in Scotland;

     (ii) arrested under the Immigration and Asylum Act 1999, section 142(3) in order to have their fingerprints taken;

   (iii) whose detention is authorised by an immigration officer under the Immigration Act 1971;

   (iv) who are convicted or remanded prisoners held in police cells on behalf of the Prison Service under the Imprisonment (Temporary Provisions) Act 1980;

    (v) detained for examination under the Terrorism Act 2000, Schedule 7 and to whom the Code of Practice issued under that Act, Schedule 14, paragraph 6 applies;

   (vi) detained for searches under stop and search powers except as required by Code A.

The provisions on conditions of detention and treatment in sections 8 and 9 must be considered as the minimum standards of treatment for such detainees.

1.13   In this Code:

    (a)   'designated person' means a person other than a police officer, designated under the Police Reform Act 2002, Part 4 who has specified powers and duties of police officers conferred or imposed on them;

    (b)   reference to a police officer includes a designated person acting in the exercise or performance of the powers and duties conferred or imposed on them by their designation.

1.14   Designated persons are entitled to use reasonable force as follows:

    (a)   when exercising a power conferred on them which allows a police officer exercising that power to use reasonable force, a designated person has the same entitlement to use force; and

    (b)   at other times when carrying out duties conferred or imposed on them that also entitle them to use reasonable force, for example:

- when at a police station carrying out the duty to keep detainees for whom they are responsible under control and to assist any other police officer or designated person to keep any detainee under control and to prevent their escape.
- when securing, or assisting any other police officer or designated person in securing, the detention of a person at a police station.
- when escorting, or assisting any other police officer or designated person in escorting, a detainee within a police station.
- for the purpose of saving life or limb; or
- preventing serious damage to property.

1.15   Nothing in this Code prevents the custody officer, or other officer given custody of the detainee, from allowing police staff who are not designated persons to carry out individual procedures or tasks at the police station if the law allows. However, the officer remains responsible for making sure the procedures and tasks are carried out correctly in accordance with the Codes of Practice. Any such civilian must be:

    (a)   a person employed by a police authority maintaining a police force and under the control and direction of the Chief Officer of that force;

    (b)   employed by a person with whom a police authority has a contract for the provision of services relating to persons arrested or otherwise in custody.

1.16   Designated persons and other police staff must have regard to any relevant provisions of the Codes of Practice.

1.17   References to pocket books include any official report book issued to police officers or other police staff.

Notes for Guidance

1A   Although certain sections of this Code apply specifically to people in custody at police stations, those there voluntarily to assist with an investigation should be treated with no less consideration, e.g. offered refreshments at appropriate times, and enjoy an absolute right to obtain legal advice or communicate with anyone outside the police station.

1B   A person, including a parent or guardian, should not be an appropriate adult if they:

- *are*
  - ~ *suspected of involvement in the offence*
  - ~ *the victim*
  - ~ *a witness*

~ *involved in the investigation*

- *received admissions prior to attending to act as the appropriate adult.*

Note: If a juvenile's parent is estranged from the juvenile, they should not be asked to act as the appropriate adult if the juvenile expressly and specifically objects to their presence.

1C   If a juvenile admits an offence to, or in the presence of, a social worker or member of a youth offending team other than during the time that person is acting as the juvenile's appropriate adult, another appropriate adult should be appointed in the interest of fairness.

1D   In the case of people who are mentally disordered or otherwise mentally vulnerable, it may be more satisfactory if the appropriate adult is someone experienced or trained in their care rather than a relative lacking such qualifications. But if the detainee prefers a relative to a better qualified stranger or objects to a particular person their wishes should, if practicable, be respected.

1E   A detainee should always be given an opportunity, when an appropriate adult is called to the police station, to consult privately with a solicitor in the appropriate adult's absence if they want.

1F   A solicitor or independent custody visitor (formerly a lay visitor) present at the police station in that capacity may not be the appropriate adult.

1G   'Mentally vulnerable' applies to any detainee who, because of their mental state or capacity, may not understand the significance of what is said, of questions or of their replies. 'Mental disorder' is defined in the Mental Health Act 1983, section 1(2) as 'mental illness, arrested or incomplete development of mind, psychopathic disorder and any other disorder or disability of mind'. When the custody officer has any doubt about the mental state or capacity of a detainee, that detainee should be treated as mentally vulnerable and an appropriate adult called.

1H   Paragraph 1.1A is intended to cover delays which may occur in processing detainees e.g. if:

- *a large number of suspects are brought into the station simultaneously to be placed in custody;*
- *interview rooms are all being used;*
- *there are difficulties contacting an appropriate adult, solicitor or interpreter.*

1I   The custody officer must remind the appropriate adult and detainee about the right to legal advice and record any reasons for waiving it in accordance with section 6.

1J   The designation of police staff custody officers applies only in police areas where an order commencing the provisions of the Police Reform Act 2002, section 38 and Schedule 4A, for designating police staff custody officers is in effect.

1K   This Code does not affect the principle that all citizens have a duty to help police officers to prevent crime and discover offenders. This is a civic rather than a legal duty; but when a police officer is trying to discover whether, or by whom, an offence has been committed he is entitled to question any person from whom he thinks useful information can be obtained, subject to the restrictions imposed by this Code. A person's declaration that he is unwilling to reply does not alter this entitlement.

2   CUSTODY RECORDS

2.1A   When a person is brought to a police station:

- under arrest;
- is arrested at the police station having attended there voluntarily; or

- attends a police station to answer bail

they should be brought before the custody officer as soon as practicable after their arrival at the station or, if appropriate, following arrest after attending the police station voluntarily. This applies to designated and non-designated police stations. A person is deemed to be 'at a police station' for these purposes if they are within the boundary of any building or enclosed yard which forms part of that police station.

2.1   A separate custody record must be opened as soon as practicable for each person brought to a police station under arrest or arrested at the station having gone there voluntarily or attending a police station in answer to street bail. All information recorded under this Code must be recorded as soon as practicable in the custody record unless otherwise specified. Any audio or video recording made in the custody area is not part of the custody record.

2.2   If any action requires the authority of an officer of a specified rank, subject to paragraph 2.6A, their name and rank must be noted in the custody record.

2.3   The custody officer is responsible for the custody record's accuracy and completeness and for making sure the record or copy of the record accompanies a detainee if they are transferred to another police station. The record shall show the:

- time and reason for transfer;
- time a person is released from detention.

2.4   A solicitor or appropriate adult must be permitted to consult a detainee's custody record as soon as practicable after their arrival at the station and at any other time whilst the person is detained. Arrangements for this access must be agreed with the custody officer and may not unreasonably interfere with the custody officer's duties.

2.4A   When a detainee leaves police detention or is taken before a court they, their legal representative or appropriate adult shall be given, on request, a copy of the custody record as soon as practicable. This entitlement lasts for 12 months after release.

2.5   The detainee, appropriate adult or legal representative shall be permitted to inspect the original custody record after the detainee has left police detention provided they give reasonable notice of their request. Any such inspection shall be noted in the custody record.

2.6   Subject to paragraph 2.6A, all entries in custody records must be timed and signed by the maker. Records entered on computer shall be timed and contain the operator's identification.

2.6A   Nothing in this Code requires the identity of officers or other police staff to be recorded or disclosed:

   (a)   in the case of enquiries linked to the investigation of terrorism; or
   (b)   if the officer or police staff reasonably believe recording or disclosing their name might put them in danger.

In these cases, they shall use their warrant or other identification numbers and the name of their police station. See Note 2A.

2.7   The fact and time of any detainee's refusal to sign a custody record, when asked in accordance with this Code, must be recorded.

Note for Guidance

2A The purpose of paragraph 2.6A(b) is to protect those involved in serious organ-ised crime investigations or arrests of particularly violent suspects when there is re-liable information that those arrested or their associates may threaten or cause harm to those involved. In cases of doubt, an officer of inspector rank or above should be consulted.

3 INITIAL ACTION

(a) Detained persons – normal procedure

3.1 When a person is brought to a police station under arrest or arrested at the station having gone there voluntarily, the custody officer must make sure the person is told clearly about the following continuing rights which may be exercised at any stage during the period in custody:

(i) the right to have someone informed of their arrest as in section 5;

(ii) the right to consult privately with a solicitor and that free independent legal advice is available;

(iii) the right to consult these Codes of Practice. See Note 3D.

3.2 The detainee must also be given:

- a written notice setting out:
  ~ the above three rights;
  ~ the arrangements for obtaining legal advice;
  ~ the right to a copy of the custody record as in paragraph 2.4A;
  ~ the caution in the terms prescribed in section 10.
- an additional written notice briefly setting out their entitlements while in custody, see Notes 3A and 3B.

Note: The detainee shall be asked to sign the custody record to acknowledge receipt of these notices. Any refusal must be recorded on the custody record.

3.3 A citizen of an independent Commonwealth country or a national of a foreign country, including the Republic of Ireland, must be informed as soon as practicable about their rights of communication with their High Commission, Embassy or Consulate. See section 7.

3.4 The custody officer shall:

- record the offence(s) that the detainee has been arrested for and the reason(s) for the arrest on the custody record. See paragraph 10.3 and Code G para-graphs 2.2 and 4.3.
- note on the custody record any comment the detainee makes in relation to the arresting officer's account but shall not invite comment. If the arresting officer is not physically present when the detainee is brought to a police station, the arresting officer's account must be made available to the custody officer remotely or by a third party on the arresting officer's behalf. If the custody officer authorises a person's detention the detainee must be informed of the grounds as soon as practicable and before they are questioned about any offence;
- note any comment the detainee makes in respect of the decision to detain them but shall not invite comment;
- not put specific questions to the detainee regarding their involvement in any offence, nor in respect of any comments they may make in response to the

arresting officer's account or the decision to place them in detention. Such an exchange is likely to constitute an interview as in paragraph 11.1A and require the associated safeguards in section 11.

See paragraph 11.13 in respect of unsolicited comments.

3.5   The custody officer shall:

(a)   ask the detainee, whether at this time, they:

(i)   would like legal advice, see paragraph 6.5;
(ii) want someone informed of their detention, see section 5;

(b)   ask the detainee to sign the custody record to confirm their decisions in respect of (a);

(c)   determine whether the detainee:

(i)   is, or might be, in need of medical treatment or attention, see section 9;
(ii) requires:

- an appropriate adult;
- help to check documentation;
- an interpreter;

(d)   record the decision in respect of (c).

3.6   When determining these needs the custody officer is responsible for initiating an assessment to consider whether the detainee is likely to present specific risks to custody staff or themselves. Such assessments should always include a check on the Police National Computer, to be carried out as soon as practicable, to identify any risks highlighted in relation to the detainee. Although such assessments are primarily the custody officer's responsibility, it may be necessary for them to consult and involve others, e.g. the arresting officer or an appropriate health care professional, see paragraph 9.13. Reasons for delaying the initiation or completion of the assessment must be recorded.

3.7   Chief Officers should ensure that arrangements for proper and effective risk assessments required by paragraph 3.6 are implemented in respect of all detainees at police stations in their area.

3.8   Risk assessments must follow a structured process which clearly defines the categories of risk to be considered and the results must be incorporated in the detainee's custody record. The custody officer is responsible for making sure those responsible for the detainee's custody are appropriately briefed about the risks. If no specific risks are identified by the assessment, that should be noted in the custody record. See Note 3E and paragraph 9.14.

3.9   The custody officer is responsible for implementing the response to any specific risk assessment, e.g.:

- reducing opportunities for self harm;
- calling a health care professional;
- increasing levels of monitoring or observation.

3.10   Risk assessment is an ongoing process and assessments must always be subject to review if circumstances change.

3.11   If video cameras are installed in the custody area, notices shall be prominently displayed showing cameras are in use. Any request to have video cameras switched off shall be refused.

(b) Detained persons – special groups

3.12   If the detainee appears deaf or there is doubt about their hearing or speaking ability or ability to understand English, and the custody officer cannot establish effective communication, the custody officer must, as soon as practicable, call an interpreter for assistance in the action under paragraphs 3.1–3.5. See section 13.

3.13   If the detainee is a juvenile, the custody officer must, if it is practicable, ascertain the identity of a person responsible for their welfare. That person:

- may be:
  - ~ the parent or guardian;
  - ~ if the juvenile is in local authority or voluntary organisation care, or is otherwise being looked after under the Children Act 1989, a person appointed by that authority or organisation to have responsibility for the juvenile's welfare;
  - ~ any other person who has, for the time being, assumed responsibility for the juvenile's welfare.
- must be informed as soon as practicable that the juvenile has been arrested, why they have been arrested and where they are detained. This right is in addition to the juvenile's right in section 5 not to be held incommunicado. See Note 3C.

3.14   If a juvenile known to be subject to a court order under which a person or organisation is given any degree of statutory responsibility to supervise or otherwise monitor them, reasonable steps must also be taken to notify that person or organisation (the 'responsible officer'). The responsible officer will normally be a member of a Youth Offending Team, except for a curfew order which involves electronic monitoring when the contractor providing the monitoring will normally be the responsible officer.

3.15   If the detainee is a juvenile, mentally disordered or otherwise mentally vulnerable, the custody officer must, as soon as practicable:

- inform the appropriate adult, who in the case of a juvenile may or may not be a person responsible for their welfare, as in paragraph 3.13, of:
  - ~ the grounds for their detention;
  - ~ their whereabouts.
- ask the adult to come to the police station to see the detainee.

3.16   It is imperative a mentally disordered or otherwise mentally vulnerable person, detained under the Mental Health Act 1983, section 136, be assessed as soon as possible. If that assessment is to take place at the police station, an approved social worker and a registered medical practitioner shall be called to the station as soon as possible in order to interview and examine the detainee. Once the detainee has been interviewed, examined and suitable arrangements made for their treatment or care, they can no longer be detained under section 136. A detainee must be immediately discharged from detention under section 136 if a registered medical practitioner, having examined them, concludes they are not mentally disordered within the meaning of the Act.

3.17   If the appropriate adult is:

- already at the police station, the provisions of paragraphs 3.1 to 3.5 must be complied with in the appropriate adult's presence;

- not at the station when these provisions are complied with, they must be complied with again in the presence of the appropriate adult when they arrive.

3.18 The detainee shall be advised that:

- the duties of the appropriate adult include giving advice and assistance;
- they can consult privately with the appropriate adult at any time.

3.19 If the detainee, or appropriate adult on the detainee's behalf, asks for a solicitor to be called to give legal advice, the provisions of section 6 apply.

3.20 If the detainee is blind, seriously visually impaired or unable to read, the custody officer shall make sure their solicitor, relative, appropriate adult or some other person likely to take an interest in them and not involved in the investigation is available to help check any documentation. When this Code requires written consent or signing the person assisting may be asked to sign instead, if the detainee prefers. This paragraph does not require an appropriate adult to be called solely to assist in checking and signing documentation for a person who is not a juvenile, or mentally disordered or otherwise mentally vulnerable (see paragraph 3.15).

(c) Persons attending a police station voluntarily

3.21 Anybody attending a police station voluntarily to assist with an investigation may leave at will unless arrested. See Note 1K. If it is decided they shall not be allowed to leave, they must be informed at once that they are under arrest and brought before the custody officer, who is responsible for making sure they are notified of their rights in the same way as other detainees. If they are not arrested but are cautioned as in section 10, the person who gives the caution must, at the same time, inform them they are not under arrest, they are not obliged to remain at the station but if they remain at the station they may obtain free and independent legal advice if they want. They shall be told the right to legal advice includes the right to speak with a solicitor on the telephone and be asked if they want to do so.

3.22 If a person attending the police station voluntarily asks about their entitlement to legal advice, they shall be given a copy of the notice explaining the arrangements for obtaining legal advice. See paragraph 3.2.

(d) Documentation

3.23 The grounds for a person's detention shall be recorded, in the person's presence if practicable.

3.24 Action taken under paragraphs 3.12 to 3.20 shall be recorded.

(e) Persons answering street bail

3.25 When a person is answering street bail, the custody officer should link any documentation held in relation to arrest with the custody record. Any further action shall be recorded on the custody record in accordance with paragraphs 3.23 and 3.24 above.

Notes for Guidance

3A The notice of entitlements should:

- *list the entitlements in this Code, including:*

~ *visits and contact with outside parties, including special provisions for Commonwealth citizens and foreign nationals;*

~ *reasonable standards of physical comfort;*

~ *adequate food and drink;*

~ *access to toilets and washing facilities, clothing, medical attention, and exercise when practicable.*

• *mention the:*

~ *provisions relating to the conduct of interviews;*

~ *circumstances in which an appropriate adult should be available to assist the detainee and their statutory rights to make representation whenever the period of their detention is reviewed.*

3B   In addition to notices in English, translations should be available in Welsh, the main minority ethnic languages and the principal European languages, whenever they are likely to be helpful. Audio versions of the notice should also be made available.

3C   If the juvenile is in local authority or voluntary organisation care but living with their parents or other adults responsible for their welfare, although there is no legal obligation to inform them, they should normally be contacted, as well as the authority or organisation unless suspected of involvement in the offence concerned. Even if the juvenile is not living with their parents, consideration should be given to informing them.

3D   The right to consult the Codes of Practice does not entitle the person concerned to delay unreasonably any necessary investigative or administrative action whilst they do so. Examples of action which need not be delayed unreasonably include:

• *procedures requiring the provision of breath, blood or urine specimens under the Road Traffic Act 1988 or the Transport and Works Act 1992*

• *searching detainees at the police station*

• *taking fingerprints, footwear impressions or non-intimate samples without consent for evidential purposes.*

3E   Home Office Circular 32/2000 provides more detailed guidance on risk assessments and identifies key risk areas which should always be considered.

4   DETAINEE'S PROPERTY

(a)   Action

4.1   The custody officer is responsible for:

(a)   ascertaining what property a detainee:

(i)   has with them when they come to the police station, whether on:

• arrest or re-detention on answering to bail;

• commitment to prison custody on the order or sentence of a court;

• lodgement at the police station with a view to their production in court from prison custody;

• transfer from detention at another station or hospital;

• detention under the Mental Health Act 1983, section 135 or 136;

• remand into police custody on the authority of a court

(ii)   might have acquired for an unlawful or harmful purpose while in custody;

(b)   the safekeeping of any property taken from a detainee which remains at the police station.

The custody officer may search the detainee or authorise their being searched to the extent they consider necessary, provided a search of intimate parts of the body or involving the removal of more than outer clothing is only made as in Annex A. A search may only be carried out by an officer of the same sex as the detainee. See Note 4A.

4.2   Detainees may retain clothing and personal effects at their own risk unless the custody officer considers they may use them to cause harm to themselves or others, interfere with evidence, damage property, effect an escape or they are needed as evidence. In this event the custody officer may withhold such articles as they consider necessary and must tell the detainee why.

4.3   Personal effects are those items a detainee may lawfully need, use or refer to while in detention but do not include cash and other items of value.

(b)   Documentation

4.4   It is a matter for the custody officer to determine whether a record should be made of the property a detained person has with him or had taken from him on arrest. Any record made is not required to be kept as part of the custody record but the custody record should be noted as to where such a record exists. Whenever a record is made the detainee shall be allowed to check and sign the record of property as correct. Any refusal to sign shall be recorded.

4.5   If a detainee is not allowed to keep any article of clothing or personal effects, the reason must be recorded.

Notes for Guidance

4A   PACE, Section 54(1) and paragraph 4.1 require a detainee to be searched when it is clear the custody officer will have continuing duties in relation to that detainee or when that detainee's behaviour or offence makes an inventory appropriate. They do not require every detainee to be searched, e.g. if it is clear a person will only be detained for a short period and is not to be placed in a cell, the custody officer may decide not to search them. In such a case the custody record will be endorsed 'not searched', paragraph 4.4 will not apply, and the detainee will be invited to sign the entry. If the detainee refuses, the custody officer will be obliged to ascertain what property they have in accordance with paragraph 4.1.

4B   Paragraph 4.4 does not require the custody officer to record on the custody record property in the detainee's possession on arrest if, by virtue of its nature, quantity or size, it is not practicable to remove it to the police station.

4C   Paragraph 4.4 does not require items of clothing worn by the person be recorded unless withheld by the custody officer as in paragraph 4.2.

5   RIGHT NOT TO BE HELD INCOMMUNICADO

(a)   Action

5.1   Any person arrested and held in custody at a police station or other premises may, on request, have one person known to them or likely to take an interest in their welfare informed at public expense of their whereabouts as soon as practicable. If the person cannot be contacted the detainee may choose up to two alternatives. If they cannot be contacted, the person in charge of detention or the investigation has discretion to allow further attempts until the information has been conveyed. See Notes 5C and 5D.

5.2 The exercise of the above right in respect of each person nominated may be delayed only in accordance with Annex B.

5.3 The above right may be exercised each time a detainee is taken to another police station.

5.4 The detainee may receive visits at the custody officer's discretion. See Note 5B.

5.5 If a friend, relative or person with an interest in the detainee's welfare enquires about their whereabouts, this information shall be given if the suspect agrees and Annex B does not apply. See Note 5D.

5.6 The detainee shall be given writing materials, on request, and allowed to telephone one person for a reasonable time, see Notes 5A and 5E. Either or both these privileges may be denied or delayed if an officer of inspector rank or above considers sending a letter or making a telephone call may result in any of the consequences in:

   (a) Annex B paragraphs 1 and 2 and the person is detained in connection with an indictable offence; or
   (b) Annex B paragraphs 8 and 9 and the person is detained under the Terrorism Act 2000, Schedule 7 or section 41.

Nothing in this paragraph permits the restriction or denial of the rights in paragraphs 5.1 and 6.1.

5.7 Before any letter or message is sent, or telephone call made, the detainee shall be informed that what they say in any letter, call or message (other than in a communication to a solicitor) may be read or listened to and may be given in evidence. A telephone call may be terminated if it is being abused. The costs can be at public expense at the custody officer's discretion.

5.7A Any delay or denial of the rights in this section should be proportionate and should last no longer than necessary.

(b) Documentation

5.8 A record must be kept of any:

   (a) request made under this section and the action taken;
   (b) letters, messages or telephone calls made or received or visit received;
   (c) refusal by the detainee to have information about them given to an outside enquirer. The detainee must be asked to countersign the record accordingly and any refusal recorded.

Notes for Guidance

5A   A person may request an interpreter to interpret a telephone call or translate a letter.

5B   At the custody officer's discretion, visits should be allowed when possible, subject to having sufficient personnel to supervise a visit and any possible hindrance to the investigation.

5C   If the detainee does not know anyone to contact for advice or support or cannot contact a friend or relative, the custody officer should bear in mind any local voluntary

373

bodies or other organisations who might be able to help. Paragraph 6.1 applies if legal advice is required.

5D   In some circumstances it may not be appropriate to use the telephone to disclose information under paragraphs 5.1 and 5.5.

5E   The telephone call at paragraph 5.6 is in addition to any communication under paragraphs 5.1 and 6.1.

6   RIGHT TO LEGAL ADVICE

(a)   Action

6.1   Unless Annex B applies, all detainees must be informed that they may at any time consult and communicate privately with a solicitor, whether in person, in writing or by telephone, and that free independent legal advice is available from the duty solicitor. See paragraph 3.1, Note 6B and Note 6J.

6.2   Not Used.

6.3   A poster advertising the right to legal advice must be prominently displayed in the charging area of every police station. See Note 6H.

6.4   No police officer should, at any time, do or say anything with the intention of dissuading a detainee from obtaining legal advice.

6.5   The exercise of the right of access to legal advice may be delayed only as in Annex B. Whenever legal advice is requested, and unless Annex B applies, the custody officer must act without delay to secure the provision of such advice. If, on being informed or reminded of this right, the detainee declines to speak to a solicitor in person, the officer should point out that the right includes the right to speak with a solicitor on the telephone. If the detainee continues to waive this right the officer should ask them why and any reasons should be recorded on the custody record or the interview record as appropriate. Reminders of the right to legal advice must be given as in paragraphs 3.5, 11.2, 15.4, 16.4, 2B of Annex A, 3 of Annex K and 16.5 and Code D, paragraphs 3.17(ii) and 6.3. Once it is clear a detainee does not want to speak to a solicitor in person or by telephone they should cease to be asked their reasons. See Note 6K.

6.5A   In the case of a juvenile, an appropriate adult should consider whether legal advice from a solicitor is required. If the juvenile indicates that they do not want legal advice, the appropriate adult has the right to ask for a solicitor to attend if this would be in the best interests of the person. However, the detained person cannot be forced to see the solicitor if he is adamant that he does not wish to do so.

6.6   A detainee who wants legal advice may not be interviewed or continue to be interviewed until they have received such advice unless:

    (a)   Annex B applies, when the restriction on drawing adverse inferences from silence in Annex C will apply because the detainee is not allowed an opportunity to consult a solicitor; or

    (b)   an officer of superintendent rank or above has reasonable grounds for believing that:

        (i)   the consequent delay might:

- lead to interference with, or harm to, evidence connected with an offence;
- lead to interference with, or physical harm to, other people;
- lead to serious loss of, or damage to, property;

- lead to alerting other people suspected of having committed an offence but not yet arrested for it;
- hinder the recovery of property obtained in consequence of the commission of an offence.

(ii) when a solicitor, including a duty solicitor, has been contacted and has agreed to attend, awaiting their arrival would cause unreasonable delay to the process of investigation.

Note: In these cases the restriction on drawing adverse inferences from silence in Annex C will apply because the detainee is not allowed an opportunity to consult a solicitor;

(c) the solicitor the detainee has nominated or selected from a list:

(i) cannot be contacted;
(ii) has previously indicated they do not wish to be contacted; or
(iii) having been contacted, has declined to attend; and

the detainee has been advised of the Duty Solicitor Scheme but has declined to ask for the duty solicitor.

In these circumstances the interview may be started or continued without further delay provided an officer of inspector rank or above has agreed to the interview proceeding.

Note: The restriction on drawing adverse inferences from silence in Annex C will not apply because the detainee is allowed an opportunity to consult the duty solicitor;

(d) the detainee changes their mind, about wanting legal advice.

In these circumstances the interview may be started or continued without delay provided that:

(i) the detainee agrees to do so, in writing or on the interview record made in accordance with Code E and F; and
(ii) an officer of inspector rank or above has inquired about the detainee's reasons for their change of mind and gives authority for the interview to proceed.

Confirmation of the detainee's agreement, their change of mind, the reasons for it if given and, subject to paragraph 2.6A, the name of the authorising officer shall be recorded in the written interview record or the interview record made in accordance with Code E or F. See Note 6I.

Note: In these circumstances the restriction on drawing adverse inferences from silence in Annex C will not apply because the detainee is allowed an opportunity to consult a solicitor if they wish.

6.7 If paragraph 6.6(b)(i) applies, once sufficient information has been obtained to avert the risk, questioning must cease until the detainee has received legal advice unless paragraph 6.6(a), (b)(ii), (c) or (d) applies.

6.8 A detainee who has been permitted to consult a solicitor shall be entitled on request to have the solicitor present when they are interviewed unless one of the exceptions in paragraph 6.6 applies.

6.9 The solicitor may only be required to leave the interview if their conduct is such that the interviewer is unable properly to put questions to the suspect. See Notes 6D and 6E.

6.10 If the interviewer considers a solicitor is acting in such a way, they will stop the interview and consult an officer not below superintendent rank, if one is readily available, and otherwise an officer not below inspector rank not connected with the investigation. After speaking to the solicitor, the officer consulted will decide if the interview should continue in the presence of that solicitor. If they decide it should not, the suspect will be given the opportunity to consult another solicitor before the interview continues and that solicitor given an opportunity to be present at the interview. See Note 6E.

6.11   The removal of a solicitor from an interview is a serious step and, if it occurs, the officer of superintendent rank or above who took the decision will consider if the incident should be reported to the Law Society. If the decision to remove the solicitor has been taken by an officer below superintendent rank, the facts must be reported to an officer of superintendent rank or above who will similarly consider whether a report to the Law Society would be appropriate. When the solicitor concerned is a duty solicitor, the report should be both to the Law Society and to the Legal Services Commission.

6.12   'Solicitor' in this Code means:

- a solicitor who holds a current practising certificate
- an accredited or probationary representative included on the register of representatives maintained by the Legal Services Commission.

6.12A   An accredited or probationary representative sent to provide advice by, and on behalf of, a solicitor shall be admitted to the police station for this purpose unless an officer of inspector rank or above considers such a visit will hinder the investigation and directs otherwise. Hindering the investigation does not include giving proper legal advice to a detainee as in Note 6D. Once admitted to the police station, paragraphs 6.6 to 6.10 apply.

6.13   In exercising their discretion under paragraph 6.12A, the officer should take into account in particular:

- whether:
    - ~ the identity and status of an accredited or probationary representative have been satisfactorily established;
    - ~ they are of suitable character to provide legal advice, e.g. a person with a criminal record is unlikely to be suitable unless the conviction was for a minor offence and not recent.
- any other matters in any written letter of authorisation provided by the solicitor on whose behalf the person is attending the police station. See Note 6F.

6.14   If the inspector refuses access to an accredited or probationary representative or a decision is taken that such a person should not be permitted to remain at an interview, the inspector must notify the solicitor on whose behalf the representative was acting and give them an opportunity to make alternative arrangements. The detainee must be informed and the custody record noted.

6.15   If a solicitor arrives at the station to see a particular person, that person must, unless Annex B applies, be so informed whether or not they are being interviewed and asked if they would like to see the solicitor. This applies even if the detainee has declined legal advice or, having requested it, subsequently agreed to be interviewed without receiving advice. The solicitor's attendance and the detainee's decision must be noted in the custody record.

(b) Documentation

6.16   Any request for legal advice and the action taken shall be recorded.

6.17   A record shall be made in the interview record if a detainee asks for legal advice and an interview is begun either in the absence of a solicitor or their representative, or they have been required to leave an interview.

Notes for Guidance

6A   In considering if paragraph 6.6(b) applies, the officer should, if practicable, ask the solicitor for an estimate of how long it will take to come to the station and relate this to the time detention is permitted, the time of day (i.e. whether the rest period under paragraph 12.2 is imminent) and the requirements of other investigations. If the solicitor is on their way or is to set off immediately, it will not normally be appropriate to begin an interview before they arrive. If it appears necessary to begin an interview before the solicitor's arrival, they should be given an indication of how long the police would be able to wait before 6.6(b) applies so there is an opportunity to make arrangements for someone else to provide legal advice.

6B   A detainee who asks for legal advice should be given an opportunity to consult a specific solicitor or another solicitor from that solicitor's firm or the duty solicitor. If advice is not available by these means, or they do not want to consult the duty solicitor, the detainee should be given an opportunity to choose a solicitor from a list of those willing to provide legal advice. If this solicitor is unavailable, they may choose up to two alternatives. If these attempts are unsuccessful, the custody officer has discretion to allow further attempts until a solicitor has been contacted and agrees to provide legal advice. Apart from carrying out these duties, an officer must not advise the suspect about any particular firm of solicitors.

6C   Not Used.

6D   A detainee has a right to free legal advice and to be represented by a solicitor. The solicitor's only role in the police station is to protect and advance the legal rights of their client. On occasions this may require the solicitor to give advice which has the effect of the client avoiding giving evidence which strengthens a prosecution case. The solicitor may intervene in order to seek clarification, challenge an improper question to their client or the manner in which it is put, advise their client not to reply to particular questions, or if they wish to give their client further legal advice. Paragraph 6.9 only applies if the solicitor's approach or conduct prevents or unreasonably obstructs proper questions being put to the suspect or the suspect's response being recorded. Examples of unacceptable conduct include answering questions on a suspect's behalf or providing written replies for the suspect to quote.

6E   An officer who takes the decision to exclude a solicitor must be in a position to satisfy the court the decision was properly made. In order to do this they may need to witness what is happening.

6F   If an officer of at least inspector rank considers a particular solicitor or firm of solicitors is persistently sending probationary representatives who are unsuited to provide legal advice, they should inform an officer of at least superintendent rank, who may wish to take the matter up with the Law Society.

6G   Subject to the constraints of Annex B, a solicitor may advise more than one client in an investigation if they wish. Any question of a conflict of interest is for the solicitor under their professional code of conduct. If, however, waiting for a solicitor to give advice to one client may lead to unreasonable delay to the interview with another, the provisions of paragraph 6.6(b) may apply.

377

6H   In addition to a poster in English, a poster or posters containing translations into Welsh, the main minority ethnic languages and the principal European languages should be displayed wherever they are likely to be helpful and it is practicable to do so.

6I   Paragraph 6.6(d) requires the authorisation of an officer of inspector rank or above to the continuation of an interview when a detainee who wanted legal advice changes their mind. It is permissible for such authorisation to be given over the telephone, if the authorising officer is able to satisfy themselves about the reason for the detainee's change of mind and is satisfied it is proper to continue the interview in those circumstances.

6J   Whenever a detainee exercises their right to legal advice by consulting or communicating with a solicitor, they must be allowed to do so in private. This right to consult or communicate in private is fundamental. Except as allowed by the Terrorism Act 2000, Schedule 8, paragraph 9, if the requirement for privacy is compromised because what is said or written by the detainee or solicitor for the purpose of giving and receiving legal advice is overheard, listened to, or read by others without the informed consent of the detainee, the right will effectively have been denied. When a detainee chooses to speak to a solicitor on the telephone, they should be allowed to do so in private unless this is impractical because of the design and layout of the custody area or the location of telephones. However, the normal expectation should be that facilities will be available, unless they are being used, at all police stations to enable detainees to speak in private to a solicitor either face to face or over the telephone.

6K   A detainee is not obliged to give reasons for declining legal advice and should not be pressed to do so.

7   CITIZENS OF INDEPENDENT COMMONWEALTH COUNTRIES OR FOREIGN NATIONALS

(a)   Action

7.1   Any citizen of an independent Commonwealth country or a national of a foreign country, including the Republic of Ireland, may communicate at any time with the appropriate High Commission, Embassy or Consulate. The detainee must be informed as soon as practicable of:

- this right;
- their right, upon request, to have their High Commission, Embassy or Consulate told of their whereabouts and the grounds for their detention. Such a request should be acted upon as soon as practicable.

7.2   If a detainee is a citizen of a country with which a bilateral consular convention or agreement is in force requiring notification of arrest, the appropriate High Commission, Embassy or Consulate shall be informed as soon as practicable, subject to paragraph 7.4. The countries to which this applies as at 1st April 2003 are listed in Annex F.

7.3   Consular officers may visit one of their nationals in police detention to talk to them and, if required, to arrange for legal advice. Such visits shall take place out of the hearing of a police officer.

7.4   Notwithstanding the provisions of consular conventions, if the detainee is a political refugee whether for reasons of race, nationality, political opinion or religion, or is seeking political asylum, consular officers shall not be informed of the arrest of one of their nationals or given access or information about them except at the detainee's express request.

(b) Documentation

7.5   A record shall be made when a detainee is informed of their rights under this section and of any communications with a High Commission, Embassy or Consulate.

Note for Guidance

7A   The exercise of the rights in this section may not be interfered with even though Annex B applies.

8   CONDITIONS OF DETENTION

(a) Action

8.1   So far as it is practicable, not more than one detainee should be detained in each cell.

8.2   Cells in use must be adequately heated, cleaned and ventilated. They must be adequately lit, subject to such dimming as is compatible with safety and security to allow people detained overnight to sleep. No additional restraints shall be used within a locked cell unless absolutely necessary and then only restraint equipment, approved for use in that force by the Chief Officer, which is reasonable and necessary in the circumstances having regard to the detainee's demeanour and with a view to ensuring their safety and the safety of others. If a detainee is deaf, mentally disordered or otherwise mentally vulnerable, particular care must be taken when deciding whether to use any form of approved restraints.

8.3   Blankets, mattresses, pillows and other bedding supplied shall be of a reasonable standard and in a clean and sanitary condition. See Note 8A.

8.4   Access to toilet and washing facilities must be provided.

8.5   If it is necessary to remove a detainee's clothes for the purposes of investigation, for hygiene, health reasons or cleaning, replacement clothing of a reasonable standard of comfort and cleanliness shall be provided. A detainee may not be interviewed unless adequate clothing has been offered.

8.6   At least two light meals and one main meal should be offered in any 24 hour period. See Note 8B. Drinks should be provided at meal times and upon reasonable request between meals. Whenever necessary, advice shall be sought from the appropriate health care professional, see Note 9A, on medical and dietary matters. As far as practicable, meals provided shall offer a varied diet and meet any specific dietary needs or religious beliefs the detainee may have. The detainee may, at the custody officer's discretion, have meals supplied by their family or friends at their expense. See Note 8A.

8.7   Brief outdoor exercise shall be offered daily if practicable.

8.8   A juvenile shall not be placed in a police cell unless no other secure accommodation is available and the custody officer considers it is not practicable to supervise them if they are not placed in a cell or that a cell provides more comfortable accommodation than other secure accommodation in the station. A juvenile may not be placed in a cell with a detained adult.

(b) Documentation

8.9   A record must be kept of replacement clothing and meals offered.

8.10   If a juvenile is placed in a cell, the reason must be recorded.

8.11   The use of any restraints on a detainee whilst in a cell, the reasons for it and, if appropriate, the arrangements for enhanced supervision of the detainee whilst so restrained, shall be recorded. See paragraph 3.9.

Notes for Guidance

8A   The provisions in paragraph 8.3 and 8.6 respectively are of particular importance in the case of a person detained under the Terrorism Act 2000, immigration detainees and others likely to be detained for an extended period. In deciding whether to allow meals to be supplied by family or friends, the custody officer is entitled to take account of the risk of items being concealed in any food or package and the officer's duties and responsibilities under food handling legislation.

8B   Meals should, so far as practicable, be offered at recognised meal times, or at other times that take account of when the detainee last had a meal.

9   CARE AND TREATMENT OF DETAINED PERSONS

(a) General

9.1   Nothing in this section prevents the police from calling the police surgeon or, if appropriate, some other health care professional, to examine a detainee for the purposes of obtaining evidence relating to any offence in which the detainee is suspected of being involved. See Note 9A.

9.2   If a complaint is made by, or on behalf of, a detainee about their treatment since their arrest, or it comes to notice that a detainee may have been treated improperly, a report must be made as soon as practicable to an officer of inspector rank or above not connected with the investigation. If the matter concerns a possible assault or the possibility of the unnecessary or unreasonable use of force, an appropriate health care professional must also be called as soon as practicable.

9.3   Detainees should be visited at least every hour. If no reasonably foreseeable risk was identified in a risk assessment, see paragraphs 3.6–3.10, there is no need to wake a sleeping detainee. Those suspected of being intoxicated through drink or drugs or having swallowed drugs, see Note 9CA, or whose level of consciousness causes concern must, subject to any clinical directions given by the appropriate health care professional, see paragraph 9.13:

- be visited and roused at least every half hour
- have their condition assessed as in Annex H
- and clinical treatment arranged if appropriate

See Notes 9B, 9C and 9H.

9.4   When arrangements are made to secure clinical attention for a detainee, the custody officer must make sure all relevant information which might assist in the treatment of the detainee's condition is made available to the responsible health care professional. This applies whether or not the health care professional asks for such information. Any officer or police staff with relevant information must inform the custody officer as soon as practicable.

(b)   Clinical treatment and attention

9.5   The custody officer must make sure a detainee receives appropriate clinical attention as soon as reasonably practicable if the person:

   (a)   appears to be suffering from physical illness; or
   (b)   is injured; or
   (c)   appears to be suffering from a mental disorder;
   (d)   appears to need clinical attention.

9.5A   This applies even if the detainee makes no request for clinical attention and whether or not they have already received clinical attention elsewhere. If the need for attention appears urgent, e.g. when indicated as in Annex H, the nearest available health care professional or an ambulance must be called immediately.

9.5B   The custody officer must also consider the need for clinical attention as set out in Note for Guidance 9C in relation to those suffering the effects of alcohol or drugs.

9.6   Paragraph 9.5 is not meant to prevent or delay the transfer to a hospital if necessary of a person detained under the Mental Health Act 1983, section 136. See Note 9D. When an assessment under that Act takes place at a police station, see paragraph 3.16, the custody officer must consider whether an appropriate health care professional should be called to conduct an initial clinical check on the detainee. This applies particularly when there is likely to be any significant delay in the arrival of a suitably qualified medical practitioner.

9.7   If it appears to the custody officer, or they are told, that a person brought to a station under arrest may be suffering from an infectious disease or condition, the custody officer must take reasonable steps to safeguard the health of the detainee and others at the station. In deciding what action to take, advice must be sought from an appropriate health care professional. See Note 9E. The custody officer has discretion to isolate the person and their property until clinical directions have been obtained.

9.8   If a detainee requests a clinical examination, an appropriate health care professional must be called as soon as practicable to assess the detainee's clinical needs. If a safe and appropriate care plan cannot be provided, the police surgeon's advice must be sought. The detainee may also be examined by a medical practitioner of their choice at their expense.

9.9   If a detainee is required to take or apply any medication in compliance with clinical directions prescribed before their detention, the custody officer must consult the appropriate health care professional before the use of the medication. Subject to the restrictions in paragraph 9.10, the custody officer is responsible for the safekeeping of any medication and for making sure the detainee is given the opportunity to take or apply prescribed or approved medication. Any such consultation and its outcome shall be noted in the custody record.

9.10   No police officer may administer or supervise the self-administration of medically prescribed controlled drugs of the types and forms listed in the Misuse of Drugs Regulations 2001, Schedule 2 or 3. A detainee may only self-administer such drugs under the personal supervision of the registered medical practitioner authorising their use. Drugs listed in Schedule 4 or 5 may be distributed by the custody officer for self-administration if they have consulted the registered medical practitioner authorising their use, this may be done by telephone, and both parties are satisfied self-administration will not expose the detainee, police officers or anyone else to the risk of harm or injury.

9.11   When appropriate health care professionals administer drugs or other medications, or supervise their self-administration, it must be within current medicines legislation and the scope of practice as determined by their relevant professional body.

9.12   If a detainee has in their possession, or claims to need, medication relating to a heart condition, diabetes, epilepsy or a condition of comparable potential seriousness then, even though paragraph 9.5 may not apply, the advice of the appropriate health care professional must be obtained.

9.13   Whenever the appropriate health care professional is called in accordance with this section to examine or treat a detainee, the custody officer shall ask for their opinion about:

- any risks or problems which police need to take into account when making decisions about the detainee's continued detention;
- when to carry out an interview if applicable; and
- the need for safeguards.

9.14   When clinical directions are given by the appropriate health care professional, whether orally or in writing, and the custody officer has any doubts or is in any way uncertain about any aspect of the directions, the custody officer shall ask for clarification. It is particularly important that directions concerning the frequency of visits are clear, precise and capable of being implemented. See Note 9F.

(c)   Documentation

9.15   A record must be made in the custody record of:

(a)   the arrangements made for an examination by an appropriate health care professional under paragraph 9.2 and of any complaint reported under that paragraph together with any relevant remarks by the custody officer;

(b)   any arrangements made in accordance with paragraph 9.5;

(c)   any request for a clinical examination under paragraph 9.8 and any arrangements made in response;

(d)   the injury, ailment, condition or other reason which made it necessary to make the arrangements in (a) to (c), see Note 9G;

(e)   any clinical directions and advice, including any further clarifications, given to police by a health care professional concerning the care and treatment of the detainee in connection with any of the arrangements made in (a) to (c), see Note 9F;

(f)   if applicable, the responses received when attempting to rouse a person using the procedure in Annex H, see Note 9H.

9.16   If a health care professional does not record their clinical findings in the custody record, the record must show where they are recorded. See Note 9G. However, information which is necessary to custody staff to ensure the effective ongoing care and well being of the detainee must be recorded openly in the custody record, see paragraph 3.8 and Annex G, paragraph 7.

9.17   Subject to the requirements of Section 4, the custody record shall include:

- a record of all medication a detainee has in their possession on arrival at the police station;
- a note of any such medication they claim to need but do not have with them.

Notes for Guidance

9A   A 'health care professional' means a clinically qualified person working within the scope of practice as determined by their relevant professional body. Whether a health care professional is 'appropriate' depends on the circumstances of the duties they carry out at the time.

9B   Whenever possible juveniles and mentally vulnerable detainees should be visited more frequently.

9C   A detainee who appears drunk or behaves abnormally may be suffering from illness, the effects of drugs or may have sustained injury, particularly a head injury which is not apparent. A detainee needing or dependent on certain drugs, including alcohol, may experience harmful effects within a short time of being deprived of their supply. In these circumstances, when there is any doubt, police should always act urgently to call an appropriate health care professional or an ambulance. Paragraph 9.5 does not apply to minor ailments or injuries which do not need attention. However, all such ailments or injuries must be recorded in the custody record and any doubt must be resolved in favour of calling the appropriate health care professional.

9CA   Paragraph 9.3 would apply to a person in police custody by order of a magistrates' court under the Criminal Justice Act 1988, section 152 (as amended by the Drugs Act 2005, section 8) to facilitate the recovery of evidence after being charged with drug possession or drug trafficking and suspected of having swallowed drugs. In the case of the healthcare needs of a person who has swallowed drugs, the custody officer subject to any clinical directions, should consider the necessity for rousing every half hour. This does not negate the need for regular visiting of the suspect in the cell.

9D   Whenever practicable, arrangements should be made for persons detained for assessment under the Mental Health Act 1983, section 136 to be taken to a hospital. There is no power under that Act to transfer a person detained under section 136 from one place of safety to another place of safety for assessment.

9E   It is important to respect a person's right to privacy and information about their health must be kept confidential and only disclosed with their consent or in accordance with clinical advice when it is necessary to protect the detainee's health or that of others who come into contact with them.

9F   The custody officer should always seek to clarify directions that the detainee requires constant observation or supervision and should ask the appropriate health care professional to explain precisely what action needs to be taken to implement such directions.

9G   Paragraphs 9.15 and 9.16 do not require any information about the cause of any injury, ailment or condition to be recorded on the custody record if it appears capable of providing evidence of an offence.

9H   The purpose of recording a person's responses when attempting to rouse them using the procedure in Annex H is to enable any change in the individual's consciousness level to be noted and clinical treatment arranged if appropriate.

10   CAUTIONS

(a)   When a caution must be given

10.1   A person whom there are grounds to suspect of an offence, see Note 10A, must be cautioned before any questions about an offence, or further questions if the answers provide the grounds for suspicion, are put to them if either the suspect's answers or silence, (i.e. failure or refusal to answer or answer satisfactorily) may be given in evidence to a court in a prosecution. A person need not be cautioned if questions are for other necessary purposes, e.g.:

    (a)   solely to establish their identity or ownership of any vehicle;

    (b)   to obtain information in accordance with any relevant statutory requirement, see paragraph 10.9;

    (c)   in furtherance of the proper and effective conduct of a search, e.g. to determine the need to search in the exercise of powers of stop and search or to seek co-operation while carrying out a search;

    (d)   to seek verification of a written record as in paragraph 11.13;

    (e)   when examining a person in accordance with the Terrorism Act 2000, Schedule 7 and the Code of Practice for Examining Officers issued under that Act, Schedule 14, paragraph 6.

10.2   Whenever a person not under arrest is initially cautioned, or reminded they are under caution, that person must at the same time be told they are not under arrest and are free to leave if they want to. See Note 10C.

10.3   A person who is arrested, or further arrested, must be informed at the time, or as soon as practicable thereafter, that they are under arrest and the grounds for their arrest, see paragraph 3.4, Note 10B and Code G, paragraphs 2.2 and 4.3.

10.4   As per Code G, section 3, a person who is arrested, or further arrested, must also be cautioned unless:

    (a)   it is impracticable to do so by reason of their condition or behaviour at the time;

    (b)   they have already been cautioned immediately prior to arrest as in paragraph 10.1.

(b) Terms of the cautions

10.5   The caution which must be given on:

    (a)   arrest;

    (b)   all other occasions before a person is charged or informed they may be prosecuted, see section 16,

should, unless the restriction on drawing adverse inferences from silence applies, see Annex C, be in the following terms:

'You do not have to say anything. But it may harm your defence if you do not mention when questioned something which you later rely on in Court. Anything you do say may be given in evidence.'

See Note 10G.

10.6   Annex C, paragraph 2 sets out the alternative terms of the caution to be used when the restriction on drawing adverse inferences from silence applies.

10.7   Minor deviations from the words of any caution given in accordance with this Code do not constitute a breach of this Code, provided the sense of the relevant caution is preserved. See Note 10D.

10.8   After any break in questioning under caution, the person being questioned must be made aware they remain under caution. If there is any doubt the relevant caution should be given again in full when the interview resumes. See Note 10E.

10.9   When, despite being cautioned, a person fails to co-operate or to answer particular questions which may affect their immediate treatment, the person should be informed of any relevant consequences and that those consequences are not affected by the caution. Examples are when a person's refusal to provide:

- their name and address when charged may make them liable to detention;
- particulars and information in accordance with a statutory requirement, e.g. under the Road Traffic Act 1988, may amount to an offence or may make the person liable to a further arrest.

(c) Special warnings under the Criminal Justice and Public Order Act 1994, sections 36 and 37

10.10   When a suspect interviewed at a police station or authorised place of detention after arrest fails or refuses to answer certain questions, or to answer satisfactorily, after due warning, see Note 10F, a court or jury may draw such inferences as appear proper under the Criminal Justice and Public Order Act 1994, sections 36 and 37. Such inferences may only be drawn when:

(a)   the restriction on drawing adverse inferences from silence, see Annex C, does not apply; and

(b)   the suspect is arrested by a constable and fails or refuses to account for any objects, marks or substances, or marks on such objects found:

- on their person;
- in or on their clothing or footwear;
- otherwise in their possession; or
- in the place they were arrested;

(c)   the arrested suspect was found by a constable at a place at or about the time the offence for which that officer has arrested them is alleged to have been committed, and the suspect fails or refuses to account for their presence there.

When the restriction on drawing adverse inferences from silence applies, the suspect may still be asked to account for any of the matters in (b) or (c) but the special warning described in paragraph 10.11 will not apply and must not be given.

10.11   For an inference to be drawn when a suspect fails or refuses to answer a question about one of these matters or to answer it satisfactorily, the suspect must first be told in ordinary language:

(a)   what offence is being investigated;
(b)   what fact they are being asked to account for;
(c)   this fact may be due to them taking part in the commission of the offence;
(d)   a court may draw a proper inference if they fail or refuse to account for this fact;
(e)   a record is being made of the interview and it may be given in evidence if they are brought to trial.

(d) Juveniles and persons who are mentally disordered or otherwise mentally vulnerable

10.12   If a juvenile or a person who is mentally disordered or otherwise mentally vulnerable is cautioned in the absence of the appropriate adult, the caution must be repeated in the adult's presence.

(e) Documentation

10.13   A record shall be made when a caution is given under this section, either in the interviewer's pocket book or in the interview record.

Notes for Guidance

10A   There must be some reasonable, objective grounds for the suspicion, based on known facts or information which are relevant to the likelihood the offence has been committed and the person to be questioned committed it.

10B   An arrested person must be given sufficient information to enable them to understand that they have been deprived of their liberty and the reason they have been arrested, e.g. when a person is arrested on suspicion of committing an offence they must be informed of the suspected offence's nature, when and where it was committed. The suspect must also be informed of the reason or reasons why the arrest is considered necessary. Vague or technical language should be avoided.

10C   The restriction on drawing inferences from silence, see Annex C, paragraph 1, does not apply to a person who has not been detained and who therefore cannot be prevented from seeking legal advice if they want, see paragraph 3.21.

10D   If it appears a person does not understand the caution, the person giving it should explain it in their own words.

10E   It may be necessary to show to the court that nothing occurred during an interview break or between interviews which influenced the suspect's recorded evidence. After a break in an interview or at the beginning of a subsequent interview, the interviewing officer should summarise the reason for the break and confirm this with the suspect.

10F   The Criminal Justice and Public Order Act 1994, sections 36 and 37 apply only to suspects who have been arrested by a constable or Customs and Excise officer and are given the relevant warning by the police or customs officer who made the arrest or who is investigating the offence. They do not apply to any interviews with suspects who have not been arrested.

10G   Nothing in this Code requires a caution to be given or repeated when informing a person not under arrest they may be prosecuted for an offence. However, a court will not be able to draw any inferences under the Criminal Justice and Public Order Act 1994, section 34, if the person was not cautioned.

11   INTERVIEWS – GENERAL

(a)   Action

11.1A   An interview is the questioning of a person regarding their involvement or suspected involvement in a criminal offence or offences which, under paragraph 10.1, must be carried out under caution. Whenever a person is interviewed they must be informed of the nature of the offence, or further offence. Procedures under the Road Traffic Act 1988, section 7 or the Transport and Works Act 1992, section 31 do not constitute interviewing for the purpose of this Code.

11.1   Following a decision to arrest a suspect, they must not be interviewed about the relevant offence except at a police station or other authorised place of detention, unless the consequent delay would be likely to:

    (a)   lead to:

        • interference with, or harm to, evidence connected with an offence;
        • interference with, or physical harm to, other people; or
        • serious loss of, or damage to, property;

    (b)   lead to alerting other people suspected of committing an offence but not yet arrested for it; or

(c)   hinder the recovery of property obtained in consequence of the commission of an offence.

Interviewing in any of these circumstances shall cease once the relevant risk has been averted or the necessary questions have been put in order to attempt to avert that risk.

11.2   Immediately prior to the commencement or re-commencement of any interview at a police station or other authorised place of detention, the interviewer should remind the suspect of their entitlement to free legal advice and that the interview can be delayed for legal advice to be obtained, unless one of the exceptions in paragraph 6.6 applies. It is the interviewer's responsibility to make sure all reminders are recorded in the interview record.

11.3   Not Used.

11.4   At the beginning of an interview the interviewer, after cautioning the suspect, see section 10, shall put to them any significant statement or silence which occurred in the presence and hearing of a police officer or other police staff before the start of the interview and which have not been put to the suspect in the course of a previous interview. See Note 11A. The interviewer shall ask the suspect whether they confirm or deny that earlier statement or silence and if they want to add anything.

11.4A   A significant statement is one which appears capable of being used in evidence against the suspect, in particular a direct admission of guilt. A significant silence is a failure or refusal to answer a question or answer satisfactorily when under caution, which might, allowing for the restriction on drawing adverse inferences from silence, see Annex C, give rise to an inference under the Criminal Justice and Public Order Act 1994, Part III.

11.5   No interviewer may try to obtain answers or elicit a statement by the use of oppression. Except as in paragraph 10.9, no interviewer shall indicate, except to answer a direct question, what action will be taken by the police if the person being questioned answers questions, makes a statement or refuses to do either. If the person asks directly what action will be taken if they answer questions, make a statement or refuse to do either, the interviewer may inform them what action the police propose to take provided that action is itself proper and warranted.

11.6   The interview or further interview of a person about an offence with which that person has not been charged or for which they have not been informed they may be prosecuted, must cease when:

(a)   the officer in charge of the investigation is satisfied all the questions they consider relevant to obtaining accurate and reliable information about the offence have been put to the suspect, this includes allowing the suspect an opportunity to give an innocent explanation and asking questions to test if the explanation is accurate and reliable, e.g. to clear up ambiguities or clarify what the suspect said;

(b)   the officer in charge of the investigation has taken account of any other available evidence; and

(c)   the officer in charge of the investigation, or in the case of a detained suspect, the custody officer, see paragraph 16.1, reasonably believes there is sufficient evidence to provide a realistic prospect of conviction for that offence. See Note 11B.

This paragraph does not prevent officers in revenue cases or acting under the confiscation provisions of the Criminal Justice Act 1988 or the Drug Trafficking Act 1994 from inviting suspects to complete a formal question and answer record after the interview is concluded.

(b)   Interview records

11.7   (a)   An accurate record must be made of each interview, whether or not the interview takes place at a police station;

      (b)   The record must state the place of interview, the time it begins and ends, any interview breaks and, subject to paragraph 2.6A, the names of all those present; and must be made on the forms provided for this purpose or in the interviewer's pocket book or in accordance with the Codes of Practice E or F;

      (c)   Any written record must be made and completed during the interview, unless this would not be practicable or would interfere with the conduct of the interview, and must constitute either a verbatim record of what has been said or, failing this, an account of the interview which adequately and accurately summarises it.

11.8   If a written record is not made during the interview it must be made as soon as practicable after its completion.

11.9   Written interview records must be timed and signed by the maker.

11.10   If a written record is not completed during the interview the reason must be recorded in the interview record.

11.11   Unless it is impracticable, the person interviewed shall be given the opportunity to read the interview record and to sign it as correct or to indicate how they consider it inaccurate. If the person interviewed cannot read or refuses to read the record or sign it, the senior interviewer present shall read it to them and ask whether they would like to sign it as correct or make their mark or to indicate how they consider it inaccurate. The interviewer shall certify on the interview record itself what has occurred. See Note 11E.

11.12   If the appropriate adult or the person's solicitor is present during the interview, they should also be given an opportunity to read and sign the interview record or any written statement taken down during the interview.

11.13   A written record shall be made of any comments made by a suspect, including unsolicited comments, which are outside the context of an interview but which might be relevant to the offence. Any such record must be timed and signed by the maker. When practicable the suspect shall be given the opportunity to read that record and to sign it as correct or to indicate how they consider it inaccurate. See Note 11E.

11.14   Any refusal by a person to sign an interview record when asked in accordance with this Code must itself be recorded.

(c)   Juveniles and mentally disordered or otherwise mentally vulnerable people

11.15   A juvenile or person who is mentally disordered or otherwise mentally vulnerable must not be interviewed regarding their involvement or suspected involvement in a criminal offence or offences, or asked to provide or sign a written statement under caution or record of interview, in the absence of the appropriate adult unless paragraphs 11.1, 11.18 to 11.20 apply. See Note 11C.

11.16   Juveniles may only be interviewed at their place of education in exceptional circumstances and only when the principal or their nominee agrees. Every effort should be made to notify the parent(s) or other person responsible for the juvenile's welfare and the appropriate adult, if this is a different person, that the police want to interview the juvenile and reasonable time should be allowed to enable the appropriate adult to be present at the interview. If awaiting the appropriate adult would cause unreasonable delay, and unless the juvenile is suspected of an offence against the educational establishment, the principal or their nominee can act as the appropriate adult for the purposes of the interview.

11.17 If an appropriate adult is present at an interview, they shall be informed:

- they are not expected to act simply as an observer; and
- the purpose of their presence is to:
  - ~ advise the person being interviewed;
  - ~ observe whether the interview is being conducted properly and fairly;
  - ~ facilitate communication with the person being interviewed.

(d) Vulnerable suspects – urgent interviews at police stations

11.18 The following persons may not be interviewed unless an officer of superintendent rank or above considers delay will lead to the consequences in paragraph 11.1(a) to (c), and is satisfied the interview would not significantly harm the person's physical or mental state (see Annex G):

(a) a juvenile or person who is mentally disordered or otherwise mentally vulnerable if at the time of the interview the appropriate adult is not present;

(b) anyone other than in (a) who at the time of the interview appears unable to:
  - appreciate the significance of questions and their answers; or
  - understand what is happening because of the effects of drink, drugs or any illness, ailment or condition;

(c) a person who has difficulty understanding English or has a hearing disability, if at the time of the interview an interpreter is not present.

11.19 These interviews may not continue once sufficient information has been obtained to avert the consequences in paragraph 11.1(a) to (c).

11.20 A record shall be made of the grounds for any decision to interview a person under paragraph 11.18.

Notes for Guidance

11A Paragraph 11.4 does not prevent the interviewer from putting significant statements and silences to a suspect again at a later stage or a further interview.

11B The Criminal Procedure and Investigations Act 1996 Code of Practice, paragraph 3.4 states 'In conducting an investigation, the investigator should pursue all reasonable lines of enquiry, whether these point towards or away from the suspect. What is reasonable will depend on the particular circumstances.' Interviewers should keep this in mind when deciding what questions to ask in an interview.

11C Although juveniles or people who are mentally disordered or otherwise mentally vulnerable are often capable of providing reliable evidence, they may, without knowing or wishing to do so, be particularly prone in certain circumstances to provide information that may be unreliable, misleading or self-incriminating. Special care should always be taken when questioning such a person, and the appropriate adult should be involved if there is any doubt about a person's age, mental state or capacity. Because of the risk of unreliable evidence it is also important to obtain corroboration of any facts admitted whenever possible.

11D   Juveniles should not be arrested at their place of education unless this is unavoidable. When a juvenile is arrested at their place of education, the principal or their nominee must be informed.

11E   Significant statements described in paragraph 11.4 will always be relevant to the offence and must be recorded. When a suspect agrees to read records of interviews and other comments and sign them as correct, they should be asked to endorse the record with, e.g. 'I agree that this is a correct record of what was said' and add their signature. If the suspect does not agree with the record, the interviewer should record the details of any disagreement and ask the suspect to read these details and sign them to the effect that they accurately reflect their disagreement. Any refusal to sign should be recorded.

12   INTERVIEWS IN POLICE STATIONS

(a)   Action

12.1   If a police officer wants to interview or conduct enquiries which require the presence of a detainee, the custody officer is responsible for deciding whether to deliver the detainee into the officer's custody.

12.2   Except as below, in any period of 24 hours a detainee must be allowed a continuous period of at least 8 hours for rest, free from questioning, travel or any interruption in connection with the investigation concerned. This period should normally be at night or other appropriate time which takes account of when the detainee last slept or rested. If a detainee is arrested at a police station after going there voluntarily, the period of 24 hours runs from the time of their arrest and not the time of arrival at the police station. The period may not be interrupted or delayed, except:

    (a)   when there are reasonable grounds for believing not delaying or interrupting the period would:

        (i)   involve a risk of harm to people or serious loss of, or damage to, property;

        (ii)   delay unnecessarily the person's release from custody;

        (iii)   otherwise prejudice the outcome of the investigation;

    (b)   at the request of the detainee, their appropriate adult or legal representative;

    (c)   when a delay or interruption is necessary in order to:

        (i)   comply with the legal obligations and duties arising under section 15;

        (ii)   to take action required under section 9 or in accordance with medical advice.

If the period is interrupted in accordance with (a), a fresh period must be allowed. Interruptions under (b) and (c), do not require a fresh period to be allowed.

12.3   Before a detainee is interviewed the custody officer, in consultation with the officer in charge of the investigation and appropriate health care professionals as necessary, shall assess whether the detainee is fit enough to be interviewed. This means determining and considering the risks to the detainee's physical and mental state if the interview took place and determining what safeguards are needed to allow the interview to take place. See Annex G. The custody officer shall not allow a detainee to be interviewed if the custody officer considers it would cause significant harm to the detainee's physical or mental state. Vulnerable suspects listed at paragraph 11.18 shall be treated as always being at some risk during an interview and these persons may not be interviewed except in accordance with paragraphs 11.18 to 11.20.

12.4   As far as practicable interviews shall take place in interview rooms which are adequately heated, lit and ventilated.

12.5   A suspect whose detention without charge has been authorised under PACE, because the detention is necessary for an interview to obtain evidence of the offence for which they have been arrested, may choose not to answer questions but police do not require the suspect's consent or agreement to interview them for this purpose. If a suspect takes steps to prevent themselves being questioned or further questioned, e.g. by refusing to leave their cell to go to a suitable interview room or by trying to leave the interview room, they shall be advised their consent or agreement to interview is not required. The suspect shall be cautioned as in section 10, and informed if they fail or refuse to co-operate, the interview may take place in the cell and that their failure or refusal to co-operate may be given in evidence. The suspect shall then be invited to co-operate and go into the interview room.

12.6   People being questioned or making statements shall not be required to stand.

12.7   Before the interview commences each interviewer shall, subject to paragraph 2.6A, identify themselves and any other persons present to the interviewee.

12.8   Breaks from interviewing should be made at recognised meal times or at other times that take account of when an interviewee last had a meal. Short refreshment breaks shall be provided at approximately two hour intervals, subject to the interviewer's discretion to delay a break if there are reasonable grounds for believing it would:

   (i)   involve a:
      • risk of harm to people;
      • serious loss of, or damage to, property;
   (ii)   unnecessarily delay the detainee's release;
   (iii)   otherwise prejudice the outcome of the investigation.

See Note 12B.

12.9   If during the interview a complaint is made by or on behalf of the interviewee concerning the provisions of this Code, the interviewer should:

   (i)   record it in the interview record;
   (ii)   inform the custody officer, who is then responsible for dealing with it as in section 9.

(b)   Documentation

12.10   A record must be made of the:
   • time a detainee is not in the custody of the custody officer, and why
   • reason for any refusal to deliver the detainee out of that custody

12.11   A record shall be made of:
   (a)   the reasons it was not practicable to use an interview room; and
   (b)   any action taken as in paragraph 12.5.

The record shall be made on the custody record or in the interview record for action taken whilst an interview record is being kept, with a brief reference to this effect in the custody record.

12.12   Any decision to delay a break in an interview must be recorded, with reasons, in the interview record.

12.13   All written statements made at police stations under caution shall be written on forms provided for the purpose.

12.14   All written statements made under caution shall be taken in accordance with Annex D. Before a person makes a written statement under caution at a police station they shall be reminded about the right to legal advice. See Note 12A.

Notes for Guidance

12A   It is not normally necessary to ask for a written statement if the interview was recorded in writing and the record signed in accordance with paragraph 11.11 or audibly or visually recorded in accordance with Code E or F. Statements under caution should normally be taken in these circumstances only at the person's express wish. A person may however be asked if they want to make such a statement.

12B   Meal breaks should normally last at least 45 minutes and shorter breaks after two hours should last at least 15 minutes. If the interviewer delays a break in accordance with paragraph 12.8 and prolongs the interview, a longer break should be provided. If there is a short interview, and another short interview is contemplated, the length of the break may be reduced if there are reasonable grounds to believe this is necessary to avoid any of the consequences in paragraph 12.8(i) to (iii).

13   INTERPRETERS

(a)   General

13.1   Chief officers are responsible for making sure appropriate arrangements are in place for provision of suitably qualified interpreters for people who:

- are deaf;
- do not understand English.

Whenever possible, interpreters should be drawn from the National Register of Public Service Interpreters (NRPSI) or the Council for the Advancement of Communication with Deaf People (CADCP) Directory of British Sign Language/English Interpreters.

(b)   Foreign languages

13.2   Unless paragraphs 11.1, 11.18 to 11.20 apply, a person must not be interviewed in the absence of a person capable of interpreting if:

(a)   they have difficulty understanding English;
(b)   the interviewer cannot speak the person's own language;
(c)   the person wants an interpreter present.

13.3   The interviewer shall make sure the interpreter makes a note of the interview at the time in the person's language for use in the event of the interpreter being called to give evidence, and certifies its accuracy. The interviewer should allow sufficient time for the interpreter to note each question and answer after each is put, given and interpreted. The person should be allowed to read the record or have it read to them and sign it as correct or indicate the respects in which they consider it inaccurate. If the interview is audibly recorded or visually recorded, the arrangements in Code E or F apply.

13.4   In the case of a person making a statement to a police officer or other police staff other than in English:

(a)   the interpreter shall record the statement in the language it is made;
(b)   the person shall be invited to sign it;
(c)   an official English translation shall be made in due course.

(c) Deaf people and people with speech difficulties

13.5 If a person appears to be deaf or there is doubt about their hearing or speaking ability, they must not be interviewed in the absence of an interpreter unless they agree in writing to being interviewed without one or paragraphs 11.1, 11.18 to 11.20 apply.

13.6 An interpreter should also be called if a juvenile is interviewed and the parent or guardian present as the appropriate adult appears to be deaf or there is doubt about their hearing or speaking ability, unless they agree in writing to the interview proceeding without one or paragraphs 11.1, 11.18 to 11.20 apply.

13.7 The interviewer shall make sure the interpreter is allowed to read the interview record and certify its accuracy in the event of the interpreter being called to give evidence. If the interview is audibly recorded or visually recorded, the arrangements in Code E or F apply.

(d) Additional rules for detained persons

13.8 All reasonable attempts should be made to make the detainee understand that interpreters will be provided at public expense.

13.9 If paragraph 6.1 applies and the detainee cannot communicate with the solicitor because of language, hearing or speech difficulties, an interpreter must be called. The interpreter may not be a police officer or any other police staff when interpretation is needed for the purposes of obtaining legal advice. In all other cases a police officer or other police staff may only interpret if the detainee and the appropriate adult, if applicable, give their agreement in writing or if the interview is audibly recorded or visually recorded as in Code E or F.

13.10 When the custody officer cannot establish effective communication with a person charged with an offence who appears deaf or there is doubt about their ability to hear, speak or to understand English, arrangements must be made as soon as practicable for an interpreter to explain the offence and any other information given by the custody officer.

(e) Documentation

13.11 Action taken to call an interpreter under this section and any agreement to be interviewed in the absence of an interpreter must be recorded.

14 QUESTIONING – SPECIAL RESTRICTIONS

14.1 If a person is arrested by one police force on behalf of another and the lawful period of detention in respect of that offence has not yet commenced in accordance with PACE, section 41 no questions may be put to them about the offence while they are in transit between the forces except to clarify any voluntary statement they make.

14.2 If a person is in police detention at a hospital they may not be questioned without the agreement of a responsible doctor. See Note 14A.

Note for Guidance

14A If questioning takes place at a hospital under paragraph 14.2, or on the way to or from a hospital, the period of questioning concerned counts towards the total period of detention permitted.

15   REVIEWS AND EXTENSIONS OF DETENTION

(a)   Persons detained under PACE

15.1   The review officer is responsible under PACE, section 40 for periodically deter-mining if a person's detention, before or after charge, continues to be necessary. This requirement continues throughout the detention period and except as in paragraph 15.10, the review officer must be present at the police station holding the detainee. See Notes 15A and 15B.

15.2   Under PACE, section 42, an officer of superintendent rank or above who is responsible for the station holding the detainee may give authority any time after the second review to extend the maximum period the person may be detained without charge by up to 12 hours. Further detention without charge may be authorised only by a magistrates' court in accordance with PACE, sections 43 and 44. See Notes 15C, 15D and 15E.

15.2A   Section 42(1) of PACE as amended extends the maximum period of de-tention for indictable offences from 24 hours to 36 hours. Detaining a juvenile or mentally vulnerable person for longer than 24 hours will be dependent on the circumstances of the case and with regard to the person's:

  (a)   special vulnerability;
  (b)   the legal obligation to provide an opportunity for representations to be made prior to a decision about extending detention;
  (c)   the need to consult and consider the views of any appropriate adult; and
  (d)   any alternatives to police custody.

15.3   Before deciding whether to authorise continued detention the officer respon-sible under paragraphs 15.1 or 15.2 shall give an opportunity to make representations about the detention to:

  (a)   the detainee, unless in the case of a review as in paragraph 15.1, the detainee is asleep;
  (b)   the detainee's solicitor if available at the time; and
  (c)   the appropriate adult if available at the time.

15.3A   Other people having an interest in the detainee's welfare may also make representations at the authorising officer's discretion.

15.3B   Subject to paragraph 15.10, the representations may be made orally in person or by telephone or in writing. The authorising officer may, however, refuse to hear oral representations from the detainee if the officer considers them unfit to make repre-sentations because of their condition or behaviour. See Note 15C.

15.3C   The decision on whether the review takes place in person or by telephone or by video conferencing (see Note 15G) is a matter for the review officer. In determin-ing the form the review may take, the review officer must always take full account of the needs of the person in custody. The benefits of carrying out a review in person should always be considered, based on the individual circumstances of each case with specific additional consideration if the person is:

  (a)   a juvenile (and the age of the juvenile); or
  (b)   mentally vulnerable; or
  (c)   has been subject to medical attention for other than routine minor ailments; or
  (d)   there are presentational or community issues around the person's detention.

15.4   Before conducting a review or determining whether to extend the maximum period of detention without charge, the officer responsible must make sure the detainee is reminded of their entitlement to free legal advice, see paragraph 6.5, unless in the case of a review the person is asleep.

15.5 If, after considering any representations, the officer decides to keep the detainee in detention or extend the maximum period they may be detained without charge, any comment made by the detainee shall be recorded. If applicable, the officer responsible under paragraph 15.1 or 15.2 shall be informed of the comment as soon as practicable. See also paragraphs 11.4 and 11.13.

15.6 No officer shall put specific questions to the detainee:

- regarding their involvement in any offence; or
- in respect of any comments they may make:

  ~ when given the opportunity to make representations; or
  ~ in response to a decision to keep them in detention or extend the maximum period of detention.

Such an exchange could constitute an interview as in paragraph 11.1A and would be subject to the associated safeguards in section 11 and, in respect of a person who has been charged, paragraph 16.5. See also paragraph 11.13.

15.7 A detainee who is asleep at a review, see paragraph 15.1, and whose continued detention is authorised must be informed about the decision and reason as soon as practicable after waking.

(b) Persons detained under the Terrorism Act 2000

15.8 In terrorism cases:

(a) the powers and duties of the review officer are in the Terrorism Act 2000, Schedule 8, Part II;

(b) a police officer of at least superintendent rank may apply to a judicial authority for a warrant of further detention under the Terrorism Act 2000, Schedule 8, Part III.

(c) Telephone review of detention

15.9 PACE, section 40A provides that the officer responsible under section 40 for reviewing the detention of a person who has not been charged, need not attend the police station holding the detainee and may carry out the review by telephone.

15.9A PACE, section 45A(2) provides that the officer responsible under section 40 for reviewing the detention of a person who has not been charged, need not attend the police station holding the detainee and may carry out the review by video conferencing facilities (See Note 15G).

15.9B A telephone review is not permitted where facilities for review by video conferencing exist and it is practicable to use them.

15.9C The review officer can decide at any stage that a telephone review or review by video conferencing should be terminated and that the review will be conducted in person. The reasons for doing so should be noted in the custody record.

See Note 15F.

15.10 When a telephone review is carried out, an officer at the station holding the detainee shall be required by the review officer to fulfil that officer's obligations under PACE section 40 or this Code by:

(a) making any record connected with the review in the detainee's custody record;

(b) if applicable, making a record in (a) in the presence of the detainee; and

(c) giving the detainee information about the review.

15.11 When a telephone review is carried out, the requirement in paragraph 15.3 will be satisfied:

(a) if facilities exist for the immediate transmission of written representations to the review officer, e.g. fax or email message, by giving the detainee an opportunity to make representations:

(i) orally by telephone; or

(ii) in writing using those facilities; and

(b) in all other cases, by giving the detainee an opportunity to make their representations orally by telephone.

(d) Documentation

15.12 It is the officer's responsibility to make sure all reminders given under paragraph 15.4 are noted in the custody record.

15.13 The grounds for, and extent of, any delay in conducting a review shall be recorded.

15.14 When a telephone review is carried out, a record shall be made of:

(a) the reason the review officer did not attend the station holding the detainee;

(b) the place the review officer was;

(c) the method representations, oral or written, were made to the review officer, see paragraph 15.11.

15.15 Any written representations shall be retained.

15.16 A record shall be made as soon as practicable about the outcome of each review or determination whether to extend the maximum detention period without charge or an application for a warrant of further detention or its extension. If paragraph 15.7 applies, a record shall also be made of when the person was informed and by whom. If an authorisation is given under PACE, section 42, the record shall state the number of hours and minutes by which the detention period is extended or further extended. If a warrant for further detention, or extension, is granted under section 43 or 44, the record shall state the detention period authorised by the warrant and the date and time it was granted.

Notes for Guidance

15A Review officer for the purposes of:

- *PACE, sections 40 and 40A means, in the case of a person arrested but not charged, an officer of at least inspector rank not directly involved in the investigation and, if a person has been arrested and charged, the custody officer;*

- *the Terrorism Act 2000, means an officer not directly involved in the investigation connected with the detention and of at least inspector rank, for reviews within 24 hours of the detainee's arrest or superintendent for all other reviews.*

15B The detention of persons in police custody not subject to the statutory review requirement in paragraph 15.1 should still be reviewed periodically as a matter of good practice. Such reviews can be carried out by an officer of the rank of sergeant or above.

The purpose of such reviews is to check the particular power under which a detainee is held continues to apply, any associated conditions are complied with and to make sure appropriate action is taken to deal with any changes. This includes the detainee's prompt release when the power no longer applies, or their transfer if the power requires the detainee be taken elsewhere as soon as the necessary arrangements are made. Examples include persons:

(a) arrested on warrant because they failed to answer bail to appear at court;

(b) arrested under the Bail Act 1976, section 7(3) for breaching a condition of bail granted after charge;

(c) in police custody for specific purposes and periods under the Crime (Sentences) Act 1997, Schedule 1;

(d) convicted, or remand prisoners, held in police stations on behalf of the Prison Service under the Imprisonment (Temporary Provisions) Act 1980, section 6;

(e) being detained to prevent them causing a breach of the peace;

(f) detained at police stations on behalf of the Immigration Service;

(g) detained by order of a magistrates' court under the Criminal Justice Act 1988, section 152 (as amended by the Drugs Act 2005, section 8) to facilitate the recovery of evidence after being charged with drug possession or drug trafficking and suspected of having swallowed drugs.

The detention of persons remanded into police detention by order of a court under the Magistrates' Courts Act 1980, section 128 is subject to a statutory requirement to review that detention. This is to make sure the detainee is taken back to court no later than the end of the period authorised by the court or when the need for their detention by police ceases, whichever is the sooner.

[. . .]

15C In the case of a review of detention, but not an extension, the detainee need not be woken for the review. However, if the detainee is likely to be asleep, e.g. during a period of rest allowed as in paragraph 12.2, at the latest time a review or authorisation to extend detention may take place, the officer should, if the legal obligations and time constraints permit, bring forward the procedure to allow the detainee to make representations. A detainee not asleep during the review must be present when the grounds for their continued detention are recorded and must at the same time be informed of those grounds unless the review officer considers the person is incapable of understanding what is said, violent or likely to become violent or in urgent need of medical attention.

15D An application to a Magistrates' Court under PACE, sections 43 or 44 for a warrant of further detention or its extension should be made between 10am and 9pm, and if possible during normal court hours. It will not usually be practicable to arrange for a court to sit specially outside the hours of 10am to 9pm. If it appears a special sitting may be needed outside normal court hours but between 10am and 9pm, the clerk to the justices should be given notice and informed of this possibility, while the court is sitting if possible.

15E In paragraph 15.2, the officer responsible for the station holding the detainee includes a superintendent or above who, in accordance with their force operational policy or police regulations, is given that responsibility on a temporary basis whilst the appointed long-term holder is off duty or otherwise unavailable.

15F The provisions of PACE, section 40A allowing telephone reviews do not apply to reviews of detention after charge by the custody officer or to reviews under the Terrorism Act 2000, Schedule 8, Part II in terrorism cases. When video conferencing is not required, they allow the use of a telephone to carry out a review of detention before charge. The procedure under PACE, section 42 must be done in person.

15G The use of video conferencing facilities for decisions about detention under section 45A of PACE is subject to the introduction of regulations by the Secretary of State.

16 CHARGING DETAINED PERSONS

(a) Action

16.1 When the officer in charge of the investigation reasonably believes there is sufficient evidence to provide a realistic prospect of the detainee's conviction for the offence, see paragraph 11.6, they shall without delay, and subject to the following qualification, inform the custody officer who will be responsible for considering whether the detainee should be charged. See Notes 11B and 16A. When a person is detained in respect of more than one offence it is permissible to delay informing the custody officer until the above conditions are satisfied in respect of all the offences, but see paragraph 11.6. If the detainee is a juvenile, mentally disordered or otherwise mentally vulnerable, any resulting action shall be taken in the presence of the appropriate adult if they are present at the time. See Note 16B and 16C.

16.1A Where guidance issued by the Director of Public Prosecutions under section 37A is in force the custody officer must comply with that Guidance in deciding how to act in dealing with the detainee. See Notes 16AA and 16AB.

16.1B Where in compliance with the DPP's Guidance the custody officer decides that the case should be immediately referred to the CPS to make the charging decision, consultation should take place with a Crown Prosecutor as soon as is reasonably practicable. Where the Crown Prosecutor is unable to make the charging decision on the information available at that time, the detainee may be released without charge and on bail (with conditions if necessary) under section 37(7)(a). In such circumstances, the detainee should be informed that they are being released to enable the Director of Public Prosecutions to make a decision under section 37B.

16.2 When a detainee is charged with or informed they may be prosecuted for an offence, see Note 16B, they shall, unless the restriction on drawing adverse inferences from silence applies, see Annex C, be cautioned as follows:

> 'You do not have to say anything. But it may harm your defence if you do not mention now something which you later rely on in court. Anything you do say may be given in evidence.'

Annex C, paragraph 2 sets out the alternative terms of the caution to be used when the restriction on drawing adverse inferences from silence applies.

16.3 When a detainee is charged they shall be given a written notice showing particulars of the offence and, subject to paragraph 2.6A, the officer's name and the case reference number. As far as possible the particulars of the charge shall be stated in simple terms, but they shall also show the precise offence in law with which the detainee is charged. The notice shall begin:

> 'You are charged with the offence(s) shown below.' Followed by the caution.

If the detainee is a juvenile, mentally disordered or otherwise mentally vulnerable, the notice should be given to the appropriate adult.

16.4 If, after a detainee has been charged with or informed they may be prosecuted for an offence, an officer wants to tell them about any written statement or interview with another person relating to such an offence, the detainee shall either be handed a true copy of the written statement or the content of the interview record brought to their attention. Nothing shall be done to invite any reply or comment except to:

(a) caution the detainee, 'You do not have to say anything, but anything you do say may be given in evidence.'; and

(b) remind the detainee about their right to legal advice.

16.4A If the detainee:

- cannot read, the document may be read to them
- is a juvenile, mentally disordered or otherwise mentally vulnerable, the appropriate adult shall also be given a copy, or the interview record shall be brought to their attention.

16.5 A detainee may not be interviewed about an offence after they have been charged with, or informed they may be prosecuted for it, unless the interview is necessary:

- to prevent or minimise harm or loss to some other person, or the public;
- to clear up an ambiguity in a previous answer or statement;
- in the interests of justice for the detainee to have put to them, and have an opportunity to comment on, information concerning the offence which has come to light since they were charged or informed they might be prosecuted.

Before any such interview, the interviewer shall:

(a) caution the detainee, 'You do not have to say anything, but anything you do say may be given in evidence.';

(b) remind the detainee about their right to legal advice.

See Note 16B.

16.6 The provisions of paragraphs 16.2 to 16.5 must be complied with in the appropriate adult's presence if they are already at the police station. If they are not at the police station then these provisions must be complied with again in their presence when they arrive unless the detainee has been released. See Note 16C.

16.7 When a juvenile is charged with an offence and the custody officer authorises their continued detention after charge, the custody officer must try to make arrangements for the juvenile to be taken into the care of a local authority to be detained pending appearance in court unless the custody officer certifies it is impracticable to do so or, in the case of a juvenile of at least 12 years old, no secure accommodation is available and there is a risk to the public of serious harm from that juvenile, in accordance with PACE, section 38(6). See Note 16D.

(b) Documentation

16.8 A record shall be made of anything a detainee says when charged.

16.9 Any questions put in an interview after charge and answers given relating to the offence shall be recorded in full during the interview on forms for that purpose and the record signed by the detainee or, if they refuse, by the interviewer and any third parties present. If the questions are audibly recorded or visually recorded the arrangements in Code E or F apply.

16.10 If it is not practicable to make arrangements for a juvenile's transfer into local authority care as in paragraph 16.7, the custody officer must record the reasons and complete a certificate to be produced before the court with the juvenile. See Note 16D.

Notes for Guidance

16A   The custody officer must take into account alternatives to prosecution under the Crime and Disorder Act 1998, reprimands and warning applicable to persons under 18, and in national guidance on the cautioning of offenders, for persons aged 18 and over.

16AA When a person is arrested under the provisions of the Criminal Justice Act 2003 which allow a person to be re-tried after being acquitted of a serious offence which is a qualifying offence specified in Schedule 5 to that Act and not precluded from further prosecution by virtue of section 75(3) of that Act the detention provisions of PACE are modified and make an officer of the rank of superintendent or above who has not been directly involved in the investigation responsible for determining whether the evidence is sufficient to charge.

16AB Where Guidance issued by the Director of Public Prosecutions under section 37B is in force, a custody officer who determines in accordance with that Guidance that there is sufficient evidence to charge the detainee, may detain that person for no longer than is reasonably necessary to decide how that person is to be dealt with under PACE, section 37(7)(a) to (d), including, where appropriate, consultation with the Duty Prosecutor. The period is subject to the maximum period of detention before charge determined by PACE, sections 41 to 44. Where in accordance with the Guidance the case is referred to the CPS for decision, the custody officer should ensure that an officer involved in the investigation sends to the CPS such information as is specified in the Guidance.

16B The giving of a warning or the service of the Notice of Intended Prosecution required by the Road Traffic Offenders Act 1988, section 1 does not amount to informing a detainee they may be prosecuted for an offence and so does not preclude further questioning in relation to that offence.

16C There is no power under PACE to detain a person and delay action under paragraphs 16.2 to 16.5 solely to await the arrival of the appropriate adult. After charge, bail cannot be refused, or release on bail delayed, simply because an appropriate adult is not available, unless the absence of that adult provides the custody officer with the necessary grounds to authorise detention after charge under PACE, section 38.

16D Except as in paragraph 16.7, neither a juvenile's behaviour nor the nature of the offence provides grounds for the custody officer to decide it is impracticable to arrange the juvenile's transfer to local authority care. Similarly, the lack of secure local authority accommodation does not make it impracticable to transfer the juvenile. The availability of secure accommodation is only a factor in relation to a juvenile aged 12 or over when the local authority accommodation would not be adequate to protect the public from serious harm from them. The obligation to transfer a juvenile to local authority accommodation applies as much to a juvenile charged during the daytime as to a juvenile to be held overnight, subject to a requirement to bring the juvenile before a court under PACE, section 46.

17 TESTING PERSONS FOR THE PRESENCE OF SPECIFIED CLASS A DRUGS

(a) Action

17.1 This section of Code C applies only in selected police stations in police areas where the provisions for drug testing under section 63B of PACE (as amended by section 5 of the Criminal Justice Act 2003 and section 7 of the Drugs Act 2005) are in force and in respect of which the Secretary of State has given a notification to the relevant chief officer of police that arrangements for the taking of samples have been made. Such a notification will cover either a police area as a whole or particular stations within a police area. The notification indicates whether the testing applies to those arrested or charged or under the age of 18 as the case may be and testing can only take place in respect of the persons so indicated in the notification. Testing cannot be carried out unless the relevant notification has been given and has not been withdrawn. See Note 17F.

17.2   A sample of urine or a non-intimate sample may be taken from a person in police detention for the purpose of ascertaining whether he has any specified Class A drug in his body only where they have been brought before the custody officer and:

(a)   either the arrest condition, see paragraph 17.3, or the charge condition, see paragraph 17.4 is met;

(b)   the age condition see paragraph 17.5, is met;

(c)   the notification condition is met in relation to the arrest condition, the charge condition, or the age condition, as the case may be. (Testing on charge and/or arrest must be specifically provided for in the notification for the power to apply. In addition, the fact that testing of under 18s is author-ised must be expressly provided for in the notification before the power to test such persons applies.). See paragraph 17.1; and

(d)   a police officer has requested the person concerned to give the sample (the request condition).

17.3   The arrest condition is met where the detainee:

(a)   has been arrested for a trigger offence, see Note 17E, but not charged with that offence; or

(b)   has been arrested for any other offence but not charged with that offence and a police officer of inspector rank or above, who has reasonable grounds for suspecting that their misuse of any specified Class A drug caused or contributed to the offence, has authorised the sample to be taken.

17.4   The charge condition is met where the detainee:

(a)   has been charged with a trigger offence, or

(b)   has been charged with any other offence and a police officer of inspector rank or above, who has reasonable grounds for suspecting that the detainee's misuse of any specified Class A drug caused or contributed to the offence, has authorised the sample to be taken.

17.5   The age condition is met where:

(a)   in the case of a detainee who has been arrested but not charged as in para-graph 17.3, they are aged 18 or over;

(b)   in the case of a detainee who has been charged as in paragraph 17.4, they are aged 14 or over.

17.6   Before requesting a sample from the person concerned, an officer must:

(a)   inform them that the purpose of taking the sample is for drug testing under PACE. This is to ascertain whether they have a specified Class A drug present in their body;

(b)   warn them that if, when so requested, they fail without good cause to provide a sample they may be liable to prosecution;

(c)   where the taking of the sample has been authorised by an inspector or above in accordance with paragraph 17.3(b) or 17.4(b) above, inform them that the authorisation has been given and the grounds for giving it;

(d)   remind them of the following rights, which may be exercised at any stage during the period in custody:

(i)   the right to have someone informed of their arrest [see section 5];

(ii)   the right to consult privately with a solicitor and that free independent legal advice is available [see section 6]; and

(iii)   the right to consult these Codes of Practice [see section 3].

17.7   In the case of a person who has not attained the age of 17:

   (a)   the making of the request for a sample under paragraph 17.2(d) above;
   (b)   the giving of the warning and the information under paragraph 17.6 above; and
   (c)   the taking of the sample, may not take place except in the presence of an appropriate adult. (see Note 17G)

17.8   Authorisation by an officer of the rank of inspector or above within paragraph 17.3(b) or 17.4(b) may be given orally or in writing but, if it is given orally, it must be confirmed in writing as soon as practicable.

17.9   If a sample is taken from a detainee who has been arrested for an offence but not charged with that offence as in paragraph 17.3, no further sample may be taken during the same continuous period of detention. If during that same period the charge condition is also met in respect of that detainee, the sample which has been taken shall be treated as being taken by virtue of the charge condition, see paragraph 17.4, being met.

17.10   A detainee from whom a sample may be taken may be detained for up to six hours from the time of charge if the custody officer reasonably believes the detention is necessary to enable a sample to be taken. Where the arrest condition is met, a detainee whom the custody officer has decided to release on bail without charge may continue to be detained, but not beyond 24 hours from the relevant time (as defined in section 41(2) of PACE), to enable a sample to be taken.

17.11   A detainee in respect of whom the arrest condition is met, but not the charge condition, see paragraphs 17.3 and 17.4, and whose release would be required before a sample can be taken had they not continued to be detained as a result of being arrested for a further offence which does not satisfy the arrest condition, may have a sample taken at any time within 24 hours after the arrest for the offence that satisfies the arrest condition.

(b)   Documentation

17.12   The following must be recorded in the custody record:

   (a)   if a sample is taken following authorisation by an officer of the rank of inspector or above, the authorisation and the grounds for suspicion;
   (b)   the giving of a warning of the consequences of failure to provide a sample;
   (c)   the time at which the sample was given; and
   (d)   the time of charge or, where the arrest condition is being relied upon, the time of arrest and, where applicable, the fact that a sample taken after arrest but before charge is to be treated as being taken by virtue of the charge condition, where that is met in the same period of continuous detention. See paragraph 17.9.

(c)   General

17.13   A sample may only be taken by a prescribed person. See Note 17C.

17.14   Force may not be used to take any sample for the purpose of drug testing.

17.15   The terms 'Class A drug' and 'misuse' have the same meanings as in the Misuse of Drugs Act 1971. 'Specified' (in relation to a Class A drug) and 'trigger offence' have the same meanings as in Part III of the Criminal Justice and Court Services Act 2000.

17.16   Any sample taken:

    (a)   may not be used for any purpose other than to ascertain whether the person concerned has a specified Class A drug present in his body; and

    (b)   must be retained until the person concerned has made their first appearance before the court.

(d) Assessment of misuse of drugs

17.17   Under the provisions of Part 3 of the Drugs Act 2005, where a detainee has tested positive for a specified Class A drug under section 63B of PACE a police officer may, at any time before the person's release from the police station, impose a requirement for them to attend an initial assessment of their drug misuse by a suitably qualified person and to remain for its duration. The requirement may only be imposed on a person if:

    (a)   they have reached the age of 18

    (b)   notification has been given by the Secretary of State to the relevant chief officer of police that arrangements for conducting initial assessments have been made for those from whom samples for testing have been taken at the police station where the detainee is in custody.

17.18   When imposing a requirement to attend an initial assessment the police officer must:

    (a)   inform the person of the time and place at which the initial assessment is to take place;

    (b)   explain that this information will be confirmed in writing; and

    (c)   warn the person that he may be liable to prosecution if he fails without good cause to attend the initial assessment and remain for its duration

17.19   Where a police officer has imposed a requirement to attend an initial assessment in accordance with paragraph 17.17, he must, before the person is released from detention, give the person notice in writing which:

    (a)   confirms that he is required to attend and remain for the duration of an initial assessment; and

    (b)   confirms the information and repeats the warning referred to in paragraph 17.18.

17.20   The following must be recorded in the custody record:

    (a)   that the requirement to attend an initial assessment has been imposed; and

    (b)   the information, explanation, warning and notice given in accordance with paragraphs 17.17 and 17.19.

17.21   Where a notice is given in accordance with paragraph 17.19, a police officer can give the person a further notice in writing which informs the person of any change to the time or place at which the initial assessment is to take place and which repeats the warning referred to in paragraph 17.18(c).

17.22   Part 3 of the Drugs Act 2005 also requires police officers to have regard to any guidance issued by the Secretary of State in respect of the assessment provisions.

Notes for Guidance

17A   When warning a person who is asked to provide a urine or non-intimate sample in accordance with paragraph 17.6(b), the following form of words may be used:

> *'You do not have to provide a sample, but I must warn you that if you fail or refuse without good cause to do so, you will commit an offence for which you may be imprisoned, or fined, or both'.*

17B   A sample has to be sufficient and suitable. A sufficient sample is sufficient in quantity and quality to enable drug-testing analysis to take place. A suitable sample is one which by its nature, is suitable for a particular form of drug analysis.

17C   A prescribed person in paragraph 17.13 is one who is prescribed in regulations made by the Secretary of State under section 63B(6) of the Police and Criminal Evidence Act 1984. [The regulations are currently contained in regulation SI 2001 No. 2645, the Police and Criminal Evidence Act 1984 (Drug Testing Persons in Police Detention) (Prescribed Persons) Regulations 2001.]

17D   The retention of the sample in paragraph 17.16(b) allows for the sample to be sent for confirmatory testing and analysis if the detainee disputes the test. But such samples, and the information derived from them, may not be subsequently used in the investigation of any offence or in evidence against the persons from whom they were taken.

17E   Trigger offences are:

1.   Offences under the following provisions of the Theft Act 1968:

> *section 1 (theft)*
> *section 8 (robbery)*
> *section 9 (burglary)*
> *section 10 (aggravated burglary)*
> *section 12 (taking a motor vehicle or other conveyance without authority)*
> *section 12A (aggravated vehicle-taking)*
> *section 15 (obtaining property by deception)*
> *section 22 (handling stolen goods)*
> *section 25 (going equipped for stealing etc.)*

2.   Offences under the following provisions of the Misuse of Drugs Act 1971, if committed in respect of a specified Class A drug:

> *section 4 (restriction on production and supply of controlled drugs)*
> *section 5(2) (possession of a controlled drug)*
> *section 5(3) (possession of a controlled drug with intent to supply)*

3.   An offence under section 1(1) of the Criminal Attempts Act 1981 if committed in respect of an offence under any of the following provisions of the Theft Act 1968:

> *section 1 (theft)*
> *section 8 (robbery)*
> *section 9 (burglary)*
> *section 15 (obtaining property by deception)*
> *section 22 (handling stolen goods)*

4.   Offences under the following provisions of the Vagrancy Act 1824:

> *section 3 (begging)*
> *section 4 (persistent begging)*

17F   The power to take samples is subject to notification by the Secretary of State that appropriate arrangements for the taking of samples have been made for the police area as a whole or for the particular police station concerned for whichever of the following is specified in the notification:

> *(a)   persons in respect of whom the arrest condition is met;*
> *(b)   persons in respect of whom the charge condition is met;*
> *(c)   persons who have not attained the age of 18.*

Note: Notification is treated as having been given for the purposes of the charge condi-

tion in relation to a police area, if testing (on charge) under section 63B(2) of PACE was in force immediately before section 7 of the Drugs Act 2005 was brought into force; and for the purposes of the age condition, in relation to a police area or police station, if immediately before that day, notification that arrangements had been made for the taking of samples from persons under the age of 18 (those aged 14–17) had been given and had not been withdrawn.

17G   *Appropriate adult in paragraph 17.7 means the person's:*

  (a)   parent or guardian or, if they are in the care of a local authority or voluntary organisation, a person representing that authority or organisation; or

  (b)   a social worker of, in England, a local authority or, in Wales, a local authority social services department; or

  (c)   if no person falling within (a) or (b) above is available, any responsible person aged 18 or over who is not a police officer or a person employed by the police.

ANNEX A – INTIMATE AND STRIP SEARCHES

A   INTIMATE SEARCH

1.   An intimate search consists of the physical examination of a person's body orifices other than the mouth. The intrusive nature of such searches means the actual and potential risks associated with intimate searches must never be underestimated.

(a)   Action

2.   Body orifices other than the mouth may be searched only:

  (a)   if authorised by an officer of inspector rank or above who has reasonable grounds for believing that the person may have concealed on themselves:

    (i)   anything which they could and might use to cause physical injury to themself or others at the station; or

    (ii)   a Class A drug which they intended to supply to another or to export;

    and the officer has reasonable grounds for believing that an intimate search is the only means of removing those items; and

  (b)   if the search is under paragraph 2(a)(ii) (a drug offence search), the detainee's appropriate consent has been given in writing.

2A.   Before the search begins, a police officer, designated detention officer or staff custody officer, must tell the detainee:

  (a)   that the authority to carry out the search has been given;

  (b)   the grounds for giving the authorisation and for believing that the article cannot be removed without an intimate search.

2B.   Before a detainee is asked to give appropriate consent to a search under paragraph 2(a)(ii) (a drug offence search) they must be warned that if they refuse without good cause their refusal may harm their case if it comes to trial, see Note A6. This warning may be given by a police officer or member of police staff. A detainee who is not legally represented must be reminded of their entitlement to have free legal advice, see *Code C, paragraph 6.5*, and the reminder noted in the custody record.

3.   An intimate search may only be carried out by a registered medical practitioner or registered nurse, unless an officer of at least inspector rank considers this is not

practicable and the search is to take place under paragraph 2(a)(i), in which case a police officer may carry out the search. See Notes A1 to A5.

3A.   Any proposal for a search under paragraph 2(a)(i) to be carried out by someone other than a registered medical practitioner or registered nurse must only be considered as a last resort and when the authorising officer is satisfied the risks associated with allowing the item to remain with the detainee outweigh the risks associated with removing it. See Notes A1 to A5.

4.   An intimate search under:

- paragraph 2(a)(i) may take place only at a hospital, surgery, other medical premises or police station;
- paragraph 2(a)(ii) may take place only at a hospital, surgery or other medical premises and must be carried out by a registered medical practitioner or a registered nurse.

5.   An intimate search at a police station of a juvenile or mentally disordered or otherwise mentally vulnerable person may take place only in the presence of an appropriate adult of the same sex, unless the detainee specifically requests a particular adult of the opposite sex who is readily available. In the case of a juvenile the search may take place in the absence of the appropriate adult only if the juvenile signifies in the presence of the appropriate adult they do not want the adult present during the search and the adult agrees. A record shall be made of the juvenile's decision and signed by the appropriate adult.

6.   When an intimate search under paragraph 2(a)(i) is carried out by a police officer, the officer must be of the same sex as the detainee. A minimum of two people, other than the detainee, must be present during the search. Subject to paragraph 5, no person of the opposite sex who is not a medical practitioner or nurse shall be present, nor shall anyone whose presence is unnecessary. The search shall be conducted with proper regard to the sensitivity and vulnerability of the detainee.

(b)   Documentation

7.   In the case of an intimate search the custody officer shall as soon as practicable, record:

(a)   for searches under paragraphs 2(a)(i) and (ii);

- the authorisation to carry out the search;
- the grounds for giving the authorisation;
- the grounds for believing the article could not be removed without an intimate search
- which parts of the detainee's body were searched
- who carried out the search
- who was present
- the result.

(b)   for searches under paragraph 2(a)(ii):

- the giving of the warning required by paragraph 2B;
- the fact that the appropriate consent was given or (as the case may be) refused, and if refused, the reason given for the refusal (if any).

8.   If an intimate search is carried out by a police officer, the reason why it was impracticable for a registered medical practitioner or registered nurse to conduct it must be recorded.

B STRIP SEARCH

9. A strip search is a search involving the removal of more than outer clothing. In this Code, outer clothing includes shoes and socks.

(a) Action

10. A strip search may take place only if it is considered necessary to remove an article which a detainee would not be allowed to keep, and the officer reasonably considers the detainee might have concealed such an article. Strip searches shall not be routinely carried out if there is no reason to consider that articles are concealed.

The conduct of strip searches

11. When strip searches are conducted:
    (a) a police officer carrying out a strip search must be the same sex as the detainee;
    (b) the search shall take place in an area where the detainee cannot be seen by anyone who does not need to be present, nor by a member of the opposite sex except an appropriate adult who has been specifically requested by the detainee;
    (c) except in cases of urgency, where there is risk of serious harm to the detainee or to others, whenever a strip search involves exposure of intimate body parts, there must be at least two people present other than the detainee, and if the search is of a juvenile or mentally disordered or otherwise mentally vulnerable person, one of the people must be the appropriate adult. Except in urgent cases as above, a search of a juvenile may take place in the absence of the appropriate adult only if the juvenile signifies in the presence of the appropriate adult that they do not want the adult to be present during the search and the adult agrees. A record shall be made of the juvenile's decision and signed by the appropriate adult. The presence of more than two people, other than an appropriate adult, shall be permitted only in the most exceptional circumstances;
    (d) the search shall be conducted with proper regard to the sensitivity and vulnerability of the detainee in these circumstances and every reasonable effort shall be made to secure the detainee's co-operation and minimise embarrassment. Detainees who are searched shall not normally be required to remove all their clothes at the same time, e.g. a person should be allowed to remove clothing above the waist and redress before removing further clothing;
    (e) if necessary to assist the search, the detainee may be required to hold their arms in the air or to stand with their legs apart and bend forward so a visual examination may be made of the genital and anal areas provided no physical contact is made with any body orifice;
    (f) if articles are found, the detainee shall be asked to hand them over. If articles are found within any body orifice other than the mouth, and the detainee refuses to hand them over, their removal would constitute an intimate search, which must be carried out as in Part A;
    (g) a strip search shall be conducted as quickly as possible, and the detainee allowed to dress as soon as the procedure is complete.

(b) Documentation

12. A record shall be made on the custody record of a strip search including the reason it was considered necessary, those present and any result.

Notes for Guidance

A1   Before authorising any intimate search, the authorising officer must make every reasonable effort to persuade the detainee to hand the article over without a search. If the detainee agrees, a registered medical practitioner or registered nurse should whenever possible be asked to assess the risks involved and, if necessary, attend to assist the detainee.

A2   If the detainee does not agree to hand the article over without a search, the authorising officer must carefully review all the relevant factors before authorising an intimate search. In particular, the officer must consider whether the grounds for believing an article may be concealed are reasonable.

A3   If authority is given for a search under paragraph 2(a)(i), a registered medical practitioner or registered nurse shall be consulted whenever possible. The presumption should be that the search will be conducted by the registered medical practitioner or registered nurse and the authorising officer must make every reasonable effort to persuade the detainee to allow the medical practitioner or nurse to conduct the search.

A4   A constable should only be authorised to carry out a search as a last resort and when all other approaches have failed. In these circumstances, the authorising officer must be satisfied the detainee might use the article for one or more of the purposes in paragraph 2(a)(i) and the physical injury likely to be caused is sufficiently severe to justify authorising a constable to carry out the search.

A5   If an officer has any doubts whether to authorise an intimate search by a constable, the officer should seek advice from an officer of superintendent rank or above.

A6   In warning a detainee who is asked to consent to an intimate drug offence search, as in paragraph 2B, the following form of words may be used:

> *'You do not have to allow yourself to be searched, but I must warn you that if you refuse without good cause, your refusal may harm your case if it comes to trial.'*

ANNEX B – DELAY IN NOTIFYING ARREST OR ALLOWING ACCESS TO LEGAL ADVICE

A   PERSONS DETAINED UNDER PACE

1. The exercise of the rights in Section 5 or Section 6, or both, may be delayed if the person is in police detention, as in PACE, section 118(2), in connection with an indictable offence, has not yet been charged with an offence and an officer of superintendent rank or above, or inspector rank or above only for the rights in Section 5, has reasonable grounds for believing their exercise will:

(i) lead to:
- interference with, or harm to, evidence connected with a serious arrestable offence; or
- interference with, or physical harm to, other people; or

(ii) lead to alerting other people suspected of having committed an indictable offence but not yet arrested for it; or

    (iii) hinder the recovery of property obtained in consequence of the commission of such an offence.

2.   These rights may also be delayed if the officer has reasonable grounds to believe that:

    (i) the person detained for an indictable offence has benefited from their criminal conduct (decided in accordance with Part 2 of the Proceeds of Crime Act 2002); and

    (ii) the recovery of the value of the property constituting that benefit will be hindered by the exercise of either right.

3.   Authority to delay a detainee's right to consult privately with a solicitor may be given only if the authorising officer has reasonable grounds to believe the solicitor the detainee wants to consult will, inadvertently or otherwise, pass on a message from the detainee or act in some other way which will have any of the consequences specified under paragraphs 1 or 2. In these circumstances the detainee must be allowed to choose another solicitor. See Note B3.

4.   If the detainee wishes to see a solicitor, access to that solicitor may not be delayed on the grounds they might advise the detainee not to answer questions or the solicitor was initially asked to attend the police station by someone else. In the latter case the detainee must be told the solicitor has come to the police station at another person's request, and must be asked to sign the custody record to signify whether they want to see the solicitor.

5.   The fact the grounds for delaying notification of arrest may be satisfied does not automatically mean the grounds for delaying access to legal advice will also be satisfied.

6.   These rights may be delayed only for as long as grounds exist and in no case beyond 36 hours after the relevant time as in PACE, section 41. If the grounds cease to apply within this time, the detainee must, as soon as practicable, be asked if they want to exercise either right, the custody record must be noted accordingly, and action taken in accordance with the relevant section of the Code.

7.   A detained person must be permitted to consult a solicitor for a reasonable time before any court hearing.

B PERSONS DETAINED UNDER THE TERRORISM ACT 2000

8.   The rights as in sections 5 or 6, may be delayed if the person is detained under the Terrorism Act 2000, section 41 or Schedule 7, has not yet been charged with an offence and an officer of superintendent rank or above has reasonable grounds for believing the exercise of either right will:

    (i) lead to:

       • interference with, or harm to, evidence connected with an indictable offence;

       • interference with, or physical harm to, other people; or

    (ii) lead to the alerting of other people suspected of having committed an indictable offence but not yet arrested for it; or

    (iii) hinder the recovery of property:

       • obtained in consequence of the commission of such an offence; or

       • in respect of which a forfeiture order could be made under that Act, section 23;

(iv) lead to interference with the gathering of information about the commission, preparation or instigation of acts of terrorism; or

(v) by alerting any person, make it more difficult to prevent an act of terrorism or secure the apprehension, prosecution or conviction of any person in connection with the commission, preparation or instigation of an act of terrorism.

9. These rights may also be delayed if the officer has reasonable grounds for believing that:

(i) the person detained has benefited from their criminal conduct (decided in accordance with Part 2 of the Proceeds of Crime Act 2002), and

(ii) the recovery of the value of the property constituting that benefit will be hindered by the exercise of either right.

10. In these cases paragraphs 3 (with regards to the consequences specified at paragraphs 8 and 9), 4 and 5 apply.

11. These rights may be delayed only for as long as is necessary but not beyond 48 hours from the time of arrest if arrested under section 41, or if detained under the Terrorism Act 2000, Schedule 7 when arrested under section 41, from the beginning of their examination. If the above grounds cease to apply within this time the detainee must as soon as practicable be asked if they wish to exercise either right, the custody record noted accordingly, and action taken in accordance with the relevant section of this Code.

12. In this case paragraph 7 applies.

C DOCUMENTATION

13. The grounds for action under this Annex shall be recorded and the detainee informed of them as soon as practicable.

14. Any reply given by a detainee under paragraphs 6 or 11 must be recorded and the detainee asked to endorse the record in relation to whether they want to receive legal advice at this point.

D CAUTIONS AND SPECIAL WARNINGS

When a suspect detained at a police station is interviewed during any period for which access to legal advice has been delayed under this Annex, the court or jury may not draw adverse inferences from their silence.

Notes for Guidance

B1 Even if Annex B applies in the case of a juvenile, or a person who is mentally disordered or otherwise mentally vulnerable, action to inform the appropriate adult and the person responsible for a juvenile's welfare if that is a different person, must nevertheless be taken as in paragraph 3.13 and 3.15.

B2 In the case of Commonwealth citizens and foreign nationals, see Note 7A.

B3 A decision to delay access to a specific solicitor is likely to be a rare occurrence and only when it can be shown the suspect is capable of misleading that particular solicitor and there is more than a substantial risk that the suspect will succeed in causing information to be conveyed which will lead to one or more of the specified consequences.

ANNEX C – RESTRICTION ON DRAWING ADVERSE INFERENCES FROM SILENCE AND TERMS OF THE CAUTION WHEN THE RESTRICTION APPLIES

(a) The restriction on drawing adverse inferences from silence

1. The Criminal Justice and Public Order Act 1994, sections 34, 36 and 37 as amended by the Youth Justice and Criminal Evidence Act 1999, section 58 describe the conditions under which adverse inferences may be drawn from a person's failure or refusal to say anything about their involvement in the offence when interviewed, after being charged or informed they may be prosecuted. These provisions are subject to an overriding restriction on the ability of a court or jury to draw adverse inferences from a person's silence. This restriction applies:

    (a)   to any detainee at a police station, see Note 10C who, before being interviewed, see section 11 or being charged or informed they may be prosecuted, see section 16, has:

        (i)   asked for legal advice, see section 6, paragraph 6.1;

        (ii) not been allowed an opportunity to consult a solicitor, including the duty solicitor, as in this Code: and

        (iii) not changed their mind about wanting legal advice, see section 6, paragraph 6.6(d)

        Note the condition in (ii) will

        ~ apply when a detainee who has asked for legal advice is interviewed before speaking to a solicitor as in section 6, paragraph 6.6(a) or (b);

        ~ not apply if the detained person declines to ask for the duty solicitor, see section 6, paragraphs 6.6(c) and (d);

    (b)   to any person charged with, or informed they may be prosecuted for, an offence who:

        (i)   has had brought to their notice a written statement made by another person or the content of an interview with another person which relates to that offence, see section 16, paragraph 16.4;

        (ii) is interviewed about that offence, see section 16, paragraph 16.5; or

        (iii) makes a written statement about that offence, see Annex D paragraphs 4 and 9.

(b) Terms of the caution when the restriction applies

2. When a requirement to caution arises at a time when the restriction on drawing adverse inferences from silence applies, the caution shall be:

    'You do not have to say anything, but anything you do say may be given in evidence.'

3. Whenever the restriction either begins to apply or ceases to apply after a caution has already been given, the person shall be re-cautioned in the appropriate terms. The changed position on drawing inferences and that the previous caution no longer applies shall also be explained to the detainee in ordinary language. See Note C2.

Notes for Guidance

C1   The restriction on drawing inferences from silence does not apply to a person who has not been detained and who therefore cannot be prevented from seeking legal advice if they want to, see paragraphs 10.2 and 3.15.

C2   The following is suggested as a framework to help explain changes in the position on drawing adverse inferences if the restriction on drawing adverse inferences from silence:

(a) begins to apply:

    'The caution you were previously given no longer applies. This is because after that caution:

      (i) you asked to speak to a solicitor but have not yet been allowed an opportunity to speak to a solicitor. See paragraph 1(a); or

      (ii) you have been charged with/informed you may be prosecuted.' See paragraph 1(b).

      'This means that from now on, adverse inferences cannot be drawn at court and your defence will not be harmed just because you choose to say nothing. Please listen carefully to the caution I am about to give you because it will apply from now on. You will see that it does not say anything about your defence being harmed.'

(b) ceases to apply before or at the time the person is charged or informed they may be prosecuted, see paragraph 1(a);

    'The caution you were previously given no longer applies. This is because after that caution you have been allowed an opportunity to speak to a solicitor. Please listen carefully to the caution I am about to give you because it will apply from now on. It explains how your defence at court may be affected if you choose to say nothing.'

ANNEX D – WRITTEN STATEMENTS UNDER CAUTION

(a) Written by a person under caution

1.   A person shall always be invited to write down what they want to say.

2.   A person who has not been charged with, or informed they may be prosecuted for, any offence to which the statement they want to write relates, shall:

    (a) unless the statement is made at a time when the restriction on drawing adverse inferences from silence applies, see Annex C, be asked to write out and sign the following before writing what they want to say:

      'I make this statement of my own free will. I understand that I do not have to say anything but that it may harm my defence if I do not mention when questioned something which I later rely on in court. This statement may be given in evidence.';

    (b) if the statement is made at a time when the restriction on drawing adverse inferences from silence applies, be asked to write out and sign the following before writing what they want to say:

      'I make this statement of my own free will. I understand that I do not have to say anything. This statement may be given in evidence.'

3.   When a person, on the occasion of being charged with or informed they may be prosecuted for any offence, asks to make a statement which relates to any such offence and wants to write it they shall:

(a)   unless the restriction on drawing adverse inferences from silence, see Annex C, applied when they were so charged or informed they may be prosecuted, be asked to write out and sign the following before writing what they want to say:

'I make this statement of my own free will. I understand that I do not have to say anything but that it may harm my defence if I do not mention when questioned something which I later rely on in court. This statement may be given in evidence.';

(b)   if the restriction on drawing adverse inferences from silence applied when they were so charged or informed they may be prosecuted, be asked to write out and sign the following before writing what they want to say:

'I make this statement of my own free will. I understand that I do not have to say anything. This statement may be given in evidence.'

4.   When a person, who has already been charged with or informed they may be prosecuted for any offence, asks to make a statement which relates to any such offence and wants to write it they shall be asked to write out and sign the following before writing what they want to say:

'I make this statement of my own free will. I understand that I do not have to say anything. This statement may be given in evidence.';

5.   Any person writing their own statement shall be allowed to do so without any prompting except a police officer or other police staff may indicate to them which matters are material or question any ambiguity in the statement.

(b)   Written by a police officer or civilian interviewer

6.   If a person says they would like someone to write the statement for them, a police officer, or other police staff shall write the statement.

7.   If the person has not been charged with, or informed they may be prosecuted for, any offence to which the statement they want to make relates they shall, before starting, be asked to sign, or make their mark, to the following:

(a)   unless the statement is made at a time when the restriction on drawing adverse inferences from silence applies, see Annex C:

'I, ..., wish to make a statement. I want someone to write down what I say. I understand that I do not have to say anything but that it may harm my defence if I do not mention when questioned something which I later rely on in court. This statement may be given in evidence.';

(b)   if the statement is made at a time when the restriction on drawing adverse inferences from silence applies:

'I, ..., wish to make a statement. I want someone to write down what I say. I understand that I do not have to say anything. This statement may be given in evidence.'

8.   If, on the occasion of being charged with or informed they may be prosecuted for any offence, the person asks to make a statement which relates to any such offence they shall before starting be asked to sign, or make their mark to, the following:

(a) unless the restriction on drawing adverse inferences from silence applied, see Annex C, when they were so charged or informed they may be prosecuted:

'I, ..., wish to make a statement. I want someone to write down what I say. I understand that I do not have to say anything but that it may harm my defence if I do not mention when questioned something which I later rely on in court. This statement may be given in evidence.';

(b) if the restriction on drawing adverse inferences from silence applied when they were so charged or informed they may be prosecuted:

'I, ..., wish to make a statement. I want someone to write down what I say. I understand that I do not have to say anything. This statement may be given in evidence.'

9. If, having already been charged with or informed they may be prosecuted for any offence, a person asks to make a statement which relates to any such offence they shall before starting, be asked to sign, or make their mark to:

'I, ..., wish to make a statement. I want someone to write down what I say. I understand that I do not have to say anything. This statement may be given in evidence.'

10. The person writing the statement must take down the exact words spoken by the person making it and must not edit or paraphrase it. Any questions that are necessary, e.g. to make it more intelligible, and the answers given must be recorded at the same time on the statement form.

11. When the writing of a statement is finished the person making it shall be asked to read it and to make any corrections, alterations or additions they want. When they have finished reading they shall be asked to write and sign or make their mark on the following certificate at the end of the statement:

'I have read the above statement, and I have been able to correct, alter or add anything I wish. This statement is true. I have made it of my own free will.'

12. If the person making the statement cannot read, or refuses to read it, or to write the above mentioned certificate at the end of it or to sign it, the person taking the statement shall read it to them and ask them if they would like to correct, alter or add anything and to put their signature or make their mark at the end. The person taking the statement shall certify on the statement itself what has occurred.

ANNEX E – SUMMARY OF PROVISIONS RELATING TO MENTALLY DISORDERED AND OTHERWISE MENTALLY VULNERABLE PEOPLE

1. If an officer has any suspicion, or is told in good faith, that a person of any age may be mentally disordered or otherwise mentally vulnerable, or mentally incapable of understanding the significance of questions or their replies that person shall be treated as mentally disordered or otherwise mentally vulnerable for the purposes of this Code. See paragraph 1.4.

2. In the case of a person who is mentally disordered or otherwise mentally vulnerable, 'the appropriate adult' means:

(a) a relative, guardian or other person responsible for their care or custody;
(b) someone experienced in dealing with mentally disordered or mentally vulnerable people but who is not a police officer or employed by the police;

(c)   failing these, some other responsible adult aged 18 or over who is not a police officer or employed by the police.

See paragraph 1.7(b) and Note 1D.

3.   If the custody officer authorises the detention of a person who is mentally vulnerable or appears to be suffering from a mental disorder, the custody officer must as soon as practicable inform the appropriate adult of the grounds for detention and the person's whereabouts, and ask the adult to come to the police station to see them. If the appropriate adult:

- is already at the station when information is given as in paragraphs 3.1 to 3.5 the information must be given in their presence
- is not at the station when the provisions of paragraph 3.1 to 3.5 are complied with these provisions must be complied with again in their presence once they arrive.

See paragraphs 3.15 to 3.17.

4.   If the appropriate adult, having been informed of the right to legal advice, considers legal advice should be taken, the provisions of section 6 apply as if the mentally disordered or otherwise mentally vulnerable person had requested access to legal advice. See paragraph 3.19 and Note E1.

5.   The custody officer must make sure a person receives appropriate clinical attention as soon as reasonably practicable if the person appears to be suffering from a mental disorder or in urgent cases immediately call the nearest health care professional or an ambulance. It is not intended these provisions delay the transfer of a detainee to a place of safety under the Mental Health Act 1983, section 136 if that is applicable. If an assessment under that Act is to take place at a police station, the custody officer must consider whether an appropriate health care professional should be called to conduct an initial clinical check on the detainee. See paragraph 9.5 and 9.6.

6.   It is imperative a mentally disordered or otherwise mentally vulnerable person detained under the Mental Health Act 1983, section 136 be assessed as soon as possible. If that assessment is to take place at the police station, an approved social worker and registered medical practitioner shall be called to the station as soon as possible in order to interview and examine the detainee. Once the detainee has been interviewed, examined and suitable arrangements been made for their treatment or care, they can no longer be detained under section 136. A detainee should be immediately discharged from detention if a registered medical practitioner having examined them, concludes they are not mentally disordered within the meaning of the Act. See paragraph 3.16.

7.   If a mentally disordered or otherwise mentally vulnerable person is cautioned in the absence of the appropriate adult, the caution must be repeated in the appropriate adult's presence. See paragraph 10.12.

8.   A mentally disordered or otherwise mentally vulnerable person must not be interviewed or asked to provide or sign a written statement in the absence of the appropriate adult unless the provisions of paragraphs 11.1 or 11.18 to 11.20 apply. Questioning in these circumstances may not continue in the absence of the appropriate adult once sufficient information to avert the risk has been obtained. A record shall be made of the grounds for any decision to begin an interview in these circumstances. See paragraphs 11.1, 11.15 and 11.18 to 11.20.

9.   If the appropriate adult is present at an interview, they shall be informed they are not expected to act simply as an observer and the purposes of their presence are to:

- advise the interviewee
- observe whether or not the interview is being conducted properly and fairly
- facilitate communication with the interviewee

See paragraph 11.17.

10.   If the detention of a mentally disordered or otherwise mentally vulnerable person is reviewed by a review officer or a superintendent, the appropriate adult must, if available at the time, be given an opportunity to make representations to the officer about the need for continuing detention. See paragraph 15.3.

11.   If the custody officer charges a mentally disordered or otherwise mentally vulnerable person with an offence or takes such other action as is appropriate when there is sufficient evidence for a prosecution this must be done in the presence of the appropriate adult. The written notice embodying any charge must be given to the appropriate adult. See paragraphs 16.1 to 16.4A.

12.   An intimate or strip search of a mentally disordered or otherwise mentally vulnerable person may take place only in the presence of the appropriate adult of the same sex, unless the detainee specifically requests the presence of a particular adult of the opposite sex. A strip search may take place in the absence of an appropriate adult only in cases of urgency when there is a risk of serious harm to the detainee or others. See Annex A, paragraphs 5 and 11(c).

13.   Particular care must be taken when deciding whether to use any form of approved restraints on a mentally disordered or otherwise mentally vulnerable person in a locked cell. See paragraph 8.2.

Notes for Guidance

E1   The purpose of the provision at paragraph 3.19 is to protect the rights of a mentally disordered or otherwise mentally vulnerable detained person who does not understand the significance of what is said to them. If the detained person wants to exercise the right to legal advice, the appropriate action should be taken and not delayed until the appropriate adult arrives. A mentally disordered or otherwise mentally vulnerable detained person should always be given an opportunity, when an appropriate adult is called to the police station, to consult privately with a solicitor in the absence of the appropriate adult if they want.

E2   Although people who are mentally disordered or otherwise mentally vulnerable are often capable of providing reliable evidence, they may, without knowing or wanting to do so, be particularly prone in certain circumstances to provide information that may be unreliable, misleading or self-incriminating. Special care should always be taken when questioning such a person, and the appropriate adult should be involved if there is any doubt about a person's mental state or capacity. Because of the risk of unreliable evidence, it is important to obtain corroboration of any facts admitted whenever possible.

E3   Because of the risks referred to in Note E2, which the presence of the appropriate adult is intended to minimise, officers of superintendent rank or above should exercise their discretion to authorise the commencement of an interview in the appropriate adult's absence only in exceptional cases, if it is necessary to avert an immediate risk of serious harm. See paragraphs 11.1, 11.18 to 11.20.

ANNEX F – COUNTRIES WITH WHICH BILATERAL CONSULAR CONVENTIONS OR AGREEMENTS REQUIRING NOTIFICATION OF THE ARREST AND DETENTION OF THEIR NATIONALS ARE IN FORCE AS AT 1 APRIL 2003

Armenia	Kazakhstan
Austria	Macedonia
Azerbaijan	Mexico
Belarus	Moldova
Belgium	Mongolia
Bosnia-Herzegovina	Norway
Bulgaria	Poland
China*	Romania
Croatia	Russia
Cuba	Slovak Republic
Czech Republic	Slovenia
Denmark	Spain
Egypt	Sweden
France	Tajikistan
Georgia	Turkmenistan
German Federal Republic	Ukraine
Greece	USA
Hungary	Uzbekistan
Italy	Yugoslavia
Japan	

*Police are required to inform Chinese officials of arrest/detention in the Manchester consular district only. This comprises Derbyshire, Durham, Greater Manchester, Lancashire, Merseyside, North South and West Yorkshire, and Tyne and Wear.

ANNEX G – FITNESS TO BE INTERVIEWED

1. This Annex contains general guidance to help police officers and health care professionals assess whether a detainee might be at risk in an interview.

2. A detainee may be at risk in an interview if it is considered that:
   (a) conducting the interview could significantly harm the detainee's physical or mental state;
   (b) anything the detainee says in the interview about their involvement or suspected involvement in the offence about which they are being interviewed **might** be considered unreliable in subsequent court proceedings because of their physical or mental state.

3. In assessing whether the detainee should be interviewed, the following must be considered:
   (a) how the detainee's physical or mental state might affect their ability to understand the nature and purpose of the interview, to comprehend

417

what is being asked and to appreciate the significance of any answers given and make rational decisions about whether they want to say anything;

(b) the extent to which the detainee's replies may be affected by their physical or mental condition rather than representing a rational and accurate explanation of their involvement in the offence;

(c) how the nature of the interview, which could include particularly probing questions, might affect the detainee.

4. It is essential health care professionals who are consulted consider the functional ability of the detainee rather than simply relying on a medical diagnosis, e.g. it is possible for a person with severe mental illness to be fit for interview.

5. Health care professionals should advise on the need for an appropriate adult to be present, whether reassessment of the person's fitness for interview may be necessary if the interview lasts beyond a specified time, and whether a further specialist opinion may be required.

6. When health care professionals identify risks they should be asked to quantify the risks. They should inform the custody officer:

- whether the person's condition:
  ~ is likely to improve
  ~ will require or be amenable to treatment; and
- indicate how long it may take for such improvement to take effect

7. The role of the health care professional is to consider the risks and advise the custody officer of the outcome of that consideration. The health care professional's determination and any advice or recommendations should be made in writing and form part of the custody record.

8. Once the health care professional has provided that information, it is a matter for the custody officer to decide whether or not to allow the interview to go ahead and if the interview is to proceed, to determine what safeguards are needed. Nothing prevents safeguards being provided in addition to those required under the Code. An example might be to have an appropriate health care professional present during the interview, in addition to an appropriate adult, in order constantly to monitor the person's condition and how it is being affected by the interview.

ANNEX H – DETAINED PERSON: OBSERVATION LIST

1. If any detainee fails to meet any of the following criteria, an appropriate health care professional or an ambulance must be called.

2. When assessing the level of rousability, consider:

Rousability – can they be woken?

- go into the cell
- call their name
- shake gently

Response to questions – can they give appropriate answers to questions such as:

- What's your name?
- Where do you live?
- Where do you think you are?

Response to commands – can they respond appropriately to commands such as:

- Open your eyes!
- Lift one arm, now the other arm!

3. Remember to take into account the possibility or presence of other illnesses, injury, or mental condition, a person who is drowsy and smells of alcohol may also have the following:

- Diabetes
- Epilepsy
- Head injury
- Drug intoxication or overdose
- Stroke

ANNEX I – NOT USED

ANNEX J – NOT USED

ANNEX K – X-RAYS AND ULTRASOUND SCANS

(a) Action

1. PACE, section 55A allows a person who has been arrested and is in police detention to have an x-ray taken of them or an ultrasound scan to be carried out on them (or both) if:

- (a) authorised by an officer of inspector rank or above who has reasonable grounds for believing that the detainee:
    - (a) may have swallowed a Class A drug; and
    - (b) was in possession of that Class A drug with the intention of supplying it to another or to export; and
- (b) the detainee's appropriate consent has been given in writing.

2. Before an x-ray is taken or an ultrasound scan carried out, a police officer, designated detention officer or staff custody officer must tell the detainee:

- (a) that the authority has been given; and
- (b) the grounds for giving the authorisation.

3. Before a detainee is asked to give appropriate consent to an x-ray or an ultrasound scan, they must be warned that if they refuse without good cause their refusal may harm their case if it comes to trial, see Notes K1 and K2. This warning may be given by a police officer or member of police staff. A detainee who is not legally represented must be reminded of their entitlement to have free legal advice, see Code C, paragraph 6.5, and the reminder noted in the custody record.

4. An x-ray may be taken, or an ultrasound scan may be carried out, only by a registered medical practitioner or registered nurse, and only at a hospital, surgery or other medical premises.

(b) Documentation

5. The following shall be recorded as soon as practicable in the detainee's custody record:

- (a) the authorisation to take the x-ray or carry out the ultrasound scan (or both);
- (b) the grounds for giving the authorisation;
- (c) the giving of the warning required by paragraph 3; and

(d) the fact that the appropriate consent was given or (as the case may be) refused, and if refused, the reason given for the refusal (if any); and

(e) if an x-ray is taken or an ultrasound scan carried out:
- where it was taken or carried out
- who took it or carried it out
- who was present
- the result

Paragraphs 1.4–1.7 of this Code apply and an appropriate adult should be present when consent is sought to any procedure under this Annex

Notes for Guidance

K1   If authority is given for an x-ray to be taken or an ultrasound scan to be carried out (or both), consideration should be given to asking a registered medical practitioner or registered nurse to explain to the detainee what is involved and to allay any concerns the detainee might have about the effect which taking an x-ray or carrying out an ultrasound scan might have on them. If appropriate consent is not given, evidence of the explanation may, if the case comes to trial, be relevant to determining whether the detainee had a good cause for refusing.

K2   In warning a detainee who is asked to consent to an x-ray being taken or an ultrasound scan being carried out (or both), as in paragraph 3, the following form of words may be used:

'You do not have to allow an x-ray of you to be taken or an ultrasound scan to be carried out on you, but I must warn you that if you refuse without good cause, your refusal may harm your case if it comes to trial.'

CODE D: FOR THE IDENTIFICATION OF PERSONS BY POLICE OFFICERS

Commencement – Transitional Arrangements

This code has effect in relation to any identification procedure carried out after midnight on 31 December 2005.

1 INTRODUCTION

1.1 This Code of Practice concerns the principal methods used by police to identify people in connection with the investigation of offences and the keeping of accurate and reliable criminal records.

1.2 Identification by witnesses arises, e.g., if the offender is seen committing the crime and a witness is given an opportunity to identify the suspect in a video identification, identification parade or similar procedure. The procedures are designed to:

- test the witness' ability to identify the person they saw on a previous occasion
- provide safeguards against mistaken identification.

While this Code concentrates on visual identification procedures, it does not preclude the police making use of aural identification procedures such as a 'voice identification parade', where they judge that appropriate.

1.3 Identification by fingerprints applies when a person's fingerprints are taken to:

- compare with fingerprints found at the scene of a crime
- check and prove convictions
- help to ascertain a person's identity.

1.3A Identification using footwear impressions applies when a person's footwear impressions are taken to compare with impressions found at the scene of the crime.

1.4 Identification by body samples and impressions includes taking samples such as blood or hair to generate a DNA profile for comparison with material obtained from the scene of a crime, or a victim.

1.5 Taking photographs of arrested people applies to recording and checking identity and locating and tracing persons who:

- are wanted for offences
- fail to answer their bail.

1.6 Another method of identification involves searching and examining detained suspects to find, e.g., marks such as tattoos or scars which may help establish their identity or whether they have been involved in committing an offence.

1.7 The provisions of the Police and Criminal Evidence Act 1984 (PACE) and this Code are designed to make sure fingerprints, samples, impressions and photographs are taken, used and retained, and identification procedures carried out, only when justified and necessary for preventing, detecting or investigating crime. If these provisions are not observed, the application of the relevant procedures in particular cases may be open to question.

2 GENERAL

2.1 This Code must be readily available at all police stations for consultation by:

- police officers and police staff
- detained persons
- members of the public

421

2.2   The provisions of this Code:
- include the Annexes
- do not include the Notes for guidance.

2.3   Code C, paragraph 1.4, regarding a person who may be mentally disordered or otherwise mentally vulnerable and the Notes for guidance applicable to those provisions apply to this Code.

2.4   Code C, paragraph 1.5, regarding a person who appears to be under the age of 17 applies to this Code.

2.5   Code C, paragraph 1.6, regarding a person who appears blind, seriously visually impaired, deaf, unable to read or speak or has difficulty orally because of a speech impediment applies to this Code.

2.6   In this Code:
- 'appropriate adult' means the same as in Code C, paragraph 1.7,
- 'solicitor' means the same as in Code C, paragraph 6.12

and the Notes for guidance applicable to those provisions apply to this Code.

2.7   References to custody officers include those performing the functions of custody officer, see paragraph 1.9 of Code C.

2.8   When a record of any action requiring the authority of an officer of a specified rank is made under this Code, subject to paragraph 2.18, the officer's name and rank must be recorded.

2.9   When this Code requires the prior authority or agreement of an officer of at least inspector or superintendent rank, that authority may be given by a sergeant or chief inspector who has been authorised to perform the functions of the higher rank under PACE, section 107.

2.10   Subject to paragraph 2.18, all records must be timed and signed by the maker.

2.11   Records must be made in the custody record, unless otherwise specified. References to 'pocket book' include any official report book issued to police officers or police staff.

2.12   If any procedure in this Code requires a person's consent, the consent of a:
- mentally disordered or otherwise mentally vulnerable person is only valid if given in the presence of the appropriate adult
- juvenile, is only valid if their parent's or guardian's consent is also obtained unless the juvenile is under 14, when their parent's or guardian's consent is sufficient in its own right. If the only obstacle to an identification procedure in section 3 is that a juvenile's parent or guardian refuses consent or reasonable efforts to obtain it have failed, the identification officer may apply the provisions of paragraph 3.21. See Note 2A.

2.13   If a person is blind, seriously visually impaired or unable to read, the custody officer or identification officer shall make sure their solicitor, relative, appropriate adult or some other person likely to take an interest in them and not involved in the investigation is available to help check any documentation. When this Code requires written consent or signing, the person assisting may be asked to sign instead, if the detainee prefers. This paragraph does not require an appropriate adult to be called solely to assist in checking and signing documentation for a person who is not a juvenile, or mentally disordered or otherwise mentally vulnerable (see Note 2B and Code C paragraph 3.15).

2.14 If any procedure in this Code requires information to be given to or sought from a suspect, it must be given or sought in the appropriate adult's presence if the suspect is mentally disordered, otherwise mentally vulnerable or a juvenile. If the appropriate adult is not present when the information is first given or sought, the procedure must be repeated in the presence of the appropriate adult when they arrive. If the suspect appears deaf or there is doubt about their hearing or speaking ability or ability to understand English, and effective communication cannot be established, the information must be given or sought through an interpreter.

2.15 Any procedure in this Code involving the participation of a suspect who is mentally disordered, otherwise mentally vulnerable or a juvenile must take place in the presence of the appropriate adult. See Code C paragraph 1.4.

2.15A Any procedure in this Code involving the participation of a witness who is or appears to be mentally disordered, otherwise mentally vulnerable or a juvenile should take place in the presence of a pre-trial support person. However, the support-person must not be allowed to prompt any identification of a suspect by a witness. See Note 2AB.

2.16 References to:

- 'taking a photograph', include the use of any process to produce a single, still or moving, visual image
- 'photographing a person', should be construed accordingly
- 'photographs', 'films', 'negatives' and 'copies' include relevant visual images recorded, stored, or reproduced through any medium
- 'destruction' includes the deletion of computer data relating to such images or making access to that data impossible.

2.17 Except as described, nothing in this Code affects the powers and procedures:

(i) for requiring and taking samples of breath, blood and urine in relation to driving offences, etc, when under the influence of drink, drugs or excess alcohol under the:

- Road Traffic Act 1988, sections 4 to 11
- Road Traffic Offenders Act 1988, sections 15 and 16
- Transport and Works Act 1992, sections 26 to 38;

(ii) under the Immigration Act 1971, Schedule 2, paragraph 18, for taking photographs and fingerprints from persons detained under that Act, Schedule 2, paragraph 16 (Administrative Controls as to Control on Entry etc.); for taking fingerprints in accordance with the Immigration and Asylum Act 1999; sections 141 and 142(3), or other methods for collecting information about a person's external physical characteristics provided for by regulations made under that Act, section 144;

(iii) under the Terrorism Act 2000, Schedule 8, for taking photographs, fingerprints, skin impressions, body samples or impressions from people:

- arrested under that Act, section 41,
- detained for the purposes of examination under that Act, Schedule 7, and to whom the Code of Practice issued under that Act, Schedule 14, paragraph 6, applies ('the terrorism provisions')

See Note 2C;

(iv) for taking photographs, fingerprints, skin impressions, body samples or impressions from people who have been:

- arrested on warrants issued in Scotland, by officers exercising powers under the Criminal Justice and Public Order Act 1994, section 136(2)

- arrested or detained without warrant by officers from a police force in Scotland exercising their powers of arrest or detention under the Criminal Justice and Public Order Act 1994, section 137(2), (Cross Border powers of arrest etc.).

Note: In these cases, police powers and duties and the person's rights and entitlements whilst at a police station in England and Wales are the same as if the person had been arrested in Scotland by a Scottish police officer.

2.18   Nothing in this Code requires the identity of officers or police staff to be recorded or disclosed:

(a)   in the case of enquiries linked to the investigation of terrorism;

(b)   if the officers or police staff reasonably believe recording or disclosing their names might put them in danger.

In these cases, they shall use warrant or other identification numbers and the name of their police station. See Note 2D.

2.19   In this Code:

(a)   'designated person' means a person other than a police officer, designated under the Police Reform Act 2002, Part 4, who has specified powers and duties of police officers conferred or imposed on them;

(b)   any reference to a police officer includes a designated person acting in the exercise or performance of the powers and duties conferred or imposed on them by their designation.

2.20   If a power conferred on a designated person:

(a)   allows reasonable force to be used when exercised by a police officer, a designated person exercising that power has the same entitlement to use force;

(b)   includes power to use force to enter any premises, that power is not exercisable by that designated person except:

(i)   in the company, and under the supervision, of a police officer; or

(ii)   for the purpose of:

- saving life or limb; or
- preventing serious damage to property.

2.21   Nothing in this Code prevents the custody officer, or other officer given custody of the detainee, from allowing police staff who are not designated persons to carry out individual procedures or tasks at the police station if the law allows. However, the officer remains responsible for making sure the procedures and tasks are carried out correctly in accordance with the Codes of Practice. Any such civilian must be:

(a)   a person employed by a police authority maintaining a police force and under the control and direction of the Chief Officer of that force;

(b)   employed by a person with whom a police authority has a contract for the provision of services relating to persons arrested or otherwise in custody.

2.22   Designated persons and other police staff must have regard to any relevant provisions of the Codes of Practice.

Notes for Guidance

2A   For the purposes of paragraph 2.12, the consent required from a parent or guardian may, for a juvenile in the care of a local authority or voluntary organisation, be given by that authority or organisation. In the case of a juvenile, nothing in paragraph 2.12 requires the parent, guardian or representative of a local authority or voluntary organisation to be present to give their consent, unless they are acting as the appropriate adult under paragraphs 2.14 or 2.15. However, it is important that a parent or guardian not present is fully informed before being asked to consent. They must be given the same information about the procedure and the juvenile's suspected involvement in the offence as the juvenile and appropriate adult. The parent or guardian must also be allowed to speak to the juvenile and the appropriate adult if they wish. Provided the consent is fully informed and is not withdrawn, it may be obtained at any time before the procedure takes place.

2AB   The Youth Justice and Criminal Evidence Act 1999 guidance 'Achieving Best Evidence in Criminal Proceedings' indicates that a pre-trial support person should accompany a vulnerable witness during any identification procedure. It states that this support person should not be (or not be likely to be) a witness in the investigation.

2B   People who are seriously visually impaired or unable to read may be unwilling to sign police documents. The alternative, i.e. their representative signing on their behalf, seeks to protect the interests of both police and suspects.

2C   Photographs, fingerprints, samples and impressions may be taken from a person detained under the terrorism provisions to help determine whether they are, or have been, involved in terrorism, as well as when there are reasonable grounds for suspecting their involvement in a particular offence.

2D   The purpose of paragraph 2.18(b) is to protect those involved in serious organised crime investigations or arrests of particularly violent suspects when there is reliable information that those arrested or their associates may threaten or cause harm to the officers. In cases of doubt, an officer of inspector rank or above should be consulted.

3   IDENTIFICATION BY WITNESSES

3.1   A record shall be made of the suspect's description as first given by a potential witness. This record must:

(a)   be made and kept in a form which enables details of that description to be accurately produced from it, in a visible and legible form, which can be given to the suspect or the suspect's solicitor in accordance with this Code; and

(b)   unless otherwise specified, be made before the witness takes part in any identification procedures under paragraphs 3.5 to 3.10, 3.21 or 3.23.

A copy of the record shall where practicable, be given to the suspect or their solicitor before any procedures under paragraphs 3.5 to 3.10, 3.21 or 3.23 are carried out. See Note 3E.

(a)   Cases when the suspect's identity is not known

3.2   In cases when the suspect's identity is not known, a witness may be taken to a particular neighbourhood or place to see whether they can identify the person they saw. Although the number, age, sex, race, general description and style of clothing of other people present at the location and the way in which any identification is made cannot be controlled, the principles applicable to the formal procedures under paragraphs 3.5 to 3.10 shall be followed as far as practicable. For example:

(a)   where it is practicable to do so, a record should be made of the witness' description of the suspect, as in paragraph 3.1(a), before asking the witness to make an identification;

(b) care must be taken not to direct the witness' attention to any individual unless, taking into account all the circumstances, this cannot be avoided. However, this does not prevent a witness being asked to look carefully at the people around at the time or to look towards a group or in a particular direction, if this appears necessary to make sure that the witness does not overlook a possible suspect simply because the witness is looking in the opposite direction and also to enable the witness to make comparisons between any suspect and others who are in the area; see Note 3F;

(c) where there is more than one witness, every effort should be made to keep them separate and witnesses should be taken to see whether they can identify a person independently;

(d) once there is sufficient information to justify the arrest of a particular individual for suspected involvement in the offence, e.g., after a witness makes a positive identification, the provisions set out from paragraph 3.4 onwards shall apply for any other witnesses in relation to that individual. Subject to paragraphs 3.12 and 3.13, it is not necessary for the witness who makes such a positive identification to take part in a further procedure;

(e) the officer or police staff accompanying the witness must record, in their pocket book, the action taken as soon as, and in as much detail, as possible. The record should include: the date, time and place of the relevant occasion the witness claims to have previously seen the suspect; where any identification was made; how it was made and the conditions at the time (e.g., the distance the witness was from the suspect, the weather and light); if the witness's attention was drawn to the suspect; the reason for this; and anything said by the witness or the suspect about the identification or the conduct of the procedure.

3.3 A witness must not be shown photographs, computerised or artist's composite likenesses or similar likenesses or pictures (including 'E-fit' images) if the identity of the suspect is known to the police and the suspect is available to take part in a video identification, an identification parade or a group identification. If the suspect's identity is not known, the showing of such images to a witness to obtain identification evidence must be done in accordance with Annex E.

(b) Cases when the suspect is known and available

3.4 If the suspect's identity is known to the police and they are available, the identification procedures set out in paragraphs 3.5 to 3.10 may be used. References in this section to a suspect being 'known' mean there is sufficient information known to the police to justify the arrest of a particular person for suspected involvement in the offence. A suspect being 'available' means they are immediately available or will be within a reasonably short time and willing to take an effective part in at least one of the following which it is practicable to arrange;

- video identification;
- identification parade; or
- group identification.

Video identification

3.5 A 'video identification' is when the witness is shown moving images of a known suspect, together with similar images of others who resemble the suspect. Moving images must be used unless:

- the suspect is known but not available (see paragraph 3.21 of this Code); or
- in accordance with paragraph 2A of Annex A of this Code, the identification officer does not consider that replication of a physical feature can be achieved or that it is not possible to conceal the location of the feature on the image of the suspect.

The identification officer may then decide to make use of video identification but using still images.

3.6   Video identifications must be carried out in accordance with Annex A.

Identification parade

3.7   An 'identification parade' is when the witness sees the suspect in a line of others who resemble the suspect.

3.8   Identification parades must be carried out in accordance with Annex B.

Group identification

3.9   A 'group identification' is when the witness sees the suspect in an informal group of people.

3.10   Group identifications must be carried out in accordance with Annex C.

Arranging identification procedures

3.11   Except for the provisions in paragraph 3.19, the arrangements for, and conduct of, the identification procedures in paragraphs 3.5 to 3.10 and circumstances in which an identification procedure must be held shall be the responsibility of an officer not below inspector rank who is not involved with the investigation, 'the identification officer'. Unless otherwise specified, the identification officer may allow another officer or police staff, see paragraph 2.21, to make arrangements for, and conduct, any of these identification procedures. In delegating these procedures, the identification officer must be able to supervise effectively and either intervene or be contacted for advice. No officer or any other person involved with the investigation of the case against the suspect, beyond the extent required by these procedures, may take any part in these procedures or act as the identification officer. This does not prevent the iden-tification officer from consulting the officer in charge of the investigation to determine which procedure to use. When an identification procedure is required, in the interest of fairness to suspects and witnesses, it must be held as soon as practicable.

Circumstances in which an identification procedure must be held

3.12   Whenever:

(i)   a witness has identified a suspect or purported to have identified them prior to any identification procedure set out in paragraphs 3.5 to 3.10 having been held; or

(ii)   there is a witness available, who expresses an ability to identify the suspect, or where there is a reasonable chance of the witness being able to do so, and they have not been given an opportunity to identify the suspect in any of the procedures set out in paragraphs 3.5 to 3.10,

and the suspect disputes being the person the witness claims to have seen, an identification procedure shall be held unless it is not practicable or it would serve

427

no useful purpose in proving or disproving whether the suspect was involved in committing the offence. For example, when it is not disputed that the suspect is already well known to the witness who claims to have seen them commit the crime.

3.13   Such a procedure may also be held if the officer in charge of the investigation considers it would be useful.

Selecting an identification procedure

3.14   If, because of paragraph 3.12, an identification procedure is to be held, the suspect shall initially be offered a video identification unless:

    (a)   a video identification is not practicable; or

    (b)   an identification parade is both practicable and more suitable than a video identification; or

    (c)   paragraph 3.16 applies.

The identification officer and the officer in charge of the investigation shall consult each other to determine which option is to be offered. An identification parade may not be practicable because of factors relating to the witnesses, such as their number, state of health, availability and travelling requirements. A video identification would normally be more suitable if it could be arranged and completed sooner than an identification parade.

3.15   A suspect who refuses the identification procedure first offered shall be asked to state their reason for refusing and may get advice from their solicitor and/or if present, their appropriate adult. The suspect, solicitor and/or appropriate adult shall be allowed to make representations about why another procedure should be used. A record should be made of the reasons for refusal and any representations made. After considering any reasons given, and representations made, the identification officer shall, if appropriate, arrange for the suspect to be offered an alternative which the officer considers suitable and practicable. If the officer decides it is not suitable and practicable to offer an alternative identification procedure, the reasons for that decision shall be recorded.

3.16   A group identification may initially be offered if the officer in charge of the investigation considers it is more suitable than a video identification or an identification parade and the identification officer considers it practicable to arrange.

Notice to suspect

3.17   Unless paragraph 3.20 applies, before a video identification, an identification parade or group identification is arranged, the following shall be explained to the suspect:

    (i)   the purposes of the video identification, identification parade or group identification;

    (ii)   their entitlement to free legal advice; see Code C, paragraph 6.5;

    (iii) the procedures for holding it, including their right to have a solicitor or friend present;

    (iv)   that they do not have to consent to or co-operate in a video identification, identification parade or group identification;

    (v)   that if they do not consent to, and co-operate in, a video identification, identification parade or group identification, their refusal may be given in evidence in any subsequent trial and police may proceed covertly without their consent or make other arrangements to test whether a witness can identify them, see paragraph 3.21;

(vi)   whether, for the purposes of the video identification procedure, images of them have previously been obtained, see paragraph 3.20, and if so, that they may co-operate in providing further, suitable images to be used instead;

(vii)   if appropriate, the special arrangements for juveniles;

(viii) if appropriate, the special arrangements for mentally disordered or otherwise mentally vulnerable people;

(ix)   that if they significantly alter their appearance between being offered an identification procedure and any attempt to hold an identification procedure, this may be given in evidence if the case comes to trial, and the identification officer may then consider other forms of identification, see paragraph 3.21 and Note 3C;

(x)   that a moving image or photograph may be taken of them when they attend for any identification procedure;

(xi)   whether, before their identity became known, the witness was shown photographs, a computerised or artist's composite likeness or similar likeness or image by the police; see Note 3B;

(xii)   that if they change their appearance before an identification parade, it may not be practicable to arrange one on the day or subsequently and, because of the appearance change, the identification officer may consider alternative methods of identification; see Note 3C;

(xiii) that they or their solicitor will be provided with details of the description of them as first given by any witnesses who are to attend the video identification, identification parade, group identification or confrontation, see paragraph 3.1.

3.18   This information must also be recorded in a written notice handed to the suspect. The suspect must be given a reasonable opportunity to read the notice, after which, they should be asked to sign a second copy to indicate if they are willing to co-operate with the making of a video or take part in the identification parade or group identification. The signed copy shall be retained by the identification officer.

3.19   The duties of the identification officer under paragraphs 3.17 and 3.18 may be performed by the custody officer or other officer not involved in the investigation if:

(a)   it is proposed to release the suspect in order that an identification procedure can be arranged and carried out and an inspector is not available to act as the identification officer, see paragraph 3.11, before the suspect leaves the station; or

(b)   it is proposed to keep the suspect in police detention whilst the procedure is arranged and carried out and waiting for an inspector to act as the identification officer, see paragraph 3.11, would cause unreasonable delay to the investigation.

The officer concerned shall inform the identification officer of the action taken and give them the signed copy of the notice. See Note 3C.

3.20   If the identification officer and officer in charge of the investigation suspect, on reasonable grounds that if the suspect was given the information and notice as in paragraphs 3.17 and 3.18, they would then take steps to avoid being seen by a witness in any identification procedure, the identification officer may arrange for images of the suspect suitable for use in a video identification procedure to be obtained before giving the information and notice. If suspect's images are obtained in these circumstances, the suspect may, for the purposes of a video identification procedure, co-operate in providing new images which if suitable, would be used instead, see paragraph 3.17(vi).

(c) Cases when the suspect is known but not available

3.21 When a known suspect is not available or has ceased to be available, see paragraph 3.4, the identification officer may make arrangements for a video identification (see Annex A). If necessary, the identification officer may follow the video identification procedures but using **still** images. Any suitable moving or still images may be used and these may be obtained covertly if necessary. Alternatively, the identification officer may make arrangements for a group identification. See Note 3D. These provisions may also be applied to juveniles where the consent of their parent or guardian is either refused or reasonable efforts to obtain that consent have failed (see paragraph 2.12).

3.22 Any covert activity should be strictly limited to that necessary to test the ability of the witness to identify the suspect.

3.23 The identification officer may arrange for the suspect to be confronted by the witness if none of the options referred to in paragraphs 3.5 to 3.10 or 3.21 are practicable. A 'confrontation' is when the suspect is directly confronted by the witness. A confrontation does not require the suspect's consent. Confrontations must be carried out in accordance with Annex D.

3.24 Requirements for information to be given to, or sought from, a suspect or for the suspect to be given an opportunity to view images before they are shown to a witness, do not apply if the suspect's lack of co-operation prevents the necessary action.

(d) Documentation

3.25 A record shall be made of the video identification, identification parade, group identification or confrontation on forms provided for the purpose.

3.26 If the identification officer considers it is not practicable to hold a video identification or identification parade requested by the suspect, the reasons shall be recorded and explained to the suspect.

3.27 A record shall be made of a person's failure or refusal to co-operate in a video identification, identification parade or group identification and, if applicable, of the grounds for obtaining images in accordance with paragraph 3.20.

(e) Showing films and photographs of incidents and information released to the media

3.28 Nothing in this Code inhibits showing films or photographs to the public through the national or local media, or to police officers for the purposes of recognition and tracing suspects. However, when such material is shown to potential witnesses, including police officers, see Note 3A, to obtain identification evidence, it shall be shown on an individual basis to avoid any possibility of collusion, and, as far as possible, the showing shall follow the principles for video identification if the suspect is known, see Annex A, or identification by photographs if the suspect is not known, see Annex E.

3.29 When a broadcast or publication is made, see paragraph 3.28, a copy of the relevant material released to the media for the purposes of recognising or tracing the suspect, shall be kept. The suspect or their solicitor shall be allowed to view such material before any procedures under paragraphs 3.5 to 3.10, 3.21 or 3.23 are carried out, provided it is practicable and would not unreasonably delay the investigation. Each witness involved in the procedure shall be asked, after they have taken part, whether they have seen any broadcast or published films or photographs relating to the offence or any description of the suspect and their replies shall be recorded. This paragraph does not affect any separate requirement under the Criminal Procedure and Investigations Act 1996 to retain material in connection with criminal investigations.

(f) Destruction and retention of photographs and images taken or used in identification procedures

3.30 PACE, section 64A, see paragraph 5.12, provides powers to take photographs of suspects and allows these photographs to be used or disclosed only for purposes related to the prevention or detection of crime, the investigation of offences or the conduct of prosecutions by, or on behalf of, police or other law enforcement and prosecuting authorities inside and outside the United Kingdom or the enforcement of a sentence. After being so used or disclosed, they may be retained but can only be used or disclosed for the same purposes.

3.31 Subject to paragraph 3.33, the photographs (and all negatives and copies), of suspects taken in accordance with the provisions in paragraph 5.12 which are taken for the purposes of, or in connection with, the identification procedures in paragraphs 3.5 to 3.10, 3.21 or 3.23 must be destroyed unless the suspect:

(a) is charged with, or informed they may be prosecuted for, a recordable offence;

(b) is prosecuted for a recordable offence;

(c) is cautioned for a recordable offence or given a warning or reprimand in accordance with the Crime and Disorder Act 1998 for a recordable offence; or

(d) gives informed consent, in writing, for the photograph or images to be retained for purposes described in paragraph 3.30.

3.32 When paragraph 3.31 requires the destruction of any photograph, the person must be given an opportunity to witness the destruction or to have a certificate confirming the destruction if they request one within five days of being informed that the destruction is required.

3.33 Nothing in paragraph 3.31 affects any separate requirement under the Criminal Procedure and Investigations Act 1996 to retain material in connection with criminal investigations.

Notes for Guidance

3A   Except for the provisions of Annex E, paragraph 1, a police officer who is a witness for the purposes of this part of the Code is subject to the same principles and procedures as a civilian witness.

3B   When a witness attending an identification procedure has previously been shown photographs, or been shown or provided with computerised or artist's composite likenesses, or similar likenesses or pictures, it is the officer in charge of the investigation's responsibility to make the identification officer aware of this.

3C   The purpose of paragraph 3.19 is to avoid or reduce delay in arranging identification procedures by enabling the required information and warnings, see sub-paragraphs 3.17(ix) and 3.17(xii), to be given at the earliest opportunity.

3D   Paragraph 3.21 would apply when a known suspect deliberately makes themself 'unavailable' in order to delay or frustrate arrangements for obtaining identification evidence. It also applies when a suspect refuses or fails to take part in a video identification, an identification parade or a group identification, or refuses or fails to take part in the only practicable options from that list. It enables any suitable images of the suspect, moving or still, which are available or can be obtained, to be used in an identification procedure. Examples include images from custody and other CCTV systems and from visually recorded interview records, see Code F Note for Guidance 2D.

3E   When it is proposed to show photographs to a witness in accordance with Annex E, it is the responsibility of the officer in charge of the investigation to confirm to the officer responsible for supervising and directing the showing, that the first description of the suspect given by that witness has been recorded. If this description has not been recorded, the procedure under Annex E must be postponed. See Annex E paragraph 2.

3F   The admissibility and value of identification evidence obtained when carrying out the procedure under paragraph 3.2 may be compromised if:

> *(a)   before a person is identified, the witness' attention is specifically drawn to that person; or*
>
> *(b)   the suspect's identity becomes known before the procedure.*

4   IDENTIFICATION BY FINGERPRINTS AND FOOTWEAR IMPRESSIONS

(A)   TAKING FINGERPRINTS IN CONNECTION WITH A CRIMINAL INVESTIGATION

(a)   General

4.1   References to 'fingerprints' means any record, produced by any method, of the skin pattern and other physical characteristics or features of a person's:

> (i)   fingers; or
>
> (ii)   palms.

(b)   Action

4.2   A person's fingerprints may be taken in connection with the investigation of an offence only with their consent or if paragraph 4.3 applies. If the person is at a police station consent must be in writing.

4.3   PACE, section 61, provides powers to take fingerprints without consent from any person over the age of ten years:

> (a)   under section 61(3), from a person detained at a police station in consequence of being arrested for a recordable offence, see Note 4A, if they have not had their fingerprints taken in the course of the investigation of the offence unless those previously taken fingerprints are not a complete set or some or all of those fingerprints are not of sufficient quality to allow satisfactory analysis, comparison or matching.
>
> (b)   under section 61(4), from a person detained at a police station who has been charged with a recordable offence, see Note 4A, or informed they will be reported for such an offence if they have not had their fingerprints taken in the course of the investigation of the offence unless those previously taken fingerprints are not a complete set or some or all of those fingerprints

are not of sufficient quality to allow satisfactory analysis, comparison or matching.

(c) under section 61(4A), from a person who has been bailed to appear at a court or police station if the person:

    (i) has answered to bail for a person whose fingerprints were taken previously and there are reasonable grounds for believing they are not the same person; or

    (ii) who has answered to bail claims to be a different person from a person whose fingerprints were previously taken;

and in either case, the court or an officer of inspector rank or above, authorises the fingerprints to be taken at the court or police station;

(d) under section 61(6), from a person who has been:

    (i) convicted of a recordable offence;

    (ii) given a caution in respect of a recordable offence which, at the time of the caution, the person admitted; or

    (iii) warned or reprimanded under the Crime and Disorder Act 1998, section 65, for a recordable offence.

4.4 PACE, section 27, provides power to:

(a) require the person as in paragraph 4.3(d) to attend a police station to have their fingerprints taken if the:

    (i) person has not been in police detention for the offence and has not had their fingerprints taken in the course of the investigation of that offence; or

    (ii) fingerprints that were taken from the person in the course of the investigation of that offence, do not constitute a complete set or some, or all, of the fingerprints are not of sufficient quality to allow satisfactory analysis, comparison or matching; and

(b) arrest, without warrant, a person who fails to comply with the requirement.

Note: The requirement must be made within one month of the date the person is convicted, cautioned, warned or reprimanded and the person must be given a period of at least 7 days within which to attend. This 7 day period need not fall during the month allowed for making the requirement.

4.5 A person's fingerprints may be taken, as above, electronically.

4.6 Reasonable force may be used, if necessary, to take a person's fingerprints without their consent under the powers as in paragraphs 4.3 and 4.4.

4.7 Before any fingerprints are taken with, or without, consent as above, the person must be informed:

(a) of the reason their fingerprints are to be taken;

(b) of the grounds on which the relevant authority has been given if the powers mentioned in paragraph 4.3(c) applies;

(c) that their fingerprints may be retained and may be subject of a speculative search against other fingerprints, see Note 4B, unless destruction of the fingerprints is required in accordance with Annex F, Part (a); and

(d) that if their fingerprints are required to be destroyed, they may witness their destruction as provided for in Annex F, Part (a).

(c)   Documentation

4.8   A record must be made as soon as possible, of the reason for taking a person's fingerprints without consent. If force is used, a record shall be made of the circumstances and those present.

4.9   A record shall be made when a person has been informed under the terms of paragraph 4.7(c), of the possibility that their fingerprints may be subject of a speculative search.

(B)   TAKING FINGERPRINTS IN CONNECTION WITH IMMIGRATION ENQUIRIES

Action

4.10   A person's fingerprints may be taken for the purposes of Immigration Service enquiries in accordance with powers and procedures other than under PACE and for which the Immigration Service (not the police) are responsible, only with the person's consent in writing or if paragraph 4.11 applies.

4.11   Powers to take fingerprints for these purposes without consent are given to police and immigration officers under the:

  (a)   Immigration Act 1971, Schedule 2, paragraph 18(2), when it is reasonably necessary for the purposes of identifying a person detained under the Immigration Act 1971, Schedule 2, paragraph 16 (Detention of person liable to examination or removal);

  (b)   Immigration and Asylum Act 1999, section 141(7)(a), from a person who fails to produce, on arrival, a valid passport with a photograph or some other document satisfactorily establishing their identity and nationality if an immigration officer does not consider the person has a reasonable excuse for the failure;

  (c)   Immigration and Asylum Act 1999, section 141(7)(b), from a person who has been refused entry to the UK but has been temporarily admitted if an immigration officer reasonably suspects the person might break a condition imposed on them relating to residence or reporting to a police or immigration officer, and their decision is confirmed by a chief immigration officer;

  (d)   Immigration and Asylum Act 1999, section 141(7)(c), when directions are given to remove a person:

- as an illegal entrant,
- liable to removal under the Immigration and Asylum Act 1999, section 10,
- who is the subject of a deportation order from the UK;

  (e)   Immigration and Asylum Act 1999, section 141(7)(d), from a person arrested under UK immigration laws under the Immigration Act 1971, Schedule 2, paragraph 17;

  (f)   Immigration and Asylum Act 1999, section 141(7)(e), from a person who has made a claim:

- for asylum
- under Article 3 of the European Convention on Human Rights; or

  (g)   Immigration and Asylum Act 1999, section 141(7)(f), from a person who is a dependant of someone who falls into (b) to (f) above.

4.12   The Immigration and Asylum Act 1999, section 142(3), gives a police and immigration officer power to arrest, without warrant, a person who fails to comply with a requirement imposed by the Secretary of State to attend a specified place for fingerprinting.

4.13   Before any fingerprints are taken, with or without consent, the person must be informed:

    (a)   of the reason their fingerprints are to be taken;

    (b)   the fingerprints, and all copies of them, will be destroyed in accordance with Annex F, Part B.

4.14   Reasonable force may be used, if necessary, to take a person's fingerprints without their consent under powers as in paragraph 4.11.

4.15   Paragraphs 4.1 and 4.8 apply.

(C)   TAKING FOOTWEAR IMPRESSIONS IN CONNECTION WITH A CRIMINAL INVESTIGATION

(a)   Action

4.16   Impressions of a person's footwear may be taken in connection with the investigation of an offence only with their consent or if paragraph 4.17 applies. If the person is at a police station consent must be in writing.

4.17   PACE, section 61A, provides power for a police officer to take footwear impressions without consent from any person over the age of ten years who is detained at a police station:

    (a)   in consequence of being arrested for a recordable offence, see Note 4A; or if the detainee has been charged with a recordable offence, or informed they will be reported for such an offence; and

    (b)   the detainee has not had an impression of their footwear taken in the course of the investigation of the offence unless the previously taken impression is not complete or is not of sufficient quality to allow satisfactory analysis, comparison or matching (whether in the case in question or generally).

4.18   Reasonable force may be used, if necessary, to take a footwear impression from a detainee without consent under the power in paragraph 4.17.

4.19   Before any footwear impression is taken with, or without, consent as above, the person must be informed:

    (a)   of the reason the impression is to be taken;

    (b)   that the impression may be retained and may be subject of a speculative search against other impressions, see Note 4B, unless destruction of the impression is required in accordance with Annex F, Part (a); and

    (c)   that if their footwear impressions are required to be destroyed, they may witness their destruction as provided for in Annex F, Part (a).

(b)   Documentation

4.20   A record must be made as soon as possible, of the reason for taking a person's footwear impressions without consent. If force is used, a record shall be made of the circumstances and those present.

4.21   A record shall be made when a person has been informed under the terms of paragraph 4.19(b), of the possibility that their footwear impressions may be subject of a speculative search.

Notes for Guidance

4A   References to 'recordable offences' in this Code relate to those offences for which convictions, cautions, reprimands and warnings may be recorded in national police records. See PACE, section 27(4). The recordable offences current at the time when this Code was prepared, are any offences which carry a sentence of imprisonment on conviction (irrespective of the period, or the age of the offender or actual sentence passed) as well as the non-imprisonable offences under the Vagrancy Act 1824, sections 3 and 4 (begging and persistent begging), the Street Offences Act 1959, section 1 (loitering or soliciting for purposes of prostitution), the Road Traffic Act 1988, section 25 (tampering with motor vehicles), the Criminal Justice and Public Order Act 1994, section 167 (touting for hire car services) and others listed in the National Police Records (Recordable Offences) Regulations 2000 as amended.

4B   Fingerprints, footwear impressions or a DNA sample (and the information derived from it) taken from a person arrested on suspicion of being involved in a recordable offence, or charged with such an offence, or informed they will be reported for such an offence, may be subject of a speculative search. This means the fingerprints, footwear impressions or DNA sample may be checked against other fingerprints, footwear impressions and DNA records held by, or on behalf of, the police and other law enforcement authorities in, or outside, the UK, or held in connection with, or as a result of, an investigation of an offence inside or outside the UK. Fingerprints, footwear impressions and samples taken from a person suspected of committing a recordable offence but not arrested, charged or informed they will be reported for it, may be subject to a speculative search only if the person consents in writing. The following is an example of a basic form of words:

> *'I consent to my fingerprints, footwear impressions and DNA sample and information derived from it being retained and used only for purposes related to the prevention and detection of a crime, the investigation of an offence or the conduct of a prosecution either nationally or internationally.*
>
> *I understand that my fingerprints, footwear impressions or DNA sample may be checked against other fingerprint, footwear impressions and DNA records held by or on behalf of relevant law enforcement authorities, either nationally or internationally.*
>
> *I understand that once I have given my consent for my fingerprints, footwear impressions or DNA sample to be retained and used I cannot withdraw this consent.'*

See Annex F regarding the retention and use of fingerprints and footwear impressions taken with consent for elimination purposes.

5   EXAMINATIONS TO ESTABLISH IDENTITY AND THE TAKING OF PHOTOGRAPHS

(A)   DETAINEES AT POLICE STATIONS

(a)   Searching or examination of detainees at police stations

5.1   PACE, section 54A (1), allows a detainee at a police station to be searched or examined or both, to establish:

(a)   whether they have any marks, features or injuries that would tend to identify them as a person involved in the commission of an offence and to photograph any identifying marks, see paragraph 5.5; or

(b)   their identity, see Note 5A.

A person detained at a police station to be searched under a stop and search power, see Code A, is not a detainee for the purposes of these powers.

5.2   A search and/or examination to find marks under section 54A (1) (a) may be carried out without the detainee's consent, see paragraph 2.12, only if authorised by an officer of at least inspector rank when consent has been withheld or it is not practicable to obtain consent, see Note 5D.

5.3   A search or examination to establish a suspect's identity under section 54A (1) (b) may be carried out without the detainee's consent, see paragraph 2.12, only if authorised by an officer of at least inspector rank when the detainee has refused to identify themselves or the authorising officer has reasonable grounds for suspecting the person is not who they claim to be.

5.4   Any marks that assist in establishing the detainee's identity, or their identification as a person involved in the commission of an offence, are identifying marks. Such marks may be photographed with the detainee's consent, see paragraph 2.12; or without their consent if it is withheld or it is not practicable to obtain it, see Note 5D.

5.5   A detainee may only be searched, examined and photographed under section 54A, by a police officer of the same sex.

5.6   Any photographs of identifying marks, taken under section 54A, may be used or disclosed only for purposes related to the prevention or detection of crime, the investigation of offences or the conduct of prosecutions by, or on behalf of, police or other law enforcement and prosecuting authorities inside, and outside, the UK. After being so used or disclosed, the photograph may be retained but must not be used or disclosed except for these purposes, see Note 5B.

5.7   The powers, as in paragraph 5.1, do not affect any separate requirement under the Criminal Procedure and Investigations Act 1996 to retain material in connection with criminal investigations.

5.8   Authority for the search and/or examination for the purposes of paragraphs 5.2 and 5.3 may be given orally or in writing. If given orally, the authorising officer must confirm it in writing as soon as practicable. A separate authority is required for each purpose which applies.

5.9   If it is established a person is unwilling to co-operate sufficiently to enable a search and/or examination to take place or a suitable photograph to be taken, an officer may use reasonable force to:

(a)   search and/or examine a detainee without their consent; and

(b)   photograph any identifying marks without their consent.

5.10   The thoroughness and extent of any search or examination carried out in accordance with the powers in section 54A must be no more than the officer considers necessary to achieve the required purpose. Any search or examination which involves the removal of more than the person's outer clothing shall be conducted in accordance with Code C, Annex A, paragraph 11.

5.11   An intimate search may not be carried out under the powers in section 54A.

(b)   Photographing detainees at police stations and other persons elsewhere than at a police station

5.12   Under PACE, section 64A, an officer may photograph:

(a)   any person whilst they are detained at a police station; and

(b)   any person who is elsewhere than at a police station and who has been:

   (i)   arrested by a constable for an offence;
   (ii)   taken into custody by a constable after being arrested for an offence by a person other than a constable;
   (iii)   made subject to a requirement to wait with a community support officer under paragraph 2(3) or (3B) of Schedule 4 to the Police Reform Act 2002;
   (iv)   given a penalty notice by a constable in uniform under Chapter 1 of Part 1 of the Criminal Justice and Police Act 2001, a penalty notice by a constable under section 444A of the Education Act 1996, or a fixed penalty notice by a constable in uniform under section 54 of the Road Traffic Offenders Act 1988;
   (v)   given a notice in relation to a relevant fixed penalty offence (within the meaning of paragraph 1 of Schedule 4 to the Police Reform Act 2002) by a community support officer by virtue of a designation applying that paragraph to him; or
   (vi)   given a notice in relation to a relevant fixed penalty offence (within the meaning of paragraph 1 of Schedule 5 to the Police Reform Act 2002) by an accredited person by virtue of accreditation specifying that that paragraph applies to him.

5.12A   Photographs taken under PACE, section 64A:

(a)   may be taken with the person's consent, or without their consent if consent is withheld or it is not practicable to obtain their consent, see Note 5E; and

(b)   may be used or disclosed only for purposes related to the prevention or detection of crime, the investigation of offences or the conduct of prosecutions by, or on behalf of, police or other law enforcement and prosecuting authorities inside and outside the United Kingdom or the enforcement of any sentence or order made by a court when dealing with an offence. After being so used or disclosed, they may be retained but can only be used or disclosed for the same purposes. See Note 5B.

5.13   The officer proposing to take a detainee's photograph may, for this purpose, require the person to remove any item or substance worn on, or over, all, or any part of, their head or face. If they do not comply with such a requirement, the officer may remove the item or substance.

5.14   If it is established the detainee is unwilling to co-operate sufficiently to enable a suitable photograph to be taken and it is not reasonably practicable to take the photograph covertly, an officer may use reasonable force, see Note 5F:

(a) to take their photograph without their consent; and

(b) for the purpose of taking the photograph, remove any item or substance worn on, or over, all, or any part of, the person's head or face which they have failed to remove when asked.

5.15 For the purposes of this Code, a photograph may be obtained without the person's consent by making a copy of an image of them taken at any time on a camera system installed anywhere in the police station.

(c) Information to be given

5.16 When a person is searched, examined or photographed under the provisions as in paragraph 5.1 and 5.12, or their photograph obtained as in paragraph 5.15, they must be informed of the:

(a) purpose of the search, examination or photograph;

(b) grounds on which the relevant authority, if applicable, has been given; and

(c) purposes for which the photograph may be used, disclosed or retained.

This information must be given before the search or examination commences or the photograph is taken, except if the photograph is:

(i) to be taken covertly;

(ii) obtained as in paragraph 5.15, in which case the person must be informed as soon as practicable after the photograph is taken or obtained.

(d) Documentation

5.17 A record must be made when a detainee is searched, examined, or a photograph of the person, or any identifying marks found on them, are taken. The record must include the:

(a) identity, subject to paragraph 2.18, of the officer carrying out the search, examination or taking the photograph;

(b) purpose of the search, examination or photograph and the outcome;

(c) detainee's consent to the search, examination or photograph, or the reason the person was searched, examined or photographed without consent;

(d) giving of any authority as in paragraphs 5.2 and 5.3, the grounds for giving it and the authorising officer.

5.18 If force is used when searching, examining or taking a photograph in accordance with this section, a record shall be made of the circumstances and those present.

(B) PERSONS AT POLICE STATIONS NOT DETAINED

5.19 When there are reasonable grounds for suspecting the involvement of a person in a criminal offence, but that person is at a police station **voluntarily** and not detained, the provisions of paragraphs 5.1 to 5.18 should apply, subject to the modifications in the following paragraphs.

5.20 References to the 'person being detained' and to the powers mentioned in paragraph 5.1 which apply only to detainees at police stations shall be omitted.

5.21 Force may not be used to:

(a) search and/or examine the person to:

(i) discover whether they have any marks that would tend to identify them as a person involved in the commission of an offence; or

(ii) establish their identity, see Note 5A;

(b) take photographs of any identifying marks, see paragraph 5.4; or

(c) take a photograph of the person.

5.22 Subject to paragraph 5.24, the photographs of persons or of their identifying marks which are not taken in accordance with the provisions mentioned in paragraphs 5.1 or 5.12, must be destroyed (together with any negatives and copies) unless the person:

(a) is charged with, or informed they may be prosecuted for, a recordable offence;

(b) is prosecuted for a recordable offence;

(c) is cautioned for a recordable offence or given a warning or reprimand in accordance with the Crime and Disorder Act 1998 for a recordable offence; or

(d) gives informed consent, in writing, for the photograph or image to be retained as in paragraph 5.6.

5.23 When paragraph 5.22 requires the destruction of any photograph, the person must be given an opportunity to witness the destruction or to have a certificate confirming the destruction provided they so request the certificate within five days of being informed the destruction is required.

5.24 Nothing in paragraph 5.22 affects any separate requirement under the Criminal Procedure and Investigations Act 1996 to retain material in connection with criminal investigations.

Notes for Guidance

5A The conditions under which fingerprints may be taken to assist in establishing a person's identity, are described in Section 4.

5B Examples of purposes related to the prevention or detection of crime, the investigation of offences or the conduct of prosecutions include:

(a) checking the photograph against other photographs held in records or in connection with, or as a result of, an investigation of an offence to establish whether the person is liable to arrest for other offences;

(b) when the person is arrested at the same time as other people, or at a time when it is likely that other people will be arrested, using the photograph to help establish who was arrested, at what time and where;

(c) when the real identity of the person is not known and cannot be readily ascertained or there are reasonable grounds for doubting a name and other personal details given by the person, are their real name and personal details. In these circumstances, using or disclosing the photograph to help to establish or verify their real identity or determine whether they are liable to arrest for some other offence, e.g. by checking it against other photographs held in records or in connection with, or as a result of, an investigation of an offence;

(d) when it appears any identification procedure in section 3 may need to be arranged for which the person's photograph would assist;

(e) when the person's release without charge may be required, and if the release is:

(i) on bail to appear at a police station, using the photograph to help verify the person's identity when they answer their bail and if the person does not answer their bail, to assist in arresting them; or

(ii) *without bail, using the photograph to help verify their identity or assist in locating them for the purposes of serving them with a summons to appear at court in criminal proceedings;*

(f) *when the person has answered to bail at a police station and there are reasonable grounds for doubting they are the person who was previously granted bail, using the photograph to help establish or verify their identity;*

(g) *when the person arrested on a warrant claims to be a different person from the person named on the warrant and a photograph would help to confirm or disprove their claim;*

(h) *when the person has been charged with, reported for, or convicted of, a recordable offence and their photograph is not already on record as a result of (a) to (f) or their photograph is on record but their appearance has changed since it was taken and the person has not yet been released or brought before a court.*

5C *There is no power to arrest a person convicted of a recordable offence solely to take their photograph. The power to take photographs in this section applies only where the person is in custody as a result of the exercise of another power, e.g. arrest for fingerprinting under PACE, section 27.*

5D *Examples of when it would not be practicable to obtain a detainee's consent, see paragraph 2.12, to a search, examination or the taking of a photograph of an identifying mark include:*

(a) *when the person is drunk or otherwise unfit to give consent;*

(b) *when there are reasonable grounds to suspect that if the person became aware a search or examination was to take place or an identifying mark was to be photographed, they would take steps to prevent this happening, e.g. by violently resisting, covering or concealing the mark etc and it would not otherwise be possible to carry out the search or examination or to photograph any identifying mark;*

(c) *in the case of a juvenile, if the parent or guardian cannot be contacted in sufficient time to allow the search or examination to be carried out or the photograph to be taken.*

5E *Examples of when it would not be practicable to obtain the person's consent, see paragraph 2.12, to a photograph being taken include:*

(a) *when the person is drunk or otherwise unfit to give consent;*

(b) *when there are reasonable grounds to suspect that if the person became aware a photograph, suitable to be used or disclosed for the use and disclosure described in paragraph 5.6, was to be taken, they would take steps to prevent it being taken, e.g. by violently resisting, covering or distorting their face etc, and it would not otherwise be possible to take a suitable photograph;*

(c) *when, in order to obtain a suitable photograph, it is necessary to take it covertly; and*

(d) *in the case of a juvenile, if the parent or guardian cannot be contacted in sufficient time to allow the photograph to be taken.*

5F *The use of reasonable force to take the photograph of a suspect elsewhere than at a police station must be carefully considered. In order to obtain a suspect's consent and co-operation to remove an item of religious headwear to take their photograph, a constable should consider whether in the circumstances of the situation the removal of the headwear and the taking of the photograph should be by an officer of the same sex as the person. It would be appropraite for these actions to be conducted out of public view.*

6 IDENTIFICATION BY BODY SAMPLES AND IMPRESSIONS

(A) GENERAL

6.1 References to:

(a) an 'intimate sample' mean a dental impression or sample of blood, semen or any other tissue fluid, urine, or pubic hair, or a swab taken from a person's body orifice other than the mouth;

(b) a 'non-intimate sample' means:

(i) a sample of hair, other than pubic hair, which includes hair plucked with the root, see Note 6A;

(ii) a sample taken from a nail or from under a nail;

(iii) a swab taken from any part of a person's body other than a part from which a swab taken would be an intimate sample;

(iv) saliva;

(v) a skin impression which means any record, other than a fingerprint, which is a record, in any form and produced by any method, of the skin pattern and other physical characteristics or features of the whole, or any part of, a person's foot or of any other part of their body.

(B) ACTION

(a) Intimate samples

6.2 PACE, section 62, provides that intimate samples may be taken under:

(a) section 62(1), from a person in police detention only:

(i) if a police officer of inspector rank or above has reasonable grounds to believe such an impression or sample will tend to confirm or disprove the suspect's involvement in a recordable offence, see Note 4A, and gives authorisation for a sample to be taken; and

(ii) with the suspect's written consent;

(b) section 62(1A), from a person not in police detention but from whom two or more non-intimate samples have been taken in the course of an investigation of an offence and the samples, though suitable, have proved insufficient if:

(i) a police officer of inspector rank or above authorises it to be taken; and

(ii) the person concerned gives their written consent. See Notes 6B and 6C.

6.3 Before a suspect is asked to provide an intimate sample, they must be warned that if they refuse without good cause, their refusal may harm their case if it comes to trial, see Note 6D. If the suspect is in police detention and not legally represented, they must also be reminded of their entitlement to have free legal advice, see Code C, paragraph 6.5, and the reminder noted in the custody record. If paragraph 6.2(b) applies and the person is attending a station voluntarily, their entitlement to free legal advice as in Code C, paragraph 3.21 shall be explained to them.

6.4 Dental impressions may only be taken by a registered dentist. Other intimate samples, except for samples of urine, may only be taken by a registered medical practitioner or registered nurse or registered paramedic.

(b) Non-intimate samples

6.5 A non-intimate sample may be taken from a detainee only with their written consent or if paragraph 6.6 applies.

6.6 (a) under section 63, a non-intimate sample may not be taken from a person without consent and the consent must be in writing

    (aa) A non-intimate sample may be taken from a person without the appropriate consent in the following circumstances:

        (i) under section 63(2A) where the person is in police detention as a consequence of his arrest for a recordable offence and he has not had a non-intimate sample of the same type and from the same part of the body taken in the course of the investigation of the offence by the police or he has had such a sample taken but it proved insufficient.

        (ii) under section 63(3) (a) where he is being held in custody by the police on the authority of a court and an officer of at least the rank of inspector authorises it to be taken.

    (b) under section 63(3A), from a person charged with a recordable offence or informed they will be reported for such an offence: and

        (i) that person has not had a non-intimate sample taken from them in the course of the investigation; or

        (ii) if they have had a sample taken, it proved unsuitable or insufficient for the same form of analysis, see Note 6B; or

    (c) under section 63(3B), from a person convicted of a recordable offence after the date on which that provision came into effect. PACE, section 63A, describes the circumstances in which a police officer may require a person convicted of a recordable offence to attend a police station for a non-intimate sample to be taken.

6.7 Reasonable force may be used, if necessary, to take a non-intimate sample from a person without their consent under the powers mentioned in paragraph 6.6.

6.8 Before any intimate sample is taken with consent or non-intimate sample is taken with, or without, consent, the person must be informed:

    (a) of the reason for taking the sample;

    (b) of the grounds on which the relevant authority has been given;

    (c) that the sample or information derived from the sample may be retained and subject of a speculative search, see Note 6E, unless their destruction is required as in Annex F, Part A.

6.9 When clothing needs to be removed in circumstances likely to cause embarrassment to the person, no person of the opposite sex who is not a registered medical practitioner or registered health care professional shall be present, (unless in the case of a juvenile, mentally disordered or mentally vulnerable person, that person specifically requests the presence of an appropriate adult of the opposite sex who is readily available) nor shall anyone whose presence is unnecessary. However, in the case of a juvenile, this is subject to the overriding proviso that such a removal of clothing may take place in the absence of the appropriate adult only if the juvenile signifies, in their presence, that they prefer the adult's absence and they agree.

(c) Documentation

6.10   A record of the reasons for taking a sample or impression and, if applicable, of its destruction must be made as soon as practicable. If force is used, a record shall be made of the circumstances and those present. If written consent is given to the taking of a sample or impression, the fact must be recorded in writing.

6.11   A record must be made of a warning given as required by paragraph 6.3.

6.12   A record shall be made of the fact that a person has been informed as in paragraph 6.8(c) that samples may be subject of a speculative search.

Notes for guidance

6A   When hair samples are taken for the purpose of DNA analysis (rather than for other purposes such as making a visual match), the suspect should be permitted a reasonable choice as to what part of the body the hairs are taken from. When hairs are plucked, they should be plucked individually, unless the suspect prefers otherwise and no more should be plucked than the person taking them reasonably considers necessary for a sufficient sample.

6B   (a)   An insufficient sample is one which is not sufficient either in quantity or quality to provide information for a particular form of analysis, such as DNA analysis. A sample may also be insufficient if enough information cannot be obtained from it by analysis because of loss, destruction, damage or contamination of the sample or as a result of an earlier, unsuccessful attempt at analysis.

(b)   An unsuitable sample is one which, by its nature, is not suitable for a particular form of analysis.

6C   Nothing in paragraph 6.2 prevents intimate samples being taken for elimination purposes with the consent of the person concerned but the provisions of paragraph 2.12 relating to the role of the appropriate adult, should be applied. Paragraph 6.2(b) does not, however, apply where the non-intimate samples were previously taken under the Terrorism Act 2000, Schedule 8, paragraph 10.

6D   In warning a person who is asked to provide an intimate sample as in paragraph 6.3, the following form of words may be used:

'You do not have to provide this sample/allow this swab or impression to be taken, but I must warn you that if you refuse without good cause, your refusal may harm your case if it comes to trial.'

6E   Fingerprints or a DNA sample and the information derived from it taken from a person arrested on suspicion of being involved in a recordable offence, or charged with such an offence, or informed they will be reported for such an offence, may be subject of a speculative search. This means they may be checked against other fingerprints and DNA records held by, or on behalf of, the police and other law enforcement authorities in or outside the UK or held in connection with, or as a result of, an investigation of an offence inside or outside the UK. Fingerprints and samples taken from any other person, e.g. a person suspected of committing a recordable offence but who has not been arrested, charged or informed they will be reported for it, may be subject to a speculative search only if the person consents in writing to their fingerprints being subject of such a search. The following is an example of a basic form of words:

'I consent to my fingerprints/DNA sample and information derived from it being retained and used only for purposes related to the prevention and detection of a crime, the investigation of an offence or the conduct of a prosecution either nationally or internationally.

I understand that this sample may be checked against other fingerprint/DNA records held by or on behalf of relevant law enforcement authorities, either nationally or internationally.

I understand that once I have given my consent for the sample to be retained and used I cannot withdraw this consent.'

See Annex F regarding the retention and use of fingerprints and samples taken with consent for elimination purposes.

6   Samples of urine and non-intimate samples taken in accordance with sections 63B and 63C of PACE may not be used for identification purposes in accordance with this Code. See Code C note for guidance 17D.

ANNEX A – VIDEO IDENTIFICATION

(a)   General

1.   The arrangements for obtaining and ensuring the availability of a suitable set of images to be used in a video identification must be the responsibility of an identification officer, who has no direct involvement with the case.

2.   The set of images must include the suspect and at least eight other people who, so far as possible, resemble the suspect in age, general appearance and position in life. Only one suspect shall appear in any set unless there are two suspects of roughly similar appearance, in which case they may be shown together with at least twelve other people.

2A   If the suspect has an unusual physical feature, e.g., a facial scar, tattoo or distinctive hairstyle or hair colour which does not appear on the images of the other people that are available to be used, steps may be taken to:

(a)   conceal the location of the feature on the images of the suspect and the other people; or

(b)   replicate that feature on the images of the other people.

For these purposes, the feature may be concealed or replicated electronically or by any other method which it is practicable to use to ensure that the images of the suspect and other people resemble each other. The identification officer has discretion to choose whether to conceal or replicate the feature and the method to be used. If an unusual physical feature has been described by the witness, the identification officer should, if practicable, have that feature replicated. If it has not been described, concealment may be more appropriate.

2B   If the identification officer decides that a feature should be concealed or replicated, the reason for the decision and whether the feature was concealed or replicated in the images shown to any witness shall be recorded.

2C   If the witness requests to view an image where an unusual physical feature has been concealed or replicated without the feature being concealed or replicated, the witness may be allowed to do so.

3.   The images used to conduct a video identification shall, as far as possible, show the suspect and other people in the same positions or carrying out the same sequence of movements. They shall also show the suspect and other people under identical conditions unless the identification officer reasonably believes:

(a)   because of the suspect's failure or refusal to co-operate or other reasons, it is not practicable for the conditions to be identical; and

(b) any difference in the conditions would not direct a witness' attention to any individual image.

4. The reasons identical conditions are not practicable shall be recorded on forms provided for the purpose.

5. Provision must be made for each person shown to be identified by number.

6. If police officers are shown, any numerals or other identifying badges must be concealed. If a prison inmate is shown, either as a suspect or not, then either all, or none of, the people shown should be in prison clothing.

7. The suspect or their solicitor, friend, or appropriate adult must be given a reasonable opportunity to see the complete set of images before it is shown to any witness. If the suspect has a reasonable objection to the set of images or any of the participants, the suspect shall be asked to state the reasons for the objection. Steps shall, if practicable, be taken to remove the grounds for objection. If this is not practicable, the suspect and/or their representative shall be told why their objections cannot be met and the objection, the reason given for it and why it cannot be met shall be recorded on forms provided for the purpose.

8. Before the images are shown in accordance with paragraph 7, the suspect or their solicitor shall be provided with details of the first description of the suspect by any witnesses who are to attend the video identification. When a broadcast or publication is made, as in paragraph 3.28, the suspect or their solicitor must also be allowed to view any material released to the media by the police for the purpose of recognising or tracing the suspect, provided it is practicable and would not unreasonably delay the investigation.

9. The suspect's solicitor, if practicable, shall be given reasonable notification of the time and place the video identification is to be conducted so a representative may attend on behalf of the suspect. If a solicitor has not been instructed, this information shall be given to the suspect. The suspect may not be present when the images are shown to the witness(es). In the absence of the suspect's representative, the viewing itself shall be recorded on video. No unauthorised people may be present.

(b) Conducting the video identification

10. The identification officer is responsible for making the appropriate arrangements to make sure, before they see the set of images, witnesses are not able to communicate with each other about the case, see any of the images which are to be shown, see, or be reminded of, any photograph or description of the suspect or be given any other indication as to the suspect's identity, or overhear a witness who has already seen the material. There must be no discussion with the witness about the composition of the set of images and they must not be told whether a previous witness has made any identification.

11. Only one witness may see the set of images at a time. Immediately before the images are shown, the witness shall be told that the person they saw on a specified earlier occasion may, or may not, appear in the images they are shown and that if they cannot make a positive identification, they should say so. The witness shall be advised that at any point, they may ask to see a particular part of the set of images or to have a particular image frozen for them to study. Furthermore, it should be pointed out to the witness that there is no limit on how many times they can view the whole set of images or any part of them. However, they should be asked not to make any decision as to whether the person they saw is on the set of images until they have seen the whole set at least twice.

12.   Once the witness has seen the whole set of images at least twice and has indicated that they do not want to view the images, or any part of them, again, the witness shall be asked to say whether the individual they saw in person on a specified earlier occasion has been shown and, if so, to identify them by number of the image. The witness will then be shown that image to confirm the identification, see paragraph 17.

13.   Care must be taken not to direct the witness' attention to any one individual image or give any indication of the suspect's identity. Where a witness has previously made an identification by photographs, or a computerised or artist's composite or similar likeness, the witness must not be reminded of such a photograph or composite likeness once a suspect is available for identification by other means in accordance with this Code. Nor must the witness be reminded of any description of the suspect.

14.   After the procedure, each witness shall be asked whether they have seen any broadcast or published films or photographs, or any descriptions of suspects relating to the offence and their reply shall be recorded.

(c)   Image security and destruction

15.   Arrangements shall be made for all relevant material containing sets of images used for specific identification procedures to be kept securely and their movements accounted for. In particular, no-one involved in the investigation shall be permitted to view the material prior to it being shown to any witness.

16.   As appropriate, paragraph 3.30 or 3.31 applies to the destruction or retention of relevant sets of images.

(d)   Documentation

17.   A record must be made of all those participating in, or seeing, the set of images whose names are known to the police.

18.   A record of the conduct of the video identification must be made on forms provided for the purpose. This shall include anything said by the witness about any identifications or the conduct of the procedure and any reasons it was not practicable to comply with any of the provisions of this Code governing the conduct of video identifications.

ANNEX B – IDENTIFICATION PARADES

(a)   General

1.   A suspect must be given a reasonable opportunity to have a solicitor or friend present, and the suspect shall be asked to indicate on a second copy of the notice whether or not they wish to do so.

2.   An identification parade may take place either in a normal room or one equipped with a screen permitting witnesses to see members of the identification parade without being seen. The procedures for the composition and conduct of the identification parade are the same in both cases, subject to paragraph 8 (except that an identification parade involving a screen may take place only when the suspect's solicitor, friend or appropriate adult is present or the identification parade is recorded on video).

3.   Before the identification parade takes place, the suspect or their solicitor shall be provided with details of the first description of the suspect by any witnesses who are

attending the identification parade. When a broadcast or publication is made as in paragraph 3.28, the suspect or their solicitor should also be allowed to view any material released to the media by the police for the purpose of recognising or tracing the suspect, provided it is practicable to do so and would not unreasonably delay the investigation.

(b) Identification parades involving prison inmates

4.   If a prison inmate is required for identification, and there are no security problems about the person leaving the establishment, they may be asked to participate in an identification parade or video identification.

5.   An identification parade may be held in a Prison Department establishment but shall be conducted, as far as practicable under normal identification parade rules. Members of the public shall make up the identification parade unless there are serious security, or control, objections to their admission to the establishment. In such cases, or if a group or video identification is arranged within the establishment, other inmates may participate. If an inmate is the suspect, they are not required to wear prison clothing for the identification parade unless the other people taking part are other inmates in similar clothing, or are members of the public who are prepared to wear prison clothing for the occasion.

(c) Conduct of the identification parade

6.   Immediately before the identification parade, the suspect must be reminded of the procedures governing its conduct and cautioned in the terms of Code C, paragraphs 10.5 or 10.6, as appropriate.

7.   All unauthorised people must be excluded from the place where the identification parade is held.

8.   Once the identification parade has been formed, everything afterwards, in respect of it, shall take place in the presence and hearing of the suspect and any interpreter, solicitor, friend or appropriate adult who is present (unless the identification parade involves a screen, in which case everything said to, or by, any witness at the place where the identification parade is held, must be said in the hearing and presence of the suspect's solicitor, friend or appropriate adult or be recorded on video).

9.   The identification parade shall consist of at least eight people (in addition to the suspect) who, so far as possible, resemble the suspect in age, height, general appearance and position in life. Only one suspect shall be included in an identification parade unless there are two suspects of roughly similar appearance, in which case they may be paraded together with at least twelve other people. In no circumstances shall more than two suspects be included in one identification parade and where there are separate identification parades, they shall be made up of different people.

10.   If the suspect has an unusual physical feature, e.g., a facial scar, tattoo or distinctive hairstyle or hair colour which cannot be replicated on other members of the identification parade, steps may be taken to conceal the location of that feature on the suspect and the other members of the identification parade if the suspect and their solicitor, or appropriate adult, agree. For example, by use of a plaster or a hat, so that all members of the identification parade resemble each other in general appearance.

11.   When all members of a similar group are possible suspects, separate identification parades shall be held for each unless there are two suspects of similar appearance when they may appear on the same identification parade with at least twelve other

members of the group who are not suspects. When police officers in uniform form an identification parade any numerals or other identifying badges shall be concealed.

12.   When the suspect is brought to the place where the identification parade is to be held, they shall be asked if they have any objection to the arrangements for the identification parade or to any of the other participants in it and to state the reasons for the objection. The suspect may obtain advice from their solicitor or friend, if present, before the identification parade proceeds. If the suspect has a reasonable objection to the arrangements or any of the participants, steps shall, if practicable, be taken to remove the grounds for objection. When it is not practicable to do so, the suspect shall be told why their objections cannot be met and the objection, the reason given for it and why it cannot be met, shall be recorded on forms provided for the purpose.

13.   The suspect may select their own position in the line, but may not otherwise interfere with the order of the people forming the line. When there is more than one witness, the suspect must be told, after each witness has left the room, that they can, if they wish, change position in the line. Each position in the line must be clearly numbered, whether by means of a number laid on the floor in front of each identification parade member or by other means.

14.   Appropriate arrangements must be made to make sure, before witnesses attend the identification parade, they are not able to:

   (i)   communicate with each other about the case or overhear a witness who has already seen the identification parade;
   (ii) see any member of the identification parade;
   (iii) see, or be reminded of, any photograph or description of the suspect or be given any other indication as to the suspect's identity; or
   (iv) see the suspect before or after the identification parade.

15.   The person conducting a witness to an identification parade must not discuss with them the composition of the identification parade and, in particular, must not disclose whether a previous witness has made any identification.

16.   Witnesses shall be brought in one at a time. Immediately before the witness inspects the identification parade, they shall be told the person they saw on a specified earlier occasion may, or may not, be present and if they cannot make a positive identification, they should say so. The witness must also be told they should not make any decision about whether the person they saw is on the identification parade until they have looked at each member at least twice.

17.   When the officer or civilian support staff (see paragraph 3.11) conducting the identification procedure is satisfied the witness has properly looked at each member of the identification parade, they shall ask the witness whether the person they saw on a specified earlier occasion is on the identification parade and, if so, to indicate the number of the person concerned, see paragraph 28.

18.   If the witness wishes to hear any identification parade member speak, adopt any specified posture or move, they shall first be asked whether they can identify any person(s) on the identification parade on the basis of appearance only. When the request is to hear members of the identification parade speak, the witness shall be reminded that the participants in the identification parade have been chosen on the basis of physical appearance only. Members of the identification parade may then be asked to comply with the witness' request to hear them speak, see them move or adopt any specified posture.

19.   If the witness requests that the person they have indicated remove anything used for the purposes of paragraph 10 to conceal the location of an unusual physical feature, that person may be asked to remove it.

20. If the witness makes an identification after the identification parade has ended, the suspect and, if present, their solicitor, interpreter or friend shall be informed. When this occurs, consideration should be given to allowing the witness a second opportunity to identify the suspect.

21. After the procedure, each witness shall be asked whether they have seen any broadcast or published films or photographs or any descriptions of suspects relating to the offence and their reply shall be recorded.

22. When the last witness has left, the suspect shall be asked whether they wish to make any comments on the conduct of the identification parade.

(d) Documentation

23. A video recording must normally be taken of the identification parade. If that is impracticable, a colour photograph must be taken. A copy of the video recording or photograph shall be supplied, on request, to the suspect or their solicitor within a reasonable time.

24. As appropriate, paragraph 3.30 or 3.31, should apply to any photograph or video taken as in paragraph 23.

25. If any person is asked to leave an identification parade because they are interfering with its conduct, the circumstances shall be recorded.

26. A record must be made of all those present at an identification parade whose names are known to the police.

27. If prison inmates make up an identification parade, the circumstances must be recorded.

28. A record of the conduct of any identification parade must be made on forms provided for the purpose. This shall include anything said by the witness or the suspect about any identifications or the conduct of the procedure, and any reasons it was not practicable to comply with any of this Code's provisions.

ANNEX C – GROUP IDENTIFICATION

(a) General

1. The purpose of this Annex is to make sure, as far as possible, group identifications follow the principles and procedures for identification parades so the conditions are fair to the suspect in the way they test the witness' ability to make an identification.

2. Group identifications may take place either with the suspect's consent and co-operation or covertly without their consent.

3. The location of the group identification is a matter for the identification officer, although the officer may take into account any representations made by the suspect, appropriate adult, their solicitor or friend.

4. The place where the group identification is held should be one where other people are either passing by or waiting around informally, in groups such that the suspect is able to join them and be capable of being seen by the witness at the same time as others in the group. For example people leaving an escalator, pedestrians walking through a shopping centre, passengers on railway and bus stations, waiting in queues or groups or where people are standing or sitting in groups in other public places.

5. If the group identification is to be held covertly, the choice of locations will be limited by the places where the suspect can be found and the number of other people present at that time. In these cases, suitable locations might be along regular routes travelled by the suspect, including buses or trains or public places frequented by the suspect.

6. Although the number, age, sex, race and general description and style of clothing of other people present at the location cannot be controlled by the identification officer, in selecting the location the officer must consider the general appearance and numbers of people likely to be present. In particular, the officer must reasonably expect that over the period the witness observes the group, they will be able to see, from time to time, a number of others whose appearance is broadly similar to that of the suspect.

7. A group identification need not be held if the identification officer believes, because of the unusual appearance of the suspect, none of the locations it would be practicable to use satisfy the requirements of paragraph 6 necessary to make the identification fair.

8. Immediately after a group identification procedure has taken place (with or without the suspect's consent), a colour photograph or video should be taken of the general scene, if practicable, to give a general impression of the scene and the number of people present. Alternatively, if it is practicable, the group identification may be video recorded.

9. If it is not practicable to take the photograph or video in accordance with paragraph 8, a photograph or film of the scene should be taken later at a time determined by the identification officer if the officer considers it practicable to do so.

10. An identification carried out in accordance with this Code remains a group identification even though, at the time of being seen by the witness, the suspect was on their own rather than in a group.

11. Before the group identification takes place, the suspect or their solicitor shall be provided with details of the first description of the suspect by any witnesses who are to attend the identification. When a broadcast or publication is made, as in paragraph 3.28, the suspect or their solicitor should also be allowed to view any material released by the police to the media for the purposes of recognising or tracing the suspect, provided that it is practicable and would not unreasonably delay the investigation.

12. After the procedure, each witness shall be asked whether they have seen any broadcast or published films or photographs or any descriptions of suspects relating to the offence and their reply recorded.

(b) Identification with the consent of the suspect

13. A suspect must be given a reasonable opportunity to have a solicitor or friend present. They shall be asked to indicate on a second copy of the notice whether or not they wish to do so.

14. The witness, the person carrying out the procedure and the suspect's solicitor, appropriate adult, friend or any interpreter for the witness, may be concealed from the sight of the individuals in the group they are observing, if the person carrying out the procedure considers this assists the conduct of the identification.

15. The person conducting a witness to a group identification must not discuss with them the forthcoming group identification and, in particular, must not disclose whether a previous witness has made any identification.

16. Anything said to, or by, the witness during the procedure about the identification should be said in the presence and hearing of those present at the procedure.

17. Appropriate arrangements must be made to make sure, before witnesses attend the group identification, they are not able to:

    (i) communicate with each other about the case or overhear a witness who has already been given an opportunity to see the suspect in the group;

    (ii) see the suspect; or

    (iii) see, or be reminded of, any photographs or description of the suspect or be given any other indication of the suspect's identity.

18. Witnesses shall be brought one at a time to the place where they are to observe the group. Immediately before the witness is asked to look at the group, the person conducting the procedure shall tell them that the person they saw may, or may not, be in the group and that if they cannot make a positive identification, they should say so. The witness shall be asked to observe the group in which the suspect is to appear. The way in which the witness should do this will depend on whether the group is moving or stationary.

Moving group

19. When the group in which the suspect is to appear is moving, e.g. leaving an escalator, the provisions of paragraphs 20 to 24 should be followed.

20. If two or more suspects consent to a group identification, each should be the subject of separate identification procedures. These may be conducted consecutively on the same occasion.

21. The person conducting the procedure shall tell the witness to observe the group and ask them to point out any person they think they saw on the specified earlier occasion.

22. Once the witness has been informed as in paragraph 21 the suspect should be allowed to take whatever position in the group they wish.

23. When the witness points out a person as in paragraph 21 they shall, if practicable, be asked to take a closer look at the person to confirm the identification. If this is not practicable, or they cannot confirm the identification, they shall be asked how sure they are that the person they have indicated is the relevant person.

24. The witness should continue to observe the group for the period which the person conducting the procedure reasonably believes is necessary in the circumstances for them to be able to make comparisons between the suspect and other individuals of broadly similar appearance to the suspect as in paragraph 6.

Stationary groups

25. When the group in which the suspect is to appear is stationary, e.g. people waiting in a queue, the provisions of paragraphs 26 to 29 should be followed.

26. If two or more suspects consent to a group identification, each should be subject to separate identification procedures unless they are of broadly similar appearance when they may appear in the same group. When separate group identifications are held, the groups must be made up of different people.

27. The suspect may take whatever position in the group they wish. If there is more than one witness, the suspect must be told, out of the sight and hearing of any witness, that they can, if they wish, change their position in the group.

28.   The witness shall be asked to pass along, or amongst, the group and to look at each person in the group at least twice, taking as much care and time as possible according to the circumstances, before making an identification. Once the witness has done this, they shall be asked whether the person they saw on the specified earlier occasion is in the group and to indicate any such person by whatever means the person conducting the procedure considers appropriate in the circumstances. If this is not practicable, the witness shall be asked to point out any person they think they saw on the earlier occasion.

29.   When the witness makes an indication as in paragraph 28, arrangements shall be made, if practicable, for the witness to take a closer look at the person to confirm the identification. If this is not practicable, or the witness is unable to confirm the identification, they shall be asked how sure they are that the person they have indicated is the relevant person.

All cases

30.   If the suspect unreasonably delays joining the group, or having joined the group, deliberately conceals themselves from the sight of the witness, this may be treated as a refusal to co-operate in a group identification.

31.   If the witness identifies a person other than the suspect, that person should be informed what has happened and asked if they are prepared to give their name and address. There is no obligation upon any member of the public to give these details. There shall be no duty to record any details of any other member of the public present in the group or at the place where the procedure is conducted.

32.   When the group identification has been completed, the suspect shall be asked whether they wish to make any comments on the conduct of the procedure.

33.   If the suspect has not been previously informed, they shall be told of any identifications made by the witnesses.

(c)   Identification without the suspect's consent

34.   Group identifications held covertly without the suspect's consent should, as far as practicable, follow the rules for conduct of group identification by consent.

35.   A suspect has no right to have a solicitor, appropriate adult or friend present as the identification will take place without the knowledge of the suspect.

36.   Any number of suspects may be identified at the same time.

(d)   Identifications in police stations

37.   Group identifications should take place in police stations only for reasons of safety, security or because it is not practicable to hold them elsewhere.

38.   The group identification may take place either in a room equipped with a screen permitting witnesses to see members of the group without being seen, or anywhere else in the police station that the identification officer considers appropriate.

39.   Any of the additional safeguards applicable to identification parades should be followed if the identification officer considers it is practicable to do so in the circumstances.

(e) Identifications involving prison inmates

40.   A group identification involving a prison inmate may only be arranged in the prison or at a police station.

41.   When a group identification takes place involving a prison inmate, whether in a prison or in a police station, the arrangements should follow those in paragraphs 37 to 39. If a group identification takes place within a prison, other inmates may participate. If an inmate is the suspect, they do not have to wear prison clothing for the group identification unless the other participants are wearing the same clothing.

(f) Documentation

42.   When a photograph or video is taken as in paragraph 8 or 9, a copy of the photograph or video shall be supplied on request to the suspect or their solicitor within a reasonable time.

43.   Paragraph 3.30 or 3.31, as appropriate, shall apply when the photograph or film taken in accordance with paragraph 8 or 9 includes the suspect.

44.   A record of the conduct of any group identification must be made on forms provided for the purpose. This shall include anything said by the witness or suspect about any identifications or the conduct of the procedure and any reasons why it was not practicable to comply with any of the provisions of this Code governing the conduct of group identifications.

ANNEX D – CONFRONTATION BY A WITNESS

1.   Before the confrontation takes place, the witness must be told that the person they saw may, or may not, be the person they are to confront and that if they are not that person, then the witness should say so.

2.   Before the confrontation takes place the suspect or their solicitor shall be provided with details of the first description of the suspect given by any witness who is to attend. When a broadcast or publication is made, as in paragraph 3.28, the suspect or their solicitor should also be allowed to view any material released to the media for the purposes of recognising or tracing the suspect, provided it is practicable to do so and would not unreasonably delay the investigation.

3.   Force may not be used to make the suspect's face visible to the witness.

4.   Confrontation must take place in the presence of the suspect's solicitor, interpreter or friend unless this would cause unreasonable delay.

5.   The suspect shall be confronted independently by each witness, who shall be asked 'Is this the person?'. If the witness identifies the person but is unable to confirm the identification, they shall be asked how sure they are that the person is the one they saw on the earlier occasion.

6.   The confrontation should normally take place in the police station, either in a normal room or one equipped with a screen permitting a witness to see the suspect without being seen. In both cases, the procedures are the same except that a room equipped with a screen may be used only when the suspect's solicitor, friend or appropriate adult is present or the confrontation is recorded on video.

7.   After the procedure, each witness shall be asked whether they have seen any broadcast or published films or photographs or any descriptions of suspects relating to the offence and their reply shall be recorded.

ANNEX E – SHOWING PHOTOGRAPHS

(a) Action

1. An officer of sergeant rank or above shall be responsible for supervising and directing the showing of photographs. The actual showing may be done by another officer or police staff, see paragraph 3.11.

2. The supervising officer must confirm the first description of the suspect given by the witness has been recorded before they are shown the photographs. If the supervising officer is unable to confirm the description has been recorded they shall postpone showing the photographs.

3. Only one witness shall be shown photographs at any one time. Each witness shall be given as much privacy as practicable and shall not be allowed to communicate with any other witness in the case.

4. The witness shall be shown not less than twelve photographs at a time, which shall, as far as possible, all be of a similar type.

5. When the witness is shown the photographs, they shall be told the photograph of the person they saw may, or may not, be amongst them and if they cannot make a positive identification, they should say so. The witness shall also be told they should not make a decision until they have viewed at least twelve photographs. The witness shall not be prompted or guided in any way but shall be left to make any selection without help.

6. If a witness makes a positive identification from photographs, unless the person identified is otherwise eliminated from enquiries or is not available, other witnesses shall not be shown photographs. But both they, and the witness who has made the identification, shall be asked to attend a video identification, an identification parade or group identification unless there is no dispute about the suspect's identification.

7. If the witness makes a selection but is unable to confirm the identification, the person showing the photographs shall ask them how sure they are that the photograph they have indicated is the person they saw on the specified earlier occasion.

8. When the use of a computerised or artist's composite or similar likeness has led to there being a known suspect who can be asked to participate in a video identification, appear on an identification parade or participate in a group identification, that likeness shall not be shown to other potential witnesses.

9. When a witness attending a video identification, an identification parade or group identification has previously been shown photographs or computerised or artist's composite or similar likeness (and it is the responsibility of the officer in charge of the investigation to make the identification officer aware that this is the case), the suspect and their solicitor must be informed of this fact before the identification procedure takes place.

10. None of the photographs shown shall be destroyed, whether or not an identification is made, since they may be required for production in court. The photographs shall be numbered and a separate photograph taken of the frame or part of the album from which the witness made an identification as an aid to reconstituting it.

(b) Documentation

11. Whether or not an identification is made, a record shall be kept of the showing of photographs on forms provided for the purpose. This shall include anything said by the witness about any identification or the conduct of the procedure, any reasons

it was not practicable to comply with any of the provisions of this Code governing the showing of photographs and the name and rank of the supervising officer.

12. The supervising officer shall inspect and sign the record as soon as practicable.

ANNEX F – FINGERPRINTS, FOOTWEAR IMPRESSIONS AND SAMPLES – DESTRUCTION AND SPECULATIVE SEARCHES

(a) Fingerprints, footwear impressions and samples taken in connection with a criminal investigation

1. When fingerprints, footwear impressions or DNA samples are taken from a person in connection with an investigation and the person is not suspected of having committed the offence, see Note F1, they must be destroyed as soon as they have fulfilled the purpose for which they were taken unless:

(a) they were taken for the purposes of an investigation of an offence for which a person has been convicted; and

(b) fingerprints, footwear impressions or samples were also taken from the convicted person for the purposes of that investigation.

However, subject to paragraph 2, the fingerprints, footwear impressions and samples, and the information derived from samples, may not be used in the investigation of any offence or in evidence against the person who is, or would be, entitled to the destruction of the fingerprints, footwear impressions and samples, see Note F2.

2. The requirement to destroy fingerprints, footwear impressions and DNA samples, and information derived from samples, and restrictions on their retention and use in paragraph 1 do not apply if the person gives their written consent for their fingerprints, footwear impressions or sample to be retained and used after they have fulfilled the purpose for which they were taken, see Note F1.

3. When a person's fingerprints, footwear impressions or sample are to be destroyed:

(a) any copies of the fingerprints and footwear impressions must also be destroyed;

(b) the person may witness the destruction of their fingerprints, footwear impressions or copies if they ask to do so within five days of being informed destruction is required;

(c) access to relevant computer fingerprint data shall be made impossible as soon as it is practicable to do so and the person shall be given a certificate to this effect within three months of asking; and

(d) neither the fingerprints, footwear impressions, the sample, or any information derived from the sample, may be used in the investigation of any offence or in evidence against the person who is, or would be, entitled to its destruction.

4. Fingerprints, footwear impressions or samples, and the information derived from samples, taken in connection with the investigation of an offence which are not required to be destroyed, may be retained after they have fulfilled the purposes for which they were taken but may be used only for purposes related to the prevention or detection of crime, the investigation of an offence or the conduct of a prosecution in, as well as outside, the UK and may also be subject to a speculative search. This includes checking them against other fingerprints, footwear impressions and DNA records held by, or on behalf of, the police and other law enforcement authorities in, as well as outside, the UK.

(b)   Fingerprints taken in connection with Immigration Service enquiries

5.   Fingerprints taken for Immigration Service enquiries in accordance with powers and procedures other than under PACE and for which the Immigration Service, not the police, are responsible, must be destroyed as follows:

(a)   fingerprints and all copies must be destroyed as soon as practicable if the person from whom they were taken proves they are a British or Commonwealth citizen who has the right of abode in the UK under the Immigration Act 1971, section 2(1)(b);

(b)   fingerprints taken under the power as in paragraph 4.11(g) from a dependant of a person in 4.11 (b) to (f) must be destroyed when that person's fingerprints are to be destroyed;

(c)   fingerprints taken from a person under any power as in paragraph 4.11 or with the person's consent which have not already been destroyed as above, must be destroyed within ten years of being taken or within such period specified by the Secretary of State under the Immigration and Asylum Act 1999, section 143(5).

Notes for Guidance

F1   Fingerprints, footwear impressions and samples given voluntarily for the purposes of elimination play an important part in many police investigations. It is, therefore, important to make sure innocent volunteers are not deterred from participating and their consent to their fingerprints, footwear impressions and DNA being used for the purposes of a specific investigation is fully informed and voluntary. If the police or volunteer seek to have the fingerprints, footwear impressions or samples retained for use after the specific investigation ends, it is important the volunteer's consent to this is also fully informed and voluntary.

Examples of consent for:

- *DNA/fingerprints/footwear impressions – to be used only for the purposes of a specific investigation;*
- *DNA/fingerprints/footwear impressions – to be used in the specific investigation **and** retained by the police for future use.*

*To minimise the risk of confusion, each consent should be physically separate and the volunteer should be asked to sign **each consent**.*

(a) DNA:

(i)   DNA sample taken for the purposes of elimination or as part of an intelligence-led screen and to be used only for the purposes of that investigation and destroyed afterwards:

'I consent to my DNA/mouth swab being taken for forensic analysis. I understand that the sample will be destroyed at the end of the case and that my profile will only be compared to the crime stain profile from this enquiry. I have been advised that the person taking the sample may be required to give evidence and/or provide a written statement to the police in relation to the taking of it.'

(ii)   DNA sample to be retained on the National DNA database and used in the future:

'I consent to my DNA sample and information derived from it being retained and used only for purposes related to the prevention and detection of a crime, the investigation of an offence or the conduct of a prosecution either nationally or internationally.'

'I understand that this sample may be checked against other DNA records held by, or on behalf of, relevant law enforcement authorities, either nationally or internationally.'

'I understand that once I have given my consent for the sample to be retained and used I cannot withdraw this consent.'

(b) Fingerprints:

    (i) Fingerprints taken for the purposes of elimination or as part of an intelligence-led screen and to be used only for the purposes of that investigation and destroyed afterwards:

    'I consent to my fingerprints being taken for elimination purposes. I understand that the fingerprints will be destroyed at the end of the case and that my fingerprints will only be compared to the fingerprints from this enquiry. I have been advised that the person taking the fingerprints may be required to give evidence and/or provide a written statement to the police in relation to the taking of it.'

    (ii) Fingerprints to be retained for future use:

    'I consent to my fingerprints being retained and used only for purposes related to the prevention and detection of a crime, the investigation of an offence or the conduct of a prosecution either nationally or internationally.'

    'I understand that my fingerprints may be checked against other records held by, or on behalf of, relevant law enforcement authorities, either nationally or internationally.'

    'I understand that once I have given my consent for my fingerprints to be retained and used I cannot withdraw this consent.'

(c) Footwear impressions:

    (i) Footwear impressions taken for the purposes of elimination or as part of an intelligence-led screening and to be used only for the purposes of that investigation and destroyed afterwards:

    'I consent to my footwear impressions being taken for elimination purposes. I understand that the footwear impressions will be destroyed at the end of the case and that my footwear impressions will only be compared to the footwear impressions from this enquiry. I have been advised that the person taking the footwear impressions may be required to give evidence and/or provide a written statement to the police in relation to the taking of it.'

    (ii) Footwear impressions to be retained for future use:

    'I consent to my footwear impressions being retained and used only for purposes related to the prevention and detection of a crime, the investigation of an offence or the conduct of a prosecution, either nationally or internationally'.

    'I understand that my footwear impressions may be checked against other records held by, or on behalf of, relevant law enforcement authorities, either nationally or internationally.'

'I understand that once I have given my consent for my footwear impressions to be retained and used I cannot withdraw this consent.'

F2 The provisions for the retention of fingerprints, footwear impressions and samples in paragraph 1 allow for all fingerprints, footwear impressions and samples in a case to be available for any subsequent miscarriage of justice investigation.

CODE E: ON AUDIO RECORDING INTERVIEWS WITH SUSPECTS

Commencement – Transitional Arrangements

This code applies to interviews carried out after midnight on 31 December 2005, notwithstanding that the interview may have commenced before that time.

1 GENERAL

1.1 This Code of Practice must be readily available for consultation by:
- police officers
- police staff
- detained persons
- members of the public.

1.2 The Notes for Guidance included are not provisions of this Code.

1.3 Nothing in this Code shall detract from the requirements of Code C, the Code of Practice for the detention, treatment and questioning of persons by police officers.

1.4 This Code does not apply to those people listed in Code C, paragraph 1.12.

1.5 The term:
- 'appropriate adult' has the same meaning as in Code C, paragraph 1.7
- 'solicitor' has the same meaning as in Code C, paragraph 6.12.

1.6 In this Code:
- (aa) 'recording media' means any removable, physical audio recording medium (such as magnetic type, optical disc or solid state memory) which can be played and copied;
- (a) 'designated person' means a person other than a police officer, designated under the Police Reform Act 2002, Part 4 who has specified powers and duties of police officers conferred or imposed on them;
- (b) any reference to a police officer includes a designated person acting in the exercise or performance of the powers and duties conferred or imposed on them by their designation.

1.7 If a power conferred on a designated person:
- (a) allows reasonable force to be used when exercised by a police officer, a designated person exercising that power has the same entitlement to use force;
- (b) includes power to use force to enter any premises, that power is not exercisable by that designated person except:
  - (i) in the company, and under the supervision, of a police officer; or
  - (ii) for the purpose of:
    - saving life or limb; or
    - preventing serious damage to property.

1.8 Nothing in this Code prevents the custody officer, or other officer given custody of the detainee, from allowing police staff who are not designated persons to carry out individual procedures or tasks at the police station if the law allows. However, the officer remains responsible for making sure the procedures and tasks are carried out correctly in accordance with these Codes. Any such police staff must be:
- (a) a person employed by a police authority maintaining a police force and under the control and direction of the Chief Officer of that force; or

(b)   employed by a person with whom a police authority has a contract for the provision of services relating to persons arrested or otherwise in custody.

1.9   Designated persons and other police staff must have regard to any relevant provisions of the Codes of Practice.

1.10   References to pocket book include any official report book issued to police officers or police staff.

1.11   References to a custody officer include those performing the functions of a custody officer as in paragraph 1.9 of Code C.

2   RECORDING AND SEALING MASTER RECORDINGS

2.1   Recording of interviews shall be carried out openly to instil confidence in its reliability as an impartial and accurate record of the interview.

2.2   One recording, the master recording, will be sealed in the suspect's presence. A second recording will be used as a working copy. The master recording is either of the two recordings used in a twin deck/drive machine or the only recording in a single deck/drive machine. The working copy is either the second/third recording used in a twin/triple deck/drive machine or a copy of the master recording made by a single deck/drive machine. See Notes 2A and 2B.

2.3   Nothing in this Code requires the identity of officers or police staff conducting interviews to be recorded or disclosed:

(a)   in the case of enquiries linked to the investigation of terrorism; or

(b)   if the interviewer reasonably believes recording or disclosing their name might put them in danger.

In these cases interviewers should use warrant or other identification numbers and the name of their police station. See Note 2C.

Notes for Guidance

2A   The purpose of sealing the master recording in the suspect's presence is to show the recording's integrity is preserved. If a single deck/drive machine is used the working copy of the master recording must be made in the suspect's presence and without the master recording leaving their sight. The working copy shall be used for making further copies if needed.

2B   Not used.

2C   The purpose of paragraph 2.3(b) is to protect those involved in serious organised crime investigations or arrests of particularly violent suspects when there is reliable information that those arrested or their associates may threaten or cause harm to those involved. In cases of doubt, an officer of inspector rank or above should be consulted.

3   INTERVIEWS TO BE AUDIO RECORDED

3.1   Subject to paragraphs 3.3 and 3.4, audio recording shall be used at police stations for any interview:

(a)   with a person cautioned under Code C, section 10 in respect of any indictable offence, including an offence triable either way; see Note 3A;

(b)   which takes place as a result of an interviewer exceptionally putting further questions to a suspect about an offence described in paragraph 3.1(a) after

461

they have been charged with, or told they may be prosecuted for, that offence, see Code C, paragraph 16.5;

(c) when an interviewer wants to tell a person, after they have been charged with, or informed they may be prosecuted for, an offence described in paragraph 3.1(a), about any written statement or interview with another person, see Code C, paragraph 16.4.

3.2 The Terrorism Act 2000 makes separate provision for a Code of Practice for the audio recording of interviews of those arrested under Section 41 or detained under Schedule 7 of the Act. The provisions of this Code do not apply to such interviews.

3.3 The custody officer may authorise the interviewer not to audio record the interview when it is:

(a) not reasonably practicable because of equipment failure or the unavailability of a suitable interview room or recorder and the authorising officer considers, on reasonable grounds, that the interview should not be delayed; or

(b) clear from the outset there will not be a prosecution.

Note: In these cases the interview should be recorded in writing in accordance with Code C, section 11. In all cases the custody officer shall record the specific reasons for not audio recording. See Note 3B.

3.4 If a person refuses to go into or remain in a suitable interview room, see Code C paragraph 12.5, and the custody officer considers, on reasonable grounds, that the interview should not be delayed the interview may, at the custody officer's discretion, be conducted in a cell using portable recording equipment or, if none is available, recorded in writing as in Code C, section 11. The reasons for this shall be recorded.

3.5 The whole of each interview shall be audio recorded, including the taking and reading back of any statement.

Notes for Guidance

3A Nothing in this Code is intended to preclude audio recording at police discretion of interviews at police stations with people cautioned in respect of offences not covered by paragraph 3.1, or responses made by persons after they have been charged with, or told they may be prosecuted for, an offence, provided this Code is complied with.

3B A decision not to audio record an interview for any reason may be the subject of comment in court. The authorising officer should be prepared to justify that decision.

4 THE INTERVIEW

(a) General

4.1 The provisions of Code C:

• sections 10 and 11, and the applicable Notes for Guidance apply to the conduct of interviews to which this Code applies
• paragraphs 11.7 to 11.14 apply only when a written record is needed.

4.2 Code C, paragraphs 10.10, 10.11 and Annex C describe the restriction on drawing adverse inferences from a suspect's failure or refusal to say anything about their involvement in the offence when interviewed or after being charged or informed they may be prosecuted, and how it affects the terms of the caution and determines if and by whom a special warning under sections 36 and 37 can be given.

(b) Commencement of interviews

4.3   When the suspect is brought into the interview room the interviewer shall, without delay but in the suspect's sight, load the recorder with new recording media and set it to record. The recording media must be unwrapped or opened in the suspect's presence.

4.4   The interviewer should tell the suspect about the recording process. The interviewer shall:

(a)   say the interview is being audibly recorded

(b)   subject to paragraph 2.3, give their name and rank and that of any other interviewer present

(c)   ask the suspect and any other party present, e.g. a solicitor, to identify themselves

(d)   state the date, time of commencement and place of the interview

(e)   state the suspect will be given a notice about what will happen to the copies of the recording.

See Note 4A.

4.5   The interviewer shall:

- caution the suspect, see Code C, section 10
- remind the suspect of their entitlement to free legal advice, see Code C, paragraph 11.2.

4.6   The interviewer shall put to the suspect any significant statement or silence; see Code C, paragraph 11.4.

(c) Interviews with deaf persons

4.7   If the suspect is deaf or is suspected of having impaired hearing, the interviewer shall make a written note of the interview in accordance with Code C, at the same time as audio recording it in accordance with this Code. See Notes 4B and 4C.

(d) Objections and complaints by the suspect

4.8   If the suspect objects to the interview being audibly recorded at the outset, during the interview or during a break, the interviewer shall explain that the interview is being audibly recorded and that this Code requires the suspect's objections to be recorded on the audio recording. When any objections have been audibly recorded or the suspect has refused to have their objections recorded, the interviewer shall say they are turning off the recorder, give their reasons and turn it off. The interviewer shall then make a written record of the interview as in Code C, section 11. If, however, the interviewer reasonably considers they may proceed to question the suspect with the audio recording still on, the interviewer may do so. This procedure also applies in cases where the suspect has previously objected to the interview being visually recorded, see Code F 4.8, and the investigating officer has decided to audibly record the interview. See Note 4D.

4.9   If in the course of an interview a complaint is made by or on behalf of the person being questioned concerning the provisions of this Code or Code C, the interviewer shall act as in Code C, paragraph 12.9. See Notes 4E and 4F.

4.10   If the suspect indicates they want to tell the interviewer about matters not directly connected with the offence and they are unwilling for these matters to be audio recorded, the suspect should be given the opportunity to tell the interviewer at the end of the formal interview.

(e) Changing recording media

4.11   When the recorder shows the recording media have only a short time left, the interviewer shall tell the suspect the recording media are coming to an end and round off that part of the interview. If the interviewer leaves the room for a second set of recording media, the suspect shall not be left unattended. The interviewer will remove the recording media from the recorder and insert the new recording media which shall be unwrapped or opened in the suspect's presence. The recorder should be set to record on the new media. To avoid confusion between the recording media, the interviewer shall mark the media with an identification number immediately they are removed from the recorder.

(f) Taking a break during interview

4.12   When a break is taken, the fact that a break is to be taken, the reason for it and the time shall be recorded on the audio recording.

4.12A   When the break is taken and the interview room vacated by the suspect, the recording media shall be removed from the recorder and the procedures for the conclusion of an interview followed; see paragraph 4.18.

4.13   When a break is a short one and both the suspect and an interviewer remain in the interview room, the recording may be stopped. There is no need to remove the recording media and when the interview recommences the recording should continue on the same recording media. The time the interview recommences shall be recorded on the audio recording.

4.14   After any break in the interview the interviewer must, before resuming the interview, remind the person being questioned that they remain under caution or, if there is any doubt, give the caution in full again. See Note 4G.

(g) Failure of recording equipment

4.15   If there is an equipment failure which can be rectified quickly, e.g. by inserting new recording media, the interviewer shall follow the appropriate procedures as in paragraph 4.11. When the recording is resumed the interviewer shall explain what happened and record the time the interview recommences. If, however, it will not be possible to continue recording on that recorder and no replacement recorder is readily available, the interview may continue without being audibly recorded. If this happens, the interviewer shall seek the custody officer's authority as in paragraph 3.3. See Note 4H.

(h) Removing recording media from the recorder

4.16   When recording media is removed from the recorder during the interview, they shall be retained and the procedures in paragraph 4.18 followed.

(i) Conclusion of interview

4.17   At the conclusion of the interview, the suspect shall be offered the opportunity to clarify anything he or she has said and asked if there is anything they want to add.

4.18   At the conclusion of the interview, including the taking and reading back of any written statement, the time shall be recorded and the recording shall be stopped. The interviewer shall seal the master recording with a master recording label and treat it as an exhibit in accordance with force standing orders. The interviewer shall sign the label and ask the suspect and any third party present during the interview to sign it. If the suspect or third party refuse to sign the label an officer of at least inspector rank, or if not available the custody officer, shall be called into the interview room and asked, subject to paragraph 2.3, to sign it.

4.19   The suspect shall be handed a notice which explains:

- how the audio recording will be used
- the arrangements for access to it
- that if the person is charged or informed they will be prosecuted, a copy of the audio recording will be supplied as soon as practicable or as otherwise agreed between the suspect and the police.

Notes for Guidance

4A   For the purpose of voice identification the interviewer should ask the suspect and any other people present to identify themselves.

4B   This provision is to give a person who is deaf or has impaired hearing equivalent rights of access to the full interview record as far as this is possible using audio recording.

4C   The provisions of Code C, section 13 on interpreters for deaf persons or for interviews with suspects who have difficulty understanding English continue to apply. However, in an audibly recorded interview the requirement on the interviewer to make sure the interpreter makes a separate note of the interview applies only to paragraph 4.7 (interviews with deaf persons).

4D   The interviewer should remember that a decision to continue recording against the wishes of the suspect may be the subject of comment in court.

4E   If the custody officer is called to deal with the complaint, the recorder should, if possible, be left on until the custody officer has entered the room and spoken to the person being interviewed. Continuation or termination of the interview should be at the interviewer's discretion pending action by an inspector under Code C, paragraph 9.2.

4F   If the complaint is about a matter not connected with this Code or Code C, the decision to continue is at the interviewer's discretion. When the interviewer decides to continue the interview, they shall tell the suspect the complaint will be brought to the custody officer's attention at the conclusion of the interview. When the interview is concluded the interviewer must, as soon as practicable, inform the custody officer about the existence and nature of the complaint made.

4G   The interviewer should remember that it may be necessary to show to the court that nothing occurred during a break or between interviews which influenced the suspect's recorded evidence. After a break or at the beginning of a subsequent interview, the interviewer should consider summarising on the record the reason for the break and confirming this with the suspect.

4H   Where the interview is being recorded and the media or the recording equipment fails the officer conducting the interview should stop the interview immediately. Where part of the interview is unaffected by the error and is still accessible on the media, that media shall be copied and sealed in the suspect's presence and the interview recommenced using new equipment/media as required. Where the content of the interview has been lost in its entirety the media should be sealed in the suspect's presence and the interview begun again. If the recording equipment cannot be fixed or no replacement is immediately available the interview should be recorded in accordance with Code C, section 11.

5 AFTER THE INTERVIEW

5.1 The interviewer shall make a note in their pocket book that the interview has taken place, was audibly recorded, its time, duration and date and the master recording's identification number.

5.2 If no proceedings follow in respect of the person whose interview was recorded, the recording media must be kept securely as in paragraph 6.1 and Note 6A.

Note for Guidance

5A   Any written record of an audibly recorded interview should be made in accordance with national guidelines approved by the Secretary of State.

6 MEDIA SECURITY

6.1 The officer in charge of each police station at which interviews with suspects are recorded shall make arrangements for master recordings to be kept securely and their movements accounted for on the same basis as material which may be used for evidential purposes, in accordance with force standing orders. See Note 6A.

6.2 A police officer has no authority to break the seal on a master recording required for criminal trial or appeal proceedings. If it is necessary to gain access to the master recording, the police officer shall arrange for its seal to be broken in the presence of a representative of the Crown Prosecution Service. The defendant or their legal adviser should be informed and given a reasonable opportunity to be present. If the defendant or their legal representative is present they shall be invited to reseal and sign the master recording. If either refuses or neither is present this should be done by the representative of the Crown Prosecution Service. See Notes 6B and 6C.

6.3 If no criminal proceedings result or the criminal trial and, if applicable, appeal proceedings to which the interview relates have been concluded, the chief officer of police is responsible for establishing arrangements for breaking the seal on the master recording, if necessary.

6.4 When the master recording seal is broken, a record must be made of the procedure followed, including the date, time, place and persons present.

Notes for Guidance

6A   This section is concerned with the security of the master recording sealed at the conclusion of the interview. Care must be taken of working copies of recordings because their loss or destruction may lead to the need to access master recordings.

6B   If the recording has been delivered to the crown court for their keeping after committal for trial the crown prosecutor will apply to the chief clerk of the crown court centre for the release of the recording for unsealing by the crown prosecutor.

6C   Reference to the Crown Prosecution Service or to the crown prosecutor in this part of the Code should be taken to include any other body or person with a statutory responsibility for prosecution for whom the police conduct any audibly recorded interviews.

CODE F: ON VISUAL RECORDING WITH SOUND OF INTERVIEWS WITH SUSPECTS

Commencement – Transitional Arrangements

The contents of this code should be considered if an interviewing officer decides to make a visual recording with sound of an interview with a suspect after midnight on 31 December 2005

There is no statutory requirement to visually record interviews.

1 GENERAL

1.1 This code of practice must be readily available for consultation by police officers and other police staff, detained persons and members of the public.

1.2 The notes for guidance included are not provisions of this code. They form guidance to police officers and others about its application and interpretation.

1.3 Nothing in this code shall be taken as detracting in any way from the requirements of the Code of Practice for the Detention, Treatment and Questioning of Persons by Police Officers (Code C). See Note 1A.

1.4 The interviews to which this Code applies are set out in paragraphs 3.1–3.3.

1.5 In this code, the term 'appropriate adult', 'solicitor' and 'interview' have the same meaning as those set out in Code C. The corresponding provisions and Notes for Guidance in Code C applicable to those terms shall also apply where appropriate.

1.6 Any reference in this code to visual recording shall be taken to mean visual recording with sound.

1.7 References to 'pocket book' in this Code include any official report book issued to police officers.

Note for Guidance

1A As in paragraph 1.9 of Code C, references to custody officers include those carrying out the functions of a custody officer.

2 RECORDING AND SEALING OF MASTER TAPES

2.1 The visual recording of interviews shall be carried out openly to instil confidence in its reliability as an impartial and accurate record of the interview. See Note 2A.

2.2 The camera(s) shall be placed in the interview room so as to ensure coverage of as much of the room as is practicably possible while the interviews are taking place.

2.3 The certified recording medium will be of a high quality, new and previously unused. When the certified recording medium is placed in the recorder and switched on to record, the correct date and time, in hours, minutes and seconds, will be superimposed automatically, second by second, during the whole recording. See Note 2B.

2.4 One copy of the certified recording medium, referred to in this code as the master copy, will be sealed before it leaves the presence of the suspect. A second copy will be used as a working copy. See Notes 2C and 2D.

2.5 Nothing in this code requires the identity of an officer to be recorded or disclosed if:

(a) the interview or record relates to a person detained under the Terrorism Act 2000; or

   (b)   otherwise where the officer reasonably believes that recording or disclosing their name might put them in danger.

In these cases, the officer will have their back to the camera and shall use their warrant or other identification number and the name of the police station to which they are attached. Such instances and the reasons for them shall be recorded in the custody record. See Note 2E.

Notes for Guidance

2A   Interviewing officers will wish to arrange that, as far as possible, visual recording arrangements are unobtrusive. It must be clear to the suspect, however, that there is no opportunity to interfere with the recording equipment or the recording media.

2B   In this context, the certified recording media will be of either a VHS or digital CD format and should be capable of having an image of the date and time superimposed upon them as they record the interview.

2C   The purpose of sealing the master copy before it leaves the presence of the suspect is to establish their confidence that the integrity of the copy is preserved.

2D   The recording of the interview is not to be used for identification procedures in accordance with paragraph 3.21 or Annex E of Code D.

2E   The purpose of the paragraph 2.5 is to protect police officers and others involved in the investigation of serious organised crime or the arrest of particularly violent suspects when there is reliable information that those arrested or their associates may threaten or cause harm to the officers, their families or their personal property.

3   INTERVIEWS TO BE VISUALLY RECORDED

3.1   Subject to paragraph 3.2 below, if an interviewing officer decides to make a visual recording these are the areas where it might be appropriate:

   (a)   with a suspect in respect of an indictable offence (including an offence triable either way); see Notes 3A and 3B;

   (b)   which takes place as a result of an interviewer exceptionally putting further questions to a suspect about an offence described in sub-paragraph (a) above after they have been charged with, or informed they may be prosecuted for, that offence; see Note 3C;

   (c)   in which an interviewer wishes to bring to the notice of a person, after that person has been charged with, or informed they may be prosecuted for an offence described in sub-paragraph (a) above, any written statement made by another person, or the content of an interview with another person; see Note 3D;

   (d)   with, or in the presence of, a deaf or deaf/blind or speech impaired person who uses sign language to communicate;

   (e)   with, or in the presence of anyone who requires an 'appropriate adult'; or

   (f)   in any case where the suspect or their representative requests that the interview be recorded visually.

3.2   The Terrorism Act 2000 makes separate provision for a code of practice for the video recording of interviews in a police station of those detained under Schedule 7 or section 41 of the Act. The provisions of this code do not therefore apply to such interviews. See Note 3E.

3.3   The custody officer may authorise the interviewing officer not to record the interview visually:

(a) where it is not reasonably practicable to do so because of failure of the equipment, or the non-availability of a suitable interview room, or recorder, and the authorising officer considers on reasonable grounds that the interview should not be delayed until the failure has been rectified or a suitable room or recorder becomes available. In such cases the custody officer may authorise the interviewing officer to audio record the interview in accordance with the guidance set out in Code E;

(b) where it is clear from the outset that no prosecution will ensue; or

(c) where it is not practicable to do so because at the time the person resists being taken to a suitable interview room or other location which would enable the interview to be recorded, or otherwise fails or refuses to go into such a room or location, and the authorising officer considers on reasonable grounds that the interview should not be delayed until these conditions cease to apply.

In all cases the custody officer shall make a note in the custody records of the reasons for not taking a visual record. See Note 3F.

3.4   When a person who is voluntarily attending the police station is required to be cautioned in accordance with Code C prior to being interviewed, the subsequent interview shall be recorded, unless the custody officer gives authority in accordance with the provisions of paragraph 3.3 above for the interview not to be so recorded.

3.5   The whole of each interview shall be recorded visually, including the taking and reading back of any statement.

3.6   A visible illuminated sign or indicator will light and remain on at all times when the recording equipment is activated or capable of recording or transmitting any signal or information.

Notes for Guidance

3A   Nothing in the code is intended to preclude visual recording at police discretion of interviews at police stations with people cautioned in respect of offences not covered by paragraph 3.1, or responses made by interviewees after they have been charged with, or informed they may be prosecuted for, an offence, provided that this code is complied with.

3B   Attention is drawn to the provisions set out in Code C about the matters to be considered when deciding whether a detained person is fit to be interviewed.

3C   Code C sets out the circumstances in which a suspect may be questioned about an offence after being charged with it.

3D   Code C sets out the procedures to be followed when a person's attention is drawn after charge, to a statement made by another person. One method of bringing the content of an interview with another person to the notice of a suspect may be to play him a recording of that interview.

3E   When it only becomes clear during the course of an interview which is being visually recorded that the interviewee may have committed an offence to which paragraph 3.2 applies, the interviewing officer should turn off the recording equipment and the interview should continue in accordance with the provisions of the Terrorism Act 2000.

3F   A decision not to record an interview visually for any reason may be the subject of comment in court. The authorising officer should therefore be prepared to justify their decision in each case.

4 THE INTERVIEW

(a) General

4.1 The provisions of Code C in relation to cautions and interviews and the Notes for Guidance applicable to those provisions shall apply to the conduct of interviews to which this Code applies.

4.2 Particular attention is drawn to those parts of Code C that describe the restrictions on drawing adverse inferences from a suspect's failure or refusal to say anything about their involvement in the offence when interviewed, or after being charged or informed they may be prosecuted and how those restrictions affect the terms of the caution and determine whether a special warning under sections 36 and 37 of the Criminal Justice and Public Order Act 1994 can be given.

(b) Commencement of interviews

4.3 When the suspect is brought into the interview room the interviewer shall without delay, but in sight of the suspect, load the recording equipment and set it to record. The recording media must be unwrapped or otherwise opened in the presence of the suspect. See Note 4A.

4.4 The interviewer shall then tell the suspect formally about the visual recording. The interviewer shall:

    (a) explain the interview is being visually recorded;
    (b) subject to paragraph 2.5, give his or her name and rank, and that of any other interviewer present;
    (c) ask the suspect and any other party present (e.g. his solicitor) to identify themselves.
    (d) state the date, time of commencement and place of the interview; and
    (e) state that the suspect will be given a notice about what will happen to the recording.

4.5 The interviewer shall then caution the suspect, which should follow that set out in Code C, and remind the suspect of their entitlement to free and independent legal advice and that they can speak to a solicitor on the telephone.

4.6 The interviewer shall then put to the suspect any significant statement or silence (i.e. failure or refusal to answer a question or to answer it satisfactorily) which occurred before the start of the interview, and shall ask the suspect whether they wish to confirm or deny that earlier statement or silence or whether they wish to add anything. The definition of a 'significant' statement or silence is the same as that set out in Code C.

(c) Interviews with the deaf

4.7 If the suspect is deaf or there is doubt about their hearing ability, the provisions of Code C on interpreters for the deaf or for interviews with suspects who have difficulty in understanding English continue to apply.

(d) Objections and complaints by the suspect

4.8 If the suspect raises objections to the interview being visually recorded either at the outset or during the interview or during a break in the interview, the interviewer shall explain the fact that the interview is being visually recorded and that the provisions of this code require that the suspect's objections shall be recorded on the visual recording. When any objections have been visually recorded or the suspect has refused to have their objections recorded, the interviewer shall say that they are turning off the recording equipment, give their reasons and turn it off. If a separate audio recording is being maintained, the officer shall ask the person to record the reasons for refusing to agree to visual recording of the interview. Paragraph 4.8 of Code E will apply if the person objects to audio recording of the interview. The officer shall then make a written record of the interview. If the interviewer reasonably considers they may proceed to question the suspect with the visual recording still on, the interviewer may do so. See Note 4G.

4.9   If in the course of an interview a complaint is made by the person being questioned, or on their behalf, concerning the provisions of this code or of Code C, then the interviewer shall act in accordance with Code C, record it in the interview record and inform the custody officer. See Notes 4B and 4C.

4.10   If the suspect indicates that they wish to tell the interviewer about matters not directly connected with the offence of which they are suspected and that they are unwilling for these matters to be recorded, the suspect shall be given the opportunity to tell the interviewer about these matters after the conclusion of the formal interview.

(e)   Changing the recording media

4.11   In instances where the recording medium is not of sufficient length to record all of the interview with the suspect, further certified recording medium will be used. When the recording equipment indicates that the recording medium has only a short time left to run, the interviewer shall advise the suspect and round off that part of the interview. If the interviewer wishes to continue the interview but does not already have further certified recording media with him, they shall obtain a set. The suspect should not be left unattended in the interview room. The interviewer will remove the recording media from the recording equipment and insert the new ones which have been unwrapped or otherwise opened in the suspect's presence. The recording equipment shall then be set to record. Care must be taken, particularly when a number of sets of recording media have been used, to ensure that there is no confusion between them. This could be achieved by marking the sets of recording media with consecutive identification numbers.

(f)   Taking a break during the interview

4.12   When a break is to be taken during the course of an interview and the interview room is to be vacated by the suspect, the fact that a break is to be taken, the reason for it and the time shall be recorded. The recording equipment must be turned off and the recording media removed. The procedures for the conclusion of an interview set out in paragraph 4.19, below, should be followed.

4.13   When a break is to be a short one, and both the suspect and a police officer are to remain in the interview room, the fact that a break is to be taken, the reasons for it and the time shall be recorded on the recording media. The recording equipment may be turned off, but there is no need to remove the recording media. When the interview is recommenced the recording shall continue on the same recording media and the time at which the interview recommences shall be recorded.

4.14   When there is a break in questioning under caution, the interviewing officer must ensure that the person being questioned is aware that they remain under caution.

If there is any doubt, the caution must be given again in full when the interview resumes. See Notes 4D and 4E.

(g) Failure of recording equipment

4.15   If there is a failure of equipment which can be rectified quickly, the appropriate procedures set out in paragraph 4.12 shall be followed. When the recording is resumed the interviewer shall explain what has happened and record the time the interview recommences. If, however, it is not possible to continue recording on that particular recorder and no alternative equipment is readily available, the interview may continue without being recorded visually. In such circumstances, the procedures set out in paragraph 3.3 of this code for seeking the authority of the custody officer will be followed. See Note 4F.

(h) Removing used recording media from recording equipment

4.16   Where used recording media are removed from the recording equipment during the course of an interview, they shall be retained and the procedures set out in paragraph 4.18 below followed.

(i) Conclusion of interview

4.17   Before the conclusion of the interview, the suspect shall be offered the opportunity to clarify anything he or she has said and asked if there is anything that they wish to add.

4.18   At the conclusion of the interview, including the taking and reading back of any written statement, the time shall be recorded and the recording equipment switched off. The master tape or CD shall be removed from the recording equipment, sealed with a master copy label and treated as an exhibit in accordance with the force standing orders. The interviewer shall sign the label and also ask the suspect and any appropriate adults or other third party present during the interview to sign it. If the suspect or third party refuses to sign the label, an officer of at least the rank of inspector, or if one is not available, the custody officer, shall be called into the interview room and asked to sign it.

4.19   The suspect shall be handed a notice which explains the use which will be made of the recording and the arrangements for access to it. The notice will also advise the suspect that a copy of the tape shall be supplied as soon as practicable if the person is charged or informed that he will be prosecuted.

Notes for Guidance

4A   The interviewer should attempt to estimate the likely length of the interview and ensure that an appropriate quantity of certified recording media and labels with which to seal the master copies are available in the interview room.

4B   Where the custody officer is called immediately to deal with the complaint, wherever possible the recording equipment should be left to run until the custody officer has entered the interview room and spoken to the person being interviewed. Continuation or termination of the interview should be at the discretion of the interviewing officer pending action by an inspector as set out in Code C.

4C   Where the complaint is about a matter not connected with this code of practice or Code C, the decision to continue with the interview is at the discretion of the interview-

ing officer. Where the interviewing officer decides to continue with the interview, the person being interviewed shall be told that the complaint will be brought to the attention of the custody officer at the conclusion of the interview. When the interview is concluded, the interviewing officer must, as soon as practicable, inform the custody officer of the existence and nature of the complaint made.

4D   In considering whether to caution again after a break, the officer should bear in mind that he may have to satisfy a court that the person understood that he was still under caution when the interview resumed.

4E   The officer should bear in mind that it may be necessary to satisfy the court that nothing occurred during a break in an interview or between interviews which influenced the suspect's recorded evidence. On the re-commencement of an interview, the officer should consider summarising on the tape or CD the reason for the break and confirming this with the suspect.

4F   If any part of the recording media breaks or is otherwise damaged during the interview, it should be sealed as a master copy in the presence of the suspect and the interview resumed where it left off. The undamaged part should be copied and the original sealed as a master tape in the suspect's presence, if necessary after the interview. If equipment for copying is not readily available, both parts should be sealed in the suspect's presence and the interview begun again.

4G   The interviewer should be aware that a decision to continue recording against the wishes of the subject may be the subject of comment in court.

5   AFTER THE INTERVIEW

5.1   The interviewer shall make a note in his or her pocket book of the fact that the interview has taken place and has been recorded, its time, duration and date and the identification number of the master copy of the recording media.

5.2   Where no proceedings follow in respect of the person whose interview was recorded, the recording media must nevertheless be kept securely in accordance with paragraph 6.1 and Note 6A.

Note for Guidance

5A   Any written record of a recorded interview shall be made in accordance with national guidelines approved by the Secretary of State, and with regard to the advice contained in the Manual of Guidance for the preparation, processing and submission of files.

6   MASTER COPY SECURITY

(a)   General

6.1   The officer in charge of the police station at which interviews with suspects are recorded shall make arrangements for the master copies to be kept securely and their movements accounted for on the same basis as other material which may be used for evidential purposes, in accordance with force standing orders. See Note 6A.

(b)   Breaking master copy seal for criminal proceedings

6.2   A police officer has no authority to break the seal on a master copy which is required for criminal trial or appeal proceedings. If it is necessary to gain access to the master copy, the police officer shall arrange for its seal to be broken in the presence of a representative of the Crown Prosecution Service. The defendant or their legal adviser shall be informed and given a reasonable opportunity to be present. If the defendant or their legal representative is present they shall be invited to reseal and sign the master copy. If either refuses or neither is present, this shall be done by the representative of the Crown Prosecution Service. See Notes 6B and 6C.

(c) Breaking master copy seal: other cases

6.3   The chief officer of police is responsible for establishing arrangements for breaking the seal of the master copy where no criminal proceedings result, or the criminal proceedings, to which the interview relates, have been concluded and it becomes necessary to break the seal. These arrangements should be those which the chief officer considers are reasonably necessary to demonstrate to the person interviewed and any other party who may wish to use or refer to the interview record that the master copy has not been tampered with and that the interview record remains accurate. See Note 6D.

6.4   Subject to paragraph 6.6, a representative of each party must be given a reasonable opportunity to be present when the seal is broken, the master copy copied and re-sealed.

6.5   If one or more of the parties is not present when the master copy seal is broken because they cannot be contacted or refuse to attend or paragraph 6.6 applies, arrangements should be made for an independent person such as a custody visitor, to be present. Alternatively, or as an additional safeguard, arrangement should be made for a film or photographs to be taken of the procedure.

6.6   Paragraph 6.5 does not require a person to be given an opportunity to be present when:

(a)   it is necessary to break the master copy seal for the proper and effective further investigation of the original offence or the investigation of some other offence; and

(b)   the officer in charge of the investigation has reasonable grounds to suspect that allowing an opportunity might prejudice any such an investigation or criminal proceedings which may be brought as a result or endanger any person. See Note 6E.

(e) Documentation

6.7   When the master copy seal is broken, copied and re-sealed, a record must be made of the procedure followed, including the date time and place and persons present.

Notes for Guidance

6A   This section is concerned with the security of the master copy which will have been sealed at the conclusion of the interview. Care should, however, be taken of working copies since their loss or destruction may lead unnecessarily to the need to have access to master copies.

6B   If the master copy has been delivered to the Crown Court for their keeping after committal for trial the Crown Prosecutor will apply to the Chief Clerk of the Crown Court Centre for its release for unsealing by the Crown Prosecutor.

6C   Reference to the Crown Prosecution Service or to the Crown Prosecutor in this part of the code shall be taken to include any other body or person with a statutory responsibility for prosecution for whom the police conduct any recorded interviews.

6D   The most common reasons for needing access to master copies that are not required for criminal proceedings arise from civil actions and complaints against police and civil actions between individuals arising out of allegations of crime investigated by police.

6E   Paragraph 6.6 could apply, for example, when one or more of the outcomes or likely outcomes of the investigation might be: (i) the prosecution of one or more of the original suspects, (ii) the prosecution of someone previously not suspected, including someone who was originally a witness; and (iii) any original suspect being treated as a prosecution witness and when premature disclosure of any police action, particularly through contact with any parties involved, could lead to a real risk of compromising the investigation and endangering witnesses.

CODE G: FOR THE STATUTORY POWER OF ARREST BY POLICE OFFICERS

Commencement

This Code applies to any arrest made by a police officer after midnight on 31 December 2005

1 INTRODUCTION

1.1   This Code of Practice deals with statutory power of police to arrest persons suspected of involvement in a criminal offence.

1.2   The right to liberty is a key principle of the Human Rights Act 1998. The exercise of the power of arrest represents an obvious and significant interference with that right.

1.3   The use of the power must be fully justified and officers exercising the power should consider if the necessary objectives can be met by other, less intrusive means. Arrest must never be used simply because it can be used. Absence of justification for exercising the powers of arrest may lead to challenges should the case proceed to court. When the power of arrest is exercised it is essential that it is exercised in a non-discriminatory and proportionate manner.

1.4   Section 24 of the Police and Criminal Evidence Act 1984 (as substituted by section 110 of the Serious Organised Crime and Police Act 2005) provides the statutory power of arrest. If the provisions of the Act and this Code are not observed, both the arrest and the conduct of any subsequent investigation may be open to question.

1.5   This code of practice must be readily available at all police stations for consultation by police officers and police staff, detained persons and members of the public.

1.6   The notes for guidance are not provisions of this code.

2 ELEMENTS OF ARREST UNDER SECTION 24 PACE

2.1   A lawful arrest requires two elements:

A person's involvement or suspected involvement or attempted involvement in the commission of a criminal offence;

AND

Reasonable grounds for believing that the person's arrest is necessary.

2.2   Arresting officers are required to inform the person arrested that they have been arrested, even if this fact is obvious, and of the relevant circumstances of the arrest in relation to both elements and to inform the custody officer of these on arrival at the police station. See Code C paragraph 3.4.

Involvement in the commission of an offence

2.3   A constable may arrest without warrant in relation to any offence, except for the single exception listed in Note for Guidance 1. A constable may arrest anyone:

- who is about to commit an offence or is in the act of committing an offence
- whom the officer has reasonable grounds for suspecting is about to commit an offence or to be committing an offence

- whom the officer has reasonable grounds to suspect of being guilty of an offence which he or she has reasonable grounds for suspecting has been committed
- anyone who is guilty of an offence which has been committed or anyone whom the officer has reasonable grounds for suspecting to be guilty of that offence.

Necessity criteria

2.4　The power of arrest is only exercisable if the constable has reasonable grounds for believing that it is necessary to arrest the person. The criteria for what may constitute necessity are set out in paragraph 2.9. It remains an operational decision at the discretion of the arresting officer as to:

- what action he or she may take at the point of contact with the individual;
- the necessity criterion or criteria (if any) which applies to the individual; and
- whether to arrest, report for summons, grant street bail, issue a fixed penalty notice or take any other action that is open to the officer.

2.5　In applying the criteria, the arresting officer has to be satisfied that at least one of the reasons supporting the need for arrest is satisfied.

2.6　Extending the power of arrest to all offences provides a constable with the ability to use that power to deal with any situation. However applying the necessity criteria requires the constable to examine and justify the reason or reasons why a person needs to be taken to a police station for the custody officer to decide whether the person should be placed in police detention.

2.7　The criteria below are set out in section 24 of PACE as substituted by section 110 of the Serious Organised Crime and Police Act 2005. The criteria are exhaustive. However, the circumstances that may satisfy those criteria remain a matter for the operational discretion of individual officers. Some examples are given below of what those circumstances may be.

2.8　In considering the individual circumstances, the constable must take into account the situation of the victim, the nature of the offence, the circumstances of the suspect and the needs of the investigative process.

2.9　The criteria are that the arrest is necessary:

(a)　to enable the name of the person in question to be ascertained (in the case where the constable does not know, and cannot readily ascertain, the person's name, or has reasonable grounds for doubting whether a name given by the person as his name is his real name)

(b)　correspondingly as regards the person's address

an address is a satisfactory address for service of summons if the person will be at it for a sufficiently long period for it to be possible to serve him or her with a summons; or, that some other person at that address specified by the person will accept service of the summons on their behalf.

(c)　to prevent the person in question–

(i)　causing physical injury to himself or any other person;

(ii)　suffering physical injury ;

(iii)　causing loss or damage to property;

(iv)　committing an offence against public decency (only applies where members of the public going about their normal business cannot reasonably be expected to avoid the person in question); or

(v)　causing an unlawful obstruction of the highway;

(d)   to protect a child or other vulnerable person from the person in question

(e)   to allow the prompt and effective investigation of the offence or of the conduct of the person in question.

This may include cases such as:

   (i)   Where there are reasonable grounds to believe that the person:

- has made false statements;
- has made statements which cannot be readily verified;
- has presented false evidence;
- may steal or destroy evidence;
- may make contact with co-suspects or conspirators;
- may intimidate or threaten or make contact with witnesses;
- where it is necessary to obtain evidence by questioning; or

   (ii)   when considering arrest in connection with an indictable offence, there is a need to:

- enter and search any premises occupied or controlled by a person
- search the person
- prevent contact with others
- take fingerprints, footwear impressions, samples or photographs of the suspect

   (iii) ensuring compliance with statutory drug testing requirements.

(f)   to prevent any prosecution for the offence from being hindered by the disappearance of the person in question.

This may arise if there are reasonable grounds for believing that

- if the person is not arrested he or she will fail to attend court
- street bail after arrest would be insufficient to deter the suspect from trying to evade prosecution

3   INFORMATION TO BE GIVEN ON ARREST

(a)   Cautions – when a caution must be given (taken from Code C section 10)

3.1   A person whom there are grounds to suspect of an offence (see Note 2) must be cautioned before any questions about an offence, or further questions if the answers provide the grounds for suspicion, are put to them if either the suspect's answers or silence, (i.e. failure or refusal to answer or answer satisfactorily) may be given in evidence to a court in a prosecution. A person need not be cautioned if questions are for other necessary purposes e.g.:

(a)   solely to establish their identity or ownership of any vehicle;

(b)   to obtain information in accordance with any relevant statutory requirement;

(c)   in furtherance of the proper and effective conduct of a search, e.g. to determine the need to search in the exercise of powers of stop and search or to seek co-operation while carrying out a search;

(d)   to seek verification of a written record as in Code C paragraph 11.13;

(e)   when examining a person in accordance with the Terrorism Act 2000, Schedule 7 and the Code of Practice for Examining Officers issued under that Act, Schedule 14, paragraph 6.

3.2   Whenever a person not under arrest is initially cautioned, or reminded they are under caution, that person must at the same time be told they are not under arrest and are free to leave if they want to.

3.3   A person who is arrested, or further arrested, must be informed at the time, or as soon as practicable thereafter, that they are under arrest and the grounds for their arrest, see Note 3.

3.4   A person who is arrested, or further arrested, must also be cautioned unless:

(a)   it is impracticable to do so by reason of their condition or behaviour at the time;

(b)   they have already been cautioned immediately prior to arrest as in paragraph 3.1.

(c)   Terms of the caution (Taken from Code C section 10)

3.5   The caution, which must be given on arrest, should be in the following terms:

'You do not have to say anything. But it may harm your defence if you do not mention when questioned something which you later rely on in Court. Anything you do say may be given in evidence.'

See Note 5

3.6   Minor deviations from the words of any caution given in accordance with this Code do not constitute a breach of this Code, provided the sense of the relevant caution is preserved. See Note 6.

3.7   When, despite being cautioned, a person fails to co-operate or to answer particular questions which may affect their immediate treatment, the person should be informed of any relevant consequences and that those consequences are not affected by the caution. Examples are when a person's refusal to provide:

• their name and address when charged may make them liable to detention;

• particulars and information in accordance with a statutory requirement, e.g. under the Road Traffic Act 1988, may amount to an offence or may make the person liable to a further arrest.

4   RECORDS OF ARREST

(a)   General

4.1   The arresting officer is required to record in his pocket book or by other methods used for recording information:

• the nature and circumstances of the offence leading to the arrest
• the reason or reasons why arrest was necessary
• the giving of the caution
• anything said by the person at the time of arrest

4.2   Such a record should be made at the time of the arrest unless impracticable to do. If not made at that time, the record should then be completed as soon as possible thereafter.

4.3   On arrival at the police station, the custody officer shall open the custody record (see paragraph 1.1A and section 2 of Code C). The information given by the arresting officer on the circumstances and reason or reasons for arrest shall be recorded as part of the custody record. Alternatively, a copy of the record made by the officer in accordance with paragraph 4.1 above shall be attached as part of the custody record. See paragraph 2.2 and Code C paragraphs 3.4 and 10.3.

4.4   The custody record will serve as a record of the arrest. Copies of the custody record will be provided in accordance with paragraphs 2.4 and 2.4A of Code C and access for inspection of the original record in accordance with paragraph 2.5 of Code C.

(b)   Interviews and arrests

4.5   Records of interview, significant statements or silences will be treated in the same way as set out in sections 10 and 11 of Code C and in Code E (tape recording of interviews).

Notes for Guidance

1   The powers of arrest for offences under sections 4(1) and 5(1) of the Criminal Law Act 1967 require that the offences to which they relate must carry a sentence fixed by law or one in which a first time offender aged 18 or over could be sentenced to 5 years or more imprisonment

2   There must be some reasonable, objective grounds for the suspicion, based on known facts or information which are relevant to the likelihood the offence has been committed and the person to be questioned committed it.

3   An arrested person must be given sufficient information to enable them to understand they have been deprived of their liberty and the reason they have been arrested, e.g. when a person is arrested on suspicion of committing an offence they must be informed of the suspected offence's nature, when and where it was committed. The suspect must also be informed of the reason or reasons why arrest is considered necessary. Vague or technical language should be avoided.

4   Nothing in this Code requires a caution to be given or repeated when informing a person not under arrest they may be prosecuted for an offence. However, a court will not be able to draw any inferences under the Criminal Justice and Public Order Act 1994, section 34, if the person was not cautioned.

5   If it appears a person does not understand the caution, the people giving it should explain it in their own words.

6   The powers available to an officer as the result of an arrest – for example, entry and search of premises, holding a person incommunicado, setting up road blocks – are only available in respect of indictable offences and are subject to the specific requirements on authorisation as set out in the 1984 Act and relevant PACE Code of Practice.

Criminal Defence Service duty solicitor arrangements 2001 (as amended 21 July 2003 and 30 April 2005)

1. PURPOSE

1.1 The Legal Services Commission shall operate two Duty Solicitor schemes as part of the Criminal Defence Service. These are:

(a) the Police Station Duty Solicitor scheme;

(b) the Magistrates' Court Duty Solicitor scheme.

1.2 The primary objective of these schemes is to ensure that individuals requiring Advice and Assistance (including Advocacy Assistance) at a Police Station or a magistrates' court, and who choose not, or are not able, to obtain such help from an Own Solicitor, may have access to the services of a Duty Solicitor.

1.3 These Arrangements are made by the Commission under section 3(4) of the Access to Justice Act 1999.

2. DEFINITIONS

2.1 The following terms are defined as follows:

"Accreditation" means accreditation under Parts One and Two of Stage One of the Law Society's Criminal Litigation Accreditation Scheme.

"Accredited Representative" means an individual (including a solicitor or a barrister) whose name is included on the Police Station Register and who is accredited by a body recognised by us as competent to do so.

"Act" means the Access to Justice Act 1999.

"Advice and Assistance" means advice and assistance within the meaning of section 13 of the Act.

"Advocacy Assistance" means Advice and Assistance by way of advocacy within the meaning of Section 13 of the Act.

"Back-up" means a system by which the Call Centre Service (when a Duty Solicitor on a Rota is unable to accept a request for Police Station Advice and Assistance) seeks to contact another Duty Solicitor.

"Busy Scheme" means a Local Scheme serving a magistrates' court dealing with 1,250 or more defendants per annum prosecuted for non-motoring offences.

"Call Centre Service" means the telephone service established by the Commission to receive initial requests for Advice and Assistance from individuals at Police Stations.

"Call In" is a scheme in which the court Duty Solicitor is required to attend at the magistrates' court's request. This may operate as a Rota or a list.

"CDS" means the Criminal Defence Service established by the Commission under Section 12 of the Act.

"CDS Supplier" means an office of a firm of solicitors in respect of which it holds a General Criminal Contract or an office of the Public Defender Service.

"Commission" means the Legal Services Commission established under Section 1 of the Act and includes its Regional CDS Managers.

"CPD" means continuing professional development as defined in the Law Society Training Regulations 1990.

"Duty Solicitor" means a solicitor, or employed barrister, who is admitted to a Local Scheme under these Arrangements.

"Designated Fee Earner" is defined in Part D of the General Criminal Contract Specification.

"Less Busy Scheme" means a Local Scheme serving a magistrates' court dealing with less than 1,250 defendants per annum prosecuted for non-motoring offences.

"Local Committee" means a Committee established by the Commission under these Arrangements for consultation about a Local Scheme.

"Local Scheme" and "Scheme" means a scheme covering one or more magistrates' courts or one or more Police Stations within a geographical area defined by us, which is usually a petty sessions area.

"Own Solicitor" means a solicitor who provides Advice and Assistance to a client other than as a Duty Solicitor.

"Panel" and "Panel Case" means an arrangement by which the Call Centre Service telephones Duty Solicitors in sequence to identify a Duty Solicitor available to provide Advice and Assistance at a Police Station.

"Police Station" means a police station or any other place where a constable is present and, except where expressly excluded by the General Criminal Contract or these Arrangements, any place where a Services Person is assisting with an investigation by Services Police.

"Police Station Register" is the list of Accredited and Probationary Representatives maintained by the Commission or the Law Society.

"Public Defender Service" means the service provided by employed lawyers, funded directly by the Commission as part of the CDS, to provide Advice and Assistance and Representation to individuals.

"Regional CDS Manager" means an employee of the Commission with responsibility for the management of the Local Schemes within the geographic area covered by a Regional Office.

"Region" has the meaning given in Schedule 1 to these Arrangements.

"Regional Director" and "Regional Office" have the meanings given in the Legal Services Commission Regional Arrangements 2000.

"Regional Committee" means the Committee appointed by the Commission for each Region for the purpose of determining appeals under these Arrangements and facilitating consultation.

"Rota" means a rota of Duty Solicitors to provide Advice and Assistance or Advocacy Assistance at magistrates' courts and Advice and Assistance at Police Stations.

"Services Person" means a person assisting with an investigation by the Services Police.

"Services Police" means members of the Royal Navy Regulating Branch, members of the Royal Military Police, Royal Air Force Provost Officers or members of the Royal Air Force Police.

3. REGIONS AND LOCAL SCHEMES

3.1   For the purposes of these Arrangements, England and Wales shall be divided into the Regions which are set out in Schedule 1.

3.2   The Commission shall establish Local Schemes within each Region and shall identify which magistrates' courts and Police Stations will be covered by a particular scheme.

3.3   The Commission may change the magistrates' courts and Police Stations covered by a Local Scheme if it considers it appropriate to do so.

4. MEMBERSHIP OF LOCAL SCHEMES

4.1   The Commission shall determine, in accordance with these Arrangements, the membership of each Local Scheme.

Applications

4.2   Applications for Local Scheme membership shall be made to the appropriate Regional Office of the Commission, on a form approved by the Commission, and will be judged on the criteria set out in these Arrangements.

Competence

4.3   The Commission is responsible for ensuring that all members of Local Schemes are competent to undertake Duty Solicitor work.

4.4   An applicant for membership of a Local Scheme must provide the Commission with evidence of his or her competence to undertake Duty Solicitor work in accordance with paragraph 4.6 of these Arrangements.

4.5   An applicant shall have comprehensive experience of criminal defence work, including the provision of advice in the Police Station and advocacy in the Crown Court or magistrates' courts throughout the 12 months prior to the application for membership of the Local Scheme. However:

    (a) if an applicant has been in full time employment as a prosecuting solicitor, justices' clerk or in another similar position for a period of 18 months, he or she must have had comprehensive experience of criminal defence work throughout the six months immediately prior to the application;

    (b) any interval of up to 12 months, during or at the end of the periods of experience required by this paragraph, when the applicant was absent from work due to sickness, injury, pregnancy, maternity leave or for other good reason may be disregarded.

4.6   An applicant shall provide evidence of competence to the Commission in one of the following ways:

For membership of a Magistrates' Court Local Scheme

(a)   Previous selection by a local duty solicitor committee as a court Duty Solicitor (in accordance with the Legal Aid Board Duty Solicitor Arrangements 2000 or a former version of those Arrangements), provided that the applicant was a court Duty Solicitor for all or part of the period from 1 January to 1 April 2001 or selected under paragraph 8.1; or

(b)   Accreditation as defined in these Arrangements and satisfaction of the criteria in paragraph 4.7.

For membership of a Police Station Local Scheme

(c)   Previous selection by a local duty solicitor committee as a Police Station Duty Solicitor (in accordance with the Legal Aid Board Duty Solicitor Arrangements 2000 or a former version of those Arrangements), provided that the applicant was a Police Station Duty Solicitor for all or part of the period from 1 January to 1 April 2001 or selected under paragraph 8.1; or

(d)   Accreditation as defined in these Arrangements and satisfaction of the criteria in paragraph 4.7.

4.7   Where accredited status was achieved more than 12 months before the date of application to the Local Scheme, the applicant shall demonstrate the regular satisfactory performance of Police Station and magistrates' court work since that time.

Location – General Rules

Membership of a first Scheme

4.8   An applicant shall notify the Commission of the location of the CDS Supplier's office at which he or she is normally in attendance, i.e. at which he or she is normally based for the majority of the working week. An applicant may only notify one such office.

4.9   Subject to meeting the other membership criteria, an applicant is entitled to join the Police Station and magistrates' court Local Schemes covering the area in which his or her office notified in accordance with paragraph 4.8 is located. Alternatively an applicant may apply to join a Police Station Scheme and a magistrates' court Scheme other than the ones covering the area in which his or her office is located, if the Police Stations and courts covered by the alternative Schemes are more readily accessible to the applicant's office.

Membership of additional Schemes

4.10   The Commission may, subject to paragraph 4.19, permit an applicant to join more than one Police Station Local Scheme and more than one magistrates' court Local Scheme provided that:

(a)   in the case of a Police Station Local Scheme, the applicant can demonstrate that he or she is able to attend the Police Station within 45 minutes of receiving a call – whether in or out of normal office hours;

(b) for Police Station and magistrates' court Local Schemes, the applicant is located at an office of a CDS Supplier for whom he or she undertakes criminal work and that office:

i) for a Busy Scheme, is the office identified under paragraph 4.8 and that office is readily accessible to the court covered by the Local Scheme which the applicant wishes to join; or

ii) for a Less Busy Scheme, is the office identified under paragraph 4.8 or another office of the same CDS Supplier which is accessible to the court covered by the Local Scheme which the applicant wishes to join and arrangements will be made to see clients at that office.

4.11 Where a strict application of the criteria set out in paragraphs 4.10(a) and (b) would prevent individuals wishing to receive Duty Solicitor services from doing so by restricting the membership of a particular Local Scheme to an unacceptably low level, the Commission may relax the requirements of those paragraphs in respect of applications to join a Scheme.

Special rules

4.12 The Commission may introduce special rules for a particular Local Scheme or Schemes which differ from the general rule where the particular local conditions of the Scheme mean that an alternative approach would be more appropriate.

4.13 Where the Commission plans to introduce special rules for a Local Scheme or Schemes it shall consult the relevant Regional Committee and Local Committee or Local Committees. Details of any rules introduced will be published and made available to all affected CDS Suppliers within the area covered by the Local Scheme or Schemes. The Commission shall provide six weeks notice of the introduction of any such special rules.

CDS Supplier

4.14 An applicant shall be a full or part time Designated Fee Earner employed by, or a partner in, a CDS Supplier and shall notify the appropriate Regional Office of the CDS Supplier for which he or she will undertake Duty Solicitor work, i.e. which will submit claims to the Commission for the work and which will be contractually responsible for the performance of the applicant's Duty Solicitor work.

Status

4.15 An applicant shall hold a current practising certificate which may (in the discretion of the Commission) be conditional.

4.16 An applicant shall not be a special constable.

4.17 An applicant may not apply for Local Scheme membership during any period of suspension or exclusion from membership imposed under paragraphs 5.2 or 5.4 of these Arrangements.

4.18 Where:

(a) an applicant is under investigation, faces an outstanding criminal charge or has been convicted of a criminal offence which is not treated as spent under the Rehabilitation of Offenders Act 1974; or

(b) an applicant has been the subject of any adverse findings by the Adjudication Committee of the Office for the Supervision of Solicitors or by the

Solicitors' Disciplinary Tribunal, or where any complaint or application to either body has not been determined; or

(c) some other good reason arises which makes an applicant's scheme membership incompatible with the standards expected of a Duty Solicitor,

the Commission may refuse the application, provided that it gives the applicant written reasons for its decision.

General requirement

4.19 The Commission shall normally require Duty Solicitors to serve on both the Local Police Station and Local magistrates' court Schemes.

Approval of applications

4.20 Where an application for Local Scheme membership is approved by the Commission, it shall notify the applicant within 30 days of the date of receipt of the application.

Refusal of applications

4.21 If the Commission refuses the application it shall notify the applicant and provide a statement of reasons for the decision within 30 days of receipt of the application.

4.22 Any applicant whose application is refused under paragraph 4.21 may appeal to the Regional Committee in accordance with Section 7 of these Arrangements.

4.23 There is no right of appeal to the Commission against a refusal, revocation or suspension of Accreditation by the Law Society. Such appeals should be directed to the relevant Accreditation assessment organisation or to the Law Society.

5. CONTINUED MEMBERSHIP OF LOCAL SCHEMES

5.1 Continued membership of a Local Scheme is dependent on a Duty Solicitor:

(a) undertaking at least two hours CPD annually on issues relevant to the law, practice and procedure in the Police Station or magistrates' courts;

(b) undertaking personally a number equivalent to the majority of:

i) Court Duty Solicitor Rota turns allocated to that solicitor; and
ii) Police Station Duty Solicitor slots allocated; and

(c) continuing to undertake criminal defence work generally and Duty Solicitor work in particular as evidenced by accepting at least 12 Police Station Duty Solicitor or Own Solicitor cases annually involving attendance at the Police Station or, where fewer than this number of cases are offered, all cases so offered (or a number equivalent to those offered).

5.2 The Commission shall have power to suspend for a period of up to 12 months or remove a Duty Solicitor from the Local Scheme or Schemes of which he or she is a member if he or she fails to meet any of the criteria in paragraph 5.1 in relation to a Scheme. On suspension, the Commission may impose conditions which must be met before the Duty Solicitor resumes his or her membership of the relevant Scheme or Schemes.

5.3 The Commission shall not suspend or remove a Duty Solicitor from membership of a Local Scheme or Schemes where any of the criteria in paragraph 5.1 are not met because of an absence from work of up to 12 months due to sickness, injury, pregnancy, maternity leave or for other good reason.

5.4   The Commission may also suspend or remove a Duty Solicitor from a Local Scheme or Schemes where in relation to a Scheme he or she:

(a)   unreasonably failed to attend a Police Station when he or she should have done so;

(b)   sent a representative to the Police Station when he or she should have attended personally;

(c)   failed to accept a reasonable number of Panel calls;

(d)   failed to accept Rota cases;

(e)   unreasonably failed to carry out a duty or duties or failed to comply with the requirements set out in these Arrangements including local instructions drawn up under paragraphs 6.12 to 6.14 or any contract between the Commission and the CDS Supplier;

(f)   is under investigation, faces an outstanding criminal charge or has been convicted of a criminal offence or is the subject of an investigation by the Office for the Supervision of Solicitors;

(g)   does not demonstrate the level of competence required for Accreditation or Accreditation has been suspended or revoked;

(h)   no longer complies with the "location" rules set out in paragraphs 4.8 to 4.13;

(i)   is no longer a Designated Fee Earner with a CDS Supplier;

(j)   does not comply with, and the Commission has not waived, the requirement in paragraph 4.19; or

(k)   some other good reason arises which makes his or her continuing scheme membership incompatible with the standards expected of a Duty Solicitor.

5.5   Where a Duty Solicitor is suspended from membership of a Local Scheme under paragraphs 5.2 or 5.4 and is unable to fulfil any conditions imposed under paragraph 5.2, he or she may apply to the Commission in writing for restoration to the Scheme or Schemes concerned once the suspension period has expired.

5.6   Where a Duty Solicitor is removed from a Scheme under paragraph 5.4, a fresh application for Scheme membership will be considered against all of the criteria in Section 4 of these Arrangements. The reasons for the applicant's removal may be a factor considered by the Commission under paragraph 4.18 (c) of these Arrangements.

5.7   A Duty Solicitor who has been suspended or removed under this Section may appeal to the Regional Committee in accordance with the provisions of Section 7 of these Arrangements.

5.8   The Commission shall postpone a suspension or removal until any appeal is heard unless it considers that there is good reason for suspending or removing the Duty Solicitor prior to the appeal hearing which shall be notified to the appellant.

5.9   Where the Commission is considering suspension or removal it must notify the Duty Solicitor of its reasons in writing and must offer him or her the opportunity to make written representations which must be submitted within 14 days of the date of notification. Where the Commission is considering suspension or removal under paragraphs 5.4 (e), (f), (g), (i) (j) or (k) it may suspend or remove immediately if it considers it necessary to do so.

Changes in circumstances

5.10   It is the responsibility of a Duty Solicitor, and the CDS Supplier for which he or she acts as a Duty Solicitor, to notify the Commission immediately in any of the following circumstances:

(a)   if the Duty Solicitor leaves the CDS Supplier in which he or she is employed as a Duty Solicitor;

(b)   if the Duty Solicitor's practising address changes;

(c)   if the Duty Solicitor is no longer able to comply with any of the qualifying or continuing membership criteria (set out in Sections 4 and 5 of these Arrangements);

(d)   if the Duty Solicitor wishes voluntarily to withdraw from a Scheme or Schemes in accordance with paragraph 6.10 of these Arrangements;

(e)   on resignation from a Local Scheme, giving at least one month's notice;

(f)   if he or she is under investigation for or is charged with a criminal offence;

(g)   if any proceedings have been instituted before the Adjudication Committee of the Office for the Supervision of Solicitors or by the Solicitors' Disciplinary Tribunal; or

(h)   if the Adjudication Committee of the Office for the Supervision of Solicitors or the Solicitors' Disciplinary Tribunal has made an adverse finding.

6.   MANAGEMENT OF LOCAL SCHEMES

6.1   The Commission shall manage each Local Scheme. Generally, responsibility for management will lie with the Regional CDS Manager in the Commission's Regional Office which covers the area in which the Local Scheme operates.

Rotas, Panels and Call Ins

6.2   The Commission shall decide:

(a)   in consultation with the appropriate magistrates' courts, whether there should be attendance or Call In (whether by Rota or list) cover, or a combination of both, for each magistrates' court Local Scheme;

(b)   whether there should be Rota or Panel cover, or a combination of both, for each Police Station Local Scheme,

and the times during which such arrangements shall be in operation. In both instances the Commission shall also consult with the relevant Regional Committees and with CDS Suppliers through any local consultation mechanism established under paragraph 7.23 of these Arrangements.

Scheme lists

6.3   For each Local Scheme the Commission shall maintain a list of slots. CDS Suppliers will be allocated one slot on the Local Scheme list for every Duty Solicitor employed by that CDS Supplier who is a member of that Scheme.

6.4   Rota, Panel and Call In Schemes will be based on the Local Scheme lists. Rota slots will be allocated to CDS Suppliers in accordance with the slots on the Local Scheme list.

Rotas

6.5   The Commission shall determine the number of Duty Solicitors to deploy at any one time in consultation with the relevant magistrates' courts, Police Stations, relevant Regional Committees and with Scheme members through any local consultation mechanism established under paragraph 7.24 of these Arrangements, and may determine that Duty Solicitors should be available or extra Duty Solicitors made available to respond to unusual demands.

6.6   The Commission shall normally produce Rotas covering a minimum period of three months, and a maximum of six months, and shall normally issue such Rotas one month before the start date.

6.7   Duty Solicitors who are new to a particular Scheme will be added to the Local Scheme list as soon as possible.

6.8   Copies of any Rota (or list for a Call In Scheme) will be sent, as appropriate, to the court, the Call Centre Service and each CDS Supplier with a Duty Solicitor on the Rota.

Voluntary or permanent withdrawal from Schemes

6.9   It is the responsibility of both the Duty Solicitor and the CDS Supplier for which he or she undertakes Duty Solicitor work to ensure that the Commission is notified that a Duty Solicitor wishes to leave a Local Scheme.

6.10   A Duty Solicitor may notify the Commission that he or she wishes to withdraw voluntarily from a Local Scheme for a period of up to three months but may only do so once within a period of 12 months. Where this is the case the Duty Solicitor will be restored to the Scheme automatically at the end of the withdrawal period. The three month withdrawal period may be extended provided that the Duty Solicitor still complies with the Accreditation and other membership requirements.

Client awareness

6.11   The Commission shall take steps to ensure that potential clients are made aware of the availability of the Duty Solicitor at Police Stations and magistrates' courts.

Local instructions

6.12   The Commission may draw up local instructions which set out how the Duty Solicitor service is to be provided at particular Police Stations or magistrates' courts.

6.13   Local instructions may also set out arrangements agreed with other criminal justice agencies to improve the overall effectiveness of the criminal justice system locally. CDS Suppliers with Duty Solicitors on the Local Scheme will be consulted using the arrangements in paragraph 7.24 before such instructions are introduced or amended. The Regional Committee may also be consulted.

6.14   Where local instructions are drawn up, Duty Solicitors on the relevant Scheme or Schemes shall comply with them.

Duty Solicitor service

6.15   If it is not possible for any Duty Solicitor to provide service on a Local Scheme the Commission may make alternative arrangements for such service to be provided.

Services cases

6.16 The Commission may introduce a special Panel for cases where Services personnel require Advice and Assistance and Advocacy Assistance.

7. COMMITTEES, APPEALS AND CONSULTATION

Regional Committees

7.1 The Commission shall establish one or more Regional Committees for each of the Regions set out in Schedule 1. The area covered by a Regional Committee may be amended by the Commission in consultation with the relevant Regional Committee. The role of a Regional Committee is to:

(a) consider appeals in accordance with these Arrangements; and
(b) facilitate consultation and communication between the members of Local Schemes, the Commission and other criminal justice agencies affected by the operation of Duty Solicitor services.

7.2 The members of each Regional Committee shall be such as the Regional Committee shall from time to time appoint and will normally be the following:

(a) at least one Duty Solicitor from each of the Local Schemes falling within the Region covered by the Regional Committee who shall normally be a member of any Local Committee in the Region or other local liaison group established by the Commission under paragraph 7.24;
(b) one or more Justices of the Peace, nominated by the Magistrates' Association;
(c) one or more Justices' Clerks, nominated by the Justices' Clerks' Society;
(d) one or more representatives of the police force or forces in the Region, nominated by the chief officer(s) of police;
(e) one or more lay members who shall, prior to appointment, be interviewed by the chair or vice chair of the Regional Committee to ascertain the applicant's understanding of the role and suitability for membership (members of court staff are ineligible for appointment under this sub-paragraph);
(f) one or more representatives of the probation service or services in the Region, nominated by that service or those services;
(g) one or more representatives of the Crown Prosecution Service in the Region, nominated by that service;
(h) a district judge (magistrates' court); and
(i) such other members as the Committee decides to appoint.

7.3 The members of a Regional Committee shall not be fewer than 10 nor more than 35. The majority of members shall be solicitors appointed under paragraph 7.2 (a) above.

7.4 Each member shall be appointed for a term of up to three years and may be appointed for successive periods not exceeding three years, provided that the total period of service shall not exceed ten years, until he or she attains the age of 70. A member shall be reappointed only if he or she has attended at least half of all the meetings which were held during his or her membership unless there are special circumstances to permit reappointment despite a lower level of attendance.

7.5 A member of a Regional Committee may resign by giving notice in writing to the appropriate Regional Office. Any vacancy on a Regional Committee so arising shall be filled in accordance with the provisions in this Section.

7.6   A member of the Regional Committee shall be disqualified from membership if:
   (a)   a receiving order in bankruptcy is made against him or her;
   (b)   he or she becomes a patient within the meaning of the Mental Health Act 1983;
   (c)   he or she fails to attend meetings without leave of the Committee for six months;
   (d)   he or she ceases to be a nominee of any body or organisation he or she was nominated to represent; or
   (e)   there is some other good reason to disqualify him or her.

7.7   The Committee shall at the first meeting after its appointment and then annually elect a member to act as chair of the Committee and another to act as vice chair. A chair or vice chair shall be eligible for reappointment at the expiration of such period provided that no chair or vice chair shall hold office for more than three years.

7.8   A Regional Committee may appoint a sub-committee of at least three members to whom it may delegate all decisions excluding appeals, provided that the full Regional Committee shall meet at least twice a year. A sub-committee shall consist of at least one Duty Solicitor and one lay member.

7.9   A Regional Committee or its chair may appoint a sub-committee of at least three members appointed under 7.2 (a) or (e) (provided that there are at least two members appointed under 7.2 (a)) to whom it may delegate the determination of appeals.

7.10   A quorum shall consist of not less than one third of the members of the committee or sub-committee and in any event shall consist of a minimum of two members.

7.11   A Regional Committee or a sub-committee shall keep minutes of its proceedings and such minutes shall be signed by the Chair.

7.12   The ruling of the chair of a Regional Committee or a sub-committee shall be final on any matter of procedure arising at a meeting.

Appeals

7.13   The following decisions of the Commission under these Arrangements may be the subject of appeal by an applicant for membership of a Local Scheme or by a Duty Solicitor:
   (a)   a decision to refuse an applicant membership of a Local Scheme under Section 4 of these Arrangements;
   (b)   a decision to remove or suspend a Duty Solicitor from a Local Scheme under paragraphs 5.2 or 5.4;
   (c)   a decision to refuse to register a police station representative under paragraph 2.2 of the Police Station Register Arrangements 2001;
   (d)   a decision to suspend or remove a police station representative under paragraph 6.4 of the Police Station Register Arrangements 2001;
   (e)   a decision to suspend a solicitor from acting as a supervising solicitor for probationary representatives under Part B, Rule 3.3 of the General Criminal Contract Specification.

7.14   All appeals shall be made in writing within 30 days of receipt of the decision against which the appeal is to be made, subject to the Regional Committee having discretion to accept an appeal outside that period for good reason. The appellant shall submit written representations when giving notice of appeal. The Commission's staff may obtain and provide information relating to the appeal provided that the appellant receives a copy.

7.15   On receipt of an appeal under paragraph 7.13 the Commission may reconsider its decision, but if it decides not to do so it shall refer the matter to the Regional Committee or to another Regional Committee if no suitable members of the Regional Committee are available to consider the appeal.

7.16   The Regional Committee will normally consider appeals at the latest within three months of the date on which the appeal was received. The appellant shall have the right to make oral representations and the Committee may, in any event, require personal appearance. The Commission may also be represented at the appeal.

7.17   If oral representations or written representations subsequently submitted include matters not mentioned in the written representations referred to in paragraph 7.14 above, the Regional Committee has a discretion not to consider such additional matters unless the appellant has given 14 days notice to the Commission's staff and the Regional Committee.

7.18   The Regional Committee shall consider the application afresh in accordance with the relevant criteria in these Arrangements using the most current guidance available and the decision of the Regional Committee will replace the decision of the Commission.

7.19   A Duty Solicitor member of the Regional Committee who is a member of the Local Scheme to which the appeal relates shall not participate in the hearing and determination of such appeal.

7.20   The Regional Committee may exclude the appellant from any other Scheme or Schemes on the basis of its appeal findings and shall provide reasons for doing so.

7.21   The Regional Committee may allow an appeal subject to such conditions as it considers appropriate.

7.22   Appellants will be notified of the decision of the Regional Committee in writing. The Regional Committee shall provide reasons for its decision.

Local Committees

7.23   The Commission will use its best endeavours to establish arrangements for consulting and discussing the operation of a Local Scheme with representatives of that Scheme.

7.24   This may be achieved through the establishment of:

    (a)   a Local Committee, membership of which shall be open to:

        i)   one representative from each CDS Supplier with a member on the Local Scheme;

        ii)   a representative of the Justices' Clerk of each magistrates' court covered by the Scheme;

        iii)   a Justice of the Peace;

        iv)   a representative of the police force covering the area concerned;

        v)   a nominee of the Local Law Society;

        vi)   one or more lay members; and

        vii)   such other members as the Local Committee decides to appoint; or

    (b)   liaison arrangements with the criminal law sub-committee, or equivalent, of the Local Law Society; or

    (c)   such other local arrangements as appear effective to the Commission.

7.25 Where the Commission considers that a Local Committee established under paragraph 7.24 (a) above would be too large to facilitate effective consultation and liaison and having consulted all CDS Suppliers with a Duty Solicitor on the Local Scheme as to whether they all wish to be represented it may restrict the number of representatives under paragraph 7.24 (a)(i) to a maximum of 10 in which case those appointments shall be made by the Commission after inviting nominations from all firms.

Committee fees

7.26 There shall be paid to any Regional Committee members attending meetings under these Arrangements such fees and such travelling and other proper expenses and subsistence allowances as the Lord Chancellor may from time to time authorise.

8. TRANSITIONAL ARRANGEMENTS

8.1 Applications by solicitors wishing to become Duty Solicitors made before 1 February 2001 shall be determined under the provisions of the Duty Solicitor Arrangements 2000 (as amended). Any application not determined by a Local Committee by 1 April 2001 shall be referred to the relevant Regional Committee appointed either under the Duty Solicitor Arrangements 2000 or under these Arrangements. Any appeal to or review by the Duty Solicitor Committee shall, after 2 April 2001, be undertaken by a committee drawn from members of Regional Committees appointed either under the Duty Solicitor Arrangements 2000 or these Arrangements. No appeal or review may be considered under the Duty Solicitor Arrangements 2000 (as amended) after 30 September 2002.

[Schedule 1 omitted]

APPENDIX C

Sentencing toolkit

This appendix contains the following:
- Magistrates' Court Association sentencing guidelines
- Overview of Youth Court sentencing powers
- Sentencing authorities
  - *R.* v. *Page* (shoplifting)
  - *R.* v. *Kefford* (appropriate use of custodial sentences)
  - *R.* v. *Mills* (custodial sentences for dishonesty where previous good character and single mother)
  - *R.* v. *Kelly* (drug treatment and testing orders)
  - *R.* v. *Baldwin* (use of fines)
  - *R.* v. *Banks* (discharge of fines within 12 months)
  - *R.* v. *Ghafoor* (sentencing of adults where offence committed whilst a youth)
  - *R.* v. *McInerney* (domestic burglary)
  - *R.* v. *Oliver* (indecent images)
  - *R.* v. *Webbe and others* (handling stolen goods)
  - *R.* v. *Czyzewski* (fraudulent evasion of duty on tobacco and alcohol)
  - *R.* v. *Poulton and Celaire* (offensive weapons)
  - *R.* v. *Williams* (ASBO for driving offences)
  - *R.* v. *Morrison* (ASBO, sentencing for breach of)
  - *R. (Mills)* v. *Birmingham Magistrates' Court* (ASBO following conviction)
  - *R.* v. *Boness* (ASBO – principle of proportionality)

MAGISTRATES' COURT ASSOCIATION SENTENCING GUIDELINES: (ISSUED OCTOBER 2003 FOR IMPLEMENTATION FROM JANUARY 2004)

Reproduced by kind permission of the Magistrates' Association

Offence/Guideline	Aggravating factors	Mitigating factors
Affray *Commit*	Busy public place Group action Injuries caused People actually put in fear Vulnerable victim(s)	Did not start trouble Provocation Single offender Stopped on police arriving

494

Offence/Guideline	Aggravating factors	Mitigating factors
Aggravated vehicle-taking *Custody*	Avoiding detection or apprehension Competitive driving: Racing, showing off Disregard of warnings, e.g. from passengers or others in vicinity Excessive speed Evidence of alcohol or drugs Group action Police pursuit Premeditated Serious injury/damage Serious risk Vehicle destroyed	No alcohol or drugs involved Passenger only Single incident Speed not excessive Very minor damage/injury
Animal cruelty *Community Penalty*	Adult involving children Animal(s) kept for livelihood Committed over a period or involving several animals Deriving pleasure from torturing or pleasuring Disregarded warnings of others Group action Offender in position of special responsibility towards the animal Premeditated/deliberate Prolonged neglect Serious injury or death Use of weapon	Ignorance of appropriate care Impulsive Minor injury Offender induced by others Single incident
Assault – actual bodily harm *Commit*	Deliberate kicking Extensive injuries (incl. psychiatric) Group action Headbutting Offender in position of authority On hospital/medical or school premises Premeditated Victim particularly vulnerable Victim serving public Weapon	Minor injury Provocation Single blow
Assault on a police officer *Custody*	Any injuries caused Gross disregard for police authority Group action Premeditated	Impulsive action Unaware that person was a police officer
Burglary (dwelling) *Commit (Consider guidelines in R. v. McInerney)*	Forced entry Group offence Night time Occupants frightened People in house Professional operation Repeat victimisation Soiling, ransacking, damage	Low value Nobody frightened No damage or disturbance No forcible entry Opportunist
Burglary (non-dwelling) *Community penalty*	Forcible entry Group offence Harm to business Occupants frightened Professional operation Repeat victimisation School premises Soiling, ransacking, damage	Low value Nobody frightened No damage or disturbance No forcible entry

Offence/Guideline	Aggravating factors	Mitigating factors
Careless driving *Discharge/fine*	Excessive speed High degree of carelessness Serious risk Hand-held mobile phone	Minor risk Momentary lapse Negligible/parking damage Sudden change in weather conditions
Common assault *Community penalty* *Custody if racially or* *religiously aggravated*	Group action Injury Offender in position of authority On hospital/medical premises Premeditated Victim particularly vulnerable Victim public servant Weapon	Impulsive action Minor injury Provocation Single blow
Criminal damage *Discharge/fine.* *Community penalty if* *racially or religiously* *aggravated*	Deliberate Group offence Serious damage	Impulsive action Minor damage Provocation
Dangerous driving *Commit*	Avoiding detection or apprehension Competitive driving, racing, showing off Disregard of warnings, e.g. from passengers or others in vicinity Evidence of alchohol or drugs Excessive speed Prolonged, persistent, deliberate bad driving Serious risk Hand-held mobile phone	Emergency Single incident Speed not excessive
Driving: Failing to stop Failing to report *Discharge/fine*	Evidence of drinking Serious injury Serious damage	Believed identity to be known Failed to stop but reported Negligible damage No one at scene but failed to report Stayed at scene but failed to give/left before giving full particulars
Driving – no insurance *Discharge/fine*	Deliberate driving without insurance LGV, HGV, PCV or minicabs No reference to insurance ever having been held	Accidental oversight Genuine mistake Responsibility for providing insurance resting with another – the parent/owner/lender/hirer Smaller vehicle, e.g. moped
Driving while disqualified by Court Order *Community penalty*	Efforts to avoid detection Long distance drive Planned, long-term evasion Recent disqualification	Emergency established Full period expired but test not re-taken Short distance driven
Drugs: Class A drugs – possession *Community penalty*	An amount other than a very very small quantity	Very small quantity

Offence/Guideline	Aggravating factors	Mitigating factors
Drugs: Class A drugs – production, supply, possession with intent to supply *Commit*	Commercial production Deliberate adulteration Large amount Sophisticated operation Supply to children Venue (prison, school, etc.)	Small amount
Drugs: Class B drugs – possession *Discharge/fine*	Large amount	Small amount
Drugs: Class B drugs – supply: possession with intent to supply *Commit*	Commercial production Deliberate adulteratiaon Large amount Venue (prison, school, etc.)	No commecial motive Small amount
Drugs: Cultivation of cannabis *Discharge/fine*	Commercial cultivation Large quantity	For personal use Not commercial Not responsible for planting Small scale cultivation
Drunk and disorderly *Discharge/fine*	Offensive language or behaviour On hospital/medical premises With group	Induced by others No significant disturbance Not threatening
Fear or provocation of violence POA 1986 s.4A *Custody*	Football hooliganism Group action High degree of planning Night time offence Victims specifically targeted Weapon	Short duration
Handling stolen goods *Community penalty*	Adult involving children High value Organiser or distributor	For personal use Impulsive action Low value No financial gain Single item Unsophisticated
Harassment, alarm or distress POA 1986 s.5 *Discharge/fine. Community penalty if racially or religiously aggravated (only community rehabilitation and curfew orders are available for this offence)*	Group action Vulnerable victim	Stopped as soon as police arrived Trivial accident
Harassment alarm or distress with intent POA 1986 s.4A *Custody. Commit for sentence if racially or religiously aggravated*	Football hooliganism Group action High degree of planning Night time offence Victims specifically targeted Weapon	Short duration

Offence/Guideline	Aggravating factors	Mitigating factors
Harassment – conduct causing fear of violence PFHA s.4 *Custody. Commit for sentence if racially or religiously aggravated*	Disregard of warning Excessive persistence Interference with employment/business Invasion of victim's home Involvement of others Threat to use weapon or substance (including realistic imitations) Use of violence or grossly offensive material Where photographs or images of a personal nature are involved	Initial provocation Short duration
Harassment – conduct causing harassment PFHA s.2 *Community penalty. Custody if racially or religiously aggravated*	Disregard of warning Excessive persistence Interference with employment/business Invasion of victim's home Involvement of others Threat to use weapon or substance (including realistic imitations) Use of violence or grossly offensive material Where photographs or images of a personal nature are involved	Initial provocation Short duration
Indecent assult *Custody*	Age differential Breach of trust Injury (may be psychiatric) Prolonged assault Very young victim Victim deliberately targeted Victim serving public Vulnerable victim	Slight contact
Making off without payment *Discharge/fine*	Deliberate plan High value Two or more involved Victim particularly vulnerable	Impulsive action Low value
Obstructing a police officer *Discharge/fine*	Group action Premeditated	Genuine misjudgement Impulsive action Minor obstruction
Obtaining by deception *Community penalty*	Committed over lengthy period Large sums or valuable goods Two or more involved Victim particularly vulnerable	Impulsive action Short period Small sum
Possession of a bladed instrument *Custody*	Group action or joint possession Location of offence People put in fear/weapon brandished Planned use	Acting out of genuine fear No attempt to use Not premeditated
Possession of an offensive weaon *Custody*	Group action or joint possession Location of offence People put in fear/weapon brandished Planned use Very dangerous weapon	Acting out of genuine fear No attempt to use Not premeditated

Offence/Guideline	Aggravating factors	Mitigating factors
Social Security – false representation to obtain benefit *Community penalty*	Fraudulent claims over a long period Large amount Organised group offence Planned deception	Misunderstanding of regulations Pressurised by others Small amount
Taking vehicle without consent *Community penalty*	Group action Premeditated Professional hallmarks Related damage Vulnerable victim	Misunderstanding with owner Soon returned Vehicle belonged to family or friend
Theft (general) *Community penalty*	Adult involving children High value Organised team Planned Related damage Sophisticated Vulnerable victim	Impulsive action Low value
Theft in breach of trust *Community penalty*	Casting suspicion on others Committed over a period High value Planned Senior employee Sophisticated Vulnerable victim	Impulsive action Low value Previous inconsistent attitude by employer Single item Unsupported junior
Threatening behaviour POA s.4 *Community penalty.* *Custody if racially or religiously aggravated*	Group action On hospital/medical premises Public put in fear Victim serving the public Vulnerable victim	Minor matter Short duration
TV licence evasion *Discharge/fine*	Failure to respond to payment opportunities	Accidental oversight Confusion of responsibility Licence immediately obtained Very short unlicensed use
Violent disorder *Commit*	Busy public place Fighting between rival groups Large group People put in fear Planned Vulnerable victims Weapon	Impulsive No one put in fear Provocation
Wounding – grievous bodily harm *Commit.*	Deliberate kicking/biting Extensive injuries Group action Offender in position of authority Premeditated Victim particularly vulnerable Victim serving public Weapon	Minor wound Provocation Single blow

499

Excess alcohol offences

Breath	Blood	Urine	Disqualify for not less than	Guideline
36–55	80–125	107–170	12 months	B
56–70	126–160	171–214	16 months	C
71–85	161–195	215–260	24 months	C
86–100	196–229	261–308	24 months	Comm. Pen
101–115	230–264	309–354	30 months	Comm. Pen
116–130	265–300	355–400	30 months	Custody
131+	301+	401+	36 months	Custody

OVERVIEW OF YOUTH COURT SENTENCING POWERS

Youth Court sentencing options

Type of sentence	Must the offence be imprisonable	Age	Minimum	Maximum	PSR	SSR	Other requirements/ comments
Absolute discharge	No	10–17	–	–	No	No	Suitable where the Court does not want to punish the defendant and furthermore feels that the defendant is morally blameless.
Referral order	No	10–17	3 months	12 months	No	No	Available from April 2002. Refers to first time offenders pleading guilty. Refer to the Youth Offender Panel where contract drawn up to prevent re-offending. See separate guidance for length.
Conditional discharge	No	10–17	None	3 years	No	No	Appropriate where inexpedient to punish. But may not be made where offender has received a Final Warning within previous 2 years. If defendant commits offence during currency of order then liable to sentence for subsequent AND original offence.
Fine	No	10–13 14–17	None None	£250 £1000	No	No	Seriousness of offence(s) is reflected in the amount of the fine imposed. The financial circumstances of the offender/parent must be taken into account.
Reparation order	No	10–17	None	24 hours over 3 months	No	Yes	To take into account feelings and wishes of victims of crime, confront offenders with consequences of their criminal behaviour and allowing them to make amends.
Action plan order	No	10–17	3 months	3 months	No	Yes	Short intensive individually tailored response to offending behaviour, addressing causes of offending and offending itself. Can include specified activities.

Type of sentence	Must the offence be imprisonable	Age	Minimum	Maximum	PSR	SSR	Other requirements/ comments
Attendance centre order	Yes	10–13 14–15 16–17	12 hours ^{m} 12 hours 12 hours	12 hours 24 hours^G 36 hours	No	No	Centre must be reasonably accessible m – Can be reduced if 12 hours excessive. G – Can be increased to 24 hours only if 12 are inadequate.
Supervision order	No	10–17	None	3 years	No*	No*	To encourage and assist offenders towards a responsible and law-abiding life, secure rehabilitation, protect public from harm. Prevent further offences. Requirements can be included.
Community rehabilitation order	No	16–17	6 months	3 years	No*	No*	Defendant will be supervised by probation officer. Purpose is to rehabilitate, protect the public and prevent further offences.
Community punishment order	Yes	16–17	40 hours	240 hours	No	Yes	Defendant will be allocated tasks of benefit to the community.
Community punishment & rehabilitation order:	Yes	16–17	1 year	3 years	No*	No*	This Order combines rehabilitation with punishment in the community.
Rehabilitation element: Punishment element:			40 hours	100 hours			Reserved for the most serious offences within the community bracket.
Drug treatment and testing order J	No	16–17	6 months	3 years	Yes	No	Defendant must be dependent on or have propensity to misuse drugs, which requires, and may be susceptible to, treatment. Will be treatment and testing requirements and periodic reviews by court.
Curfew order	No	10–17	Up to 6 months in length (3 months if under 16) 2–12 hours per day		No*	No	Court must obtain and consider information about proposed curfew address including the attitude of others affected by the Order. Order must take account of religious beliefs: for example the Jewish Sabbath runs from Friday sunset to Saturday sunset and special consideration may be appropriate, employment, education and requirement of other Community Orders.
Detention and training order	Yes	12–17	4 months NB. 4,6,8,10,12,18,24 months	24 months	Yes	No	Where offence(s) are so serious a period of custody is required. A period of detention and training followed by a period of supervision. If offender is under 15 years at the date of conviction must be a 'persistent offender'.

* No legal requirement for a PSR (pre-sentence report) to be obtained and SSR (specific sentence report) inappropriate

Parents

These orders may be made in addition to the above disposals:

Type of sentence	Must the offence be imprisonable	Age	Minimum	Maximum	PSR	SSR	Other requirements/ comments
Parenting order	No	10–15 must 16&17 may	–	12 months°	No	Yes	Prevent offending by providing help, support, encouragement and direction to parents in: • taking responsibility • providing proper care/control to their children. 2 elements: (1) ° guidance/ counselling 3 months max, 1 × per week; (2) requirements regarding exercising control over child's behaviour up to 12 months. • Age 10–15 reasons if no Order made.
Parental bind over	No	10–15 must 16–17 may	–	£1,000 3 years or 18th	No	No	An Order binding over the parent(s) where court satisfied in circumstances of the case that to do so would prevent re-offending. Age 10–15 reasons if no Order made.

SENTENCING AUTHORITIES

R. v. *Page* [2004] EWCA Crim 3358, Court of Appeal

Shoplifting

The court gave guidelines on the level of sentence appropriate to cases of shoplifting.

1. When dealing with adult shoplifters:

   (i) it is a classic offence for which custody should be the sentence of last resort and will almost never be appropriate for a first offence (in so far as older authorities suggest to the contrary, they should no longer be regarded as authoritative, except where the aggravating feature of the use of a child was involved, in which case immediate custody was, and still is, merited) and a community penalty may in some cases be appropriate on a plea by a first-time offender even where other adults were involved and the offence was organised;

   (ii) when the offence or offences are attributable to drug addiction, a drug treatment and testing order will often be appropriate;

   (iii) a short custodial term of not more than one month may be appropriate for a defendant who persistently offends on a minor scale and, if that persistence also involves preparation of equipment by the defendant to facilitate the offence, two months might be called for; and

   (iv) even when a defendant has been sentenced for a large number of such offences or where he or she has a history of persistent similar offending on a significant scale, the comparative lack of seriousness of the offence and the need for proportionality between the sentence and the particular offence

will, on a plea of guilty, rarely require a total sentence of more than two years and will often merit no more than 12 to 18 months.
2. Young offenders will usually be dealt with appropriately by a non-custodial penalty, where there is no evidence that they are being used by adults.
3. Nothing is intended to affect the level of sentence appropriate for shoplifting by organised gangs. Where this occurs repeatedly or on a large scale sentences of the order of four years may well be appropriate, even on a plea of guilty.
4. If violence is used on a shopkeeper after theft, so a charge of robbery is inapt, a sentence in excess of four years is likely to be appropriate.

R. v. Kefford [2002] Crim LR 432, Court of Appeal

Appropriate use of custodial sentences

Lord Woolf CJ: This is the judgment of the Court.

The constitution of this Court, consisting of three of the most senior judges in England and Wales who sit in the Court of Appeal (Criminal Division), demonstrates the general importance of this judgment which is on an appeal against sentence.

The judgment has to be seen against the background of a further recent upsurge in the prison population. The latest figures available to the court indicate that the population is at the highest figure yet recorded. The latest figure which we have is 69,892. This increase is over 2,000 inmates higher than the figure forecast in November 2001. That figure has to be compared with the figure at the time of the Strangeways prison disturbances in 1990 when the population was just over 45,000 and falling. The present prison population has also to be compared with the uncrowded capacity of the prison estate which is 63,653 and is worryingly close to the overcrowded capacity of 70,834 inmates.

The prison system should not have to operate so close to its overcrowded capacity. This is because at any one time there will be a number of cells out of commission for operational reasons. In addition, frequently the places where prison space is available are not where the accommodation is required. The stage has now been reached when it would be highly undesirable if the prison population were to continue to rise.

The overcrowding of the prison system is not only a matter for grave concern for the Prison Service, is also a matter of grave concern for the criminal justice system as a whole. Prison sentences are imposed by the courts normally for three purposes: to punish the offender concerned, to deter other offenders and to stop the offender committing further offences in the future. The ability of the Prison Service to tackle a prisoner's offending behaviour and so reduce reoffending is adversely affected if a prison is overcrowded. The ability of the Prison Service to service the courts is impeded if prisons are overcrowded, since the Prison Service is unable to ensure that prisoners arrive at courts at the appropriate time. In the past attempts have been made to relieve overcrowding by using police cells but this is a wholly unsatisfactory remedy. Apart from being extremely expensive, it prevents the police performing their duties in tackling crime.

The present situation has arisen notwithstanding a significant prison building programme. The cost of that programme has been substantial. In the three years ending April 2002, the cost has been respectively, £155 million, £135 million and £175 million. Next year the budgeted cost is £240 million. It is to be hoped that the planned programme of prison building in the future will alleviate this situation.

However any relief will be short lived if the prison population continues to grow. In addition to the prison building expenditure, there is the cost of a prison place which is £36,651 per annum.

Those who are responsible for imposing sentences have to take into account the impact on the prison system of the number of prisoners the prison estate is being required to accommodate at the present time. The courts are not responsible for providing prison places. That is the responsibility of the government. However, the courts must accept the realities of the situation. Providing a new prison takes a substantial period of time and in the present situation it is of the greatest importance to the criminal justice system as a whole and the public who depend upon the criminal justice system for their protection against crime, that only those who need to be sent to prison are sent to prison and that they are not sent to prison for any longer than is necessary.

Nothing that we say in this judgment is intended to deter courts from sending to prison for the appropriate period those who commit offences involving violence or intimidation or other grave crimes. Offences of this nature, particularly if they are committed against vulnerable members of the community undermine the public's sense of safety and the courts must play their part in protecting the public from these categories of offences. There are, however, other categories of offences where a community punishment or a fine can be sometimes a more appropriate form of sentence than imprisonment.

What we have said here is of particular importance to magistrates because they deal with a great many cases where the decision as to whether a prison sentence is necessary is frequently made. When this category of offending comes before the Crown Court, what we have said is equally relevant. We are not breaking new ground in saying this. The same message has been given repeatedly since at least 1980. In *R.* v. *Bibi* [1980] 1 WLR 1193 at p. 1195 Lord Lane CJ said: 'but this case opens up wider horizons because it is no secret that our prisons at the moment are dangerously overcrowded. So much so that sentencing courts must be particularly careful to examine each case to ensure, if an immediate custodial sentence is necessary, that the sentence is as short as possible, consistent only with the duty to protect the interests of the public and to punish and deter the criminal.'

Very much the same thing was said more recently by Rose VP in *R.* v. *Ollerenshaw* [1999] 1 Cr App R (S) 65. We also draw attention to the even more recent decision of this Court in *R.* v. *Mills* (unreported, 14 January 2002) where the same guidance was repeated in the context of the dramatic increase of the female prison population.

In the case of economic crimes, for example obtaining undue credit by fraud, prison is not necessarily the only appropriate form of punishment. Particularly in the case of those who have no record of previous offending, the very fact of having to appear before a court can be a significant punishment. Certainly, having to perform a form of community punishment can be a very salutary way of making it clear that crime does not pay, particularly if a community punishment order is combined with a curfew order. In the appropriate cases, it can be better that an offender repays his debt to society by performing some useful task for the public than spending a short time in prison. The recent Halliday Report makes clear the limits of what can be achieved during a short period of custody. It is preferable that the prison service is in a position to deal effectively, uninhibited by the corrosive effects of overcrowding, with those cases for whom imprisonment is necessary.

R. v. *Mills* [2002] Crim LR 331, Court of Appeal

Custodial sentences for dishonesty where previous good character and single mother

[. . .]

15. In our judgment, a judge also has to take into account the reality of sentencing policy in respect of offences of this nature. The first factor that he has to take into account in doing so is that it is now clear that apart from 'the clang of the prison door' type of sentence, which gives a prisoner the opportunity of knowing what is involved in imprisonment, the ability of the prison service to achieve anything positive in the case of a short prison sentence is very limited. Secondly, with a mother who is the sole support of two young children, as is the case here, the judge has to bear in mind the consequences to those children if the sole carer is sent to prison. Finally, he should take into account the current situation in relation to the female prison population. Since 1993 there has been a remarkable increase. The female prison population has always been substantially lower than that of the male prison population. But the annual increase since 1993 is as follows. It increased from 1,560 to 2,260 in 1996, and then to 3,350 in the year 2000. In November 2001 the total number of females in prison had risen again to 4,020. Females currently comprise 5.9 per cent of the total prison population. The proportion has increased from an average of 4.4 per cent in 1997, to 5 per cent in 1999, and 5.2 per cent in the year 2000. Between November 2000 and November 2001 the number of females held increased by 19 per cent, from 3,380 to 4,020. That 19 per cent increase in the female prison population has to be compared with an increase of 6 per cent in the male prison population. The male prison population is substantially larger. There the increase is from 60,690 to 64,430.

16. Short prison sentences are always difficult for the prison service to accommodate. The rise in the female prison population means that two male prison establishments have now had to be converted to female prisons. Because of the smaller percentage of the prison population, the ability to imprison mothers close to their homes in the community is difficult. The difficulties in the prison population to which we have referred does not mean that if an offence is such that it is necessary to send an offender to prison, they should not be sent to prison for the appropriate time. But in a borderline case, in a case where the offence does not in particular involve violence but is one with financial consequences to a commercial concern, it is very important that those who have responsibilities for sentencing take into account the facts to which we have referred with regard to the prison population as well as the other matters. In a case of a person such as this appellant who is of previous good character, who has been performing useful acts in the community, where there is every reason to think that she will not offend again, and where the offending behaviour is out of character with her normal behaviour, the courts should strive to avoid sending her to prison and instead use punishments in the community which enable offenders to repay the harm they have done. It is true that obtaining credit, as this appellant did, is easy for those who resort to dishonesty. The courts should deter those sort of offences, albeit some would say that the credit companies should do more to check references which are given by those who attempt to commit offences of this nature. Be that as it may, commercial concerns are entitled to the protection of the courts. What we have said merely indicates the course which where possible the courts should take to impose a punishment which is fitting and appropriate for that nature of offence.

R. v. *Baldwin*, *The Times*, 22 November 2002, Court of Appeal

Use of fines

Fines were, in the judgment of the court underused. Where there was evidence that the offender was unlikely to re-offend and had stability in his life (employment, etc.), it was desirable to explore the use of a financial or other non-custodial penalty, particularly in light of the present state of prison overcrowding.

R. v. *Kelly*, 30 July 2002, unreported, Court of Appeal

Drug treatment and testing order

[. . .]
7.   The appellant is now 28. He has an appalling record, having been convicted of some 87 offences, 59 of which are for theft or kindred offences. He has spent a total of six years in custody. The pre-sentence report noted that prior to the appellant's arrest he was using half a gramme of heroin a day at a cost of £35. The report proposed that the appellant be assessed for a drug treatment and testing order (DTTO) and Mr Recorder Axtell adjourned sentencing to allow an assessment for such an order to be undertaken. That assessment reported that the substances that caused the most difficulty for the appellant were heroin and Benzodiazepines. The DTTO team was of the opinion that the appellant required an intensive and structured programme of work to overcome his addiction. The appellant was assessed suitable for a DTTO for eighteen months, during which he should attend a residential rehabilitation programme. However, no such appropriate programme was then available, which meant that if he was sentenced to a DTTO he would have to spend the first two weeks on a community programme, which it was thought would be less intensive.

8.   When the appellant came back to be sentenced, His Honour Judge Price said that the totality of his offending was too great and that there was no alternative but to impose a sentence of immediate imprisonment. He accordingly proceeded to pass the sentences we have already referred to, amounting to a total of three years six months' imprisonment with two additional months consecutive for breach of licence.
[. . .]
15.   With respect to the learned sentencing judge, we are of the view that he gave too great importance to the appellant's scale of offending and therefore gave too little consideration to the appropriateness of a DTTO disposal. The sad fact is that it will often be the case that a candidate for a DTTO has been guilty of acquisitive offending on a significant scale to fund his drug addiction. DTTOs provide a chance for the offender to break his addiction and therefore cease offending. Thus a sentencing judge must be careful not to give disproportionate weight to the scale of offending and thereby diminish the usefulness both to the offender and to the community of a DTTO.

R. v. *Banks*, 15 January 2003, unreported, Court of Appeal

Discharge of fines within 12 months

The court once again stated that fines should be set at a level which allowed for their complete discharge within a period of 12 months, taking into account the offender's financial circumstances and the seriousness of the offence.

R. v. Ghafoor, **19 July 2002, unreported, Court of Appeal**

Sentencing of adults where offence committed whilst a youth

The approach to be adopted where a defendant crosses a relevant age threshold between the date of the commission of the offence and the date of conviction should now be clear. The starting point is the sentence that the defendant would have been likely to receive if he had been sentenced at the date of the commission of the offence. It has been described as 'a powerful factor'. That is for the obvious reason that, as Mr Emmerson points out, the philosophy of restricting sentencing powers in relation to young persons reflects both (a) society's acceptance that young offenders are less responsible for their actions and therefore less culpable than adults, and (b) the recognition that, in consequence, sentencing them should place greater emphasis on rehabilitation, and less on retribution and deterrence than in the case of adults. It should be noted that the 'starting point' is not the maximum sentence that could lawfully have been imposed, but the sentence that the offender would have been likely to receive.

So the sentence that would have been passed at the date of the commission of the offence is a 'powerful factor'. It is the starting point, and other factors may have to be considered. But in our judgment, there have to be good reasons for departing from the starting point. An examination of the authorities to which we have been referred shows that, although the court has looked at other factors to see whether there should be a departure from the starting point, it is not obvious that there has in fact been a departure in any of them. This serves to demonstrate how powerful a factor the starting point is. That is because justice requires there to be good reason to pass a sentence higher than would have been passed at the date of the commission of the offence.

That is not to say that the starting point may not be tempered somewhat in certain cases. We have in mind in particular cases where there is a long interval between the date of commission of the offence and the date of conviction. By the date of conviction, circumstances may have changed significantly. The offender may now have been revealed as a dangerous criminal, whereas at the date of the offence that was not so. By the date of conviction, the tariff for the offence in question may have increased. These are factors that can be taken into account, and can, in an appropriate case, properly lead to the passing of a sentence somewhat higher than the sentence that would have been passed at the date of the commission of the offence. It will rarely be necessary for a court even to consider passing a sentence that is more severe than the maximum that it would have had jurisdiction to pass at the date of commission of the offence.

But in a case such as the present where the date of conviction is only a few months after the date of the offence, we think that it would rarely be appropriate to pass a longer sentence than that which would have been passed at the date of the offence. In this case, then, if the appellant had been sentenced at the time of the offence, having regard to his plea of guilty, he should have received a sentence of 18 months detention and training. The maximum permissible sentence would have been 24 months: he would have been entitled to credit for his plea of guilty which could not have been less than 6 months (see section 101(1) of the Powers of Criminal Court (Sentencing) Act 2000). The equivalent sentence for an 18 year old is 18 months detention in a young offender institution. The judge should, therefore, have arrived at this sentence as the correct starting point. He should then have considered whether there were any good reasons for departing from it. In our view, there were plainly none. The interval of time between the date of the offence and the date of conviction was relatively short. The judge identified no reasons for passing a higher sentence than the starting point sentence, let alone one which was three times as long.

R. v. *McInerney and others* [2003] 1 Cr App R 627, Court of Appeal

Domestic burglary

[. . .]

The Panel's Proposals

A standard burglary

17.   In making their proposals relating to domestic burglaries of the classes identified in paragraph 1 of this judgment, the Panel helpfully make clear that although they 'have not adopted the results of the public opinion survey' they have taken into account public attitudes in deciding what is for sentencing purposes a 'typical' or as they prefer to say a 'standard' domestic burglary. A standard domestic burglary is a burglary which has the following features:

(i)   it is committed by a repeat offender;
(ii)   it involves the theft of electrical goods such as a television or video;
(iii)   the theft of personal items such as jewellery;
(iv)   damage is caused by the break-in itself;
(v)   some turmoil in the house, such as drawers upturned or damage to some items occurs;
(vi)   no injury or violence, but some trauma is caused to the victim.

18.   Although the Panel do not say this specifically, we assume that the theft of the electrical goods or the personal items are alternative and the standard burglary does not need to have all of the listed features. Some of the features can be sufficient to bring the offence within the same category. It is in this sense that we use the term 'standard burglary' in this judgment.

19.   The width of the definition of burglary in section 9 of the Theft Act 1968 underlines the fact that this court can do no more than provide guidelines. The application of the guidelines must be subject to all the circumstances of the particular case and sentencers in applying the guidelines must tailor their sentence to meet those circumstances.

Aggravating and mitigating features

20.   Having established what they regarded and what we also treat as a standard burglary the Panel went on in the conventional way to identify what they regarded as being aggravating and mitigating factors. In doing so the Panel took into account the responses from the Report. These factors were not the same as those laid down by this court in *Brewster*. Nonetheless we consider that the factors identified by the Panel should be the ones that courts should now apply. Though they are to be treated as examples and not as an exhaustive list.

21.   The Panel divided the aggravating factors into two categories. We consider this is helpful as long as it appreciated there is no clear line between the categories and they can overlap. The high-level aggravating factors are:

• force used or threatened against the victim;
• a victim injured (as a result of force used or threatened);

- the especially traumatic effect on the victim, in excess of the trauma generally associated with a standard burglary;
- professional planning, organisation or execution;
- vandalism of the premises, in excess of the damage generally associated with a standard burglary;
- the offence was racially aggravated;
- a vulnerable victim deliberately targeted (including cases of 'deception' or 'distraction' of the elderly).

22.   The medium-level aggravating features are:

- a vulnerable victim, although not targeted as such;
- the victim was at home (whether daytime or night-time burglary);
- goods of high value were taken (economic or sentimental);
- the burglars worked in a group.

23.   An example of a case that could overlap the two categories, would be a case where the victim is especially old, say in his 90s but was not shown to have been targeted because of this. The Panel does not refer specifically to the number of offences in relation to which the offender is to be sentenced. The number of offences may indicate that the offender is a professional burglar which would be a high level aggravating feature but even if they do not fall within this category the number could still be at least a mid-level aggravating feature. The fact that the offender is on bail or licence can also be an aggravating feature as can the fact that the offence was committed out of spite.

24.   The Panel, rightly in our view, did not seek to indicate what percentage uplift should result from the presence of either the high-level or medium-level factors. They did, however, indicate, and again we would agree, that it is appropriate for the sentencer 'to reflect the degree of harm done, including the impact of the burglary upon the victim whether or not the offender foresaw that result or the extent of that impact'. If, of course the offender foresees a result of the offending behaviour then that increases the seriousness of the offence.

25.   The Panel also identified features (again they should not be regarded as an exhaustive list) which obviously are appropriate to take into account in mitigating the seriousness of the offence. They are:

- a first offence;
- nothing, or only property of very low value, is stolen;
- the offender played only a minor part in the burglary;
- there is no damage or disturbance to property.

The fact that the crime is committed on impulse may also be a mitigating factor.

26.   The Panel drew attention to the fact that the survey showed that for the public the time of the commission of the burglary was not itself significant. However, if it is committed at night, that makes it more likely that the premises are occupied. In addition, we would suggest that an intrusion into an occupied home must be more frightening to the occupants, if they find that they have intruders at a time when they are in the dark, particularly if they are woken from their sleep. A confrontation of the householder, by the burglar, could in our judgment amount to an aggravating feature.

27.   We also agree with the Panel that it is necessary to take into account other factors including a timely plea of guilty. Where section 111 of the 2000 Act [PCCSA] applies, the reduction is limited to 20 per cent of the determinate sentence of at least three years.

28.   In addition, the offender's age or state of health, both physical and mental can be a mitigating fact, so can evidence of genuine remorse, response to previous sentences and ready co-operation with the police.

29.   We have already agreed that the fact that it is a first offence should be regarded as a mitigating factor. In the case of burglary so far as sentencing is concerned, we do consider that the offender's criminal record is, as was indicated in *Brewster*, of more particular significance. In judging the record it is of course necessary to take into account the type of offence for which the offender has previously been convicted and the number of offences which were considered on any particular occasion. It is of importance that the efforts which an offender has or has not made to rehabilitate himself. In the case of offences committed because the offender is an alcoholic or a drug addict, while the taking of drink or drugs is no mitigation, the sentencing process must recognise the fact of the addiction and the importance of breaking the drug or drink problem. This is not only in the interests of the offender but also in the public interest since so commonly the addiction results in a vicious circle of imprisonment followed by re-offending. When an offender is making or prepared to make a real effort to break his addiction, it is important for the sentencing court to make allowances if the process of rehabilitation proves to be irregular. What may be important is the overall progress that the offender is making. This is part of the thinking behind drug and treatment orders.

30.   As the Panel pointed out, in relation to section 111 of the 2000 Act, there 'are some first time burglaries which on their facts are so serious that a sentence of three years or more might be appropriate but, conversely some third, fourth or fifth time burglaries where a sentence lower than three years could properly be justified'. (The lower sentence being achieved by the reliance on the exception to section 111.)

31.   As to the appropriate sentencing under section 111 it has also to be borne in mind (again as the Panel observes) that an offender convicted of a single domestic burglary will accrue a qualifying conviction. Equally an offender convicted on one occasion of three burglaries who asked for another three burglaries to be taken into consideration will also only accrue one qualifying offence. The totality of the actual criminal behaviour is important.

The starting points suggested by the Panel after a trial

32.   In relation to adult offenders, not taking into account any aggravating or personal mitigating factors or the discount for a guilty plea, in relation to a completed, as opposed to an attempted, burglary of domestic premises, the panel divided their recommendations into four categories. We set out what they recommended in relation to each category (omitting the references to earlier cases since on examination we did not regard them as throwing additional light on the issues in relation to which they were cited):

   (a)   For a low level burglary committed by a first-time domestic burglar (and for some second-time domestic burglars), where there is no damage to property and no property (or only property of very low value) is stolen, the starting point should be a community sentence . . . Other types of cases at this level would include thefts (provided they are of items of low value) from attached garages or from vacant property . . . .

   (b)   For a domestic burglary displaying most of the features of the standard domestic burglary [see paragraph 17] above (theft of electrical goods and/or personal items, damage caused by the break-in, some turmoil in the house and some trauma to the victim), but committed by a first-time domestic burglar, the starting point should be a custodial sentence of 9 months. A case at this level would, on a guilty plea, be suitable for disposal in a magistrates' court . . . The starting point for a second-time domestic burglar committing such an offence should be a custodial sentence of 18 months. When the offence is committed by an offender with two or more previous qualifying convictions for domestic burglary, the starting point is a custodial sentence of three years – i.e. the presumptive minimum now prescribed by law in these circumstances.

(c) In the case of a standard domestic burglary which additionally displays any one of the 'medium relevance' factors referred to in paragraph [22 above], but committed by a first-time domestic burglar, the starting point should be a custodial sentence of 12 months. The starting point for a second-time domestic burglar committing such an offence should be a custodial sentence of two years. When the offence is committed by an offender with two or more previous convictions for domestic burglary the starting point is a custodial sentence of three and a half years (42 months).

(d) In the case of a standard domestic burglary which additionally displays any one of the 'high relevance' factors mentioned in [paragraph 21], but committed by a first-time domestic burglar, the starting point should be a custodial sentence of 18 months. The starting point for a second-time domestic burglar committing such an offence should be a custodial sentence of three years. When the offence is committed by an offender with two or more previous convictions for domestic burglary the starting point is a custodial sentence of 4 and a half years (54 months). The presence of more than one 'high relevance' factor could bring the sentence for an offence at this level significantly above the suggested starting points.

33. The suggested starting points in paragraphs (b) to (d) indicate a substantial increase in the length of the custodial sentence each time the offender commits a further qualifying burglary. However, the Panel proposes that this incremental increase in sentencing levels should slow significantly after the third qualifying conviction in order to retain a degree of proportionality. In addition, it will be observed that although divided into sub-paragraphs the Panel's starting points actually include more than four recommendations. We draw attention in particular to sub-paragraph (b). It will be seen that the starting points rise in clear stages until they reach the statutory minimum presumed under section 111. The process then continues in sub-paragraph (c) and (d).

Our starting points

34. As to the starting points contained in (d), we would endorse the recommendation of the Panel. We also endorse the non-custodial approach recommended in (a).

35. In relation to (b) and (c) we adopt a different approach. It is not so much a question of our parting company with the approach of the Panel that fits in conveniently with the automatic sentence provided for by section 111 of the 2000 Act, (while recognising that hitherto their approach would be regarded as being an appropriate approach to adopt), but our adopting a difference of emphasis.

36. An unqualified approach under sub-paragraphs (b) and (c) will reinforce the flaws in our present sentencing policies. Its effect on the present deeply depressing pattern of re-offending will be limited. That its effect should be limited is not

surprising when the reality behind a prison sentence of 12 or for that matter 18 months is taken into account. The prisoner will be statutorily entitled to release after half of the sentence. Before the prisoner reaches that point release will in fact have occurred in accordance with the practice quoted by Lord Falconer in the passage from Hansard which we have cited.

37. We fully accept that there are some cases where the clang of the prison cell door for the first time may have a deterrent effect but the statistics of re-offending suggest that the numbers who will be deterred by their first experience of incarceration are not substantial. If they are not deterred by their first period of incarceration, then it becomes even less likely that a moderately longer sentence (which equally gives no opportunity for tackling re-offending behaviour) will achieve anything. We therefore have reservations to a ladder of increasing sentences with starting points nine, 12 and 18 months.

38. In saying what we have, we have not forgotten the importance of maintaining the public's confidence in the criminal justice system and protecting the public from offending behaviour particularly offending behaviour such as domestic burglary which causes the public great distress. On the contrary, it is our intention that the guidance that we give should provide greater protection than is provided at present. Here we refer to the report of the Social Exclusion Unit dated July 2002. The Summary sets out the following picture:

1. Prison sentences are not succeeding in turning the majority of offenders away from crime. Of those prisoners released in 1997, 58 per cent were convicted of another crime within two years. 36 per cent were back inside on another prison sentence. The system struggles particularly to reform younger offenders. 18–20-year-old male prisoners were reconvicted at a rate of 72 per cent over the same period; 47 per cent received another prison sentence.

2. Despite falling in the 1980s, the reconviction rate rose again in the 1990s and has remained obstinately high in recent years. The factors behind this are complex, but it is possible to single out a number of changes over that period which may have contributed: these include an erosion in post-release support for short-term prisoners – those sentenced to less than 12 months; a change in benefit rules for prisoners; and the sharp rise in social exclusion, in areas such as child poverty, drug use, school exclusion and inequality.

3. In fact, the headline reconviction figure masks a far greater problem for public safety. We know, for instance, that of those reconvicted in the two years following release, each will actually have received three further convictions on average. For each reconviction, it is estimated that five recorded offences are committed. At a conservative estimate, released prisoners are responsible for at least 1 million crimes per year – 18 per cent of recorded, notifiable crimes. And this takes no account of the amount of unrecorded crime that ex-prisoners, reconvicted or otherwise, will have committed.

The cost

4. Many of the costs of re-offending by ex-prisoners are not quantifiable, but can be devastating and long-term, and are frequently felt by the most vulnerable in society. Most obviously, there is the impact on victims, many of whom will be repeat victims, and on their families; also on communities, predominantly the most disadvantaged. In turn, where re-offenders are caught and imprisoned, a heavy toll is taken on their families and on their own lives.

5. The financial cost of re-offending by ex-prisoners, calculated from the overall costs of crime, is staggering and widely felt. In terms of the cost to the criminal justice system of dealing with the consequences of crime, recorded crime alone committed by ex-prisoners comes to at least £11 billion per year.

6. An ex-prisoner's path back to prison is extremely costly for the criminal justice system. A re-offending ex-prisoner is likely to be responsible for crime costing the criminal justice system an average of £65,000. Prolific offenders will cost even more. When re-offending leads to a further prison sentence, the costs soar. The average cost of a prison sentence imposed at a Crown Court is roughly £30,500, made up of court and other legal costs. The costs of actually keeping prisoners within prison vary significantly, but average £37,500 per year.

7. And yet these costs are only a fraction of the overall cost of re-offending. First, recorded crime accounts for between only a quarter and a tenth of total crime, and ex-prisoners are likely to be prolific offenders. They may, therefore, be responsible for a large proportion of unrecorded crime and its costs as well. Second, there are high financial costs to: the police and the criminal justice system more widely; the victims of the crimes; other public agencies who also have to pick up the pieces; the national economy through loss of income; the communities in which they live; and, of course, prisoners themselves and their families.

39. We also refer to two of the paragraphs dealing with the causes.

12. Many prisoners' basic skills are very poor. 80 per cent have the writing skills, 65 per cent the numeracy skills and 50 per cent the reading skills at or below the level of an 11-year-old child. 60 to 70 per cent of prisoners were using drugs before imprisonment. Over 70 per cent suffer from at least two mental disorders. And 20 per cent of male and 37 per cent of female sentenced prisoners have attempted suicide in the past. The position is often even worse for 18–20-year-olds, whose basic skills, unemployment rate and school exclusion background are all over a third worse than those of older prisoners.

[. . .]

14. There is a considerable risk that a prison sentence might actually make the factors associated with re-offending worse. For example, a third lose their house while in prison, two-thirds lose their job, over a fifth face increased financial problems and over two-fifths lose contact with their family. There are also real dangers of mental and physical health deteriorating further, of life and thinking skills being eroded, and of prisoners being introduced to drugs. By aggravating the factors associated with re-offending, prison sentences can prove counter-productive as a contribution to crime reduction and public safety.

40. To maintain a situation, which makes no contribution to changing this picture, will not increase but reduce the confidence of the public in the criminal justice system.

41. There is another aspect of the problem of which the Panel were acutely aware and that is the fact that as a result of the prison system being so grossly over-crowded, the Prison Service cannot achieve the limited assistance which could otherwise be provided during a short sentence particularly if it is coupled with continued training and supervision after release from prison. The Panel referred to a global increase of around 10,800 and the fact that they had been informed that the long term prison projections 'currently assume that the domestic burglary provision will lead to a 4,500 increase in the prison population, although this figure will have to be revised over time.' In relation to that figure the Panel appropriately comment: 'This must be a matter of grave concern given the current unprecedented numbers in prison'. Now it is being projected that the prison population

will reach almost 110,000 by the end of the decade (Home Office statistics published December 2002).

42. The Panel in an annexe set out figures from the 2000 British Crime Survey which show that it is estimated that there were 760,000 incidents in 1999 in which a burglar gained entry into a home and just under three quarters of those involved theft of property. These are very high figures but they actually represent a fall in the number of burglaries by 21 per cent between 1997 and 1999. The annexe also gives figures as to the pattern of sentencing in 2000. Figures indicate that in the magistrates' court of the 4,800 offenders who were sentenced, 29 per cent were sentenced to immediate custody and the average sentence length was 5.3 months. In the Crown Court of the 10,227 offenders who were sentenced, 77 per cent were given immediate custody and the average sentence was 20.9 months in 2000, 90 per cent of the sentences being between six months and three years.

43. Against those gloomy statistics, there is positive evidence emerging as to what can be achieved by punishment in the community. Here the Panel said:

> 29. But reform of sentences would not, of itself, be enough. Major changes to the way in which those inside and outside the criminal justice system operate are necessary to ensure that the system is focusing resources sufficiently to deal with the right people, using robust systems of accountability and joint working, and delivering in innovative ways. Long-term change is needed to ensure that all those dealing with prisoners and ex-prisoners make the maximum possible impact on re-offending.

Guidance

44. We therefore propose that instead of adopting a stepped approach as suggested by the Panel in sub-paragraphs (b) and (c) in cases in which courts would otherwise be looking to starting point of up to 18 months imprisonment, the initial approach of the courts should be to impose a community sentence subject to conditions that ensure that the sentence is (a) an effective punishment; and (b) one which offers action on the part of the Probation Service to tackle the offender's criminal behaviour; and (c) when appropriate, will tackle the offender's underlying problems such as drug addiction. If, and only if, the court is satisfied the offender has demonstrated by his or her behaviour that punishment in the community is not practicable, should the court resort to a custodial sentence. It will be pointless to try and identify all the factors that will indicate that a community disposal is not a practical option but they may relate to the effect of the offence on the victim, the nature of the offence or the offender's record.

45. The increased use of community punishment that this approach involves will set the Probation Service a real challenge but this is a challenge that they are now in a position to accept. The public will benefit from this approach as it requires appropriate action to tackle the offending behaviour of the offender. It will also result in a saving in the expense of imprisonment. The public will also benefit because it should help to reduce the demands placed on the Prison Service by ever increasing numbers.

46. The new approach to sentencing we are setting out (in relation to cases in which otherwise a sentence of 18 months imprisonment or less would have been imposed following a trial) should and is intended to provide better protection for the public and to result in some reduction in the use of custody. Its ability to do this will be increased when the Criminal Justice Bill, which is now before

Parliament, is passed and a greater number of sentencing options are available to magistrates and judges.

47.   If, of course, a prisoner does not comply with the requirements of a community punishment and, in particular, if he commits further offences during the currency of that sentence, then he should be re-sentenced. We accept the fact that if an offender has not complied with the requirements of a community punishment this will be a strong indicator that a custodial sentence and possibly a substantial sentence is necessary.

48.   Where a custodial sentence is necessary, then it should be no longer than necessary. In the case of repeat offenders and aggravated offences long sentences will still be necessary as indicated by the Panel in sub-paragraphs (b) (c) and (d) above. As to the incremental increases, we agree with the Panel, that the increase in sentencing levels should slow significantly after the third qualifying conviction. It is necessary to retain a degree of proportionality between the level of sentence for burglary and other serious offences.

Juvenile offenders

49.   As to juvenile offenders, the Panel stated its advice in the following terms:

> 36.   Exceptionally, since domestic burglary is one of the offences which may attract a sentence of long-term detention under s.91 of the Powers of Criminal Courts (Sentencing) Act 2000, a young offender may be committed by the youth court for trial in the Crown Court with a view to such a sentence being passed. A sentence of long-term detention is available in respect of any offender aged 10 to 17 inclusive who is convicted of domestic burglary.
>
> 37.   Where an offender who is now aged 18 or over has two qualifying previous convictions for domestic burglary as a juvenile, a third alleged domestic burglary must be tried in the Crown Court, and the presumptive minimum sentence is a custodial sentence of three years. Although section 111 does not apply until the offender has attained the age of 18, it would seem to follow that for an offender who is under 18 but is charged with a third domestic burglary, a custodial sentence in excess of 24 months (the maximum term available for a detention and training order) will be the likely sentence and so the youth court should generally commit the case to Crown Court for trial with a view to sentence under section 91.

50.   We generally endorse this approach subject to reiterating more strongly in relation to juveniles what we have already said. The Youth Justice Board is spearheading effective punishment in the community and it is important that, where appropriate, juvenile offenders are dealt with in Youth Court and not the Crown Court.

Generally

51.   We draw attention to the important powers of court to make restitution and compensation orders. When appropriate, those orders should always be made.

52.   The final point we make before turning to the two specific appeals which are before us, is to remind magistrates' courts and their clerks that, because of the provisions of section 111 of the 2000 Act, when a defendant charged with domestic burglary has two or more qualifying previous convictions, then the latest charge is only triable on indictment.

R. v. *Oliver*, unreported, 21 November 2002

Indecent images

[. . .]

We categorise the relevant levels as:

1. images depicting erotic posing with no sexual activity;
2. sexual activity between children, or solo masturbation by a child;
3. non-penetrative sexual activity between adults and children;
4. penetrative sexual activity between children and adults;
5. sadism or bestiality.

[. . .]

11. As to the nature of the offender's activity, the seriousness of an individual offence increases with the offender's proximity to, and responsibility for, the original abuse. Any element of commercial gain will place an offence at a high level of seriousness. In our judgment, swapping of images can properly be regarded as a commercial activity, albeit without financial gain, because it fuels demand for such material. Wide-scale distribution, even without financial profit, is intrinsically more harmful than a transaction limited to two or three individuals, both by reference to the potential use of the images by active paedophiles, and by reference to the shame and degradation to the original victims.

12. Merely locating an image on the internet will generally be less serious than downloading it. Downloading will generally be less serious than taking an original film or photograph of indecent posing or activity. We agree with the Panel that the choice between a custodial and non-custodial sentence is particularly difficult. On the one hand, there is considerable pressure, demonstrated by Parliament increasing the maximum permissible sentence, to mark society's abhorrence of child sexual abuse and child pornography by the use of custody. On the other hand, there is evidence that sex offender treatment programmes can be effective in controlling offenders' behaviour and thus preventing the commission of further offences. We agree with the Panel's recommendation that, in any case which is close to the custody threshold, the offender's suitability for treatment should be assessed with a view to imposing a community rehabilitation order with a requirement to attend a sex offender treatment programme. We also agree with the Panel that the appropriate sentence should not be determined by the availability of additional orders, or by the availability of treatment programmes for offenders in custody.

13. That said, we turn to the particular factors relevant to the level of sentence. We stress that the proposals we make are guidelines intended to help sentencers. They are not to be construed as providing sentencers with a straitjacket from which they cannot escape. We bear in mind the current state of overcrowding in our prisons, and that a custodial sentence should only be imposed when necessary. We also bear in mind the public concern in this area to which we have already referred.

14. In our judgment, a fine will normally be appropriate in a case where the offender was merely in possession of material solely for his own use, including cases where material was downloaded from the internet but was not further distributed, and either the material consisted entirely of pseudo-photographs, the making of which had involved no abuse or exploitation of children, or there was no more than a small quantity of material at Level 1. A conditional discharge may be appropriate in such a case if the defendant pleads guilty and has no previous

convictions. But a discharge should not be granted, as we have earlier indicated, for the purpose of avoiding the requirement of registration under the Sex Offenders Act 1997.

15. Possession, including downloading, of artificially created pseudo-photographs and the making of such images, should generally be treated as being at a lower level of seriousness than possessing or making photographic images of real children. But there may be exceptional cases in which the possession of a pseudo-photograph is as serious as the possession of a photograph of a real child: for example, where the pseudo-photograph provides a particularly grotesque image generally beyond the scope of a photograph. It is also to be borne in mind that, although pseudo-photographs lack the historical element of likely corruption of real children depicted in photographs, pseudo-photographs may be as likely as real photographs to fall into the hands of, or to be shown to, the vulnerable, and there to have equally corrupting effect. It will usually be desirable that a charge or count in an indictment specifies whether photographs or pseudo-photographs are involved.

16. We agree with the Panel that a community sentence may be appropriate in a case where the offender was in possession of a large amount of material at Level 1 and/or no more than a small number of images at Level 2, provided the material had not been distributed or shown to others. For an offender with the necessary level of motivation and co-operation, the appropriate sentence would be a community rehabilitation order with a sex offender programme. We agree with the Panel that the custody threshold will usually be passed where any of the material has been shown or distributed to others, or, in cases of possession, where there is a large amount of material at Level 2, or a small amount at Level 3 or above. A custodial sentence of up to six months will generally be appropriate in a case where (a) the offender was in possession of a large amount of material at Level 2 or a small amount at Level 3; or (b) the offender has shown, distributed, or exchanged indecent material at Level 1 or 2 on a limited scale, without financial gain. A custodial sentence of between six and 12 months will generally be appropriate for (a) showing or distributing a large number of images at Level 2 or 3; or (b) possessing a small number of images at Levels 4 or 5.

17. In relation to more serious offences, a custodial sentence between 12 months and three years will generally be appropriate for (a) possessing a large quantity of material at Levels 4 or 5, even if there was no showing or distribution of it to others; or (b) showing or distributing a large number of images at Level 3; or (c) producing or trading in material at Levels 1 to 3. Sentences longer than three years should be reserved for cases where (a) images at Levels 4 or 5 have been shown or distributed; or (b) the offender was actively involved in the production of images at Levels 4 or 5, especially where that involvement included a breach of trust, and whether or not there was an element of commercial gain; or (c) the offender had commissioned or encouraged the production of such images. An offender whose conduct merits more than three years will merit a higher sentence if his conduct is within more than one of categories (a), (b) and (c) than one where conduct is within only one such category.

18. Sentences approaching the 10-year maximum will be appropriate in very serious cases where the defendant has a previous conviction either for dealing in child pornography, or for abusing children sexually or with violence. Previous such convictions in less serious cases may result in the custody threshold being passed and will be likely to give rise to a higher sentence where the custody threshold has been passed. An extended sentence may be appropriate in some

cases, even where the custodial term is quite short: see *R.* v. *Nelson* [2002] 1 Cr App R(S) 565.

19. The levels of sentence which we have indicated are appropriate for adult offenders after a contested trial and without (save to the extent that we have referred to them) previous convictions.

20. There are specific factors which are capable of aggravating the seriousness of a particular offence. We identify these as follows:

(i) If the images have been shown or distributed to a child.

(ii) If there are a large number of images. It is impossible to specify precision as to numbers. Sentencers must make their own assessment of whether the numbers are small or large. Regard must be had to the principles presently applying by virtue of *R.* v. *Canavan, Kidd and Shaw* [1998] 1 Cr App R 79.

(iii) The way in which a collection of images is organised on a computer may indicate a more or less sophisticated approach on the part of the offender to trading, or a higher level of personal interest in the material. An offence will be less serious if images have been viewed but not stored.

(iv) Images posted on a public area of the internet, or distributed in a way making it more likely they will be found accidentally by computer users not looking for pornographic material, will aggravate the seriousness of the offence.

(v) The offence will be aggravated if the offender was responsible for the original production of the images, particularly if the child or children involved were members of the offender's own family, or were drawn from particularly vulnerable groups, such as those who have left or have been taken from their home or normal environment, whether for the purposes of exploitation or otherwise, or if the offender has abused a position of trust, as in the case of a teacher, friend of the family, social worker, or youth group leader.

(vi) The age of the children involved may be an aggravating feature. In many cases it will be difficult to quantity the effect of age by reference to the impact on the child. But in some cases that impact may be apparent. For example, assaults on babies or very young children attract particular repugnance and may, by the conduct depicted in the image, indicate the likelihood of physical injury to the private parts of the victim. Some conduct may manifestly (that is to say, apparently from the image) have induced fear or distress in the victim, and some conduct which might not cause fear or distress to an adolescent child, might cause fear or distress to a child of, say, 6 or 7.

21. So far as mitigation is concerned, we agree with the Panel that some, but not much, weight should be attached to good character. A plea of guilty, by virtue of section 152 of the Powers of Criminal Courts (Sentencing) Act 2000, is a statutory mitigating factor. The extent of the sentencing discount to be allowed for a plea of guilty will vary according to the timing and circumstances of the plea. The sooner it is tendered, the greater is likely to be the discount: see, for example, *R.* v. *Barber* [2002] 1 Cr App R(S) 548.

22. These kind of offences very rarely result in the prosecution or cautioning of offenders under the age of 18. When such a person has to be sentenced, the appropriate sentence is likely to be a supervision order with a relevant treatment programme. We draw attention, however, as did the Panel, to the apparent present shortage of adequate treatment programmes for young sex offenders.

R. v. Webbe and others **[2001] Crim LR 668, Court of Appeal**

Handling stolen goods

1.   The sentencing panel, in paragraph 14, go on to identify nine factors, which may be regarded as aggravating the offence. With each of those factors we agree. They are as follows:

   1.   The closeness of the handler to the primary offence. (We add that closeness may be geographical, arising from presence at or near the primary offence when it was committed, or temporal, where the handler instigated or encouraged the primary offence beforehand, or, soon after, provided a safe haven or route for disposal).
   2.   Particular seriousness in the primary offence.
   3.   High value of the goods to the loser, including sentimental value.
   4.   The fact that the goods were the proceeds of a domestic burglary.
   5.   Sophistication in relation to the handling.
   6.   A high level of profit made or expected by the handler.
   7.   The provision by the handler of a regular outlet for stolen goods.
   8.   Threats of violence or abuse of power by the handler over others, for example, an adult commissioning criminal activity by children, or a drug dealer pressurizing addicts to steal in order to pay for their habit.
   9.   As is statutorily provided by section 151(2) of the Powers of Criminal Courts (Sentencing) Act 2000, the commission of an offence while on bail.

2.   We also agree with the mitigating factors identified as being among those relevant by the sentencing panel: namely, low monetary value of the goods, the fact that the offence was a one-off offence, committed by an otherwise honest defendant, the fact that there is little or no benefit to the defendant, and the fact of voluntary restitution to the victim.

3.   We also agree with the panel that other factors to be taken into account include personal mitigation, ready co-operation with the police, previous convictions, especially for offences of dishonesty and, as statutorily provided by section 152 of the Powers of Criminal Courts (Sentencing) Act 2000, a timely plea of guilty.

4.   The panel, in paragraph 21 of their advice, helpfully identify four possible levels of seriousness of the offence. They suggest that a distinction can be drawn between offences first, for which a fine or a discharge is appropriate; second, for which a community sentence is appropriate; third, for those which cross the custody threshold and, fourth, more serious offences.

5.   We agree that offences do fall into those four categories. We do not, however, take the view that it is always possible to draw a distinction between the first two categories of offence with quite the clarity which the panel suggest.

6.   In our judgment, the panel are right to say that, where the property handled is of low monetary value and was acquired for the receiver's own use, the starting point should generally be a moderate fine or, in some cases (particularly, of course, if a fine cannot be paid by a particular defendant) a discharge. Such an outcome would, in our judgment be appropriate in relation to someone of previous good character handling low value domestic goods for his own use. By low value we mean less than four figures.

7.   We agree that, irrespective of value, the presence of any one of the aggravating features to which we have referred is likely to result in a community sentence rather than a fine or discharge. We agree that a community sentence may be

appropriate where property worth less than four figures is acquired for resale, or where more valuable goods are acquired for the handler's own use. Such a sentence may well be appropriate in relation to a young offender with little criminal experience, playing a peripheral role. But adult defendants with a record of dishonesty are likely to attract a custodial sentence.

8.   Thus far, as we have indicated, we agree with the factors which the panel identifies in relation to the sentencing process for less serious offences. But we do not believe that a clear dividing line is capable of being drawn between those offences which, appropriately attract, on the one hand, a discharge or fine and, on the other, a community sentence.

9.   So far as the custody threshold is concerned, we agree that a defendant either with a record of offences of dishonesty, or who engages in sophisticated law breaking, will attract a custodial sentence. It is in relation to the length of that sentence that the aggravating and mitigating features which we have earlier identified will come into play, as will the personal mitigation of the offender, who may appropriately, in accordance with *Ollerenshaw* [1991] 1 Cr App R(S) 65, be dealt with by a somewhat shorter sentence than might, at first blush, otherwise have seemed appropriate.

10.   We also agree with the panel that, in relation to more serious offences, there will be some for which a sentence within the range of 12 months to four years will be appropriate and there will be others for which a sentence of considerably more than four years, up to the maximum, may be appropriate. In this regard, the factors to be taken into consideration will include whether an offence is committed in the context of a business, whether the offender is acting as an organiser or distributor of the proceeds of crime and whether the offender has made himself available to other criminals as willing to handle the proceeds of thefts or burglaries.

11.   In all of these more serious cases, according to the other circumstances, sentences in the range of 12 months to four years are likely to be appropriate if the value of the goods involved is up to around £100,000. Where the value of the goods is in excess of £100,000, or where the offence is highly organised and bears the hallmarks of a professional commercial operation, a sentence of four years and upwards is likely to be appropriate, and it will be the higher where the source of the handled property is known by the handler to be a serious violent offence such as armed robbery. As we have earlier indicated, sentences significantly higher than four years also may be appropriate where a professional handler, over a substantial period of time, demonstrated by his record or otherwise, has promoted and encouraged, albeit indirectly, criminal activity by others.

12.   The sentences which we have indicated will, of course, be subject to discount in appropriate cases for a plea of guilty.

13.   We should also add that a court passing sentence in handling cases should always have in mind the power to make restitution orders under sections 148 and 149 of the Powers of Criminal Courts (Sentencing) Act 2000, to make compensation orders under section 130 of the Powers of Criminal Court (Sentencing) Act 2000, and to make confiscation orders in relation to profits, under the Criminal Justice Act 1988 and the Proceeds of Crime Act 1995. A Magistrates' Court cannot, of course, make a confiscation order in a case of handling. But it is open to magistrates, in such a case, where appropriate, to commit to the Crown Court for sentence.

R. v. Czyzewski, The Times, **25 July 2003, Court of Appeal**

Fraudulent evasion of duty on tobacco and alcohol

Principal serious factors were the level of duty evaded, the complexity and sophistication of the organisation involved, the defendant's function within the organisation and the amount of personal profit to the defendant.

An offence would be aggravated if a defendant:

- played an organisational role;
- made repeated importations, particularly in the face of a warning from the authorities;
- was a professional smuggler;
- used a legitimate business as a front;
- abused a position of privilege as a customs or police officer or as an employee (e.g. of a security firm);
- used children or vulnerable adults;
- threatened violence to those enforcing the law;
- dealt in goods with an additional health risk because of possible contamination;
- disposed of goods to under-aged purchasers.

In addition there were statutory aggravating features of offending while on bail or having previous convictions.

Evidence of professional smuggling would include:

- a complex operation with many people involved;
- financial accounting or budgets;
- obtaining goods from several different sources;
- integration of freight movements with commercial organisations;
- sophisticated concealment methods such as forged documents or specially adapted vehicles;
- varying of methods and routes;
- links with illicit overseas organisations;
- where the amount of goods smuggled was one and a half million cigarettes or came to a value of some £75,000 or where the value involved was a potential indication of professional smuggling.

Mitigating factors would include a prompt plea of guilty, co-operation with the authorities, particularly in providing information about the organisation and, to a limited extent, previous good character. Pressure from others to commit the offence may, depending on the circumstances, afford mitigation.

Appropriate starting points for sentencing, following a trial where a defendant had no relevant previous convictions and disregarding personal mitigation, were as follows.

1. Where the duty evaded was less than £1,000 and the level of personal profit was small: a moderate fine. If there was particularly strong mitigation and there had been no earlier warning, a conditional discharge may be appropriate.
2. Where the duty evaded by a first time offender was not more than £10,000 (approximately equating to 65,000 cigarettes) or the defendant's offending was at a low level, either within an organisation or persistently as an individual: a community sentence, or curfew order enforced by tagging, or a higher level of fine. The custody threshold was likely to be passed if any of the aggravating factors were present.
3. Where the duty evaded was not less than £10,000 and up to £100,000 whether the defendant operated individually or at a low level within an organisation: up to nine months' imprisonment. Some of these cases could appropriately be dealt with by

magistrates, but others, particularly if marked by any of the aggravating factors, should be dealt with by the Crown Court.
4. Where the duty evaded was in excess of £100,000: a custodial sentence, the length of which would be determined, principally, by the degree of professionalism of the defendant and the presence or absence of other aggravating factors. Subject to this, the duty evaded would indicate starting points as follows. £100,000 to £500,000: nine months' to three years' imprisonment. £500,000 to £1m: three years' to five years' imprisonment. In excess of £1m: five years' to seven years' imprisonment. Where very many millions of pounds in duty had been evaded, it may be appropriate to impose consecutive sentences or, alternatively, to charge an offence of cheating the public revenue, for which the maximum sentence was life imprisonment.

It is stressed that the proposed guidelines were not a straitjacket and sentencers could be expected to move up by reference to aggravating factors or down by reference to mitigating factors, particularly a prompt plea of guilty and co-operation. Sentencers should also remember their powers to order the confiscation of assets under the Proceeds of Crime Act 2002; compensation under s.130, and deprivation orders, particularly of vehicles, under s.143 of the Powers of Criminal Courts (Sentencing) Act 2000; and disqualification from driving where a motor vehicle had been used. The licensing authority should also be notified where licensed premises had been used for sale of smuggled goods.

R. v. Poulton and Celaire [2003] Crim LR 124, Court of Appeal

Offensive weapons

The Court of Appeal gave sentencing guidelines in relation to the possession of offensive weapons. The following were relevant:

1. *Offenders intention.* Specific plan to use or threaten violence, racially or religiously aggravated use or offence whilst under influence of alcohol or drugs would all act to aggravate the offence.
2. *Circumstances of the offence.* Court would have regard to factors such as place of use, e.g. aggravated if on school premises or in possession at a large public gathering for example. Other examples included public transport and threats toward public servants.
3. *Nature of weapon.* The custody threshold would often be met in respect of an adult of good character when aggravating factors were present. With no aggravating factors or actual threat made and if the weapon was not particularly dangerous the custody threshold may not be met, but a community penalty at the top end of the scale might be expected.

R. v. Williams [2005] EWCA Crim 1796

ASBO for driving offences

The imposition of an anti-social behaviour order on a habitual driving offender, with the underlying objective of giving the court higher sentencing powers in the event of future offending, was something which should be done only exceptionally.

R. v. Morrison [2005] EWCA Crim 2237

Sentencing for breach of ASBO

1. An anti-social behaviour order, though it may prohibit conduct which is also a distinct offence, must be justified by reference to the statutory requirements of section 1C(2)(a) and (b). Caution should be exercised in the making of an anti-social behaviour order if the behaviour in question would in any event be a criminal offence.
2. An ASBO should not be made simply for the purpose of increasing the available sentence beyond the maximum which would otherwise be laid down by statute for the conduct which is prohibited.
3. If a breach of an ASBO consists of no more than the commission of an offence for which a maximum penalty is prescribed by statute, it is wrong in principle to pass a sentence for that breach calculated by reference to the five year maximum for breach of an ASBO. Rather the tariff is determined by the statutory maximum for the offence in question.
4. We draw attention, however, in that last proposition to the words 'no more than'. There may be exceptional cases in which it can properly be said that the vice of the breach of an ASBO, although it amounts to an offence, goes beyond that offence. We do not attempt to foresee circumstances in which that may occur but we have in mind, for example, repeated offences of criminal damage directed against a particular and perhaps vulnerable victim or group of victims. We have not, however, heard any argument about such an exceptional case. Argument about it must await the occurrence of appropriate events, if they occur. We are satisfied that, absent exceptional circumstances, the proposition which we have set out as number 3 must prevail.

R. (Mills) v. Birmingham Magistrates' Court [2005] EWHC 2732 (Admin)

ASBO following conviction

Facts: D was convicted of theft and made subject to an ASBO. D had numerous like convictions and the prosecution contended that the act of theft (shoplifting) caused harassment, alarm or distress. D appealed.

Held: Theft could indeed be classed as anti-social behaviour dependent upon the facts. However, for the offence D was convicted of, no such harassment, alarm or distress had been caused. Accordingly, section 1C Crime and Disorder Act 1998 did not trigger and an ASBO should not have been made.

R. v. Boness and others [2005] EWCA Crim 2395

ASBO – principle of proportionality

An anti-social behaviour order made following conviction for a relevant offence pursuant to s.1C of the Crime and Disorder Act 1998, had to be proportionate, that is, commensurate with the risk to be guarded against.

Criminal Justice Act 2003, Schedule 15

SCHEDULE 15
Section 224
SPECIFIED OFFENCES FOR PURPOSES OF CHAPTER 5 OF PART 12
PART 1

1   Manslaughter.
2   Kidnapping.
3   False imprisonment.
4   An offence under section 4 of the Offences against the Person Act 1861 (c. 100) (soliciting murder).
5   An offence under section 16 of that Act (threats to kill).
6   An offence under section 18 of that Act (wounding with intent to cause grievous bodily harm).
7   An offence under section 20 of that Act (malicious wounding).
8   An offence under section 21 of that Act (attempting to choke, suffocate or strangle in order to commit or assist in committing an indictable offence).
9   An offence under section 22 of that Act (using chloroform etc. to commit or assist in the committing of any indictable offence).
10   An offence under section 23 of that Act (maliciously administering poison etc. so as to endanger life or inflict grievous bodily harm).
11   An offence under section 27 of that Act (abandoning children).
12   An offence under section 28 of that Act (causing bodily injury by explosives).
13   An offence under section 29 of that Act (using explosives etc. with intent to do grievous bodily harm).
14   An offence under section 30 of that Act (placing explosives with intent to do bodily injury).
15   An offence under section 31 of that Act (setting spring guns etc. with intent to do grievous bodily harm).
16   An offence under section 32 of that Act (endangering the safety of railway passengers).
17   An offence under section 35 of that Act (injuring persons by furious driving).
18   An offence under section 37 of that Act (assaulting officer preserving wreck).
19   An offence under section 38 of that Act (assault with intent to resist arrest).
20   An offence under section 47 of that Act (assault occasioning actual bodily harm).

21   An offence under section 2 of the Explosive Substances Act 1883 (c. 3) (causing explosion likely to endanger life or property).

22   An offence under section 3 of that Act (attempt to cause explosion, or making or keeping explosive with intent to endanger life or property).

23   An offence under section 1 of the Infant Life (Preservation) Act 1929 (c. 34) (child destruction).

24   An offence under section 1 of the Children and Young Persons Act 1933 (c. 12) (cruelty to children).

25   An offence under section 1 of the Infanticide Act 1938 (c. 36) (infanticide).

26   An offence under section 16 of the Firearms Act 1968 (c. 27) (possession of firearm with intent to endanger life).

27   An offence under section 16A of that Act (possession of firearm with intent to cause fear of violence).

28   An offence under section 17(1) of that Act (use of firearm to resist arrest).

29   An offence under section 17(2) of that Act (possession of firearm at time of committing or being arrested for offence specified in Schedule 1 to that Act).

30   An offence under section 18 of that Act (carrying a firearm with criminal intent).

31   An offence under section 8 of the Theft Act 1968 (c. 60) (robbery or assault with intent to rob).

32   An offence under section 9 of that Act of burglary with intent to–

   (a)   inflict grievous bodily harm on a person, or
   (b)   do unlawful damage to a building or anything in it.

33   An offence under section 10 of that Act (aggravated burglary).

34   An offence under section 12A of that Act (aggravated vehicle-taking) involving an accident which caused the death of any person.

35   An offence of arson under section 1 of the Criminal Damage Act 1971 (c. 48).

36   An offence under section 1(2) of that Act (destroying or damaging property) other than an offence of arson.

37   An offence under section 1 of the Taking of Hostages Act 1982 (c. 28) (hostage-taking).

38   An offence under section 1 of the Aviation Security Act 1982 (c. 36) (hijacking).

39   An offence under section 2 of that Act (destroying, damaging or endangering safety of aircraft).

40   An offence under section 3 of that Act (other acts endangering or likely to endanger safety of aircraft).

41   An offence under section 4 of that Act (offences in relation to certain dangerous articles).

42   An offence under section 127 of the Mental Health Act 1983 (c. 20) (ill-treatment of patients).

43   An offence under section 1 of the Prohibition of Female Circumcision Act 1985 (c. 38) (prohibition of female circumcision).

44   An offence under section 1 of the Public Order Act 1986 (c. 64) (riot).

45   An offence under section 2 of that Act (violent disorder).

46   An offence under section 3 of that Act (affray).

47   An offence under section 134 of the Criminal Justice Act 1988 (c. 33) (torture).

48   An offence under section 1 of the Road Traffic Act 1988 (c. 52) (causing death by dangerous driving).

49   An offence under section 3A of that Act (causing death by careless driving when under influence of drink or drugs).

50   An offence under section 1 of the Aviation and Maritime Security Act 1990 (c. 31) (endangering safety at aerodromes).
51   An offence under section 9 of that Act (hijacking of ships).
52   An offence under section 10 of that Act (seizing or exercising control of fixed platforms).
53   An offence under section 11 of that Act (destroying fixed platforms or endangering their safety).
54   An offence under section 12 of that Act (other acts endangering or likely to endanger safe navigation).
55   An offence under section 13 of that Act (offences involving threats).
56   An offence under Part II of the Channel Tunnel (Security) Order 1994 (S.I. 1994/570) (offences relating to Channel Tunnel trains and the tunnel system).
57   An offence under section 4 of the Protection from Harassment Act 1997 (c. 40) (putting people in fear of violence).
58   An offence under section 29 of the Crime and Disorder Act 1998 (c. 37) (racially or religiously aggravated assaults).
59   An offence falling within section 31(1)(a) or (b) of that Act (racially or religiously aggravated offences under section 4 or 4A of the Public Order Act 1986 (c. 64)).
60   An offence under section 51 or 52 of the International Criminal Court Act 2001 (c. 17) (genocide, crimes against humanity, war crimes and related offences), other than one involving murder.
61   An offence under section 1 of the Female Genital Mutilation Act 2003 (c. 31) (female genital mutilation).
62   An offence under section 2 of that Act (assisting a girl to mutilate her own genitalia).
63   An offence under section 3 of that Act (assisting a non-UK person to mutilate overseas a girl's genitalia).
64   An offence of–

   (a)   aiding, abetting, counselling, procuring or inciting the commission of an offence specified in this Part of this Schedule,
   (b)   conspiring to commit an offence so specified, or
   (c)   attempting to commit an offence so specified.

65   An attempt to commit murder or a conspiracy to commit murder.

PART 2
SPECIFIED SEXUAL OFFENCES

66   An offence under section 1 of the Sexual Offences Act 1956 (c. 69) (rape).
67   An offence under section 2 of that Act (procurement of woman by threats).
68   An offence under section 3 of that Act (procurement of woman by false pretences).
69   An offence under section 4 of that Act (administering drugs to obtain or facilitate intercourse).
70   An offence under section 5 of that Act (intercourse with girl under thirteen).
71   An offence under section 6 of that Act (intercourse with girl under 16).
72   An offence under section 7 of that Act (intercourse with a defective).
73   An offence under section 9 of that Act (procurement of a defective).
74   An offence under section 10 of that Act (incest by a man).
75   An offence under section 11 of that Act (incest by a woman).
76   An offence under section 14 of that Act (indecent assault on a woman).
77   An offence under section 15 of that Act (indecent assault on a man).

78 An offence under section 16 of that Act (assault with intent to commit buggery).

79 An offence under section 17 of that Act (abduction of woman by force or for the sake of her property).

80 An offence under section 19 of that Act (abduction of unmarried girl under eighteen from parent or guardian).

81 An offence under section 20 of that Act (abduction of unmarried girl under sixteen from parent or guardian).

82 An offence under section 21 of that Act (abduction of defective from parent or guardian).

83 An offence under section 22 of that Act (causing prostitution of women).

84 An offence under section 23 of that Act (procuration of girl under twenty-one).

85 An offence under section 24 of that Act (detention of woman in brothel).

86 An offence under section 25 of that Act (permitting girl under thirteen to use premises for intercourse).

87 An offence under section 26 of that Act (permitting girl under sixteen to use premises for intercourse).

88 An offence under section 27 of that Act (permitting defective to use premises for intercourse).

89 An offence under section 28 of that Act (causing or encouraging the prostitution of, intercourse with or indecent assault on girl under sixteen).

90 An offence under section 29 of that Act (causing or encouraging prostitution of defective).

91 An offence under section 32 of that Act (soliciting by men).

92 An offence under section 33 of that Act (keeping a brothel).

93 An offence under section 128 of the Mental Health Act 1959 (c. 72) (sexual intercourse with patients).

94 An offence under section 1 of the Indecency with Children Act 1960 (c. 33) (indecent conduct towards young child).

95 An offence under section 4 of the Sexual Offences Act 1967 (c. 60) (procuring others to commit homosexual acts).

96 An offence under section 5 of that Act (living on earnings of male prostitution).

97 An offence under section 9 of the Theft Act 1968 (c. 60) of burglary with intent to commit rape.

98 An offence under section 54 of the Criminal Law Act 1977 (c. 45) (inciting girl under sixteen to have incestuous sexual intercourse).

99 An offence under section 1 of the Protection of Children Act 1978 (c. 37) (indecent photographs of children).

100 An offence under section 170 of the Customs and Excise Management Act 1979 (c. 2) (penalty for fraudulent evasion of duty etc.) in relation to goods prohibited to be imported under section 42 of the Customs Consolidation Act 1876 (c. 36) (indecent or obscene articles).

101 An offence under section 160 of the Criminal Justice Act 1988 (c. 33) (possession of indecent photograph of a child).

102 An offence under section 1 of the Sexual Offences Act 2003 (c. 42) (rape).

103 An offence under section 2 of that Act (assault by penetration).

104 An offence under section 3 of that Act (sexual assault).

105 An offence under section 4 of that Act (causing a person to engage in sexual activity without consent).

106 An offence under section 5 of that Act (rape of a child under 13).

107 An offence under section 6 of that Act (assault of a child under 13 by penetration).

108 An offence under section 7 of that Act (sexual assault of a child under 13).

109 An offence under section 8 of that Act (causing or inciting a child under 13 to engage in sexual activity).

110 An offence under section 9 of that Act (sexual activity with a child).

111 An offence under section 10 of that Act (causing or inciting a child to engage in sexual activity).

112 An offence under section 11 of that Act (engaging in sexual activity in the presence of a child).

113 An offence under section 12 of that Act (causing a child to watch a sexual act).

114 An offence under section 13 of that Act (child sex offences committed by children or young persons).

115 An offence under section 14 of that Act (arranging or facilitating commission of a child sex offence).

116 An offence under section 15 of that Act (meeting a child following sexual grooming etc.).

117 An offence under section 16 of that Act (abuse of position of trust: sexual activity with a child).

118 An offence under section 17 of that Act (abuse of position of trust: causing or inciting a child to engage in sexual activity).

119 An offence under section 18 of that Act (abuse of position of trust: sexual activity in the presence of a child).

120 An offence under section 19 of that Act (abuse of position of trust: causing a child to watch a sexual act).

121 An offence under section 25 of that Act (sexual activity with a child family member).

122 An offence under section 26 of that Act (inciting a child family member to engage in sexual activity).

123 An offence under section 30 of that Act (sexual activity with a person with a mental disorder impeding choice).

124 An offence under section 31 of that Act (causing or inciting a person with a mental disorder impeding choice to engage in sexual activity).

125 An offence under section 32 of that Act (engaging in sexual activity in the presence of a person with a mental disorder impeding choice).

126 An offence under section 33 of that Act (causing a person with a mental disorder impeding choice to watch a sexual act).

127 An offence under section 34 of that Act (inducement, threat or deception to procure sexual activity with a person with a mental disorder).

128 An offence under section 35 of that Act (causing a person with a mental disorder to engage in or agree to engage in sexual activity by inducement, threat or deception).

129 An offence under section 36 of that Act (engaging in sexual activity in the presence, procured by inducement, threat or deception, of a person with a mental disorder).

130 An offence under section 37 of that Act (causing a person with a mental disorder to watch a sexual act by inducement, threat or deception).

131 An offence under section 38 of that Act (care workers: sexual activity with a person with a mental disorder).

132 An offence under section 39 of that Act (care workers: causing or inciting sexual activity).

133 An offence under section 40 of that Act (care workers: sexual activity in the presence of a person with a mental disorder).

134   An offence under section 41 of that Act (care workers: causing a person with a mental disorder to watch a sexual act).
135   An offence under section 47 of that Act (paying for sexual services of a child).
136   An offence under section 48 of that Act (causing or inciting child prostitution or pornography).
137   An offence under section 49 of that Act (controlling a child prostitute or a child involved in pornography).
138   An offence under section 50 of that Act (arranging or facilitating child prostitution or pornography).
139   An offence under section 52 of that Act (causing or inciting prostitution for gain).
140   An offence under section 53 of that Act (controlling prostitution for gain).
141   An offence under section 57 of that Act (trafficking into the UK for sexual exploitation).
142   An offence under section 58 of that Act (trafficking within the UK for sexual exploitation).
143   An offence under section 59 of that Act (trafficking out of the UK for sexual exploitation).
144   An offence under section 61 of that Act (administering a substance with intent).
145   An offence under section 62 of that Act (committing an offence with intent to commit a sexual offence).
146   An offence under section 63 of that Act (trespass with intent to commit a sexual offence).
147   An offence under section 64 of that Act (sex with an adult relative: penetration).
148   An offence under section 65 of that Act (sex with an adult relative: consenting to penetration).
149   An offence under section 66 of that Act (exposure).
150   An offence under section 67 of that Act (voyeurism).
151   An offence under section 69 of that Act (intercourse with an animal).
152   An offence under section 70 of that Act (sexual penetration of a corpse).
153   An offence of–
       (a)   aiding, abetting, counselling, procuring or inciting the commission of an offence specified in this Part of this Schedule,
       (b)   conspiring to commit an offence so specified, or
       (c)   attempting to commit an offence so specified.

Director of Public Prosecution's Guidance on Charging (January 2005)

GUIDANCE TO POLICE OFFICERS AND CROWN PROSECUTORS ISSUED
BY THE DIRECTOR OF PUBLIC PROSECUTIONS UNDER S37A OF THE
POLICE AND CRIMINAL EVIDENCE ACT 1984
SECOND EDITION: JANUARY 2005
[PREVENTION OF TERRORISM ACT 2005 OFFENCES ADDED]

1. Introduction

What this Guidance is for, where it applies and when it comes into effect

1.1   This Guidance[1] is to enable Custody Officers to decide how a person should be dealt with when:

- The Custody Officer determines there is sufficient evidence (in accordance with the Threshold Test) to charge a person with an offence[2], or
- A person has been arrested for breach of bail who had previously been released on bail for a charging decision[3]

1.2   This Guidance also specifies what information must be sent to a Crown Prosecutor to enable a charging or other decision to be made.[4]

1.3   This Guidance applies to those cases the Director of Public Prosecutions is required to take over in accordance with Section 3 of the Prosecution of Offences Act 1985.

1.4   This Guidance will come into effect in those Local Criminal Justice Board Areas and on the dates specified in the schedule hereto.

---

[1] Issued by the Director of Public Prosecutions under Section 37(A)(1)(a) of the Police and Criminal Evidence Act 1984, as inserted by the Criminal Justice Act 2003.
[2] PACE, Section 37(7) as amended.
[3] PACE, Section 37C.
[4] PACE, Section 37A(1)(b).

2. Key Provisions and Principles of this Guidance

Statutory provisions and key principles that under-pin this Guidance

- Crown Prosecutors will determine whether a person is to be charged in all indictable only, either way or summary offences subject to those cases specified in this Guidance which the police may continue to charge.
- Charging decisions by Crown Prosecutors will be made following a review of evidence in cases and will be in accordance with this Guidance.
- Custody Officers must comply with this Guidance in deciding how a person is to be dealt with in accordance with Section 37(7) PACE, as amended by Schedule 2 to the Criminal Justice Act 2003.
- Crown Prosecutors will seek to identify and resolve cases that are clearly not appropriate for prosecution at the earliest opportunity on consideration of whatever material is available.
- Crown Prosecutors will provide guidance and advice to investigators throughout the investigative and prosecuting process. This may include lines of enquiry, evidential requirements and assistance in any pre-charge procedures. Crown Prosecutors will be pro-active in identifying, and where possible, rectifying evidential deficiencies and in bringing to an early conclusion those cases that cannot be strengthened by further investigation.
- Crown Prosecutors will only require 'evidential reports' (see Paragraph 7.2 (i) below) where it is clear that the case will proceed to the Crown Court or is likely to be a contested summary trial or where it appears to the Crown Prosecutor that the case is so complex or sensitive that a decision to charge cannot be made without an evidential report.
- Where it is necessary, pre-charge bail arrangements will be utilised to facilitate the gathering of evidence, including, in appropriate cases, all the key evidence on which the prosecution will rely, prior to the charging decision being taken (Section 37(7)(a) and Section 47(1A) PACE).
- Crown Prosecutors will notify the officer involved in the investigation of any advice and charging or other decision in writing using the form MG3 (Section 37B(4) PACE).
- Persons may be charged whilst in police detention, or in accordance with Section 29 of the Criminal Justice Act 2003 (*charging by post*) when it is brought into force. [*The summons procedure may be used until that change in the process arrangements.*]
- Where a Crown Prosecutor notifies a Custody Officers that there is insufficient evidence to charge, or that though there is sufficient evidence to charge, a person should not be charged or given a caution, the Custody Officer shall give notice in writing to that person that he is not to be prosecuted (Section 37B(5) PACE).
- Where Crown Prosecutors decide that a person should be charged with an offence or given a caution, conditional caution, a reprimand or final warning in respect of an offence, the person shall be charged or cautioned, or conditionally cautioned, or given a reprimand or final warning accordingly (Section 37B(6) PACE).
- Where Crown Prosecutors decide that a person should be cautioned but it proves not to be possible to give the person such a caution, the person shall instead be charged with the offence (Section 37B(7) PACE.)
- In order to facilitate efficient and effective early consultations and make charging decisions, Crown Prosecutors will be deployed, as Duty Prosecutors for such hours as shall be agreed locally to provide guidance and make charging decisions. This service will be complemented by a centrally managed out of hours duty prosecutor arrangement to ensure a continuous 24 hour service.

3. Responsibility for determining charges

Duty of Crown Prosecutors to determine charge cases

3.1 *Charging by Crown Prosecutors – the principle*

    (i) Crown Prosecutors will be responsible for the decision to charge and the specifying or drafting of the charges in all indictable only, either way or summary offences where a Custody Officer determines that the Threshold Test is met in any case, except for those offences specified in this Guidance which may be charged or cautioned by the police without reference to a Crown Prosecutor.

Transitional arrangements for charging some likely guilty plea cases

3.2 *Charging by Crown Prosecutors – transitional arrangements*

    (ii) Establishment of the principle set out in Paragraph 3.1 above will be achieved incrementally and will be notified by further editions of this Guidance.

    (iii) Until such notification, the police may determine the charge in any either way or summary offences where it appears to the Custody Officer that a guilty plea is likely and that the case is suitable for sentencing in the magistrates' court, but excluding those specified in Annex A to this Guidance

    (iv) Where the Custody Officer is uncertain whether a case falls under 3.2(iii) above, early consultation with a Duty Prosecutor should be undertaken to clarify whether the charging decision is one that should be made by a Crown Prosecutor

Details, with exceptions, of cases the police may charge

3.3 *Charging by the Police*

The Police may determine the charge in the following cases:

    (i) Any offence under the Road Traffic Acts or any other offence arising from the presence of a motor vehicle, trailer, or pedal cycle on a road or other public place, *except where* (and the charge must therefore be determined by a Crown Prosecutor):

- The circumstances have resulted in the death of any person; or
- There is an allegation of dangerous driving; or
- The allegation is one of driving whilst disqualified and there has been no admission in a PACE interview to both the driving and the disqualification; or
- The statutory defence to being in charge of a motor vehicle (unfit through drink or drugs or excess alcohol) may be raised under Section 4(3) or 5(2) of the Road Traffic Act 1988; or
- There is an allegation of the unlawful taking of a motor vehicle or the aggravated unlawful taking of a motor vehicle (unless the case is suitable for disposal as an early guilty plea in the magistrates' court).

    (ii) Any offence of absconding under the Bail Act 1976 and any offence contrary to Section 5 of the Public Order Act 1986 and any offence under the Town Police Clauses Act 1847, the Metropolitan Police Act 1839, the Vagrancy Act 1824, the Street Offences Act 1959, under Section 91 of the Criminal Justice Act 1967, Section 12 of the Licensing Act 1872, any offence under any bylaw and any summary offence punishable on conviction with a term of imprisonment of 3 months or less *except where* (and the charge must therefore be determined by a Crown Prosecutor):

- The Director of Public Prosecutions publishes other arrangements for the charging and prosecution of these offences.

Cases charged by the police to be reviewed by a Crown Prosecutor

3.4   *Review by Crown Prosecutors under Section 10 of the Prosecution of Offences Act 1985*

Where by virtue of this Guidance the police determine the charge, that determination and the charge will be subject to a review by a Crown Prosecutor acting under Section 10 of the Prosecution of Offences Act 1985 and under Section 37B of the Police and Criminal Evidence Act 1984 (as amended).

CPS to charge cases delegated to police in certain circumstances

3.5   *Combinations of persons and offences*

Where the charges or joint charges to be preferred against one or more persons include a combination of offences, some of which may be determined by the police, and others that must be determined by a Crown Prosecutor, the Custody Officer shall refer all charges to a Crown Prosecutor for determination.

Application of Code for Crown Prosecutors to Custody Officers

3.6   *The application of the Code for Crown Prosecutors*

When determining charges, Crown Prosecutors and Custody Officers will apply the principles contained in the latest edition of the Code for Crown Prosecutors.

Charge selection, range and number of charges

3.7   *Number and seriousness of charge(s)*

In determining the totality of charges to proceed, the selection of charges should seek to reflect the seriousness and the extent of the offending. It should also provide the court with adequate sentencing powers, and enable the case to be presented in a clear and simple way. Where appropriate, a schedule of other admitted offences may be listed on an MG18 for the charged person to ask the Court to take into consideration.

General application of full Code Test

3.8   *Application of the Full Code Test*

In any case where the charging decision is to be made, and the information required to be considered under Paragraph 7.2 (below) of this Guidance is available for review, the standard to be applied in reaching the charging decision will be the Full Test under the Code for Crown Prosecutors: namely (following a review of the evidential material provided) that there is enough evidence to provide a realistic prospect of conviction and that it is in the public interest to proceed.

3.9   *Application of the Threshold Test to Charging decisions*

In cases where it is determined that it would not be appropriate for the person to be released on bail after charge and where the information referred to in Paragraph 7.2

(below) of this Guidance is not available at the time the charging decision has to be taken, a staged approach will then apply:

The Threshold Test for charging in custody cases where an evidential file is unavailable

    (i)   Where the evidential material required under Paragraph 7.2 (below) is not available, the Crown Prosecutor (or Custody Officer) will assess the case against the Threshold Test set out in Paragraph 3.10. This should be noted on the MG3 and a review date for a Full Code Test agreed as part of the action plan.

When to apply a Full Code Test for Crown Prosecutors in custody cases

    (ii)   Subsequently, upon receipt of further evidence or a Report to Crown Prosecutor for a Charging Decision (MG3) accompanied by the information required in accordance with Paragraph 7.2 of this Guidance, the Crown Prosecutor will review the case in accordance with the Full Code Test before deciding whether it is appropriate to continue with the offence(s) charged or prefer additional or alternative charges.

A decision to charge and withhold bail must be kept under review. The evidence gathered must be regularly assessed to ensure the charge is still appropriate and that continued objection to bail is justified. Crown Prosecutors will only apply the Threshold Test for a limited period. The Full Code Test must be applied as soon as reasonably practicable, taking into account the progress of the investigation.

Where however the information specified in Paragraph 7.2 is available at the time that the initial Report to Crown Prosecutor is made, the Full Code Test will be applied.

The Threshold Test

3.10   *The Threshold Test*

Application of the Threshold Test will require an overall assessment of whether in all the circumstances of the case there is at least a reasonable suspicion against the person of having committed an offence (in accordance with Article 5 of the European Convention on Human Rights) and that at that stage it is in the public interest to proceed.

The evidential decision in each case will require consideration of a number of factors including: the evidence available at the time and the likelihood and nature of further evidence being obtained; the reasonableness for believing that evidence will become available; the time that will take and the steps being taken to gather it; the impact of the expected evidence on the case, and the charges the totality of the evidence will support.

The public interest means the same as under the Full Code Test, but will be based on the information available at the time of charge, which will often be limited.

Application of the above Tests to police charged cases

3.11   Where, in accordance with this Guidance, Custody Officers make the charging decision without referral to Crown Prosecutors, they will apply the Full Code Test. Where the case is one in which it is not proposed to release the person on bail after charge and the evidential material required to apply the Full Code Test is not available, the Custody Officer will proceed to apply the Threshold Test in accordance with Paragraph 3.10 above.

Emergency charging by the police of CPS cases

3.12   *Emergency Cases – Expiry of PACE Time Limits*

In cases where the charging responsibility lies with a Crown Prosecutor in accordance with this Guidance and it is proposed to withhold bail for the purposes of making an application to a court for a remand in custody (or for bail conditions that may only be imposed by a court) but it proves not to be possible to consult with a Crown Prosecutor in person or by telephone before the expiry of any PACE custody time limit applicable before charge, a Custody Officer may proceed to charge, but only on the authority of a Duty Inspector. The Duty Inspector shall note the custody record and MG3 to confirm that it is appropriate to charge under this emergency provision. The case must be referred to a Crown Prosecutor as soon as is practicable for authority to proceed with the prosecution.

4.   Decisions ancillary to the charging decision

Consultations prior to applications to withhold bail at court and short remands to police custody

4.1   *Consultations where it is proposed to withhold bail or impose conditions*

Whilst decisions to detain or bail persons are exclusively matters for a Custody Officer, where it appears that a person in police detention should not be released and should be detained for the purposes of an application being made to a court for a remand in custody, including short periods in police custody for the purpose of enquiries into other offences, the Custody Officer may wish to consult a Duty Prosecutor to confirm that any proposed application for a remand in custody or the imposition of bail conditions which can only be imposed by a court is justified in accordance with the Bail Act 1976, is proportionate, is likely to be ordered by the court and that sufficient detail to support any such application is recorded on the MG7.

Court selection

4.2   *Determination of the court for first appearance*

When Crown Prosecutors make charging decisions concerning cases that are to be bailed directly to an initial hearing, the Crown Prosecutor will determine whether the case is appropriate for an Early First Hearing Court or an Early Administrative Hearing Court. This will be indicated on the form MG3 with the charge decision.

Special provisions for PYO cases

4.3   *Special procedure for Persistent Young Offenders*

Crown Prosecutors will be responsible for the decision to charge in all cases involving Persistent Young Offenders unless the charge is one specified in Paragraph 3.3 of this Guidance.

Whenever a person who is, or appears to be, under 18 years of age is taken into custody, the Custody Officer will undertake an immediate check to ascertain whether the person is a Persistent Young Offender.

Where it appears to an Investigating or Custody Officer that the person under investigation may be a Persistent Young Offender, early consultation will be undertaken with the Duty Prosecutor to confirm the likely charges and the evidential requirements in the case. Early consultation will be utilised to proactively manage all Persistent Young Offender cases to secure consistent performance in progressing these cases.

Where it appears that the case will be contested, the Duty Prosecutor and Investigating Officer will agree, as soon as practicable and in any case within 3 days of the arrest on the evidential requirements to progress the case and on a date for the completion of the agreed work, including any pre-charge bail period, taking into account the 71 day target from arrest to sentence for concluding such cases.

5. Deployment of and role of Duty Prosecutor

Deployment and duty of Crown Prosecutors

5.1 Deployment

Chief Crown Prosecutors will make arrangements for the deployment of Crown Prosecutors to act as Duty Prosecutor in locally agreed locations having regard to the area business and wherever possible on a face-to-face basis, or to be otherwise available for the purposes of fulfilling the CPS's statutory duty. Duty Prosecutors will be available for consultation and will render such early legal advice and guidance, including where appropriate the making of charging decisions as will facilitate the efficient and effective preparation and disposal of criminal prosecutions.

When early advice may be sought by the police

5.2 Early Consultations

Early consultation and advice may be sought and given in any case (including those in which the police may themselves determine the charge) and may include lines of enquiry, evidential requirements and any pre-charge procedures. In exercising this function, Crown Prosecutors will be pro-active in identifying and, where possible, rectifying evidential deficiencies and identify those cases that can proceed to court for an early guilty plea as an expedited report.

Stopping weak cases early

5.3   Early consultation should also seek to identify evidentially weak cases, which cannot be rectified by further investigation, either at that stage or at all, so that these investigations may, where appropriate, be brought to an early conclusion.

Duty Prosecutor's action on receipt of a case

5.4   *Reviewing the Report to Crown Prosecutor for a Charging Decision (MG3) and evidence.*

Where Crown Prosecutors receive a 'Report to Crown Prosecutor for a Charging Decision' (MG3) accompanied by the information specified in Paragraph 7.2 below, it is the duty of the Crown Prosecutor to review the evidence as soon as is practicable, having regard to any bail return dates, and decide whether it is appropriate or not, at that stage, to charge the person with an offence or divert them from the criminal justice system.

Written notice of charging or other decision

5.5   Once a charging (or other) decision has been made, Crown Prosecutors will give written notice of the decision by completing the second part of the Report to Crown Prosecutor for a Charging Decision (MG3) which will be provided to an officer involved in the investigation of the offence. A copy will be retained by the Crown Prosecutor.

Agreeing an action plan to build a case file

5.6   Where during the course of a consultation or following receipt of the Report to Crown Prosecutor for a Charging Decision (MG3) it is clear that a charging decision in the case cannot be reached at that stage, the Crown Prosecutor consulted will advise on the further steps to be taken, including the evidence to be gathered or the statements to be obtained before the decision can be reached and will agree with the investigating officer the action to be taken and the time in which that is to be achieved. This agreement will be recorded on the MG3 and a copy will be provided to an officer involved in the investigation. A copy will be retained by the Crown Prosecutor. In providing such advice, Crown Prosecutors should avoid simply requiring full files to be produced but will specify the precise evidence required or to be sought in accordance with Paragraph 7.2 below. Persons will not be charged until all agreed actions have been completed.

Referrals of cases in special circumstances

5.7   Where it appears at an early consultation that the case is of such complexity or sensitivity that it is more appropriate for referral to a specialist unit or prosecutor, or for an individual prosecutor to be allocated to the case from the outset, the Duty Prosecutor, or any Crown Prosecutor consulted, will contact the appropriate Area Unit Head forthwith to make the necessary arrangements.

Building evidential files: use of police pre-charge bail

5.8   In cases identified as likely to be contested or to be sent to the Crown Court, Crown Prosecutors will detail the requirements for preparation of an evidential report where that information is not immediately available before a full charging decision can be taken. Where the person is suitable for release on bail the Custody Officer will then bail the person for such a period as is sufficient to allow any agreed action to be completed and the case to be reported to a Crown Prosecutor for a charging decision.

6.   Decisions not to prosecute

Written notice by Custody Officer of no prosecution

6.1   *Insufficient evidence or not in the public interest to charge*

Where the Crown Prosecutor notifies a Custody Officer that there is not sufficient evidence to charge the person with an offence or that there is sufficient evidence but the public interest does not require the person to be charged or given a caution in respect of an offence, the Custody Officer will notify the person in writing to that effect.

Written notice by Custody Officer of no prosecution, but possible further action

6.2   Where however it appears to the Crown Prosecutor that should further evidence or information come to light in the future the case may be re-considered under the Code for Crown Prosecutors, the Crown Prosecutor will notify the Custody Officer to that effect who will notify the person in writing accordingly.

7.   Information to be sent to Crown Prosecutors for charging decisions

Evidence needed to make a charging decision

7.1   In making charging decisions, Crown Prosecutors will examine and assess the evidence available before reaching a decision. Wherever possible, Crown Prosecutors will seek to make the decision on the evidence presented to them by the investigator. Where however this is not possible, Custody Officers will arrange for persons to be released on bail, if it is necessary and appropriate to do so, to permit the required information to be provided as soon as is practicable.

Form of reports

7.2   The information to be provided by an officer involved in the investigation to a Crown Prosecutor to determine charges will be in the form of the 'Report to a Crown Prosecutor for a Charging Decision' (MG3) and must be accompanied by the following:

Crown Court and likely not guilty cases

   (i)   *All cases proceeding to the Crown Court or expected to be contested: Evidential Report.*

   Where it is clear that the case is likely to or will proceed to the Crown Court or is likely to be contested, the Report to Crown Prosecutor for a Charging Decision (MG3) must be accompanied by an Evidential Report containing the key evidence upon which the prosecution will rely together with any unused material which may undermine the prosecution case or assist the defence (including crime reports, initial descriptions and any previous convictions of key witnesses).

   The Evidential Report must also be accompanied by suggested charge(s), a record of convictions and cautions of the person, and any observations of the reporting or supervising officer.

All other cases

   (ii)   *Other cases referred to a Crown Prosecutor for a charging decision*

   In any other case to be referred to a Crown Prosecutor for a charging decision, the Report to Crown Prosecutor must be accompanied by an Expedited Report containing key witness statements, any other compelling evidence[5] and a summary of an interview. Where the offence has been witnessed by no more than 4 police officers, a key witness statement and a summary of the other evidence may suffice. Whether the summary of the

---

[5] For example, visually recorded evidence of the crime taking place from which it is possible to clearly identify the offender

interview or of other police witnesses is to be oral or written will be at the discretion of the Duty Prosecutor concerned.

The Expedited Report must be accompanied by any other information that may have a bearing on the evidential or public interest test, a record of convictions and cautions and any observations of the reporting or supervising officer.

File information in custody cases

7.3   *Custody cases – Threshold Test – expedited report*

Where in accordance with this Guidance and in order to facilitate the making of an application to a court for a remand in custody, a charging decision is to be taken in accordance with Paragraph 3.9(i) above, the Report to Crown Prosecutor (MG3) must be accompanied by an Expedited Report containing sufficient material then available and brief details of any previous convictions or cautions of the person to allow the Threshold Test to be applied. The Manual of Guidance remand file will be provided for the first and subsequent interim hearings, until the completed Report to Crown Prosecutor, or further evidence referred to in Paragraph 3.9(ii) above is submitted.

Early consultation in evidential report cases

7.4   *Requirement for early consultation in Evidential Report Cases*

Early consultation with a Duty Prosecutor should be undertaken to identify those cases in which an evidential file will be required and to agree the timescales for the completion and submission of the Report to Crown Prosecutor for a Charging Decision (MG3). An officer involved in the investigation must submit the completed Report to Crown Prosecutor for a Charging Decision (MG3) within the agreed timescale together with the evidential material referred to in Paragraphs 5.6 and 7.2(i) above.

Complex or sensitive cases

7.5   *Complex or sensitive cases – evidential report*

In any case where it appears to a Duty Prosecutor that the case is so complex or sensitive that a decision to charge, or not as the case may be, cannot be made without fuller information, the Report to Crown Prosecutor for a Charging Decision (MG3) must be accompanied by an evidential file and the material mentioned in Paragraphs 5.6 and 7.2(i) above.

When police uncertain about the information required

7.6   *Case requirements unclear – consult with a Duty Prosecutor*

Where an Investigating Officer considers that a defence may have been raised by a person in interview, or is uncertain whether a person has fully admitted an offence and requires clarification of the information required to accompany the report for a charging decision, early consultation with a Duty Prosecutor should occur to determine whether the case is likely to proceed and to establish the report requirements to facilitate the making of the charging decision.

8. Roles and Responsibilities of Custody Officers under Section 37(7) (a) to (d) PACE, as amended by Schedule 2 to the Criminal Justice Act 2003

Early consultation where offence to be charged by CPS

8.1 *Requirement for early consultations*

Where it appears likely that a charge will be determined by Crown Prosecutors, Custody Officers must direct investigating officers to consult a Duty Prosecutor as soon as is practicable after a person is taken into custody. This will enable early agreement to be reached as to the Report and evidential requirements and, where appropriate, for any period of bail to be determined to permit submission of the Report to the Crown Prosecutor for a Charging Decision (MG3).

Early decisions

8.2 Early consultation with a Duty Prosecutor will allow the early identification of weak cases and those where the charging decision may be made upon consideration of limited information.

Referrals where police do not wish to prosecute where sufficient to charge on Threshold Test

8.3 *Referrals where the police do not wish to proceed*

In any indictable only case in which the Threshold Test is met and in which an investigating or supervisory officer decides that he does not wish to proceed with a prosecution, the case must be referred to a Crown Prosecutor to confirm whether or not the case is to proceed. Early consultation in such a case may allow the investigation and preparation of case papers to be curtailed unless the complexity or sensitivity of the case determines otherwise.

Stage at which cases must be referred to a Crown Prosecutor

8.4 *The standard to be applied in determining whether the case is to be referred to a Crown Prosecutor or the person released on bail*

In determining whether there is sufficient evidence to charge in accordance with Section 37(7) PACE, Custody Officers will apply the Threshold Test set out in Paragraph 3.10 above. Where, in any case, it appears that there is manifestly no evidence and the Threshold Test is not met in respect of a detained person, the Custody Officer need not refer the case to a Crown Prosecutor before releasing that person, whether on bail or otherwise. In any case where this Guidance requires charges to be determined by Crown Prosecutors and a Custody Officer concludes that the Threshold Test is met, the Custody Officer will ensure that the case is referred to a Crown Prosecutor as soon as is practicable, or, where the person is suitable for bail, release the person detained on pre-charge bail, with or without conditions, in accordance with Section 37(7)(a).

Application of police pre-charge bail

8.5 *Delaying charging and releasing persons suitable on bail*

In any case where this Guidance requires charging decisions to be made by Crown Prosecutors and the required information is not then available, Custody Officers will release those persons suitable for bail (with or without conditions as appropriate) to allow for consultation with a Crown Prosecutor and the submission of an evidential report for a Charging Decision (MG3) in accordance with this Guidance.

Early disclosure to defence

8.6   The period of bail should be such as to allow the completion of the investigation, submission of a Report to a Crown Prosecutor for a Charging Decision (MG3), for the person to be charged, and for early disclosure of the evidence and any unused material referred to in Paragraph 7.2 to be provided to the defence prior to the first appearance.

Delayed charges – other reasons

8.7   Where a Custody Officer determines that there is sufficient evidence to charge a person but concludes that it is not appropriate at that stage to charge the person with an offence or to seek a charging decision from a Crown Prosecutor and proposes to release the person from police custody in accordance with Section 37(7)(b) PACE, the person may only be released on unconditional bail. The Custody Officer should record the reasons for so acting.

9.   Cautions, reprimands and final warnings

Diversion from prosecution, police to caution, reprimand etc

9.1   Where the police consider that the Threshold Test is met in a case, other than an indictable only offence, and determine that it is in the public interest instead to administer a simple caution, or to administer a reprimand or final warning in the case of a youth, the police may issue that caution, reprimand or final warning as appropriate, without referring the case to a Crown Prosecutor.

Consultation on decision to caution

9.2   Notwithstanding the above, an investigating officer may wish to consult with a Crown Prosecutor in respect of any case in which it is proposed to deal with a person by way of a caution, reprimand or final warning.

Actions on conditional caution cases

9.3   Where a conditional cautioning scheme is in force locally and the police wish to conditionally caution any person for an offence, the Custody Officer must refer the case to a Crown Prosecutor for decision.

Review by Crown Prosecutors

9.4   Where in accordance with this Guidance, the police have determined to initiate proceedings against a person by way of a charge, and a Crown Prosecutor, acting under Section 10 of the Prosecution of Offences Act 1985 and Section 37B of the Police and Criminal Evidence Act 1984 (as amended) notifies a Custody Officer that it is more appropriate to proceed by way of a conditional caution (if a scheme is in force locally), simple caution, reprimand or final warning, the Custody Officer will ensure that the person is given a conditional caution, simple caution, reprimand or final warning as appropriate.

Decisions to charge or caution by Crown Prosecutors

9.5   Crown Prosecutors, when undertaking a charging review in accordance with this Guidance, may determine that a charge, conditional caution (if a scheme is in force locally), simple caution, reprimand or final warning is appropriate. Written notice of the decision will be given to the Custody Officer on an MG3. Where it subsequently proves not to be possible to give the person a conditional caution (if this scheme is enforced locally), simple caution, reprimand, or final warning, the matter will be referred back to the Crown Prosecutor to determine whether the person is instead to be charged with the offence.

10.   Breach of Pre-Charge Bail Conditions

Action on breach of bail conditions pending CPS charging decision

10.1   Where a person is released on bail pending a CPS decision on charge or re-released following arrest for breach of a condition of bail for that purpose [under Section 37(7)(a) or 37C(2)(b) PACE,] and that person is subsequently arrested under Section 46A(1A) PACE on reasonable grounds of having broken any of the conditions of bail, or for failing to surrender to bail at the police station, and a Custody Officer concludes that the person should be detained in custody for the purpose of an application to the court for a remand in custody, the Custody Officer will consult a Crown Prosecutor for a decision as to whether to charge with the offence for which the person had previously been released on bail or with any other offence or be released without charge either on bail or without bail.

Charging breach of bail – emergency situations

10.2   In any such case where it has proved not to be possible to consult with a Crown Prosecutor in person or by telephone before the expiry of any PACE custody time limit and it is proposed to withhold bail for the purposes of an application for a remand into custody (or for bail conditions that may only be imposed by the court) a Custody Officer may proceed to charge, but only on the authority of a Duty Inspector. The Duty Inspector shall note the custody record and MG3 to confirm that it is appropriate to charge under the emergency provisions. The case must be referred to a Crown Prosecutor as soon as is practicable for authority to proceed with the prosecution.

11.   Police action post referral and escalation procedure

Police action post referral

11.1   In any case where the Threshold is met and the case has been referred to a Crown Prosecutor for a charging decision, and the decision of the Crown Prosecutor is to charge, caution, obtain additional evidence, or take no action, the police will not proceed in any other way without first referring the matter back to a Crown Prosecutor.

Dispute resolution

11.2   Where in any case an Investigating or Custody Officer is not in agreement with the charging decision, the Report requirements or any diversion proposal of a Crown Prosecutor and wishes to have the case referred for further review, the case must be referred to the BCU Crime Manager (normally Detective Chief Inspector), or appointed Deputy, for consultation with a CPS Unit Head, or appointed Deputy for resolution. If further escalation is required, the involvement of the Divisional Commander and the Level E Unit Head or Chief Crown Prosecutor should be obtained. Procedures should be in place for this review to be conducted speedily.

12.   Form of Report to Crown Prosecutor for a Charging Decision (MG3)

Form of MG3

12.1   The Report to Crown Prosecutor for a Charging Decision to be used will be the form MG3, a copy of which is attached at Annex B to this Guidance. The Manual of Guidance Editorial Board may vary this form from time to time.

13.   Requirements to Comply with the Manual of Guidance Provisions

Compliance with Manual of Guidance

13.1   All consultation arrangements and procedures for the preparation, processing and submission of prosecution files and the disclosure of unused material will be carried out in accordance with the provisions of the latest edition of the Manual of Guidance as agreed between the Home Office, Association of Chief Police Officers and the Crown Prosecution Service.

KEN MACDONALD QC
DIRECTOR OF PUBLIC PROSECUTIONS

Schedule

This Guidance is to come into operation in the following Areas with effect from 4 January 2005; Avon & Somerset, Cleveland, Greater Manchester, Humberside, Kent, Lancashire, London, Merseyside, Northumbria, Nottinghamshire, South Yorkshire, Thames Valley, West Midlands & West Yorkshire.

This Guidance is to come into effect in the following Areas on the dates specified below:

Local Criminal Justice Board Area	Date of coming into effect	Authorisation of Director of Public Prosecutions
Bedfordshire		
Cambridgeshire		
Cheshire		
Cumbria	5 December 2005	[Ken Macdonald]
Derbyshire		
Dorset		
Devon & Cornwall		
Durham	22 August 2005	[Ken Macdonald]
Dyfed Powys		
Essex		
Gloucestershire	17 October 2005	[Ken Macdonald]
Gwent		
Hampshire	19 April 2005	[Ken Macdonald]
Hertfordshire	14 November 2005	[Ken Macdonald]
Leicestershire		
Lincolnshire	14 November 2005	[Ken Macdonald]
Norfolk	24 October 2005	[Ken Macdonald]
North Wales	12 September 2005	[Ken Macdonald]
North Yorkshire	8 November 2005	[Ken Macdonald]
Northamptonshire		
South Wales	3 October 2005	[Ken Macdonald]
Staffordshire		
Suffolk	3 October 2005	[Ken Macdonald]
Surrey		
Sussex	14 November 2005	[Ken Macdonald]
Warwickshire		
West Mercia	11 July 2005	[Ken Macdonald]
Wiltshire		

Annex A

OFFENCES OR CIRCUMSTANCES, WHICH MUST ALWAYS BE REFERRED TO A CROWN PROSECUTOR FOR EARLY CONSULTATION AND CHARGING DECISION – WHETHER ADMITTED OR NOT

- Offences requiring the Attorney General's or Director of Public Prosecution's consent.
- Any indictable only offence.
- Any either way offence triable only on indictment due to the surrounding circumstances of the commission of the offence or the previous convictions of the person.

In so far as not covered by the above:

- Offences under the Terrorism Act 2000, the Prevention of Terrorism Act 2005 or any other offence linked with terrorist activity.
- Offences under the Anti-Terrorism, Crime and Security Act 2001.
- Offences under the Explosive Substances Act 1883
- Offences under any of the Official Secrets Acts.
- Offences involving any racial, religious or homophobic aggravation.
- Offences classified as Domestic Violence.
- Offences under the Sexual Offences Act 2003 committed by or upon persons under the age of 18 years.
- Offences involving Persistent Young Offenders, unless chargeable by the police under Paragraph 3.3.
- Offences arising directly or indirectly out of activities associated with hunting wild mammals with dogs under the Hunting Act 2004.
- The following specific offences[6]:
  - Wounding or inflicting grievous bodily harm, contrary to Section 20 of the Offences Against the Person Act 1861
  - Assault occasioning actual bodily harm, contrary to Section 47 of the Offences Against the Person Act 1861
  - Violent Disorder contrary to Section 2 of the Public Order Act 1986.
  - Affray, contrary to Section 3 of the Public Order Act 1986
  - Offences involving deception, contrary to the Theft Acts 1968 & 1978
  - Handling stolen goods, contrary to Section 22 of the Theft Act 1968

---

[6] File requirements for these cases will be in accordance with the Manual of Guidance expedited file, to include key witness statements or other compelling evidence and a short descriptive note of any interview conducted.

Annex B

Annex
B

REPORT TO CROWN PROSECUTOR FOR CHARGING DECISION
DECISION LOG & ACTION PLAN   Page .... of ......
Not Disclosable

URN

REPORT TO CROWN PROSECUTOR (FOR POLICE COMPLETION)

Suspect 1: PO/PYO/YO♦ M/F♦	**Proposed charge(s):**
Surname:	....
Forename(s):	....
D.O.B:....................... Custody Ref:........................	....
Ethnicity code (self-defined):	....
Suspect 2: PO/PYO/YO♦ M/F♦	**Proposed charge(s):**
Surname:	....
Forename(s):	....
D.O.B:....................... Custody Ref:........................	....
Ethnicity code (self-defined):	....

Officer seeking advice: .... Supervisor's name: .... Consulted Y / N♦

Material provided to CPS (*indicate if attached*)

	Date of item		Date of item
Statement of:		Pocket note book/Incident report book:	
Statement of:		Police incident log:	
Statement of:		Video/photographs:	
Interview record:		Previous convictions/disposals:	
Forensic/expert evidence:		Other:	

Outline of circumstances and decision/advice sought (*unless verbal report given*)
(Consider: time limit on proceedings (if applicable); strengths and weaknesses of case; possible lines of defence; witness assessment; public safety/bail issues; disclosure; any financial or asset recovery issues; orders on conviction; public interest.)

Continue on separate sheet if necessary

Officer completing: .... Rank & No./Job title: .... Date: ....

Contact details (station, tel, mobile, e-mail): .... Signature:..

RESTRICTED
FOR POLICE AND PROSECUTION ONLY (when complete)

Page......... of ....

CHARGING DECISION/ADVICE & CASE ACTION PLAN (FOR CPS COMPLETION)   URN: ....

Charging decision and advice, specifying or attaching charges (*refer to documents/evidence seen, decision on offences*)

Continue on separate sheet if necessary

Prosecutor to indicate general nature of decision and advice (*Tick one box only*)

Code	Advice	Suspect 1	Suspect 2	Code	Advice	Suspect 1	Suspect 2
A	Charge + request Full File			H	Request Evidential File		
B	Charge + request Expedited File			I	Request Expedited File		
C	Simple caution			J	Further investigation - resubmit		
D	Conditional caution			K	NFA – Evidential		
E	Reprimand			L	NFA – Public Interest		
F	Final warning			M	Other (*please specify*)		
G	TIC			N	Refer for financial investigation		
If 'K', enter Evidential code:				If 'C, D, E, F or L', enter Public Interest code:			

Further action agreed:

1.

2.

3.

4.

Action date by:

1.

2.

3.

4.

Asset recovery case: Yes/No◆

Return bail date:...

Charging review/action date: ....

PYO Provisional trial date: ....

Further consultation needed pre-charge: Y /N◆   (*If further consultation necessary, use continuation sheet MG3 A*)

Prosecutor name (*print*): ....

Contact details: ....   Date:......................

Investigation stage at which advice sought:

Pre arrest ☐   Post Arrest ☐   Post Interview ☐   Post bail for further enqs ☐   Bail for charging decision ☐

How advice delivered:

Face to Face ☐   Video Conferencing ☐   Telephone ☐   CPS Direct ☐   Written ☐

Index

Immigration Advice at the Police Station

3rd Edition

Rosie Brennan

Providing essential coverage of both immigration and criminal practice it takes the reader through the situations that clients may face, offering advice on practice and conduct, illustrated using case studies.

Key revisions and new material includes:

- updated information on the system of immigration enforcement action
- chapter on criminal offences introduced by the Asylum and Immigration (Treatment of Claimants) Act 2004, updated information on other immigration offences and discussion of the immigration aspects of these criminal cases
- the amended immigration appeal system
- updates on detention and bail in the police station
- changes to the funding regime.

Available from Marston Book Services:
Tel. 01235 465 656.

1 85328 948 5
408 pages
£34.95
January 2006

The Law Society

Key Criminal Cases 2005

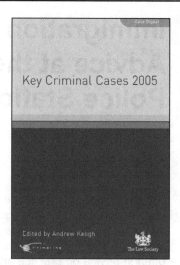

Edited by Andrew Keogh

This excellent new collection provides you with a quick and easy way to access the key criminal cases from 2005 and bring yourself up to date with the latest in criminal litigation.

Encompassing many of the reforms introduced by the Criminal Justice Act 2003, this portable guide brings together digests of over 150 of the most relevant and topical cases of 2005. Key cases include:

- *R.* v. *Hanson* (bad character)
- *R.* v. *Lang* (dangerous offenders)
- *R.* v. *Morrison* (ASBOs)

The cases are organised alphabetically within subject areas for swift navigation, enabling the reader to quickly find the most up to date cases. Each case contains a concise digest of the essential ruling and is supported by electronic updates via Crimeline (www.crimeline.info).

Available from Marston Book Services:
Tel. 01235 465 656.

1 85328 578 1
176 pages
£29.95
April 2006

The Law Society